Language Files

Tenth Edition

Editors of Previous Editions

9th edition, 2004

Georgios Tserdanelis
Wai Yi Peggy Wong

8th edition, 2001

Thomas W. Stewart, Jr.
Nathan Vaillette

7th edition, 1998

Nick Cipollone
Steven Hartman Keiser
Shravan Vasishth

6th edition, 1994

Stefanie Jannedy
Robert Poletto
Tracey L. Weldon

5th edition, 1991

Monica Crabtree
Joyce Powers

4th edition, 1987

Carolyn McManis
Deborah Stollenwerk
Zhang Zheng-Sheng

3rd edition, 1985

Anette S. Bissantz
Keith A. Johnson

2nd edition, 1982

Carol Jean Godby
Rex Wallace
Catherine Jolley

1st compilations, 1977–79

Deborah B. Schaffer
John W. Perkins
F. Christian Latta
Sheila Graves Geoghegan

Language Files

Materials for an Introduction to Language and Linguistics

Tenth Edition

Editors

Anouschka Bergmann
Kathleen Currie Hall
Sharon Miriam Ross

Department of Linguistics
The Ohio State University

The Ohio State University Press
Columbus

"How Adults Talk to Children" from *Psychology and Language,* by Herbert H. Clark and Eve V. Clark, copyright © 1977 by Harcourt Brace Jovanovich, Inc., reprinted by permission of the publisher.

"The Birds and the Bees" from *An Introduction to Language,* Second Edition, by Victoria A. Fromkin and Robert Rodman, copyright © 1978 by Holt, Rinehart and Winston, Inc., reprinted by permission of the publisher.

Excerpts from *An Introduction to Descriptive Linguistics,* Revised Edition, by Henry A. Gleason, copyright © 1961 by Holt, Rinehart and Winston, Inc., and renewed 1989 by H. A. Gleason, Jr., reprinted by permission of the publisher.

Excerpts from *Descriptive Linguistics,* Workbook by Henry A. Gleason, Jr., copyright © 1955 and renewed 1983 by Holt, Rinehart and Winston, Inc., reprinted by permission of the publisher.

"Variations in Speech Style," adapted from sections of Ann D. Zwicky, "Style," in *Styles and Variables in English,* edited by Timothy Shopen and Joseph M. Williams, © 1981. Cambridge, MA: Winthrop Publishers (Prentice-Hall).

Library of Congress Cataloging-in-Publication Data

Language files : materials for an introduction to language and linguistics / editors, Anouschka Bergmann, Kathleen Currie Hall, Sharon Miriam Ross (Department of Linguistics, The Ohio State University). — 10th ed.
   p. cm.
  Includes bibliographical references and index.
  ISBN 978-0-8142-5163-8 (pbk. : alk. paper)
   1. Linguistics. I. Bergmann, Anouschka. II. Hall, Kathleen Currie. III. Ross, Sharon Miriam.

P121.L3855 2007
410—dc22

2007004479

Cover design by Graphic Composition, Inc.
Typesetting by Graphic Composition, Inc.

The paper used in this publication meets the minimum requirements of the American National Standard for Information Sciences—Permanence of Paper for Printed Library Materials. ANSI Z39.48–1992.

9 8 7 6 5 4 3 2 1

Contents

Chapter 5: Syntax   193

Chapter 6: Semantics   231

Chapter 7: Pragmatics   267

Chapter 8: Language Acquisition   309

Chapter 9: Language Storage and Processing   351

Preface to the Tenth Edition

An Introduction to *Language Files*

Since its inception thirty years ago, the *Language Files* has grown from a collection of materials designed simply as a supplement for undergraduate courses into a full-fledged introductory textbook. The scope of the text makes it suitable for use in a wide range of courses, while its unique organization into instructor-friendly files allows for tremendous flexibility in course design.

The *Language Files* was originally the idea of Arnold Zwicky, who was among its first authors. Since the first edition, many editors have contributed to the development of the *Language Files;* the current edition is the result of this cumulative effort.

Changes in the Current Edition

In honor of the publication of this 10th edition, we have incorporated a number of major changes. These are outlined below and divided in the following way: first, we introduce new tools for using the book; second, we give an overview of the global contentful changes; finally, we present a list of specific changes by chapter.

New Tools for Using the Book

- Continuing a trend from the 9th edition, we have increased the use of an outline numbering system, ensuring that it is used consistently in each chapter. For example, in Chapter 8, the first full file is File 8.1, and within that file, distinct topics are divided into sections labeled as 8.1.1, 8.1.2, and so on. This system is now used uniformly in every file and chapter. All text within a file is contained within one of these numbered sections. In this way, instructors can choose to assign very specific topics with ease, increasing the book's modularity. Students will also be aided in taking organized and hierarchical notes.
- Also in an attempt to increase the modularity of the book, and following the editors of the 9th edition, we have added a number of cross references throughout the book, indicating where information can be found about related topics.
- Each chapter has a new file at the beginning (numbered, for example, 8.0) that provides a brief introduction to the topic covered in the chapter. Unlike the introductory files in the 9th edition, the introductory files in this edition are designed to introduce each topic in broad terms; significant concepts and more complex ideas are introduced in later files in the chapter.
- Following each chapter's introduction is an annotated table of contents for that chapter, providing a brief outline of the contents that can be found in each file of that chapter. This allows instructors to have a guide as to which files will be most applicable to their curricula, and it allows students to gain a bird's-eye view of the topic that they are about to study.

- The exercises for each chapter (which previously appeared file by file) have been compiled into a single file at the end of the chapter (titled Practice). Exercises are still organized by the file that they refer to. We hope that by placing all of the exercises for a chapter together, we will aid both instructors in choosing exercises to assign and students in finding the exercises that they have been assigned.
- In addition to this consolidation of the practice exercises, we have expanded the number of exercises: there are now exercises available for every file in each chapter.
- There are three kinds of exercise in the Practice files. "Exercises" give students an opportunity to practice applying concepts from the chapter in relatively straightforward ways by answering basic questions, examining data, generating novel sentences that meet certain criteria, and so on. "Discussion Questions" ask for further consideration of some particular issue. They may be used to spark in-class discussions or may be assigned to students to discuss in small groups or to write short-essay-type responses. "Activities" require that students engage in further work by undertaking more involved linguistic analysis, collecting their own linguistic data, using materials available on the Internet, and so on.
- A selected bibliography has been added to the back of the book.
- Vocabulary items in the glossary are now marked with the file(s) in which they are first introduced.
- The IPA chart has been updated to the 2005 edition.
- We have put several reference tools on the inside front and back covers of the textbook, so as to make it easier for students to locate certain often-used materials. On the inside front cover is a list of symbols used in the text. On the inside back cover is a copy of the official IPA chart. On the page facing the inside back cover, we have added copies of the charts for American English consonants and vowels, and on the reverse side of this page, we have listed IPA symbols for the sounds of American English and example words containing those sounds.

Global Contentful Changes

- Material about signed languages, which previously appeared in its own chapter, has now been incorporated where relevant throughout the book. File 1.5, Language Modality, introduces signed languages in comparison with spoken languages.
- The chapter on animal communication has moved to the second half of the book (Chapter 14). In this way, we are able to focus on the structure of human language first and later show animal communication systems in contrast with this structure. Furthermore, animal communication is now adjacent to other chapters that also pertain to how language relates to other fields of study.
- The chapter on psycholinguistics has been split into two chapters, Language Acquisition (Chapter 8) and Language Storage and Processing (Chapter 9).
- Each chapter begins with a comic that gives some insight into the subfield of linguistics covered in that chapter. It is the hope of the editors that these comics will spark discussion in classrooms and demonstrate to students that linguistic concepts do arise in daily life. Questions in each practice file refer to the comic and ask students to draw on the linguistic content of the chapter in order to analyze it.
- The 9th edition saw a shift to the International Phonetic Alphabet (IPA) in the phonetics and phonology chapters; in the 10th edition, the use of the IPA has been extended consistently to the rest of the book.
- A new chapter (Chapter 16, Practical Applications) helps to answer a question with which most linguistics instructors quickly become familiar: What can you do with a degree in linguistics? It provides overviews of six practical ways that a linguistics education can be applied. Of course, students should note that there are many more than these six!
- In cases too numerous to mention individually, discussions of various topics have been

clarified, expanded upon, and—where appropriate—condensed. We have also added more examples and illustrations of concepts.

Additionally, the following changes affect particular chapters.

Chapter 1: Introduction

- File 1.1 (Introducing the Study of Language) combines the old files Why Study Language and Pre-Course Objectives into a single introductory file.
- The pre-course survey has been changed into separate lists of "surprising but true" facts about language and "common misconceptions" about language, which could be combined into a "survey" for students to examine initial thoughts, beliefs, and attitudes about language.
- File 1.2 (What You Know When You Know a Language) now covers the basic concepts involved in knowing a language, including a discussion of the distinction between competence and performance; a description of the communication chain and a discussion of how each aspect of linguistic study fits into this chain (serving as an overview to the contents of the book); a discussion of mental grammar; and the introduction of descriptive rules. This file is designed to stand on its own, separate from File 1.3.
- File 1.3 (What You Don't (Necessarily) Know When You Know a Language) is the corollary to File 1.2. It includes discussion of two popular misconceptions about what it means to know a language, namely, writing and prescriptive grammar. By creating this as a separate file rather than integrating these concepts in with actual features of language, we hope to highlight their status as things that are commonly misconstrued as part of linguistic study.
- File 1.4 (Design Features of Language) contains the discussion of the design features of language that in previous editions appeared in the chapter on Animal Communication. These have been extracted and expanded so as to be presented as actual features of human languages instead of simply differences between human and animal communication. Note that the chapter on Animal Communication (now Chapter 14) also contains the file Communication and Language, which revisits the design features with respect to animal communication systems.
- File 1.5 (Language Modality) contains a discussion of language modality, focusing on the differences between signed and spoken languages. Much of this file used to appear in the old chapter on Visual Languages. We introduce the concepts here, however, in order to establish the differences up front and allow us to integrate the discussion of signed languages in the rest of the text.

Chapter 2: Phonetics

- The old file on experimental methods in phonetics has been deleted; sections on how to investigate particular phenomena are now integrated into the chapter where they are relevant to the discussion. (There is also a new general file on experimental techniques in Chapter 9 (File 9.7).)
- The use of IPA symbols has been brought more in line with the usage described for various languages in the *Journal of the International Phonetic Alphabet*.
- File 2.5 (Suprasegmental Features) has been updated to reflect more recent thinking on suprasegmentals.
- File 2.6 (Acoustic Phonetics) has been shortened so that it covers both general acoustics and acoustic phonetics in a single file; it does not repeat as much content from articulatory phonetics.
- File 2.7 (The Phonetics of Signed Languages) has been added.
- In File 2.8 (Practice), new exercises take advantage of easily available phonetics analysis software.

Chapter 3: Phonology

- Data throughout the chapter have been updated to be more accurate and to use the IPA more consistently.
- File 3.1 (The Value of Sounds: Phonemes and Allophones) has been updated to include a discussion of the importance of alternations in phonological analysis.
- Information about the relevant language families has been added to the data analysis questions.
- File 3.5 (How to Solve Phonology Problems) now immediately precedes File 3.6 (Practice).

Chapter 4: Morphology

- This chapter has seen minor reorganization: there is a new file division between morphological processes and morphological typology.
- File 4.2 (Morphological Processes) contains a discussion of simultaneous affixation in signed languages.
- File 4.4 (The Hierarchical Structure of Derived Words) now follows the introduction of affixation in File 4.2 (Morphological Processes).

Chapter 5: Syntax

- As in the 9th edition, File 5.1 (Basic Ideas of Syntax) provides a general overview of syntax that can serve as a unit unto itself in isolation from the rest of the chapter; in the 10th edition, this file introduces more aspects of syntax, including lexical categories and agreement.
- Lexical categories are now discussed in their own file (File 5.3) rather than appearing as a section of the file about phrases; in this way students can easily refer to information about lexical categories when it becomes relevant in other disciplines (such as morphology and language change).
- While the chapter about syntax in the 9th edition was rich with examples, the 10th edition has added a significant amount of prose both explicating these examples and fitting syntax into a wider context.

Chapter 6: Semantics

- Although the content of this chapter is by and large quite similar to that of the 9th edition, there has been a general restructuring of the chapter to further highlight the distinction between lexical and compositional semantics. Content from the file in previous editions titled Theories of Meaning has been divided and moved according to the lexical/compositional split. There are now two files about lexical semantics and two about compositional semantics.
- Reference and sense are introduced relative to one another; these two ideas are contrasted throughout the chapter.
- Explanations of set theory have been expanded and clarified.
- The discussion of antonymy (in File 6.3, Lexical Semantics: Word Relations) has been revised.
- Entailment is now introduced in the discussion of compositional semantics (whereas in previous editions it was introduced in the chapter about pragmatics).

Chapter 7: Pragmatics

- The chapter has been restructured to highlight the centrality of Gricean maxims in most introductory studies of pragmatics.
- File 7.1 (Language in Context) is entirely new material, introducing ways in which context affects language use.

- File 7.3 (Drawing Conclusions) includes a new discussion about the nature of implicature and draws an explicit connection between conversational implicature and the Gricean maxims.
- File 7.4 (Speech Acts) has been restructured such that it now emphasizes felicity and the use of speech acts relative to context.
- File 7.5 (Presupposition) is a new file introducing presupposition as an element for pragmatic investigation.
- Information about entailment has moved to Chapter 6 (Semantics); information about discourse analysis has been condensed and moved to Chapter 10 (Language Variation).

Chapter 8: Language Acquisition

- This chapter includes the files on language acquisition that were previously part of the chapter entitled Psycholinguistics.
- File 8.1 (Theories of Language Acquisition) includes an expanded discussion of the critical period hypothesis. Connectionist Theories and Social Interaction Theory are added to the theories of language acquisition discussed in the file.
- File 8.2 (First-Language Acquisition: The Acquisition of Speech Sounds and Phonology) includes an expanded discussion of how infants perceive speech.
- The previous file entitled Milestones in Motor and Language Development has been split up and incorporated into File 8.2 (First-Language Acquisition: The Acquisition of Speech Sounds and Phonology) and File 8.3 (First-Language Acquisition: The Acquisition of Morphology, Syntax, and Word Meaning) as a subsection at the end of each file.
- File 8.5 (Bilingual Language Acquisition) is a new file introducing bilingual first- and second-language acquisition.

Chapter 9: Language Storage and Processing

- This chapter includes the old files Language and the Brain and Language Processing (including production and perception errors) that were previously part of the chapter entitled Psycholinguistics.
- The previous file Language and the Brain has been split into two files: File 9.1 (Language and the Brain) and File 9.2 (Aphasia).
- File 9.3 (Speech Production) includes the sections on production errors from the previous file Errors in Speech Production and Perception. Sections on models of speech production and slips of the hands have also been added to the file.
- File 9.4 (Speech Perception) is a new file discussing a number of phenomena related to how humans perceive speech sounds.
- File 9.5 (Lexical Processing) includes the sections on word recognition and lexical ambiguity from the previous file Adult Language Processing. A section on how words are stored in the mental lexicon has been added to the file.
- File 9.6 (Sentence Processing) includes information on syntactic parsing from the previous file Adult Language Processing. Discussions about structural ambiguity, late closure, and the effects of intonation on disambiguation have been added.
- File 9.7 (Experimental Methods in Psycholinguistics) is a new file introducing some common experimental techniques used in psycholinguistic research.

Chapter 10: Language Variation

- This chapter has been restructured so that each file is on a more equal footing: one describes language varieties, one looks at variation at different levels of linguistic structure, and two give reasons for language variation (regional and social). The focus of the chapter is solely on language variation; other topics relevant to sociolinguistics, such as language and identity and language and power, have been moved to Chapter 13 (Language and Culture).

- File 10.1 (Language Varieties) now includes all the information on different types of language varieties that had been scattered throughout previous versions of the chapter.
- File 10.2 (Variation at Different Levels of Linguistic Structure) has been expanded and now includes more examples and discussion.
- File 10.3 (Factors Influencing Variation: Regional and Geographic Factors) has been expanded to include an in-depth case study of American English dialects, looking at particular features of six major U.S. dialect areas.
- File 10.4 (Factors Influencing Variation: Social Factors) now combines the discussion of all the social factors influencing dialect variation into one section, so that they can be more easily compared. Each section has been updated to include more-recent studies. The section on ethnic variation now includes Chicano and Lumbee English in addition to African-American English.
- The case studies that used to appear as a separate file have now been integrated into the text. Labov's study on /ɹ/-lessness in department stores now appears in Section 10.4.2; his study of Martha's Vineyard now appears in File 13.1 (Language and Identity).
- File 10.5 (Practice) now includes exercises that involve analyzing collected data from variationist studies with respect to the factors discussed in the chapter.

Chapter 11: Language Contact

- File 11.1 (Language Contact) now includes a short section introducing intertwined (bilingual mixed) languages.
- File 11.2 (Borrowings into English) now appears before the files on pidgins and creoles. This file's outline format was changed to a more text-like format. Information about external events that led to lexical borrowing into English has been added (taken from material that used to appear in the Language Change chapter).
- File 11.5 (Societal Multilingualism) is a new file introducing societal multilingualism, code-switching, and diglossia.
- File 11.6 (Language Endangerment and Language Death) is a new file introducing issues related to language endangerment and language death.

Chapter 12: Language Change

- The IPA has been incorporated into the chapter.
- File 12.2 (Language Relatedness) now presents a more comprehensive look at language relatedness in addition to presenting the family tree and wave models. The wave model diagram has been updated.
- The discussion in File 12.3 (Sound Change) on conditioned versus unconditioned sound change has been clarified.
- File 12.7 (Reconstruction: Internal Reconstruction vs. Comparative Reconstruction) now encompasses both internal and comparative reconstruction (parts of old Files 12.4 and 12.9) and appears directly before File 12.8 (Practice).
- A flowchart, similar to those that appear in the phonology and morphology chapters, has been added to the discussion of solving comparative reconstruction problems in File 12.7.
- The comparative reconstruction exercises are now part of File 12.8.
- The file on milestones in the internal and external history of English has been removed. Much of the discussion of particular events that have influenced English historically now appears in Chapter 11 on Language Contact. The information on internal reconstruction appears in File 12.7.

Chapter 13: Language and Culture

- This chapter is an expanded version of the old chapter Language in a Wider Context.
- File 13.1 (Language and Identity) has been added as a discussion of how language can be used as a marker and an element of identity. In addition, it includes information on how identity can be studied, and it contains the case study of Martha's Vineyard that used to appear in the Language Variation chapter.
- File 13.2 (Language and Power) has been added. It includes elements of the discussion of language and power that used to appear in the files on Gender Variation and An Official Language for the United States.
- File 13.3 (Language and Thought) consolidates and updates the previous files on the Whorf Hypothesis and Color Terms, and it explores modern conceptions of the principle of linguistic relativity.
- File 13.4 (Writing Systems) now includes discussion of the role of writing in developing culture. It also has been reorganized to make the distinction between meaning-based versus sound-based writing systems clearer. Some terminology has been updated to better reflect current thought on writing systems.

Chapter 14: Animal Communication

- The chapter has been restructured in order to clarify the distinction between natural animal communication systems and attempts to teach animals to use human language.
- File 14.1 (Communication and Language) now covers the design features only with respect to animal communication systems. A general introduction of design features is now found in Chapter 1. Examples from a variety of animals have been added.
- File 14.2 (Animal Communication in the Wild) contains content from the old file The Birds and the Bees. Primate communication in the wild has been added to the file. The section on bird communication has been expanded.
- File 14.3 (Can Animals Be Taught Language?) contains material from the previous file Primate Studies.

Chapter 15: Language and Computers

- File 15.1 (Speech Synthesis) has been updated and now includes a discussion of concatenative synthesis.
- File 15.2 (Automatic Speech Recognition) is a new file covering the noisy channel model and components of automatic speech recognition systems as well as applications and issues in automatic speech recognition.

Chapter 16: Practical Applications

- This is a new chapter that contains material explaining how a background in linguistics can be applied to language education, speech-language pathology, audiology, law, advertising, code-breaking, and the further study of linguistics.

Further Resources for Using *Language Files*

The *Language Files* home page can be found at http://www.ling.ohio-state.edu/publications/files/. This home page provides up-to-date links and language- and linguistics-related Web sites, organized by topic.

A password for instructors to access the instructor's guide and answer key can be obtained through The Ohio State University Press at http://www.ohiostatepress.org by locating the Web page for the 10th edition of *Language Files* and filling out the online form provided there.

In order to facilitate the receipt of feedback from users of the *Language Files*, we also provide an e-mail address, files@ling.ohio-state.edu, to which any suggestions, questions, or requests for clarification concerning this edition may be directed.

The home page for the Department of Linguistics at The Ohio State University can be found at http://www.ling.ohio-state.edu.

Contributors to the 10th Edition

Many people have contributed to this edition, including students and faculty of the Department of Linguistics at The Ohio State University and colleagues in other departments and at other institutions.

We are particularly appreciative of those who have contributed substantial new material to this edition: Kirk Baker, Chris Brew, Ilana Bromberg, Angelo Costanzo, David Durian, Brian Joseph, Julia Porter Papke, Anton Rytting, and E. Allyn Smith (OSU, Department of Linguistics); Laura Slocum (OSU, Department of Speech and Hearing); Wayne Smith (Learning Unlimited Language School); and Bill Vicars (Sacramento State College, Department of ASL and ASL University: Lifeprint.com).

We would additionally like to thank the following individuals for their contributions of data, examples, and exercises; and for their advice regarding both the structure and content of the book: Mary Beckman, Adriane Boyd, Cynthia Clopper, Jirka Hana, Eunjong Kong, Yusuke Kubota, Fangfang Li, Jianguo Li, Ila Nagar, David Odden, Craige Roberts, Andrea Sims, Shari Speer, Judith Tonhauser, and Don Winford (OSU, Department of Linguistics); Jean Ann (SUNY Oswego); Amanda Boomershine (University of North Carolina, Wilmington); Graham Fraser (The *Toronto Star*/Carleton University); Ellen Furlong (OSU, Department of Psychology); Carolyn Currie Hall; Daniel Currie Hall (University of Toronto); Edith Hernandez (OSU, Department of Spanish and Portuguese); Alexei Kochetov (Simon Fraser University); Rina Kreitman (Cornell University); Rozenn Le Calvez (Laboratoire de Sciences Cognitives et Psycholinguistique); Caitlin Mahaffey (University of Southern California); Scott H. Mellon; Panayiotis Pappas (Simon Fraser University); Melissa A. Rinehart, Ph.D.; Aaron Shield (University of Texas at Austin); Giorgos Tserdanelis (Stony Brook University); Inga Vendelin (Laboratoire de Sciences Cognitives et Psycholinguistique); Laura Wagner (OSU, Department of Psychology); Ruth Weinschenk-Vennor (OSU, Department of Near Eastern Languages and Cultures); Peggy Wong (University of Wisconsin); and anonymous contributors to the OSU linguistics questions database. Thanks also go to Carolyn Sherayko, Sherayko Indexing Service, for her careful work in preparing the index.

We are also grateful to our department chair and the supervisor for this edition, Beth Hume, who has provided insight and feedback throughout the process of preparing the book.

Finally we would like to thank the people at The Ohio State University Press, especially Maggie Diehl, Malcolm Litchfield, Eugene O'Connor, and Jason Stauter, for their care and attention in this project. We appreciate their advice, patience, flexibility, and cooperation throughout the production of this edition.

Anouschka Bergmann
Kathleen Currie Hall
Sharon Miriam Ross

Department of Linguistics
The Ohio State University

Acknowledgments

The editors and publisher are grateful to the following sources for permission to include the following previously copyrighted material.

File 1.5

Figure (2) from *Signing: How to Speak with Your Hands* by Elaine Costello. Copyright 1983 by Elaine Costello. Used by permission of Bantam Books, a division of Bantam Doubleday Dell Publishing Group, Inc.

Figure (3) © 2006, William Vicars, www.Lifeprint.com. Used with permission.

File 1.6

Picture of ASL in Exercise 29 © 2006, William Vicars, www.Lifeprint.com. Used with permission.

Picture of TSL in Exercise 29 © 1979, W. H. Smith and L. Ting, *Shou neng sheng chyau (your hands can become a bridge)*. Used with permission.

File 2.0

Comic © HILARY B. PRICE. KING FEATURES SYNDICATE

File 2.2

Figure (1) from Lieberman, Philip, and Sheila E. Blumstein. 1990. *Speech Physiology, Speech Perception, and Acoustic Phonetics*. New York: Cambridge University Press.

File 2.6

Figure (2) adapted with permission from Ladefoged, Peter. 1962. *Elements of Acoustic Phonetics*. Chicago: University of Chicago Press.

File 2.7

Figure (1) from *Signing: How to Speak with Your Hands* by Elaine Costello. Copyright 1983 by Elaine Costello. Used by permission of Bantam Books, a division of Bantam Doubleday Dell Publishing Group, Inc.

Figures (2), (3), (4), (6), (7), and (8) © 2006, William Vicars, www.Lifeprint.com. Used and/or adapted with permission.

Figure (5) ©1979, W. H. Smith & L. Ting, *Shou neng sheng chyau (your hands can become a bridge)*. Used with permission.

File 2.8

Images of ASL in Exercise 38 from *Signing: How to Speak with Your Hands* by Elaine Costello. Copyright 1983 by Elaine Costello. Used by permission of Bantam Books, a division of Bantam Doubleday Dell Publishing Group, Inc.

Images of ASL in Exercises 39 and 40 © 2006, William Vicars, www.Lifeprint.com. Used with permission.

File 3.0

FOR BETTER OR FOR WORSE © 1990 Lynn Johnston Productions. Dist. By Universal Press Syndicate. Reprinted with permission. All rights reserved.

File 3.2

Figures (10), (11), and (17) © 2006, William Vicars, www.Lifeprint.com. Used with or adapted by permission.

File 3.3

Figures (3), (4), and (5) © 2006, William Vicars, www.Lifeprint.com. Used with or adapted by permission.

File 3.6

Photographs in Exercise 21 (ASL) © 2006, William Vicars, www.Lifeprint.com. Used with permission.

Exercise 23 (Mokilese) adapted from O'Grady, William, and Michael Dobrovolsky. 1989. *Contemporary Linguistics: An Introduction*. New York: Saint Martin's Press, Inc.

Exercise 24 (Sindhi) adapted from Ladefoged, Peter. 1971. *Preliminaries of Linguistic Phonetics*. Chicago: University of Chicago Press.

Exercises 26 (Standard Spanish), 27 (Russian), 33 (Spanish), and 34 (Canadian French) adapted from Cowan, William, and Jaromira Rakusan. 1980. *Source Book for Linguistics*. Amsterdam: John Benjamins B.V.

Exercise 30 (English) adapted from Akmajian, Adrian, David P. Demers, and Robert M. Harnish. 1984. *Linguistics: An Introduction to Language and Communication*. Cambridge, MA: MIT Press.

Excerpts of Exercises 31 (Totonac), 32 (Tojolabal), and 36 (Farsi) adapted from *Descriptive Linguistics,* Workbook by Henry A. Gleason, Jr., copyright © 1955 and renewed 1983 by Holt, Rinehart and Winston, Inc., Orlando, FL, reprinted by permission of the publisher.

Exercise 38 (Modern Greek) adapted from Pearson, Bruce L. 1977. *Workbook in Linguistic Concepts*. New York: McGraw-Hill, Inc. Reproduced with permission of McGraw-Hill.

File 4.0

Comic © DAN PIRARO. KING FEATURES SYNDICATE

File 4.2

Figures (2), (3), (4), and (6) © 2006, William Vicars, www.Lifeprint.com. Adapted by permission.

File 4.6

Excerpts of Exercises 8 (Bontoc), 38 (Swahili), and 42 (Hanunoo) from *Descriptive Linguistics,* Workbook by Henry A. Gleason, Jr., © 1966 and renewed 1983 by Holt, Rinehart and Winston, Inc., Orlando, FL, reprinted by permission of the publisher.

Images in Exercises 13 and 33 © 2006, William Vicars, www.Lifeprint.com. Used with or adapted by permission.

Exercises 29 (Isthmus Zapotec), 40 (Zoque), and 44 (Popoluca) from Nida, Eugene A. 1949. *Morphology: The Descriptive Analysis of Words*. 2nd edition. Ann Arbor: University of Michigan Press.

Exercise 30 (Turkish) from Akmajian, Adrian, David P. Demers, and Robert M. Harnish. 1984. *Linguistics: An Introduction to Language and Communication*. Cambridge, MA: MIT Press.

Exercise 35 (Cebuano) from Pearson, Bruce L. 1997. New York: McGraw-Hill, Inc. Reproduced with permission of McGraw-Hill.

Exercise 39 (Cree) from Cowan, William, and Jaromira Rakusan. 1980. *Source Book for Linguistics*. Amsterdam: John Benjamins B.V.

File 5.0

FRANK & ERNEST: © Thaves/Dist. by Newspaper Enterprise Association, Inc.

File 6.0

Comic © KING FEATURES SYNDICATE

File 6.2

Portions of this file have been adapted from unpublished material by William Badecker and Thomas Ernst.

File 6.4

Small portions of this file are remnants of unpublished material by William Badecker and Thomas Ernst.

File 7.0

GET FUZZY: © Darby Conley/Dist. by United Feature Syndicate, Inc.

File 8.0

Cartoon by Mike Baldwin, available at www.CartoonStock.com.

File 8.1

List in (1) adapted from Lenneberg's characteristics in Aitchison, Jean. 1976. *The Articulate Mammal: An Introduction to Psycholinguistics.* London: Hutchison and Co.

File 8.2

Chart in (2) adapted from Lenneberg, Eric H. 1967. *Biological Foundations of Language.* New York: John Wiley & Sons, Inc.

File 8.3

Chart in (2) adapted from Lenneberg, Eric H. 1967. *Biological Foundations of Language.* New York: John Wiley & Sons, Inc.

File 9.0

Comic © HILARY B. PRICE. KING FEATURES SYNDICATE

File 9.1

Figure (1), "Map of the Human Cortex," by Carol Donner from "Specializations of the Human Brain" by Norman Geschwind. Copyright © September 1979 by Scientific American, Inc. All rights reserved.

File 9.8

Figures in Exercise 1 adapted from illustration by Carol Donner from "Specializations of the Human Brain" by Norman Geschwind. Copyright © September, 1979 by Scientific American, Inc. All rights reserved.

Exercise (8b) is from Avrutin, S. 2001. "Linguistics and agrammatism." *GLOT International* 5:3–11.

Exercises (8c) and (8d) are adapted from Gardner, H. 1975. *The shattered mind.* New York: Knopf.

File 10.0

FOR BETTER OR FOR WORSE © 2004 Lynn Johnston Productions. Dist. By Universal Press Syndicate. Reprinted with permission. All rights reserved.

File 10.1

Sections adapted from Zwicky, Ann D. "Styles." *Styles and Variables in English.* Timothy Shopen and Joseph M. Williams, eds. 1981. Cambridge, MA: Winthrop Publishers (Prentice-Hall).

File 10.2

Figure (1) © 2006, William Vicars, www.Lifeprint.com. Used with permission.

Figure (2) © 1979, W. H. Smith and L. Ting, *Shou neng sheng chyau (your hands can become a bridge).* Used with permission.

File 10.3
Figure (1) reproduced by permission of Gallaudet College Press, from Shroyer and Shroyer, *Signs across America* (1984), pp. 96, 97.
Figure (2) from Carver, Craig M. 1987. *American Regional Dialects*. Ann Arbor, MI: University of Michigan Press.

File 10.5
Figure in Exercise 11 reproduced by permission of Gallaudet College Press, from Shroyer, Edgar, and Susan Shroyer, *Signs across America* (1984), p. 3.

File 11.0
Comic © ZITS PARTNERSHIP. KING FEATURES SYNDICATE

File 12.0
NON SEQUITUR © 2004 Wiley Miller. Dist. By UNIVERSAL PRESS SYNDICATE. Reprinted with permission. All rights reserved.

File 12.2
Figure (3) adapted from Jeffers, Robert R., and Ilse Lehiste. 1979. *Principles and Methods for Historical Linguistics*. Cambridge, MA: MIT Press. All rights reserved.
Figure (4) adapted from descriptions in Gordon, Raymond G., Jr. (ed.). 2005. *Ethnologue: Languages of the World,* Fifteenth edition. Dallas, Tex.: SIL International. Online version: http://www.ethnologue.com/.

File 12.8
Figures in Exercise 17 from *Signing: How to Speak with Your Hands* by Elaine Costello. Copyright 1983 by Elaine Costello. Used by permission of Bantam Books, a division of Bantam Doubleday Dell Publishing Group, Inc.
Excerpts of Exercise 38 (Proto-Western Turkic) adapted from Columbus, Frederick. 1974. *Introductory Workbook in Historical Phonology.* 5th edition. Cambridge, MA: Slavica.

File 13.0
Cartoon by Gordon Gurvan, available at www.CartoonStock.com.

File 14.0
Marmaduke: © United Feature Syndicate, Inc.

File 14.2
Figure (1) reprinted with permission from Fromkin and Rodman, *An Introduction to Language,* 2nd edition (1978), p. 42.
Figure (2) reprinted with permission from Fromkin and Rodman, *An Introduction to Language,* 2nd edition (1978), p. 43.
Figure (3) reproduced by permission by © 2003 Nature Publishing Group, "Neuroperception: Facial expressions linked to monkey calls" by Asif A. Ghazanfar & Nikos K. Logothetis, et al. *Nature,* Vol. 423, pp. 937–938.
Additions to Section 14.2.2 are based on O'Grady W. et al., *Contemporary Linguistics: An Introduction,* 2nd ed., New York: St. Martin's Press, 1993, pp. 508–509.
Section 14.2.1 and parts of Section 14.2.2 are adapted from Fromkin, Victoria, and Robert Rodman. 1978. "The Birds and the Bees." *An Introduction to Language,* 2nd Edition. New York: Holt, Rinehart and Winston, 41–45.

File 15.0
Comic © HILARY B. PRICE. KING FEATURES SYNDICATE

Inside Back Cover
IPA chart reprinted by permission from International Phonetic Association (Department of Theoretical and Applied Linguistics, School of English, Aristotle University of Thessaloniki, Thessaloniki 54124, GREECE) http://www.arts.gla.ac.uk/IPA/IPA_chart_(C)2005.pdf

CHAPTER
1

Introduction

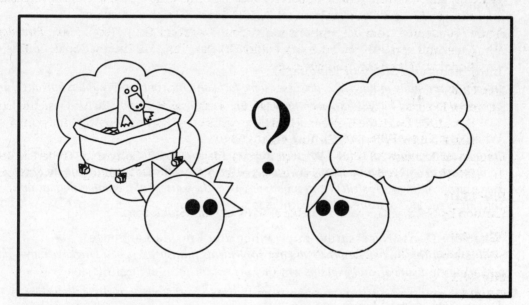

What Is Language?

Language touches every part of our lives: it gives words to our thoughts, voice to our ideas, and expression to our feelings. It is a rich and varied human ability—one that we can use effortlessly, that children seem to acquire automatically, and that linguists have found to be complex yet systematic and describable. This, language, will be the object of our study.

Contents

Introducing the Study of Language

1.1.1 Why Study Language?

Language makes us uniquely human. While many species have the capacity to communicate using sounds and gestures, and a few can even acquire certain aspects of human language, no other species is comparable to humans with respect to the creativity and complexity of the systems that humans use to express thoughts and to communicate. We can manipulate elements in our language to create complex thoughts, and we can understand words and sentences that we have never spoken or heard. This capacity is shared by hearing people and deaf people, and it emerges very early in the development of children, who acquire adult linguistic competence in an astonishingly short period of time. It is the human language faculty that makes this possible. Used as a probe into the human mind, language provides us with a unique window through which we can investigate a fundamental aspect of what it is to be human.

Language also reflects one's self-identity and is indispensable for social interactions in a society. We perform different roles at different times in different situations in society. Consciously or subconsciously, we speak differently depending on where we come from, whom we talk to, where the conversation is carried out, what purposes we have, etc. For example, southerners in America tend to speak with an accent different from, say, that of native New Yorkers; a conversation between two buddies would not be the same as a conversation between business associates; two lawyers in a café would speak differently than they would in a courtroom; to sound younger, a middle-aged person, being aware of linguistic change in progress, might imitate younger speakers; etc. All languages are variable, and they reflect our individual identity, as well as social and cultural aspects of a society.

Not only does studying language reveal something interesting about human society, but there are also many practical applications of the study of language that can have a significant effect on people's everyday lives. For example, studying languages allows us to develop better teaching tools for language instruction, design computers that can interact with humans using language, and more effectively treat people with speech and language disorders.

1.1.2 Some Surprising but True Things about Language

You have been speaking one or more languages for most of your life, and therefore you may think that you know most of what there is to know about language. However, you will likely find some of the following facts about language surprising.

(1) Grammar is actually a much more complex phenomenon than anything that could ever be taught in school, but nevertheless every human being masters the grammar of some language.

(2) There are languages that don't have words for *right* and *left* but use words for cardinal directions (like *north* and *west*) instead.

(3) Some aspects of language appear to be innate.

(4) There are more than 6,000 languages spoken in the world, but 90% of the population speaks only 10% of them.

(5) Turkish, among other languages, has a special verb tense used for gossip and hearsay.

(6) Most sentences that you hear and utter are novel; they have never been uttered before.

(7) No language is intrinsically easier or harder to learn than any other.

(8) Some languages structure sentences by putting the object first and the subject last.

(9) There are communities, such as the Al-Sayyid Bedouin tribe, in which all members of the community can use a signed language.

(10) There is nothing inherent about most words that gives them their meaning: any group of speech sounds could have any meaning.

(11) There are specific structures in your brain designed to process language.

(12) The language you speak affects whether or not you distinguish between certain sounds.

(13) Rules like "don't split infinitives" were invented by people in the eighteenth century who believed that English should be more like Latin.

(14) The same words in the same order don't always mean the same thing.

(15) No language is more or less logical than any other.

(16) Certain sounds that you could make with your mouth are never used as speech sounds in any language.

1.1.3 Some Common Misconceptions about Language

In addition to not knowing some of the facts in the list above, you may also hold beliefs about language that are not true. The following is a list of common misconceptions. It's understandable that people might have come to hold some of these beliefs, because they are often propagated in our society (and a few of them even have an element of truth to them); however, the scientific investigation of language has revealed them to be false.

(1) People who say *Nobody ain't done nothin'* aren't thinking logically.

(2) Swearing degrades a language.

(3) Many animals have languages much like human languages.

(4) Writing is more perfect than speech.

(5) The more time parents spend teaching their children English, the better their children will speak.

(6) You can almost always recognize someone's background by the way he talks.

(7) The rules in grammar textbooks are guidelines for correct language use and should be followed whenever possible.

(8) Women tend to talk more than men.

(9) There are "primitive" languages that cannot express complex ideas effectively.

(10) People from the East Coast talk nasally.

(11) Some people can pick up a language in a couple of weeks.

(12) It's easier to learn Chinese if your ancestry is Chinese.

(13) Native Americans all speak dialects of the same language.

(14) Every language has a way to mark verbs for the past tense.

(15) Correct spelling preserves a language.

(16) Nouns can be used to refer only to people, places, or things.

1.1.4 Underlying Themes of Linguistic Study

The two previous lists illustrate that there is much more to know about language than one knows merely by being a language user. Human language is an enormously complex phenomenon. The task of a linguist is to tease apart the patterns of various aspects of human language, thereby discovering the way that language works.

Below is a list of some very general principles of human language that will be explained and illustrated throughout this book. We present them here not because we expect you to see the full significance of each of these ideas all at once, but rather because they are underlying themes in much of the study of linguistics and will come up repeatedly throughout the book. During your studies, you may find it useful to refer to this list to see how these ideas interact with the topic that you are currently studying.

(1) Language is systematic in spite of its enormous complexity, and it can therefore be studied scientifically.

(2) Not only is language systematic, but it is systematic on many levels, from the system of individual sounds to the organization of entire discourses.

(3) These systematic rules allow us to express an infinite number of ideas in an infinite number of ways.

(4) Language varies systematically from person to person, region to region, and situation to situation. There is variation at every level of structure.

(5) Languages are diverse, often astonishingly so.

(6) Despite this diversity, there are a great many universal properties of languages. That is, there are characteristics shared by all languages as well as characteristics that no language has.

(7) Many properties of language are arbitrary, in the sense that they cannot be predicted from other properties or from general principles.

(8) Although a great many complex rules govern our speech, we are no more aware of them than we are of the principles that govern walking or picking up an object.

(9) Children acquire language without being taught; language acquisition is (at least partly) innate.

(10) All languages change over time, whether speakers desire change or not.

This book will introduce you to some of the properties of language and basic principles of linguistic research. We hope to lead you to examine your own beliefs and attitudes about language, to make you more aware of the diversity of language systems as well as their fundamental similarities, and to introduce you to some of the applications of linguistic investigation. The study of language and linguistics will not disappoint the challenge seekers, the scientific discovers, or those who are simply inquisitive.

What You Know When You Know a Language

1.2.1 Linguistic Competence and Linguistic Performance

As a speaker of English (or any other language that you may be a speaker of), you know a great deal about your language. Suppose, however, that someone were to ask you to put all of that knowledge into a textbook that would be used to teach English to others. You would soon find that although you know perfectly well how to speak English, you are not consciously aware of most of that knowledge.

If you think about it, we are really unaware of many things we do every day. For example, most people know how to walk and do so without thinking about it. Most of us can describe walking as well: we pick up one foot and put it in front of the other. However, there are many nuances and individual motor tasks involved in walking that we don't ever think about and that only a very small set of people (kinesiologists, for example) understand: for example, exactly how you shift your balance between steps, how speed affects your stride, and so on. You modulate these things all the time when you walk without thinking about them, and you probably don't know exactly how you do so. The same holds true for our knowledge of language: for the most part, it is hidden. Linguists are interested in this "hidden" knowledge, which they refer to as linguistic **competence.**

On the other hand, not all of your knowledge is hidden. People reveal some of their knowledge through their linguistic **performance**—the way that they produce and comprehend language. You can think of linguistic competence as a person's unseen potential to speak a language, and linguistic performance as the observable realization of that potential: our performance is what we do with our linguistic competence. Put another way, linguistic competence resides in your mind, and linguistic performance is revealed in your speech (though keep in mind that revealing it does not mean that we are conscious of how it works!).

Consider again the case of walking. If you are able to walk, you have that ability even when you are sitting down (and not actively using it). That ability is your walking competence. When you stand up and walk across the room, that's walking performance. Now, suppose that you stumble or trip on occasion. That doesn't mean that you aren't a competent walker: you still have your walking competence, but your performance was impaired. Maybe you just weren't paying attention to where you were going, or the ground was uneven, or it was dark and you couldn't see clearly; perhaps there was nothing unusual at all but for some reason you simply lost your balance. In the same way, you may make **performance errors** when you use language, such as being unable to remember a word, mispronouncing something, or jumbling the words in a sentence. Sometimes there is an apparent reason (you may be tired or distracted, or you may be trying to produce a particularly difficult utterance), and other times there is no apparent reason at all: you simply make a mistake. Nonetheless, your linguistic competence remains unimpaired.

Since competence can't be observed directly, linguists must use linguistic performance as a basis for making hypotheses and drawing conclusions about what linguistic competence must be like. However, in most cases they try to disregard imperfections in performance (the inevitable speech errors, incomplete utterances, and so on) and focus on consistent patterns in their study of linguistic competence.

1.2.2   The Speech Communication Chain

When you use language, you use it to communicate an idea from your mind to the mind of someone else. Of course, language is not the only way to do this: there are many types of communication systems (e.g., honking a horn on a car, drawing a picture, screaming wordlessly at the top of your lungs, using Semaphore flags, etc.). The key elements in any communication system (as outlined by Claude Shannon and Warren Weaver in 1949) are an information source, a transmitter, a signal, a receiver, and a destination. When we use language as our communication system, one person acts as the information source and the transmitter, sending a signal to another person, who acts as a receiver and the destination. In order to act either as a source and transmitter or as a receiver and destination, you must have a great deal of information stored as part of your linguistic competence: that is, you know a lot about your language. The diagram in (1) outlines the **communication chain** as it relates to language.

(1) The speech communication chain

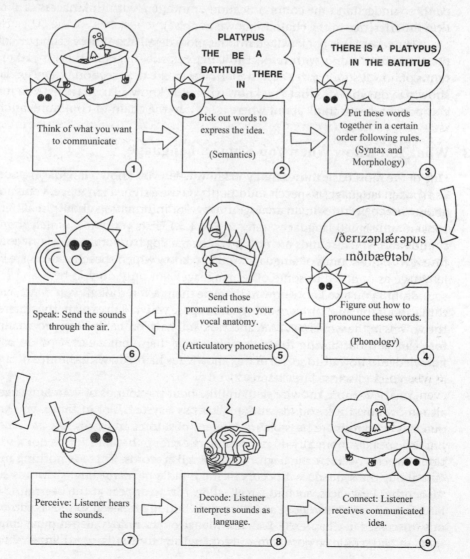

Basically, this illustration shows that for an idea to be communicated from one person to another, numerous steps must be carried out. First, an idea of something to be communicated must be thought of; this is not necessarily a function of language per se, but it is certainly the first step in communicating any idea. Once the idea is there, you have to put the idea into words that have meaning and that are expressed in a particular way. These steps form the backbone of much traditional linguistic research. Note that these first four steps represent the "information source" in the communication system. Step 5 is the transmitter; in this step, the speaker actually gives physical expression to the mental representation of the message to be conveyed. Step 6 is the signal itself; here, the sounds generated by the speaker travel through the air to the listener. The listener acts as the receiver in step 7, sensing the sound signal and sending it to her own brain. Step 8 in the diagram is particularly simplified, in that it really encompasses steps 2–4 in reverse. That is, to "decode" the signal that has been perceived, the listener must **also** use mental knowledge of phonology, morphology, syntax, and semantics (concepts that will be further explained below) to interpret the sounds as language. Finally, step 9 represents the destination: the listener has received the communicated idea.

Note that in the diagram, the listener in fact receives exactly the same idea that the listener tried to convey. This, as you have probably experienced, is an idealization: all of these steps take place in a particular context that can either add to the ability of all participants to understand the communication or interfere with the success of the communication (interference in the chain is known as **noise**).

The rest of this book will go into far more detail about how each part of this communication chain works with respect to language; the diagram in (1) is rather simplified in terms of how it summarizes each step. However, the next section briefly explains each part, showing you what it is that you know when you know a language. As you read about each component, try to think about where it fits into the chain-of-communication diagram.

1.2.3   What You Know When You Know a Language

One of the most basic things that you know when you know a language, assuming that you use spoken language, is speech sounds. (If you use a signed language, you know a great deal about speech gestures in an analogous way. For information about the difference between spoken and signed languages, refer to File 1.5.) First, you know which sounds are speech sounds and which sounds are not; if you hear a dog bark or a door slam, you will not confuse it with the sounds of language. You also know which speech sounds are sounds of your language as opposed to some other language. Not only do you hear and recognize these sounds, but you also know how to produce them, even though you may have never had to think about the mechanics of doing so. Suppose you had to explain the differences between the vowels in the words *bat, beat,* and *boot.* You have probably been producing these sounds for years without having to think twice about them, but clearly you do have competent knowledge of how to do so. All of this knowledge has to do with the area of language known as **phonetics** (discussed in Chapter 2).

You have more knowledge than this about the sounds of your language, though: you also know how these sounds work together as a system. For instance, you know which sequences of sounds are possible in different positions. In words like *pterodactyl* or *Ptolemy,* English speakers normally do not pronounce the /p/ because /pt/ is not a sound combination that can occur at the beginning of English words. There is nothing inherently difficult about the sequence; it occurs in the middle of many English words such as *captive.* Also, other languages, such as Greek, allow /pt/ to appear at the beginning of words. This language-specific knowledge about the distribution of speech sounds is part of your **phonology** (discussed in Chapter 3). Your knowledge of phonology also allows you to identify that *spaff* and *blig* could be possible words of English but that *fsap* and *libg* could not. Additionally, phonology allows you to recognize sounds and words spoken by different speakers, even though most people do not pronounce them in exactly the same way.

For the most part, speech consists of a continuous stream of sound; there are few if any pauses between words. Speakers of a language, however, have little trouble breaking this stream of sound down into words. For example, an English speaker can easily analyze the sequence in (2a) as containing the individual words in (2b); this is what we must do all the time when we hear speech.

(2) a. thedogisplayinginthebackyard
    b. the dog is playing in the back yard

You also know how to break individual words down into smaller parts that have a particular meaning or function (how many parts are there in the word *unbelievability?*), and how to create words by combining these smaller parts. That is, you can both produce and comprehend newly composed words that you haven't heard before, for example, *ungiraffelike.* You also know which combinations are words and which ones aren't: *baker* is a word, but **erbake* is not. *Nicely* is a word, but **bookly* is not. (The * is used to mark that something is ungrammatical—in this case, it indicates that these are not possible words of English.) Your knowledge of these and other facts about word formation comprises your knowledge of **morphology** (discussed in Chapter 4).

You also know a great deal about your language's **syntax** (discussed in Chapter 5): how words combine to form phrases and sentences. This fact is evidenced by your ability to construct and use sentences that you have never heard before, and to recognize when a sentence is well formed.

(3) a. I will pick the package up at eight o'clock.
    b. At eight o'clock, I will pick up the package.
    c. * Package up pick at o'clock will the eight I.
    d. * I will picks the package up at eight o'clock.

In (3) above, sentences (a) and (b) are both **grammatical,** even though they have different word orders. On the other hand, (c) and (d) are **ungrammatical:** (c) is nonsense, and (d) violates a rule of verb agreement. It's possible that you have thought at some point about the fact that verbs must agree with their subject and that random orderings of words don't make sentences. But what about the sentences in (4)?

(4) a. I have a cup of pebbles.
    b. * I have a cup of pebble.
    c. * I have a cup of gravels.
    d. I have a cup of gravel.

Your internal knowledge of English syntax gives you the information necessary to know that (4a) and (4d) are grammatical while (4b) and (4c) are not, although it is likely (especially if you are a native speaker of English) that you have never thought explicitly about this fact.

Part of your linguistic competence also has to do with your ability to determine the meaning of sentences. When you interpret meanings, you are appealing to your knowledge of **semantics** (discussed in Chapter 6). When you hear a word, such as *platypus* or *green* or *dawdle,* you have some idea of a meaning that goes with that word. You know when two words mean the same thing—e.g., *sofa* and *couch*—and when one word has two (or more) meanings—e.g., *duck.* You also know how words combine together to form larger meanings out of the meanings of their parts.

(5) a. The green duck dawdled around the cactus.
     b. The duck dawdled around the green cactus.

(6) a. The platypus ducked under the sofa.
     b. !The sofa ducked under the platypus.

The two sentences in (5) each contain the same words, yet they have different meanings. The same is true of the pair of sentences in (6), but here the second seems semantically anomalous (this anomaly is indicated by the exclamation point), because part of your knowledge of English semantics includes the fact that a sofa is not the sort of thing that is able to duck.

Your understanding of the meaning of sentences also involves an understanding of how the context of those utterances influences their meaning. Suppose that, while you are sitting in class, your instructor says to you, "Can you close the door?" Taken quite literally, you have been asked a yes-no question about your door-closing abilities, but you would probably not even think of interpreting the question in that way; instead, you would understand it as a request to close the door. Your ability to use context in order to interpret an utterance's meaning is part of your knowledge of **pragmatics** (discussed in Chapter 7). Your knowledge of pragmatics also helps you figure out which utterances are appropriate or inappropriate in any given situation.

Each of these elements of language—phonetics, phonology, morphology, syntax, semantics, and pragmatics—is part of your linguistic competence and is therefore an integral part of the way that you communicate linguistically. These are the things that you know when you say that you know a language.

1.2.4 How You Store Your Linguistic Competence

Now that we have considered some of the kinds of knowledge involved in knowing a language, it is appropriate to give some thought to the question of **where** this knowledge is. This is a difficult question to answer, because although people produce language all the time, it isn't tangible. If I make a hammer, then afterwards I can pick it up and show it to you. I cannot, on the other hand, show you a sentence that I have created. That sentence exists only in my mind (and, after I have uttered it, it exists in your mind as well). Although I may write it down, the string of letters that appear on the page is only a visual representation of the sentence: they aren't the sentence itself (a concept that will be further elaborated on in File 1.3). So, then, where does language exist? It exists only in the minds of its speakers. In some ways, you can think of your linguistic competence not only as your ability to use language but also as being language itself!

There are two parts of this knowledge. The first part is called the **lexicon**, which consists of the collection of all the words that you know: what functions they serve, what they refer to, how they are pronounced, and how they are related to other words.

The second part of your knowledge is made up of all the **rules** you know about your language, which are stored in the form of a **mental grammar**. A word of caution may be in order here: The words *grammar* and *rule* mean something rather different to a linguist than they do to most people in casual conversation (for more on the common understanding of the term *grammar,* see File 1.3). For a linguist, a **grammar** is a language system. It is the set of all the elements and rules (about phonetics, phonology, morphology, syntax, and semantics) that make up a language. A rule, then, is just a statement of some pattern that occurs in language. The rules in your mental grammar help you to produce well-formed utterances and to interpret the utterances of others.

The rules in your mental grammar are not necessarily the sorts of rules that are written down or taught anywhere; rather, they are the rules in your head that tell you how to combine sounds and words to create well-formed utterances. In the first years of their lives, children work very hard to acquire these rules by paying attention to the language being used around them. All humans (excepting those with the most severe cases of mental retardation or significant brain damage) are capable of acquiring the language that they are exposed to as children, and they will do so naturally, without being taught. In Chapter 8, you will find considerably more information about **language acquisition** and how children go about constructing mental grammars of their native languages.

Although everyone becomes a fully competent speaker of their native language, with a complete mental grammar that allows them to communicate effectively with other people in their speech community, the details of mental grammars do vary among speakers. Variation occurs among speakers from different language and dialect groups and even among speakers of the same dialect. No two speakers have exactly the same mental grammar, and therefore no two speakers will find exactly the same set of sentences well formed. However, our mental grammars are similar enough that we disagree very seldom and are able to understand one another most of the time. More information about **language variation** can be found in Chapter 10.

In sum, your linguistic competence is stored in a lexicon and a mental grammar, which you access in order to both produce and comprehend utterances. Though you may not be actively aware of all of the linguistic knowledge that you have stored away, you nonetheless use it all the time; it forms the backbone of the communication chain.

1.2.5 Uncovering and Describing What You Know

One of the jobs of linguists is to figure out all of the hidden knowledge that speakers have stored in their mental grammars: to objectively describe speakers' performance of language and, from their performance, deduce the rules that form the speakers' competence. This process is analogous to a situation in which you see nurses, doctors, ambulances, people in wheelchairs, and so on, coming from a building you are unfamiliar with and hypothesize that the building is a hospital. You use the evidence you can see in order to draw conclusions about the internal structure of what you cannot see.

In order to discover the internal structure of language—that is, the lexicon and the mental rules—linguists must first describe language as it is used. This involves listening to spoken language, finding generalizations, and then making descriptive statements about what has been observed. For example, a linguist describing English might make the observations in (7).

(7) Examples of descriptive observations about English
   a. The vowel sound in the word *suit* is produced with rounded lips.
   b. The sequence of sounds [bɪt] is a possible word in English.
   c. The plural of many nouns is the same as the singular but with an *–s* at the end.
   d. Adjectives come before the nouns they describe: *green shirt,* not **shirt green.*
   e. The words *sofa* and *couch* mean roughly the same thing.

These generalizations and others like them describe what English speakers do. By analyzing such collections of generalizations, known as **descriptive grammars**, linguists can begin to determine what the mental grammar must consist of. That is, a mental grammar contains all of the rules that an individual speaker uses to produce and comprehend utterances, while a descriptive grammar contains the rules that someone has deduced based on observing speakers' linguistic performance.

What You Don't (Necessarily) Know When You Know a Language

1.3.1 What Language Is and Is Not

In File 1.2, we talked about what it means to know a language: you have a lot of mental knowledge, or competence, about how to use speech to communicate ideas. We said that a linguist's job is to describe language use and deduce competence from performance. But there are a number of other ideas that are often so closely linked with language use that they sometimes cloud the issue of what you know when you know a language.

Two of those ideas—writing and prescriptive grammar—are discussed in this file. Our goal is to help you see that, while these topics are both interesting and related to knowledge of language, they are not part of "what you know" when you know a language—and therefore not part of the study of linguistics or the topic of this book.

1.3.2 Language Is Not Writing

Speaking and signing, on the one hand, and writing, on the other, are two different forms of communication that serve different functions, both related to language. Neither is superior or inferior to the other. Language, as we saw in File 1.2, consists of the knowledge in speakers' minds of a lexicon and a mental grammar. In order to reveal her knowledge of language, a speaker must perform it in some way. While speech and writing are both expressions of linguistic competence, speech is a more immediate manifestation of language. One of the basic assumptions of modern linguistics (as opposed to linguistics before the beginning of the twentieth century), therefore, is that speech—whether it be spoken orally or signed manually (see File 1.5)—is primary and writing is secondary.

Writing is the representation of language in a physical medium different from sound. Spoken language encodes thought into a physically transmittable form, while writing, in turn, encodes spoken language into a physically preservable form. Writing is a three-stage process: thinking of an idea, expressing it using mental grammar, and then transferring it to written form. All units of writing, whether letters or characters, are based on units of speech, i.e., words, syllables, or sounds (more on writing systems will be discussed in File 13.4): so, for a thought to be written, it must first be processed by the speech system and then put into writing. Because linguists are attempting to use performed language to understand mental language competence, it makes sense to get as close to the original as possible. When linguists study language, therefore, they take the spoken language as their best source of data and their object of description (except in instances of languages like Latin, for which there are no longer any speakers, so that the written form **is** the closest they can come). We will be concerned with spoken language throughout this book. Though ideally we would prefer to give our examples in audio form, for practical reasons we will instead use conventional written transcriptions of the audio form, with the understanding that it is always the spoken form that is intended (the conventions used for such transcription are given in Chapter 2).

You may think that, with the advent of so many "instant messaging" programs, writing can now be just as immediate as speech. But it is important to remember that even though the written form can be **nearly** immediate these days, there is still an extra step between conceptualizing the message you want to communicate and the reception of that idea, if you have to write it—regardless of whether you do so longhand or type it into a computer.

There are several reasons for maintaining that speech is primary/basic and writing is secondary. The most important ones are the following:

a. Archeological evidence indicates that writing is a later historical development than spoken language. Writing was first used in Sumer (modern-day Iraq) about 6,000 years ago. The Sumerians probably devised written characters for the purpose of maintaining inventories of livestock and merchandise. As far as physical and cultural anthropologists can tell, spoken language, on the other hand, has probably been used by humans for hundreds of thousands of years.

b. Writing does not exist everywhere that spoken language does. This may seem hard to imagine in our highly literate society. But the fact is that there are still many communities in the world where a written form of language is not used. According to SIL International, among the approximately 6,900 languages in the world today, a rough estimate of 3,900 languages (or 57%) are unwritten (*Ethnologue,* 2004). Note that this estimate says nothing about literacy percentages, fluency, or whether the system is indigenous to the language users; it says only whether a writing system exists. Even in cultures that use a writing system there are individuals who fail to learn the written form of their language. In fact, the majority of human beings are illiterate, though quite capable of spoken communication. However, no naturally occurring society uses only a written language with no spoken form.

c. Writing must be taught, whereas spoken language is acquired automatically. All children (except children with serious learning disabilities) naturally learn to speak the language of the community in which they are brought up. They acquire the basics of their native language before they enter school, and even if they never attend school, they become fully competent speakers. Spoken languages can even develop spontaneously in societies where a full language does not exist (see File 8.1). Writing systems vary in complexity, but regardless of their level of sophistication, they must all be taught explicitly.

d. Neurolinguistic evidence (studies of the brain "in action" during language use) demonstrates that the processing and production of written language is overlaid on the spoken language centers in the brain. Spoken language involves several distinct areas of the brain; writing uses these areas and others as well.

e. Writing can be edited before it is shared with others in most cases, while speech is usually much more spontaneous. This is further evidence of the immediacy of speech as a communication signal, compared to the delayed nature of writing.

Despite all of this evidence, however, there is a widely held misconception that writing is more perfect than speech. To many people, writing somehow seems more correct and more stable, whereas speech can be careless, corrupted, and susceptible to change. Some people even go so far as to identify 'language' with writing and to regard speech as a secondary form of language used imperfectly to approximate the ideals of the written language. What gives rise to the misconception that writing is more perfect than speech? There are several reasons for this misconception, many of which ironically are the same as the ones listed above for why writing is secondary to speech from the point of view of a linguist:

a. Writing can be edited, and so the product of writing is usually more aptly worded and better organized, containing fewer errors, hesitations, and incomplete sentences than are found in speech. This "perfection of writing" can be explained by the fact that writing is the result of deliberation, correction, and revision, while speech is the spontaneous and simultaneous formulation of ideas; writing is therefore less subject to the constraint of time than speech is.

b. Writing must be taught and is therefore intimately associated with education and educated speech. Since the speech of the educated is more often than not perceived as the "standard language," writing is associated indirectly with the varieties of language that people tend to view as "correct." (However, the association of writing with the standard variety is not a necessary one, as evidenced by the attempts of writers to transcribe faithfully the speech of their characters. Mark Twain's *Huckleberry Finn* and John Steinbeck's *Of Mice and Men* contain examples of this.)

c. Writing is more physically stable than spoken language, which consists of nothing more than sound waves traveling through the air and is therefore ephemeral and transient. Writing tends to last, because of its physical medium (characters on some surface), and can be preserved for a very long time. Spelling, especially in the modern era, does not seem to vary from individual to individual or from place to place as easily as pronunciation does. Thus writing has the appearance of being more stable. (Of course, spelling does vary, as exemplified by the differences between the British and the American ways of spelling *gray* and words with the suffixes *-ize* and *-ization.* The British spellings are *grey* and *-ise* and *-isation.*) Writing could also change if it were made to follow changes in speech. The fact that people at various times try to carry out spelling reforms amply illustrates this possibility. (For instance, *through* is sometimes spelled as *thru,* or *night* as *nite,* to reflect their modern pronunciations more closely.)

While these characteristics of writing may make it seem more polished and permanent, they clearly do not make it a more primary indication of a speaker's linguistic competence. It is for these reasons that linguists focus on spoken language as the object of their study and why we say that writing is not necessarily something you know when you know a language.

1.3.3   Language Is Not Prescriptive Grammar

We said in File 1.2 that part of knowing a language is having a system of rules about phonetics, phonology, morphology, syntax, and semantics that tell you how to combine sounds and words into well-formed, meaningful utterances that someone else can understand. Linguists try to discover these mental rules by observing, describing, and analyzing speech as it is performed.

There are, therefore, several uses of the term *grammar* that need to be clarified. Linguists recognize three distinct things called "grammar": (a) what the linguist is actually trying to understand—the mental grammar, (b) the linguist's description of the rules of a language as it is spoken—the descriptive grammar, and (c) the socially embedded notion of the "correct" or "proper" ways to use a language—the so-called **prescriptive grammar.**

The first two have been described in detail in the previous file and will be explored in the rest of this book. Because the third meaning of *grammar* is the most common in everyday speech, however, it is worth taking the time to first explain what prescriptive grammar really is and then to show why it is not part of what you know when you know a language.

To most people, the word *grammar* means the sort of thing they learned in English class or in other language classes, when they were taught about subjects and predicates and parts of speech and were told not to dangle participles or strand prepositions, etc. (1) shows some examples of this sort of grammar.

(1) Examples of prescriptive rules
   a. Never end a sentence with a preposition.
       NO: Where do you come <u>from</u>?
       YES: <u>From</u> where do you come?

b. Never split an infinitive.
   NO: . . . <u>to</u> boldly <u>go</u> where no one has gone before
   YES: . . . <u>to go</u> boldly where no one has gone before

c. Never use double negatives.
   NO: I <u>don't</u> have <u>nothing</u>.
   YES: I <u>don't</u> have <u>anything</u>. I have <u>nothing</u>.

As you can see from these examples, prescriptive rules tell you how to speak or write, according to someone's idea of what is "good" or "bad." This is why it is called "prescriptive": it is being **prescribed** like a doctor's prescription of a medicine. Of course, there is nothing inherently good or bad about any use of language; prescriptive rules serve only to mold your spoken and written English to some norm.

Notice that the prescriptive rules make a value judgment about the correctness of an utterance and try to enforce a usage that conforms to one formal norm. On the other hand, the rules in a mental grammar are, of course, what actually exist as the foundation of language and **cannot**—by definition—be incorrect. Descriptive rules, meanwhile, simply describe what happens in spoken language and therefore accept the patterns a speaker uses, without judgment. Descriptive rules allow for different varieties of a language; they don't ignore a construction simply because some prescriptive grammarian doesn't like it, and they don't describe what a speaker "should" or "shouldn't" do—just what they actually do. For example, some descriptive rules of English would include those in (2).

(2) Examples of descriptive rules
    a. Some English speakers end a sentence with a preposition.
    b. Some English speakers split infinitives.
    c. Some English speakers use double negatives for negation.

These "rules" are simply descriptions of what happens, not guidelines for what ought to happen. They are a much closer picture of a speaker's competence than prescriptive rules. After all, just like writing, prescriptive rules must be taught, and they often conflict with what native speakers of a language (who are clearly competent language users) really do.

If prescriptive rules are not based on actual use, how did they arise? Many of these rules were actually invented by someone. During the seventeenth and eighteenth centuries, scholars became preoccupied with the art, ideas, and language of ancient Greece and Rome. The classical period was regarded as a golden age and Latin as the perfect language. The notion that Latin was somehow better or purer than contemporary languages was strengthened by the fact that Latin was by then strictly a written language and had long ceased to undergo the changes natural to spoken language. One such scholar was John Dryden, whose preoccupation with Latin led him to write: "I am often put to a stand in considering whether what I write be the idiom of the tongue . . . and have no other way to clear my doubts but by translating my English into Latin" (Scott, 1808: 235). For many writers of the seventeenth and eighteenth centuries, the rules of Latin became, whenever remotely feasible, the rules of English. The rules in (1a) and (1b) above are results of this phenomenon.

Speakers of English have been freely ending sentences with prepositions since the beginning of the Middle English period (about 1100 c.e.). There are even some instances of this construction in Old English. Speakers who attempt to avoid it often sound stilted and stuffy. The fact that ending sentences with prepositions is perfectly natural in English did not stop John Dryden from forbidding it because he found it to be non-Latin. His rule has been with us ever since (see (1a)).

Also since the early Middle English period, English has had a two-word infinitive composed of *to* plus an uninflected verb (e.g., *to write*). English speakers have always been able to split this two-word infinitive by inserting words (usually adverbs) between *to* and the verb (e.g., *to quickly write*). There have been periods in English literary history when splitting infinitives was very fashionable. However, eighteenth-century grammarians noticed that Latin infinitives were never split. Of course, it was impossible to split a Latin infinitive because it was a single word (e.g., *describere*, 'to write down'). But that fact did not prevent the early grammarians from formulating another prescriptive rule of English grammar (see (1b)).

The double negative rule (see (1c)) has a different source. In Old and Middle English, double and triple negatives were common, and even quadruple negatives existed, usually for the purposes of emphasis. The sentence in (3) from Old English illustrates this. It contains two negative words and was entirely grammatical.

(3) The use of the double negative in Old English

ne	bið	ðær	**nænig**	ealo	gebrowen	mid	Estum
not	*is*	*there*	*not-any*	*ale*	*brewed*	*among*	*Estonians*

'No ale is brewed among the Estonians.'

By Shakespeare's time, however, the double negative was rarely used by educated speakers, although it was still common in many dialects. In 1762, Bishop Robert Lowth attempted to argue against the double negative by invoking rules of logic: "Two negatives in English destroy one another or are equivalent to an affirmative" (204). Of course, language and formal logic are different systems, and there are many languages (e.g., Russian and Spanish) in which multiple negation is required in some cases for grammaticality. Certainly no one misunderstands the English-speaking child or adult who says, "I don't want none." But Lowth ignored the fact that it is **usage,** not logic, that must determine the descriptive rules of a grammar—and his prescriptive rule has persisted in classrooms and "grammar" books today.

You may think it somewhat surprising that rules that do not reflect actual language use should survive. One of the most important reasons that they do survive is that such rules are associated with a particular social status. Nonstandard dialects are still frowned upon by many groups and can inhibit one's progress in society: for example, trying to get a job while speaking with a nonstandard, stigmatized dialect may be difficult. The existence of prescriptive rules allows a speaker of a nonstandard dialect to explicitly learn the rules of the standard and employ them in appropriate social circumstances (for more discussion of language varieties, see Chapter 10; for a discussion of language and identity, see File 13.1). Therefore, prescriptive rules are used as an aid in social identity marking and mobility. This does not mean, however, that these judgments about dialects are linguistically valid. The idea that one dialect of a language is intrinsically better than another is simply false; from a strictly linguistic point of view all dialects are equally good and equally valid. To look down on nonstandard dialects is to exercise a form of social and linguistic prejudice. It is for these reasons that linguists do not make use of prescriptive grammars, but rather only descriptive grammars, which are used as a tool for discovering mental grammars.

FILE **1.4**

Design Features of Language

1.4.1 How to Identify Language When We Come across It

Before we discuss language in any more depth, it will be useful if we first have some idea of what people mean when they say "language." So far, we have talked a great deal about language. We have discussed what language comprises (that is, what you know when you know a language), and we have talked briefly about how language is stored in the brain. We have also explored various commonly held ideas about language that are both true and untrue. We haven't yet defined language, though.

Defining language turns out to be a remarkably difficult task: nobody seems to be able to find a definition of *language* that captures its fundamental nature. But if we cannot define *language,* then we must come up with some other solution: we still must have some way to identify language when we come across it. One possibility is to identify the features that something must have in order to be a language. Linguist Charles Hockett designed one such list that identifies descriptive characteristics of language.

While his list does not tell us the fundamental nature of language, it does tell us a great deal about what language is like and what we can do with it. Hockett's list of descriptive characteristics of language is known as the **design features** of language. It has been modified over the years, but a standard version is provided below. While there are many kinds of communication systems in the world, all of which follow some form of the communication chain outlined in File 1.2, only communication systems that display these nine design features can be called a "language."

The order in which the design features are presented is also significant: the features proceed from most universal to most particular. All communication systems have the first three design features, while human language alone has the final two.

1.4.2 Mode of Communication

The very nature of a system of communication is that messages must be sent and received. The term **mode of communication** refers to the means by which these messages are transmitted and received. For most human languages, speakers transmit messages using their voices; however, a significant number of human languages are also transmitted gesturally: via hand, arm, head, and face movement. Both are viable systems for transmitting the complex sorts of messages required of language. Language **modality** will be discussed in considerably more depth in File 1.5.

1.4.3 Semanticity

The second aspect of language that is universal across all communication systems is **semanticity.** Semanticity is the property requiring that all signals in a communication system have a meaning or a function. It is critically important to successful linguistic communication that, for example, if your friend says to you "pizza," you both have a similar idea of what he

17

is talking about. It would never do if your friend said "pizza" and you thought, "There's that word with the /p/ sound again. Wonder why he keeps saying it all the time."

Even if you hear a word you don't know, you nevertheless assume that it must have some meaning. For example, if you heard the sentence *There was a large amount of frass in the tubes with the fruit flies,* you might not recognize the word *frass*,[1] but you would not assume that it was meaningless. If words or sentences didn't have meaning, then, of course, we would be unable to use them to communicate!

1.4.4 Pragmatic Function

Communication systems must also have a **pragmatic function:** that is, they must serve some useful purpose. Examples of functions that human language has include helping individuals to stay alive, influencing others' behavior, and finding out more about the world. For example, a person who needs food might use language to ask for more mashed potatoes; more dramatically, a person trapped in a burning house might stay alive by calling for help. A politician communicates certain messages to try to influence people's voting behavior. People ask questions all the time in order to learn the information they need to get through their days.

Sometimes people may question the usefulness of a certain communicative act, for example, in the case of gossip. However, even gossip fulfills a useful purpose in societies. It helps us to understand our social environment and plays an important role in social bonding and establishing social relationships. The same is true of set phrases such as "nice weather today" or the question "Hey, what's up?" that receives the so-called answer "What's up?" These set phrases serve to acknowledge the other person or initiate a conversation, which are both necessary tasks for the maintenance of our social structure.

1.4.5 Interchangeability

Interchangeability denotes the ability of individuals to both transmit and receive messages. Each individual human can both produce messages (by speaking or signing) and comprehend the messages of others (by listening or watching).

1.4.6 Cultural Transmission

Another important feature of human language is that there are aspects of language that we can acquire only through communicative interaction with other users of the system. This aspect of language is referred to as **cultural transmission.** Even though children's ability to learn language seems to be innate, they must still learn all of the specific signals of their language through interaction with other speakers. In fact, a child who is never spoken to will not learn language (see File 8.1). Furthermore, children will learn the language(s) or dialect(s) that other people use to interact with them. Thus, children of Russian parents will learn Russian if their parents interact with them in Russian, but they will learn English if their parents interact with them in English. Our genetic or hereditary background in and of itself has no influence whatsoever on the language that we acquire as children.

1.4.7 Arbitrariness

a. Arbitrariness in Language. It is generally recognized that the words of a language represent a connection between a group of sounds or signs, which give the word its **form,**

---

[1]The word *frass* means 'the debris or excrement of insects.'

and a **meaning,** which the sound can be said to represent. The combination of a form and a meaning is called a **linguistic sign**: Form + Meaning = Linguistic Sign. For example, one word for 'the inner core of a peach' is represented in English by the sounds [pɪt][2] (which we spell as <pit>), occurring in that order to give the sound (i.e., the form) that we make when we say the word *pit*.

(1) [pɪt] + = the word *pit*

An important fact about linguistic signs is that, typically in language, the connection between form and meaning is **arbitrary.** The term *arbitrary* here refers to the fact that the meaning is not in any way predictable from the form; nor is the form dictated by the meaning. Note that there **is** a relationship between form and meaning: you don't have a different meaning in mind every time that you say [pɪt]. (If there were no relationship at all, then you could say [pɪt] one time and mean 'licorice' and another time and mean 'courageous' and another time and mean 'mandolin.' Clearly language doesn't work this way.) That relationship is an arbitrary **convention** of English, which tells you that a certain group of sounds goes with a particular meaning.

The opposite of arbitrariness in this sense is nonarbitrariness, and the most extreme examples of nonarbitrary form-meaning connections are said to be **iconic** (or "picture-like"). Iconic forms represent their meanings directly. For linguistic signs in general, however, the connection between form and meaning is not a matter of logic or reason; nor is it derivable from laws of nature.

b. Evidence for Arbitrariness. The fact that the inner core of a peach may be called a *stone* or even a *seed* as well as a *pit* points to arbitrariness. If the connection between the form and the meaning here were nonarbitrary (because the form determined the meaning, or vice versa), there would not be many possible forms to express a single simple meaning. Likewise, there is nothing intrinsic in the combination of the sounds represented by [pɪt] that suggests the meaning 'inner core of a peach'; the same sequence of sounds can represent 'a large, deep hole in the ground.'

Evidence of arbitrariness in language can also be seen in cross-linguistic comparisons. For instance, words with the same meaning usually have different forms in different languages, and similar forms usually express different meanings, as the examples in (2) illustrate. If there were an inherent, nonarbitrary connection between forms and meanings, with the meaning being determined by the form or vice versa, then such cross-linguistic differences should not occur. There would be universally correct and recognized forms for each meaning.

---

[2]Symbols in square brackets "[ ]" are transcriptions in the International Phonetic Alphabet (or IPA), which is a standardized set of symbols devised to indicate pronunciations for all languages. For more details, see Chapter 2 ("Phonetics") and the inside back cover of the book (a guide to the sounds of English and the IPA Chart).

(2) Arbitrary form-meaning connections of linguistic signs as seen cross-linguistically

Form	Meaning	Language
[wɑtɹ] [o] [vasɐ] [søy]	'water'	English French German Cantonese
[li]	proper name, 'Lee' 'bed' 'borrowed/lent' 'this'	English French German Cantonese

Finally, arbitrariness in language is shown in names for inventions and new products. For example, new cars come on the market every year. Many of them are very similar to each other: they all have four tires, a cabin that can seat some number of people, an engine, and so on. Yet despite their similarities, makes of car have startlingly different names. Some of them are very long words; others are quite short; they begin with all kinds of different sounds. A person naming a new car will certainly think of a sequence of sounds that she likes, but she won't be constrained in any way by the nature of the car or the nature of the sounds themselves—only by her own arbitrary preferences.

c. Onomatopoeia. It is clear that arbitrariness is the norm in language, at least as far as the basic relationship between the form of a word and its meaning is concerned. At the same time, though, it turns out that there are some nonarbitrary aspects to language. In the vocabulary of all languages, a small degree of nonarbitrariness involves items whose forms are largely determined by their meanings. Most notable and obvious are the so-called onomatopoetic (or onomatopoeic) words, i.e., words that are imitative of natural sounds or have meanings that are associated with such sounds of nature.

Examples of onomatopoetic words in English include noise-words such as [bɑʊwɑʊ] for *bow-wow* for the noise a dog makes, [splæt] for *splat* for the sound of a rotten tomato hitting a wall, [br̩bl̩] for *burble,* a verb for the making of a rushing noise by running water derived from the sound itself, and so on. In all of these words, the match-up between the form of the word and the meaning of the word is very close: the meaning is very strongly suggested by the sound of the word itself.

But even in such onomatopoetic words, an argument for arbitrariness is to be found. While the form is *largely* determined by the meaning, the form is not an exact copy of the natural noise; roosters, for instance, do not actually say [kɑkədudl̩du]—English speakers have just arbitrarily **conventionalized** this noise in that form. Different languages can have different onomatopoetic words for the same sounds. For example, a rooster says [kɑkədudl̩du] in English but [kukuku] in Mandarin Chinese, even though (presumably) roosters sound the same in China as in America. If there were an inherent and determined connection between the meaning and the form of onomatopoetic words, we would expect the same meaning to be represented by the same sounds in different languages. The table in (3), which lists eleven natural sounds represented by onomatopoetic words in nine languages, shows that this is not the case.

(3) Cross-linguistic examples of onomatopoeia (see Chapter 2 and the IPA chart in the back of the book for aid on IPA symbols)

Sound	English	German	French	Spanish	Hebrew	Hindi	Mandarin	Japanese	Greek
Dog barking	[baʊwaʊ]	[vaʊvaʊ]	[wafwaf]	[waʊwaʊ]	[haʊhaʊ]	[bʰɔbʰɔ]	[waŋwaŋ]	[waɴwaɴ]	[ɣavɣav]
Rooster crowing	[kakə-dudḷdu]	[kikəʁiki]	[kokoʁiko]	[kikiriki] or [kokoriko]	[kukuɣikuku]	[kukukuku]	[kukuku]	[kokekokkoː]	[kikiriku]
Cat meowing	[miaʊ]	[miaʊ]	[miaʊ]	[miaʊ]	[miaʊ]	[miaʊ]	[miaʊ]	[niaɯ]	[ɲaʊ]
Cow lowing	[muː]	[mu]	[mɵ]	[mu]	[mu]	[mũː]	[mər]	[mo:mo:]	[muː]
Sheep bleating	[baː]	[mɛ]	[bɛː]	[be]	[mɛ̃ː]	[mɛ̃ːmɛ̃ː]	[miɛ]	[me:me:]	[be:]
Bird chirping	[twittwit]	[pippip]	[kɥikɥi]	[piopio] or [pippip]	[tˤuitˤtˤuitˤ]	[tʃiːtʃiː]	[tɕitɕi]	[tʃitʃi]	[tsiutsiu]
Bomb exploding	[bum]	[bum] or [vʁum]	[bum]	[bum]	[bum]	[bʰɔɖaːm]	[bɔ̃ŋ]	[baɴ]	[bum]
Laughing	[haha]	[haha]	[haha]	[xaxa]	[haha]	[haha]	[xaxa]	[haha]	[xaxa]
Sneezing	[atʃu]	[hatʃi]	[atʃum]	[atʃu]	[aptʃi]	[atʃũː]	[aʔtʰi]	[hakɯʃoɴ]	[apsu]
Something juicy hitting a hard surface	[splæt]	[platʃ]	[flɔk]	—	—	—	[pyaʔ]	[guʃaʔ]	[plats]
Clock	[tɪktɑk]	[tɪktak]	[tiktak]	[tɪktak]	[tɪktak]	[tiktik]	[tiʔtaʔ]	[tʃɪktakɯ]	[tiktak]

d. Sound Symbolism. A second apparent counterexample to arbitrariness is **sound symbolism**: certain sounds occur in words not by virtue of being directly imitative of some sound but rather simply by being evocative of a particular meaning. That is, these words more abstractly suggest some physical characteristics by the way they sound. For instance, in many languages, words for 'small' and small objects or words that have smallness as part of their meaning often contain the vowel [i], which occurs in English *teeny* 'extra small,' *petite* and *wee* 'small,' and dialectal *leetle* for 'little,' in Greek *mikros* 'small,' in Spanish diminutive nouns (i.e., those with the meaning 'little X') such as *perrito* 'little dog,' where *-ito* is a suffix indicating 'little,' and so on. Such universal sound symbolism—with the sound [i] suggesting 'smallness'—seems to be motivated because [i] is a high-pitched vowel and so more like the high-pitched sounds given off by small objects. Thus the use of [i] in 'small' words creates a situation in which an aspect of the form, i.e., the occurrence of [i], is determined by an aspect of the meaning, i.e., 'smallness.' We may thus characterize the appearance of [i] in such words as somewhat iconic—the "small" vowel [i] is an icon for the meaning 'small(ness).'

e. Nonarbitrary Aspects of Language. All in all, the above examples show that nonarbitrariness or iconicity have at best a somewhat marginal place in language. At the same time, though, it cannot be denied that they do play a role in language and moreover that speakers are aware of their potential effects. Poets often manipulate onomatopoeia and sound symbolism in order to achieve the right phonic impression in their poetry. For example, Alfred Tennyson in his poem *The Princess* utilized nasal consonants to mimic the noise made by the bees he refers to:

(4) The *m*oa*n* of doves i*n* i*mmm*e*m*orial el*m*s
And *m*ur*m*uring of i*nn*u*m*erable bees (v. 11.206–7)

1.4.8 Discreteness

Consider the English sentence *He is fast.* It is not one unified sign that always appears exactly as it is. Rather, it is composed of many discrete units: the independent words *he, is,* and *fast.* These words, in turn, are composed of even smaller discrete units: the individual sounds [h], [i], [ɪ], [z], [f], [æ], [s], and [t]. (Refer to the back page of the book for help with these symbols.) The property of language (among other communication systems) that allows us to combine together discrete units in order to create larger communicative units is called **discreteness.**

Every language has a limited number of sounds, between roughly 10 and 100. English, for example, has about 50 sounds. The sounds themselves are for the most part meaningless—the sound [f] in *fish* or *foot* does not have any meaning by itself—but we can combine a very small number of sounds to create a very large number of meaningful words. For example, we can combine the sounds [f], [u] and [l] to create the word *fool;* [t], [u], and [l] to create the word *tool;* [p], [u], and [l] to create the word *pool;* [k], [u], and [l] to create the word *cool,* etc. We can then reorder the sounds in [kul] *cool* to get [klu] *clue* or [luk] *Luke.* The fact that we can generate a large number of meaningful elements (words) from few meaningless units (sounds) is called **duality of patterning.**

We can further combine words into phrases and sentences. Thus, from a selection of only 100 or fewer units, we can create a very large number of meanings (an infinite number, actually). A communication system that can put pieces together in different ways has much more expressive capability than one that does not. If we were limited to only 100 or so meanings, then language would not be nearly so useful as it turns out to be!

1.4.9 Displacement

Displacement is the ability of a language to communicate about things, actions, ideas, and so on, that are not present in space or time while speakers are communicating. We can, for example, talk about the color red when we are not actually seeing it, or we can talk about a friend who lives in another state when he is not with us. We can talk about a class we had last year or the class we will take next year.

1.4.10 Productivity

Earlier we described discreteness: the capacity of a communication system to combine discrete pieces in various ways in order to have more meanings than do the discrete pieces alone. There is another feature—this one also unique to human language—that piggybacks on discreteness, and that is productivity. **Productivity** refers to a language's capacity for novel messages to be built up out of discrete units. Note how productivity differs from discreteness. For a communication system to have discreteness, the only requirement is that there be recombinable units; however, it would be possible for there to be a fixed set of ways in which these units could combine. Indeed, some communication systems do work that way. Because language is productive, though, there is no fixed set of ways in which units can combine.

The productivity of human language grants people the ability to produce and understand any number of novel sentences that they may have never heard before, thereby expressing propositions that may never have been expressed before. In fact, in any language it is possible to produce an infinite number of sentences, so most of the sentences that you hear are ones you have never heard before. For example, you probably have never read the following sentence before, but you can still understand what it means: *Funky potato farmers dissolve glass.* You understand what it means even though you may not know why the potato farmers are funky or how glass can be dissolved, and even though you have never seen or heard it before.

We are able to construct and understand novel forms such as this one based on the fact that the discrete units of language (sounds, morphemes, and words) can be put together in regular, systematic, and rule-governed ways. The way that you come to understand the meaning of a new sentence is by applying what you know about rules for how words combine in your language to the words themselves.

Rules at all levels of linguistic structure are productive. That is, they allow creation of new forms, tell which new forms are allowed, and tell how they can be used. The rules of language, rather than limiting us, in fact are what grant us the ability to communicate about such a broad range of ideas.

1.4.11 What the Design Features Tell Us, and What They Don't Tell Us

All languages exhibit all nine design features: any communication system that does not is therefore not a language. Furthermore, as far as we know, only human communication systems display all nine design features. (File 14.1 discusses Hockett's design features with respect to animal communication.)

Clearly, any language will exhibit all nine of the design features discussed in this file. Does this necessarily mean that any communication system that exhibits all nine features should be considered a language? There are so-called "formal" languages such as the formal logic that may be used to write mathematical proofs and various computer languages which display all of the design features but which seem to differ in some critical ways from languages such as English, Spanish, Mandarin, and Apache. (No child could ever acquire a computer language like C++ as his native language!) Furthermore, a number of people engage in constructing languages as a hobby: designing languages that imitate human language. There are many reasons that people might choose to construct languages. These reasons range from designing a language to be used in some sort of fictional universe such as the novels of J. R. R. Tolkien or the television series *Star Trek,* on the one hand, to designing a language to facilitate international communication, which was the goal of the designers of the language Esperanto, on the other. Other people work on constructing artificial languages just for fun.

Do we want to make a distinction between languages such as English, Spanish, Mandarin, and Apache, on the one hand, and Esperanto, Elvish, and Klingon, on the other? And how should we classify "formal" languages? Although many of these questions are still open to debate and research, we will make the following distinctions for the purposes of this book. The object of our linguistic study here will be confined to what we call **natural languages**, those languages that have evolved naturally in a speech community. The lexicon and grammar of a natural language have developed through generations of native speakers of that language. A **constructed language**, on the other hand, is one that has been specifically invented by a human and that may or may not imitate all the properties of a natural language. Some constructed languages have the potential to become a natural language, if they are learned by native speakers and adopted by a speech community; this is the case with Modern Hebrew, which was reconstructed from ancient Hebrew and then adopted by a particular community. The distinction between constructed languages and formal languages is that formal languages are not the sort of system that a child can acquire naturally. Because we want to confine most of our discussion to natural languages, we will often shorten the term to "language" in the rest of the book. You should keep in mind, however, that other types of language do, in fact, exist. Thus the design features help us distinguish language from other nonlinguistic communication systems, but we need more criteria to ensure that a system is a natural language and not either an artificial language or a man-made code.

Language Modality

1.5.1 Auditory-Vocal and Visual-Gestural Languages

In File 1.2, we saw that language is a cognitive system. That is, language exists only insofar as that people who use a particular language have a set of grammatical rules for it in their heads. However, it isn't good enough to say merely that we have grammatical rules in our heads. In order for language to be a system of communication—a system that allows us to share our thoughts with others—we have to be able to use it to transmit messages. We must be able to use those grammatical rules to produce something in the world: something that others are able to perceive and interpret. Therefore, every language must have a mode of communication or a **modality.** A language's modality tells us two things: how it is produced, and how it is perceived.

It is likely that most of the languages with which you are familiar are **auditory-vocal** (sometimes also called **aural-oral**), which means that they are perceived via hearing and produced via speech. Auditory-vocal languages include English, Russian, Portuguese, Navajo, Korean, and Swahili, among many others. Auditory-vocal languages may also be referred to as **spoken languages.** Throughout history there has been a commonly held— though entirely incorrect—view that language is inseparable from speech. This misconception is often spread when the terms *speech* and *language* are used interchangeably. From this confusion, people may conclude that only spoken languages may properly be described as being languages. Nothing could be further from the truth.

There are also human languages that are **visual-gestural.** In fact, there are hundreds of visual-gestural languages in use all over the world. Visual-gestural languages, which may also be referred to as **signed languages**, are those which are perceived visually and produced via hand and arm movements, facial expressions, and head movements.[1] Although visual-gestural languages are often used by individuals who are deaf or hard of hearing, many hearing people also communicate via one of the world's many signed languages. And, as with spoken languages, signed languages may be acquired in childhood as a person's first language or much later, either through instruction in school or via immersion in a culture that uses a particular signed language.

---

[1]Auditory-vocal and visual-gestural languages represent the two most predominant modes of communication for human language. There are, however, some less commonly used language modalities. For example, individuals who are deaf-blind may use a tactile-gestural modality. That is, they use their hands to feel another person's signing. Within a particular signed language, there may be certain conventions or modifications to signs when they are being interpreted tactilely, creating a different dialect of the signed language for use among the visually impaired. When two individuals, each of whom is both deaf and blind and communicates in this way, have a conversation, the entire conversation will take place using the tactile-gestural modality. But this alteration in modality does not represent a new type of language. Thus we may say that signed languages have a primary modality which is visual-gestural and a secondary modality which is tactile-gestural.

With the exception of their modality, signed languages are similar to spoken languages in every way. (See File 1.2, "What You Know When You Know a Language.") Sign languages are made up of words which can be put together in sentences according to particular grammatical rules. In fact, every kind of linguistic analysis that may be performed on spoken languages may also be performed on signed languages. Examples of linguistic phenomena from various signed languages will be presented throughout the rest of *Language Files*.

1.5.2 Some Common Misconceptions about Visual-Gestural Languages

Unfortunately, there is a large amount of misinformation that has been spread about the nature of visual-gestural languages. Few if any people believe all of these misconceptions—indeed some of the misconceptions contradict one another—but each is repeated often enough to bear mentioning here.

a. Signed Language vs. Manual Codes. There is a myth that rather than being languages in their own right, signed languages instead derive from spoken languages. According to this myth, one would expect that deaf signers in America would have a signed language that was structurally identical to English while deaf signers in Japan would have a signed language that was structurally similar to Japanese and so on. In other words, this myth suggests that signed languages are merely codes for the languages spoken in the surrounding area.

Codes and languages are radically different kinds of systems in several ways. A **code** is an artificially constructed system for representing a natural language; it has no structure of its own but instead borrows its structure from the natural language that it represents. Morse code is a well-known example of a code. Signed languages, on the other hand, evolve naturally and independently of spoken languages. They are structurally distinct from each other and from spoken languages. Note, in addition, that codes never have native speakers (people who learn them as children as their primary form of communication) because they are artificial systems. Languages, of course, do have native speakers. Signed languages are learned natively by both hearing and deaf people all over the world.

A strong piece of evidence that sign languages do not derive from the surrounding spoken language is that British Sign Language and American Sign Language are unrelated; someone who is fluent in only one of these languages cannot understand a person using the other. This is true despite the fact that speakers of American English and British English can generally understand each other quite well.

It is worth noting that manual codes for spoken languages do exist. These codes use certain gestures to represent letters, morphemes, or words of a spoken language and follow the grammar of that spoken language. For example, to communicate the concept 'indivisible' in American Sign Language (ASL) requires only one gesture, as seen in (1b), whereas a manual code for English, Signed Exact English II (SEE II) requires three separate gestures, as seen in (1a), because of the way that it mirrors English morphology.

(1) The meaning 'indivisible' represented in two manual systems
    a. SEE II: 'indivisible'   b. American Sign Language: INDIVISIBLE

in-   divide   -ible

The differences between the two systems shown in example (1) address morphemes (parts of words), but there are also differences in word order, since the word order for versions of signed English mirror those of English, while ASL has its own rules for word order.

An indication that signed codes are unnatural is the striking difference between manually coded English and a natural language in the rate of transmission of information. These rates can be measured by rendering the same proposition into different languages or codes and measuring the time it takes for someone to produce the proposition in each language or code. A comparison of these rates showed an average seconds-per-proposition rate of 1.5 for both English and American Sign Language, a signed language used by the deaf in the United States and Canada, whereas SEE II, a manual code, scored at a distant 2.8. This suggests that true language, be it spoken or signed, is a much more efficient means of communicating than signed codes.

Both manual codes and signed languages have been used for communication with and among deaf individuals. However, because codes are merely based on natural languages rather than being languages themselves, they do not share many of the properties of language that linguists study, so they will generally be ignored in this book.

b. Signed Language vs. Pantomime. There is a second belief which is entirely counter to the argument that signed languages are manual codes, but which is equally incorrect. This second myth states that signed languages don't consist of words at all but rather involve signers using their hands to draw pictures in the air or to act out what they are talking about. There are two misconceptions here masquerading as one.

The first misconception is that sign languages do not have any internal structure. In fact, sign languages are governed by the same sorts of phonological, morphological, and syntactic rules that govern spoken languages.

The second misconception is that the words in a signed language are completely iconic. Were this the case, one would expect that it would not be necessary to learn sign languages at all; we would be innately able to understand them because every word would clearly show its meaning. Like spoken languages, however, the forms of words in signed language are predominantly arbitrary in their relationship to meaning (see File 1.4). The sound sequence /hugar/ means 'to play' in Spanish and 'he lives' in Hebrew and has no meaning at all in English. Similarly, there is a gesture (2) which means 'possible' in American Sign Language (ASL) and 'weigh' in Finnish Sign Language. There is no obvious reason why the ideas of 'possible' and 'weigh' should be represented in the same way; furthermore, if you look at the form of this sign, there is no particular reason that this gesture should or shouldn't be associated with either of these meanings. They are merely arbitrary conventions of the language users: one convention for one linguistic community, and a different convention for the other.

(2) POSSIBLE (ASL) and WEIGH (Finnish SL)

 (repeat movement)

From *Signing: How to Speak with Your Hands* by Elaine Costello. Copyright 1983 by Elaine Costello. Used by permission of Bantam Books, a division of Bantam Doubleday Dell Publishing Group, Inc., p. 196.

This point is made more explicit when we consider the signs for 'possible' in a different Language. In Taiwan Sign Language, the sign for 'possible' is made entirely with one hand: first the pinky touches the chin, and then a bent hand touches one side of the chest and then the other. As you can see, this is nothing like the sign for 'possible' in ASL!

There are signs in any given sign language that appear to have a certain degree of iconicity. For example, (3) shows the ASL sign for KNOW. The form in (3a) is the version generally shown in dictionaries and taught in classrooms. Notice how the speaker's hand touches his forehead, where one may think of thought occurring. However, this iconicity does not extend to regular use of the sign by the signing community; the form in (3b) is a common pronunciation of KNOW in which the hand instead touches the cheek. (Just as with spoken languages, signed languages are often pronounced slightly differently in casual conversation.)

(3) a. KNOW (indexical form)   b. KNOW (casual pronunciation)

© 2006, William Vicars, www.Lifeprint.com. Used with permission.

The key point here is that the way that the sign is modified makes the sign less iconic and more arbitrary. In fact, there is a general trend across signs in signed languages that, while they may be somewhat iconic when introduced into the language, over time they change to become more arbitrary.

In any event, were sign language about drawing pictures or pantomime, then signers would have their communication restricted to concrete objects and events. In reality, signed languages can convey abstract concepts as well. Displacement is every bit as available to signers as to those who use a spoken language.

c. Universality of Signed Languages. A third myth, which is related to the myth that signed languages are pantomime, is that there is only one signed language that is used by deaf speakers all over the world. One might expect a certain degree of universality in pantomime; after all, pantomime must be iconic. Signed languages, however, are arbitrary. There are many distinct sign languages, and they are not mutually intelligible.

In fact, there are more than 150 documented sign languages, each of which is as distinct from every other as are the various spoken languages that you may have heard of. Two individuals who knew two different sign languages would have as much trouble communicating with one another as you would have communicating with someone who spoke a language that you did not speak.

1.5.3 Who Uses Signed Languages?

Signed languages are used all over the world. Wherever there is a sizable community of deaf individuals, there is a sign language in use. In some cases, when deaf children are born to deaf parents, the children learn a sign language from their parents. More often, when a deaf child is born to hearing parents who do not sign, the child may learn a signed language at an institution such as a school for the deaf.

Interestingly, there have been multiple times throughout history when the deaf population has composed such a large percentage of some community's overall population that the entire community—both hearing and deaf individuals—have used a sign language to communicate. One such case was the northern part of Martha's Vineyard Island during the eighteenth and early nineteenth centuries: although English was used as well, everyone in the community signed, regardless of whether they were deaf or had deaf family members. Hearing individuals would at times have conversations with one another in Martha's Vineyard Sign Language even if there were no deaf individuals present—the signed language was that pervasive in the community. (The sign language that they used was one which was spoken only on Martha's Vineyard Island; since that time, that language has been completely lost; see File 11.6 for more information about language death.) Something similar is going on today in the Al Sayyid Bedouin tribe in Israel: again, such a large portion of the community is deaf that many hearing individuals sign fluently as well, even if they do not have deaf family members. In fact, the ability to sign fluently is considered a kind of status symbol among the hearing individuals. So a person need not be deaf in order to be a signer.

Furthermore, just because a person has a hearing loss does not mean that that person will necessarily choose to communicate using a signed language. In the United States, the Deaf community (notice the capital <D>) comprises individuals who are deaf or hard of hearing and who further identify themselves as Deaf, subscribe to a particular Deaf culture with its own values and customs, and use ASL to communicate. These individuals take pride in their language and in being Deaf, just as people from many other cultural backgrounds feel pride for their own languages and cultures. However, there are numerous other deaf individuals who do not associate themselves with Deaf culture, instead communicating in some other way, for example, by reading lips. There is no outside compulsion for deaf individuals to become signers or members of the Deaf community, and whether they do or don't will be determined by diverse and complicated social and practical factors.

Thus, while signed languages are by and large associated with deaf people, it is neither the case that only deaf individuals sign nor the case that deaf individuals must sign. Rather, both auditory-vocal and visual-gestural modalities are viable options for human language, and the choice between them will depend in any given circumstance on both physical and social parameters.

1.5.4 Representing Signs in a Two-Dimensional Format

There is a point worth making here that is not about signed languages per se but rather about the way that we present the signs themselves. Of course, a sign cannot be written straightforwardly using the Roman alphabet (the characters that English is written in and that you are reading right now) because these characters represent sounds: an irrelevant property for signed languages. We therefore adopt the convention that you have already seen above of using capitalized letters spelling out an English word to represent the sign for that word. For example, we might say that the sign for 'dog' is DOG.

Sometimes, however, it is not sufficient merely to tell the meaning of a sign. Often it will also be necessary to specify the form of a sign: the way that it is produced. There are three kinds of images used throughout this book to accomplish that task: photographs of signers, drawings of people producing signs, and drawings that show only the hands (but not the signer). Each of these types of illustration is useful in a different way and highlights a different aspect of the sign being illustrated. However, none of them completely captures the way that a sign is produced in three-dimensional space and in real time. Thus, while the images are a useful guide to various linguistic properties of the signs being discussed, they cannot be taken to be a completely reliable guide for how to produce the signs.

1.5.5 The Importance of Studying Different Modalities

Often certain linguistic principles exhibit themselves differently in signed languages than they do in spoken languages, but they are there! With the exception of the physical principles of how the languages are articulated and perceived, both visual-gestural and auditory-vocal languages behave in the same way. This similarity says something remarkable about the nature of human language and its universality. On the other hand, the fact that the physical principles of how spoken and signed languages are articulated and perceived differ allows us to investigate which aspects of language are universal and which are modality specific.

For example, studies of spoken language have found that pauses in continuous spontaneous speech have a certain minimum length, even when people are told to speak rapidly. To find out whether this is because of the need to breathe (and the minimum amount of time required to take a breath) or whether this is related to cognitive processes (maybe we pause because we haven't yet planned the next part of our utterance), we can study pause length in the production of signed languages compared with pause length in spoken languages (since breathing doesn't interfere with signing as it does with speech). Studies on pause duration in signed languages (e.g., Grosjean, 1979) showed that pauses do exist in signed languages but that they do not have a certain minimum length. So we can conclude that the minimum pause length in spoken languages is not a fact about linguistic processing ability.

The majority of examples in this book will come from spoken languages (most often English) only because we are assured that our readers are familiar with English. However, in terms of linguistic research more generally, considering languages with different modalities is of the utmost importance. By observing the sorts of effects that different modalities do and do not have on languages, we can come to learn profound truths about language itself.

FILE **1.6**

Practice

File 1.1—Introducing the Study of Language

Discussion Questions

1. Look at the list of "surprising but true" facts about language given in Section 1.1.2. Which items on the list were things you had heard before, and which were new to you? Which really were surprising? What about those items surprised you?

2. Look at the list of "common misconceptions" about language given in Section 1.1.3. How many of these beliefs are ones you have held at some point or have heard other people express? For each, how do you think that it came to be widely believed? What sort of evidence do you think linguists might have that causes them to say that each is false?

File 1.2—What You Know When You Know a Language

Exercises

3. Why do linguists tend to ignore speech performance errors in their study of linguistic competence?

4. Look back at the illustration at the beginning of this chapter. What is missing from this picture from a communication standpoint? What has to happen in order for the person on the right to receive the message "There is a platypus in the bathtub"?

5. Look back at the illustration at the beginning of this chapter. What sorts of noise might have interrupted the communication of the idea that there is a platypus in the bathtub?

6. Look back at the illustration at the beginning of this chapter. List at least three messages other than "There is a platypus in the bathtub" that the person on the left might be trying to convey, based on the illustration of the concept he has in his mind.

7. What are five descriptive rules of your native language?

Discussion Questions

8. Look back at the illustration at the beginning of this chapter. We have already talked about how language can be used to convey the message "There is a platypus in the bathtub." What other sorts of ways could this message be communicated? Do you think they would be less effective or more effective than using language? Explain.

30

9. We said with regard to the data given in example (4) in File 1.2 that it's more likely that you have thought explicitly about such examples if you are a non-native speaker of English than if you are a native speaker. Why would a non-native speaker be more likely to have thought about a particular grammatical rule of English than a native speaker? What does this tell you about the relationship between mental grammar and the sorts of grammars that we learn in school (either for a first language or for a second language)?

10. Suppose that you are chaperoning a group of kindergarten students on a trip to the zoo. One of these children walks up to you, pulls on your sleeve, and exclaims, "Look at all the **aminals**!" (Please note: the spelling of "aminal" is intended to indicate the child's pronunciation.) Has this child necessarily made a speech performance error? How do you know? If you do not know, how might you find out? What sort of additional evidence might you need? What would you do to test your hypothesis?

11. What might be some of the difficulties linguists encounter given that speech is used as the primary data for finding out the grammatical rules of a language?

File 1.3—What You Don't (Necessarily) Know When You Know a Language
Exercises

12. For each of the following statements:
    i. Identify which ones are prescriptive rules and which are descriptive.
    ii. Give an example of how the rule could be written the other way (that is, write the prescriptive rules as descriptive and the descriptive rules as prescriptive).

    a. *It's me* is ungrammatical; *it's I* is the correct way to express this idea.
    b. People who say *ain't* may suffer some negative social consequences, because many speakers of English associate *ain't* with lack of education.
    c. In casual styles of speaking, English speakers frequently end sentences with prepositions; ending sentences with prepositions is avoided in formal styles.
    d. *Between you and me* is correct; *between you and I* is ungrammatical.
    e. Some speakers of English accept the sentence *My mother loved.*

13. "I don't say *my car needs washed;* I say *my car needs to be washed.*"
    i. Try to give at least one descriptive grammatical rule that appears to be part of this speaker's linguistic competence as reflected by the above statement.
    ii. Given the rule(s) you gave in (i), what would the speaker be likely to say if she sees that the street is dirty, using the verb *seems* instead of *needs*? Do you think this is likely to be what she would actually say?

Discussion Questions

14. Some of the reasons that speech is primary and writing is secondary to linguists overlap with the reasons that some people think writing is primary. Explain how this could be, keeping in mind that linguists might have goals different from those of other members of society.

15. "E-mail writings and instant messaging can be equated with speech, because people often use contractions like *I'm, won't, isn't* or spellings like *c ya* or *where r u* that reflect the spoken form." Do you agree with this statement? Why or why not?

16. "Since speech is primary/basic and writing is secondary, it is not worthwhile to study writing in any way." Do you agree with this statement? Why or why not?

17. Give a prescriptive rule and a descriptive rule for the placement of adjectives with respect to the nouns they modify in English. Explain how each type of rule might change if, at some point in the future, younger speakers of English began saying things like *shirt green* or *idea brilliant*.

18. Would language change if we put effort into advocating prescriptive rules? Give evidence from what you have learned in this file, and/or from your personal experience, to support your view.

File 1.4—Design Features of Language

Exercises

19. You are given the following information: the word for ❁ is pronounced as [xua] (written as 花) in Mandarin Chinese. Can you fill out the formula below with the two elements "[xua]" and "❁"?

Form + Meaning = Linguistic Sign

_____ + _____ = the word 花

20. Consider this sign ⊘ meaning "no-smoking." The sign has two components: ⊘ meaning "no," and the picture of a cigarette meaning "cigarette/smoking." Does each of the components have an arbitrary or an iconic relation with its meaning? Please briefly explain your answer. Be sure to discuss each of the two elements separately.

21. Consider the compound words *blackboard* and *outfox* and the relationship of their meanings to the meanings of the words that make them up. In what ways do these compound words show a degree of nonarbitrariness in their form-meaning connection? Will this be true for all compound words? (*Hint:* Think about the color of objects we call *blackboards*.)

22. Onomatopoetic words often show a resistance to change in their pronunciation over time; for example, in earlier stages of English the word *cuckoo* had roughly the same pronunciation as it has now, and it failed to undergo a regular change in the pronunciation of vowels that would have made it sound roughly like *cowcow*; similarly, the word *babble* has had *b* sounds in it for over 2,000 years and did not undergo the sound shift characteristic of all the Germanic languages by which original *b* came to be pronounced as *p*. Can you suggest a reason for this resistance to change with respect to these (and similar) words?

23. In Chinese, expressions for moving from one city to another by way of yet another city must take the form 'from X pass-through Y to Z' and cannot be expressed as 'from X to Z pass-through Y'; this is illustrated in the examples below (the * indicates that a sentence is unacceptable).

a. ta   cong   Sanfanshi   jingguo   Zhijiage   dao   Niuyue
he   from   San Francisco   pass-through   Chicago   to   New York
'He went from San Francisco through Chicago to New York'

b. *ta cong Sanfanshi dao   New York jingguo   Zhijiage
he from San Francisco to   Niuyue   pass-through   Chicago
'He went from San Francisco to New York through Chicago'

How would you characterize the form-meaning relationship exhibited by these Chinese expressions? (*Hint:* Look at the ordering of places in the sentences.)

24. Traffic signals and signs are an example of a communication system that combines both arbitrary and nonarbitrary elements. Give examples of two traffic signs that are arbitrary and two that are nonarbitrary. Explain why you think that each of your examples is or is not arbitrary.

Discussion Questions

25. Try to imagine what would happen if we suddenly lost one of the design features of language. How would our communication change? What abilities would we lose? Discuss each of the following design features with respect to these questions.

    a. Displacement
    b. Interchangeability
    c. Productivity
    d. Pragmatic Function
    e. Discreteness

Activities

26. Productivity refers to our ability to produce and understand messages that have never been expressed before. To understand how frequently we deal with messages that have never been expressed before or that we have never heard or uttered before, go to <http://www.google.com>, and type in a number of sentences, using quotation marks around the sentence. For example, you could type in <"People can produce and understand messages that have never been expressed before."> Type in at least 10 sentences. For each sentence, write down the number of documents that Google found containing your sentence. How many of your sentences have not been expressed at least once on the World Wide Web? Try to use sentences of different lengths and compare the results. With short sentences, you may get more hits—but be sure to see whether you have in fact found the same sentence in each case, rather than just part of a sentence. Longer sentences, like the sentence you're reading right now, are less likely to result in as many hits.

27. One piece of evidence for sound symbolism is the often quite consistent responses that speakers of a language give when asked the relative meanings of pairs of nonsense words, where the only clue to work from is the sound (i.e., the form) of the words. For example, speakers of English typically judge the nonsense word *feeg* to refer to something smaller than the nonsense word *foag*. Try the following experiment on a friend and then compare your friend's responses with your own and compare your results with those of others in your class. Based on your experiment, which sounds do you think are suggestive of something heavy and which sounds are suggestive of something light?

    Pronounce the words below according to regular English spelling, and for each pair of words decide which member of the pair could refer to something heavy and which to something light.

a. lat—loat   e. fleen—feen
b. foon—feen   f. seeg—sleeg
c. mobe—meeb   g. poas—poat
d. toos—tace   h. toos—tood

File 1.5—Language Modality

Exercises

28. Over the years, many people have (mistakenly) associated signed languages with pantomime. Give three arguments that this association is unwarranted.

29. The following are illustrations of the signs for 'me' in both American Sign Language and Taiwan Sign Language. What about these signs is similar, and what is different? To what extent is each sign iconic, and to what extent is it arbitrary?

    a. ME in American Sign Language   b. ME in Taiwan Sign Language
       (The signer is touching his chest.)   (The signer is touching his nose.)

© 2006, William Vicars, www.LifePrint.com.   © 1979, W. H. Smith and L. Ting, *Shou neng sheng*
Used with permission.   *chyau* (*your hands can become a bridge*). Used with
                                             permission.

Discussion Questions

30. Consider again the list from File 1.2 of what you know when you know a language. Speculate about how each of the items in this list might be manifested in the same way for spoken and signed languages and how its manifestation might be different.

Activities

31. The following is the URL for the British Deaf Association's Sign Community: <http://www.signcommunity.org.uk/>. On this Web page, you have the opportunity to watch several short video clips of speakers of British Sign Language (using Flash Player software). When you move your mouse over the picture of a person, you will see him or her sign a single word, but if you click on the person, you will be able to see a longer clip. Watch one or two of these clips.
    i. Describe your impressions of watching these signers. In general terms, describe how they use their hands, their bodies, and their faces.
    ii. Based on what you have observed in the videos, discuss why static images (such as those we use in this book) are inadequate for describing the way that a signed language is produced.

iii. Do you understand any of what the signers are saying? If so, how do you know (what cues are you using)? If not, why do you not know?

Further Readings

Crystal, D. (1987). *The Cambridge encyclopedia of language.* Cambridge: Cambridge University Press.

Gordon, R. G. (Ed.). (2005). *Ethnologue: Languages of the world* (15th ed.). Dallas, TX: SIL International. Online version: http://www.ethnologue.com/.

Groce, N. E. (1985). *Everyone here spoke sign language: Hereditary deafness on Martha's Vineyard.* Cambridge, MA: Harvard University Press.

CHAPTER

2

========================

Phonetics

© HILARY B. PRICE. KING FEATURES SYNDICATE

FILE **2.0**

What Is Phonetics?

Phonetics is the study of the minimal units that make up language.[1] For spoken language, these are the sounds of speech—the consonants, vowels, melodies, and rhythms. As described in File 1.2, the process of communicating has several steps. Within this chain, there are three aspects to the study of speech sounds: **articulatory phonetics,** the study of the production of speech sounds; **acoustic phonetics,** the study of the transmission and the physical properties of speech sounds; and **auditory phonetics,** the study of the perception of speech sounds. In this chapter, we focus on the articulation and acoustics of speech sounds, as these branches are better understood than auditory phonetics at this point.

One of the most basic aspects of phonetics is figuring out which sounds are possible in speech. You can make a plethora of different noises with your mouth, but only a subset of these noises are used in human language. In this chapter, we will describe some of the features that characterize the speech sounds of the world's languages. We'll see that breaking speech sounds into their component parts reveals similarities among even the most exotic-seeming sounds.

Contents

---

[1]While phonetics is traditionally the study of the **sounds** of speech, the study of phonetics is not actually limited to spoken modalities (see File 1.5). Because *phonetics* has come to refer to the study of the minimal units that make up language in general, phoneticians may also study the minimal units (the phonetics) of signed languages (see File 2.7).

FILE **2.1**

Representing Speech Sounds

2.1.1 Studying Pronunciation

"You're not from around here, are you?" Sometimes you can tell by the way a person pronounces words that he or she speaks a dialect that is different from yours. For example, some people do not pronounce *pin* differently from *pen*. In some parts of Ohio the word *push* is pronounced with a vowel sound like the one in *who*. If you hear someone say *poosh* you can guess where they are from. Such pronunciation differences have been noted for many thousands of years. For example, there is a story in the Bible (Judges 12:4–6) about a group who used a password that their enemies could not pronounce correctly. The password they used was *shibboleth,* since their enemies couldn't say the <sh> sound. This group would kill anyone with the telltale pronounciation *sibboleth*. These illustrations show that pronunciation is a part of what we know when we know a language.

There are numerous ways of studying pronunciation in spoken language. In recent years, phoneticians have begun to employ some very sophisticated instrumental techniques to study spoken language.

In articulatory phonetics, we want to know the way in which speech sounds are produced—what parts of the mouth are used and in what sorts of configurations. To investigate these aspects of sound production, phoneticians have used **X-ray photography** and cinematography, among other techniques. More recently, to avoid methods that expose talkers to dangerous amounts of radiation, phoneticians have used point-tracking devices such as the X-ray microbeam or the electromagnetic articulograph to track the locations of small receptors glued onto the lips, tongue, and jaw. Articulatory phonetics is also done with **palatography** (see Section 2.2.6) to observe contact between the tongue and the roof of the mouth, and instruments to measure airflow and air pressure during speech.

In acoustic phonetics, we are more interested in the characteristics of the sounds produced by these articulations. To study acoustic phonetics, phoneticians use pictures of the sounds, using tools such as the **sound spectrograph.** These pictures help acoustic phoneticians explore the physical properites of sounds. These days, you can download sound editing and analysis software from the Web. Try searching for a "waveform editor" or an "audio spectrograph," or simply for "phonetics analysis software," and see if you find any free software to enable you to look at and edit speech sounds on your computer.

The third branch of phonetics, auditory phonetics, focuses on how humans process speech sounds: how we perceive pronunciation. While the fundamentals of perception can be explored by using fairly simple experimental methods that look at human responses to particular stimuli, advanced study of this field depends on more modern equipment such as magnetic resonance imaging (MRI) and computerized tomography (CT).

All of these techniques give us great insight into the details of phonetics. But the simplest and most basic method of phonetic analysis—**impressionistic phonetic transcription**—is still a vital tool for phoneticians. An example of phonetic transcription is the line "you say tomato, I say tomahto" from Ira Gershwin's lyrics to the song "Let's Call the Whole Thing Off." The word *tomato* is pronounced differently by different people, and we can symbolize two of the pronunciations as "tomato" and "tomahto" as Gershwin did. Or we could follow the pronunciation guide in *Webster's Third New International Dictionary* and write the two pronunciations as tə'mātō and tə'måto. Or we could refer to the *American Heritage Dictionary*, where the two pronunciations are written təmā'tō and təmä'tō. Confusing, isn't it? Yet we need to use phonetic transcription because the normal spelling of the word doesn't tell us enough about how it is pronounced by different people.

Spelling	Gershwin	Webster's	Amer. Heritage
tomato	tomato	tə'mātō	təmā'tō
tomato	tomahto	tə'måtō	təmä'tō

2.1.2   The "Right" Phonetic Alphabet

Did Gershwin write the two pronunciations of *tomato* correctly? Or does one of the dictionaries have the right way to symbolize the difference? It should be clear that there is no one "right" answer about how to write pronunciation in a phonetic transcription. The choices we make are largely arbitrary or influenced by typographical or historical considerations. However, it is absolutely crucial that both the reader and the author agree on the sound qualities that are assigned to the symbols in a phonetic alphabet. This is why almost all dictionaries give some guide to the pronunciation symbols where they list familiar words as examples of the sounds. For example, *father* is used to illustrate the sound intended by <å> in *Webster's* and by <ä> in the *American Heritage*. Whether the <a> has one mark or two is an arbitrary decision. This is fine, so long as we have a pronunciation guide.

If the goal of having a phonetic transcription system is to be able to unambiguously convey the important aspects of the pronunciation of a given set of sounds, using a written system of symbols, then such a system must have certain characteristics.

First, each symbol should represent one sound (or **phone**) only, and there should be only one symbol for each sound. The letter <c> violates this principle in English spelling because it represents two sounds (the [k] sound in *cat,* and the [s] sound in *cymbal,* and both the [k] and [s] in *cynic,* for example). Hence using a <c> does not unambiguously tell the reader which sound is intended.

Second, if two sounds can distinguish one word from another, they should be represented by different symbols. The letters <th> in English violate this principle because the difference between the <th> sounds in *thy* and *thigh* is not captured by using <th> for both words. That is, there is an important difference in pronunciation that is not captured with these letters.

Third, if two sounds are very similar and their difference arises only from the context they are in, we should be able to represent that similarity. For example, the [k] sounds in *keep* and *cool* are different from each other in that the exact places they are articulated are dependent on the following vowel. The [k] in *keep* is produced farther forward in the mouth than the [k] in *cool.* But if we are not interested in this variation, because it is reasonably predictable, we want to make sure that these [k] sounds are not written with different symbols in our transcription system.

Based on the criteria above, the English spelling system is not a good phonetic alphabet because:

- sometimes the same sound is spelled using different letters, such as the [i] sound in *sea, see, scene, receive, thief, amoeba, machine,* and *Aesop;*
- sometimes the same letters can stand for different sounds, as in *sign, pleasure,* and *resign,* or *charter* and *character,* or *father, all, about, apple, any,* and *age;*

- sometimes a single sound is spelled by a combination of letters, as in lo_ck_, _th_at, b_oo_k, b_oa_st, mount_ai_n, _sh_op, app_le_, or _s_pe_ci_al;
- sometimes a single letter represents a combination of sounds, as in e_x_it or _u_se;
- sometimes letters stand for no sound at all, as in _k_now, dou_b_t, thoug_h_, _i_sland, r_h_ubarb, or moos_e_.

A good phonetic transcription system is consistent and unambiguous because there is always a one-to-one correspondence between sounds and symbols. This is even true across languages, so that the symbols you will be learning can be used to transcribe the sounds of any language.

In this book we use the International Phonetic Alphabet (IPA for short). For our purposes this phonetic alphabet is the right one to use because it is applicable to all spoken human languages, rather than just English, and it has all of the properties of a "useful phonetic alphabet" discussed above. Here's what Anthony Burgess (the author of *A Clockwork Orange* and other novels) had to say about the IPA. "I propose that the reader become familiar with the International Phonetic Alphabet, or IPA. The reader may shudder in advance, but we have to do something about the accurate visualization of speech. I have the idealistic vision of phonetic symbols being added to our daily stock of alphabetic signs, so that I may tap the symbol /ə/ on my typewriter or word processor when I want to represent the sound that begins *apart* or ends *Asia*" (*A Mouthful of Air* [New York: Quill, 1992], pp. 26–27).

2.1.3 Types of Speech Sounds

In order to create a good phonetic transcription system, we need to know what types of sounds we are trying to transcribe. Phoneticians divide the speech stream into two main categories: **segments** and **suprasegmentals**. Segments are the discrete units of the speech stream and can be further subdivided into the categories consonants (File 2.2) and vowels (File 2.3). These sounds are transcribed easily using discrete symbols like [p] and [i]. Suprasegmentals, on the other hand, can be said to "ride on top of" segments in that they apply to entire strings of consonants and vowels—these are properties such as stress, tone, and intonation (File 2.5). These properties are somewhat more difficult to represent using an alphabetic-like transcription system, and there are many different ways they can be transcribed.

From an articulatory point of view, consonants and vowels are both made by positioning the vocal tract in a particular configuration. However, consonants are distinguished from vowels in that consonants are produced with a constriction somewhere in the vocal tract that impedes airflow, while vowels have at most only a slight narrowing and allow air to flow freely through the oral cavity. We can also distinguish consonants and vowels acoustically, based on the type of sounds they produce: consonants are much quieter than vowels and usually cannot function as the **nucleus** of a syllable. The syllable nucleus is the "heart" of the syllable, carrying suprasegmental information such as stress, loudness, and pitch, which vowels are much better suited to do than consonants.

Vowels in turn are often divided into two categories: **monophthongs** ([mɑnɔpθɑŋz]) and **diphthongs** ([dɪfθɑŋz] or [dɪpθɑŋz]). You can think of monophthongs as simple vowels, composed of a single configuration of the vocal tract, while diphthongs are complex vowels, composed of a sequence of two different configurations. We consider diphthongs to be "single" vowels, however, because the sequence of two configurations acts as the nucleus to a single syllable. To conceptualize this better, think of the two words *knives* and *naive*. The actual vowel sounds in these two words are essentially the same, but in *knives*, there is just one syllable nucleus (the diphthong [ɑɪ]), while in *naive*, there are two separate nuclei (the monophthong [ɑ] in the first syllable, followed by the monophthong [i] in the second syllable). The differences between monophthongs and diphthongs will be discussed in more detail in File 2.3.

2.1.4 Phonetic Symbols for English

This section lists the IPA symbols for English segments that we will be using in this book. Phonetic symbols are written in square brackets, [ ], to distinguish them from letters or words written in ordinary spelling. It is important to remember that these symbols are not the same as letters of English. Rather, they represent the sounds of language. The following table gives the phonetic symbols for the sound inventory of Standard American English, and the example words make use of Standard American English pronunciations. (Other sounds and symbols will be introduced in File 2.4.)

Symbol	Sample Words	Name of Symbol
Consonants:		
[p]	pit, tip, spit, hiccough, appear	
[b]	ball, globe, amble, brick, bubble	
[t]	tag, pat, stick, pterodactyl, stuffed	
[d]	dip, card, drop, loved, batted	
[k]	kit, scoot, character, critique, exceed	
[g]	guard, bag, finger, designate, Pittsburgh	
[ʔ]	uh-oh, hatrack, Batman	glottal stop
[f]	foot, laugh, philosophy, coffee, carafe	
[v]	vest, dove, gravel, anvil, average	
[θ]	through, wrath, thistle, ether, teeth	theta
[ð]	the, their, mother, either, teethe	eth, [εð]
[s]	soap, psychology, packs, descent, peace, excruciating	
[z]	zip, roads, kisses, Xerox, design	
[ʃ]	shy, mission, nation, glacial, sure	esh, [εʃ]
[ʒ]	measure, vision, azure, casualty, decision	yogh, [joʊg] or ezh, [εʒ]
[h]	who, hat, rehash, hole, whole	
[tʃ]	choke, match, feature, constituent	
[dʒ]	judge, George, Jell-O, region, residual	
[m]	moose, lamb, smack, amnesty, ample	
[n]	nap, design, snow, know, mnemonic	
[ŋ]	lung, think, finger, singer, ankle	engma or eng
[l]	leaf, feel, Lloyd, mild, applaud	
[ɹ]	reef, fear, Harris, prune, carp	
[ɾ]	writer, butter, udder, clutter, cuter	flap
[w]	with, swim, mowing, queen, twilight	
[ʍ]	which, where, what, whale, why (for those dialects in which *witch* and *which* do not sound the same)	voiceless 'w'
[j]	you, beautiful, feud, use, yell	lower-case 'j'

Symbol	Sample Words	Name of Symbol
Syllabic Consonants:		
[m̩]	poss<u>um</u>, chas<u>m</u>, Ad<u>am</u>, bott<u>om</u>less	syllabic 'm'
[n̩]	but<u>ton</u>, chick<u>en</u>, less<u>on</u>, kitt<u>en</u>ish	syllabic 'n'
[l̩]	litt<u>le</u>, sing<u>le</u>, simp<u>le</u>, stab<u>il</u>ize	syllabic 'l'
[ɹ̩]	ladd<u>er</u>, sing<u>er</u>, b<u>ur</u>p, p<u>er</u>cent	syllabic 'r'

Vowels
i. Monophthongs (Simple Vowels)

[i]	b<u>ea</u>t, w<u>e</u>, bel<u>ie</u>ve, p<u>eo</u>ple, mon<u>ey</u>	
[ɪ]	b<u>i</u>t, cons<u>i</u>st, <u>i</u>njury, mal<u>i</u>gnant, b<u>u</u>siness	small capital 'i'
[ɛ]	b<u>e</u>t, rec<u>e</u>ption, s<u>ay</u>s, g<u>ue</u>st	epsilon
[æ]	b<u>a</u>t, l<u>au</u>gh, <u>a</u>nger, comr<u>a</u>de, r<u>a</u>lly	ash
[u]	b<u>oo</u>t, wh<u>o</u>, s<u>ew</u>er, d<u>u</u>ty, thr<u>ough</u>	
[ʊ]	p<u>u</u>t, f<u>oo</u>t, b<u>u</u>tcher, c<u>ou</u>ld, b<u>oo</u>gie-w<u>oo</u>gie	upsilon
[ɔ]	b<u>ou</u>ght, c<u>au</u>ght, wr<u>o</u>ng, st<u>a</u>lk, c<u>o</u>re	open 'o'
[ɑ]	p<u>o</u>t, f<u>a</u>ther, s<u>e</u>rgeant, h<u>o</u>nor, h<u>o</u>spital	script 'a'
[ʌ]	b<u>u</u>t, t<u>ou</u>gh, an<u>o</u>ther, <u>o</u>ven	wedge or turned 'v'
[ə]	<u>a</u>mong, sof<u>a</u>, Asi<u>a</u>	schwa

ii. Diphthongs (Complex Vowels)

[ɑɪ]	b<u>i</u>te, St<u>ei</u>n, <u>ai</u>sle, ch<u>oir</u>, <u>i</u>sland	
[ɑʊ]	b<u>ou</u>t, br<u>ow</u>n, d<u>ou</u>bt, fl<u>ow</u>er, l<u>ou</u>d	
[ɔɪ]	b<u>oy</u>, d<u>oi</u>ly, rej<u>oi</u>ce, perestr<u>oi</u>ka, ann<u>oy</u>	
[oʊ]	b<u>oa</u>t, b<u>eau</u>, gr<u>ow</u>, th<u>ough</u>, <u>o</u>ver	
[eɪ]	b<u>ai</u>t, r<u>ei</u>gn, gr<u>ea</u>t, th<u>ey</u>, g<u>au</u>ge	

In the list in the table above, we have given you examples of individual sounds in individual words. When we actually use language on a day-to-day basis, however, we speak in phrases and sentences, with all the words run together. This type of speech is known as **running speech** or **continuous speech**, and, although as linguists we sometimes need to break speech into its component parts of words and sounds, you should bear in mind that most everyday speech is not separated out into these pieces. In running speech, the pronunciations of words may be affected by the surrounding words (see Section 2.2.6 on phonetic coarticulation or File 3.2 on phonological assimilation), and one of the open research questions in the study of language processing is how the human mind processes running speech into its meaningful component parts (see Chapter 9).

Articulation: English Consonants

2.2.1 Introducing Articulatory Phonetics

Say the word *hiss* and hold the [s]. Now inhale while holding the tongue position of [s]. What part of your tongue is cooled by the incoming airstream? What part of the roof of your mouth is cooled? Simple, intuitive observations such as these (bolstered by careful X-ray and palatography studies) lead to an **articulatory description** of speech sounds like the consonants of English. **Articulation** is the motion or positioning of some part of the vocal tract (often, but not always, a muscular part like the tongue and/or lips) with respect to some other vocal tract surface in the production of a speech sound (more on this below).

English speech sounds are formed by forcing a stream of air out of the lungs through the oral or nasal cavities, or both. This airstream provides the energy for sound production in the mouth—either by making the vocal folds vibrate or by making hissing or popping noises as air escapes through narrow openings in the mouth. Sounds created by exhaling are said to be made by using a **pulmonic** (=lung) **egressive** (=blowing out) **airstream mechanism**. Other **airstream mechanisms** are used in other languages but are discussed only briefly in Section 2.4.6.

The focus of this file is the articulation of English consonants (refer to Section 2.1.3 for a description of the different types of speech sounds). When describing a consonant it is necessary to provide information about three different aspects of the articulation of the consonant:

- Is the sound voiced or voiceless?
- Where is the airstream constricted (i.e., the place of articulation)?
- How is the airstream constricted (i.e., the manner of articulation)?

The voicing, place, and manner of articulation are known as **segmental features.** We will discuss each of these aspects in turn. Please note that in this file and elsewhere, whenever we say things like "[p] is voiceless" or "the [p] in *pan,*" what we really mean is "the sound represented by the symbol [p]." Remember that we are talking about speech sounds symbolized by phonetic transcription, but not <p> as in the spelling of the word.

2.2.2 Anatomy of Human Speech Production

In order to answer the three questions listed above, we first need to know more about the anatomy of speech production. There are three basic components of the human anatomy that are involved in the production of speech (see (1)). One is the **larynx** (sometimes called the voice box), which contains the vocal folds and the glottis; another is the **vocal tract** above the larynx, which is composed of the oral and nasal cavities. The third is the **sub-glottal system,** which is the part of the respiratory system located below the larynx. When air is inhaled, it is channeled through the nasal or oral cavity, or both, through the larynx

(1) The speech production mechanism.

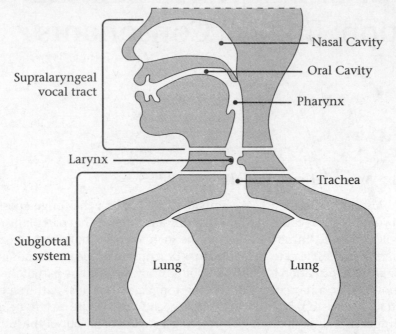

into the lungs. English speech sounds are produced while exhaling, as a stream of air is moved out of the lungs and through the larynx and the vocal tract.

2.2.3 States of the Glottis: Voicing

Humans have a larynx at the top of the **trachea** (or windpipe). Within the larynx are folds of muscle called **vocal folds** (these are popularly known as vocal cords, but they are not really cords). In the display in (2) we are viewing the larynx as if looking down a person's throat. A flap of tissue called the epiglottis is attached at the front of the larynx and can fold down and back to cover and protect the vocal folds, which are stretched horizontally along the open center of the larynx. The opening between these folds is called the **glottis.** At the front of the larynx, the vocal folds are attached to cartilage and can't be moved, but at the back of the larynx, the vocal folds are attached to two small movable cartilages that can close or open the glottis. When the two free ends are brought together, the vocal folds can be nearly or completely closed, impeding airflow through the glottis (2b). When the folds are wide open, the glottis has roughly the shape of a triangle, as can be seen in (2a).

The vocal folds can be opened so that the flow of air coming up from the lungs passes through freely, or the folds may be held close together so that they vibrate as air passes through. Try putting your hand lightly on your throat, or putting your fingers in your ears, and then making a drawn-out [s]. Your vocal folds are separated to open the glottis, as in (2a), so you should feel no vibration. But now make a [z] (again, draw it out), and you will feel a vibration or buzzing feeling. This is due to the vibration of the vocal folds—your glottis is now as in the shape of (2b).

Sounds made with the vocal folds vibrating are called **voiced** sounds, and sounds made without such vibration are called **voiceless** sounds. The underlined sounds in the following pairs of words (see (3)) differ only in that the sound is voiceless in the first word of each pair and voiced in the second. Try saying these words, but don't whisper when you do, because the vocal folds don't vibrate when you whisper.

(2) Three states of the glottis. The view is of the larynx (from above) looking down the throat.

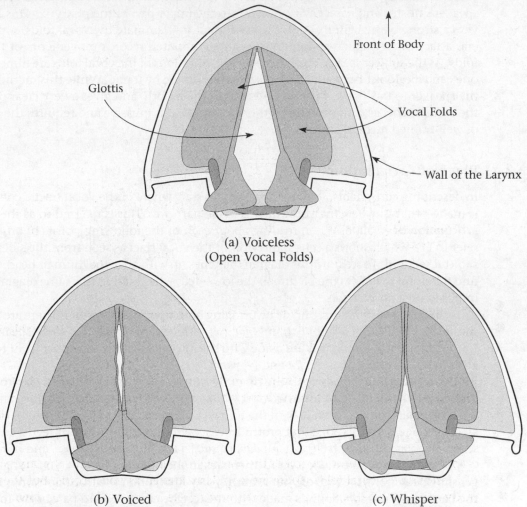

(a) Voiceless
(Open Vocal Folds)

(b) Voiced
(Approximated Vocal Folds)

(c) Whisper
(Partially Closed Vocal Folds)

(3) Voiced versus voiceless sounds

a. [f] <u>f</u>at	c. [θ] <u>th</u>igh	e. [s] <u>s</u>ip	g. [ʃ] dilu<u>ti</u>on
[v] <u>v</u>at	[ð] <u>th</u>y	[z] <u>z</u>ip	[ʒ] delu<u>si</u>on
b. [tʃ] ri<u>ch</u>	d. [p] <u>p</u>at	f. [t] <u>t</u>ab	h. [k] <u>k</u>ill
[dʒ] ri<u>dge</u>	[b] <u>b</u>at	[d] <u>d</u>ab	[g] <u>g</u>ill

In making an articulatory description of a consonant, it is first necessary to state whether a sound is voiced (there is vocal fold vibration) or voiceless (there is no vocal fold vibration). A chart of the voiced and voiceless consonants of English is provided in Section 2.2.7.

Phoneticians can determine if a given segment is voiced or voiceless using a number of different techniques. The simplest is one we described earlier: feeling for vibration of the vocal folds while you produce a sound. This technique, however, is very limited in its ability to determine voicing in running speech (try saying *ice cream* while placing your fingers lightly on your throat—is it obvious that the [s] and [k] in the middle are both voiceless?). One alternative is to examine a picture of the acoustic signal called a **spectrogram,** which will be discussed in more detail in File 2.6. Spectrograms can indicate whether vocal fold vibrations are present in a sound. Another method of studying voicing is to look at the vocal folds directly, using high-speed video. A very thin fiberoptic line is inserted through the speaker's nostril and nasal cavity, down into the upper part of the pharynx. This line conveys a strong white light through the vocal tract to illuminate the vocal folds. A tiny camera, attached to the line and connected to a computer, records movements of the vocal folds. As the subject speaks, the extremely fast vibrations of the vocal folds are filmed so that one can later look at and analyze the recordings frame by frame. While this method allows the speaker to talk freely, with no obstacles in the mouth, and gives a very clear picture of the adjustments and movements of the vocal folds, it is invasive and requires the presence of well-trained medical personnel.

2.2.4 Place of Articulation

In describing consonants, it is also necessary to state where in the vocal tract a constriction is made—that is, where the vocal tract is made narrower. This is referred to as the **place of articulation** of a sound. When reading about each of the following points of articulation, refer to (4), which shows a schematic view of the vocal tract as seen from the side (called a **sagittal section**). To see how this diagram matches up with an actual human head, you may find it helpful to refer to the picture to the lower left, which shows this same diagram superimposed on a photograph.

Bilabial consonants are made by bringing both lips closer together. There are five such sounds in English: [p] *pat*, [b] *bat*, [m] *mat*, [w] *with*, and [ʍ] *where* (for some speakers).

Labiodental consonants are made with the lower lip against the upper front teeth. English has two labiodentals: [f] *fat* and [v] *vat*.

Interdentals are made with the tip of the tongue protruding between the front teeth. There are two interdental sounds in most varieties of American English: [θ] *thigh* and [ð] *thy*.

Alveolar sounds are made with the tongue tip at or near the **alveolar** [ælvilɹ̩] **ridge.** The alveolar ridge is a small ridge that protrudes just behind your upper front teeth. English has seven alveolar consonants: [t] *tab*, [d] *dab*, [s] *sip*, [z] *zip*, [n] *noose*, [l] *loose*, and [ɹ] *red*.

Palatal sounds are made a bit further back in the mouth. If you let your tongue or finger slide back along the roof of your mouth, you will find that the front portion is hard and the back portion is soft. Sounds made with the tongue near the hard part of the roof of the mouth (the "hard **palate**") are called palatal sounds. English makes five sounds in the region of the hard palate: [ʃ] *leash*, [ʒ] *measure*, [tʃ] *church*, [dʒ] *judge*, [j] *yes*. (More precisely, [ʃ, ʒ, tʃ], and [dʒ] are "alveo-palatal" sounds, because they are made in the area between the alveolar ridge and the hard palate. We'll use the shorter term "palatal" to describe these sounds of English, however.)

Velar consonants are produced at the soft part of the roof of the mouth behind the hard palate—the **velum.** Sounds made with the tongue near the velum are said to be velar. There are three velar sounds in English: [k] *kill*, [g] *gill*, and [ŋ] *sing*.

Glottal sounds are produced at the larynx. The space between the vocal folds is the glottis. English has two sounds made at the glottis. One is easy to hear: [h], as in *high* and *history*. The other is called a glottal stop and is transcribed phonetically as [ʔ]. This sound occurs before each of the vowel sounds in *uh-oh*.

2.2.5 Manner of Articulation

Besides stating whether a consonant is voiced or voiceless and giving the consonant's point of articulation, it is necessary to describe its **manner of articulation,** that is, how the airstream is modified by the vocal tract to produce the sound. The manner of articulation of a sound depends largely on the degree of closure of the articulators (how close together or far apart they are).

(4) Sagittal section of the vocal tract

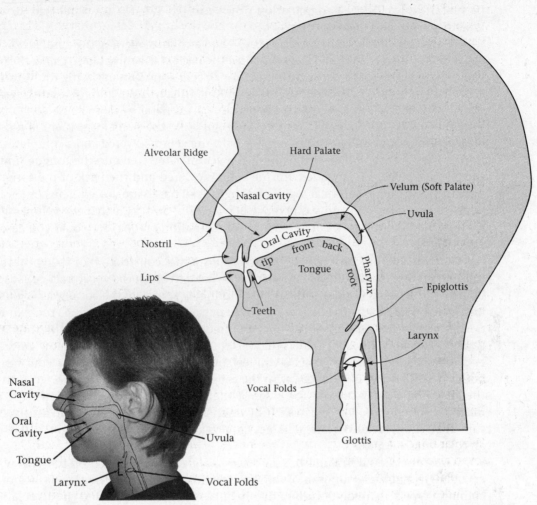

Stops are made by obstructing the airstream completely in the oral cavity. Notice that when you say [p] and [b] your lips are closed together for a moment, stopping the airflow. [p] and [b] are bilabial stops. [b] is a voiced bilabial stop, while [p] is a voiceless bilabial stop. [t], [d], [k], and [g] are also stops. What is the three-part description (voicing, place, and manner) of each?

The glottal stop, [ʔ], is made by momentarily closing the vocal folds. If you stop halfway through *uh-oh* and hold the articulators in position for the second half, you should be able to feel yourself making the glottal stop. (It will feel like a catch in your throat.) Nasal consonants are also stops in terms of their oral articulation; see descriptions of nasals below.

Fricatives are made by forming a nearly complete obstruction of the vocal tract. The opening through which the air escapes is very small, and as a result a turbulent noise is produced (much as air escaping from a punctured tire makes a hissing noise). Such a turbulent, hissing mouth noise is called **frication**, hence the name of this class of speech sounds. [ʃ], as in *ship*, is made by almost stopping the air with the tongue near the palate. It is a voiceless palatal fricative. How would you describe each of the following fricatives: [f], [v], [θ], [ð], [s], [z], and [ʒ]?

Affricates are made by briefly stopping the airstream completely and then releasing the articulators slightly so that frication noise is produced. This is why phoneticians describe affricates as a sequence of a stop followed by a fricative. English has only two affricates, [tʃ], as in *church*, and [dʒ], as in *judge*. [tʃ] is pronounced like [t] followed by [ʃ]. It is a voiceless palatal affricate. [dʒ] is a combination of [d] and [ʒ]. What is the three-part description (voicing, place, and manner) of [dʒ]?

Nasals are produced by lowering the velum and thus opening the nasal passage to the vocal tract. When the velum is raised against the back of the throat (also called the **pharynx wall**), no air can escape through the nasal passage. Sounds made with the velum raised are called oral sounds. The sounds [m], as in *Kim*, [n], as in *kin*, and [ŋ], as in *king*, are produced with the velum lowered and hence are called nasal sounds. These consonants are sometimes classified as nasal stops because, just like the oral stops, there is a complete obstruction in the oral cavity. [m] is made with the velum lowered and a complete obstruction of the airstream at the lips. For [n], the velum is lowered and the tongue tip touches the alveolar ridge. [ŋ] is made with the velum lowered and the back of the tongue stopping the airstream in the velar region. In English, all nasals are voiced. Thus [m] is a voiced bilabial nasal (stop); the only difference between [m] and [b] is that the velum is lowered for the articulation of [m], but raised for the articulation of [b]. How would you describe [n] and [ŋ]?

Liquids, like all consonants, involve a substantial constriction of the vocal tract, but the constrictions for liquids are not narrow enough to block the vocal tract or cause turbulence. For the lateral (= side) liquid [l] the midline, or center, of the vocal tract is completely obstructed, like in a stop, but there is a side passage around the tongue. You can feel this positioning by first starting to say *leaf* and "freezing" your tongue at the [l], then inhaling sharply. The air will cool the side(s) of your tongue, showing you the airflow pattern. (Not everyone has the same pattern: do you feel air on the left or right side of your tongue? or both?) The [l] sound is produced with the tongue touching the alveolar ridge as in [t], but the airstream escapes around the sides of the tongue. The presence of this side passage makes [l] sound more like the nasal [n] (which also has a side passage and an alveolar closure) than [t]. [l] is called a lateral liquid. Liquids are usually voiced in English: [l] is a voiced alveolar lateral liquid.

The other liquid in English is [ɹ]. There is a great deal of variation in the ways speakers of English make r-sounds; most are voiced and articulated in the alveolar region, and a common type also involves curling the tip of the tongue back behind the alveolar ridge to make a **retroflex** sound. For our purposes [ɹ] as in *red* may be considered a voiced alveolar retroflex liquid.

Nasals and liquids are classified as consonants, so we would not normally expect them to be syllabic. However, they sometimes act like vowels in that they can function as syllable nuclei. Pronounce the following words out loud, and listen to the liquids and nasals in them: *prism*, *prison*, *table*, and *hiker*. In these words the nucleus of the second syllable consists only of a syllabic nasal or liquid; there is no vowel in these second syllables. In order to indicate that these are **syllabic consonants,** a short vertical line is placed below the phonetic symbol. The final n of *prison* would be transcribed [n̩]; likewise [m̩], [l̩], and [ɹ̩] in *prism*, *table*, and *hiker*.

Glides are made with only a slight closure of the articulators, so that if the vocal tract were any more open, the result would be a vowel sound. [w] is made by raising the back of the tongue toward the velum while rounding the lips at the same time, so it is classified as a voiced bilabial glide. (Notice the similarity in the way you articulate the [w] and the vowel [u] in the word *woo:* the only change is that you open your lips a little more for [u].) [w̥] is produced just like [w], except that it is voiceless; not all speakers of English use this sound. Speakers who use it say it in the word *which* [w̥ɪtʃ], making it distinct from *witch* [wɪtʃ]. [j] is made with a slight closure in the palatal region. It is a voiced palatal glide. Compare the pronunciation of *yawn* [jɔn] and *eon* [iɔn], and notice the similarity between [j] and the vowel [i].

The last manner of articulation that we will discuss here is the **flap.** A flap (sometimes called a tap) is similar to a stop in that it involves the complete obstruction of the oral cavity. The closure, however, is much faster than that of a stop: the articulators strike each other very quickly. In American English, we have an alveolar flap, in which the tip of the tongue is brought up and simply allowed to quickly strike the roof of the mouth as it is returned to its rest position. This voiced sound is symbolized by the IPA character [ɾ] and occurs as the middle sound in the words *writer* and *ladder*.

2.2.6 Investigating Place and Manner of Articulation: Palatography

In addition to the ability of the average speaker to feel at least approximately where and how particular consonant sounds are made, phoneticians have developed a number of methods for looking more precisely at the place and manner of articulation. One of the most common methods is **palatography.** In palatography, a picture is made that shows where the tongue touches the roof of the mouth during a particular articulation.

One way to do this, **static palatography,** involves painting the tongue black with a (tasteless) mixture of olive oil and charcoal powder. When the speaker produces a word like *see,* the tongue leaves a black trace on the alveolar ridge and the hard palate, where it touched to make closure. The speaker can then produce another word like *she* (after rinsing off and repainting the tongue), so that the place of articulation for [s] versus [ʃ] can be studied. This method, in addition to being rather messy, works only if the speaker produces a single isolated sound and the contact pattern is photographed or examined immediately.

In order to observe the interplay between articulations, that is, how one consonant's place of articulation affects another consonant's place of articulation, you can use **dynamic palatography** (also called EPG, which is the abbreviation for electropalatography). This method is similar to static palatography but more sophisticated because it allows the experimenter to record sequences of contacts that the tongue makes with the hard palate in the course of the production of an utterance. The places where contact is made are directly recorded into a computer. Once the recordings are made, you can align a specific point in time of the acoustic display of the utterance with a specific EPG display. This way you can measure exactly where, how much, and how long contact between the tongue and the roof of the mouth is produced at any given time in the utterance.

The speaker in such a study is required to use an artificial hard palate (similar to a retainer) that is custom made to fit his or her hard palate exactly. This artificial palate has many small embedded electrodes that record contact as soon as the tongue moves against them. So for any given moment in time during the recording, the researcher knows exactly where the tongue contacts the roof of the mouth. Since the retainer covers only the hard palate, the exact amount of contact made in the soft palate region for velar consonants, such as /g/or /k/, is sometimes hard to see. Nevertheless, this method provides fairly exact data about where and at what point in time within an utterance the tongue touches the hard palate.

You can compare the two types of images made using static versus dynamic palatography in (5). Both of these images show the contact pattern for a [d], spoken by different speakers. The one on the left is the result of static palatography; the one on the right is from dynamic palatography. In both cases, the speaker's teeth are toward the top of the page, and we are looking at the roof of the mouth. In the static palatography picture, the black marks indicate where the tongue touched the roof of the mouth during the production of the nonsense word *ahdah* [ɑdɑ]. In the dynamic palatography picture, the cross-marks indicate the locations of all the sensors on the artificial hard palate; the black boxes indicate sensors that were contacted by the tongue during the [d] of the phrase *bad guy* [bædɡaɪ].

(5) Comparing images from static and dynamic palatography for the production of [d]

In both cases, it is clear that the tongue made full contact with the roof of the mouth, completely closing off the airflow. This is consistent with how we have described the manner of articulation of [d], as a stop.

The contact was made at the front of the mouth in both cases—right along the alveolar ridge, as expected from our description of the place of articulation for [d]. There are differences in the two pictures, however: the one on the left also clearly shows that this speaker produced the word with the tongue far enough forward that it also partly touched the teeth—hence this particular production could be characterized as somewhat **dental**, not purely alveolar. Meanwhile, the speaker on the right has contact that extends much further back along the sides of the mouth. This is very likely because this person was saying the whole phrase *bad guy*, where the [d] is followed by a velar [g]. The two sounds are made using a single flowing action: we don't stop between the two words to reposition the tongue. In this picture, we can see that the back of the tongue is already making contact with the sides of the mouth, in preparation for the velar closure. This kind of **co-articulation** of segments is not something that we can capture using our standard transcriptions, which simply list each segment separately.

Notice that palatography tells you only about the relation of the tongue and the mouth: the pictures in (5) say nothing about the voicing or nasality of the sounds produced. These pictures are completely consistent with the articulations we expect for not only [d] but also [t] (a voiceless alveolar stop) and [n] (a voiced alveolar nasal stop).

2.2.7 The Consonant Chart

The chart of the consonants of English in (6) can be used for easy reference. The three-part articulatory description of consonants is conventionally given in this order: Voicing-Place-Manner, e.g., voiced palatal glide or voiceless bilabial stop. To find the description of a sound, first locate the phonetic symbol on the chart. You can find out the state of the glottis by checking whether the sound is in the shaded part of the box or not—the shaded boxes show voiced consonants, while the nonshaded ones show voiceless consonants. Then check the label at the top of the vertical column that contains the sound to see what its place of articulation is. Finally, check the manner of articulation label at the far left of the sound's horizontal row. Locate [ð], for example. It lies in a shaded region, indicating that this sound is voiced. Now look above [ð]. It is in the vertical column marked "interdental." Looking to the far left you see it is a fricative. [ð], then, is the voiced interdental fricative.

You can also use the chart to find a symbol that corresponds to a particular phonetic description by essentially reversing the above procedure. If you want to find the voiced

(6) The consonants of English classified by voicing, place of articulation, and manner of articulation.

		Place of Articulation												
		Bilabial		Labio-dental		Inter-dental		Alveolar		Palatal		Velar		Glottal
Stop		p	b					t	d			k	g	ʔ	
Fricative				f	v	θ	ð	s	z	ʃ	ʒ			h	
Affricate										tʃ	dʒ				
Flap									ɾ						
Nasal			m						n				ŋ		
Lateral Liquid									l						
Retroflex Liquid									ɹ						
Glide		w̥	w										j		

State of the Glottis: | Voiceless | Voiced |

palatal fricative, first look in the fricative row, then under the palatal column, and locate the symbol in the shaded part of the box: this is [ʒ].

The chart can also be used to find classes of sounds—that is, groups of sounds that share one or more characteristics. For instance, to find all the alveolars, just read off all the sounds under the "alveolar" column. Or, to find all the stops, read off all the sounds in the "stop" row.

You should familiarize yourself with the chart so that you can easily recognize the phonetic symbols. The list of phonetic symbols for consonants, which was presented in File 2.1.4, should also help you remember which symbol represents which consonant. This chart and the list are also printed on the very last page of this book, for easy reference. Remember that we are talking about *speech sounds* and not letters in the English spelling system.

Articulation: English Vowels

2.3.1 Articulatory Properties of Vowels

In Section 2.1.3, we explained the difference between consonants and vowels, and in File 2.2, we discussed the articulation of consonants. Vowels are the most sonorant, or intense, and the most audible of sounds in speech. Unlike consonants, they usually function as syllable nuclei, and the consonants that surround them often depend on the vowel for their audibility. For example, in the word *pop,* neither [p] has much sound of its own; the [p]s are heard mainly because of the way they affect the beginning and end of the vowel sound.

Because vowels are produced with a relatively open vocal tract, they do not have a consonant-like point of articulation (place of constriction) or manner of articulation (type and degree of constriction). They are also almost always voiced. This means that the three standard descriptors for consonants (place, manner, and voicing) are not helpful when we want to describe vowels. What should we use instead?

Hold your jaw lightly in your hand. Now say *he* [hi], *who* [hu], and *ha* [hɑ]. Did your jaw move for *ha?* The tendency for the jaw to open for [ɑ] is why we will call [ɑ] a **low** vowel. It is usually pronounced with the jaw quite open—lowering the tongue body away from the roof of the mouth. The contrast in jaw position between [i] and [u] as opposed to [ɑ] is large because both [i] and [u] are pronounced with the tongue body close to the roof of the mouth—hence they are called **high** vowels.

Vocal fold vibration is the sound source for vowels. The vocal tract above the glottis acts as an acoustic resonator affecting the sound made by the vocal folds. The shape of this resonator determines the quality of the vowel: [i] versus [u] versus [ɑ], for example.

There are four main ways in which speakers can change the shape of the vocal tract and thus change vowel quality:

- raising or lowering the body of the tongue
- advancing or retracting the body of the tongue
- rounding or not rounding the lips
- making these movements with a tense or a lax gesture

Therefore, when describing a vowel, it is necessary to provide information about these four aspects of the articulation of the vowel. Refer to the chart in (1) as each aspect is discussed in the following section.[1]

Broadly speaking, there are two types of vowels in English, namely, monophthongs and diphthongs. Diphthongs are two-part vowels, whereas monophthongs have only one part (see Section 2.1.3). We will discuss the four aspects of the articulation of the vowels using monophthongs; articulation of diphthongs will be discussed in the next section.

---

[1]Although this textbook uses IPA symbols for transcription, the classification of vowels is presented in a more traditional style, with only three levels of height and a tense-lax distinction. The standard IPA vowel chart is printed on the inside back cover of the book for comparison purposes.

(1) The vowels (monophthongs) of English

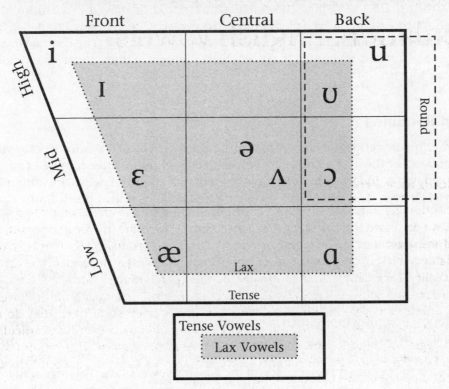

2.3.2 Tongue Height

If you repeat to yourself the vowel sounds of *seat, set, sat*—transcribed [i], [ɛ], [æ]—you will find that you open your mouth a little wider as you change from [i] to [ɛ], and then a little wider still as you change from [ɛ] to [æ]. These varying degrees of openness correspond to different degrees of tongue height: high for [i], mid for [ɛ], and low for [æ].

High vowels like [i] are made with the front of the mouth less open because the tongue body is raised, or high. The **high** vowels of English are [i], [ɪ], [u], and [ʊ], as in l*ea*k, l*i*ck, L*u*ke, l*oo*k, respectively. Conversely, **low** vowels like the [æ] in s*a*t are pronounced with the front of the mouth open and the tongue lowered. The low vowels of English are [æ] as in c*a*t and [ɑ] as in c*o*t. **Mid** vowels like the [ɛ] of *set* are produced with an intermediate tongue height. In the inventory of English monophthongs, these mid vowels are [ɛ, ʌ, ɔ], as in D*e*ll, d*u*ll, d*o*ll, respectively. Note that an unstressed vowel in English is often pronounced as the mid vowel [ə], as in *a*bove and *a*tomic.

In many American dialects, words like *caught* and *cot*, or *dawn* and *Don*, are pronounced differently, with an [ɔ] and [ɑ], respectively. In other American dialects, these words are pronounced the same. If you pronounce these pairs the same, you probably use the unrounded vowel [ɑ] in all of these words. For most speakers of English, however, even those who pronounce *caught* and *cot* the same, the vowel [ɔ] appears in words such as c*o*re, m*o*re, b*o*re.

2.3.3 Tongue Advancement

Besides being held high or mid or low, the tongue can also be moved forward or pulled back within the oral cavity. For example, in the high **front** vowel [i] as in *beat*, the body of the tongue is raised and pushed forward so it is just under the hard palate. The high **back** vowel

[u] of *boot,* on the other hand, is made by raising the body of the tongue in the back of the mouth, toward the velum. The tongue is advanced or moved forward for all the front monophthongs, [i], [ɪ], [ɛ], [æ], as in *seek, sick, sec, sack,* and retracted or pulled back for the back monophthongs, [u], [ʊ], [ɔ], [ɑ], as in *ooze, look, hall, dot.* The central vowels, [ʌ] as in *luck* or [ə] as the first vowel in the word *another,* require neither advancement nor retraction of the tongue.

2.3.4 Lip Rounding

Vowel quality also depends on lip position. When you say the [u] in *two,* your lips are **rounded**. For the [i] in *tea,* they are **unrounded**. English has three rounded monophthongs: [u], [ʊ], [ɔ], as in *loop, foot, fall;* all other monophthongs in English are unrounded. In the vowel chart in (1), the rounded vowels are enclosed in a dotted line forming a rectangle.

2.3.5 Tenseness

Vowels that are called **tense** have more extreme positions of the tongue or the lips than vowels that are **lax**. The production of tense vowels involves bigger changes from a mid-central position in the mouth. Additionally, tense vowels in English usually have longer duration (in milliseconds) than lax vowels. On the vowel chart you can clearly see that the distance between the tense vowels [i] and [u] is bigger than the distance between the lax vowels [ɪ] and [ʊ]. For example, tense vowels are made with a more extreme tongue gesture to reach the periphery (outer edges) of the possible **vowel space**. This means that the tongue position for the tense high front vowel [i] is higher and fronter than for the lax high front vowel [ɪ]. Lax vowels, then, are not peripheral to the degree that tense vowels are. Compare tense [i] in *meet* with lax [ɪ] in *mitt,* or tense [u] in *boot* with lax [ʊ] in *put.* In the latter case you will find that the tense rounded vowel [u] is also produced with more and tighter lip rounding than the lax counterpart [ʊ].

   Now we can consider some sample descriptions of English vowels:

(2) Sample descriptions of English vowels
   a. [i], as in *beat,* is high, front, unrounded, and tense.
   b. [ɔ], as in *caught,* is mid, back, rounded, and lax.
   c. [ɑ], as in *cot,* is low, back, unrounded, and lax.
   d. [ʌ], as in *cut,* is mid, central, unrounded, and lax. (Note that "central" and "mid" refer to the same general area in the vocal tract but along different dimensions.)

2.3.6 Describing Vowels: Diphthongs

You may have noticed that there are a number of vowel sounds in English that have not yet been discussed. For example, the vowels in the words *buy, bay, bow* (as in "bow down"), *bow* (as in "bow and arrow"), and *boy,* or the exclamations *ow!, oh!,* and *oy!* have not yet been described. These vowels are **diphthongs** ([dɪfθɑɪŋz] or [dɪpθɑɪŋz]), which, as mentioned in Section 2.1.3, are complex vowel sounds as opposed to monophthongs, which are simple vowel sounds. Diphthongs are "complex" because they are two-part vowel sounds, consisting of a transition from one vowel to the other in the same syllable.

   If you try saying the word *eye* slowly, concentrating on how you make this vowel sound, you should find that your tongue starts out in the low back position for [ɑ] and then moves toward the high front position for [ɪ] (see (3)). If you have a hard time perceiving this as two sounds, try laying a finger on your tongue and saying *eye.* This should help you feel the upward tongue movement.

(3) Two-part articulations of the diphthongs of English (the arrows indicate the transitions)

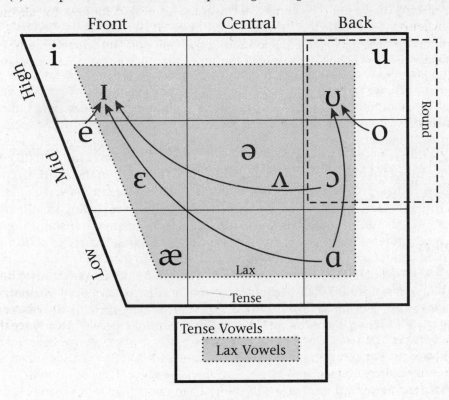

Tense Vowels

    Lax Vowels

This diphthong, which consists of two articulations and the two corresponding sounds, is written with two symbols: [ɑɪ], as in [bɑɪ] *buy*.[2] To produce the vowel in the word *bow (down)*, the tongue and the lips start in the low back position for [ɑ] and move toward the high back position for [ʊ]; so this diphthong is written [ɑʊ], as in [bɑʊ] *bow (down)*.[2] In the vowel of the word *boy*, the tongue moves from the mid back position for the rounded vowel [ɔ] toward the high front position for [ɪ]; so the diphthong of *boy* is written [ɔɪ], as in [bɔɪ].[3] To say the vowel in the word *bow (and arrow)*, the tongue and the lips start in the mid back position for the rounded vowel [o] and move toward the high back position for the rounded vowel; so the diphthong is written [oʊ], as in [boʊ] *bow (and arrow)*. As for the production of the vowel of the word *bay*, the tongue starts in the mid front position for [e] and moves toward the position for [ɪ]; so this diphthong is written [eɪ], as in [beɪ] *bay*. The chart in (3) illustrates the tongue movements involved in the production of these diphthongs.

2.3.7 Investigating Vowel Articulations

In Section 2.2.6, we described several ways to determine the place and manner of articula-

---

[2] There are other analyses of the structure of diphthongs. The most common alternative to the one presented here views diphthongs as two-part vowel sounds consisting of a vowel and a glide (see Section 2.2.5) within the same syllable. The correspondence for [ɪ], as in [ɑɪ], is then the palatal glide [j]; hence, [ɑj]. The diphthongs we present as [ɑɪ], [ɑʊ], [ɔɪ], [oʊ], and [eɪ] would be written as [ɑj], [ɑw], [ɔj], [ow], and [ej], respectively, in this system.

[3] We should point out that there is, of course, variation in the pronunciation of all speech, even if we are talking about "Standard American English" (see Chapter 10 on language variation). Some speakers, for example, may produce the vowel in *eye* more like [ai], or the vowel in *bow (down)* more like [əʊ]. If your pronunciations don't exactly match those presented here, you're certainly not wrong! For consistency, however, we will be using the transcriptions given here to represent these sounds.

tion of consonants, using different types of palatography. These methods won't tell us much about vowel articulations, however, because, of course, vowels are produced with a relatively open vocal tract, and the tongue doesn't touch the roof of the mouth. Instead, studying vowels usually involves imaging techniques that allow investigators to look at the whole mouth and the tongue's position in it.

One technique is to use X-ray movies of people talking. These X-ray films can be played over and over again to see tongue, lip, and jaw movements as they occur over time. Although you can find some old example films of X-ray speech by searching online, this methodology is not used anymore because it turned out to be harmful for the speakers.

Instead, researchers now use safer methods such as ultrasound, Magnetic Resonance Imaging (MRI), or Electromagnetic Articulography (EMA). Ultrasound and MRI (like X-rays) both make use of invisible rays that "bounce off" hard structures in their path to create visual images of those structures (in the case of ultrasound, these are sound waves; in the case of MRI, these are radio waves). EMA, on the other hand, involves placing small sensors on a subject's tongue, teeth, and other articulators; these sensors then transmit information back to a computer about their relative locations, allowing researchers to collect precise information about how the articulators move and interact in speech.

Of course, all of the techniques mentioned here can be also used to study consonant articulations, and all are especially useful for consonants that are produced without contact on the hard palate (e.g., [b] or [g]). This makes these techniques particularly well suited for studying the interaction of consonants and vowels in running speech.

Beyond English: Speech Sounds of the World's Languages

2.4.1 Beyond English?

In File 2.1, it was claimed that the phonetic alphabet used in this book can be used for any language. The parts of the phonetic alphabet that we have employed up to this point may seem Anglocentric—no different really from *Webster's* pronunciation symbols for English, or any other reasonably consistent method of writing English sounds. To "de-anglicize" our phonetic alphabet so that it is truly useful for describing the pronunciation of other languages, we must add new symbols to it.

It is not the goal of this file, however, to review all of the speech sounds that can be used in human language. Rather, we restrict ourselves to some of the common phonetic symbols that you may encounter. Yet, even this partial look at phonetic diversity highlights the fact that English uses only a small subset of the possible sounds found in human language. We should note that, if you run across a symbol you are not familiar with, you are now in a position to interpret it using the IPA chart on the inside back cover of this book.

2.4.2 Vowels

The most straightforward additions to our phonetic alphabet can be made by filling in some holes. There are certainly other sounds that are possible given the features we've identified for English sounds, but these correspond to combinations of the features that happen not to occur in English. Consider, for example, the vowel chart in File 2.3. In connection with that chart we noted that the only rounded vowels in English are the back vowels [u], [ʊ], and [ɔ] and the diphthong [oʊ] (as in *who'd*, *hood*, *awed*, and *owed*, respectively). You might have thought that these are the only rounded vowels in other languages as well. But if you have studied German or French, you know that this is not true. In addition to the back rounded vowels [u] and [o], German and French both have **front rounded vowels,** such as [y] and [ø]. The high front rounded vowel [y] is pronounced with a tongue position very similar to that for [i], but instead of spread lips, the vowel is pronounced with rounded lips. Similarly, the mid front rounded vowel [ø] is produced with a tongue position as in [e], but with rounded lips. (1) gives some examples of the contrast between front and back rounded vowels in French and in German.

Another vowel distinction that does not come up in English is the distinction between [ɑ] and [a]. [ɑ] is used for low back unrounded vowels, which may contrast with [a], a somewhat more front low unrounded vowel.

All of the vowels we have discussed so far have been oral vowels—that is, they are produced with the velum raised and hence the nasal passage closed. All languages have oral vowels, and many have only oral vowels. Some languages, however, also have **nasalized vowels.**

A nasalized vowel is in nearly every respect identical to its oral vowel counterpart—the only exception is that the nasal passage is open in nasalized vowels (cf. Section 2.2.5 in File 2.2). This is very much like the distinction between an oral stop [b] and a nasal stop [m].

(1) Examples of the contrast between front and back rounded vowels

Front		Back	
French			
[ty]	'you (familiar)'	[tu]	'all'
[vy]	'seen'	[vu]	'you (formal)'
[nø]	'knot'	[no]	'our (plural)'
[fø]	'fire'	[fo]	'false'
German			
[gytə]	'benevolence'	[gutə]	'good (masc. sg.)'
[grys]	'greet'	[grus]	'greeting'
[ʃøn]	'beautiful'	[ʃon]	'already'
[bøgen]	'arches'	[bogen]	'arch'

Nasalized vowels are written with a tilde [~] over the corresponding oral vowel symbol. So, a nasalized mid front vowel is written [ẽ], and a nasalized mid back rounded vowel is written [õ].

We don't have to look very far to find vowel nasalization used as the only feature to distinguish words in language, as the following examples from French illustrate (see (2)).

(2) Examples of the contrast between oral and nasal vowels in French

Oral		Nasalized	
[mɛ]	'but'	[mɛ̃]	'hand'
[ʃas]	'hunt'	[ʃãs]	'luck'
[bo]	'beautiful' (masc.)	[bɔ̃]	'good' (masc.)

2.4.3 Fricatives

Take a look at the fricative row of the English consonant chart in File 2.2. In this row there are five empty cells—bilabial voiceless and voiced, velar voiceless and voiced, and glottal voiced. It turns out that all five of these possible sounds occur in other languages. The symbols that belong in those cells are shown below in (3):

(3) Examples of fricatives

Description	Symbol	Example	Gloss	Language
voiceless bilabial fricative	[ɸ]	éɸá	'he polished'	Ewe
voiced bilabial fricative	[β]	ɛ̀βɛ̀	'Ewe'	Ewe
voiceless velar fricative	[x]	xɔma	'soil'	Modern Greek
voiced velar fricative	[ɣ]	ɣɔma	'eraser'	Modern Greek
voiced glottal fricative	[ɦ]	pluɦ	'plough'	Ukrainian

Though English does not contrast voiced and voiceless glottal fricatives, we do have the voiced glottal fricative [ɦ] when the *h* sound comes between vowels, as it does in the word *ahead*.

In theory it should be easy to say the other fricatives in this list because they simply combine features that already exist in English. [ɸ] is a bilabial sound like [p], and a fricative with a noise sounding much like [f]. Voilà, now you can say [ɸ], right? Well, not if you are like most people. It takes practice to master these new, non-English sounds. However, you may have some experience with some of them if you've studied other languages. The voiceless velar fricative [x] is found in German, Yiddish, and Mandarin Chinese. It is the last sound in the German pronunciation of *Bach* [bɑx], the first sound in the Yiddish word [xʊtspə] 'brazenness, utter nerve,' and the first sound in the Mandarin Chinese word [xɑu ²¹⁴] 'good.' The voiced bilabial fricative [β] is found in Spanish (*Cuba* [kuβa]), as is the voiced velar fricative [ɣ] (*amigo* [amiɣo] 'friend').

2.4.4 Filling in Other Blanks in the Consonant Chart

We can fill in some other empty cells in the English consonant chart. For example, looking at the affricate row, you will notice that English has only palatal affricates. As you might guess, others are possible. For example, the voiceless alveolar affricate [tˢ] occurs in a variety of languages including Canadian French ('ended' [abutˢi]). Similarly, a voiceless labial affricate [pf] is a familar sound from German ('penny' [pfɛnɪk]). The phonetic symbols for these sounds give a good indication of how to say them because we already know how to say [t], [s], [p] and [f].

In addition to the palatal fricatives and affricates of English, it should come as no surprise that some languages make use of palatal stops and nasals. For example, the voiceless palatal stop [c] is used in Greek ('candle' [ceri]), and the voiced palatal nasal [ɲ] is a familiar consonant in Spanish ('pipe' [kaɲa]). These palatal sounds are made with the body of the tongue, like a [k] or [ŋ], but with the tongue touching farther forward in the mouth. You can get the feel of palatal sounds by contrasting your pronunciation of *key*, in which the tongue is fronted, versus *coo*, in which the tongue contact is farther back. It is reasonable to transcribe English *key* as [ci] and *coo* as [ku].

Now, with this description of how to make a palatal stop, we see that the English affricates that we called "palatal" earlier are actually pronounced with a constriction that is somewhere in between alveolar and palatal. This is why we said earlier that [ʃ], [ʒ], [tʃ], and [dʒ] are alveo-palatal consonants. True palatal fricatives do exist, and one example is the voiceless palatal fricative [ç] which is found in Greek ('hand' [çeri]). The five new sounds that we discussed in this section are listed in (4).

(4) Sounds and examples

Description	Symbol	Example	Gloss	Language
voiceless alveolar affricate	[tˢ]	[abutˢi]	'ended'	Canadian French
voiceless labial affricate	[pf]	[pfenik]	'penny'	German
voiceless palatal stop	[c]	[ceri]	'candle'	Modern Greek
voiced palatal nasal stop	[ɲ]	[kaɲa]	'pipe'	Spanish
voiceless palatal fricative	[ç]	[çeri]	'hand'	Modern Greek

2.4.5 Places of Articulation Not Used in English

So far we have seen that the phonetic alphabet contains symbols for non-English sounds that are composed of the same basic phonetic features that are found in English. We now turn to some consonants that are made at places of articulation that we don't find in English.

The voiceless uvular stop [q] is used in Farsi, for example, in the word meaning 'a little bit' [qædri]. The **uvula** is at the very back of the roof of the mouth—that thing that hangs down in your throat. Uvular stops are produced by making a stop closure between the back of the tongue and the uvula. This is like a [k] but with the tongue pulled farther back than normal. The voiced counterpart of [q] is [ɢ].

The voiceless pharyngeal fricative [ħ] is used in Maltese, for example in the word meaning 'clouds' [sħab]. The voiced pharyngeal fricative [ʕ] is used in some dialects of Hebrew, as in the word [ʕor] 'skin.' The pharyngeal place of articulation seems exotic indeed if you thought that the uvular stop had a back tongue position, because the **pharynx** is even further back and lower in the vocal tract. However, it is fairly easy to say a pharyngeal fricative if you start with the vowel [ɑ] of _father_ and just open your jaw wider to pull the tongue back in the mouth. For many people this maneuver causes a frication noise—a voiced pharyngeal fricative. The new sounds that we discussed in this section are listed in (5).

(5) Sounds and examples

Description	Symbol	Example	Gloss	Language
voiceless uvular stop	[q]	[qædri]	'little bit'	Farsi
voiceless pharyngeal fricative	[ħ]	[sħab]	'clouds'	Maltese
voiced uvular stop	[ɢ]	[ihipɢeoqteq]	'explore'	Inuktitut
voiced pharyngeal fricative	[ʕ]	[ʕor]	'skin'	Hebrew

2.4.6 Manners of Articulation Not Used in English

Just as some languages use places of articulation that are not used in English, some languages use manners of articulation not found in English. In this section we will describe four non-English manners of articulation.

The American English [ɹ] sound is an exotic speech sound. This sound is very unusual in the languages of the world. It is also very difficult for children to master (e.g., many children pronounce the word _train_ as [tweɪn] instead of [tɹeɪn]), and it is also a cause of difficulty for adult learners of English. Most languages that have an /r/ sound have a tongue-tip trilled [r]. If you have studied a language other than English, you may have run into the voiced alveolar **trill** [r]. For example, the sound that corresponds to the Spanish spelling <rr> is trilled ('dog' [pero]).

Another manner of articulation not used in English may be familiar from the Russian word for 'no' [nʲɛt]. The **palatalized** nasal in this word is indicated by the superscript small [ʲ]. To American ears [nʲ] sounds like the sequence [nj], but in X-ray movies of Russian we see that the tongue body position for the glide [j] is simultaneous with the tongue tip position for [n]. So instead of a sequence [nj] the Russian palatalized [nʲ] involves a secondary articulation [ʲ] which is simultaneous with the primary constriction [n]. Many consonants can be palatalized. In the exercises later in this book you will find the palatalized voiceless bilabial stop [pʲ], the palatalized voiceless alveolar stop [tʲ], the palatalized voiceless velar stop [kʲ], the palatalized voiceless alveolar fricative [sʲ], and the palatalized voiceless alveo-palatal fricative [ʃʲ].

The phenomenon of secondary articulation helps explain a difference in how [l] is pronounced in English. At the beginnings of words (and as the first sound in stressed syllables within words) [l] is pronounced with the tongue-tip touching the alveolar ridge and the tongue body held rather low in the mouth. But at the ends of words (or as the last sound in a syllable) [l] is pronounced with the tongue body higher in the mouth, and some-times the tongue-tip does not touch the roof of the mouth at all. Compare the way you say [l] in *laugh* and *Al* (before and after the vowel [æ]). Traditionally these two pronunciations of English [l] are called **clear** (tongue body down, tongue-tip up) and **dark** (tongue body up and tongue-tip down), respectively. We can add to this rough description by noting that in dark [l] (as in *Al*) there is a secondary articulation in which the tongue body moves toward the velum. The dark [l] is therefore more accurately described as **velarized**, and we write this velarized alveolar lateral liquid as [ɫ]. In Macedonian the contrast between velarized [ɫ] and plain [l] distinguishes words: for example, [bela] means 'trouble' while [beɫa] means 'white (fem. nom. sg.).'

The final non-English manner of articulation we want to discuss here is **glottalization.** In glottalized consonants, a glottal stop [ʔ] is produced simultaneously with the primary oral closure in the vocal tract. This simultaneous glottal gesture is symbolized by the small superscript glottal stop symbol [ʔ] after a symbol for whatever consonant is glottalized (e.g., [pʔ] for a glottalized voiceless bilabial stop).

At first, glottalization may seem quite comparable to a secondary articulation. The name for the phenomenon, "glottalization," parallels the names of the secondary articulations "palatalization" and "velarization." Additionally, the symbol used for glottalized consonants (e.g., [pʔ]) is similar in form to the symbols used for palatalized consonants (e.g., [pʲ]).

Unlike palatalization and other secondary articulations, however, glottalization affects the **airstream mechanism** of speech. That is, unlike all of the other sounds we have discussed, the main airstream for glottalized sounds is not the exhaled air from the lungs. Instead, the air pressure that makes the stop release noise (the pop when you release a stop closure) is made by compressing the air in the mouth cavity with the larynx. This is done by closing the glottis (and an oral closure like [k]) and then raising the larynx in the throat. This compresses the air in the mouth—you can think of the rising larynx as a piston in a car engine. Then the stop release noise is made by this compressed air when the [k] closure is released. And then the glottal stop is released. This high-pressure release may make quite a "pop," and so it may not be surprising that such consonants are also called **ejectives**. These consonants may seem very exotic, but they can be fun and easy once you learn them. They occur in 15%–20% of all languages. The sounds that we have discussed in this section are listed in (6).

(6) Sounds and examples

Description	Symbol	Example	Gloss	Language
voiced alveolar trill	[r]	[pero]	'dog'	Spanish
palatalized consonants	[pʲ] etc.	[pʲatʲ]	'five'	Russian
velarized alveolar lateral liquid	[ɫ]	[beɫa]	'white'	Macedonian
glottalized (ejective) stops	[pʔ] etc.	[pʔo]	'foggy'	Lakhota

Suprasegmental Features

2.5.1 Segmental vs. Suprasegmental Features

So far we have studied the characteristics of the **segments** (i.e., individual sounds) of speech: place and manner of articulation and voicing for consonants; tongue height and advancement, lip rounding, and tenseness for vowels. In this file we will consider other features that speech sounds may also have: length, intonation, tone, and stress. These features are called **suprasegmental** features because they are thought of as "riding on top of" other segmental features (*supra-* means 'over, above'). Suprasegmental features are different from the features we've studied so far (segmental features) in that it is often difficult or even impossible to identify the quality of a suprasegmental feature if you hear just a single segment. Instead, for suprasegmentals, you have to compare different segments and different utterances to see what the features are. In addition, some suprasegmental features can extend across numerous segments in an utterance, rather than belonging to a single phonetic segment.

2.5.2 Length

The first suprasegmental feature we will talk about is **length**: some speech sounds are longer than others. However, the actual duration of a segment may vary for a number of different reasons (e.g., speaking quickly to a friend as you run out the door versus speaking slowly as you read a story to a young child). Because of this variation, we can't just look at a particular segment and say "that was a long [i]" or "that was a short [i]." Instead, we have to compare the durations of segments within a given utterance (e.g., "this is a long [i] compared to that one").

In some languages, differences in the durations of segments can be as meaningful as the difference between having your tongue body in a high versus a mid front position ([i] versus [e]). Substituting a long segment for an otherwise identical short segment (or vice versa) can result in a different word. For example, consider the data from Finnish shown in (1). In Finnish, both vowels and consonants may be either long or short, and the difference can make a difference in the meaning of a word. (In the data in (1), long vowels and consonants are marked with a following [ː]; segments without this symbol are assumed to be short.)

(1) Examples of using length to contrast word meaning in Finnish

    a.   i. [muta]   'mud'
         ii. [muːta] 'some other'
        iii. [mutːa] 'but'

    b.   i. [tapan] 'I kill'
         ii. [tapaːn] 'I meet'

    c.   i. [tule]   'come!'
         ii. [tuleː] 'comes'
        iii. [tuːleː] 'is windy'

The difference between a long [uː] and a short [u] in Finnish is dependent on the overall speech rate; you have to compare the duration of any given segment with the durations of the other segments to figure out if it was long or short. This is what makes length a suprasegmental feature.

In addition to this type of length difference that can make the difference between two words, speech sounds also vary in duration inherently. For example, all else being equal, high vowels are shorter than low vowels, and voiceless consonants are longer than voiced consonants. Voiceless fricatives are the longest consonants of all.

The duration of a speech sound may also be influence by the sounds around it. For example, say the words *beat* and *bead* aloud. In which word is the [i] longer? In English, a vowel preceding a voiced consonant is about 1.5 times longer than the same vowel before a voiceless consonant. The place and manner of articulation of a following consonant can also affect vowel length. Try saying the word *bees*. How does the length of the [i] in *bees* compare to that in *bead?*

2.5.3 Intonation

Voiced speech sounds, particularly vowels, may be produced with different pitches. Pitch is the psychological correlate of fundamental frequency, which depends on the rate of vibration of the vocal folds (see File 2.6). The pattern of pitch movements across a stretch of speech such as a sentence is commonly known as **intonation.** The intonation contour of an utterance plays a role in determining its meaning. For example, you can read the same words with different intonations and mean different things. Try reading the words in (2) out loud with different pitch patterns, and see if you can get this effect. You might try reading them with either a rising or a falling pitch at the end, or with any other intonation patterns you can think of.

(2) a. You got an A on the test
    b. Yes

Using a rising intonation at the end of the utterance tends to make it sound more like a question, while using a falling intonation makes it sound like a statement.

Although there are multiple systems available for analyzing the intonation of an utterance, one of the most common systems assumes that there are two different intonational phenomena involved in marking the intonation contours of sentences: **pitch accents** and **edge tones.**[1]

Pitch accents usually involve a change in fundamental frequency in the middle of an utterance: a word may be produced with a pitch that is particularly higher or lower than the surrounding words. Words that receive a pitch accent are perceived as very prominent in an utterance—not all words in an utterance get a pitch accent.

Read the examples in (3) aloud. The word that receives a pitch accent, that is, the word that is especially prominent, is written in capital letters. You can see that by putting the prominence on different words, you can use the same string of words to answer different questions.

(3) a. Speaker 1: Who kissed Peter?
    b. Speaker 2: MARY kissed Peter.

    a. Speaker 1: Who did Mary kiss?
    b. Speaker 2: Mary kissed PETER.

---

[1]This system is know as the ToBI, or "Tones and Break Indices," labeling system. For more information on ToBI, see http://www.ling.ohio-state.edu/~tobi/.

a. Speaker 1: What did Mary do to Peter?
b. Speaker 2: Mary KISSED Peter.

Next we will look at how edge tones can change the meaning of a sentence. Edge tones occur at the end of a phrase. Like pitch accents, they usually involve changes in fundamental frequency, but unlike pitch accents, they represent the pitch pattern right before a perceived break instead of in the middle of an utterance. Read the examples in (4) aloud. In these examples, punctuation indicates where a break occurs. Thus, there is a perceptual break at every period, question mark, and comma. Notice that even though punctuation coincides with a break in these examples, this is not always the case.

(4) a. You got an A on the test.
     b. You got an A on the test?
     c. You got an A on the test, a C on the homework, and a B on the quiz.

In each example, how did you read the word preceding a punctuation mark? Did you read it with a falling or a rising pitch? The first sentence is a statement and is thus usually produced with falling pitch at the end. This is called sentence-final intonation. The second sentence is a yes/no question, which is usually said with rising pitch, so-called question intonation, at the end. The third example also has sentence-final intonation at the end. But there are two further breaks corresponding to each comma. The pitch before these breaks first falls and then rises again slightly. This is called continuation rise; it indicates that the speaker is not done speaking. Thus, the intonation on the word *test* determines whether the string of words *you got an A on the test* is a statement or a question, and whether the speaker is done speaking or not.

2.5.4 Tone

In many languages, the pitch at which the syllables in a word are pronounced can make a difference in the word's meaning. Such languages are called **tone languages** and include Thai; Mandarin and other "dialects" of Chinese (cf. File 10.1 for an explanation of the notion "dialect"); Vietnamese; languages in New Guinea such as Skou; many of the Bantu languages of Africa such as Zulu, Luganda, and Shona; other African languages such as Yoruba and Igbo; and many North and South American Indian languages such as Apache, Navajo, Kiowa, Mazotec, and Bora. To see how the tone of a word can make a difference in meaning, consider the words in Mandarin Chinese in (5):

(5) Examples from Mandarin Chinese: different tones, different meanings

Segments	Tone Numbers[2]	Tone Pattern	Gloss
[ma]	55	high level	'mother'
[ma]	35	high rising	'hemp'
[ma]	214	low falling rising	'horse'
[ma]	51	high falling	'scold'

As you can see, the same segments in a word (in this case, the syllable [ma]) can be pronounced with different tones and as a result correspond to different meanings.

---

[2] The tone numbers used in this table were devised by a Chinese linguist named Y. R. Chao to describe the tones of all dialects of Chinese. In this commonly used system for Chinese, '5' indicates the highest pitch and '1' indicates the lowest pitch in the pitch range.

In tone languages, tones can be of two types: either level or contour. All tone languages have level tones; in these tones a syllable is produced with a relatively steady tone such as a high tone, a mid tone, or a low tone. Some tone languages also have contour tones, where a single syllable is produced with tones that glide from one level to another. For example, a rising tone might glide from a low tone to a high tone, while a falling tone might glide from a high tone to a low tone.

There are multiple systems for transcribing tones; the choice of system often has to do with the number and type of tonal contrasts the transcriber needs to make, as well as the history of the systems traditionally used to transcribe tones in a particular set of languages. For Mandarin, for example, tone numbers are often used to indicate the different levels of tone (see (5)). In Kikerewe, on the other hand, tones are often transcribed using accent marks over the vowel in a syllable, where [´] indicates a high tone, [¯] indicates a mid tone, [`] indicates a low tone, [ˇ] indicates a rising tone, and [^] indicates a falling tone (see (6)). See the IPA chart on the inside back cover of the book for the standard IPA symbols used to mark tone.

(6) Examples of level and contour tones in Kikerewe

Word	Tone Pattern	Gloss
[kùsàlà]	low-low-low	'to be insane'
[kùsálà]	low-high-low	'to cut off meat'
[kùʃǐːngà]	low-rise-low	'to defeat, win'
[kùsìːngà]	low-low-low	'to rub, apply ointment'
[kùzúmà]	low-high-low	'to insult, scold'
[kùzùmà]	low-low-low	'to rumble, be startled'
[kùkālâːŋgà]	low-mid-fall-low	'to fry'

It is important to note that the tones in a tone language are at least to a certain degree relative, rather than absolute. This is part of what makes them suprasegmental features. For example, the pitch of a high-level tone spoken by a Mandarin speaker with a deep or low-pitched voice will be considerably lower than the pitch of the same tone spoken by a female speaker with a higher-pitched voice. To determine whether a given syllable has a high or a low tone, you must compare it to other syllables spoken by the same speaker—and even then, different utterances may be produced with different tonal ranges!

At the same time, however, there are certain constants in tone production that can help listeners process tones. Some languages tend to be "higher pitched" overall than others: for example, Cantonese tends to be spoken on a higher pitch than Taita, which gives listeners at least some sort of baseline to expect for the tonal range. And, of course, a listener's knowledge about the speaker's physical characteristics (male versus female, tall versus short, etc.) will help him correctly identify the tones he hears.

We should also point out that tone and intonation are not mutually exclusive: tone languages also use intonation.

2.5.5 Stress

The last suprasegmental feature we will examine is **stress.** Stress, like tone, is a property of entire syllables, not just segments. A stressed syllable is more prominent than an unstressed one. This prominence is due to a number of factors, including the fact that stressed syllables are longer and louder than unstressed syllables and usually contain full vowels. Full vowels are produced with more extreme positions of the tongue than reduced vowels, which are produced closer to the mid central position in the mouth and often occur in unstressed syllables.

For example, compare the first vowels in the words *photograph* and *photography;* how are they different? In *photograph,* the first syllable is the most stressed and would be transcribed with the full vowel [oʊ]. But in *photography,* the second syllable is the most stressed, and the vowel in the first syllable has been "reduced" to [ə].

English uses several stress levels, as illustrated by a word like *photography:* in this word, the second syllable is most prominent (has primary stress), the final syllable is next most prominent (has secondary stress), and the other syllables are unstressed (have tertiary stress). In IPA, we transcribe stress using a mark before the beginning of a syllable: primary stress is marked with ['], and secondary stress is marked with [,]. Tertiary stress is not marked. So, for example, the word *photography* would be transcribed as [fəˈtɑɡɹəˌfi].

In some languages the placement of stress on a word is predictable; for example, stress almost always falls on the first syllable of a word in Czech, on the next to last syllable of a word in Welsh, and on the last syllable of a phrase in French. In other languages such as Russian and English, stress placement is not predictable and must be learned for each word. In such languages the placement of stress can cause a difference in meaning. For example, what is the difference between a *bláckboard* and a *black bóard?* a *white hóuse* and the *Whíte House?* (Note that in these phrases, an acute accent is placed over the word or syllable that receives primary stress.) Consider also the words *record, perfect,* and *subject.* How are their meanings different when stress falls on the first syllable as opposed to the second? Compare also the words *incite* and *insight,* which differ phonetically only in stress placement but which mean different things.

Much of our emphasis in the previous files has been on the transcription of speech sounds with a series of symbols. Suprasegmental features, on the other hand, prove to be difficult to transcribe this way because they are "superimposed" on the other features. For example, while the symbol [a] always represents the same speech sound whenever we write it, the symbol [ː] has no meaning in isolation. Its meaning is a function of the meaning of the symbol (such as [a]) with which it is used, and even then it indicates only that a segment is long relative to the length of a similar sound transcribed without the [ː]. Similarly, marking stress indicates only that the segments of the stressed syllables are louder and longer than their neighboring sounds. And you can change the intonational pattern of an English utterance radically without changing the segments on which the intonation rides. As you can see, our transcription system doesn't express these facts very well. Perhaps because of this, suprasegmental features remain an important topic in contemporary phonetic research.

Acoustic Phonetics

2.6.1 Articulatory vs. Acoustic Phonetics

So far we have been concerned with articulatory phonetics, the study of how speech sounds are produced. In this file, we will examine many of the exact same speech sounds. This time, however, we will focus on the physical aspects of the sound wave, i.e., the acoustic characteristics of the sounds.

One of the main difficulties in studying speech is that speech is fleeting; as soon as a sound is uttered, it's gone. One of the ways to capture it is to transcribe it using phonetic symbols, as we've seen in previous files. But transcription runs the risk of involving endless debate about what a speaker actually said (e.g., did she say short [a] or long [aː]?). However, modern technology has made it possible to conquer the fleeting nature of speech, at least to some degree, by making records of the acoustic properties of sounds.

2.6.2 Simple Sound Waves

Before we look at speech sounds, it is important to understand something of the nature of sound waves. Sound waves, unlike letters on a page, are not permanent things. They are disturbances in the air set off by a movement of some sort. One kind of movement that can set off a sound wave is vibration, such as that produced by violin strings, rubber bands, and tuning forks—or vocal folds. In this kind of sound wave, a vibrating body sets the molecules of air surrounding it into vibration.

In order to understand how this works, imagine that air molecules are like people in a crowded elevator trying to keep a comfortable distance from one another: if one person moves toward another person, that second person may step back away from the first person. By stepping back, this new person may move closer to yet another person, and so the reaction continues throughout the elevator. Similarly, if one person suddenly moves away from another person, that second person may realize she could have more space on either side by moving back toward the first person. Again, the result may be a chain of movements throughout the crowd while everyone tries to stay equally far apart from everyone else.

There are two physical phenomena resulting from this tendency toward equidistance that make it possible for sound waves to move through the atmosphere. These are **compression,** in which air molecules are more crowded together than usual, and **rarefaction,** in which air molecules are spread farther apart than usual. Because there is a tendency for air molecules (like people in an elevator) to remain equidistant from one another, whenever they are placed in compression or rarefaction, certain instability is set up. Compressed molecules tend to move away from one another so that they are no longer compressed. Likewise, when air is rarefied, there is a tendency for the molecules to move nearer together, as they were before rarefaction occurred.

When the string of a guitar is vibrating, it causes a sound wave in the following way: as the string moves away from its rest position, it pushes the adjacent air molecules closer to neighboring molecules, causing compression. The neighboring, compressed molecules

(1) 440 hertz sine wave, the tone A

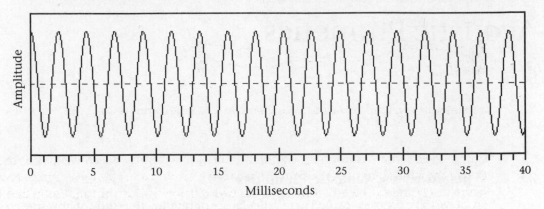

move away from the first "uncomfortably close" molecules, toward others. Those other molecules in turn do the same, and the chain reaction continues.

As the vibrating guitar string moves in the other direction, back to its rest position and beyond, a rarefaction is created. This pulls the air molecules that had been pushed away back toward the string, which creates a rarefaction between them and the molecules on their other side, which pulls those molecules back, and so on. Note that the consequences of the movement (the crowding of the molecules) may be transmitted over a large distance while each individual molecule simply vibrates in place. This chain reaction, which is the consequence of the movement of the string, is the sound wave. When the string moves back and forth at a certain frequency (that is, a certain number of times per second), a group of air molecules which are at some distance from the string will alternately be compressed and rarefied at that frequency. If this chain reaction involving compression and rarefaction is repeated at a rate of 440 times a second, we will hear a musical tone known as "A above middle C." A sound wave such as this, which repeats at regular intervals, is called a **periodic wave.**

If we plot the energy with which the air molecules press against or pull away from one another in such a sound, the resulting plot looks like the one shown in (1). You can think of the figure in (1) as a plot of the movement (vertical axis) of some air molecules across time (horizontal axis), or, more accurately, you can think of it as being the amount of pressure exerted by the air molecules across time. That is, if the dashed line in the figure represents the resting location of a molecule, you can think of the wavy line (the sine wave) as representing the molecule being pushed away from the resting position, then back toward it, and then away from it in the other direction. The plot in (1) has a frequency of 440 Hz ("hertz," abbreviated Hz, is a unit of measurement meaning 'cycles/second'), meaning that the molecule moves away from, back toward, away from in the opposite direction, and back toward its original resting position 440 times in a single second.

Air molecules can vibrate at many different frequencies. When they vibrate at rates from 20 to 20,000 times a second, the vibration is perceived as sound. It is interesting to note, however, that we don't really use this whole range for speech. In fact, the highest frequency that can be transmitted by a telephone is 3,500 Hz, and yet little essential information about the speech signal is lost by cutting off frequencies above this.

2.6.3 Complex Sound Waves

Our discussion of sound waves up to this point has been very basic and somewhat simplified. In fact, simple sound waves such as those discussed in the previous section are not produced by guitar strings or human vocal folds. It's really not too difficult to understand why

(2) Complex vibration of a string

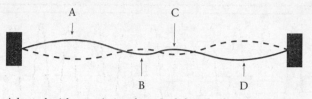

Adapted with permission from Ladefoged, *Elements of Acoustic Phonetics* (1962), p. 24.

simple sound waves could not be produced by a guitar string. When we look at the vibration of the whole length of the string, it becomes clear that a simple wave cannot result. The figure in (2) shows the vibrating string at two different points in time (solid and dashed lines); the amount of movement is exaggerated to make it easier to see.

From the figure in (2), you can see that the string vibrates one way at A, another way at B, another way at C, and yet another way at D. The result of the parts of the string vibrating in different ways simultaneously is a complex wave, such as that in (3c). Complex waves can be viewed as the combinations of a number of simple waves in the same way that the complex pattern of vibration in (2) can be seen as the combination of several simpler patterns of vibration. Thus (3a) and (3b) illustrate the simple wave components of the complex wave in (3c).

The sound wave that is produced by the vocal folds is a complex wave. This complex wave is composed of a fundamental wave which repeats itself at the frequency of the opening and closing of the vocal folds, and a set of **harmonics** which repeat at frequencies which are multiples of the fundamental. Thus, if the vocal folds open and close at a rate of 100 cycles per second, the fundamental frequency of the resulting sound wave is 100 hertz (cycles/second), the second harmonic is 200 Hz, the third harmonic is 300 Hz, and so on. Note that the first harmonic is the **fundamental frequency** (pitch).

The complex wave produced by the vocal folds is known as the source wave, because the vocal folds are the source of the sound wave; it is their movement which creates the wave. It can be represented in a histogram as in (4a), where the horizontal axis stands for cycles per second, and the vertical axis represents the amplitude of the wave. Each line represents one component wave (or harmonic) in the complex vocal wave. Note that the relative amplitude of each wave gets progressively smaller at higher frequencies.

As this sound wave passes through the vocal tract, the articulators shape it, or filter it, boosting the energy at some harmonic frequencies and damping the energy at others. This filter action is similar to the effect of room acoustics on a speaker's voice. Some rooms enhance the voice so that no amplification is needed, while others seem to absorb the voice, muffling the sound. In a similar way, the vocal tract acts as a filter on the source wave. In (4), the vocal tract positioned for the vowel [ɑ] has a filtering effect as in (4b), and harmonics at about 600 Hz, 1380 Hz, and 2500 Hz are enhanced, while harmonics at other positions are damped, yielding the output wave in (4c).

Thus a speech sound (wave) is the result of two independent things: the source wave (the contribution of the vocal folds) and the filter (the contribution of the articulators and the vocal tract).

2.6.4 Vowels

In the production of vowels, the filtering effect of the vocal tract produces amplitude peaks at certain frequencies by enhancing the harmonics (the component waves of a complex wave form, produced by the vocal folds) at those frequencies while damping harmonics at other frequencies (see (4) in Section 2.6.3). These peaks in the filter function are called

(3) Two simple waves combining to form a complex wave

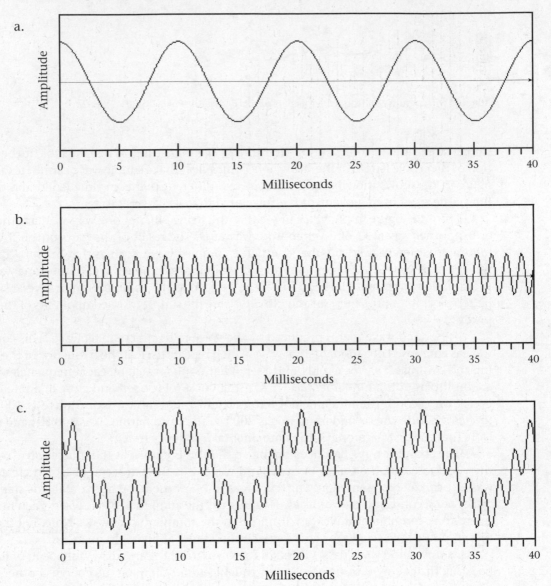

formants (resonant frequencies of the vocal tract). For example, just as a trombone has particular resonant frequencies (determined by the length of the tube) that shape the sound produced by the vibration of the lips, in vowel sounds the vocal tract has resonant frequencies (determined by the length and configuration of the vocal tract) that shape the sound produced by vocal fold vibration. These resonant frequencies of the vocal tract are the vowel formants. Vowels have several formants, the first three of which are the most important for speech perception. The values of these formants differ from vowel to vowel. The table in (5) lists typical formant frequencies for eight American English vowels.

We can plot these vowels by the frequencies of their first two formants, as shown in (6). Note that if we put the origin (0,0) in the upper right-hand corner, the resulting diagram looks strikingly similar to the vowel chart in (1) in File 2.3. Thus we can see that the first formant corresponds inversely to the height dimension (high vowels have a low F1 and low vowels have a high F1), and the second formant corresponds to the advancement (front/back) dimension (front vowels have a high F2 and back vowels have a low F2).

(4) Source plus filter equals speech sound

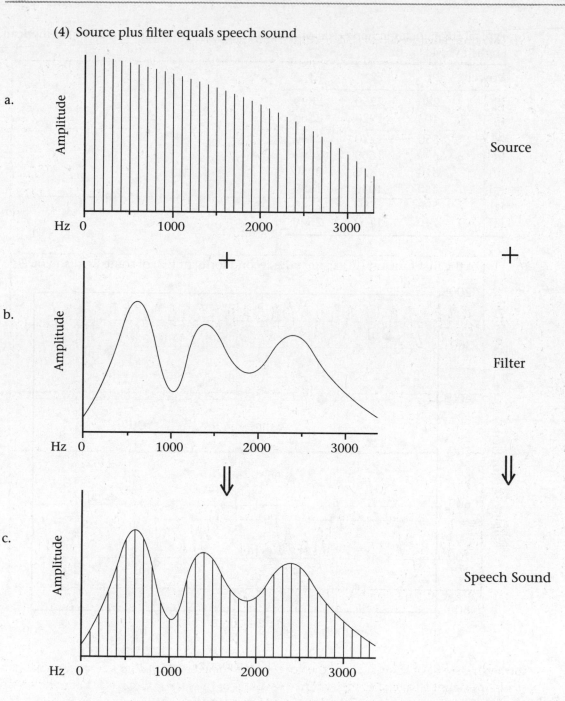

a.   Source

b.   Filter

c.   Speech Sound

A common method of representing acoustic properties of speech sounds is to use a **spectrogram.** Spectrograms are graphs that encode three acoustic dimensions: the vertical axis represents frequency, and the horizontal axis represents time. A third dimension is represented by degree of darkness that indicates the amount of acoustic energy present at a certain time and at a certain frequency. Dark horizontal bands usually represent formants because formants represent enhanced bands of energy at particular frequencies. In (7) we see spectrograms for the three vowels [i], [u], and [ɑ]. The arrows point out only the first three vowel formants, although there are more formants visible in these spectrograms. The horizontal lines in each of these displays mark off frequency in hertz by the 1000s. These spectrograms show visually the differences that we hear when we listen to these three vowels.

(5) Typical frequencies in hertz (Hz) of the first, second, and third formants for American English vowels

Vowel	F1	F2	F3
[i]	280	2250	2890
[ɪ]	400	1920	2560
[ɛ]	550	1770	2490
[æ]	690	1660	2490
[u]	310	870	2250
[ʊ]	450	1030	2380
[ɔ]	590	880	2540
[ɑ]	710	1100	2540

(6) Plot of the first formant (F1) against the second formant (F2) of some English vowels

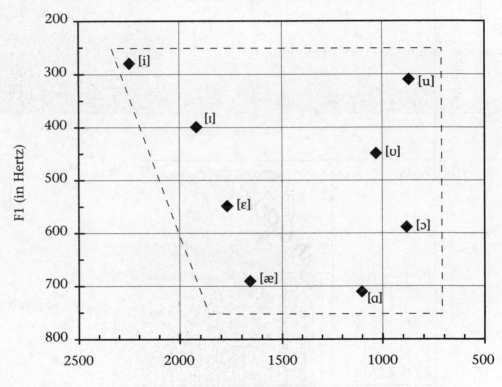

2.6.5 Stops

Spectrograms can clearly show other types of segments as well. In File 2.2, we described the articulatory properties of consonants in terms of their voicing and their manner and place of articulation. Stop consonants are produced by completely closing off the oral cavity with the lips or tongue, blocking the flow of air. This lack of airflow makes stops easy to detect on spectrograms because they are characterized by a lack of energy—hence a gap—in the display, as illustrated in (8). So, the acoustic characteristic of a stop (the silence we hear, or the blank space on the spectrogram) reflects its manner of articulation.

If a stop is voiced, the vocal folds will actually be vibrating during the closure, and some low-frequency noise is produced. This noise can be seen as the dark band at the very bottom of the spectrogram during the "silence" of the stop. This band is called the **voice bar.**

(7) Spectrograms of the vowels [i], [u], [ɑ]

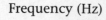

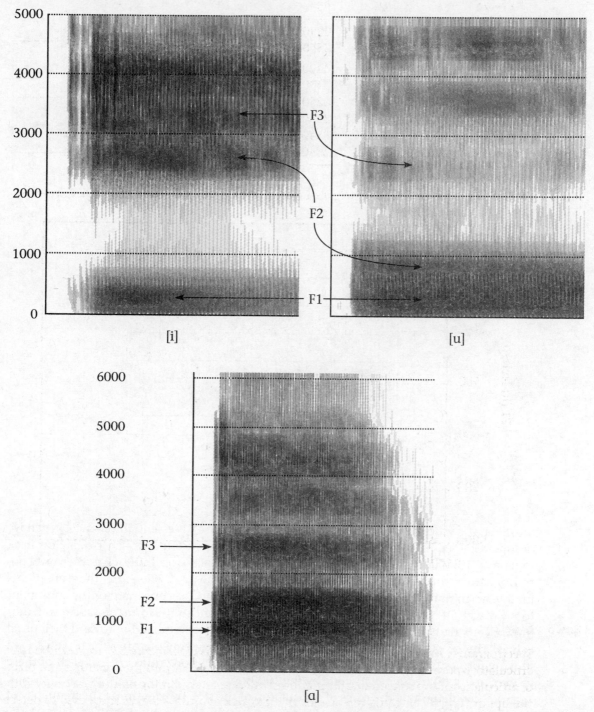

Voiceless stops never have this voice bar. In English, voiceless stops are also often further characterized by a period of **aspiration**, during which air rushes out of the mouth after the release of the stop closure and before the onset of the vowel. This aspiration is transcribed with a superscript [h], as in [pʰ] and can be clearly seen in the spectrogram in (9) of the word *pat*.

The acoustic information corresponding to place of articulation for a stop is found

(8) Spectrograms of [ɑdɑ], [ɑgɑ], [ɑbɑ]

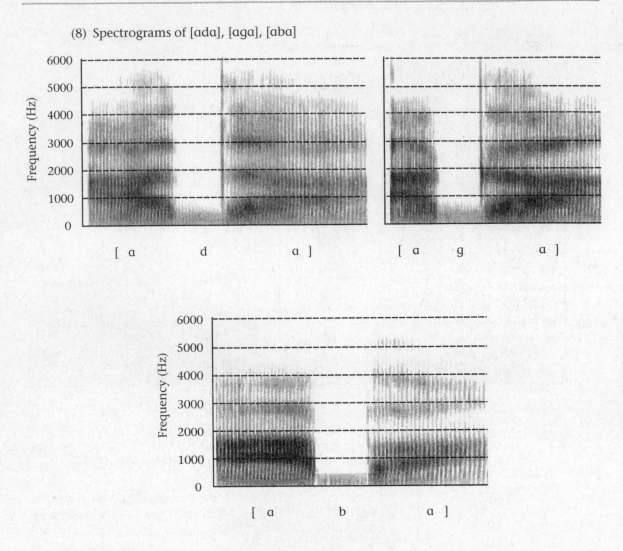

mostly in the vowels around it since, after all, the stop itself is essentially silence. When we pronounce a sequence like [ɑdɑ], the tongue can't move instantaneously from a low back tongue position to the alveolar ridge for the voiced alveolar stop and back to the vowel position. Rather, the tongue glides from one position to the next. Therefore, there are points in time when the tongue is in transition from the vowel to the consonant or the consonant to the vowel. Of course, this changing vocal tract shape affects the formants; as a result, during the early part of the second vowel the formants are also in transition toward their usual values. The spectrograms in (8) show vowel-stop-vowel sequences in which we can see moving formants reflecting the moving articulator. (The horizontal lines in each of these displays mark off frequency in hertz by the 1000s.)

We can determine the place of articulation of the stop by examining the frequency of the second formant at the juncture of the vowel and the consonant. For alveolar stops, the second formant of the vowel will be around 1700–1800 Hz going into or coming out of the consonant. For bilabial stops, F2 will be low at the juncture of the consonant and vowel, and higher in the vowel itself (so, for the sequence [ɑb], the second formant will seem to fall into the consonant, while for the sequence [bɑ], the second formant will seem to rise out of the consonant). For velar stops, the pattern will depend on what kind of vowel pre-

(9) Spectrograms of [pʰæt]

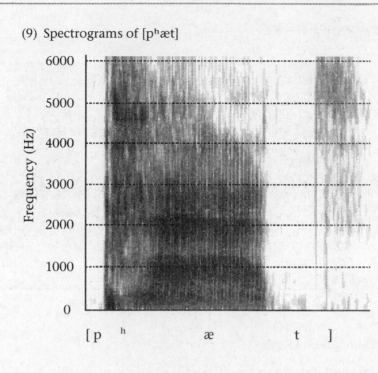

cedes or follows the consonant. For example, if the consonant is followed by a front vowel, the F2 will start high and then fall, but if the consonant is followed by a back vowel, the F2 will start fairly low, around 900 Hz or lower.

2.6.6 Fricatives

Fricatives involve a new kind of sound that we have not dealt with up to this point. The difference between the noise found in vowels and in fricatives is that the sound in vowels has its source in the periodic vibration of the vocal folds, while the sound in fricatives comes from the aperiodic, or random, turbulence of the air rushing through a small opening. Note in (10) that during the vowels there is a regular repetition (seen in the vertical stripes) while in the fricative portions there is no apparent pattern; it looks like static on a TV screen.

We find differences among English fricatives in the relative frequency of the noise (e.g., [s] has a higher frequency energy concentration in the frication noise than [ʃ]), amplitude (e.g., [s] is louder than [f]), and duration (e.g., [s] is longer than [z]). As with stops, the formant transitions from the consonant into the vowel are also used by listeners to determine the place of articulation.

Voiced fricatives are interesting in that they combine periodic noise (the vocal folds are vibrating in a regular cycle) and aperiodic noise (there is turbulence from the air being forced through a small opening). Affricates are sequences of stop plus fricative both in their articulation and in their acoustic characteristics. A spectrogram of an affricate begins with a gap in the wave form, which is immediately followed by the aperiodicity of a fricative.

2.6.7 Nasals

In the production of nasal consonants, the oral cavity is closed as if for a stop, but air escapes past the lowered velum through the nasal cavity. In acoustic terms, the nasal passage serves as the filter for the vocal source, just as the oral cavity acts as a filter in vowels. All nasal consonants have quite similar formants (see (11)), reflecting the shape of the nasal

(10) Spectrograms of [lis] and [liʃ]

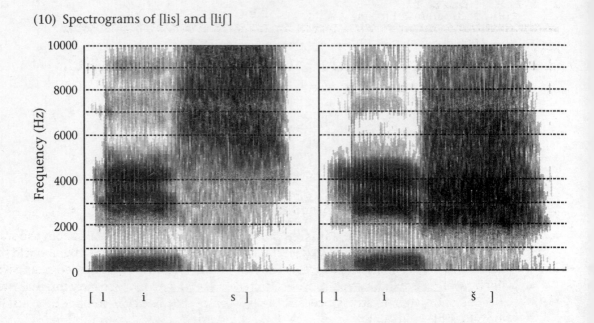

     [l   i   s]   [l   i   š]

(11) Spectrogram of [mi] and [ni]

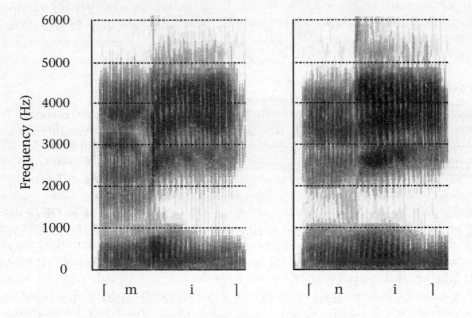

    [m   i   ]   [n   i   ]

passage, which enhances some harmonics and damps others. Nasal formants are usually somewhere around 250, 2500, and 3250 Hz. The place of articulation of nasal consonants, however, is still cued by the transitions from the nasal into the vowel. Note that in (11), there is a lighter area (a lack of energy, caused by the damping of the nasal cavity) at around 1250 Hz for [mi] and around 1750 Hz for [ni].

The Phonetics of Signed Languages

2.7.1 Extending *Phonetics* to Signed Languages

The term *phonetics* was originally coined as a term used specifically to talk about the study of the sounds of language. However, phonetics has come to be the name of the subfield that deals with how language is produced, regardless of the modality of that production. Signs, which serve the same function as words in spoken languages, likewise have internal structure. Therefore, signs in any signed language are composed of discrete components, just like words in spoken language.

As has been the case for the preceding files of this chapter, the focus of this file will be on articulatory phonetics: how signs are produced. However, in the same way that phoneticians also study acoustic phonetics—the sounds themselves—and auditory phonetics—how sounds are perceived—likewise linguists who are working on signed language phonetics may also take an interest in how signs are perceived or in the structure of the signs themselves independent of how they are articulated.

2.7.2 The Parameters of Articulation in Signed Languages

The study of the phonetics of signed languages is relatively new. Thus, whereas linguists speak fairly confidently when they say, for example, that a significant feature in describing a consonant is place or manner of articulation, there is still some discussion of which attributes of a sign are significant. Nonetheless, there is a canonical set of parameters that are generally recognized in one way or another as being linguistically significant.

How do you know that a parameter is significant? Well, in evaluating spoken languages (if you speak one), the task is relatively easy. You know, for example, that *mitt* and *bit* are different words, and therefore the feature nasal must be important (because you are able to distinguish between [m] and [b], and they differ only in nasality). When we want to know whether some particular parameter is significant in a signed language, we can do much the same thing: we look to see whether a change to the articulation of that parameter can influence the identity of a sign. (This notion of how discrete yet meaningless units of language can come to affect meaning will be readdressed in Section 3.1.3.)

By performing this set of observations, we can conclude that there are four key parameters of articulation in signed languages. These are place of articulation, movement, handshape, and hand orientation, each of which will be discussed in more detail below. The ways that these features are organized, though, does not correspond directly to the way that features like nasal or rounded are organized. Rather, they themselves are segments. In the same way that a word will have some number of vowels and some number of consonants, a sign will have some number of movements and some number of places of articulation.

One fascinating difference between signed and spoken language is the manner in which their fundamental elements (phones/**primes**) are combined into utterances. In spoken languages, owing both to the nature of the speech mechanism and to the way that our brains process auditory input, phones are organized in linear temporal order; several phones cannot be produced at the same time. (Imagine trying to produce all the phones of a word at the same time! Furthermore, think about how difficult it is to understand three different people talking to you at the same time.) In contrast, a prime in ASL always occurs simultaneously with other primes. Primes cannot stand alone but must co-occur with primes from the other parameters. For example, one could not simply have a hand movement without also having the hand in a particular hand shape or location. (Not only is it possible to produce multiple primes at the same time, but also it is possible to interpret them. Imagine that you are shown a photograph, but that it flashes in front of you and then disappears immediately. You will be able to tell many things about the photograph, because our visual processing, unlike auditory processing, does allow us to clearly perceive multiple different things going on at the same time.)

We will now describe each of the four parameters in more detail and provide several examples of each. Although the examples given in this file come from only two languages, the same parameters are relevant for all signed languages.

2.7.3 Location

The first parameter of sign articulation that we will consider is location. Clearly it is impossible to articulate a sign if the hands aren't somewhere! And we could imagine a system in which all gestures could be made anywhere at all and still have the same meaning (just as you can say a word at any volume at all and it still has the same meaning). How, then, do we know that location is important? We find pairs of words like the following. In the ASL signs for 'apple' (1a) and 'lucky' (2a), the location where the sign is made is at the chin. The sign for 'onion' in (1b) is the same in every way as the sign for 'apple' except that it is made near the eye. Similarly, the sign for 'clever' in (2b) is the same in every way as the sign for 'lucky' except that it is made starting at the forehead. Evidence like this tells us that location is significant.

(1) a. ASL: APPLE   b. ASL: ONION

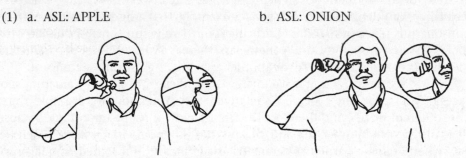

From *Signing: How to Speak with Your Hands* by Elaine Costello. Copyright 1983 by Elaine Costello. Used by permission of Bantam Books, a division of Bantam Doubleday Dell Publishing Group, Inc., pp. 67 and 222.

(2) a. ASL: LUCKY

© 2006, William Vicars, www.Lifeprint.com. Adapted by permission.

b. ASL: CLEVER

The examples in (1) and (2) have places of articulation that differ between the upper and lower halves of the face. Examples such as these are particularly clear in pictorial two-dimensional form; however, there are certainly other locations that contrast.

Every sign language has a particular "signing space": a general area in which signs may be produced. Obviously the outside range might be determined by how far away from your body you can stretch your arms, but most languages have a smaller space than this. For example, ASL has very few signs that are articulated below the waist. But place of articulation is a much more specific feature than just identifying a general area. A sign's place of articulation tells exactly where, relative to the signer's body, that sign must be articulated. Examples include [the front of the shoulder of the arm opposite from the hand making the sign], [the top of the bridge of the nose], [above the shoulder of the hand articulating the sign, but touching neither the shoulder nor the ear], and so on.

One very interesting fact about signing space is that it can be expanded or reduced. If a signer is "whispering," he will reduce the signing space, bringing all places of articulation in closer to his center. This may also involve altering the location of some signs, articulating them in places closer in front of the torso than they normally would be. However, the places of articulation will still have the same sort of positions relative to each other. That is, in whispering, signs normally produced on the forehead will be lowered, while signs normally produced on the chin will also be lowered; every sign will come in toward the signer's center an equivalent amount. If a signer is "yelling," he will increase his signing space and the amount of movement in his signs.

2.7.4 Movement

The second parameter is movement. The examples in (3) and (4) show two pairs of signs that are distinguished by the kind of movement they involve. In TOUGH, one hand begins higher than the other and moves rapidly downward until it is lower; PHYSICS is similar in many ways but involves the two hands moving toward each other.

(3) a. ASL: TOUGH (difficult)

b. ASL: PHYSICS

The signs CAN and SHOES likewise distinguish between vertical and horizontal movement (see (4)), though the vertical motion in CAN is different from the vertical motion in TOUGH. (Try to describe the difference in movement between these two signs.)

(4) a. ASL: CAN   b. ASL: SHOES

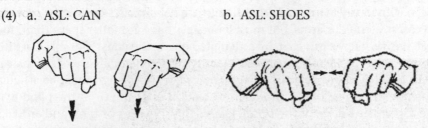

Some signs have movements that are designed to take a hand from one place of articulation to another. For example, the ASL sign for KING moves from the shoulder opposite the signing hand to the top of the hip on the same side as the signing hand. This is different from, for example, the sign for TOUGH above, because in TOUGH what matters is the type of movement itself, more than the precise starting and stopping location.

A third type of movement has to do with ways that the wrist or fingers move and does not actually require any change in place at all. For example, in the ASL sign for YES, the wrist moves up and down (as though it were a head nodding), and in the ASL sign for WAIT, the fingers waggle back and forth, but the hands do not move. Other such movements may include finger circling or one hand tapping another body part.

One interesting thing about movement is that it functions a little bit like vowels in spoken language. You can often understand a word or sentence (in its written form) without vowels; similarly, a signer can often understand a sign or sentence without movement. Nonetheless, just like vowels in spoken languages, movement is a critical part of articulation in sign languages.

2.7.5 Handshape

Third, we will look at handshape. In (5) you see five signs of Taiwan Sign Language, each with no movement and with the same place of articulation (touching the nose). What differs is the shape of the hand: which fingers are extended, whether the fingers are bent or straight, the position of the thumb, whether fingers are touching, and so on. In (5), the five different handshapes give five different meanings to the five signs that they are a part of.

(5) Examples of signs in Taiwan Sign Language differing only in handshape

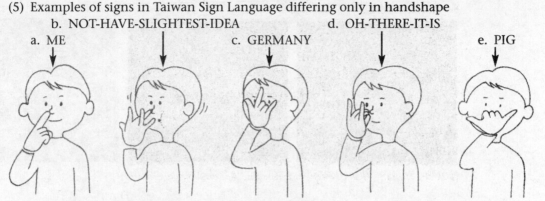

In order to see one way that handshape can interact with movement, consider the two ASL signs in (6). Here, although both LIKE and WHITE begin with the same handshape, they end with different handshapes, because the handshape changes during the movement.

(6) a. ASL: LIKE

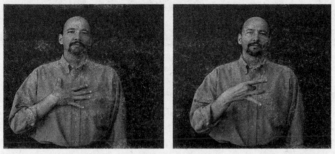

b. ASL: WHITE

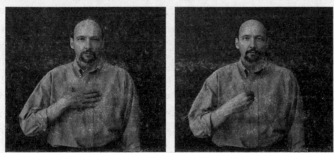

The two signs in (6) also serve to make the point that one sign can contain more than one handshape.

2.7.6 Orientation

The last parameter that has to do with the way that the hands are used is orientation: the direction that the palm of the hand is facing. In both (7a) and (7b), the hands are facing toward each other; however, in (7a) the two hands are pointing left and right, whereas in (7b) they are facing toward the speaker and away from the speaker.

(7)   a. ASL: MEET (the uninflected verb)

© 2006, William Vicars, www.Lifeprint.com. Adapted by permission.

b. ASL: I MEET YOU

© 2006, William Vicars, www.Lifeprint.com. Adapted by permission.

Of course, even in two-handed signs, the hands need not face each other; in the signs for CAN and SHOES in (4), the palm orientation is [facing down]. In the signs for LUCKY and CLEVER in (2), there is a change of orientation during the sign: these two signs begin with the palm facing the speaker and end with the palm facing away from the speaker.

2.7.7 Facial and Other Parameters of Signing

Especially because all four of the parameters of signing articulation that we have described so far are superimposed, they interact with each other in complex ways. One parameter may change while another stays the same, or two may change at the same time.

There is still more to consider in evaluating sign language articulation, though. In addition to hand and arm gestures, other elements may also play a role in signing, such as head movement or tilt and facial expression. In some cases, a facial expression may be part of a sign itself, for example, pursed lips in the ASL sign REALLY-SKINNY. The sign in question also has a manual component: two hands, each with the pinkies extended, begin with the pinkies touching and then move away from each other. However, if only this manual part is performed without the lips being pursed, then the entire word hasn't been articulated. It would be like leaving a segment out of some spoken word: saying [fut] instead of [flut] for *flute*, for example. If somebody were to say, "I play the [fut] in the school orchestra," you would know what they meant, but you would also know that they hadn't articulated the word properly. A second example would be not producing a tone change in a word that required one in a language like Mandarin, in which tones are components of word production.

In other cases, face and head movement act as more of a suprasegmental feature like intonation. For example, there is a particular intonation that we associate with questions like *Where do you live?* In ASL there is also a suprasegmental feature that indicates such a question: it includes inclining the head forward and lowering the eyebrows.

There are other possible facial features as well: squinting or a wrinkled nose, for example. For a very nice example of facial expression being used to articulate a particular sign, compare the signs for HOT in (8a) and VERY HOT in (8b). Notice how the signer's face is different when he articulates VERY HOT from when he articulates HOT. (There are other differences in the production of these two signs as well, but for now just pay attention to the signer's facial features.)

(8) a. HOT

© 2006, William Vicars, www.Lifeprint.com. Adapted by permission.

b. VERY HOT

© 2006, William Vicars, www.Lifeprint.com. Adapted by permission.

2.7.8 Phonetic Inventories in Signed Languages

In File 2.4, it became clear that different languages make use of different inventories of sounds. Some languages have front rounded vowels or consonants with a uvular place of articulation, but English has neither: English is rather unusual in having a retroflex liquid, and so on. All spoken languages have some kinds of consonants and vowels, but the sets of consonants and vowels differ from language to language. The same is true of signed languages. Every language has handshapes, kinds of movements, and places of articulation, but not every one is available in every sign language.

For example, in (5d) we saw the Taiwan Sign Language sign OH-THERE-IT-IS. The hand shape for this sign, which is called the "dragon" handshape, is formed by sticking the pinky and index finger up while bending the middle finger and ring finger in to meet the thumb. If you try to make this handshape, you will find that it is not terribly difficult to produce. Nonetheless, this handshape is not available in the inventory of handshapes that are used in ASL. A second example is the handshape formed by making a fist and extending your ring finger: TSL makes use of it, but ASL does not. Conversely, the ASL "T" handshape, which is formed by making a fist and sticking the thumb between the index finger and middle finger (as though you were playing "I got your nose" with a young child), is a handshape that is not available in TSL. There are other handshapes which appear in neither ASL nor TSL but which do occur in other sign languages. A more profound difference is that in TSL, the elbow can be an active articulator, whereas in ASL the forearm and elbow can be only used as passive articulators. (To conceptualize what this means, think about your mouth: your tongue is an active articulator because it moves, but your alveolar ridge is a passive articulator because it is involved in articulation only when your tongue touches it.)

The same sort of thing (primes that are available in one signed language but not another) occurs for kinds of movement and places of articulation. Some languages have a movement that is a side-to-side twisting of the wrist; others do not. Some sign languages have [crown of the head] as a place of articulation; others do not.

There are many things, of course, that you can do with your hands and arms—just as there are many things you can do with your mouth. Some of these, such as swallowing, whistling, throwing a ball, or brushing at a mosquito are nonlinguistic, while others may be linguistic. It is important to remember, though, that just because a certain kind of articulatory gesture may have linguistic applications does not mean that it is necessarily used in any given language.

2.7.9 Studying and Analyzing the Phonetics of Signed Languages

In the previous files, a number of innovations have been described that help researchers to discuss, describe, and research the articulation of spoken languages. There have been fewer technological innovations for the study of phonetics in signed languages, in part because the sign language articulators are large, slow, and not covered by your cheeks. In other words, they are a lot easier to study in a straightforward way than are the articulators of spoken languages!

Another reason, though, is that as we mentioned above, the study of the phonetics of signed languages is simply newer than the study of spoken language phonetics. Of course, one tool that has been very helpful is simple video recording, which allows researchers to look at the same segments over and over again. More sophisticated technology involves attaching sensors to various parts of signers hands, arms, face, and so on. The sensors' positions and movements can then be recorded and sent to a computer to allow precise measuring of, for example, amount of movement, precise tilt and orientation, exact distance between hands and between hands and the body, and so on. Of course, as this field of study continues to grow, more instruments and tools are certain to follow.

Practice

Note: Several of the activities in this chapter (e.g., 30 and 31 below) and later chapters call for the use of phonetics analysis software. These days, it is possible to find free software to download onto your computer that allows you to fairly easily record and look at speech sounds. To find some, try searching for "phonetics analysis software" or "waveform editor." Some that are available include Praat, WaveSurfer, Speech Analyzer, and Waveforms Annotations Spectrograms and Pitch (WASP), among others. None of the activities in this book crucially depend on using one or the other—all of these packages are excellent for our purposes. Occasionally, however, we think that it is helpful to beginning students to give specific instructions on how to complete an activity; when we do so, the instructions will be for Praat. You should, however, be able to complete any activity using whatever package you choose; ask your instructor for more resources if you need help.

File 2.0—What Is Phonetics?

Exercises

1. What are the three different areas of phonetics, and how do they fit into the communication chain?

File 2.1—Representing Speech Sounds

Exercises

2. Why is it useful to have a phonetic transcription system?

3. What is meant by having a "one-to-one correspondence between sounds and symbols"? Why would this property be desirable?

4. Refer to the "Rhymes with Orange" cartoon at the beginning of this chapter. How does Hilary Price (the cartoonist) represent the patient's condition? Is her system a good phonetic transcription system? Why or why not?

File 2.2—Articulation: English Consonants

Exercises

5. Refer to the "Rhymes with Orange" cartoon at the beginning of this chapter. What are the similarities and differences between a [v] and a [b], the two sounds that differentiate the words *vowel* and *bowel?* Do you think that this similarity adds to the humor of the cartoon? For example, would it have been as funny if it had been a cartoon about Irritable Trowel Syndrome or Irritable Cowl Syndrome? Explain why or why not.

6. Looking at (2) of File 2.2, explain why your vocal folds don't vibrate when you whisper.

7. Write the phonetic symbol representing each of the following sounds (don't forget to use square brackets). The first one is given as an example.

Example: voiced palatal glide: [j]

  a. voiceless palatal affricate
  b. voiced velar nasal
  c. voiceless glottal fricative
  d. voiced labiodental fricative
  e. voiced interdental fricative
  f. voiced palatal fricative
  g. voiced alveolar lateral liquid

8. Write the three-part articulatory descriptions for the consonant sounds represented by the following symbols. The first one is given as an example.

Example: [j]: voiced palatal glide

  a. [f]   **f.** [ɹ]
  b. [z]   **g.** [ʒ]
  c. [n]   **h.** [tʃ]
  d. [ŋ]   **i.** [g]
  e. [ʃ]   **j.** [ʔ]

9. This exercise is designed to help you become more familiar with the shapes of the vocal tract connected with the production of different consonant sounds. For each drawing presented on page 89, there is only one consonant sound of English that could be produced by a vocal tract positioned as shown; you are to figure out which consonant sound is represented (either by referring to the descriptions of different sounds or by experimenting with your own vocal tract—some of each is recommended). Be sure that you take into account the voicing, manner, and place of articulation of each sound. Write the phonetic symbol for that sound between the brackets below the appropriate drawing. Note that voicing is shown by two wavy or bumpy lines (representing vocal fold vibration) where the larynx would be, whereas voiceless sounds are represented by two lines shaped like an ellipse at the larynx level, indicating an open glottis. Take care also to note whether the air passage to the nasal cavity is open or closed (i.e., if the velum is lowered or raised). The first drawing is labeled to start you off.

10. Given the articulatory descriptions of consonants in this file, what would you expect the difference between a [t] and an [s] to look like in static palatography pictures? Of the two pictures below, which do you think could be an instance of [t] and which an instance of [s]? How do you know? What other sounds would make the pattern on the roof of the mouth seen in (a) and (b)?

a.   **b.**

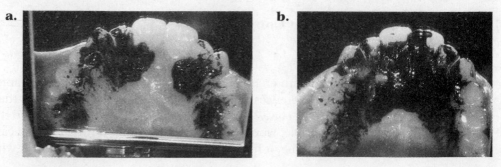

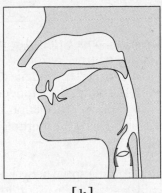

[k]

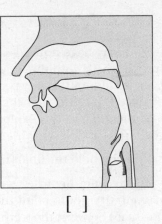

[ ]

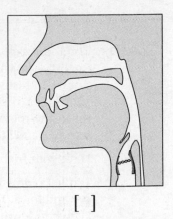

[ ]

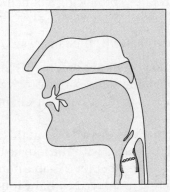

[ð]

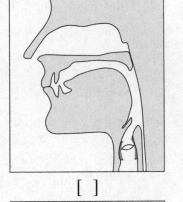

[ ]

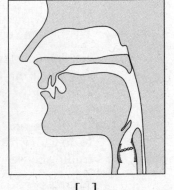

[ ]

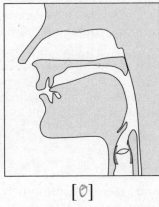

[θ]

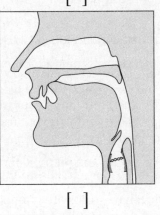

[ ]

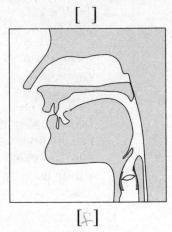

[f]

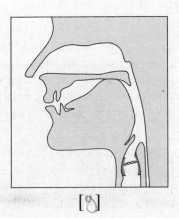

[ŋ]

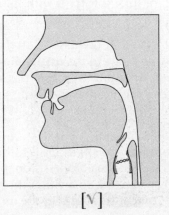

[v]

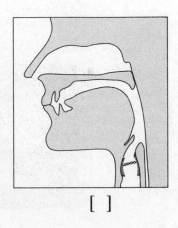

[ ]

Activities

11. The toothpick test. You may have noticed a bit of waffling about the articulation of English [ɹ]. Many people say [ɹ] with the tongue tip curled up (the "retroflex" [ɹ] mentioned in the text). But there are also many people who do not curl the tongue tip up for [ɹ]. Instead, they produce a so-called "bunched" [ɹ] with the body of the tongue pulled up to the roof of the mouth. You can explore this variation in articulation between retroflex and bunched [ɹ] by asking some friends to help you with the toothpick test.

Have your friend say *fur* and hold the final [ɹ], as in [fɹɹɹɹɹɹ].

While holding the [ɹ], have him/her insert a toothpick into the space between the upper and lower front teeth (try not to point the toothpick at an angle up or down, but keep it level with the space between the teeth).

If the toothpick pokes the top of the tongue, your friend is producing a bunched [ɹ]; if it pokes the underside of the tongue, your friend is producing a retroflex [ɹ].

Try the same test on other friends. Do all of your friends say [ɹ] the same way?

Try the same test with other words containing [ɹ]. Do you always produce [ɹ] the same way in all the words? Do you and your friends have the same patterns of variation across words? (Note that language variation is discussed in more detail in Chapter 10.)

12. One of the other complexities of English phonetics that was glossed over in this file has to do with whether [θ] and [ð] are truly interdental (produced with the tongue tip protruding between the front teeth). For many people they are, but for a sizable number of perfectly good speakers of English, [θ] and [ð] are dental (produced with the tongue tip touching the back of the upper front teeth). Ask your friends to help you look at this variation.

Make a list of words that contain [θ] and a list of words that contain [ð].

Watch while your friend reads the list (you may have to have them hold the list up at eye level).

If you can see the tongue protruding, your friend is making [θ] and [ð] interdental. If not, then they are probably dental. Is your friend consistent in making all [θ]s and [ð]s either interdental or dental?

Do all of your friends say [θ] and [ð] the same way?

13. What does toilet paper have to do with phonetics? Hold a piece of tissue loosely in front of (but not touching) your mouth and say the words *buy* and *pie*. Does the tissue flutter more for [b] or for [p]? Now try it with *spy*. Is the [p] in *spy* more like the [b] in *buy* or the [p] in *pie* in terms of how much the tissue moves?

You should have found that the tissue flutters more for [p] in *pie* than [b] in *buy*. The fluttering of the tissue is due to the **aspiration** of the sound (see the discussion of aspiration in File 2.6). An aspirated sound has a puff of air coming out of your mouth when you produce it—this causes the tissue to flutter in *pie* where the [p] is aspirated, but not in *buy* where the [b] is unaspirated. We write an aspirated [p] with a superscript [h], as in [pʰ].

You should also find that the [p] in *spy* is more like the [b] in *buy* than the [pʰ] in *pie*. This is because in English, the voiceless stop [p] is not aspirated when it comes after an [s] at the beginning of a word. So, neither the [p] in *spy* nor the [b] in *buy* should cause the tissue to flutter much, because they are unaspirated, while the aspirated [pʰ] in *pie* should cause the tissue to flutter a lot. This is a phonological phenomenon in English that is discussed in further detail in File 3.1.

File 2.3—Articulation: English Vowels

Exercises

14. Write the phonetic symbol representing each of the following sounds (don't forget to use square brackets). The first one is given as an example:

    Example: high back lax rounded vowel: [ʊ]

    a. high front tense unrounded vowel
    b. mid back lax unrounded vowel
    c. mid front lax unrounded vowel
    d. low back lax unrounded vowel

15. Write the four-part articulatory descriptions for the vowel sounds represented by the following symbols: The first one is given as an example.

    Example: [ə]: mid, central, unrounded, and lax

a. [ɪ]	**d.** [u]
b. [ʌ]	**e.** [æ]
c. [ɛ]	**f.** [ʊ]

Supplemental Exercises: Consonants and Vowels Combined

16. **i.** What is the difference between a consonant and a vowel?
    ii. Why can't we use palatography to study vowel height?

17. Refer to the "Rhymes with Orange" cartoon at the beginning of this chapter. Write out the patient's words using IPA. How did you decide which symbols to use? Do you think everyone would write it out the same way? Explain your answer.

18. Circle all the symbols below which represent voiced sounds:

    [s]   [d]   [g]   [ð]   [tʃ]   [b]   [t]   [ʔ]   [ɹ]   [θ]   [p]

    [o]   [f]   [ʃ]   [z]   [k]   [i]   [m]   [v]   [h]   [w]   [ɪ]

19. Give the conventional spelling for the following phonetically transcribed words. (Note that some may have more than one possible spelling.) The first one (a) is given as an example.

a. [sloʊp] *slope*	**k.** [peɪn]	**u.** [pitsə]	**ee.** [fɪm]
b. [bjuɾi]	**l.** [wɛnzdeɪ]	**v.** [ækʃn̩]	**ff.** [pɹɑɪd]
c. [seɪl]	**m.** [kɑnʃəs]	**w.** [sʌni]	**gg.** [ðoʊ]
d. [wɔɹm]	**n.** [θaʊzn̩d]	**x.** [ʃuleɪs]	**hh.** [gɹeɪs]
e. [ɹut]	**o.** [fʌdʒ]	**y.** [kɹɔld]	**ii.** [sɹ̩veɪ]
f. [liʒɹ̩]	**p.** [kaɪt]	**z.** [pɔɪnt]	**jj.** [lʊk]
g. [sɹ̩tʃt]	**q.** [kɹaʊd]	**aa.** [kloʊð]	**kk.** [neɪʃn̩]
h. [kɹud]	**r.** [ɹɑt]	**bb.** [ɹoʊt]	**ll.** [bæn]
i. [ɹɪdʒ]	**s.** [kɔɹl]	**cc.** [θæŋk]	**mm.** [eɪʒə]
j. [ɹitʃ]	**t.** [ɹɪtʃ]	**dd.** [ʃak]	**nn.** [bɑks]

20. Transcribe the following words. The first one (a) is given as an example.

a. touch [tʌtʃ]	**p.** punched	**ee.** leather	**tt.** cringe
b. woman	**q.** lather	**ff.** Godzilla	**uu.** pushed
c. women	**r.** Cairo	**gg.** raspberry	**vv.** isn't
d. flood	**s.** vision	**hh.** slyly	**ww.** rhythm
e. wrapped	**t.** price	**ii.** calves	**xx.** January
f. prays	**u.** monkey	**jj.** wove	**yy.** mother
g. brood	**v.** huge	**kk.** mustache	**zz.** pure
h. ghoul	**w.** cough	**ll.** carrot	**aaa.** February
i. torch	**x.** batch	**mm.** child	**bbb.** bathtub
j. stood	**y.** whale	**nn.** sugar	**ccc.** union
k. move	**z.** easy	**oo.** cane	**ddd.** hoodlum
l. breathe	**aa.** hour	**pp.** said	**eee.** icy
m. breath	**bb.** carton	**qq.** larynx	**fff.** July
n. lose	**cc.** though	**rr.** love	**ggg.** cookies
o. loose	**dd.** circus	**ss.** sewn	**hhh.** August

21. Correct the mistakes in the following phonetic transcriptions of English words, if there is a mistake.

a. [shut] *shut*   **c.** [falʊ] *follow*   **e.** [lɛft] *left*   **g.** [ðim] *theme*   **i.** [ɹæn] *rang*
b. [swit] *swift*   **d.** [tɹad] *trod*   **f.** [tʃild] *child*   **h.** [vois] *voice*   **j.** [hɛlθ] *health*

22. Read the phonetically transcribed sentences below and write them out in ordinary spelling. These transcriptions represent the pronunciation of a particular speaker on a particular occasion and thus may differ from your own pronunciation of the same passages in certain minor details, but this should not cause you any difficulty. These passages are from Woody Allen's book *Without Feathers*.

a. [dʌbz æskt hɪz bɹʌðɹ̩ wʌt ɪt wʌz laɪk ɪn ði ʌðɹ̩ wɹ̩ld n̩d hɪz bɹʌðɹ̩ sɛd ɪt wʌz nat ənlaɪk klivlṇd] ([dʌbz] "Dubbs" is a proper name.)

b. [itɹ̩n̩l̩ nʌθɪŋnɛs ɪz oʊkeɪ æz lɔŋ æz jɹ̩ dɹɛst fɹ̩ ɪt]

c. [ɪf ju aɹ sɪkstin ɔɹ ʌndɹ̩ tɹaɪ nat tə goʊ bald]

d. [ænd sun dʒoʊbz pæstʃɹ̩z dɹaɪd ʌp n̩d hɪz tʌŋ klivd tu ðə ɹuf əv hɪz maʊθ soʊ hi kʊd nat pɹənaʊns ðə wɹ̩d fɹæŋkɪnsɛns wɪθaʊt gɛɹɪŋ bɪg læfs] ([dʒoʊb] "Job" is a proper name.)

e. [mʌni ɪz nat ɛvɹiθɪŋ bʌt ɪt ɪz bɛɹ̩ ðæn hævɪŋ wʌnz hɛlθ]

f. [ðə gɹæshapɹ̩ pleɪd al sʌmɹ̩ waɪl ði ænt wɹ̩kt n̩ seɪvd wɛn wɪntɹ̩ keɪm ðə gɹæshapɹ̩ hæd nʌθɪŋ bʌt ði ðɛnt kəmpleɪnd əv tʃɛst peɪnz]

g. [ðə sæfaɹɹ̩ wʌz əɹɪdʒənəli oʊnd baɪ ə sʌltn̩ hu daɪd ʌndɹ̩ mɪstɪɹiəs sɹ̩kəmstænsəz wɛn ə hænd ɹitʃt aʊt əv ə boʊl əv sup hi wʌz itɪŋ n̩ stɹæŋgl̩d hɪm]

h. [ðə gɹeɪt ɹoʊ ɪz ə mɪθəkl̩ bist wɪθ ðə hɛd əv ə laɪn̩ ænd ðə badi ʌv ə laɪn̩ bʌt nat ðə seɪm laɪn̩] ([ɹoʊ] "Roe" is a nonsense name.)

Activities

23. How loud are vowels and consonants? For this activity, you'll need two people and a large open space with either little background noise (like a quiet woods) or steady background noise (like a beach). Stand back to back, as for a duel. One person is the speaker. His/her job is to say a speech sound at normal volume repeatedly, with minimal volume change over repetitions. The other person is the listener. His/her job is to slowly walk away from the speaker, counting the number of steps it takes until the speech sound can no longer be heard.

Write down the number of steps it takes for different speech sounds to become inaudible. Are consonants the same as vowels? Are all consonants the same as each other?

Here are some good sounds to try (be sure that you don't say a vowel with the consonants (e.g., don't say [ɛf] when you mean [f]): [f], [θ], [s], [n], [i], [ɪ], [u], [ɑ], [æ]

File 2.4—Beyond English: Speech Sounds of the World's Languages

Exercises

24. Write the IPA symbol for each of the following sounds (don't forget to use square brackets). The first one is given as an example.

    Example: voiced alveolar trill   [r]

    a. voiced bilabial fricative
    b. mid front rounded vowel
    c. voiceless palatal stop
    d. voiceless uvular stop
    e. velarized alveolar lateral liquid
    f. voiceless glottalized alveolar stop

25. Write out the description of each of the following IPA symbols or combinations of symbols. The first one is given as an example.

    Example: [x]   voiceless velar fricative

    a. [y]
    b. [ɦ]
    c. [sʲ]
    d. [ɲ]
    e. [tˢ]
    f. [ħ]

Discussion Questions

26. Refer to the IPA consonant chart on the inside back cover of the book. Note that there are two types of empty boxes in this chart: some are gray and some are white. What is the difference between the two types of empty boxes?

File 2.5—Suprasegmental Features

Exercises

27. Read the following pairs of sentences aloud. Words in capital letters indicate the presence of a pitch accent and should be said with special prominence. Both sentences in each pair contain exactly the same words, but they differ in intonation and have

different meanings. Paraphrase what the two sentences in each pair mean. How are the meanings different?

a. John called Paul a Republican and then he INSULTED him.
John called Paul a Republican and then HE insulted HIM.

b. John even gave his daughter a new BICYCLE.
John even gave his DAUGHTER a new bicycle.

c. Maxwell didn't kill the JUDGE with a silver hammer.
Maxwell didn't kill the judge with a silver HAMMER.

d. Of the three men, John hates BILL the most.
Of the three men, JOHN hates Bill the most.

28. In File 2.6, you learned that the intonation right before a break can change the meaning of a sentence. For example, rising intonation before a break indicates a question. However, where a break occurs in a sentence can also change its meaning. Turn each of the strings of words below into two sentences with different meanings by adding punctuation or other visual markers that can serve to differentiate the two meanings. Then paraphrase the different meanings.

a. when danger threatens your children call the police
b. I met Mary and Elena's mother at the mall yesterday
c. turn right here

29. Using your knowledge of English, indicate which syllable of each of the following words receives primary stress. Is the placement of English stress predictable for these words? Why or why not?

a. *cat*
b. *catsup*
c. *catarrh*
d. *catalogue*
e. *cathedral*
f. *caterwaul*
g. *caterpillar*
h. *catastrophe*
i. *catastrophic*
j. *categorical*

Activities

30. In the text, we said that the duration of a speech sound may be influenced by the sounds around it. To test this for yourself, first record the following words using a microphone and some sort of phonetics software (see the note at the beginning of File 2.8).

heat / heed / he's
hit / hid / his
hate / hayed / haze
hat / had / has
height / hide / hies
hoot / who'd / whose

Notice that in each set of three words, only the final consonant changes: it is a voiceless alveolar stop, a voiced alveolar stop, or a voiced alveolar fricative.

Measure the duration of the vowel in each word. (You can use Praat to record by clicking on *New* and *Record mono Sound . . .* or *Record stereo Sound. . . .* After you have recorded and saved your sentences, you can look at the spectrograms by opening the recording [*Read* and *Read from file*] and clicking on *Edit*. A window will open with the spectrogram of your sound in the lower section. You can highlight the vowels using the cursor and get their duration by clicking on "Query"; then "Get selection length.")

   i. For which context is each vowel the shortest? The longest? (That is, are vowels longer before voiceless or voiced alveolar stops? voiced alveolar stops or fricatives?) Is the answer the same for every vowel?

   ii. Within a context, which vowel is shortest? The longest? (That is, is the vowel in *heed* shorter or longer than the vowel in *hid*, etc.?)

   iii. Based on your observations, which of the following words do you think would have longer vowel: *boat* or *bode?*

31. Record yourself saying the sentence *Mary had a little lamb* (using a microphone and some sort of phonetics software (see the note at the beginning of File 2.8). Say the sentence with as many different intonational patterns as you can think of. You should record at least five sentences. After you have recorded and saved your sentences, you should be able to look at the pitch movements of your voice graphically in the speech editor. (You can use Praat to record by clicking on *New* and *Record mono Sound . . .* or *Record stereo Sound. . . .* After you have recorded and saved your sentences, you can look at the pitch movements by opening the file (click on *Read* and *Read from file*) and clicking on *Edit*. A window will open with the pitch movements of your utterance in the lower part of the picture represented by a blue line on top of the spectrogram. You can adjust the pitch range that is shown in the picture by clicking on *Pitch* and *Pitch settings. . . .*) Now answer the following questions.

   i. What meaning did you intend for each of the sentences you recorded? For example, the sentence could have been a question or a correction that Mary (and not someone else) had a little lamb; or it could have been sarcastic; etc.

   ii. How are the pitch movements for each of the sentences different? To answer this, just describe what you see and hear. You could, for example, write that the pitch peaks on a certain word or goes down at the end.

   iii. Can you draw any conclusions as to which pitch movement you used to convey which meaning? For example, if you said the sentence and corrected a certain word, what is your pitch movement for a correction?

File 2.6—Acoustic Phonetics

Exercises

32. Describe in your own words how vowels are "shaped" by the vocal tract.

33. What information does a spectrogram give you?

34. On the following page you will find a spectrogram showing the formants of five vowels from a language called Mazotec. (Each vowel in the spectrogram is preceded by a fricative.) Mazotec has five vowels: [i], [e], [a], [o], and [u]. Your task is to measure the vowel space. Find the center value for the first and the second formants (in hertz). Be sure to take the value from the middle of the formant (on both the time axis and the frequency axis). Then plot the first formant values against the second formant values in the graph provided below. In other words, for each vowel, its first formant

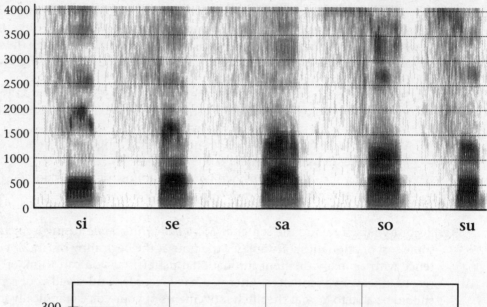

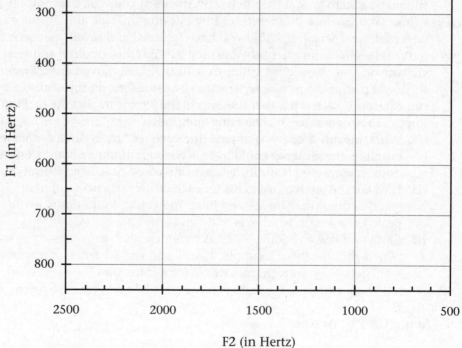

frequency will be the vertical (the "y") value, and its second formant frequency will be the horizontal (the "x") value of a point. When you have finished, compare this chart with (6) in File 2.6.

35. How does the Mazotec vowel space (described in Exercise 34) compare with the vowel space of English (cf. (6), File 2.6)? Are the vowels in the same place relative to each other, or are there differences in the way that English distributes its vowels compared to how Mazotec distributes its vowels?

36. Match each of the following words to the appropriate spectrogram.

    a. *shoe*
    b. *hippo*
    c. *ow!*

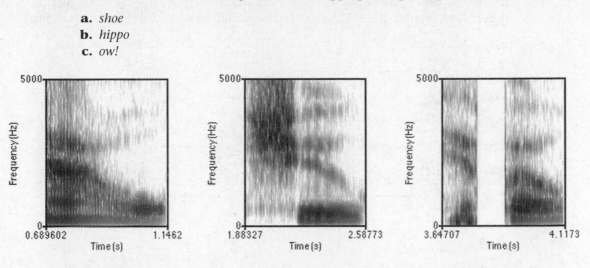

Activities

37. You may be able to learn something interesting about vowels by whistling. Whistling highlights the second vowel formant, which is highest when the tongue is in the high front position and lowest when the tongue is in the high back position. Whistle down a scale until you get to the lowest note you can whistle. Now let your vocal folds vibrate (as if you were humming while whistling). What vowel sound are you making? Try it again, but this time whistle up a scale until you get to the highest note you can make. Try unrounding your lips (smile!) and see if it sounds like a vowel of English when you hum. You may have found that your highest note has a tongue position like [i] and your lowest note has a tongue position like [u].

File 2.7—The Phonetics of Signed Languages

Exercises

38. The following two ASL signs differ in one parameter. Which parameter distinguishes them?

        THINK   WONDER

From *Signing: How to Speak with Your Hands* by Elaine Costello. Copyright 1983 by Elaine Costello. Used by permission of Bantam Books, a division of Bantam Doubleday Dell Publishing Group, Inc., pp. 200–201.

39. The following two signs, both of which are articulated in front of the torso, differ in two parameters and are the same in two parameters. Which two are the same? Which two differ? How do they differ? (Try to describe the difference as specifically as possible.)

CHOCOLATE   CHURCH

© 2006, William Vicars, www.Lifeprint.com. Used with permission.

40. Describe the four parameters of articulation for each of the following signs of ASL.

a. DEAF   b. GRANDMA   c. BAD

© 2006, William Vicars, www.Lifeprint.com. Used with permission.

Discussion Questions

41. Suppose that you were assigned to a team that was responsible for creating a sort of IPA to represent signed languages using written characters. What sorts of characters might this alphabet need to have? How might you want to organize such an alphabet? What would be some of the challenges that you would run into with this project?

42. What does signed "yelling" have in common with yelling in spoken languages; what does signed "whispering" have in common with whispering in spoken languages? Are there any differences (aside, obviously, from the modality itself)?

Further Readings

Ladefoged, P. (2001). *Vowels and consonants: An introduction to the sounds of languages.* Malden, MA: Blackwell.

Ladefoged, P., and Maddieson, I. (1996). *The sounds of the world's languages.* Oxford, UK; Cambridge, MA: Blackwell.

CHAPTER
3

Phonology

For Better or For Worse®   **by Lynn Johnston**

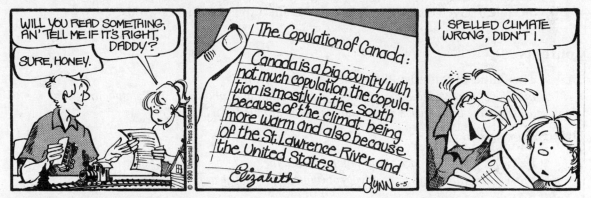

What Is Phonology?

Both phonetics and phonology can be generally described as the study of speech sounds, but they are not the same field. Phonetics (the subject of Chapter 2) is specifically the study of how speech sounds are produced, what their physical properties are, and how they are interpreted. **Phonology,** on the other hand, is the study of the distribution of sounds in a language and the interactions between those different sounds. Phonologists ask the following kinds of questions: What is the organization of sounds in a given language? Of all the sounds in a language, which are predictable and which are unpredictable in given contexts? Which sounds affect the identities of words?

Contents

The Value of Sounds: Phonemes and Allophones

3.1.1 Predicting the Occurrence of Sounds

In both Kikamba (a Bantu language spoken in Kenya) and English, we can hear the sounds [k] and [g]. The Kikamba word [kosuuŋga] 'to guard' contains both phones, as does the English word [kɑgneɪt] *cognate*. The difference between Kikamba and English lies in the way the two sounds contribute to the identity of a word. In English, the two phones can distinguish words, as shown by words like [tæk] *tack* and [tæg] *tag,* where alternating between [k] and [g] affects the message conveyed by the utterance. In this sense, phonologists say that the occurrence of these two sounds in English is unpredictable, since we cannot look at the rest of the word and determine which sound will occur. That is, if we know that a word in English begins with [tæ], we cannot predict whether the word will end with [k] or [g] since both *tack* and *tag* are different, but possible, words.

In Kikamba, on the other hand, the sounds [k] and [g] *are* predictable from their environment. Sounds are predictable when we expect to see one sound but not the other based upon the sounds that precede and/or follow it. In Kikamba, the only consonant that can come directly after an [ŋ] is [g], and [g] can only come immediately after [ŋ]. The combination [ŋk] does not occur in Kikamba (see Roberts-Kohno 2000). So, if there is a velar stop in a word in Kikamba, we can predict whether it will be a [k] or a [g]: it will be a [g] if it is immediately preceded by [ŋ]; otherwise, it will be a [k]. However, in English we cannot make this prediction: the sound [k] does appear after the sound [ŋ], as in [æŋkɹ] *anchor,* as does the sound [g], as in [æŋgɹ] *anger.*

To illustrate how strong this distribution is in Kikamba, consider the case where you have a word with a [k] such as *katala,* the base form from which conditional forms of the verb 'to count' are built. To say 'if you count,' you add an [o] to the front of the word: [okatala]. But to say 'if I count,' you add an [ŋ]. Even though this word has a [k] in it, we have seen that it is a rule in this language that [k] cannot appear after [ŋ]—so the [k] appears as a [g] instead: [ŋgatala] 'if I count.' This type of alternation does not happen in English, because there is no rule governing the distribution of [k] and [g].

So while Kikamba and English both use the phones [k] and [g], the languages differ in that in Kikamba we can predict the occurrence of one versus the other, and in English we cannot. If someone learning Kikamba were to use [k] after [ŋ], the identity of the word would not change. Instead, a native speaker of Kikamba might think that the speaker sounded funny, had an accent, or had mispronounced the word. On the other hand, if a learner of English were to make the same substitution in English, then the identity of the word is likely to change. Imagine confusing [k] and [g] and saying at a dinner party "we're having [gɹæb] for dinner tonight." Your guests might feel rather uncomfortable, especially if they were expecting crab!

The bottom line is that in Kikamba, the sounds [k] and [g] are predictably distributed, while in English they are not.

3.1.2 Allophones and Phonemes

In every language, certain sounds pattern together as if they were simply variants of the "same" sound, instead of different sounds that can be used to distinguish words, even though they may be phonetically distinct. For example, the sounds [k] and [g] are clearly different sounds: we use them to make the contrast between different words in English, as we saw in Section 3.1.1. But as we also saw, these two sounds are completely predictable in Kikamba. In Kikamba, then, these sounds can be thought of as variants of the "same" sound, because in any given context, if there is some velar stop sound, we can predict which one ([k] or [g]) it will be.

Similarly, if you ask a native speaker of English how many different sounds are represented by the underlined letters in the words *pin*, *bin*, and *spin*, they will probably say "two," grouping the aspirated [pʰ] of *pin* and unaspirated [p] of *spin* together. Though [pʰ] and [p] are phonetically different sounds, native English speakers often overlook this difference and may even consider them to be the "same" sound (see Section 2.6.5).

One of the goals of this file is to help you understand more clearly the distinction between "same" and "different" sounds. To do this, we will discuss the terms **allophone** and **phoneme**. Since these concepts are the crux of phonological analysis, it is important that they be clearly understood. Perhaps the best way to start to explain these terms is through examples. On a separate piece of paper, transcribe the following five words in IPA:

(1) top   stop   little   kitten   hunter

It is likely that you transcribed all of these words with a [t], like the following:

(2) [tap]   [stap]   [lɪtl̩]   [kɪtn̩]   [hʌntɪ̈]

This is good, since it probably reflects something that is psychologically real to you. But, in fact, the physical reality (the acoustic phonetic fact) is that the 't' you transcribed in those five examples is pronounced slightly differently from one example to the next. To illustrate this, pronounce the five words again. Concentrate on what the 't' sounds like in each example, but be sure to say them as you normally would if you were talking to a friend—that is, don't try to enunciate them abnormally clearly.

What differences did you notice? Compare, for example, the /t/ of *top* to that of *stop*. You should be able to detect a short burst or puff of air after the /t/ in *top* that is absent in *stop*. That puff of air is what we have called aspiration (see Section 2.6.5), which is transcribed with a superscripted [ʰ]. So while a native speaker might think of the 't' sound in *top* and *stop* as being the same sound, the 't' is actually pronounced differently in each word. This difference can be captured in the transcription, as in [tʰap] and [stap], respectively.

Now say the words *little* and *kitten*. We might say that the 't' in *little* sounds "softer" than the one in *stop*, and is clearly voiced. For most speakers of American English (but not of British English), the 't' in words like *little* is pronounced as a flap, [ɾ], much like the *r* in Spanish in words like [paɾa] 'for' and [toɾo] 'bull' (see Section 2.2.5). English *kitten*, on the other hand, is pronounced with the same sound we hear in the expression *uh-oh*, a glottal stop [ʔ]. So, we could transcribe *little* and *kitten* as [lɪɾl̩] and [kɪʔn̩], respectively.

For some speakers of American English, in casual speech words like *hunter* are pronounced with no 't' at all, but rather as [hʌnɾ̩]. Try to say it this way and see if it sounds like something you've heard before. In any case, while you may have initially transcribed the five words above with a /t/, they may also be transcribed in a way that reflects the different pronunciations of that sound, as in the following:

(3) [tʰap]   [stap]   [lɪɾl̩]   [kʰɪʔn̩]   [hʌnɾ̩]

To a native speaker, all of the words above may seem to have a 't' in them, at least at some psychological level.[1] Evidence of this lies in the fact that one may transcribe them all with a 't,' at least until trained in transcription. Someone who lacks linguistic training would probably not hesitate to state that all the above words have a 't' and would need to be convinced that subtle differences, like aspiration, exist among them. In this sense, the above words do have a 't.' On the other hand, we can observe that the 't' may be pronounced in several different ways.

Unlike a speaker of English, a native speaker of Hindi does not ignore the difference between aspirated and unaspirated sounds when speaking or hearing Hindi. To a speaker of Hindi, the aspirated sound [pʰ] is as different from unaspirated [p] as [pʰ] is from [b] to our ears. The difference between aspirated and unaspirated stops must be noticed by Hindi speakers because their language contains many words that are pronounced in nearly the same way, except that one word will have an aspirated stop where the other has an unaspirated stop. The data in (4) illustrate this.

(4)

Hindi	Gloss
[pʰəl]	'fruit'
[pəl]	'moment'
[bəl]	'strength'

A native speaker of English may not be aware of the difference between aspirated and unaspirated stops because aspiration will never make a difference in the meanings of English words. If we hear someone say [mæp] and [mæpʰ], we may recognize them as different pronunciations of the same word *map*, but not as different words. Because of the different ways in which [p] and [pʰ] affect meaning distinctions in English and Hindi, these sounds have different values in the phonological systems of the two languages. We say that these two sounds are **noncontrastive** in English, since interchanging the two does not result in a change of meaning. In Hindi, on the other hand, [p] and [pʰ] are **contrastive,** since replacing one sound with the other in a word can change the word's meaning. We will have more to say about this terminological distinction below.

Linguists attempt to characterize these different relations between sounds in language by grouping the sounds in a language's sound inventory into classes. Each class contains all of the sounds that a native speaker considers as the "same" sound. For example, [t] and [tʰ] in English would be members of the same class. But English [tʰ] and [d] are members of different classes because they are contrastive. That is, if you interchange one for the other in a word, you can cause a change in the word's meaning, e.g. [tʰaɪm] *time* versus [daɪm] *dime*. On the other hand, speakers of Hindi would not classify [t] and [tʰ] as members of the same class because they perceive them as different. That is, they are contrastive in Hindi.

A class of speech sounds that seem to be variants of the same sound is called a **phoneme.** Each member of a particular phoneme class is called an **allophone,** which corresponds to an actual phonetic segment produced by a speaker. That is, the various ways that a phoneme is pronounced are called allophones.

In this view, we can say that the 't' sounds in words like *stop, top, little,* and *kitten* all belong to a single class, which we will label by the symbol /t/, characterizing this particular phoneme. By saying that *stop* and *top,* for example, each have the phoneme /t/, we are saying that the sounds [t] and [tʰ] are related.

---

[1] The reasons for this may be manifold, including phonetic similarities, phonological patterning, different pronunciations across language varieties, or spelling.

In (5) we see how the phoneme /t/ is related to its allophones in English and how the Hindi phonemes /t/ and /tʰ/ are related to their allophones. In English, [t], [tʰ], [ɾ], and [ʔ] are allophones of the same phoneme, which we can label /t/. In this way, we can say that in English the phoneme /t/ has the allophones [t] as in [stɑp], [tʰ] as in [tʰɑp], [ɾ] as in [lɪɾl], and [ʔ] as in [kɪʔn̩]. On the other hand, in Hindi, [t] and [tʰ] are allophones of different phonemes. Note that symbols representing phonemes are written between slashes; this distinguishes them from symbols representing (allo)phones, which are written between square brackets.

(5)

	English				**Hindi**	
Phonemes:	/t/				/t/	/tʰ/
Allophones:	[t]	[tʰ]	[ʔ]	[ɾ]	[t]	[tʰ]

By providing a description like this, linguists attempt to show that the phonological system of a language has two levels. The more concrete level involves the physical reality of phonetic segments, the allophones, whereas phonemes are something more abstract. In fact, linguists sometimes describe phonemes as the form in which we store sounds in our minds. So, phonemes are abstract psychological concepts, and they are not directly observable in a stream of speech; only the allophones of a phoneme are.

The phoneme is a unit of linguistic structure that is just as significant to the native speaker as the word or the sentence. Native speakers reveal their knowledge of phonemes in a number of ways. When an English speaker makes a slip of the tongue and says [tʃi keɪn] for *key chain*, reversing [tʃ] and [k], he or she has demonstrated that [tʃ] functions mentally as a single unit of sound, just as [k] does. Recall from File 2.2 that [tʃ] is phonetically complex, consisting of [t] followed immediately by [ʃ]. Yet, since [tʃ] represents the pronunciation of a single phoneme /tʃ/ in English, no native speaker would make an error that would involve splitting up its phonetic components; you will never hear [ti kʃen] as a slip of the tongue (see File 9.3).

Knowledge of phonemes is also revealed in alphabetic spelling systems (see File 13.4). For example, English does not have separate letters for [pʰ] and [p]; they are both spelled with the letter *p*. Examples like this show that the English spelling system ignores differences in pronunciation that don't result in meaning distinctions. For the most part, the English spelling system attempts to provide symbols for phonemes, not phonetic segments. In general, alphabetic writing systems tend to be phonemic rather than phonetic, though they achieve this goal with varying degrees of success. As noted in File 2.1, of course, there are multiple ways to represent the same sound (e.g., the [k] sound is written with a <k> in the word *kitten* but with a <c> in the word *cool*). What's crucial here, though, is that both of these spellings represent /k/, and not, say, the difference between [k] and [kʰ].

3.1.3 Identifying Phonemes and Allophones: The Distribution of Speech Sounds

In order to determine whether sounds in a given language are allophones of a single phoneme or allophones of separate phonemes, we need to consider the distribution of the sounds involved. The **distribution** of a phone is the set of phonetic environments in which it occurs. For example, nasalized vowels in English occur only in the environment of a nasal consonant. More precisely, a linguist would describe the distribution of English [ĩ], [õ], and so on, by stating that the nasalized vowels always and only occur immediately preceding a nasal consonant. In this book we will mainly be concerned with two types of distribution—contrastive distribution and complementary distribution—though a third distribution, free variation, will also be introduced in the following section.

Let us consider **contrastive distribution** first. Recall from above that a pair of phones is contrastive if interchanging the two can change the meaning of a word. This means that the sounds can occur in the same phonetic environment. It also means that the sounds are allophones of different phonemes. Two sounds are noncontrastive if replacing one phone with another does not result in a change of meaning.

Our earlier discussion of the patterning of [p] and [pʰ] in Hindi and English provides a good example of this difference. Recall that we said that in Hindi these two sounds could affect the meaning of a word based on examples like [pəl] *moment* and [pʰəl] *fruit*, where the two meanings are distinguished by the occurrence of [p] or [pʰ]. This means that the two sounds [p] and [pʰ] are contrastive in Hindi. In English, on the other hand, simply replacing [p] for [pʰ], or vice versa, will never effect a change in the meaning of a word; the sounds are noncontrastive in English.

We just determined whether or not [p] or [pʰ] are contrastive in Hindi and English by taking into account the distribution of sounds in each individual language. We did this by identifying a **minimal pair.** A minimal pair is defined as a pair of words whose pronunciations differ by exactly one sound and that have different meanings. When you find a minimal pair, you know that the two sounds that differ are contrastive and, thus, the sounds involved are allophones of different phonemes. If you try, you can think of many minimal pairs in English, or any other language you know well. For example, the minimal pair [tʰiːm] *team* and [tʰiːn] *teen* shows that [n] and [m] are allophones of separate phonemes (that is, they are contrastive) in English since they can be used to contrast meaning. In Hindi, the words [pʰəl] 'fruit' and [bəl] 'strength' constitute a minimal pair, showing [pʰ] and [b] to be allophones of separate phonemes; [pʰəl] *fruit* and [pəl] *moment* also form a minimal pair in Hindi. But notice that there are no minimal pairs involving [pʰ] and [p] in English; these two sounds are never contrastive with respect to one another. Instead, they are allophones of the same phoneme, /p/.

Consider another example in which two languages make different distinctions using the same set of sounds. In English, [l] and [ɹ] are contrastive phonemes, as can be seen from the existence of minimal pairs such as *leaf* [lif] versus *reef* [ɹif], *alive* [əlɑɪv] versus *arrive* [əɹɑɪv], or *feel* [fil] versus *fear* [fiɹ]. In Korean, on the other hand, [l] and [ɾ] are never contrastive.[2] Consider the data in (6).

(6) Korean [l] versus [ɾ] alternations

Citation Form	Nominative Case	Gloss
[pul]	[puɾi]	'fire'
[mal]	[maɾi]	'language, speech'
[tal]	[taɾi]	'moon'
[kʰal]	[kʰaɾi]	'knife'
[pal]	[paɾi]	'foot'
[sal]	[saɾi]	'flesh'

---

[2] You will notice that the two "r" sounds in English and Korean are not the same phonetically—in English, it is a voiced alveolar retroflex liquid [ɹ], while in Korean, it is a voiced alveolar flap [ɾ] (see Section 2.2.5). Similarly, the exact articulation of /l/ in the two languages is also not identical, though we use the same symbol for both. These phonetic differences are not particularly important here, however, because we are concerned only with the distribution of the two sounds in each language (a phonological question) rather than with the quality of the two sounds (a phonetic question).

Notice that in each example, only one English translation is given. For example, the word for 'fire' has two forms: one when it is used by itself, the citation form (such as in the answer to the question "What is the Korean word for 'fire'?"); and one when it is used as the subject of a sentence, the nominative form (such as in "The fire burned brightly"). This use of different forms for different grammatical roles is similar to the use in English of, say, *atom* as the noun for the smallest unit of an element ("An atom of helium has 2 protons") as opposed to *atomic* as the adjectival form of the same word ("The atomic structure of helium is simple"). In the English case, it's clear that the ending -*ic* at the end of *atomic* is a marker of an adjective. Similarly, in Korean, the final -*i* in the second column of words in (6) indicates that these words are in the nominative case. (For more on these kinds of markers, see Chapter 4.) If we remove the special ending of the word *atomic,* you can see that the base of the word is still *atom.* But notice that the base *atom* in the word *atomic* is not pronounced the same as it is in isolation. The word *atom* by itself is pronounced ['æˌɾm̩], but in *atomic,* it's pronounced [ˌəˈtʰɑm]. Given that these two forms represent the same base word, we might expect that they would be pronounced the same way. Instead, the pronunciation of the base word alternates depending on the phonetic context it appears in. An **alternation** is simply a difference between two (or more) phonetic forms that you might otherwise expect to be related. Identifying alternations relies on the assumption that, all else being equal, the same word should be expressed by the same sounds—when we find different pronunciations of the same word that are systematically linked to particular grammatical contexts, we have an alternation. So in English, the base word *atom* is expressed alternately by the sounds ['æˌɾm̩] and [ˌəˈtʰɑm]. In Korean, the base word *fire* is expressed alternately by the sounds [pul] and [puɾ].

Why might these words have alternating pronunciations depending on what other elements they appear with? The answer to this question takes us back to looking at the distribution of the sounds [l] and [ɾ] in Korean. In the words listed in (6), we see that [l] and [ɾ] do not occur in the same phonetic environment. Even though we are looking at the "same" word (for example, the word for 'fire'), the phonetic quality of the third sound is not always the same—it alternates between [l] and [ɾ]. Specifically, as you can see from the data in (6), you use an [l] when the sound is the last sound in the word (is in "word-final" position), but you use [ɾ] when the sound is between two vowels (is in "intervocalic" position). In fact, if you were to look at all of Korean, you would find that [ɾ] appears only between two vowels, while [l] never appears in that position. Meanwhile, [l] can appear at the ends of words, but [ɾ] never does.[3] These two observations mean that if someone gave you the frame [tɑ__] in Korean, you could tell them whether an [ɾ] or an [l] goes in the blank. In Korean, it must be an [l]! Notice that you cannot do the same thing in English: either an [l] or an [ɹ] could go in the blank to form a possible English word.

The difference that has been illustrated here between English and Korean is that in English, [l] and [ɹ] are in contrastive distribution, while in Korean, [l] and [ɾ] are in **complementary distribution.** Sounds showing this type of distribution are considered to be allophones of the same phoneme. To understand better what we mean by complementary distribution, think about what the term complementary means: two complementary parts of something make up a whole. For example, the set of people in your class at any given moment can be divided into the set of people who are under 5'5" tall and the set of people who are 5'5" tall or taller. These two sets of people complement each other. They are mutually exclusive (one person can't simultaneously be both shorter and taller than 5'5"), but together they make up the whole class.

The Korean sounds [l] and [ɾ] are in complementary distribution, because they appear in different sets of environments: [ɾ] occurs between vowels, and [l] occurs word-finally.

---

[3]In some modern words that have come into Korean from other languages, [l] can also appear at the beginning of words. But it never appears as the only segment between two vowels.

Given our assumptions about alternations—that the same word should be expressed by the same sounds—we can hypothesize that even though [l] and [ɾ] are phonetically different phones in Korean, they are allophones of a single phoneme. We can represent that single phoneme as /l/. At this point, it probably seems like an arbitrary choice as to why /l/ should be the phoneme and not /ɾ/; we will talk more about how to make this choice in File 3.5.

If two sounds are in complementary distribution in a language, there will never be a minimal pair that uses them to distinguish two words. Furthermore, the appearance of one allophone or the other will always be predictable, as we saw above with the frame [tɑ__]. You can predict that [ɾ] but not [l] will appear between vowels in any word in Korean, and that [l] but not [ɾ] will appear word-finally—even if you have never studied Korean. This kind of prediction is a powerful tool in helping phonologists understand the structure of languages.

What's particularly interesting about this (and all other) phonological distributions is that it represents actual knowledge that native speakers have. For example, if you give a native speaker of Korean the new (nonsense) word *moladam* and ask them to say it out loud, they will say it with an [ɾ] between the two vowels, and not an [l]! Of course, this is not something that anyone has explicitly taught them (especially since they have never seen this word before), but the distribution of sounds is one of the things that you know when you know a language (see File 1.2).

Consider another linguistic example, namely, the distribution of the English sounds [p] and [pʰ] shown in (7).

(7) | *spat* | [spæt] | *pat* | [pʰæt] |
     |---------|--------|--------|--------|
     | *spool* | [spul] | *pool* | [pʰul] |
     | *speak* | [spik] | *peek* | [pʰik] |

As you can see in the English words in (7), [p] and [pʰ] do not occur in the same phonetic environment. As a result, there are no minimal pairs involving a [p]-[pʰ] contrast. In fact, the phones are in complementary distribution: [p] occurs after [s] but never word-initially, while [pʰ] occurs word-initially but never after [s]. Since these sounds appear in different phonetic environments, there can be no pair of words composed of identical strings of sounds except that one has [p] and the other has [pʰ]. As stated above, phones that are in complementary distribution are allophones of a single phoneme. In this case, [p] and [pʰ] are both allophones of the phoneme we can represent as /p/. Furthermore, the appearance of one allophone or another in a given context is predictable. For example, we can predict that the allophone [pʰ] (but never [p]) will appear in word-initial position. So even in words not listed in (7), we know that it will be [pʰ], rather than [p], that will occur at the beginning of a word.[4] Similarly, we can predict that [p] (but never [pʰ]) will follow [s] in other words.

3.1.4 Free Variation

Most phonological distributions can be described as either contrastive or complementary. Remember that the hallmark of a contrastive distribution is that you can't predict which of two (or more) sounds belongs in a certain context, because each will produce a different but meaningful word; the hallmark of a complementary distribution is that you can predict which of two sounds belongs in any given context. In some contexts, however, more than one pronunciation of a given sound may be possible. In these cases, you may not be able to predict exactly which sound will occur, but the choice does **not** affect the meaning of the

---

[4]In point of fact, this is true not just at the beginning of a word but at the beginning of any stressed syllable. That is, in English, [pʰ] but not [p] can appear as the first consonant of a stressed syllable.

word. Consider, for example, the pronunciations of some English words in (8) (remember that [p˺] represents an unreleased voiceless bilabial stop).

(8) *leap*   [lip]   *leap*   [lip˺]
     soap   [soʊp]   *soap*   [soʊp˺]
     troop   [trup]   *troop*   [trup˺]
     happy   [hæpi]   —   *[hæp˺i]

These words show that [p] and [p˺] both share some of the same phonetic environments; specifically, they can both appear at the ends of words. Unlike the case of English [b] versus [pʰ], or [m] versus [n], however, there are no minimal pairs involving these sounds in the language. Why not? Although there are pairs of words in (8) that differ in only one sound, none of these words contrast in meaning. Thus, the choice between [p] and [p˺] in *leap, soap,* and *troop* does not make a difference in meaning; that is, the sounds are noncontrastive. Rather, they are interchangeable in word-final position. Sounds with this type of patterning are considered to be in **free variation.** To a native speaker, sounds like [p] and [p˺] that are in free variation are perceived as being the "same" sound. We can conclude that they are allophones of the same phoneme, because they are perceived as the same and do not serve to distinguish the meanings of words.

Another term that you may encounter to describe the different types of phonological distributions in language is overlapping. If two sounds are in **overlapping distribution,** they can occur in the same environment. Both sounds that are in contrastive distribution and sounds that are in free variation are therefore considered to have an overlapping distribution; only sounds that are in complementary distribution do not overlap. For example, in English, the sounds [d] and [l] are in overlapping distribution because they can contrast: the words *lid* and *lit* form a minimal pair, and both [d] and [t] can occur after [lɪ]—that is, the environment [lɪ_] is one where [d] and [t] overlap. Similarly, [t] and [t˺] have an overlapping distribution because they can also both occur after [lɪ_], as two different pronunciations of the word *lit*. The difference between [d] and [t] on the one hand, and [t] and [t˺] on the other, is that interchanging [d] and [t] changes the identity of the words, while interchanging [t] and [t˺] does not.

3.1.5 Summary

To summarize, a phone's distribution is the collection of phonetic environments in which the phone may appear; when linguists describe a phone's distribution, they describe this collection. Relative to each other, two (or more) phones will be in contrastive distribution, in complementary distribution, or in free variation. Phones in contrastive distribution may appear in minimal pairs and are allophones of different phonemes. Phones in free variation may, like phones in contrastive distribution, also appear in the same phonetic environments, but never cause a contrast in meaning; they are allophones of the same phoneme. In either of these two types of distribution, given a particular phonetic environment, one cannot predict which of the phones will occur. If the phones are in complementary distribution, their appearance in particular phonetic environments is predictable; they never appear in minimal pairs, and they are allophones of the same phoneme.

Phonological Rules

3.2.1 Phonological Rules

In File 3.1, we discussed the fact that phonemes and (allo)phones belong to different levels of structure in language—that is, phonemes are abstract mental entities, and phones are physical events. In this file we consider the connection between these two levels. The mapping between phonemic and phonetic elements is accomplished using **phonological rules** (recall from Section 1.2.3 that a rule of grammar expresses a pattern in a language). A speaker's knowledge of phonological rules allows him or her to "translate" phonemes into actual speech sounds; knowledge of these rules forms part of the speaker's linguistic competence. This change from the phonemic underlying form to the actual phonetic form of a word by means of phonological rules can be represented with a diagram:

(1) phonemic form
    ⇓
   rules
    ⇓
phonetic form

As an example, consider the English word *can* /kæn/. This word has a final /n/ sound in its phonemic form, and in fact it is frequently pronounced with a final [n]. If we listen carefully, however, we find that the final consonant of *can* (especially in casual speech) is often [m] or [ŋ].[1] The examples in (2) illustrate this. (Here and throughout this file we use a fairly broad transcription style, recording phonetic detail only for the segments under discussion.)

(2) *I can ask*   [aɪ kæn æsk]   (or [aɪ kn̩ æsk])
     I can see   [aɪ kæn si]   (or [aɪ kn̩ si])
     I can bake   [aɪ kæm beɪk]   (or [aɪ km̩ beɪk])
     I can play   [aɪ kæm pleɪ]   (or [aɪ km̩ pleɪ])
     I can go   [aɪ kæŋ goʊ]   (or [aɪ kŋ̩ goʊ])
     I can come   [aɪ kæŋ kʌm]   (or [aɪ kŋ̩ kʌm])

As these transcriptions show, the phoneme /n/ is pronounced as the phone [m] when it precedes a labial consonant and as the phone [ŋ] when it precedes a velar consonant. We can state this fact about English as a descriptive rule:

---

[1]In linguistic analysis, we often have to distinguish between "careful" and "casual" speech. Careful speech is when a speaker speaks more slowly and clearly than usual, while casual speech is when a speaker speaks more quickly and with more co-articulation (see Section 2.2.6) than usual. Of course, these are really endpoints on a scale of speech styles (see File 10.1), and people actually talk at many different styles in between.

(3) /n/ is pronounced as   [m] before a labial consonant

[ŋ] before a velar consonant

[n] everywhere else.

(We will be adjusting this rule later on in this file.) Notice that a phonological rule has three parts: the sound(s) affected by the rule, the environment where the rule applies, and the result of the rule. Here /n/ is affected by the rule. The rule applies when /n/ is followed by a labial or velar consonant. The result of the application of the rule is that /n/ acquires the same place of articulation as the following consonant. We can write this rule using short-hand of the form X → Y / C __ D. Here, 'X' is the sound that is affected by the rule, 'Y' is the result of the application, and 'C __ D' is the environment in which the rule applies (the **conditioning environment**). By "C __ D," we mean that C comes before the sound in question, and D comes after it; the blank represents where the sound appears. You can read these rules in the following way: "X becomes Y when it comes after C and before D." Thus, if you saw the form CXD, you would know that it turns into CYD if the rule applies. So, for the rule in (3) above, we would write:

(4) [n] → [m] / ___ labial consonant

[n] → [ŋ] / ___ velar consonant

[n] → [n] / everywhere else

Now consider how the phonetic forms of some of the above examples are derived from the phonemic forms:

(5) **phonemic form:**   /kæn æsk/   /kæn beɪk/   /kæn goʊ/
    apply rule: kæn æsk   kæm beɪk   kæŋ goʊ
    phonetic form: [kæn æsk]   [kæm beɪk]   [kæŋ goʊ]

This illustrates what happens in speaking. In listening, a hearer reverses this process: he or she perceives the phonetic form of an utterance, then sends it "backwards" through the phonological rules, and finally obtains a phonemic form that matches a form stored in memory.

The rule illustrated above applies not only to /n/, but also to /t/ and /d/:

(6) *hat trick*   [hæt tɹɪk]

hit batsman   [hɪp bætsmn̩]

night class   [nɑɪk klæs]

bad dream   [bæd dɹim]

head band   [hɛb bænd]

bad guy   [bæg gɑɪ]

3.2.2 Natural Classes

Can we make one rule to state that /n/, /t/, and /d/ all change place of articulation according to what sound follows? Is it random chance that these three sounds all seem to undergo the same phonological rule? To answer these questions, let's first take a look at the articulatory descriptions of these three sounds:

(7) /t/   voiceless alveolar oral stop

/d/   voiced alveolar oral stop

/n/   voiced alveolar nasal stop

Not only are all three sounds alveolar stops, but they are the **only** alveolar stops in English. (Note that there is no such thing as a voiceless alveolar nasal stop as a phoneme of

English.) Therefore, we can make the description more general by removing some of the properties:

(8) /n/, /t/, /d/   alveolar stop

With respect to English, saying "alveolar stop" is the same as saying /n/, /t/, and /d/. These three sounds are all of the phonemes in English that are produced by stopping the flow of air at the alveolar ridge. Thus, they are the **natural class** of alveolar stops. A natural class is a group of sounds in a language that share one or more articulatory or auditory property, **to the exclusion of all other sounds in that language.** That is, in order for a group of sounds to be a natural class, it must include all of the sounds that share a particular property or set of properties, and not include any sounds that don't.

All of the properties used in Files 2.2 and 2.4 to describe individual sounds can also be used to describe natural classes. For example, in the English vowels the monophthongs [i, u] and the first part of the diphthongs [eɪ] and [oʊ] are tense vowels, and there are no other tense vowels in English. Thus, these vowels are members of the natural class of tense vowels in English. Likewise, the consonants [k, g, ŋ] are all described as velar consonants, and they are the only velar consonants used in English; thus they constitute the natural class of velar consonants in English. Notice that we already referred to the natural class of velar consonants in the formulation of our rule at the beginning of this file. You'll recall that this rule affects the natural class of alveolar stops when followed by a member of either the natural class of velar consonants or the natural class of bilabial consonants. This shows that natural classes can be used to describe both the sounds affected by a rule **and** the environments where a rule applies.

In talking about groups of sounds, we must use a few properties in addition to those needed to describe individual sounds. For example, if you look at the consonant chart on the last page of this book, you will notice that the only labiodental consonants in English are the fricatives [f] and [v], while the bilabial fricative slots are left empty. In many situations it is advantageous to refer to [f] and [v] together with [p, b, m, w] and [w̥] as belonging to the same natural class. For this purpose we use the property labial.

Another property used to describe natural classes divides the segments into two groups, **obstruents** and **sonorants.** Obstruents are produced with an obstruction of the airflow. The sounds in this category are stops, fricatives, and affricates. Sonorants, on the other hand, are segments produced with a relatively open passage for the airflow. Sonorant segments include nasals, liquids, glides, and vowels. Thus, the class of labial obstruents in English is [p, f, b, v], while the class of labial sonorant consonants is [m, w, w̥].[2] The class of labial consonants is the union of both sets: [p, f, b, v, m, w, w̥]. As we will see, being able to divide consonants into obstruents and sonorants is quite useful in stating phonological rules.

3.2.3 Classification of Phonological Rules

In addition to seeing that phonological rules apply to natural classes of segments, we can classify phonological rules according to the kind of process that they involve. Seven major kinds of processes are discussed here, along with examples from the phonology of English and other languages.

   a. Assimilation. Rules of **assimilation** cause a sound (or gesture) to become more like a neighboring sound (or gesture) with respect to some phonetic property. In other

---

[2]As already mentioned, the class of sonorants also includes vowels, because they do not have an obstruction of airflow. Some linguists treat rounded vowels as "labial," in which case the entire class of English labial sonorants would be [m, w, w̥, u, ʊ, o, ɔ], and the entire class of English labials would be [p, f, b, v, m, w, w̥, u, ʊ, o, ɔ].

words, the segment affected by the rule assimilates or takes on a property from a nearby (often adjacent) segment. Rules of assimilation are very common in languages. The first rule we considered in Section 3.2.1 falls into this category. We can call it alveolar stop assimilation because it applies to all alveolar stops (/t/, /d/, and /n/):

(9) **Alveolar stop assimilation** (English): Alveolar stops assimilate to the place of articulation of a following consonant.

Thus, when a sound having the properties alveolar and stop immediately precedes a labial consonant, this rule causes the alveolar stop to take on the property labial (thereby replacing its specification for alveolar). Similarly, this rule can apply to change the sound's place of articulation feature to dental when it precedes a dental consonant (examples such as *width* [wɪd̪θ] and *in this* [ɪn̪ ðɪs]), and so on, for the other places of articulation.

We saw examples of this sort of alveolar assimilation in (2) and (6). These examples of assimilation all took place across a word boundary (e.g., the /n/ in *can* assimilating to the /b/ in *bake*). We can see a similar sort of phenomenon taking place across word boundaries in certain ASL handshapes. We will consider the handshape that is used in the sign ME, which is a pointing index finger, as shown in (10).

(10) The unassimilated sign for ME in ASL

The sign ME may take on features of other handshapes, however, depending on the sign that follows it. For example, in order to say "I am named . . . ," a speaker of ASL would sign "ME NAME . . . ." In order to say "I know," a speaker of ASL would sign "ME KNOW." The signs NAME and KNOW have different handshapes: NAME is articulated with two fingers (index finger and middle finger) extended; KNOW is articulated with a bent hand and all four fingers extended.

When the sign ME is produced before one of these other words, it can take on the handshape of the word that follows it, as shown in (11).

(11) a. The phrase 'I am named . . .' in ASL, formed from the lexical items ME NAME

b. The sentence 'I know' in ASL, formed from the lexical items ME KNOW

Notice that in both (11a) and (11b), the signer touches his chest with his hand facing the same way as he would in the unassimilated form. That is, the place of articulation, the orientation, and the movement for ME do not change. But the handshape used for ME in (11a) is the handshape of NAME, and the handshape used in (11b) is the handshape of KNOW.

Another assimilation process is **palatalization**. Palatalization refers to a special type of assimilation in which a consonant becomes like a neighboring palatal. For example, when American English speakers say *Did you?* rapidly, they very often pronounce it as [dɪdʒu]. The sounds [d] (the alveolar stop from the end of *did*) and [j] (the palatal glide from the beginning of *you*) combine to form the palatal affricate [dʒ]. In this case, the palatal nature of the glide has been assimilated by the stop, making it a palatal affricate. Front vowels such as [i] and [e] also cause this change. The most common types of palatalization occur when alveolar, dental, and velar stops or fricatives appear before a front vowel. So the following are all common types of palatalization: [t] → [tʃ]; [d] → [dʒ]; [s] → [ʃ]; [k] → [tʃ]; [g] → [dʒ]. While there are variants on palatalization, and other sounds can be palatalized, the main things to look for are a sound becoming a palatal and/or a sound change conditioned by a front vowel.

The rules of assimilation that we've discussed so far cause sounds to assimilate to **adjacent** sounds. This is a common way that assimilation occurs. However, long-distance assimilation also exists, and a relatively common type of long-distance assimilation is called **vowel harmony.** This typically causes all the vowels in a word to "harmonize" or agree in some property such as rounding or backness.

Finnish has a common type of vowel harmony rule, which can be stated as follows:

(12) **Vowel harmony** (Finnish): A back vowel becomes front when preceded by a front vowel in the same word.

By this rule, Finnish words have, with few exceptions, either all front vowels or all back vowels, but not both in the same word. We can see the vowel harmony rule in action when a suffix is added to the end of a word. In this case, the suffix vowel changes to match the quality of vowels in the word. For example, the suffix meaning 'in' has the form [-ssɑ] when added to a word where the last vowel is back, as in [tɑlo] 'house,' [tɑlossɑ] 'in the house.' However, the suffix takes the form [-ssæ] when it attaches to a word with a final front vowel, as in [metsæ] 'forest,' [metsæssæ] 'in the forest.' In cases like this, we can say that the vowel of the suffix harmonizes, or assimilates, to the preceding vowel.

b. Dissimilation. Unlike assimilation, which makes sounds more similar, rules of **dissimilation** cause two close or adjacent sounds to become less alike with respect to some property, by means of a change in one or both sounds. An example of dissimilation in Greek is the following:

(13) **Manner dissimilation** (Greek): A stop becomes a fricative when followed by another stop.

For example, in fast speech especially, the form /epta/ 'seven' can be pronounced as [efta], and /ktizma/ 'building' can be pronounced as [xtizma] ([x] is a voiceless velar fricative).

c. Insertion. Phonological rules of **insertion** cause a segment not present at the phonemic level to be added to the phonetic form of a word. An example of this kind of rule from English is voiceless stop insertion:

(14) **Voiceless stop insertion** (English): Between a nasal consonant and a voiceless fricative, a voiceless stop with the same place of articulation as the nasal is inserted.

Thus, for instance, the voiceless stop insertion rule may apply to the words *dance* /dæns/ → [dænts], *strength* /stɹɛŋθ/ → [stɹɛŋkθ], and *hamster* /hæmstɹ/ → [hæmpstɹ].

d. Deletion. Deletion rules eliminate a sound that was present at the phonemic level. Such rules apply more frequently to unstressed syllables and in casual speech. English examples include:

(15) **/h/-Deletion** (English): /h/ may be deleted in unstressed syllables.

The /h/-deletion rule would apply to a sentence such as *He handed her his hat* /hi hændəd hɹ̩ hɪz hæt/ to yield [hi hændəd ɹ̩ ɪz hæt]. Deletion is common in fast speech because it saves time and articulatory effort. Sounds like [h] that are not very perceptible are often the "victims" of deletion because speakers can save time and effort by deleting them without sacrificing much information. That is, the listener may not be relying on these sounds in order to understand what the speaker is saying.

e. Metathesis. Rules of **metathesis** change the order of sounds. In many instances, sounds metathesize in order to make words easier to pronounce or easier to understand. In Leti, an Austronesian language, consonants and vowels switch places when a word that ends in a consonant is combined with a word that starts with two consonants. The last two sounds in the first word trade places to avoid having three consonants in a row.

(16) **CV metathesis** (Leti): When three consecutive consonants occur, the first consonant trades places with the preceding vowel.

By this rule, /danat + kviali/ 'millipede' undergoes metathesis to become [dantakviali], and /ukar + ppalu/ 'index finger' becomes [ukrappalu]. On the other hand, /ukar + lavan/ 'thumb' does not undergo metathesis and so is pronounced as [ukɑrlɑvɑn] because there are not three consecutive consonants.

Metathesis is also possible in sign languages. In these cases, the order of two signs or parts of signs is switched. For example, in ASL, several signs are articulated with a path of movement that moves from a location just beneath the ear to a location by the side of the mouth. However, many speakers of ASL will produce these words with these two places of articulation reversed. Consider the signs for DEAF in (17). These two pronunciations include the same handshape, orientation, and type of movement; however, the order of the two locations is reversed in the second pronunciation.

(17) a. DEAF (indexical form)   b. DEAF (place of articulation metathesis)

© 2006, William Vicars, www.Lifeprint.com.   © 2006, William Vicars, www.Lifeprint.com.
Used with permission.   Used with permission.

Metathesis may similarly occur between places of articulation in signs with movement along a different path, for example, between forehead and chin or from one side of the chin to the other. Other signs in ASL that allow metathesis of place of articulation include RESTAURANT, FLOWER, PARENTS, and TWINS.

f. Strengthening. Rules of **strengthening** (also called fortition) make sounds stronger. The rule of English aspiration, as stated below, provides an example:

(18) **Aspiration** (English): Voiceless stops become aspirated when they occur at the beginning of a stressed syllable.

The pronunciation of *tap* /tæp/ as [tʰæp] and *cat* /kæt/ as [kʰæt] illustrate the application of the English aspiration rule. Aspirated stops are considered to be stronger sounds than unaspirated stops because the duration of voicelessness is much longer in aspirated stops (since it extends through the period of aspiration).

g. Weakening. Rules of **weakening** (also called lenition) cause sounds to become weaker. The "flapping" rule of English is an example of weakening. [ɾ] is considered to be a weaker sound than [t] or [d] because it is shorter and it obstructs air less.

(19) **Flapping** (English): An alveolar oral stop is realized as [ɾ] when it occurs after a stressed vowel and before an unstressed vowel.

The pronunciation of *writer* /ɹaɪtɹ̩/ as [ɹaɪɾɹ̩] and *rider* /ɹaɪdɹ̩/ as [ɹaɪɾɹ̩] are examples of the application of this rule. Note that voicing assimilation is involved in the change of /t/ to [ɾ]: the /t/ takes on the "voicedness" of the vowels surrounding it.

3.2.4 Multiple Rule Application

To this point we have seen examples where one phonological rule applies. In reality there is often more than one change that occurs between a given phonemic form and a phonetic output. To illustrate this let's look at how plural nouns are formed in English. When you learned to write in English, you learned that the way to make most nouns plural is to add an <s>, which is usually pronounced [z]. There are actually three different phonetic forms of the English plural marker: [s], [z], and [əz], seen in the words *cats* [kæts], *dogs* [dɔgz], and *foxes* [fɑksəz]. We need only one phonemic form for the plural marker if we use two rules to derive the phonetic forms.

Let's assume that the single phonemic form of the plural marker is /-z/, rather than /-s/ or /-əz/.[3] Why do words like *fox, ditch, bush, orange, rouge,* and *maze* have [-əz] as their plural suffix instead of just keeping the phonemic form /-z/? The answer lies in the last sound of each of these words—they all end in sounds that have a high-pitched hissing sound quality. These sounds are called **sibilant** consonants. The English sibilants are [tʃ, ʃ, s, dʒ, ʒ, z]. Notice that the plural marker is also a sibilant /-z/. Because of the high-pitched hissing sound, it is very difficult to hear two sibilants that are next to each other. Try saying [fɑksz], [dɪtʃz], [bɹɪdʒz], etc., and you will get the idea. This difficulty is remedied by inserting a schwa between the two sibilants.

(20) **Schwa insertion** (English): Insert [ə] between two sibilants.

The schwa insertion rule makes these plurals pronounceable by separating the two sibilants: [fɑksəz], [dɪtʃəz], [bɹɪdʒəz], etc. But why do we still need two different plurals, [-s] and [-z], for words that do not end in sibilants?

Try to pronounce [kætz] or [dɔgs], in which the voicing qualities of the final two consonants differ. You will probably find that it is difficult to produce a consonant cluster if one consonant is voiced and the other is voiceless. It is for this reason that the plural marker changes its voicing specification to match the sound it follows.

(21) **Voicing assimilation** (English): /-z/ takes on the voicing specification of the preceding sound.

The voicing assimilation rule takes a phonemic form like /kæt-z/ and turns it into the pronounceable form [kæts]. With these two rules acting together, we can derive the plural

---

[3]This assumption is in fact correct for English; the arguments for picking this form, however, are beyond the scope of this discussion.

for any English noun (except, of course, for "special" or irregular plurals like *oxen, octopi,* or *cherubim*). In (22), you can see how these **derivations** work: starting with the phonemic form, we apply each rule in turn (first schwa insertion, then voicing assimilation), and we end up with the correct final phonetic form.

(22) Sample derivations of English plurals

phonemic form:	/kæt-z/	/dɔg-z/	/faks-z/	/bɹɪdʒ-z/
schwa insertion:	—	—	faksəz	bɹɪdʒəz
voicing assimilation:	kæts	—	—	—
phonetic form:	[kæts]	[dɔgz]	[faksəz]	[bɹɪdʒəz]

3.2.5 Obligatory and Optional Rules

Notice that phonological rules may be **obligatory** or **optional**. Obligatory English rules include aspiration, vowel nasalization, vowel lengthening, and liquid and glide devoicing. Such a rule always applies in the speech of all speakers of a language or dialect having the rule, regardless of style or rate of speaking. The effects of obligatory rules are often very subtle and difficult to notice, but they are an important part of a native accent. For instance, it may be difficult to tell that a vowel is nasalized in English, but not applying the rule of vowel nasalization would make someone sound like a non-native speaker of English.

The existence of obligatory rules is what causes people to have foreign accents. It is easier to learn the rules of a new language than to "turn off" the obligatory rules of your native language. The very fact that we are often unaware of these rules causes us to apply them when they are not appropriate. When speakers of American English learn other languages, they often apply rules such as flapping and vowel reduction, even though the other language may not have these rules.

Optional phonological rules, on the other hand, may or may not apply in any given utterance. Optional rules are responsible for variation in speech; for example, we can pronounce /kæn bi/ *can be* as either [kæm bi] or [kæn bi], depending on whether alveolar stop assimilation is applied or not. The use of optional rules depends in part on rate and style of speech.

Phonotactic Constraints and Foreign Accents

3.3.1 Phonotactic Constraints

In every language there are restrictions on the kinds of sounds and sound sequences possible in different positions in words (particularly at the beginning and end). These restrictions can be formulated in terms of rules stating which sound sequences are possible in a language and which are not. Restrictions on possible combinations of sounds are known as **phonotactic constraints.** Languages generally prefer syllables made up of a consonant (C) first, and a vowel (V) second, but some languages allow a syllable to begin with more than one consonant. For instance, English allows up to three consonants to start a word, provided the first is /s/, the second /p/, /t/, or /k/, and the third /l/, /ɹ/, /j/, or /w/ (see below). There is a wide variety of syllable types in English, as illustrated in (1)

(1)

V	*a*	CV	*no*	CCV	*flew*	CCCV	*spree*
VC	*at*	CVC	*not*	CCVC	*flute*	CCCVC	*spleen*
VCC	*ask*	CVCC	*ramp*	CCVCC	*flutes*	CCCVCC	*strength*
VCCC	*asked*	CVCCC	*ramps*	CCVCCC	*crafts*	CCCVCCC	*strengths*

Other languages, however, do not have such a large number of syllable structures, as the lists in (2) illustrate. (Hebrew CVCC syllables are allowed only at the end of a word, and only if the final consonant is [t].)

(2)

Hawaiian	Indonesian	Hebrew
CV	CV	CV
V	V	CCV
	VC	CCVC
	CVC	CVC
		CVCC

Notice that this means that Indonesian has clusters only in the middle of words; that is, there are no clusters initially or finally. Hawaiian does not permit clusters in any position. Meanwhile, even though Hebrew permits both initial and final clusters, it does not allow a single vowel to be a syllable by itself. Every language has its own set of permitted segmental sequences.

We can investigate examples of restrictions on consonant sequences in more detail by considering some in a language we know very well—English. To start with, any consonant of English may occur initially (at the beginning) in words except for two: [ʒ] and [ŋ]. While some speakers do pronounce these sounds in borrowed words such as *Jacques* and *Nguyen*, no native English word begins with them. A large number of two-consonant combinations also occur word-initially, with a stop or fricative being followed by a liquid or glide:

[bɹ]	*bring*	[gl]	*glean*	[mj]	*music*	[kw]	*quick*
[æɹ]	*three*	[fl]	*fly*	[hj]	*humor*	[sw]	*sweet*

In addition, [s] can also be followed by voiceless and nasal stops (as in *stay, small*) and by [f] and [v] in a small number of borrowed words (*sphere, svelte,* etc.). [ʃ] can be followed by a nasal stop or a liquid, but only [ʃɹ] is a cluster native to English (e.g., *shrink*). The others are present only in borrowings from Yiddish and German (*Schlemiel* 'clumsy person,' *Schnook*, 'fool,' *Schwinn*).

3.3.2   Phonotactic Constraints in Signed Languages

There are similar kinds of constraints on what sorts of segment combinations are and are not allowed in various signed languages. As with the phonotactic constraints for syllable structures and for consonants and vowels in spoken languages described above, constraints on syllable structure and on what sorts of handshapes and movements can appear adjacent to one another in signed languages differ from language to language. The phonotactic constraints discussed in this section are specific to ASL.

First we will consider restrictions on syllable structure; there will be two examples.[1] It was mentioned above that in Hebrew, a vowel alone cannot serve as a syllable: there is a minimum requirement that a syllable in Hebrew contain at least two segments. There is a similar minimum requirement for ASL syllables: a monosyllabic sign cannot consist of just one handshape, one location, and one orientation; at least one of these elements is required to change in order to form a grammatical syllable.

The second example we will consider is when changes of handshape are allowed. Many signs include a change of handshape during movement of the hands from one location to another; other signs involve handshape changes that occur while the hands are held stationary at some particular place. In ASL, handshape changes may always occur during movement. The sign WHITE, shown in (3), provides a good example of this.

(3) ASL: WHITE

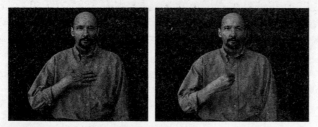

© 2006, William Vicars, www.Lifeprint.com. Adapted by permission.

Likewise, if a sign comprises only one place of articulation without movement to another place of articulation, handshape change can occur while the hand is kept at that location. However, if a sign involves the hands being at some place and then moving, or

---

[1]It probably seems very peculiar to think about signs as having syllables! Nonetheless, signs can be broken down into prosodic units just like spoken words. If you are not a signer, though, it is very difficult to figure out what might comprise a signed syllable. (We also lack intuitions about syllable structure of spoken languages that we do not know.) Therefore, we will simply take it as an underlying assumption that signed languages have syllables, and go from there.

moving and then winding up at some place, then the change of handshape must take place during the movement. It is ungrammatical in ASL for handshape to change while the hands are held at some particular location if there is a movement component of that sign.

To illustrate what this would be like, try to mimic the sign for 'white' shown in (3). Place your hand flat on your chest. Next, draw your hand away from your chest (to a distance of about 5 or 6 inches), and as you do so, bring your thumb and fingers together. (You won't be forming a fist; rather, imagine that you are holding a small object between your fingers and thumb.) This sign is perfectly acceptable in ASL. Now you are going to produce an ungrammatical sign. Again, place your hand flat on your chest. Next, move it away from your chest, again about 5 or 6 inches—this time keeping your hand flat—and once you have finished moving your hand, bring your fingers and thumb in to touch each other. Of course, there is nothing at all articulatorily difficult about making such a motion, but it is not a permitted sign in ASL; this constraint is merely an arbitrary rule built into the phonology of ASL.

Not only do signed languages have syllable structure constraints, but also there are constraints on which segments can be adjacent to one another in the same way that certain sound combinations are not allowed in some languages (like word-initial /fk/ in English). For example, in any given sign language, there may be certain handshapes which—though parts of the system of handshapes in that language—are not allowed by the grammar to appear adjacent to one another within a word.

An interesting phonotactic constraint that does not have any obvious direct parallel in spoken languages but that seems fairly uniform among signed languages pertains to the fact that in signed languages there are two possible primary articulators, namely, the right hand and the left hand. In all signed languages studied to date, a signer may be right-hand dominant or left-hand dominant (which roughly corresponds to whether the signer is right- or left-handed). The dominant hand is the one that the signer will use to perform all one-handed signs. (If a right-handed signer were to injure her right arm or happened to be carrying a large box under her right arm, she might temporarily switch and use her left hand to sign with, but no signer switches back and forth between hands as a matter of course: this would be considered extremely aberrant to any native speaker of a sign language.) Interestingly, there are very specific restrictions on what the non-dominant hand may do in any given two-handed sign. If both hands are moving, then the non-dominant hand must have the same handshape and orientation as the dominant hand and must move in the same way: that is, in signs where both hands are moving, there is a symmetry constraint. (You can think of this as the "don't pat your head and rub your belly" constraint.) An example of an ASL sign that follows the symmetry constraint is CAN, meaning 'be able to,' illustrated in (4). Although the non-dominant hand does move in this sign, it mirrors exactly the shape, orientation, and movement of the dominant hand.

(4) ASL: CAN

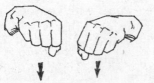

© 2006, William Vicars, www.Lifeprint.com. Used with permission.

The non-dominant hand may also participate in a sign by remaining stationary while the dominant hand moves. This is exemplified in the ASL sign CHOCOLATE in (5): the two hands have different handshapes, but the non-dominant hand (the lower hand, which is held flat) is not moving.

(5) ASL: CHOCOLATE

© 2006, William Vicars, www.Lifeprint.com. Used with permission.

A grammatical sign in any sign language cannot have both hands moving unless they both have the same handshape and orientation and are performing the same kind of movement. Interestingly, in Signed Mandarin (which is not a sign language, but rather a signed code for Mandarin Chinese; see File 1.5) there are certain signs that have been introduced by hearing (non-native signer) instructors at deaf schools that do not follow this rule. The fact that the Signed Mandarin words do not follow the universal rule for signed languages is yet more evidence that signed codes and signed languages differ! For example, in the signed Mandarin sign for 'ink,' both hands are moving, so the sign should follow the symmetry constraint. However, in this sign the dominant hand is facing toward the signer, and the non-dominant hand away from the signer, so they have different orientations; the dominant hand moves in a path away from the body while the non-dominant hand moves from side to side, so they have different movement; and the dominant hand has one finger extended while the non-dominant hand has three fingers extended, so they have different handshapes. Thus this sign is ungrammatical for three reasons.

There has been an attempt (again by non-native signers) to introduce such signs from Signed Mandarin into Taiwan Sign Language, but the reaction among the native signers is that these signs are not possible in their language. It is exactly as though somebody told you that /kpflus/ was a new word of English; you wouldn't accept it!

3.3.3   Foreign Accents

If a language has severe restrictions on its phonotactics, the restrictions will generally apply to every word in the language, native or not. Therefore, languages seek to overcome problems of borrowing a foreign word that violates their phonotactics. For instance, in English, two stops cannot come at the beginning of words, nor can stop plus nasal combinations. So, in order to pronounce the foreign words *Ptolemy* and *gnostic* more easily, English speakers simply drop the first consonant and pronounce the words [tɑləmi] and [nɑstɪk], respectively. Or, speakers may insert a vowel between the two consonants, as in the pronunciation of the words *Gdansk* and *knish* as [gədænsk] and [kənɪʃ].

As these examples from English illustrate, there are different ways of handling phonotactic problems. Japanese and Finnish provide us with additional examples. Japanese and Finnish generally avoid syllables containing sequences of consonants. When borrowing a foreign word that violates the language's syllable structure, the two languages must force it somehow to fit. There are two ways that borrowed words with consonant clusters are "repaired." One is to drop or delete one of the consonants; the other is to insert a vowel to separate the consonants. Finnish opts for deletion. In loan words, Finnish drops the first of a series of consonants that do not conform to its phonotactics. Thus, Germanic *Strand* (CCCVNC) ends up as *ranta* 'beach' (CVNCV) in Finnish, and *glass* becomes *lasi*. Note also the addition of a final vowel to avoid a consonant in syllable-final position.

The other way to break up consonant clusters is used in Japanese. Japanese inserts vowels into the cluster, so that, for example, a CCC sequence will end up as CVCVCV. The insertions are rule-governed, meaning that the insertion always works the same way; the vowel /u/ is inserted, except after /t/ and /d/, when the vowel /o/ is inserted. Thus, we can predict the shape of new words in Japanese (e.g., recent English loan words in the language).

So, for example, when the English term *birth control* was borrowed into Japanese, it became [baːsu kontoroːru]. Note that the nasals [m] and [n] are allowed syllable-finally in Japanese.

/bɹɪθ/ → /baːsu/

/kəntɹol/ → /kontoroːru/

The /u/ in [baːsu] and the last /u/ in [kontoroːru] are inserted to keep the word-final syllables from ending in a consonant. The second [o] in [kontoroːru] is inserted to prevent [t] and [r] from forming a cluster. Notice also the substitutions made by Japanese for English sounds: /Vr/ → /Vː/, /θ/ → /s/, /l/→ /r/.

Another source of foreign accents is the fact that not all sound systems are the same, as we discovered in conducting phonemic analyses of different languages. Some languages have fewer or more phonemes or allophones than English does, and we can detect this when we hear non-native speakers of English pronounce English. For instance, French speakers often pronounce English *this* [ðɪs] as [zɪs] and *thin* [θɪn] as [sɪn]. The reason for this mispronunciation is that the phonemic inventory of French does not contain /ð/ or /θ/, so French speakers substitute the nearest equivalent sounds, the fricatives /z/ and /s/, available in their phonemic inventory. This is known as **sound substitution,** a process whereby sounds that already exist in a language are used to replace sounds that do not exist in the language when borrowing or trying to pronounce a foreign word.

Another familiar example involves the pronunciation of German by some speakers of English. German has a voiceless velar fricative phoneme, represented by the symbol /x/. English, of course, lacks this sound, though we do have a voiceless velar stop /k/. Most speakers of English substitute /k/ for /x/ in a German word like *Bach* /bax/, producing [bɑk]. Another example of the same substitution is the way Americans will tend to pronounce the German word *Lebkuchen* /lebkuxən/ 'Christmas cookie' as [leɪbkukən]. Some English speakers, striving for a more "Germanlike" pronunciation, will pronounce it instead as [leɪbkuhən]. Why do you suppose an English speaker might substitute /h/ for /x/?

We can conclude by observing that substitutions by non-native speakers and strategies for handling phonotactic constraints both result in foreign accents, as well as changes in words that have been borrowed into another language. A Spanish speaker does not pronounce *student* as [ɛstudɛnt] because he or she doesn't know any better but because the consonant clusters /st/, /sk/, and /sp/ never occur at the beginning of a word in Spanish without being preceded by a vowel—for example, in the words *estudiante* 'student,' *escuela* 'school,' and *espalda* 'shoulder.' The Spanish speaker who says [ɛstudɛnt] is simply applying the phonological rules of Spanish when speaking English words.

Implicational Laws

3.4.1 Recurring Phonological Patterns

In studying phonetics, you saw that human languages use a wide variety of sounds. In spite of this variety, some sounds are more common than others. Thus, while it is true that almost all human languages use the stop consonants [p] and [t] and the vowel [a], relatively few languages use pharyngeal fricatives ([ħ] and [ʕ], the "throaty" sounds used in Arabic), voiceless vowels (like in whispered speech), and clicks (*tsk, tsk!* and horse calling sounds are American examples). So [p], [t], and [a] are **more common** in languages while pharyngeal fricatives, voiceless vowels, and clicks are **less common** speech sounds. The purpose of this file is to explain why some sounds are more common than others. Before attempting an explanation, however, we will make four observations concerning more common and less common speech sounds.

3.4.2 Sound Inventories

The first observation has to do with the inventories of sounds in languages. The observation is basically this: if a language uses a less common sound, one of its more common counterparts will also be used. Two parts of this statement need clarification. First, when we say that a language uses a particular sound, we mean that the sound is in the inventory of **phonemes** in the language. In other words, that sound is distinctive relative to other sounds in the language.

The second part of the statement that needs clarification is the phrase "one of its more common counterparts." This phrase refers to the fact that for each less common sound in the inventory there tends to be a more common sound in the inventory which is just like the less common sound except for one or two phonetic features. For instance, the more common counterpart of a voiceless vowel is a voiced vowel of the same tongue height, tongue advancement, and lip rounding. Likewise, the more common counterpart of a voiceless pharyngeal fricative is a voiceless velar fricative.

The table in (1) presents some (relatively) less common sounds and their (relatively) more common counterparts.

One thing to notice about this chart is that [s] appears both as a more common sound (as opposed to [x]) and as a less common sound (as opposed to [t]). This illustrates the fact that in using the terms "more common" and "less common" to designate the sounds in an implicational relationship, we are not referring to an absolute standard. Rather, "more common" and "less common" are used in a **relative** way. In other words, [s] is less common in relation to [t], but more common in relation to [x].

We have said that if a language uses a less common sound, one of its more common counterparts will also be included in that language's inventory of distinct sounds. In terms of the chart presented in (1), this means that any language that uses [ã] will also use [a], any language that uses [ḁ] will also use [a], any language that uses [x] will also use [k], and so on. This type of observation is called an **implicational law** because the presence of the less

(1)

Less common	More common
[ã]	[a]
[ḁ]	[a]
[x]	[k] or [s]
[s]	[t]
[d]	[t]
[ð]	[d] or [z]
voiced stops	voiceless stops
fricatives in place X	stops in place X

common sound **implies** that the more common sound will also be used in the language. Of course, the implication cannot be reversed. In other words, the fact that English uses the sound [k] does not imply that we also use [x].

Implicational laws can be stated for natural classes of sounds rather than just for individual pairs of sounds. For instance, the class of voiceless consonants is relatively more common than the class of voiced consonants. In other words, if a language makes use of voiced stops, it will also make use of voiceless ones. The reverse is not true; there are some languages that have only voiceless stops. Thus, the presence of voiced stops implies the presence of their voiceless counterparts, while the presence of voiceless stops does not imply the presence of voiced ones.

Another implicational law that can be stated in terms of a natural class of sounds is that the presence of fricatives in a language implies the presence of stops with the same place of articulation as the fricatives in that language. Thus, if a language uses an [s], then it also uses a [t].

3.4.3 Frequency and Distribution

The second observation concerning implicational laws is that they are not simply generalizations concerning inventories of sounds; they are also related to the **degree** to which sounds will be used in a particular language and to the **range of distribution** of the sounds in the words of the language. Thus, even if a language makes use of a pharyngeal fricative, this less common sound will be used in fewer words than will the more common velar fricative. In other words, the pharyngeal fricative will have limited usage compared with the velar fricative. More common sounds have a wider distribution within a language—i.e., they are used in more phonetic environments than less common sounds. So, for instance, Cantonese Chinese has both stops and fricatives in its inventory of sounds, but fricatives may occur in only one position in the syllable, as the first sound. Stops have wider distribution: they occur both syllable-initially and syllable-finally in Cantonese.

An English example of the limited usage and limited distribution of less common sounds has to do with the sound [ð]. The sound [ð] can be classified as less common because it is relatively rare in the languages of the world, and anywhere [ð] occurs in English, [z] can also occur. If you try to think of words that contain [ð], you will probably find that your list is limited to "grammatical" words like *this, that, those, them,* and *they,* and a few other words like *either* and *lathe.* Furthermore, [ð] occurs as the last sound in English words less often than [z] does. Compared with the number of words that contain [z], it is obvious that [ð] has limited use in English.

3.4.4 Acquisition of Sounds

A third type of observation related to implicational laws has to do with the order of the acquisition of sounds: children learning a language acquire the use of more common sounds before they acquire the use of less common ones. As a result, children who have not yet mastered the complete sound inventory of their native language will substitute more common sounds when trying to say less common sounds. When a little girl says [dɪs wʌn] for *this one*, she is replacing the relatively less common [ð] with [d], a much more common sound. This is an indication that the child has not yet fully acquired the use of [ð], although [d] is readily available for use. When the language development of a child is followed from babbling through maturity, a characteristic order of acquisition appears. This order in the acquisition of sounds is relatively constant for children around the world, no matter what language they are learning. Once again, the implicational laws capture a generalization about language; namely, that the acquisition of a relatively less common sound implies that its more common counterpart has already been acquired.

3.4.5 Sound Change

The fourth and last type of observation related to implicational laws involves language change: less common sounds tend to be less stable than more common ones. Thus, in the course of language change, if any sound is going to be lost, it is more likely to be a less common one rather than its more common counterpart. An illustration of this can be drawn from the history of English. In the Old English pronunciation of the word *knight* there was a voiceless velar fricative [x] between the vowel and the [t]. As you can see, the letters <gh> indicate where this consonant used to be. During the development of English, this velar fricative was lost (so *knight* now rhymes with *quite*). In fact, all instances of the velar fricative sound (as in *height, sight, fight, might,* and so on) were lost. English speakers just stopped using velar fricatives altogether, so now we find it hard to learn how to say them when we are trying to learn a language like German that uses them. This observation fits in with the implicational law that says that fricatives are less common than stops. Therefore, the fricative [x] is less stable and more likely to be lost than the corresponding stop consonant [k]. For more on sound change, see File 12.3.

3.4.6 Explaining Implicational Laws

At this point we can summarize what we have observed about common and uncommon speech sounds: the presence of a less common sound in a language implies that its more common counterpart will also be present; less common sounds have limited usage and distribution in the languages that do make use of them, as compared with common sounds; the use of common sounds is acquired before the use of less common ones; and less common sounds tend to be less stable than common ones and are thus more likely to be lost or changed over time. We might be tempted to say that the implicational laws are themselves the explanations of the observations. Thus, we might say that [x] is more likely to be lost in language change than [k] is because [k] is more common than [x]. Or we might want to say that [k] is acquired by children before [x] because [k] is more common than [x]. This type of explanation is circular, however. The circularity stems from the fact that we distinguished between common and less common sounds by making the observations.

The alternative to this circular form of explanation is to explain the above observations (and thus the implicational laws) in terms of the communicative nature of language. It is important to realize that when people use language, their goal (generally speaking) is to communicate—that is, to successfully transmit a message from a speaker to a hearer (refer to diagram (1) in File 1.2). Focusing on the function of language leads us to ask what sounds are most useful for transmitting a message from speaker to hearer.

First of all, notice that if a sound is difficult to produce, speakers will be somewhat inconsistent in pronouncing it, and this inconsistency may result in confusion on the part of the hearer. To avoid being misunderstood, speakers may avoid words with difficult sounds (resulting in limited usage), and if enough speakers avoid a difficult sound, it may disappear from the language entirely (language change). Of course, sounds that are difficult to produce (such as fricatives, whose production involves delicate control of muscles) are not likely to be mastered by children before easier sounds are. As you can see, there are at least some instances where the observation that sound X is more common than sound Y is directly tied to the fact that sound X is easier to produce than sound Y. Thus, [k] is more common than [x] because stops are easier to produce than fricatives. Alveolar fricatives are more common than pharyngeal fricatives because the tip of the tongue is more agile than the back of the tongue; hence alveolar consonants are easier to produce than pharyngeal ones. Thus, ease of production is an explanation of at least some of the implicational laws.

Another way to answer the question of what sounds are most useful for transmitting a message from speaker to hearer focuses on the hearer's point of view. It is reasonable to suppose that if a sound blends into the surrounding sounds too much, its distinctive qualities may become difficult to hear. So, for example, if Morse code were made up of long dashes and not-so-long dashes, or dots and somewhat shorter dots, rather than dots and dashes, it would be difficult to use. In the same way, the consonants and vowels which make up syllables are most usable when they are quite different from each other. So, the kind of syllable which is most useful in transmitting messages in language is composed of **maximally distinct** consonants and vowels. By this we mean that the consonants have very few qualities in common with the vowels, and the vowels are likewise very different from the consonants. The value of maximally distinct carriers of information is obvious when we think about Morse code. If you can't tell the difference between dots and dashes, then little communication can take place. In the same way, if you can't tell the difference between consonants and vowels, then communication using language is likely to be very inefficient.

Perhaps a couple of examples of the ways that consonants can be more vowel-like, or vowels can be more consonant-like, are in order. One implicational law that we noticed is that the use of voiced consonants in a language implies the use of voiceless ones (thus voiceless consonants are more common than voiced ones). The natural explanation for this implicational law is that voiceless consonants have fewer qualities in common with vowels than do voiced consonants; thus, in syllables containing consonants and vowels, voiceless consonants are perceptually more salient (or noticeable) than voiced ones. A way that vowels can be less consonant-like is to be pronounced with the mouth wide open, as in the vowel [ɑ]. Because consonants are made by obstructing the vocal tract in some way, a vowel that is pronounced with the mouth wide open will be more distinct from surrounding consonants than will be a vowel like [i] or [u] which is pronounced with the mouth somewhat closed. It just so happens that there is an implicational law corresponding to this distinction between [i], [u], and [ɑ]. The presence of a closed vowel ([i], [u]) implies the presence of an open vowel ([ɑ]). Thus, syllables with maximally distinct consonants and vowels are easier to perceive than syllables with consonants and vowels that resemble each other, and therefore some implicational laws exist for the sake of the listener, to make language easier to perceive.

3.4.7 Conclusion

In this file we have seen that although there is great variety in the sounds that can be employed in language, there are universal tendencies: to restrict the inventory of sounds to certain more common sounds, to restrict the degree of utilization and distribution of less common sounds in languages that do use them, to acquire more common sounds earlier than less common ones, and for less common sounds to be unstable in the face of language change. We have also shown that these observations concerning more common and less common sounds are related to the ease of production and ease of perception of those sounds. In addition, the implicational laws can at least sometimes be explained by assuming that people are using language in order to communicate, and that this produces a need for efficiency which leads to the use of easily produced and perceived sounds.

FILE **3.5**

How to Solve Phonology Problems

3.5.1   Goals of Phonological Analysis

Because phonemes are important units of linguistic structure, linguists must have a general method for identifying them in all languages. But the task of determining what the phonemes of a language are and what allophones are assigned to them is not always straightforward. For one thing, the set of phonemes differs from language to language, and so a different analysis is required for each language. Moreover, phonemes are psychological units of linguistic structure and are not physically present in a stream of speech. As a result, it is not possible to identify the phonemes of a language simply by taking physical measurements on a sample of language. Nor is it always easy to identify phonemes by investigating a native speaker's intuitions, since the minute phonetic details on which decisions about phonemes are made are often precisely those which speakers are not accustomed to noticing.

To get around these problems, linguists have developed an objective procedure by which the phonemes of a language can be discovered through examination of a set of words written in phonetic transcription. This procedure is based on two main observations about patterns of sounds.

First, phonemes make distinctions in meaning. If two sounds are members of separate phonemes, minimal pairs can almost always be found. For example, the minimal pair *led* and *red* is evidence that [l] and [ɹ] are members of separate phonemes in English. But if two sounds are allophones of the same phoneme, minimal pairs differing only in those sounds will not exist. For example, [bʌʔn̩] and [bʌtʰn̩] are both possible pronunciations of the English word *button* (though [bʌtʰn̩] may sound a little stilted). This is because the sounds [ʔ] and [tʰ] are both allophones of the phoneme /t/. Thus, the meaning doesn't change.

Second, the allophones of a phoneme are not a random collection of sounds but are a set of sounds that have the same psychological function. Accordingly, allophones of the same phoneme are systematically related to one another: they often share many phonetic properties, and it is possible to predict which allophone will appear in a word on the basis of phonological rules.

By analyzing the patterns of sounds that are physically present, it is possible to draw conclusions about the psychological organization of a language, which is not directly observable.

3.5.2   How to Do a Phonemic Analysis

Although a phonemic analysis can be performed successfully on any language, it is easiest to begin with a problem based on English. Look over the data in (1), which are given in a fairly detailed phonetic transcription. Recall that an open circle under a segment indicates that it is voiceless.

(1) 'pray'   [pʰɹ̥eɪ]   'fresh'   [fɹ̥ɛʃ]
    'gray'   [gɹeɪ]   'regain'   [ɹigeɪn]
    'crab'   [kʰɹ̥æb]   'shriek'   [ʃɹ̥ik]
    'par'   [pʰɑɹ]   'tar'   [tʰɑɹ]
    'broker'   [bɹoʊkɹ̩]

Beginning with the sounds [ɹ] and [ɹ̥], we attempt to answer the following question: are these sounds allophones of separate phonemes, or allophones of the same phoneme? (Of course, native speakers of English may intuitively know that they are allophones of the same phoneme. However, the procedure for doing a phonemic analysis should produce the same answer without appealing to the intuitions of speakers.)

In order to answer this question, it is necessary to examine scientifically the **distribution** of sounds within these data. That is, for each sound in question we need to determine the set of phonetic environments in which it can occur. But just what do we mean by *environment*? For the time being, we can define the **environment** of a sound as the sounds that immediately precede and follow it within a word. For example, in the word [gɹeɪ], [ɹ] is in the environment [g_eɪ]; that is, [ɹ] is preceded by [g] and followed by [eɪ].

The best way to begin a phonemic analysis is to determine whether the sounds in question are contrastive. To do this, look first for minimal pairs. Suppose for a moment we were interested in the sounds [pʰ] and [tʰ] in the data in (1). These sounds do appear in a minimal pair: [pʰɑɹ] and [tʰɑɹ] have different meanings and differ phonetically by only a single sound in the same position. This tells us that [pʰ] and [tʰ] are in overlapping distribution and, more specifically, that they are in contrastive distribution, because the difference between them causes a difference in meaning. Therefore, they are allophones of different phonemes.

Returning to the problem at hand, namely, the status of [ɹ] versus [ɹ̥], we see that there are no minimal pairs in the data that differ only by these two sounds. Since [ɹ] and [ɹ̥] are not in overlapping distribution in our data,[1] we can assume that they are in complementary distribution. However, we must prove that this is so by making a generalization about where [ɹ] (but not [ɹ̥]) may appear, and vice versa. In order to do so, we need to compare the phonetic environments of each of these sounds. The easiest way to do this is to make a list for each sound, as follows. (Note that "#" indicates a word boundary.)

(2) [ɹ]   [ɹ̥]

    [g_eɪ]   [pʰ_eɪ]
    [ɑ_#]   [kʰ_æ]
    [b_oʊ]   [f_ɛ]
    [#_i]   [ʃ_i]

Once you have collected the list of phonetic environments for each sound, you can proceed as follows:

1. *Look at the environments to find natural classes.* [ɹ̥] is preceded by [pʰ], [kʰ], [f], and [ʃ], all of which are voiceless consonants. This generalization permits us to simplify the description of the environment for [ɹ̥]; instead of listing each sound separately, it is now possible to say:

---

[1]You can always assume that the data you are given are representative of the language pattern you are asked to analyze for the purposes of solving phonology problems in this book. Sometimes we have selected a particular subset of the data from a language to illustrate a particular analytical point; this should not be taken as a sign that every word in the language will follow exactly the same pattern. However, the patterns we present are representative of basic phonological distributions.

(3) [ɪ̥] appears after voiceless consonants.

Now look at the environments in which [ɪ] appears. Are there any natural classes? Yes and no. Certainly [b] and [g] are voiced consonants, and [ɑ] is also voiced, but the set that includes [b], [g], [ɑ], the beginnings of words, and the ends of words does not form a natural class. Thus, the critical observation to make here is that there is no single natural class of environments in which [ɪ] can be found.

We have looked at the sounds preceding [ɪ] and [ɪ̥], but what about the sounds that follow them? As you can see, only [ɪ] may occur word-finally, but either [ɪ] or [ɪ̥] can occur before a vowel. Because the environment that follows either [ɪ] or [ɪ̥] can be the same (for example, [eɪ]) this alone can't tell us about when you get [ɪ] versus [ɪ̥]. Thus, the environments that condition the appearance of [ɪ] or [ɪ̥], i.e., the conditioning environments of these particular allophones, are their immediately preceding sounds.

2. *Look for complementary gaps in the environments.* So far, we have shown that [ɪ̥] appears after voiceless consonants, while [ɪ] appears in an apparently random set of environments. Yet, it is possible to make one more critical observation. [ɪ] does not appear in the environments in which [ɪ̥] appears, namely, after voiceless consonants. Moreover, [ɪ̥] does not appear where [ɪ] does; there is no [ɪ̥] after voiced consonants or at the beginnings or ends of words. Since the environments of [ɪ] and [ɪ̥] have systematic and complementary gaps, we say that [ɪ] and [ɪ̥] are in complementary distribution. Therefore, they are allophones of the same phoneme.

3. *State a generalization about the distribution of each of these sounds.* In other words, write a rule that will make predictions about where each of the sounds can occur. Actually, we've done the hard part of this already by observing that [ɪ̥] occurs following voiceless consonants. How should we state the distribution of [ɪ]? We could try formulating our rule as follows:

(4) [ɪ̥] appears following voiceless consonants;
    [ɪ] appears following voiced consonants or vowels, or at the beginning or end of
        a word.

However, that's not a very succinct formulation of the rule. To simplify it, recall that wherever [ɪ̥] occurs, [ɪ] can't, because their possible environments form complementary sets. Therefore, we can revise our rule this way:

(5) [ɪ̥] appears following voiceless consonants;
    [ɪ] appears elsewhere.

4. *Determine the identity of the phoneme and its allophones.* This next step in writing the rule involves deciding what the phoneme to which these sounds belong should be. In order to do so, we need to decide which of the allophones is the **basic allophone** and which is the **restricted allophone.** We have determined that the conditioning environment for [ɪ̥] consists of a single natural class of sounds. [ɪ̥] is restricted to occurring only there, whereas [ɪ] may appear anywhere else. Therefore, we can identify [ɪ̥] as the restricted allophone and [ɪ] as the basic one. It makes sense to name the phoneme after the basic allophone, since it is the one that can show up in a wider variety of contexts. Furthermore, the basic allophone is assumed to be the closest approximation of the mental "sound" that speakers store in memory. In choosing a name for the phoneme, we have made the leap from observable phonetic reality to unobservable psychological reality. (It is not always possible to choose one allophone as basic, however. In that case the phonology exercise's instructions will

not tell you to do so, and any of the allophones would serve equally well as the name of the phoneme.)

We can improve on our rule once more by writing it to show the process of going from the phoneme to each of the allophones, as in (6). This notation was introduced in Section 3.2.1. The arrows in the rule in (6) mean 'is pronounced as.' We use slashes around symbols that represent phonemes, and a single slash indicates the beginning of the environment specification:

(6) / ɹ / → [ɹ̥] / after voiceless consonants;
    / ɹ / → [ɹ] / elsewhere.

Now that we have formulated the necessary phonological rule, we can see which phonological process it involves (cf. File 3.2). In this rule a voiced phoneme changes into a voiceless sound when it follows another voiceless sound. In other words, /ɹ/ becomes more like a preceding sound with respect to the feature of voicelessness. Therefore, we can conclude that the process of assimilation is involved in this phonological rule.

3.5.3 Some Potential Trouble Spots

The procedure outlined in the previous section will work for any language for which reliable phonetic transcriptions exist. However, beginners are often confused by certain questions.

For instance, if you discover that no minimal pairs exist for two sounds, is it possible to automatically conclude that they are allophones of the same phoneme? No. It is still necessary to show that the sounds are in complementary distribution, since allophones are predictable variant pronunciations of the same phoneme.

Consider what happens if you make a decision too soon. Using the data presented in (1) at the beginning of the previous section, suppose you wanted to know whether [g] and [ʃ] are allophones of the same phoneme. Since there are no minimal pairs differentiated by these sounds in the data set, it might seem reasonable to conclude that they are. (Of course, a speaker of English should have no trouble thinking of a minimal pair involving these two sounds, for example, *gag* and *gash*. The exercises, however, are designed to be self-contained; that is, in all of the problems in the book, you will be given enough data **within** the problem set to solve the problem. This means that you should not rely on outside knowledge you may have of the language you are analyzing to answer the question.) But a careful examination of the data reveals that this is the wrong conclusion. Listing the data and the relevant environments, you find what is shown in (7).

(7) [g] appears in *gray* [gɹeɪ], *regain* [ɹigeɪn]
      generalization: [g] appears between vowels or at the beginning of a word;
    [ʃ] appears in *fresh* [fɹɛʃ], *shriek* [ʃɹik]
      generalization: [ʃ] appears at the beginning or end of a word.

As these data illustrate, [g] and [ʃ] are not in complementary distribution because their distributions overlap: either may occur at the beginning of a word. Furthermore, either may be followed by the phoneme /ɹ/. As a result, no phonological rule can be responsible for their distribution. In general, when no generalization can be made about where a group of sounds can occur, it is possible to conclude that they are members of separate phonemes. A conclusion based on such a demonstration is just as valid as showing that minimal pairs exist. This alternative way of showing that sounds are members of separate phonemes is useful because it's not always possible to find minimal pairs for all distinctive sounds. For example, there are no minimal pairs involving [ŋ] and [h] in English. But it is reasonable to assume that they belong to separate phonemes because they share few phonetic properties, and no phonological rule determines where they can occur.

The range of tests for identifying phonemes can be broadened somewhat by the use of **near-minimal pairs.** Recall that a minimal pair is a pair of words differing in meaning but phonetically identical except for one sound in the same position in each word. The definition of near-minimal pairs is the same, except that the words are *almost* identical except for the one sound. For example, *heard* [hɹd] and *Bert* [bɹt] form a near-minimal pair involving [h] and [b]. We are justified in saying that [h] and [b] are allophones of separate phonemes because no conceivable phonological rule would permit only [h] at the beginnings of words ending in [d], and only [b] at the beginnings of words ending in [t]. (This conclusion is partly based on extensive study of how phonological rules work: experience does play a role in being able to do phonological analysis.)

One final point about minimal pairs: notice that we have not defined them as pairs of words that rhyme. It is not necessary for two words to rhyme in order to form a minimal pair. Consider the English minimal pairs *state* [steɪt] and *steak* [steɪk], for example, or *boat* [boʊt] and *beat* [bit]. Nor is rhyming sufficient to qualify a pair of words as a minimal pair: *gray* [gɹeɪ] and pray [pʰɹeɪ] from the list of data above rhyme, but differ in two sounds. And to take another example, *glitter* and *litter* rhyme but do not form a minimal pair because they do not contain the same number of sounds.

Another question that often troubles beginners is this: when describing the environment in which a sound appears, how do you know where to look? In the problem we solved in the previous section, we considered only the sounds that preceded [ɹ] and [ɹ̥]. This is certainly not the only possibility. In fact, identifying conditioning environments is the most challenging part of doing a phonemic analysis.

Recall that in many cases, the relevant conditioning environment consists of the sounds immediately surrounding the sound in question. However, it is sometimes necessary to look beyond the sound's immediate environment. As we saw for Finnish vowels in Section 3.2.3, if you are examining the distribution of a vowel allophone, it is quite common that the conditioning environment involves a vowel in an adjacent syllable, even though consonants may intervene. It may also be necessary to consider preceding or following sounds even when they belong to another word that is adjacent in the stream of speech. However, it is best to start by examining the immediate environment of an allophone when you are trying to determine what its conditioning environment is.

Since there are many logically possible environments to consider, the task is made easier by eliminating all of those except the most plausible. This can be accomplished by using strategies like the following:

a. *Formulate hypotheses about the allophones.* Investigation of the world's languages has revealed that some sounds are more common than others (see File 3.4 for relevant discussion). For example:

- Voiced nasals and liquids are more common than voiceless ones.
- Oral vowels are more common than nasal vowels.
- Short consonants are more common than long consonants.
- "Plain" consonants are more common than those with secondary articulations like velarization, palatalization, and labialization.

On the basis of these generalizations, it is possible to speculate that if a less common sound appears in a language, it is probably a restricted allophone. But these tendencies should be used only as a guide for forming hypotheses, not as a basis for jumping to conclusions, since some languages exhibit exceptions. For example, French has both nasal and oral vowel phonemes.

b. *Keep in mind that allophonic variation results from the application of phonological rules.* Also remember that rules usually involve some phonological process, such as assimilation or deletion. Once you have a hunch about which allophone is the restricted one, check the environment in which it appears for evidence that a phonological process has applied. This may involve looking in more than one place until you have discovered a reasonable candidate. In the problem in the previous section, we were guided by the knowledge that voicing differences in consonants are often caused by voicing assimilation, and that voicing assimilation frequently occurs in consonant clusters. Since /ɹ/ is the second member of all of the clusters given, we concluded that the consonant preceding it constituted the conditioning environment. Even if it is not obvious that a phonological process has been at work, you should be able to write a phonological rule and, thus, state a generalization about where the allophones of the phoneme occur.

3.5.4 Flowchart for Discovering the Distribution of Sounds

The flowchart in (8) should help you to identify the type of distribution two (or more) sounds in a language have. The rectangular boxes ask you to do something or give you some information that your working through the flowchart has revealed. The diamond-shaped boxes pose a question. Try reading through the flowchart before you attempt to analyze the languages in the next file (File 3.6, "Practice"); it may help you to understand the relationship between the different types of distributions of sounds in a language.

(8) A flowchart for identifying the distribution of sounds

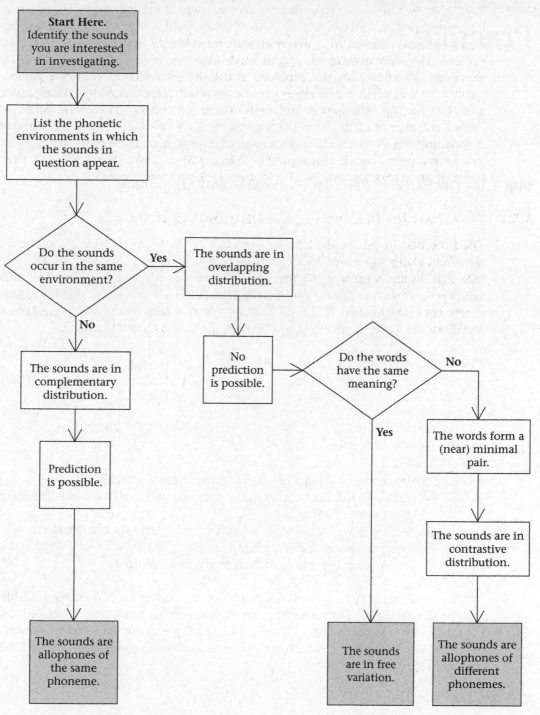

Practice

File 3.1—The Value of Sounds: Phonemes and Allophones

Exercises

1. **Ukrainian**

   Look at the following Ukrainian words containing the sounds [s], [sʲ], [ʃ], and [ʃʲ]. The sounds [sʲ] and [ʃʲ] are palatalized variants of [s] and [ʃ]; see the discussion in Section 2.4.6. The words have been arranged to help you identify minimal pairs.

[s]		[sʲ]		[ʃ]		[ʃʲ]	
a.	[lɪs]	'fox'	[lɪsʲ]	'sheen'	[lɪʃ]	'lest'		
b.	[mɪska]	'bowl'			[mɪʃka]	'little mouse'	[mɪʃʲi]	'mice'
c.	[sapka]	'little hoe'			[ʃapka]	'hat'		
d.	[sɪla]	'strength'			[ʃɪla]	'she sewed'	[ʃʲistʲ]	'six'
e.	[sum]	'sadness'			[ʃum]	'rustling'		
f.	[sudɪ]	'trials'	[sʲudɪ]	'hither'			[koʃʲi]	'baskets'
g.	[sosna]	'pine'	[sʲomɪj]	'seventh'	[ʃostɪj]	'sixth'		
h.	[posadu]	'job' (acc.)	[posʲadu]	'I will occupy'				

   i. What minimal pairs can you identify in these words?

   ii. Is there a minimal triplet (like a minimal pair, but involving three sounds and three words)? What is it?

   iii. Which three of these four sounds are in contrastive distribution?

   iv. One of these sounds occurs only before a particular vowel. What is this sound, and what is the vowel? Which words indicate this?

2. Refer to the *For Better or For Worse* cartoon at the beginning of this chapter. This cartoon hinges on the use of a minimal pair, *copulation* versus *population*. What two consonants differentiate these words? Using your knowledge of consonant articulation (see File 2.3), what are the phonetic descriptions of these two sounds? How do they differ phonetically?

Discussion Questions

3. We have said that both contrastive distribution and free variation involve a context where it is impossible to predict which of two or more sounds belongs. However, these two are not the same thing. Consider the context [pʰlɑ__]. Of the sounds [p, pʼ, b, t, tʼ, d], only one doesn't form a real word of English when inserted in this context—which one? Of the rest of these sounds, which ones are in contrastive distribution? Which ones are in free variation? How do you know?

4. Fill in the following table using the three terms "contrastive distribution," "complementary distribution," and "free variation" as defined in this chapter, with respect to two sounds in a given context. (For example, the upper left-hand cell of the table should contain the name of the type of distribution that occurs when two sounds are contrastive and predictable in a certain context.) Which cell in the table is blank? Why is it blank?

	Predictable	Nonpredictable
Contrastive		
Noncontrastive		

5. Refer to the *For Better or For Worse* cartoon at the beginning of this chapter. Elizabeth has clearly misunderstood the word *population* as *copulation*. Given what you know about the sounds [p] and [k] in English and the notion of a minimal pair, why does this challenge the notion of what it means for a pair of sounds to be "contrastive"? Do you think this is a serious challenge that undermines the phonological understanding of contrast? Why or why not?

Activities

6. Obtain a dictionary or textbook for some signed language from your library, or go to an online sign language dictionary. (You may use a search engine to find one, or you may go to www.Lifeprint.com, which is the Web site of the man whom most of the ASL pictures in this book came from.) Look through the lists of words and try to find minimal pairs. The two words that you select should be the same in three of the following parameters and should differ in only one: place of articulation, movement, handshape, and orientation. For each minimal pair, specify which parameter the two signs differ in, and describe the difference.

File 3.2—Phonological Rules

Exercises

7. List the members of the following natural classes of English sounds.

   a. alveolar obstruents   T, b, S, Z
   b. voiced labial consonants   w, m
   c. velar oral stops   k, g
   d. interdental fricatives   θ, ð
   e. high tense vowels   e
   f. low vowels   æ, a
   g. palatal sonorants   j
   h. voiced sibilants   z ʒ, dʒ

8. Describe the following natural classes of English sounds.

   a. [ɪ, l]
   b. [f, θ, s, ʃ, h]
   c. [w, j, w̥]
   d. [i, u]
   e. [p, b]
   f. [n, ɹ, l]

9. Identify the phonological rule or rules from this file operating in each of the following derivations.

a.	little	/lɪtl̩/	→	[lɪɾl̩]
b.	late bell	/leɪt bɛl/	→	[leɪp bɛl]
c.	park	/pɑɹk/	→	[pʰɑɹk]
d.	lance	/læns/	→	[lænts]
e.	it's her car	/ɪts hɹ̩ kɑɹ/	→	[ɪts ɹ̩ kʰɑɹ]
f.	ten pages	/tɛn peɪdʒz/	→	[tɛm pʰeɪdʒəz]
g.	two cups	/tu kʌpz/	→	[tʰu kʰʌps]

(handwritten annotations: "(pɪtɪk)"; "Aspiration of voiceless bilabial stop,"; "[lænts] Incretion voiceless alveolar stop"; "deletion glottal fricative voiceless, Asp"; "Incretion, Aspiration, Assim vel"; "2 Aspirations, Assimilation voicing")

10. Examine the following sets of data, and for each set write a rule to describe the derivation of the phonetic forms from the phonemic ones. (To do so, determine what sound or natural class of sounds is being altered, what it is being changed to, and what the environment is. That is, your rules should be of the form X → Y/C_D.) Where possible, also explain what kind of process (of the seven types) is involved in the rule.

a. In the speech of some New Yorkers, examples like the following are found.

there	/ðɛɹ/	→	[ðɛ]		*marry*	/mæɹi/	→	[mæɹi]
court	/kɔɹt/	→	[kɔt]		*Paris*	/pæɹɪs/	→	[pæɹɪs]
large	/lɑɹdʒ/	→	[lɑdʒ]		*for all*	/fɔɹ ɔl/	→	[fɔɹ ɔl]
stores	/stɔɹz/	→	[stɔz]		*story*	/stɔɹi/	→	[stɔɹi]
cared	/kɛɹd/	→	[kɛd]		*caring*	/kɛɹɪŋ/	→	[kɛɹɪŋ]

(handwritten annotations: "alveolar deletion of pretonic liquid"; "the sound after, consonant"; "r open during following 'r'"; "vowel after 'r' stays."")

b. Examples like the following are very common in English.

OSU	/oɛsju/	→	[oɛʃu]
did you	/dɪd ju/	→	[dɪdʒu]
capture	/kæptɹ̩/	→	[kæptʃɹ̩]
gracious	/gɹeɪsiəs/	→	[gɹeɪʃəs]

(handwritten annotations: "palatalization + deletion"; "Alveolar palatal"; "Place of articulation is palatization")

c. The following data are from German. (The symbol /tˢ/ represents a voiceless alveolar affricate.)

German	Gloss			
Bild	'picture'	/bɪld/	→	[bɪlt]
blieb	'remained'	/blib/	→	[blip]
Weg	'way'	/veg/	→	[vek]
fremd	'foreign'	/frɛmd/	→	[frɛmt]
gelb	'yellow'	/gɛlb/	→	[gɛlp]
Zug	'train'	/tˢug/	→	[tˢuk]
Vogel	'bird'	/fogl̩/	→	[fogl̩]
Baum	'tree'	/baʊm/	→	[baʊm]
schnell	'fast'	/ʃnɛl/	→	[ʃnɛl]

Discussion Questions

11. Consider the following paragraphs and answer the questions about natural classes.
    i. The English indefinite article is *a* [ə] before most words: *a car, a peanut, a tennis ball,* etc., but it is *an* [æn] before words like *apple, onion, icicle, evening, eagle,* and *honor.* To what natural classes do the sounds at the beginning of each set of words belong? (That is, before what class of sounds do you use [ə]? [æn]?)
    ii. Some American English speakers (largely in the Midwest and the South) pronounce [ɪ] in words like *then, Kenny, pen, Bengals, gem, lengthen, Remington,* and

temperature (where other speakers have [ɛ]). But, like others, they have [ɛ] in words like *pet, bell, peg,* and *tech.* What natural class of sounds follows the vowel in words where these speakers have [ɪ]?

   iii. Some midwestern American speakers in casual speech drop the unstressed vowel in the first syllable of words like *police, believe, parade, Columbus, pollution, terrific,* and *collision,* but do not drop it in words like *detective, dependent, majestic,* or *pedantic.* What natural class of sounds follows the unstressed vowel in the first syllable in the first group of words?

   iv. At some time during a child's language development, he or she might pronounce certain words as follows: *that* [dæt], *these* [diz], *this* [dɪs], and *three* [fɹi], *think* [fɪŋk], *bath* [bæf]. What natural class of sounds is being affected? Do the sounds used as replacements form a natural class?

12. In File 3.2, two rules were used to derive the three phonetic forms of the English plural. Is the order of these rules important? Show what would happen if we applied the voicing assimilation rule before the schwa insertion rule. Give examples.

13. The traditional sign for TOMATO in ASL involves one hand with the index finger extended, moving from the lips down in front of the body, while the other hand is in a flat O handshape and remains still in front of the body. Some signers now produce it without the O handshape, instead extending the index finger on the hand that stays still. What type of phonological process is this? Why do you think such a change might have happened?

File 3.3—Phonotactic Constraints and Foreign Accents

Exercises

14. According to the phonotactic constraints on English syllable structure given in Section 3.3.1, is [bljust] a possible word in English? Why or why not? Does this match with your own intuition?

15. List three different ways an English speaker might make the borrowed Polish place name Szczebrzeszynie [ʃtʃɛbʒɛʃɪɲɛ] fit in with English phonotactics.

Discussion Questions

16. If a consonant cluster occurs in a language, do you think that it should automatically be considered a legal phonotactic sequence in the language? For example, do you think that [ʃl] should be considered phonotactically legal in English because it occurs in the words *schlep* and *schlocky?* Why or why not?

17. Speculate as to why it is difficult for people to learn the phonotactics of another language. Why do people use "repair" strategies or substitutions rather than just pronouncing the foreign word the way it is pronounced by native speakers of the foreign language?

18. In File 3.3, we discussed the process by which some individuals are trying to introduce new signs into Taiwan Sign Language.

   i. Why do you think that the hearing instructors came up with signs that violate a universal principle of signed languages? If it is a universal principle, then why didn't the instructors create signs that followed it?

    ii. Now that they have been created, do you think that these signs will catch on in TSL? Why, or why not?

    iii. Do you think that if they do catch on, they will be modified in any particular way, or do you think that they will keep the same form that they had in Signed Mandarin? (Be sure to refer to the information about foreign accents also discussed in File 3.3.) If you think they will change, what are some possible sorts of changes that could take place?

    iv. What do you think about the Mandarin-speaking instructors creating new signs? In general, should people who are not speakers of a particular language be allowed to introduce new words into that language? Is this case different, since the creators of the new signs have a native language with a different modality?

File 3.4—Implicational Laws

Exercises

19. Explain why it doesn't make sense to ask the question, "Is [s] a common sound in the world's languages?"

20. Given the explanations for implicational laws given in Section 3.4.6, why do you think that clicks are relatively rare in the world's languages? Do you think it is related more to production or to perception? Why?

21. The explanations for implicational laws given in Section 3.4.6 have also been used to explain other phenomena, especially in the domains of language variation and change. Look at the following pictures of the ASL word LEARN. One set shows the formal version of the sign; the other shows a more casual version. Speculate as to why the sign might have changed from the formal version to the informal version, given considerations of perception and production.

    a. ASL LEARN (more formal register)

© 2006, William Vicars, www.Lifeprint.com. Adapted by permission.

    b. ASL LEARN (more casual register)

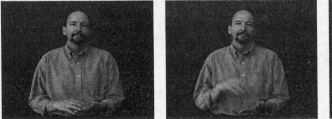

© 2006, William Vicars, www.Lifeprint.com. Adapted by permission.

Discussion Questions

22. Referring to the phonotactic constraints on syllable structure in File 3.3, do you think that there is an implicational hierarchy of syllable types? If so, what do you think it might look like? If not, why not?

File 3.5—How to Solve Phonology Problems

The exercises for this file are designed to give you practice in doing phonemic analysis at the beginning, intermediate, and more advanced levels. The instructions to each exercise are somewhat different in each case, so read them carefully before proceeding. However, each exercise requires that you follow the step-by-step procedure for doing a phonemic analysis outlined in the text of File 3.5. The exercises are designed to introduce you to problems involving minimal pairs, complementary distribution, and free variation. A linguist doing a phonemic analysis of an unknown language would, of course, examine hundreds of words in order to be sure to have enough data to find the relevant minimal pairs, complementary distributions, etc. But to save you time, the data in the exercises below have been carefully selected to give you all the relevant information you will need in a very small set of words.

Exercises

23. 🖋 **Mokilese**
   Mokilese is an Austronesian language of the Malayo-Polynesian family, spoken in Micronesia. Examine the distribution of the voiced and voiceless vowel pairs: [i, i̥] and [u, u̥] (voiceless vowels have a circle under the phonetic vowel symbol). For each pair, determine whether they are allophones of different phonemes or allophones of the same phoneme. Provide evidence for your answer. If they are allophones of one phoneme, state the contexts in which each sound occurs and decide which sound is the basic sound. Can any generalizations be made? (*Hint:* Refer to natural classes.)

a. [pi̥san]	'full of leaves'		**g.** [uduk]	'flesh'
b. [dupu̥kda]	'bought'		**h.** [kaskas]	'to throw'
c. [pu̥ko]	'basket'		**i.** [poki]	'to strike something'
d. [ki̥sa]	'we two'		**j.** [pil]	'water'
e. [su̥pwo]	'firewood'		**k.** [apid]	'outrigger support'
f. [kamwɔki̥ti]	'to move'		**l.** [ludʒuk]	'to tackle'

Beginning Exercises

24. **Sindhi**
   The following data are from Sindhi, an Indo-European language of the Indo-Aryan family, spoken in Pakistan and India. Examine the distribution of the phones [p], [pʰ], and [b]. Determine if the three are allophones of separate phonemes or allophones of the same phoneme. What is your evidence? Is the relationship among the sounds the same as in English? Why or why not?

a. [pənu]	'leaf'		**g.** [təru]	'bottom'
b. [vədʒu]	'opportunity'		**h.** [kʰəto]	'sour'
c. [ʃeki]	'suspicious'		**i.** [bədʒu]	'run'
d. [gədo]	'dull'		**j.** [bənu]	'forest'
e. [dəru]	'door'		**k.** [bətʃu]	'be safe'
f. [pʰənu]	'hood of snake'		**l.** [dʒədʒu]	'judge'

25. Standard Italian

Consider the following data from Standard Italian, an Indo-European language of the Romance family, spoken in Italy. Answer the questions that follow.

a.	[tinta]	'dye'	**g.**	[tiŋgo]	'I dye'
b.	[tɛnda]	'tent'	**h.**	[tɛŋgo]	'I keep'
c.	[dantsa]	'dance'	**i.**	[fuŋgo]	'mushroom'
d.	[neɾo]	'black'	**j.**	[bjaŋka]	'white'
e.	[dʒɛnte]	'people'	**k.**	[aŋke]	'also'
f.	[sapone]	'soap'	**l.**	[faŋgo]	'mud'

   i. Are there any minimal pairs? If so, what are they, and what can you conclude to be true of Italian from those minimal pairs?

   ii. State the phonetic environments in which the sounds [n] and [ŋ] appear. Identify any natural classes of sounds that appear in the environments you've provided.

   iii. Given what you know about the distribution of sounds and the environments you listed in (ii), are [n] and [ŋ] in complementary or contrastive distribution? Please explain your answer.

26. Standard Spanish

Standard Spanish is an Indo-European language of the Romance family. Examine the phones [d] and [ð]. Determine whether they are allophones of one phoneme or of separate phonemes. If they are allophones of one phoneme, identify the type of distribution. If they are in complementary distribution, state a rule that describes the distribution. If [d] and [ð] are allophones of separate phonemes, give minimal pairs that prove this.

a.	[dɾama]	'drama'	**g.**	[komiða]	'food'
b.	[doloɾ]	'pain'	**h.**	[anda]	'scram'
c.	[dime]	'tell me'	**i.**	[sweldo]	'salary'
d.	[kaða]	'each'	**j.**	[duɾaɾ]	'to last'
e.	[laðo]	'side'	**k.**	[toldo]	'curtain'
f.	[oðio]	'hatred'	**l.**	[falda]	'skirt'

27. Russian

Russian is an Indo-European language of the Slavic family, spoken in Russia. Determine from the following Russian data whether [a] and [ɑ] complement each other as allophones of the same phoneme or whether they are in contrast as allophones of separate phonemes. If they are allophones of separate phonemes, provide evidence for your claim. If they are in complementary distribution, pick one allophone as the basic sound, and give the conditioning phonetic contexts for its allophones. ([ł] represents a velarized [l], [sʲ] a palatalized alveolar fricative, and [mʲ] a palatalized voiced bilabial nasal.)

a.	[atəm]	'atom'	**f.**	[upał]	'he fell'
b.	[dva]	'two'	**g.**	[dɑł]	'he gave'
c.	[dar]	'gift'	**h.**	[pɑːłkə]	'stick'
d.	[masʲ]	'ointment'	**i.**	[ukrɑłə]	'she stole'
e.	[mʲatə]	'mint'	**j.**	[brał]	'he took'

28. Burmese

Burmese is a Sino-Tibetan language of the Tibeto-Burman family, spoken in Myanmar. The following Burmese data contain both voiced and voiceless nasals. The latter are indicated by a small circle placed under the phonetic symbol. Are [m] and [m̥] allophones of the same phoneme, or are they different phonemes? What about [n] and [n̩]? Is the same also true for [ŋ] and [n̠]? Give evidence for your answer. If there is a phonological process involved, state what it is and give the conditioning environment. What is it about this environment that triggers this rule? *Note:* Burmese is a tone language, where [ˊ] indicates a high-toned vowel, [ˋ] a low-toned vowel, [ˆ] a falling-toned vowel. No tone marking indicates that the vowel is mid-toned. The sequence of sounds [eɪ] is a diphthong.

a.	[ɪnî]	'fire'	**n.**	[nìè]	'fine, small'
b.	[mwêɪ]	'to give birth'	**o.**	[nwâ]	'cow'
c.	[mjiʔ]	'river'	**p.**	[ŋâ]	'five'
d.	[mjâwn]	'ditch'	**q.**	[ŋouʔ]	'stump (of tree)'
e.	[mjín]	'to see'	**r.**	[mîn]	'old (people)'
f.	[nê]	'small'	**s.**	[hm̥í]	'to lean against'
g.	[njiʔ]	'dirty'	**t.**	[hm̥wêɪ]	'fragrant'
h.	[nwè]	'to bend flexibly'	**u.**	[hm̥jajʔ]	'to cure (meat)'
i.	[hm̥jawʔ]	'to multiply'	**v.**	[hm̥òwn]	'flour, powder'
j.	[hn̥êɪ]	'slow'	**w.**	[hn̠jiʔ]	'to wring, squeeze'
k.	[hn̥wêɪ]	'to heat'	**x.**	[hn̠jeɪʔ]	'to nod the head'
l.	[hn̥jaʔ]	'to cut off (hair)'	**y.**	[hn̠â]	'to borrow'
m.	[hn̠eʔ]	'bird'	**z.**	[hîn]	'curry'

29. **Korean**

Korean is a "language isolate," meaning that it is not linguistically related to other languages. It is spoken in Korea. In the following Korean words, you will find the sounds [s] and [ʃ]. Determine whether the sounds [s] and [ʃ] are allophones of the same phoneme or separate phonemes. If the sounds are allophones of the same phoneme, give the basic and derived allophones and the environment in which the derived allophone occurs.

a.	[ʃi]	'poem'	**j.**	[sal]	'flesh'
b.	[miʃin]	'superstition'	**k.**	[kasu]	'singer'
c.	[ʃinmun]	'newspaper'	**l.**	[sanmun]	'prose'
d.	[tʰaksaŋʃige]	'table clock'	**m.**	[kasəl]	'hypothesis'
e.	[ʃilsu]	'mistake'	**n.**	[miso]	'smile'
f.	[oʃip]	'fifty'	**o.**	[susek]	'search'
g.	[paŋʃik]	'method'	**p.**	[tapsa]	'exploration'
h.	[kanʃik]	'snack'	**q.**	[so]	'cow'
i.	[kaʃi]	'thorn'			

30. **English**

English is an Indo-European language of the Germanic family. In the following dialect of English, common in Canada and parts of the United States, there is a predictable variant [əɪ] of the diphthong [aɪ]. What phonetic segments condition this change? What feature(s) characterize the class of conditioning segments?

a.	[bəɪt]	*bite*	**f.**	[fəɪt]	*fight*	**k.**	[taɪm]	*time*
b.	[taɪ]	*tie*	**g.**	[baɪ]	*buy*	**l.**	[təɪp]	*type*
c.	[ɹaɪd]	*ride*	**h.**	[ɹəɪs]	*rice*	**m.**	[naɪnθ]	*ninth*
d.	[ɹaɪz]	*rise*	**i.**	[faɪl]	*file*	**n.**	[faɪɾ]	*fire*
e.	[ɹəɪt]	*write*	**j.**	[ləɪf]	*life*	**o.**	[bəɪk]	*bike*

31. Totonac

Examine the classes of voiced versus voiceless vowels in Totonac, a Totonacan language spoken in Mexico. Are voiced and voiceless vowels in Totonac in contrast, in free variation, or in complementary distribution? If the sounds are in complementary distribution, pick one sound as the basic sound and give the phonetic contexts for its allophones. (Note that [tˢ] represents a voiceless alveolar affricate, and [ɫ] a velarized [l].)

a.	[tˢapsḁ]	'he stacks'	**g.**	[snapapḁ]	'white'
b.	[tˢilinksḁ]	'it resounded'	**h.**	[stapu̥]	'beans'
c.	[kasitti̥]	'cut it'	**i.**	[ʃumpi̥]	'porcupine'
d.	[kuku̥]	'uncle'	**j.**	[taːqhu̥]	'you plunged'
e.	[ɫkakḁ]	'peppery'	**k.**	[tihaʃɫi̥]	'he rested'
f.	[miki̥]	'snow'	**l.**	[tukʃɫi̥]	'it broke'

Intermediate Exercises

32. Tojolabal

Tojolabal is a Mayan language of the Kanjobalan-Chujean family, spoken in Mexico. Determine whether plain [k] and glottalized [kʔ] are allophones of a single phoneme, in free variation, or in contrast. Support your answer with specific examples. (*Hint:* Don't forget that near-minimal pairs can be as convincing as minimal pairs.)

a.	[kisim]	'my beard'	**g.**	[sak]	'white'
b.	[tˢakʔa]	'chop it down'	**h.**	[kʔiʃin]	'warm'
c.	[koktit]	'our feet'	**i.**	[skutʃu]	'he is carrying it'
d.	[kʔak]	'flea'	**j.**	[kʔuːtes]	'to dress'
e.	[pʔakan]	'hanging'	**k.**	[snika]	'he stirred it'
f.	[kʔaʔem]	'sugar cane'	**l.**	[ʔakʔ]	'read'

33. Spanish

Examine the following data from Spanish and answer the questions which follow. Note that [β] represents a voiced bilabial fricative, and [ɣ] a voiced velar fricative.

a.	[bino]	'he came'	**h.**	[uβa]	'grape'	**o.**	[siɣlo]	'century'
b.	[diβino]	'divine'	**i.**	[golpe]	'a hit'	**p.**	[pweβlo]	'village'
c.	[kaβo]	'end'	**j.**	[gato]	'cat'	**q.**	[laðron]	'thief'
d.	[suβteraneo]	'subterranean'	**k.**	[aɣo]	'I do'	**r.**	[kaβra]	'goat'
e.	[brotaɾ]	'to sprout'	**l.**	[iɣaðo]	'liver'	**s.**	[loɣɾaɾ]	'to achieve'
f.	[imbjeɾno]	'winter'	**m.**	[teŋgo]	'I have'			
g.	[amiɣo]	'friend'	**n.**	[leɣal]	'legal'			

   i. The allophones [b] and [β] are in complementary distribution, as are [g] and [ɣ]. Determine the conditioning environments for each pair, and state a rule that describes the distribution of the allophones.

   ii. Refer to Exercise 26 (Standard Spanish) and the rule for the distribution of the allophones [d] and [ð]. Describe the distribution of [b], [d], [g] and [β], [ð], [ɣ] in the most general terms possible, assuming each pair of allophones follows the same pattern.

34. Canadian French

In the dialect of French (an Indo-European language of the Romance family) spoken in Canada, consider the distribution of [t] and [tˢ] (a voiceless alveolar affricate) in the data below. State their distribution and determine if they are allophones of one phoneme or of separate phonemes. [y] and [ʏ] are high, front, rounded vowels, tense and lax, respectively.

a. [tu]	'all'		**g.** [telegram]	'telegram'
b. [abutˢi]	'ended'		**h.** [trɛ]	'very'
c. [tɛl]	'such'		**i.** [kʌltˢyr]	'culture'
d. [tẽb]	'stamp'		**j.** [minʏt]	'minute'
e. [tˢimɪd]	'timid'		**k.** [tˢy]	'you'
f. [tˢɪt]	'title'		**l.** [tˢɣb]	'tube'

35. German

German is an Indo-European language of the Germanic family, spoken in Germany. Examine the voiceless velar fricative represented by [x] and the voiceless palatal fricative represented by [ç] in the German data below. Are the two sounds in complementary distribution or are they contrastive? If the sounds are allophones in complementary distribution, state the phonetic contexts for each allophone.

a. [axt]	'eight'		**g.** [ɪç]	'I'
b. [buːx]	'book'		**h.** [ɛçt]	'real'
c. [lɔx]	'hole'		**i.** [ʃpreːçə]	'(he/she/it) would speak'
d. [hoːx]	'high'		**j.** [lɛçəln]	'to smile'
e. [flʊxt]	'flight'		**k.** [riːçən]	'to smell'
f. [laxən]	'to laugh'		**l.** [fɛçtən]	'to fence'

36. Farsi

Farsi is an Indo-European language of the Indo-Iranian family, which is the most widely spoken language in Iran. In the following data, do [r], [r̥], and [ɾ] belong to one, two, or three different phonemes? If they belong to different phonemes, give the pairs of forms which show this. If they are allophones of one (or two) phonemes, state the rule for their distribution. Which one would you choose to represent the phonemic form, and why?

[r] voiced trill		[r̥] voiceless trill		[ɾ] voiced flap	
a. [ærteʃ]	'army'	**g.** [ahar̥]	'starch'	**m.** [ahaɾi]	'starched'
b. [farsi]	'Persian'	**h.** [behtær̥]	'better'	**n.** [bæɾadær̥]	'brother'
c. [qædri]	'a little bit'	**i.** [hærntowr̥]	'however'	**o.** [beɾid]	'go'
d. [rah]	'road'	**j.** [tʃar̥]	'four'	**p.** [biɾæŋg]	'pale'
e. [ris]	'beard'	**k.** [tʃedʒur̥]	'what kind'	**q.** [tʃeɾa]	'why'
f. [ruz]	'day'	**l.** [ʃir̥]	'lion'	**r.** [daɾid]	'you have'

37. Bukusu

Bukusu is a Niger-Congo language of the Bantu family, spoken in Kenya. The nasal prefix [n-] indicates that the verb is in the first person ('I eat, go, sing,' etc.). Two different processes occur when [n] stands before another consonant. Look at these words and think about what is happening. The symbols [β], [ɲ], and [x] represent, respectively, a voiced bilabial fricative, a palatal nasal, and a voiceless velar fricative.

a. [ndiːla]	'I hold'		**j.** [ɲdʒina]	'I scream'
b. [seːnda]	'I move'		**k.** [suna]	'I jump'
c. [ɲdʒuːŋga]	'I watch'		**l.** [xala]	'I cut'
d. [ŋgaβa]	'I divide'		**m.** [ŋgeta]	'I pour'
e. [mbiːma]	'I weigh'		**n.** [ndasa]	'I add'
f. [xola]	'I do'		**o.** [mbula]	'I roam'
g. [mbuka]	'I perish'		**p.** [ndula]	'I trample'
h. [fuka]	'I cook'		**q.** [fwaːra]	'I dress'
i. [funa]	'I break'		**r.** [mbala]	'I count' *(cont.)*

    i. How does the behavior of a nasal differ when it stands before the different types of obstruents (stops, fricatives, and affricates)?

    ii. There are two phonological processes at work here. What are they?

    iii. Write phonological rules to capture the facts about the nasal prefix /n-/ in Bukusu.

Advanced Exercises

38. Greek

Modern Greek is an Indo-European language spoken in Greece. Examine the sounds [x], [k], [ç], and [c] in the following data. [k] represents a voiceless velar stop, [x] a voiceless velar fricative, [ç] a voiceless palatal fricative, and [c] a voiceless palatal stop. Which of these sounds are in contrastive distribution, and which are in complementary distribution? State the distribution of the allophones.

a.	[kano]	'do'	**j.**	[kori]	'daughter'
b.	[xano]	'lose'	**k.**	[xori]	'dances'
c.	[çino]	'pour'	**l.**	[xrima]	'money'
d.	[cino]	'move'	**m.**	[krima]	'shame'
e.	[kali]	'charms'	**n.**	[xufta]	'handful'
f.	[xali]	'plight'	**o.**	[kufeta]	'bonbons'
g.	[çeli]	'eel'	**p.**	[çina]	'goose'
h.	[ceri]	'candle'	**q.**	[cina]	'china'
i.	[çeri]	'hand'			

39. Ebira

Examine the sounds [e] and [a] in the following data from Ebira, a Niger-Congo language of the Nupoid family, spoken in Nigeria. Do they appear to be allophones of separate phonemes or allophones of the same phoneme? If the two sounds are in complementary distribution, state the conditioning environments for the allophones.

a.	[mezi]	'I expect'	**e.**	[mazɪ]	'I am in pain'
b.	[meze]	'I am well'	**f.**	[mazɛ]	'I agree'
c.	[meto]	'I arrange'	**g.**	[matɔ]	'I pick'
d.	[metu]	'I beat'	**h.**	[matʊ]	'I send'

40. Ukrainian

Ukrainian is an Indo-European language of the Slavic family, spoken in Ukraine. Compare the masculine nominative singular forms of nouns with the vocative forms (nominative is used for the subject of a sentence, and vocative is used when calling to or addressing someone, as in "Hey, Robin."). There is a phonological change between the nominative and the vocative, which adds the ending [-e] to the nominative form. Three pairs of sounds are in allophonic variation. What are these pairs of sounds? What sort of phonological process is at work here? (There is a special name for it; see File 3.2.) What do you think is conditioning this alternation? (The symbols [ɦ] and [x] stand for a voiced glottal fricative and a voiceless velar fricative, respectively.)

	Nominative	*Vocative*	*Gloss*
a.	[rak]	[ratʃe]	'lobster'
b.	[junak]	[junatʃe]	'young man'
c.	[ʒuk]	[ʒutʃe]	'beetle'
d.	[pastux]	[pastuʃe]	'shepherd'
e.	[ptax]	[ptaʃe]	'bird'
f.	[boɦ]	[boʒe]	'God'
g.	[pluɦ]	[pluʒe]	'plough'

41. Maltese

Maltese is an Afro-Asiatic language of the Semitic family, spoken on the island of Malta in the Mediterranean. Consider how the indefinite (*a, some*) and the definite (*the*) are formed in the following words. Maltese forms the definite of a noun by attaching either /il-/ or /l-/ to it. Examine the data below and answer the questions that follow. (The symbol [ħ] represents a voiceless pharyngeal fricative.)

a.   *Indefinite*   *Definite*

[fellus]	'chicken'	[ilfellus]	'the chicken'
[aria]	'air'	[laria]	'the air'
[mara]	'woman'	[ilmara]	'the woman'
[omm]	'mother'	[lomm]	'the mother'
[kelb]	'dog'	[ilkelb]	'the dog'
[ʔattus]	'cat'	[ilʔattus]	'the cat'
[ħitan]	'walls'	[ilħitan]	'the walls'
[abt]	'armpit'	[labt]	'the armpit'
[ispaniol]	'Spanish (language)'	[lispaniol]	'the Spanish (language)'

   i. How can you predict the form of the definite marker?
   ii. What natural classes of sounds are involved?

Now look at these nouns in the indefinite and the definite:

b.   *Indefinite*   *Definite*

[tiːn]	'a fig'	[ittiːn]	'the fig'
[dawl]	'a light'	[iddawl]	'the light'
[sħab]	'some clouds'	[issħab]	'the clouds'
[natura]	'nature'	[innatura]	'the nature'

The definite marker has the same phonemic form in these words as it had in part (a), but a phonological process has changed its phonetic form.
   iii. What type of process is responsible for the change? How did it affect the definite marker?
   iv. What natural class of sounds causes the change from the phonemic form to the various phonetic forms in part (b)?
   v. Give the definite form of the following nouns:

   Indefinite   *Definite*

[daːr]	'a house'	_____	'the house'
[zift]	'a pitch'	_____	'the pitch'
[azzar]	'a piece of steel'	_____	'the steel'
[iŋgliz]	'English'	_____	'the English (lang.)'
[belt]	'a city'	_____	'the city'

CHAPTER

4

=========================

Morphology

© DAN PIRARO. KING FEATURES SYNDICATE

What Is Morphology?

Morphology is the study of word making. Of course, words (at least in spoken languages) are made of sounds, but often there are recognizable units bigger than sounds and smaller than words. For example, *rewind, reunite,* and *reiterate* all begin with the same two sounds: [ɹi]. We wouldn't want to say that *re* is a word, but we also wouldn't want to say it's a coincidence that these words begin in the same way.

Morphology examines meaning relationships between words and the ways in which these connections are indicated, for example, the relationships between *wind, unwind, rewind, windable, windy, winder,* and so on.

Morphology is also the study of word marking: how grammatical relationships between words are indicated. Different languages focus on different kinds of word relationships and make use of different patterns of marking. In English we find such words as *winds,* which is used in the present tense with certain subjects, and *wound,* to show that the action took place in the past.

Contents

Words and Word Formation: The Nature of the Lexicon

4.1.1 What Are Words Like?

Every language has some (large) number of words available for its users to choose from as they need. This stock of words can be thought of as a sort of mental dictionary that language users—both speakers and hearers—have internalized as part and parcel of acquiring their particular language. We call this mental dictionary the **lexicon.** But what exactly are the sorts of things we might have in our lexicon?

In the study of morphology, one topic we will consider is how words are made, but first we must answer the question of what words are. Most everyone has an idea of what a word is. However, not all words are equally distinct from all other words. To begin, consider the following question:

• Are *cat* and *dog* the same word or different words?

Your answer, like that of almost anyone familiar with English, is very probably "Of course they are different words! Isn't it obvious?" The reasons that this is obvious include both differences in **form,** that is, what a word sounds like when spoken (/kæt/ is quite distinct from /dɑg/; refer to the last page of the book for help with any unfamiliar symbols) and differences in **meaning,** such as the fact that you cannot simply use *cat* and *dog* interchangeably to mean the same thing.

On the other hand, you might say *cat* and *dog* are both kinds of pets, so the words aren't 100% different; they do have something to do with each other. Likewise, and not coincidentally, both *cat* and *dog* belong to the same **lexical category,** that is, "noun" (often defined as "the name of a person, place, thing, or idea"). (For more information about lexical categories, sometimes called "parts of speech," refer to File 5.3.) These sorts of similarities, however, are not enough to lead us to claim that *cat* and *dog* are the same word.

Now consider this question:

• Are *cat* and *catalog* the same word or different words?

Based on the discussion above, some readers might hesitate before answering this question. These two words share some elements of form, the /kæt/ part, but *catalog* doesn't seem to have the meaning of *cat* anywhere in it. Similarly, the words *kid* and *kidney* may sound partly the same, but it seems that they are not actually related in their meaning. Even though it sounds like there **could** be a *cat* and a *log* in *catalog,* or a *kid* in *kidney,* and such a connection might even be used as a source of humor in a joke or cartoon, English speakers consistently distinguish these pairs as each containing two unrelated words. Thus, when looking to see whether two items are the same word, we must consider both their phonological form and their meaning. Nevertheless, the thought that one word could be found "inside" another word is an important one.

4.1.2 Derivation

In order to get at the idea of words being inside one another, consider this third question.

- Are *cat* and *catty* ('spiteful') the same word or different words?

Here, the connection is a good bit closer than in the preceding word comparisons. Cats have gained a reputation for sometimes being vicious fighters, and it is most probably in this context that the word *catty* came into existence as part of the English language, meaning something like 'behaving like a cat in a certain respect.' So the words *cat* and *catty* are similar not only in terms of their form (the /kæt/ part) but also in terms of their meaning, since both (at least potentially) engender the image of nasty fighting.

    Is this enough to say that *cat* and *catty* are instances of the same word? Recall that evaluating "sameness" and "difference" between words involves several factors. If we compare *cat* and *catty* with respect to their part of speech, for instance, we note that whereas *cat* is a noun, *catty* is an adjective (a word used to describe a noun). Even though *cat* and *catty* share elements of form and elements of meaning, the fact that the words belong to different part of speech classes is a pretty clear sign that we are in fact dealing with two different words, rather than two "versions" of one word. There remains the feeling, however, that *cat* and *catty* are related in a way that *cat* and *dog,* on the one hand, and *cat* and *catalog,* on the other, are not. What is the nature of this relation? Let's compare some of the attributes of the two words:

(1)   *CAT*   *CATTY*

    Form: /kæt/   /kæti/
    Meaning: 'domesticated feline'   'spiteful, (fighting) like a domesticated feline'
    Part of Speech: noun   adjective

With respect to form, *cat* is obviously a shorter word (i.e., contains fewer sounds) than *catty.* The meaning of *catty* also seems to be based on the meaning of *cat,* rather than the other way around. This suggests that *catty* is based on *cat* or, in other words, that *cat* is the **root** on which *catty* is built. This process of creating words out of other words is called **derivation.** Derivation takes the phonological form of one word and performs one or more "operations" on it, the result being a (possibly) new word. In the simplest case, the phonological form of the root is used "as-is," and one or more pieces of additional form are tacked onto that. We talk of the form of the root as the **stem,** and the added pieces as **affixes.** In the case of *catty,* both the root and stem are the word *cat,* /kæt/, and the affix is /i/, spelled <-y>, which is attached to the right edge of the stem.[1] We conclude that the word *catty* includes the word *cat.*

4.1.3 Inflection

At this point, there is one more question for you to consider:

- Are *cat* and *cats* the same word or different words?

In terms of phonological form, the difference between /kæt/ and /kæts/ is exactly the same in degree (that is, one additional sound) as the difference we saw between /kæt/ and /kæti/.

---

[1]If you are wondering about the second "t" in *catty,* something not present in *cat,* it is important to notice that the 't' is purely a spelling convention and is not reflected directly in the pronunciation, that is, the /t/ in *catty* is not "twice as long" as the /t/ in *cat.* Although in many cases it does not cause any problems to refer to the spelling when talking about the structure of words, there are cases where the spelling can be misleading about what is actually going on with morphological processes. By and large we will disregard spelling; see File 1.3.

With respect to meaning, however, *cat* and *cats* seem to refer to just the same kind of thing, the difference being whether we want to talk about one (singular) or more than one (plural) of that thing. Moreover, these are both of the same lexical category, noun:

(2)

	CAT	*CATS*
Form:	/kæt/	/kæts/
Meaning:	'domesticated feline'	'domesticated feline' (plural)
Part of Speech:	noun	noun

This time the answer to the "same or different" question is not as obvious as it was in the earlier cases. *Cats* represents a different grammatical form of the word *cat,* used just in case we need to talk about more than one member of the class of *cat.* The creation of different grammatical forms of words is called **inflection.** Inflection uses the same sorts of pieces, such as stems and affixes, that derivation does, but the important difference is the linguistic entity that inflection creates—forms of words, rather than entirely new words. In sum, we find that the idea of "same" or "different" with respect to words can be an unexpectedly complicated one. Words each have a number of attributes, or ways in which they can be categorized.

There are actually very few inflectional affixes in English, so it may help to collect them in one table for easy reference (see (3)). (Table (3) shows all of the functions of inflectional affixes of English and most of the common forms that those affixes take. However, there are some less common affixes that do not appear in the table. For example, the plural of *ox* is formed with the suffix -*en*, but because the plural marker -*en* appears on very few words, it is not listed below.) Notice that all of the inflectional affixes in the table—and all of the inflectional affixes of English—are attached after the stem. (Derivational affixes in English may attach either before or after the stem.) This generalization does not hold for all languages, however.

(3) Inflectional affixes of English

Function	Affix(es)	Attaches to	Example
3rd per. sing. present	-*s*	verbs	She wait**s** there at noon.
past tense	-*ed*	verbs	She wait**ed** there yesterday.
progressive aspect	-*ing*	verbs	She is wait**ing** there now.
past participle	-*en*, -*ed*	verbs	Jack has eat**en** the cookies.
			Jack has tast**ed** the cookies.
plural	-*s*	nouns	The chair**s** are in the room.
possessive	-*'s*, -*s'*	nouns	The chair**'s** leg is broken.
			The chair**s'** legs are broken.
comparative	-*er*	adjectives,	Jill is tall**er** than Joe.
		adverbs	Joe runs fast**er** than Jill.
superlative	-*est*	adjectives,	Ted is the tall**est** in his class.
		adverbs	Michael runs fast**est** of all.

4.1.4 Some Notes about Morphemes

So far we have seen words that contain only one part, like *cat* and *catalog,* and words that contain two parts, like *cats* and *catty.* These parts that words are made of are called **morphemes.** A few notes are in order about the terminology that we use to discuss morphemes. First, while a root by definition contains only one morpheme, a stem may contain one or more than one morpheme. For example, in the word *cattiness,* the root is *cat.* The stem for *cattiness,* however, is *catty,* which, contains two morphemes—the root and one affix. In *cattiness* there is also a second affix, [nɛs] spelled <ness>. Each affix must contain only one morpheme: by definition, an affix is a single morpheme. Affixes that follow a stem are called **suffixes,** whereas affixes that precede a stem are called **prefixes.**

Another thing to notice about affixes is that sometimes different meanings or functions can be marked by the same phonetic shape (note the three *-s* affixes in table (3)). Affixes that sound alike but have different meanings or functions are **homophonous.** (Different words that sound the same are likewise said to be homophonous.) Another example is the case of *-er,* which can be either inflectional or derivational. As an inflectional suffix, it marks comparative degree on adjectives and adverbs (like in *taller, faster* in the table), but the same phonetic shape can be used to derive an agent noun from a verb, as in *speak, speaker.* These two *-er* affixes are homophonous with each other, and it is therefore important to consider not only form but also meaning when you are analyzing morphological structures.

Further evidence that both form and meaning are necessary when identifying morphemes comes from cases of words that merely appear to contain multiple morphemes, but in fact do not. Look again at the word *catalog.* In terms of both its orthography and its pronunciation, it appears to contain the words *cat, a,* and *log.* Neither felines nor sections of tree limbs have anything to do with 'inventories,' though. Thus, we conclude that *catalog* is monomorphemic: it is made of only one part.

As a final caution, do not confuse word length with number of morphemes. Some words, such as *Madagascar, lugubrious,* or *pumpernickel,* are quite long but contain only one morpheme; other words, such as *ads,* are very short but contain two morphemes.

4.1.5 Classifying Elements in Morphology

In the study of word formation, that is, **morphology,** the most basic acts of analysis are comparison (e.g., *cat* compared with *catty*) and segmentation, which allow one to see what the internal constituent parts of a word are. From such analysis, it becomes apparent that words and affixes do not share the same status in language overall. Simple words like *cat, dog, book,* and *walk* do not have any affixes and cannot be broken down into smaller meaningful pieces. Single, irreducible meaningful pieces are called morphemes, and we can categorize them in several ways.

Morphemes such as the simple words above are called **free morphemes** because they can be used as words all by themselves. Affixes, on the other hand, always have to be attached to the stem of some word in order to be used. Because they cannot stand alone, affixes are called **bound morphemes.** Affixes are not the only things that can be bound. There are some roots that do not have stand-alone forms; that is, they only appear with one or more affixes attached. For example, the words *infer, confer, refer, defer, prefer,* and *transfer* all seem to have a root *-fer* (stem /fɹ/) with a prefix attached to its left. This root, however, does not correspond to any free morpheme in English. The same is true of *boysen-* and *rasp-* in *boysenberry* and *raspberry.* While *berry* is a free morpheme, neither *boysen-* nor *rasp-* can stand alone. Morphemes of this sort are called **bound roots** because although they do seem to have some associated basic meaning (in the case of *-fer,* the meaning is something like 'carry, bring'), they are unable to stand alone as words in their own right. Other examples are *-ceive* (*conceive, receive, deceive*) and *-sist* (*resist, desist, consist, subsist*). Can you think of a single basic meaning for each of these bound roots?

While we have defined morphemes as meaningful pieces, there are differing degrees of meaningfulness. Some morphemes carry semantic content. That is, some simple words have some kind of identifiable meaning (e.g., *moose, car, house,* etc.), and some affixes indicate a change in meaning with respect to the root to which they attach (e.g., *re-play* means 'play again'). Morphemes of this sort are called **content morphemes.** Any affix that, when added to a stem, produces a word that belongs to a different part of speech class, such as turning nouns into adjectives (like *-y* above) or turning verbs into nouns (like *-ment* in *establish* → *establishment*), is also considered to be part of the content morpheme class. Other morphemes serve only to provide information about grammatical function by relating certain words of a sentence to each other. Words that do this are, for example, prepositions such as *at, for,* and *by.* Articles (*a, an, the*) and conjunctions (*and, but, or*) are also words of this sort. Affixes that perform this function are the inflectional affixes, such as *-s* mentioned above, which marks noun words as plural. These grammatical morphemes are called **function morphemes.** The content/function distinction thus crosscuts the free/bound distinction. These relationships can be seen in table (4).

(4) Possible kinds of morphemes

	Content Morphemes	**Function Morphemes**
Free Morphemes	• Content words: • Nouns • Verbs • Adjectives • Adverbs	• Function words: • Determiners • Prepositions • Pronouns • Conjunctions
Bound Morphemes	• Bound roots • Derivational affixes	• Inflectional Affixes

Given any particular morpheme, the diagram in (5) may help you decide what sort of morpheme it is.

4.1.6 Derived and Inflected Words in the Lexicon

We have said that both derivation and inflection are ways of forming words, but in what sense is it meant that new words are being "formed"? Do we mean that every time a speaker uses a morphologically complex word, the brain reconstructs it? Some linguists maintain that this is the case. They claim that in a speaker's mental dictionary, the lexicon, each morpheme is listed individually along with other information such as its meaning, its part of speech (if it is a free morpheme), and rules for how and when it is allowed to attach to stems (if it is a bound morpheme). Indeed, that does seem to be what happens for some morphological processes in some languages. Thus, each time a word is used, it is re-formed from the separate entries in the lexicon of the parts that make it up. There is evidence, however, that indicates this is not the case for all languages; even morphologically complex words can apparently have a separate entry in the adult lexicon. That is, as English speakers, when we hear a morphologically complex word, such as *nonrecyclable,* we do not have to pull together the meanings of *non-, re-, cycle,* and *-able.* Rather, we by and large access the whole word together. (Refer to File 9.5 for more information about how words are stored in the lexicon.)

Even if not all language users do "build" morphologically complex words and word-forms every time they use them, there are still other reasons to consider derivation a process of word formation. In describing a language, the term *formation* refers to the systematic relationships between roots and the words derived from them on the one hand, and, on the other hand, between a word and its various inflected (i.e., grammatical) forms.

Furthermore, speakers of a given language also are often aware of these relationships. We see evidence of this when new words are formed based on patterns that exist in the lexicon. For example, a speaker of English may never have heard words such as *unsmelly, smellability,* or *smellful* before, but he or she would certainly understand what they mean. The fact that English speakers may use a word like *stick-to-it-ive-ness* illustrates that speakers

(5) A flowchart for identifying the status of morphemes

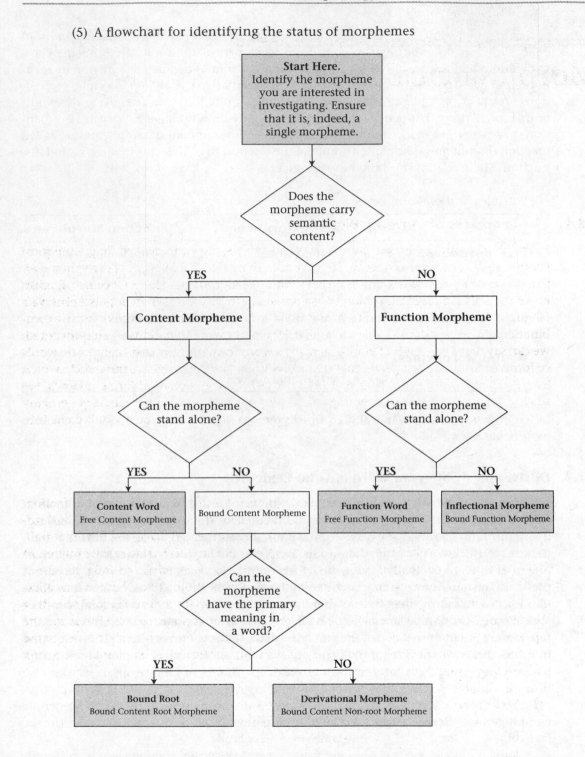

of a language have no problem accessing the patterns in their lexicons and applying them for interpreting unfamiliar words . . . and even for creating them!

Rules that speakers are able to apply to form novel words are termed **productive** rules. (Refer to File 1.4.) English has examples of both nonproductive morphemes and productive ones; for example, the suffix -*tion* is generally not used by speakers to form new nouns, whereas the suffix -*ness* is. Over long periods of time, different affixes or other morphological processes may become more or less productive (see File 12.6).

Morphological Processes

4.2.1 The Processes of Forming Words

In the previous file, we looked at how words are put together and marked for **grammatical** features such as number and tense. We have seen that English makes use of derivational affixes to create more words than would exist with free morphemes alone. Of course, English is not the only language that enlarges its vocabulary in this way. When linguists observe a language that uses affixation to form additional words, they note that the occurring combinations are systematic, i.e., rule-governed. Because these combinations are rule-governed, we can say that a process is at work—namely, a **word formation process**—since new words or forms of words are being formed. What we will consider in this file are the ways in which languages create new words from existing words, and the grammatical forms of words. We shall see that many languages employ affixation but that many other languages employ other processes. (See Files 12.6 and 12.7 for still more ways in which new words come into use in a language.)

4.2.2 Affixation

To this point, our morphological discussion has been limited to the process of **affixation.** Although English uses only **prefixes** (affixes that precede the stem they attach to) and **suffixes** (affixes that follow the stem they attach to), many other languages use **infixes** as well. Infixes are inserted within the root morpheme. Note that English has no regular infixes. At first glance, some students think that -*ful* in a word like *doubtfully* is an infix because it occurs in the middle of a word; File 4.4 will provide a more thorough account of how affixation works and show why this must be an incorrect analysis. In some colloquial speech or slang, there is some evidence of English infixes, but although some of these forms may be moderately productive, they are far from routinized. Tagalog, on the other hand, one of the major languages of the Philippines, uses infixes quite extensively. For example, the infix -*um*- is used to form the infinitive form of verbs:

(1) | *Verb Stem* | | *Infinitive* | |
|---|---|---|---|
| sulat | 'write' | sumulat | 'to write' |
| bili | 'buy' | bumili | 'to buy' |
| kuha | 'take, get' | kumuha | 'to take, to get' |

4.2.3 Affixation in Signed Languages

Signed languages make use of affixation as well: in the same way that a certain phonological form may either precede or follow a stem in spoken languages, so may a particular gesture precede or follow another gesture in a signed language. As an example, consider a suffix used in American Sign Language used to indicate negation. Recall from Section 2.7.1 that phonetic parameters of sign language gestures include place of articulation, handshape, movement, and hand orientation. This particular suffix is a movement: a rapid turning over of the hand, affixed to the end of the root sign that it is negating. The result of turning the hand is that the hand orientation in the suffix is reversed from the hand orientation in the root word. Therefore, the suffix is called the REVERSAL-OF-ORIENTATION suffix. Examples follow. Notice that in each case the two signs begin in the same way, but in the negated form, there is an additional step of turning the hand away from its original orientation.

Examples of the REVERSAL-OF-ORIENTATION suffix in ASL

(2) a. LIKE

© 2006, William Vicars, www.Lifeprint.com. Adapted by permission.

b. DON'T-LIKE

© 2006, William Vicars, www.Lifeprint.com. Adapted by permission.

(3) a. WANT

© 2006, William Vicars, www.Lifeprint.com. Adapted by permission.

b. DON'T-WANT

© 2006, William Vicars, www.Lifeprint.com. Adapted by permission.

(4) a. KNOW

© 2006, William Vicars, www.Lifeprint.com. Adapted by permission.

b. DON'T-KNOW

© 2006, William Vicars, www.Lifeprint.com. Adapted by permission.

By looking at (2)–(4), you will see that the exact form of the negation suffix differs in different environments. That is, although the movement is the same in each case (a turning of the hand(s) away from where it was originally facing), the location and orientation of the suffix are borrowed from the stem. Therefore, DON'T-LIKE and DON'T-WANT are articulated in front of the torso where LIKE and WANT are articulated, but DON'T-KNOW is articulated on the side of the head, where KNOW is articulated. This is no different from spoken languages, in which the form of an affix may assimilate to some aspect of the form of the stem. For example, in English we find the *in-* suffix which changes its form in such words as *irresponsible, impossible,* and *illogical.* Although the REVERSAL-OF-ORIENTATION suffix assimilates to a root word, the affix is clearly a second gesture which follows the root sign. Thus, so far, we have seen only cases where affixation in signed languages works very similarly to the way that it does in spoken languages.

Additionally, signed languages allow a kind of affixation that is not possible in spoken languages. For spoken languages, we considered affixes that can appear at the beginning, in the middle, and at the end of a stem. What we have not considered are affixes that are articulated at the same time as the stem. The reason is that in spoken language it is not possible to articulate two morphemes at the same time! In many cases, however, it is possible to articulate two morphemes in a visual-gestural language at the same time. (Recall from File 2.7 that phonemes in signs also routinely co-occur.) When affixes appear at the same time as each other, we say that they are **simultaneous.** Examples of simultaneous morphology have been found in every signed language that has been studied. This concept seems rather foreign to individuals who have studied only spoken languages, but it is not terribly complicated. Although signed languages allow affixation to be manifested in a way that spoken languages do not, by and large the rules for affixation are exactly the same for simultaneous morphology as for the linear morphology we have considered so far.

Most simultaneous morphology—from every signed language that has been studied—is inflectional rather than derivational. A form of simultaneous affixation that is very common across signed languages is verb inflection: morphological marking of subject and object on the verb. The general idea is that the sign for the verb originates in one location in order to mark the identity of the individual performing the action (the subject) and terminates in another location to indicate the object, while other aspects of the sign remain the same. This type of verbal inflection is used extensively in some sign languages (e.g., Idioma de Signos Nicaragense, a signed language of Nicaragua) and hardly at all in others (e.g., Kata Kolok, a signed language of Bali). In (5) is an example from American Sign Language. Although direction of movement differs depending on subject and object, hand shape and the general type of movement (an arching path from one location to another) are consistent regardless of particular inflection.

(5) GIVE (inflected for various subjects and objects)

A number of other verbs in ASL show similar patterns, including MEET, which can be found in (7) in File 2.7. Others include SHOW, ASK, and SEE. Note that while many signed languages have very similar verbal inflection systems, they are not entirely the same. Furthermore, different languages have different sets of verbs that inflect in this way: the Taiwan SL sign for 'teach' does inflect in this way, while the ASL sign for 'teach' does not.

A second example of simultaneous inflectional morphology in ASL is adverbial inflection of adjectives. For example, the sign HOT can be modified to mean VERY HOT by holding the first location of the sign for a small amount longer and then releasing it very quickly, as shown in (6). (Notice that the signer is moving his hand so quickly in the third cell of VERY HOT that the image of his hand is completely blurred!)

To articulate the VERY morpheme, hand shape, orientation, location, and path of movement remain the same, but the way that the movement is performed is different.[1] This "rapid release" morpheme can apply to many ASL adjectives.

4.2.4 Compounding

Compounding is a process that forms new words not by means of affixes but from two or more independent words. The words that are the parts of the compound can be free morphemes, words derived by affixation, or even words formed by compounding themselves. Examples in English of these three types are shown in (7).

---

[1]The signer also can use his face for emphasis; this is equivalent to a speaker using features of his voice such as pitch or volume to alter the interpretation of a word. Imagine an English speaker saying, "I accidentally touched the pot right after it came from the oven, and it was HOT!"

(6) a. HOT

© 2006, William Vicars, www.Lifeprint.com. Adapted by permission.

b. VERY HOT

© 2006, William Vicars, www.Lifeprint.com. Adapted by permission.

(7) Examples of English compounds

Compounding of Free Morphemes	Compounding of Affixed Words	Compounding of Compounded Words
girlfriend	air-conditioner	lifeguard chair
blackbird	looking-glass	aircraft carrier
textbook	watch-maker	life-insurance salesman

Notice that in English, compound words are not represented consistently in writing. Sometimes they are written together, sometimes they are written with a hyphen, and sometimes they are written separately. We know, however, that compounding forms words and not just syntactic phrases, regardless of how the compound is written, because the stress patterns are different for compounds. Think about how you would say the words *red neck* in each of the two following sentences:

(8) a. The wool sweater gave the man a red neck.
     b. If you want to make Tim really angry, call him a redneck.

Compounds that have words in the same order as phrases have primary stress on the first word only, while individual words in phrases have independent primary stress. Some other examples are listed in (9). (Primary stress is indicated by ´ on the vowel.)

(9) *Compounds*   *Phrases*
    bláckbird   bláck bírd
    mákeup   máke úp

German is one of the many other languages that use compounding to form new words. Some examples of the numerous compounds in German are listed in (10).

(10)

Compound	Meaning	Meanings of Individual Morphemes
Muttersprache	'native language'	< mother language
Schreibtisch	'desk'	< write table
stehenbleiben	'stand (still)'	< stand remain
Wunderkind	'child prodigy'	< miracle child
Parkzeitüberschreitung	'exceeding of the amount of time one is allowed to park'	< park time exceedance

4.2.5 Reduplication

Reduplication is a process of forming new words either by doubling an entire free morpheme (**total reduplication**) or part of it (**partial reduplication**). English makes no systematic use of reduplication as a part of the language's grammar. There are a very few nonsystematic cases of lexical reduplication, however, such as "bye bye." Furthermore, in colloquial speech, we may often see reduplication used to indicate intensity; this can happen with verbs, adjectives, and nouns. Consider examples (11)–(13): what does the reduplicated word mean in each case?

(11) Do you just like him as a friend, or do you like-like him?
(12) That shirt isn't what I had in mind; it's much too pale of a green. I want a shirt that is green-green.
(13) Yesterday we just went out for coffee, but this weekend we're going on a date-date.

As you can see, though, each of these uses is very restricted to the context in which it appears. We wouldn't want to say that *green-green* is a word of English. On the other hand, there are some languages that make extensive use of reduplication. In these languages, reduplication can serve some of the same functions that affixation serves in English.

Indonesian uses total reduplication to form the plurals of nouns:

(14)

Singular		Plural	
rumah	'house'	rumahrumah	'houses'
ibu	'mother'	ibuibu	'mothers'
lalat	'fly'	lalatlalat	'flies'

ASL also uses reduplication for some (though not all) of its plural formation and for other derivational and inflectional purposes.

Tagalog, on the other hand, uses partial reduplication to indicate the future tense of verbs:

(15)

Verb Stem		Future Tense	
bili	'buy'	bibili	'will buy'
kain	'eat'	kakain	'will eat'
pasok	'enter'	papasok	'will enter'

Notice that the reduplicated piece, the **reduplicant,** can be described phonologically as the first syllable of the stem.

In conjunction with the prefix *maŋ-* (which often changes the initial consonant of a following morpheme to a nasal with the same place of articulation as the original initial consonant), Tagalog also uses reduplication to derive words for occupations:[2]

---

[2]Since the phonological content of the reduplicated piece (the reduplicant) depends on the phonological shape of the stem it attaches to, the "morpheme" in reduplication is the presence of the reduplicant, rather than the phonological shape of the reduplicant.

(16) *Occupation*   *Morphemes*   *Verb*

[mamimili]	'buyer'	< /maŋ+bi+bili/	[bili]	'buy'
[manunulat]	'writer'	< /maŋ+su+sulat/	[sulat]	'write'
[maŋʔiʔisda]	'fisherman'	< /maŋ+ʔi+ʔisda/	[ʔisda]	'fish'

4.2.6 Alternations

Besides adding an affix to a morpheme or copying all or part of the morpheme to make new words or make morphological distinctions, it is also possible to make morpheme-internal modifications, called **alternations.** While alternations have to do with the sounds in a particular word pair or larger word set, these alternations mark morphological distinctions, whereas the rules in the phonology files (see Files 3.1–3.2) dealt with pronunciation independent of meaning. The following are examples of morphological alternations in English:

(17) Although the usual pattern of plural formation is to add an inflectional morpheme, some English plurals make an internal modification:

man	men	[æ]	~	[ɛ] ([æ] alternates with [ɛ] in these forms)
woman	women	[ʊ]	~	[ɪ]
goose	geese	[u]	~	[i]
foot	feet	[ʊ]	~	[i]

(18) The usual pattern of past and past participle formation is to add an affix, but some verbs show an internal alternation:

ring	rang	rung	[ɪ]~[æ]~[ʌ]
drink	drank	drunk	
swim	swam	swum	
feed	fed	fed	[i]~[ɛ]~[ɛ]
hold	held	held	[ʊ]~[ɛ]~[ɛ]

Some verbs show both an alternation and the addition of an affix to one form:

(19) *Root*   *Alternation*   *Alternation and Affixation*

break	broke	broken
speak	spoke	spoken
bite	bit	bitten
fall	fell	fallen
give	gave	given

Although the above examples are all inflectional, sometimes a derivational relation such as a change in part of speech class can be indicated by means of alternations. In the case of (20), the final consonant of a noun voices in order to become a verb.

(20) *Nouns*   *Verbs*

strife (n)	[stɹaɪf]	strive (v)	[stɹaɪv]
teeth (n)	[tiθ]	teethe (v)	[tið]
breath (n)	[brɛθ]	breathe (v)	[brið]
use (n)	[jus]	use (v)	[juz]

Alternation is also a fairly common phenomenon in languages of the world. The following data come from Hebrew and show derivational alternation between nouns and verbs:

(21) **Verbs**   **Nouns**

    [limed]   'he taught'   [limud]   'lesson'

    [sijem]   'he finished'   [sijum]   'end'

    [tijel]   'he traveled'   [tijul]   'trip'

    [bikeɣ]   'he visited'   [bikuɣ]   'visit (noun)'

    [dibeɣ]   'he spoke'   [dibuɣ]   'speech'

4.2.7 Suppletion

Languages that employ morphological processes to form words will usually have a regular, productive way of doing so according to one or more of the processes discussed above. They might also have some smaller classes of words that are irregular because they mark the same morphological distinction by another of these processes. Sometimes, however, a root will have one or more inflected forms phonetically unrelated to the shape of the root. This completely irregular situation is called **suppletion.**

    A small number of English verbs have suppletive past tenses:

(22) **Present**   **Past**

    [ɪz]   is   [wʌz]   was

    [goʊ]   go   [wɛnt]   went

Interestingly, verbs derived from the irregular *go* also show similar suppletion in their past stems: *undergo,* [past] *underwent.* Two common English adjectives—*good* and *bad*—have suppletive comparative and superlative forms.

(23) **Adj**   **Comparative**   **Superlative**

    [gʊd] good   [bɛɾɹ] better   [bɛst] best

    [bæd] bad   [wɹs] worse   [wɹst] worst

Note that there is simply no systematic similarity between the stems of these various inflected forms. That is, we could not write a productive or general rule that would account for the forms we find.

    Noun inflection in Classical Arabic provides another example of suppletion:

(24) **Singular**   **Plural**

    [marʔat]   'woman'   [nisaːʔ]   'women'

The usual plural form for Classical Arabic nouns ending in [at], however, involves the lengthening of the vowel of this ending (a morphological alternation):

(25) **Singular**   **Plural**

    [diraːsat] '(a) study'   [diraːsaːt] 'studies'

    [harakat] 'movement' [harakaːt] 'movements'

    Any given language will likely have some example(s) of suppletion, but these typically constitute a minority class within the lexicon.

Morphological Types of Languages

4.3.1 Classifying Languages by Morphological Type

So far, we have considered a number of processes that a language might utilize in order to form words: affixation, compounding, reduplication, alternation, and suppletion. Some languages make use of a number of these processes; others make use of very few; still others make use of none at all. Languages can be classified according to the way in which they use or don't use morphological processes. There are two basic morphological types, **analytic** and **synthetic,** the latter having several subtypes.

4.3.2 Analytic Languages

Analytic languages are so called because they are made up of sequences of free morphemes—each word consists of a single morpheme, used by itself with meaning and function intact. Purely analytic languages, also called **isolating** languages, do not use affixes to compose words. Semantic and grammatical concepts which are often expressed in other languages through the use of affixes are expressed by the use of separate words in analytic languages.

Mandarin Chinese is an example of a language that has a highly analytic structure. In the example sentences below, for instance, the concept of plurality and the concept of the past tense are communicated in Mandarin through the use of invariant function words rather than the use of a change of form (cf. English, *I* to *we* to indicate plurality) or the use of an affix (cf. English *-ed* for past tense).

(1) [wɔ mən tan tɕin]   (tones omitted)
    I   plural play   piano
    'We are playing the piano'

(2) [wɔ mən tan tɕin lə]   (tones omitted)
    I   plural play   piano past
    'We played the piano'

Note that the form of 'we' (I-plural) that is used in the subject position is [wɔ mən] and that the pronoun has the same form when it is used as the object, placed after the verb:

(3) [ta da   wɔ mən]   (tones omitted)
    s/he hit(s) I   plural
    'S/he hits us'

Only the position of a word in a sentence shows its function. English is unlike Mandarin in this respect, since the personal pronoun *we* is changed in form to *us* when it is used as the object of a verb. But English is like Mandarin in that word order is used to show the functions of nouns in a sentence, and in that nouns (unlike pronouns) are not marked by affixes to show their functions. For example, in the sentence *Girls like cats* the noun *girls* functions as the subject; and the noun *cats* as the direct object, but just the opposite is true of *Cats like girls;* these differences in function are signaled only by the order of words in the sentence in both English and Mandarin. Nonanalytic languages may use morphology to mark these differences.

Although only affixation has been explicitly mentioned in this section, recognize that prototypical analytic languages make use of no morphological processes at all.

4.3.3 Synthetic Languages

In **synthetic languages**, bound morphemes are attached to other morphemes, so a word may be made up of several meaningful elements. The bound morphemes may add another element of meaning to the stem (derivation) or indicate the grammatical function of the stem in a sentence (inflection). Recall that the term *stem* refers to that part of the word to which affixes are added. It may consist of one or more morphemes: for instance, in *reruns, -s* is added to the stem *rerun,* which is itself made up of two morphemes: *re-* and the root *run.*

Hungarian is a synthetic language. In the examples below, bound morphemes show the grammatical functions of nouns in their sentences:

(4) [ɔz ɛmber   laːtjɔ ɔ   kucaːt]
    the man-(subject) sees   the dog-(object)
    'The man sees the dog'

(5) [ɔ kucɔ laːtjɔ ɔz   ɛmbɛrt]
    the dog   sees   the   man-(object)
    'The dog sees the man'

As mentioned above, in English it is the position in the sentence of the noun phrase *the man* or *the dog* that tells one whether the phrase is the subject or object of the verb, but in Hungarian, a noun phrase may appear either before or after the verb in a sentence and be recognized as the subject or object in either position because it is marked with a bound morpheme (the suffix [t]) if it is the direct object. (Many synthetic languages behave similarly.) Therefore, both examples below mean the same thing, even though the position of the noun phrase meaning 'the man' is different with respect to the verb meaning 'sees.'

(6) [ɔ kucɔ laːtjɔ ɔz   ɛmbɛrt]
    the dog   sees   the   man-(object)
    'The dog sees the man'

(7) [ɔz ɛmbɛrt   laːtjɔ ɔ   kucɔ]
    the man-(object)   sees   the dog
    'The dog sees the man'

Synthetic languages like Hungarian may also use bound morphemes to indicate some concepts that English signals by means of free morphemes. For example, Hungarian indicates personal possession and location by the use of suffixes attached to the stem ([haːz], 'house'), whereas in English these concepts are expressed by the use of free morphemes. Examples are given in (8) and (9).

(8) [ɔ haːzunk   zøld]
    the house-our green
    'Our house is green'

(9) [ɔ seːkɛd   ɔ   haːzunkbɔn   vɔn]
    the chair-your the house-our-in is
    'Your chair is in our house'

4.3.4 The First Type of Synthetic Language: Agglutinating Languages

To be more specific, the kind of synthesis (putting together) of morphemes we find in Hungarian is known as **agglutination**. In agglutinating languages, like Hungarian, the morphemes are joined together relatively "loosely." That is, it is usually easy to determine where the boundaries between morphemes are, as shown in (10) and (11).

(10) [haːz-unk-bɔn]   [haːz-od-bɔn]
     house-our-in   *house-your-in*
     'in our house'   'in your house'

(11) [haːz-ɔd]   [haːz-unk]
     house-your   *house-our*
     'your house'   'our house'

Swahili is another example of an agglutinating language. Swahili verb stems take prefixes to indicate the person of the subject of the verb (first, second, or third) and also to indicate the tense of the verb, as in the following list of forms for the verb 'read':

(12) [ni-na-soma]   *I-present-read*   'I am reading'
     [u-na-soma]   *you-present-read*   'You are reading'
     [a-na-soma]   *s/he-present-read*   'S/he is reading'

     [ni-li-soma]   *I-past-read*   'I was reading'
     [u-li-soma]   *you-past-read*   'You were reading'
     [a-li-soma]   *s/he-past-read*   'S/he was reading'

     [ni-ta-soma]   *I-future-read*   'I will read'
     [u-ta-soma]   *you-future-read*   'You will read'
     [a-ta-soma]   *s/he-future-read*   'S/he will read'

A second characteristic feature of agglutinating languages is that each bound morpheme (ordinarily) carries only one meaning: *ni* = 'I,' *u* = 'you,' *a* = 's/he,' *na* = 'present,' etc.

4.3.5 The Second Type of Synthetic Language: Fusional Languages

In **fusional languages**, another subtype of synthetic language, words are formed by adding bound morphemes to stems, just as in agglutinating languages, but in fusional languages the affixes may not be easy to separate from the stem. It is often rather hard to tell where one morpheme ends and the next begins; the affixes are characteristically fused with the stem.

Spanish is a fusional language that has suffixes attached to the verb stem to indicate the person (I/you/he/she/it) and number (singular/plural) of the subject of the verb. It is often difficult to analyze a verb form into its stem and suffix, however, because there is often a fusion of the two morphemes. For example, in the following forms:

(13) [hablo]   'I am speaking'
     [habla]   'S/he is speaking'
     [hable]   'I spoke'

the morphemes in (14) can be isolated:

(14) [-o]   first person singular present tense
     [-a]   third person singular present tense
     [-e]   first person singular past tense

However, although these forms would suggest a stem *habl-* that means 'speak,' such a form never appears in isolation in Spanish. There is no Spanish free morpheme *habl.*

Fusional languages often differ from agglutinating languages in another way as well: agglutinating languages usually have only one meaning indicated by each affix, as noted above, but in fusional languages a single affix more frequently conveys several meanings simultaneously. Russian is a fusional language in which bound morphemes attached to verb stems indicate both the person and the number of the subject of the verb and the tense of the verb at the same time. For example, in (15) the bound form [-jɛt] signifies third person as well as singular and present tense:

(15) [tʃitajɛt]   's/he is reading'

In (16) the suffix [-l] means singular, masculine, and past tense, simultaneously. (Compare the Swahili examples in (12), in which person and tense are signaled by separate affixes.)

(16) [tʃital]   'he was reading'

4.3.6   The Third Type of Synthetic Language: Polysynthetic Languages

In some synthetic languages, highly complex words may be formed by combining several stems and affixes; this is usually a matter of making nouns (subjects, objects, etc.) into parts of the verb forms. Such languages are called **polysynthetic.** Sora, a language spoken in India, allows such **incorporation** of objects (subjects, instruments, etc.) into verbs:

(17) [aninɲamjɔten]   —word of Sora
     [anin - ɲam - jɔ - te   - n]   —the same word divided into morphemes
     he   catch fish   non-past do
     'He is fish-catching'
     i.e., 'He is catching fish'

(18) [ɲamkɪdtenai]   —word of Sora
     [ɲam - kɪd - te   - n - ai]   —the same word divided into morphemes
     catch tiger non-past do   first person agent
     'I will tiger-catch'
     i.e., 'I will catch a tiger'

Such verbs are roughly comparable to an English construction like *baby-sit* or *trout-fish,* but the polysynthetic constructions may be more complex, including several nouns as well as a variety of other affixes:

(19) [pɔpoʊŋkoʊntam]   —word of Sora
     [pɔ - poʊŋ - koʊn - t   - am]   —the same word divided into morphemes
     stab belly   knife   non-past you (sg.)
     '(Someone) will stab you with a knife in (your) belly'

(20) [ɲɛnədʒdʒadarsiəm]   —word of Sora

[ɲɛn- ədʒ -dʒa - dar - si - əm] —the same word divided into morphemes
I not receive cooked rice hand you (sg.)
'I will not receive cooked rice from your hands'

The incorporated or "built-in" form of the noun is not necessarily identical to its free form. For example, in Sora, the free form of 'tiger' is [kɨna], that of 'hand' is [siʔi], and that of 'knife' is [kondi].

The Hierarchical Structure of Derived Words

4.4.1 How Words Are Put Together

When we examine words composed of only two morphemes, a stem and an affix, we implicitly know something about the way in which the affix combined with its stem. That is, the word was formed via the addition of the affix to the stem. By itself, this fact seems neither particularly significant nor particularly interesting. After all, there are no other options. However, when a word comprises more than two morphemes, the order in which the morphemes are put together becomes a more significant question. In order to consider such questions, we first will note two facts about morphemes and lexical categories.

First, the stems with which a given affix may combine (its **input**) normally belong to the same part of speech class. For example, the suffix *-able* attaches freely to verbs, but not to adjectives or nouns. Thus, we can add this suffix to the verbs *adjust, break, compare,* and *debate,* but not to the adjectives *asleep, lovely, happy,* and *strong,* nor to the nouns *anger, morning, student,* and *success.* Second, the words that are formed when an affix attaches to a stem (its **output**) also normally belong to the same part of speech class. For example, the words resulting from the addition of *-able* to a verb are always adjectives. Thus, *adjustable, breakable, comparable,* and *debatable* are all adjectives.

It turns out that these two facts have an important consequence for determining the way in which words with more than one derivational affix must be formed. What it means is that you can trace the derivational history of words as though they were formed in steps, with one affix attaching to a stem at a time. Words with more than one affix can be represented as forming by means of several steps. For example, consider the word *reusable,* which is composed of a prefix *re-,* a stem *use,* and a suffix *-able.* One possible way this morphologically complex word might be formed is all at once: *re + use + able,* where the prefix and the suffix attach at the same time to the stem *use.* This cannot be the case, however, knowing what we know about how derivational affixes are restricted with respect to both their input and their output. Which attaches to *use* first, then: *re-,* or *–able?*

The prefix *re-,* meaning 'do again,' attaches to verbs and creates new words that are also verbs. (Compare with *redo, revisit,* and *rewind.*[1]) The suffix *-able* also attaches to verbs, but it forms words that are adjectives. (Compare with *stoppable, doable,* and *washable.*) When working with problems such as those described in this file, you may find it helpful to anthropomorphize the affixes a bit in your mind. For example, you can think about *re-* as the sort of thing that says, "I am looking for a verb. If you give me a verb, then I will give you another verb," and *-able* as the sort of thing that says, "I am looking for a verb. If you give me a verb, then I will give you an adjective."

---

[1]As important as considering the words that *re-* does form is considering words that it doesn't form. For example, notice that *re-* cannot grammatically combine with adjectives or with nouns:

Adjectives: *rehappy   *repurple   *replentiful
Nouns: *rekitten   *rehappiness   *repencil

We learn from examining these two rules that *re-* cannot attach to *usable*, because *usable* is an adjective, but *re-* is "looking for" a verb. However, *re-* is able to attach to the root *use*, because *use* is a verb. Since *reuse* is also a verb, it can then serve as a stem to take *-able*. Thus, the formation of the word *reusable* is a two-step process whereby *re-* and *use* attach first, and then *-able* attaches to the word *reuse*. In this way, the output of one affixation process serves as the input for the next. The restrictions that each lexical category is subject to can help us determine the sequence of derivation.

Words that are "layered" in this way have a special type of structure characterized as **hierarchical**. This hierarchical structure can be schematically represented by a tree diagram that indicates the steps involved in the formation of the word. The tree for *reusable* appears in (1).

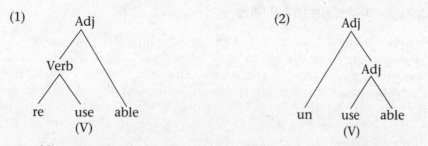

Now consider the word *unusable*. This word also contains three morphemes, so it is tempting to say that they will be put together in the same order as were the morphemes in *reusable*. However, notice that unlike *reuse*, **unuse* is not a word, because in this case, *un-* needs to have its input be an adjective. (Compare with *unhappy*, *unkind*, and *untrue*.) Fortunately, when *-able* attaches to verbs, it forms adjectives! Once the adjective *useable* has been formed, the needs of *un-* are met, and it is able to attach in order to form the target word, *unusable*. A tree for this derivation showing the hierarchical structure of *unusable* appears in (2).

Notice that these two trees, that is, the ones in (1) and (2), do not have the same shape. The shape of the tree is particular to the order in which morphemes are combined. Using the tools you have been given, though, it is possible to deduce the hierarchical structures even for very complex words. In (3) there is an example of a word with four morphemes; try to determine for yourself why this is the correct structure for the word *dehumidifier*.

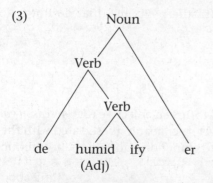

4.4.2   Ambiguous Morphemes and Words

Interestingly, some words are **ambiguous**; that is, they have more than one meaning. When we examine their internal structure, we find an explanation for this: their structure may be analyzed in more than one way. Consider, for example, the word *unlockable*. This could mean either 'not able to be locked' or 'able to be unlocked.' If we made a list to determine the parts of speech the affix *un-* attaches to, we would discover that there are actually two prefixes which have the form *un-* /ʌn/. The first combines with adjectives to form new adjectives and means 'not.' (Compare with *unaware*, *unintelligent*, or *unwise*.) The second prefix *un-* combines with verbs to form new verbs and means 'do the reverse of.' (Compare with *untie, undo,* or *undress.*)

Even though these prefixes sound alike, they are entirely different morphemes. Because of these two different sorts of *un-* in English, *unlockable* may be analyzed in two different ways. First, the suffix *-able* may join with the verb *lock* to form the adjective *lockable,* meaning 'able to be locked'; *un-* may then join with this adjective to form the new adjective *unlockable,* with the meaning 'not able to be locked.' This way of forming *unlockable* is schematized in (4).

In the second *unlockable,* the prefix *un-* joins with the verb *lock* to form the verb *unlock,* meaning 'do the reverse of lock.' The suffix *-able* then joins with this verb to form the adjective *unlockable,* with the meaning of 'able to be unlocked.' This manner of forming *unlockable* is represented in the tree in (5).

4.4.3 Morphemes That Can Attach to More than One Lexical Category

There are a few prefixes that do not attach exclusively to one part of speech. For example, consider the prefix *pre-*. *Pre-* attaches to verbs and results in a change of meaning in the words it derives, although the word class (part of speech) itself does not change, as the following examples show:

(6) preexist   preboard (an airplane)
     predetermine   predestine
     premeditate   prescreen (a movie)

However, there are examples of words with the prefix *pre-* that do not follow the same pattern as those cited above:

(7) preseason   predawn
     prewar   pregame

In these words, *pre-* attaches to a noun and forms an adjective (*the preseason game, the prewar propaganda, the pregame warm-up*). However, the meaning associated with the prefix is the same as in *preexist, preboard,* etc. (although its function is different). In addition, there are sets of words such as those in (8).

(8) prefrontal   predental
     preinvasive   prehistoric

In each of these words, *pre-* is attaching to an adjective, forming adjectives, and again the same meaning is associated with the addition of *pre-* as in *preexist, preboard,* etc. Even though it is generally the case that a given affix will be subject to one particular set of conditions on the part-of-speech class which it can attach to and on the part-of-speech class that its resulting derived words will belong to, some morphemes have a much wider range of combinatorial possibilities (historically this may represent an extension from one or two of the productive uses). Such must be the case with *pre-*. Note, however, that what *pre-* combines with and what the combination produces are not totally random or arbitrary. When *pre-* attaches to verbs, it forms only verbs. When it attaches to nouns, it forms only adjectives, and when it attaches to adjectives, it forms only adjectives. So, it is advisable to consider many examples when attempting to determine the generalization about how a given affix combines with stems.

Morphological Analysis

4.5.1 The Nature and Goals of Morphological Analysis

When a linguist comes in contact with a new language, one of his or her major tasks is to discover the meaningful units out of which the language is composed. Just as with discovering phonemes and allophones, it is important that the linguist have procedures for discovering these minimal units, since it is impossible to isolate morphemes by intuition.

For example, the Classical Greek word [grapʰɔː] means 'I write,' but if the word is considered in isolation, the linguist has no way of knowing what sound or sequence of sounds corresponds to 'I' and which sequence corresponds to 'write.' In fact, the linguist has no way of knowing even whether the word can be broken down into obvious parts or whether this form was created through alternation or suppletion. It is only by comparing [grapʰɔː] with another form, for instance, [grapʰɛː] 's/he writes,' that one is able to determine what the morphemes of these Greek words are. Looking at these two forms together allows us to hypothesize that [grapʰ] is the part that means 'write.'

Comparison, then, is the best way to begin morphological analysis. But, of course, you will not want to compare just any forms. Comparing a Greek word like [pʰɛːmi] 'to speak' with [grapʰɔː] will not provide much information, since the forms are so dissimilar and seem to have no morpheme in common. What must be compared are partially similar forms, in which it is possible to recognize recurring units. In this way we can identify the morphemes of which words are composed.

Let us consider our Classical Greek example once more. If we compare [grapʰɔː] with [grapʰɛː] 'he writes,' we note similarities between the forms. The sequence [grapʰ-] appears in both forms [grapʰ-ɛː] and [grapʰ-ɔː], and if we compare these to the English correspondences, we find that the meaning 'write' appears in both 'he writes' and 'I write.' From this, we are justified in concluding that [grapʰ-] means 'write,' since [grapʰ-] and *write* are constants in both the English and Greek. Furthermore, since the final vowels in both Greek forms contrast—and since this contrast is accompanied by a difference in meaning in our English correspondence—we can safely assume that the difference between the vowels in Classical Greek are suffixes that correspond to differences in meaning in our English translation. Therefore we determine that 'I' is marked by [-ɔː] and 'he' is marked by [-ɛː]. In sum, then, the initial step in doing morphological analysis is to compare and contrast partially similar forms.

To give yourself practice, identify and translate the morphemes in the Hungarian data in (1) and (2). ([ɟ] is a voiced palatal stop.) You should be able to identify four distinct Hungarian morphemes: two roots, one prefix, and one suffix.

(1) [hɔz]   'house'
    [ɛɟhɔz]   'a house'
    [hɔzɔ]   'his/her house'

(2) [boɾ]   'wine'
    [ɛɟboɾ]   'a wine'
    [boɾɔ]   'his/her wine'

Notice that in both the Greek and the Hungarian examples, there have been similarities in both form and meaning between the phonological forms we have considered. In order to perform a successful morphological analysis, both form and meaning similarities are necessary. To demonstrate this point, compare the following English words in (3). (We have not provided glosses because these are words of English.)

(3) work – worker   fast – faster

We notice a similarity in form: the morpheme spelled <er> and pronounced [ɹ] for both [fæstɹ] and [wɹkɹ]. However, if we think about it for a minute, it is apparent that -er has two different meanings even though phonetically it looks like the same morpheme. The -er in *worker* is the same -er that shows up in words like *painter, killer,* and *lover.* In each of these cases, -er attaches to verbs to derive a noun and means something like 'one who paints,' 'one who kills,' 'one who loves,' etc. The suffix -er in these cases is a derivational suffix known as the agentive morpheme.

The -er in *faster,* on the other hand, is the same -er that shows up in words like *wider, longer, colder, prettier,* etc. In each of these cases, -er attaches to adjective stems to create the comparative form of that adjective. The suffix -er in these cases is an inflectional suffix known as the comparative morpheme.

We will want to claim, then, that [ɹ] represents two separate morphemes—[ɹ] as an agent marker, and [ɹ] as a comparative marker—even though they are the same phonetically, i.e., homophonous morphemes. The [ɹ] that is added to verbs to yield nouns and the [ɹ] that is added to adjective stems to yield their comparative forms clearly must be distinct morphemes. This example shows us that it is not sufficient to compare words based on similarity of form alone. There must also be a similarity in meaning (in the case of derivational morphology) or function (in the case of inflectional morphology).

On the flip side, it is also important to recognize that sometimes a similarity in meaning is not matched by an exact similarity in form. Compare the set of words in (4a–e). We notice that each word has a prefix that means 'not.'

(4) a. imbalance   [ɪmbæləns]
    b. inability   [ɪnəbɪləɾi]
    c. incomplete   [ɪŋkəmplit]
    d. irresponsible   [ɪɹɪspɑnsɪbl̩]
    e. illegible   [ɪlɛdʒɪbl̩]

The problem here is the inverse of the problem in (3). Whereas in (3) we had the same phonetic forms representing two different meanings, in (4) we have five different phonetic forms with the same meaning. Since the phonetic forms of the morpheme meaning 'not' can be predicted on the basis of the phonetic environment, i.e.,

[ɪm] before labials—[p], [b], [m]
[ɪŋ] before velars—[k], [g]
[ɪɹ] before [ɹ]
[ɪl] before [l]
[ɪn] elsewhere (before vowels and other consonants),

we conclude that even though the forms differ phonetically, they belong to the same morpheme since they have the same meaning. We call [ɪm], [ɪŋ], [ɪn], [ɪɪ], and [ɪl] **allomorphs** of the same morpheme. Another example of allomorphy in English is the plural morpheme, which is realized as [s], [z], or [əz], depending on the form of the root to which it attaches (see Section 3.2.4).

4.5.2 Procedure for Performing Morphological Analysis

Now that we have considered several examples of morphological analysis, it is time to spell out exactly what we are trying to do and how we go about doing it. Our goal is this: given a set of data in phonetic representation, perform a morphological analysis of the forms in the data, identifying each morpheme, its meaning and type. You should also be able to tell where a morpheme appears with respect to other morphemes in the word. Is it a prefix, suffix, etc.? Does it attach directly to the root, or does it attach after or before another morpheme?

Now it is time to consider the procedure. It can be summed up in three steps.

1. Isolate and compare forms that are partially similar, as we did for Classical Greek [graph-ɛː] and [graph-ɔː].
2. If a single phonetic form has two distinct meanings, it must be analyzed as representing two different morphemes (as in (3)).
3. If the same function and meaning are associated with different phonetic forms, these different forms all represent the same morpheme (i.e., they are allomorphs of the morpheme), and the choice of form in each case may be predictable on the basis of the phonetic environment (as in (4)).

4.5.3 Some Cautionary Notes

People frequently assume that languages are pretty much the same in terms of what each language marks inflectionally. For example, English speakers often assume that all languages mark the plurals of nouns with an ending, or that the subject and the verb agree in person and number in other languages. This is simply not the case.

For example, Tagalog does not usually mark the plural of nouns (in most cases, the number is clear from the context). When it is necessary to be specific, a separate word, *mga*, is used to indicate plural.

(5) [aŋ bataʔ]   'the child'
    [aŋ mga bataʔ]   'the children'

When a number is specifically mentioned, no plural marker appears in Tagalog, although the plural marker is obligatory in English (**four dog* is ungrammatical). On the other hand, Tagalog has some markers that English does not. ([-ŋ] is a "linker" that links numerals and adjectives to the nouns they modify; English does not use this type of device.) Examples of both phenomena can be seen in (6).

(6) [dalawa] 'two'   [dalawaŋ bataʔ]   'two children'
    [lima]   'five'   [limaŋ bataʔ]   'five children'

English marks subject-verb agreement (e.g., *I eat* versus *he eats*), but Tagalog does not. In Tagalog, the same form of the verb is used with all subjects, as in (7).

(7) [kumakain ako]   'eat I' = 'I eat'
    [kumakain siy]   'eat he' = 'he eats'

Other languages also make distinctions that English doesn't. While English distinguishes only singular and plural verbs, some languages have a dual verb form for when just two people are involved. Consider Sanskrit *juhomi* 'I sacrifice,' *juhuvas* 'we (two) sacrifice,' and *juhumas* 'we (more than two) sacrifice.'

Some languages make another distinction in first-person plural pronouns where English has only *we*. Notice that English *we* in *we are going,* for example, may include everyone in the group the hearer is addressing (i.e., *we* = every one of us), or it may include only some hearers (i.e., *we* = 'I and (s)he,' but not 'you'). Many languages distinguish these two *we*'s: Tagalog has *tayo* (*inclusive,* i.e., 'you and I') and *kami* (*exclusive,* i.e., 'he and I').

Comanche, a Native American language of the Uto-Aztecan family, makes a number of other distinctions that English doesn't. In addition to a singular/dual/plural distinction and an inclusive/exclusive distinction, Comanche also makes a distinction between visible/not visible and near/far. Thus, if you are referring to a thing that is within your view, you use a different form than if the thing is not visible to you. Likewise, a nearby object is designated with a pronoun different from the one used for an object that is far away. Consider the following subject forms:

(8) Elements of the Comanche pronoun system

Singular/Dual/Plural Distinction

[inɨ] 'you (singular)'
[nikwɨ] 'you (two)'
[mɨɨ] 'you (plural)'

Inclusive/Exclusive Distinction

[taa] 'we (inclusive)'
[nɨnɨ] 'we (exclusive)'

Visible/Not Visible

[maʔ] 'it (visible)'
[ʔuʔ] 'it (invisible)'

Near/Far Distinction

[ʔiʔ] 'it (proximate)'
[ʔoʔ] 'it (remote)'

The lesson to be learned here is that you cannot assume that another language will make distinctions in the same way that English does. For example, while every language has some method of indicating number, not all languages do so in the same way or under the same circumstances. As we've seen, English uses an affix, Tagalog uses a separate word, and Indonesian reduplicates the word to show plurality (see File 4.2). Nor can you assume that the distinctions English makes are the only ones worth making. Languages must be examined carefully on the grounds of their own internal structures.

Finally, although the exercises for File 4.6 of this book will generally involve affixation, do not forget that often in the world's languages, morphological marking will happen through some other process.

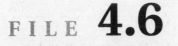
Practice

File 4.1—The Nature of the Lexicon

Exercises

1. Refer to the *Bizarro* cartoon at the beginning of the chapter and answer the following questions:
   i. How many morphemes are there in the name of the television show *Gilligan's Island*? Write each morpheme separately.
   ii. (*Optional:* If you are familiar with the IPA, then write each morpheme in *Gilligan's Island* as it would be pronounced by using the phonetic alphabet. Don't forget to put your answers in brackets.)
   iii. How many morphemes are there in the words on the sign "Gilligan's EyeLand"?
   iv. Are the word *island* and the phrase *eye land* phonologically related to each other? Are they semantically related to each other? Are they morphologically related to each other?
   v. Which component is more important to morphology: meaning (semantics) or form (phonology)? Defend your answer.
   vi. Think of two other examples of monomorphemic words (words that have only one morpheme) that sound as though they could be split up into different morphemes of English, but that aren't actually.

2. The following words are made up of either one or two morphemes. Isolate the morphemes and decide for each if it is free or bound, what kind of affix is involved (if any), and (where applicable) if the affix is inflectional or derivational.

   a. cats
   b. unhappy
   c. rejoin
   d. catsup
   e. milder
   f. hateful
   g. succotash
   h. bicycle
   i. greedy
   j. entrust
   k. signpost
   l. spacious

3. Divide the words below into their component morphemes and give the information about the morphemes as you did in (2). (*Note:* Words may consist of one, two, or more than two morphemes.)

   a. comfortable
   b. Massachusetts
   c. environmentally
   d. reconditioned
   e. unidirectional
   f. senseless
   g. thickeners
   h. nationalization
   i. unspeakably

4. In each group of words that follow, two words have the same morphological structure, one has a different suffix from those two, and one has no suffix at all. Your task is to tell which two words have the same suffix, which one has a different suffix, and which has

176

no suffix at all. Having done this, tell the meaning of each suffix. (You may find that they become more difficult as you go along.)

Example: rider   -er is a derivational suffix meaning 'one who. . . .'
          colder   -er is an inflectional suffix marking the comparative.
          silver   There is no suffix.
          smoker   This is the same -er as in rider.

a. nicer   **e.** youngster
     painter   faster
     runner   monster
     feather   gangster

b. clocks   **f.** wrestling
     Nick's   handling
     hearts   fling
     glass   duckling

c. friendly   **g.** nifty
     sadly   ducky
     softly   thrifty
     silly   lucky

d. sons   **h.** given
     lens   maven
     vans   wooden
     runs   taken

5. Are the root morphemes in each pair below pronounced the same? Different phonetic shapes of the same stem (or affix, for that matter) are called **allomorphs** (example: in *malign/malignant,* [məlɑɪn]/[məlɪgn] are (root) allomorphs). Identify any allomorphs that you uncover.

Example: malign/malignant: [məlɑɪn]/[məlɪgnənt]

a. autumn/autumnal
b. hymn/hymnal
c. damn/damnation
d. condemn/condemnation
e. divide/divisible
f. profane/profanity
g. serene/serenity
h. receive/receptive

6. The television show *The Simpsons* coined many new words by using morphology in novel ways. Two examples are *embiggens,* as in "A noble spirit embiggens the smallest man," and *introubleating,* as in "One Springfield man is treating his wife to an extra-special Valentine's Day this year, and introubleating the rest of us." Note that although these are novel words, they are similar to other words of English: *embiggens* is similar to *emboldens,* and *introubleating* is similar to *infuriating.* For each of these two words, perform the following tasks:
  i. Break it up into its component morphemes.
  ii. Provide the meaning of each morpheme and state whether it is free or bound.

Discussion Questions

7. Some people describe morphology as the study of how words are built up; others describe it as the study of how words are broken down. What assumptions does each of these two descriptions make about how words are stored in our mental lexicons? Based on what you know so far, is one of these descriptions more or less accurate? Why do you think so? Come back and revisit this question once you have read the entire chapter.

File 4.2—Morphological Processes

Exercises

8. Consider the following data from Bontoc. These data show an example of derivational morphology in which an adjectival root is turned into a verb. What type of affix is used to form the verb? Describe its placement in the word.

[fikas]	'strong'	[fumikas]	'he is becoming strong'
[kilad]	'red'	[kumilad]	'he is becoming red'
[bato]	'stone'	[bumiato]	'he is becoming stone'
[fusul]	'enemy'	[fumiusul]	'he is becoming an enemy'

9. Imagine that the English suffix *-ful* were instead an infix. Where might it attach in a morpheme like *hope?* Like *pain?* Like *beauty?* (Focus on the pronunciation of the forms, rather than their spelling.) How would you know where to place the infix? Notice that there are a limited number of pronounceable options.

10. For each of the morphological processes explained in the text—affixation, compounding, reduplication, alternation, and suppletion—give an example from English or from your native language that is not given in the text. You will need to provide both the base form and the inflected or derived form for each example.

11. For each of the following words of English, tell what the root word is and the process through which the word was formed.

a. bound   **f.** discover
b. toenail   **g.** mama
c. Sarah's   **h.** mice
d. were   **i.** ladybug
e. undomesticated **j.** rang

12. In Catalan, the form for 'to go' is [əna], and the form for 'I go' is [batʃ]. Which morphological process is this an example of? How do you know?

13. The forms for 'dancer' and 'student' in ASL are shown in (a) and (b) on the next page.
   i. What part of the **meaning** of 'student' and 'dancer' is similar? (*Hint:* Ask yourself, What is a dancer? What is a student?)
   ii. What part of the **form** of these two signs is similar?
   iii. Which morphological process is responsible for the formation of the signs DANCER and STUDENT? How do you know?

a. ASL: STUDENT

© 2006, William Vicars, www.Lifeprint.com. Adapted by permission.

b. ASL: DANCER

© 2006, William Vicars, www.Lifeprint.com. Adapted by permission.

14. Refer to image (7) in File 2.7. Explain, as carefully as you can, how the form for the un-inflected sign MEET differs from the form of the inflected sign I MEET YOU. What is the simultaneous affix that is used in the sign I MEET YOU?

15. i. In Hebrew, the following pattern is found in the derivation of color terms. (Pay particular attention to the consonants; the vowel change is not as important to this data set.) Which morphological process is this an example of? How do you know?

[lavan]	'white'	[lvanvan]	'whitish'
[kaxol]	'blue'	[kxalxal]	'bluish'
[jaɣok]	'green'	[jɣakɣak]	'greenish'
[tˢahov]	'yellow'	[tˢhavhav]	'yellowish'
[vaɣod]	'pink'	[vɣadɣad]	'pinkish'
[ʃaxor]	'black'	[ʃxarxar]	'blackish'

ii. The Hebrew word for 'red' is [adom]. Based only on the data above, what would you predict the word for 'reddish' to be?

iii. The actual Hebrew word for 'reddish' is [admumi]. Is this word at all similar to what you predicted? If so, how? Can you guess a reason for why the actual word might be different from what you predicted? (Do not attempt to explain why it takes the form that it does; just try to explain why the expected pattern may have failed.)

Discussion Questions

16. i. Look again at the data given in question 15 and consider this new fact: the Hebrew word for the color 'violet' is [sagol]. Based only on the data above, what would you expect that the word [sgalgal] would mean?   *(cont.)*

ii. The word [sgalgal] actually means 'oval.' Can you think of any examples in English or some other language where you might predict, based on morphological principles, that a form would mean one thing, but in fact it turns out to mean something else? What do these sorts of cases tell us about morphology and the lexicon of a language?

17. Assume that the English word *raspberry* can be analyzed into *rasp* + *berry* and *cranberry* into *cran* + *berry*. Discuss how these two words behave differently from other morphologically complex English words. Is this process more like affixation, or is it more like compounding? How is this process similar to each? How is it different from each?

Activities

18. There are some cases in English where a certain adjective-noun pair has become a compound noun for some speakers but is still two separate words for others. One of these is *cream cheese*. Some speakers put a stress only on the first syllable, while others treat it as two words and give each its own stress.

Construct a survey:

- Choose a number of noun-adjective pairs that are compound nouns for you or one of your classmates. Your goal will be to find out how other people pronounce these: as compounds or as separate words.
- Design questions such that you do not have to say the word yourself (thereby biasing the person responding); for example, "What do you call the white spread that people eat on bagels?"
- Collaborate with others in your class: each of you should ask your set of questions to some number of people (to be specified by your instructor).
- Afterwards, share your findings with your classmates.

File 4.3—Morphological Types of Languages
Discussion Questions

19. Often, when people are exposed to languages with properties that are different from those of languages that they already know, their immediate reaction is to think that the new type of language is much more complicated. Of course, this is true regardless of which type of language they speak to begin with. For each of the four types of language presented in File 4.3, list some attributes of that kind of language that would make it easier to learn or to understand the grammar. What are some of the attributes that would make it more difficult to learn or to understand the grammar?

Activities

20. With a group of your classmates, make up a fragment of a synthetic language. You should decide whether it will be agglutinative or fusional. Perform the following steps in order to create your language fragment. Be sure to write out the decisions that you make at each step along the way.
   i. First, come up with a name for your language.
   ii. Next, create a small lexicon. It will contain ten words; you can choose to create ten nouns, ten verbs, or five of each. For each of your lexical items, you will need to specify a phonological form (using the IPA) and a meaning (using an English gloss).

(cont.)

iii. Decide on four morphological functions that you will want to be able to perform: two should be derivational, and two should be inflectional. (Examples: marking nouns for nominal case; marking verbs as past tense, turning nouns into adjectives; turning verbs into nouns, etc.) Don't feel the need to restrict yourself to morphological functions found in English!

iv. Decide what morphological process your language will use to perform each of these functions. Don't forget to specify how—if at all—these processes will interact with your language's phonology!

v. Now, write all of the possible derived forms and inflected forms that you can make based on the words of your language and the morphological rules that you have created. For each, tell both the form (using the IPA) and the meaning (using an English gloss).

vi. Is your language fusional or agglutinative? What evidence shows that this is the case?

File 4.4—The Hierarchical Structure of Derived Words

Exercises

21. All of the words below contain two morphemes: a root and a suffix. First, identify the root in each word and the suffix. Then tell the part of speech of the root word and the part of speech of the whole word. You will need to be familiar with lexical categories, which are introduced in File 5.3. (*Hint:* In each list, the lexical categories are the same for all three words.)

    a. government
       speaker
       contemplation

    b. fictional
       childish
       colorful

    c. happiness
       rarity
       creativity

    d. messy
       bookish
       mountainous

    e. calmest
       lovelier
       sillier

22. Isolate the affixes and stems in the following groups of words. Then name the part-of-speech class of the root word to which the stem belongs, and say whether the affixation results in a word belonging to a different part-of-speech class (and if so, which class).

    a. spiteful
       healthful
       truthful

    b. unsure
       untrue
       unhappy

    c. retake
       review
       relive

    d. stoppable
       fixable
       laughable

23. From the examples given for each of the following suffixes, determine: (i) the part of speech of the word whose stem the suffix combines with, and (ii) the part of speech of the words resulting from the addition of the suffix.

    a. **-ify:** solidify, intensify, purify, clarify, rarefy *Adj → Verbs*
    b. **-ity:** rigidity, stupidity, hostility, intensity, responsibility *Adj → Noun*
    c. **-ize:** unionize, terrorize, hospitalize, crystallize, magnetize *noun → Verb*
    d. **-ive:** repressive, active, disruptive, abusive, explosive *verbs → Adj*
    e. **-ion:** invention, injection, narration, expression, pollution *verbs → Nouns*
    f. **-less:** nameless, penniless, useless, heartless, mindless *nouns → Adj*

24. Draw tree diagrams for each of the following words:

a. disappearance	**j.** international	**s.** unmistakable
b. unaffordable	**k.** misunderstandable	**t.** insincerity
c. un-American	**l.** reconstruction	**u.** dysfunctional
d. manliness	**m.** unrespectable	**v.** inconclusive
e. impersonal	**n.** nonrefundable	**w.** premeditatedly
f. irreplaceability	**o.** mismanagement	**x.** overgeneralization
g. oversimplification	**p.** underspecification	**y.** reformer
h. unhappiness	**q.** restatement	**z.** infertility
i. decommission	**r.** inflammability	**aa.** dishonesty

25. Consider the two columns of words below. What do the words in each column have in common? Come up with two more words that go in each column. Do the words in both columns have the same suffix, or do the words on the right have a different suffix from those on the left? Justify your answer.

teacher	stapler
baker	juicer
singer	copier
writer	toaster
fighter	hole-puncher
painter	lighter

26. Consider the English prefix *anti-*. Make a list of words you can think of that begin with *anti-*. Try to come up with at least ten words. (You may use a dictionary if you like.) What lexical categories contain words that can serve as root words for *anti-*? In each case, what are the lexical categories of the output?

27. The made-up words *embiggens* and *introubleating* were introduced in question 6. Draw tree diagrams for these two words.

Activities

28. Make up your own English word that you've never heard before that is composed of at least four morphemes. (If you can't think of a word right now, you are welcome to use *semiunducklike*, as in "A rhinoceros isn't like a duck at all, but a goose is only semi-unducklike." However, it's more fun to make your own word!)
  i. Indicate the morphemes that make it up.
  ii. Provide the meaning of each morpheme and state whether it is (1) free or bound; (2) a root, prefix, or suffix; and (3) derivational, inflectional, or neither.
  iii. Provide the meaning of the whole word.
  iv. Draw a tree diagram for how it was put together.

File 4.5—Morphological Analysis

Exercises

Beginning Exercises

29. &Isthmus Zapotec

Examine the following data from Isthmus Zapotec, a language spoken in Mexico. Answer the questions that follow.

a.	[palu]	'stick'	**g.**	[spalube]	'his stick'	**m.**	[spalulu]	'your stick'
b.	[kuːba]	'dough'	**h.**	[skuːbabe]	'his dough'	**n.**	[skuːbalu]	'your dough'
c.	[tapa]	'four'	**i.**	[stapabe]	'his four'	**o.**	[stapalu]	'your four'
d.	[geta]	'tortilla'	**j.**	[sketabe]	'his tortilla'	**p.**	[sketalu]	'your tortilla'
e.	[bere]	'chicken'	**k.**	[sperebe]	'his chicken'	**q.**	[sperelu]	'your chicken'
f.	[doʔo]	'rope'	**l.**	[stoʔobe]	'his rope'	**r.**	[stoʔolu]	'your rope'

i. Isolate the morphemes that correspond to the following English translations:

_____ possession (genitive)

_____ third person singular

_____ second person plural

ii. List the allomorphs for the following translations:

_____ _____ 'tortilla'   _____ _____ 'rope'

_____ _____ 'chicken'

iii. What phonological environment triggers the alternation between these allomorphs?

30. Turkish

Examine the following data from Turkish and answer the questions that follow.

a.	[deniz]	'an ocean'		**i.**	[elim]	'my hand'
b.	[denize]	'to an ocean'		**j.**	[eller]	'hands'
c.	[denizin]	'of an ocean'		**k.**	[diʃler]	'teeth'
d.	[eve]	'to a house'		**l.**	[diʃimizin]	'of our tooth'
e.	[evden]	'from a house'		**m.**	[diʃlerimizin]	'of our teeth'
f.	[evdʒɪkden]	'from a little house'		**n.**	[eldʒɪke]	'to a little hand'
g.	[denizdʒɪkde]	'in a little ocean'		**o.**	[denizlerimizde]	'in our oceans'
h.	[elde]	'in a hand'		**p.**	[evdʒɪklerimizde]	'in our little houses'

i. Give the Turkish morpheme that corresponds to each of the following translations:

_____ 'ocean'   _____ 'in'   _____ 'my'

_____ 'house'   _____ 'to'   _____ 'of'

_____ 'hand'   _____ 'from'   _____ 'our'

_____ 'tooth'   _____ 'little'   _____ (plural marker)

ii. What is the order of morphemes in a Turkish word (in terms of noun stem, plural marker, etc.)?

iii. How would one say 'of our little hands' in Turkish?

31. Luiseño

Examine the following data from Luiseño, a Uto-Aztecan language of Southern California, and answer the questions that follow.

a.	[nokaamaj]	'my son'	**m.**	[pokaamaj]	'his son'
b.	[ʔoki]	'your house'	**n.**	[poki]	'his house'
c.	[potaana]	'his blanket'	**o.**	[notaana]	'my blanket'
d.	[ʔohuukapi]	'your pipe'	**p.**	[pohuukapi]	'his pipe'
e.	[ʔotaana]	'your blanket'	**q.**	[nohuukapi]	'my pipe'
f.	[noki]	'my house'	**r.**	[ʔokaamaj]	'your son'
g.	[ʔomkim]	'your (pl.) houses'	**s.**	[pompeewum]	'their wives'
h.	[nokaamajum]	'my sons'	**t.**	[pomki]	'their house'
i.	[popeew]	'his wife'	**u.**	[tʃampeewum]	'our wives'
j.	[ʔopeew]	'your wife'	**v.**	[tʃamhuukapim]	'our pipes'
k.	[ʔomtaana]	'your (pl.) blanket'	**w.**	[ʔomtaanam]	'your (pl.) blankets'
l.	[tʃamhuukapi]	'our pipe'	**x.**	[pomkaamaj]	'their son'

i. Give the Luiseño morpheme that corresponds to each English translation. Note that the plural marker has two allomorphs; list them both.

_____	'son'	_____	'my'	_____	'their'
_____	'house'	_____	'his'	_____	(plural marker)
_____	'blanket'	_____	'your (sg.)'	_____	'pipe'
_____	'wife'	_____	'your (pl.)'	_____	'our'

ii. Are the allomorphs of the plural marker phonologically conditioned?

iii. If so, what are the conditioning environments?

32. Quiché

Some sentences from Quiché, a Native American language spoken in Guatemala, Central America, are given with their English translation in (a)–(h). Analyze the morphemes in these sentences and then fill in the exercises that follow the language data. Note that [x] is a voiceless velar fricative.

Quiché	*English*
a. [kiŋsikíx le líbr]	'I read (present tense) the book'
b. [kusikíx le líbr]	'He reads the book'
c. [kiŋwetamáx le kém]	'I learn the (art of) weaving'
d. [kataxín kiŋwetamáx le kém]	'I continually learn the (art of) weaving'
e. [kataxín kawetamáx le kém]	'You continually learn the (art of) weaving'
f. [ʃiŋwetamáx]	'I learned (it)'
g. [ʃuwetamáx le kém]	'He learned the (art of) weaving'
h. [ʃasikíx le líbr iwír]	'You read the book yesterday'

i. Fill in the blanks with the corresponding Quiché morphemes:

_____	'I'	_____	'learn'	_____	(present tense)
_____	'he'	_____	'read'	_____	(past tense)
_____	'you'	_____	'the'	_____	'continually'
_____	'book'	_____	'weaving'	_____	'yesterday'

ii. What is the order of Quiché morphemes (in terms of subject, verb, object, and tense marker)?

33. American Sign Language

Each of the four signs below includes one affix. The two signs on the left have the same affix. The two signs on the right share a different affix.

a. GRANDMOTHER   GRANDFATHER

b. MOTHER   FATHER

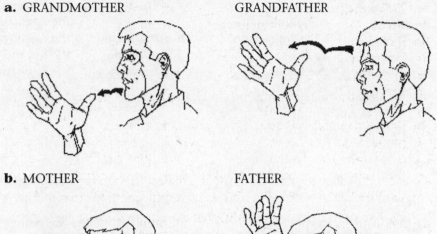

© 2006, William Vicars, www.Lifeprint.com. Used with permission.

   i. Which phonological parameter differentiates these two affixes: place of articulation, movement, hand shape, or hand orientation?

  ii. Describe the difference in form between the affix in the signs on the left and the affix in the signs on the right.

 iii. Are these two affixes prefixes, suffixes, infixes, or simultaneous affixes?

  iv. What is the meaning of the affix used on the left? What is the meaning of the affix used on the right?

34. Michoacan Aztec

Examine the following words from Michoacan Aztec, a language of Mexico, and answer the questions that follow.

a. [nokali]	'my house'		**f.** [mopelo]	'your dog'
b. [nokalimes]	'my houses'		**g.** [mopelomes]	'your dogs'
c. [mokali]	'your house'		**h.** [ikwahmili]	'his cornfield'
d. [ikali]	'his house'		**i.** [nokwahmili]	'my cornfield'
e. [nopelo]	'my dog'		**j.** [mokwahmili]	'your cornfield'

  i. Fill in the blanks with the corresponding Michoacan morphemes:

    _____ 'house'   _____ 'my'

    _____ 'dog'   _____ 'your'

    _____ 'cornfield'   _____ 'his'

    _____ (plural marker)

  ii. What is the English translation for the Michoacan word [ipelo]?

 iii. How would you say 'his cornfields' in Michoacan?

35. Cebuano

The following nouns are from Cebuano, a language of the Philippine Islands. Examine them and answer the questions that follow.

a. [bisaja]   'a Visayan'   **f.** [binisaja]   'the Visayan language'
b. [inglis]   'an Englishman'   **g.** [ininglis]   'the English language'
c. [tagalog] 'a Tagalog person'   **h.** [tinagalog] 'the Tagalog language'
d. [ilokano] 'an Ilocano'   **i.** [inilokano] 'the Ilocano language'
e. [sibwano] 'a Cebuano'   **j.** [sinibwano] 'the Cebuano language'

    i. State the rule (in words, precisely) for deriving language names from the names of ethnic groups.
    ii. What type of affixation is this?

36. Isleta

Consider the following data from Isleta, a dialect of Southern Tiwa, a Native American language spoken in New Mexico, and answer the questions that follow.

a. [temiban]   'I went'   **d.** [mimiaj]   'he was going'
b. [amiban]   'you went'   **e.** [tewanban] 'I came'
c. [temiwe]   'I am going'   **f.** [tewanhi]   'I will come'

    i. List the morphemes corresponding to the following English translations.

      _____ 'I'   _____ 'go'   _____ (present progressive)
      _____ 'you'   _____ 'come'   _____ (past progressive)
      _____ 'he'   _____ (past)   _____ (future)

    ii. What sort of affixes are the subject morphemes?
    iii. What sort of affixes are the tense morphemes?
    iv. What is the order of morphemes in Isleta?
    v. How would you say each of the following in Isleta?

      • 'He went.'
      • 'I will go.'
      • 'You were coming.'

37. German

Isolate the morphemes and word formation processes used to mark the plural in German. Don't worry about trying to describe which plural morpheme goes with which type of word. Just list the morphemes. (Note that the data below are given in normal German orthography, not IPA; vowels [ü] and [ö] are front rounded vowels and 'äu' is pronounced [ɔɪ].)

Singular	Plural	Gloss
a. Bild	Bilder	'picture'
b. Büro	Büros	'office'
c. Tüte	Tüten	'bag'
d. Loch	Löcher	'hole'
e. Uhr	Uhren	'watch'
f. Rind	Rinder	'bull/cow'
g. Wagen	Wagen	'vehicle'
h. Stift	Stifte	'pen'
i. Haus	Häuser	'house'
j. Laus	Läuse	'louse'

(cont.)

k. Hut	Hüte	'hat'
l. Hütte	Hütten	'hut'
m. Buch	Bücher	'book'
n. Dach	Dächer	'roof'
o. Kind	Kinder	'child'

Intermediate Exercises

38. Swahili

Examine the following data from Swahili, a language spoken in East Africa, and answer the questions that follow.

a. [atanipenda]	's/he will like me'	**o.** [atanipiga]	's/he will beat me'
b. [atakupenda]	's/he will like you'	**p.** [atakupiga]	's/he will beat you'
c. [atampenda]	's/he will like him/her'	**q.** [atampiga]	's/he will beat him/her'
d. [atatupenda]	's/he will like us'	**r.** [ananipiga]	's/he is beating me'
e. [atawapenda]	's/he will like them'	**s.** [anakupiga]	's/he is beating you'
f. [nitakupenda]	'I will like you'	**t.** [anampiga]	's/he is beating him/her'
g. [nitampenda]	'I will like him/her'	**u.** [amekupiga]	's/he has beaten you'
h. [nitawapenda]	'I will like them'	**v.** [amenipiga]	's/he has beaten me'
i. [utanipenda]	'you will like me'	**w.** [amempiga]	's/he has beaten him/her'
j. [utampenda]	'you will like him/her'	**x.** [alinipiga]	's/he beat me'
k. [tutampenda]	'we will like him/her'	**y.** [alikupiga]	's/he beat you'
l. [watampenda]	'they will like him/her'	**z.** [alimpiga]	's/he beat him/her'
m. [wametulipa]	'they have paid us'	**aa.** [atakusumbua]	's/he will annoy you'
n. [tulikulipa]	'we paid you'	**bb.** [unamsumbua]	'you are annoying him/her'

i. Give the Swahili morphemes corresponding to the following English translations:

_____ 'I'	_____ 'we'	_____ (past marker)
_____ 'pay'	_____ 'like'	_____ (present progressive)
_____ 's/he'	_____ 'annoy'	_____ (future marker)
_____ 'me'	_____ 'him/her'	_____ (present perfect)
_____ 'beat'	_____ 'they'	_____ 'you' (if subject)
_____ 'us'	_____ 'them'	_____ 'you' (if object)

ii. What is the order of morphemes in Swahili (in terms of subject, object, verb, and tense)?

iii. Give the Swahili word for the following English translations:

- 'I have beaten them.'
- 'They are beating me.'
- 'They have annoyed me.'
- 'You have beaten us.'
- 'We beat them.'
- 'I am paying him/her.'

iv. Give the English translation for the following Swahili words.

- [atanilipa]
- [utawapiga]
- [walikupenda]
- [nimemsumbua]

39. Cree

Examine the following data from Cree, an Algonquian language spoken in Canada, and answer the questions that follow.

a.	[tʃiːmaːn]	'canoe'	**l.**	[nitospwaːkan]	'my pipe'
b.	[nitʃiːmaːn]	'my canoe'	**m.**	[akimew]	's/he counts'
c.	[soːnija]	'money'	**n.**	[nitakimen]	'I count'
d.	[nisoːnija]	'my money'	**o.**	[apiw]	's/he sits'
e.	[wijaːʃ]	'meat'	**p.**	[nitapin]	'I sit'
f.	[niwijaːʃ]	'my meat'	**q.**	[ispelohkew]	's/he rests'
g.	[eːmihkwaːn]	'spoon'	**r.**	[nitispelohken]	'I rest'
h.	[niteːmihkwaːn]	'my spoon'	**s.**	[kaakimew]	's/he will count'
i.	[astotin]	'hat'	**t.**	[nikaakimen]	'I will count'
j.	[nitastotin]	'my hat'	**u.**	[kaapiw]	's/he will sit'
k.	[ospwaːkan]	'pipe'	**v.**	[nikaapin]	'I will sit'

   i. What are the Cree morphemes for the following?

      _____ 'I'   _____ 'my'

      _____ 's/he'   _____ (future tense)

   ii. What are the allomorphs for 'I' and 'my'?

   iii. What are the conditioning environments for the allomorphs?

   iv. How does the morpheme 'I' differ from the morpheme 'my' (with respect to form, not meaning)?

40. Zoque

Examine the following data from Zoque, a language spoken in Mexico, and answer the subsequent questions.

a.	[kenu]	'he looked'	**g.**	[kenpa]	'he looks'
b.	[sihku]	'he laughed'	**h.**	[sikpa]	'he laughs'
c.	[wihtu]	'he walked'	**i.**	[witpa]	'he walks'
d.	[kaʔu]	'he died'	**j.**	[kaʔpa]	'he dies'
e.	[cihcu]	'it tore'	**k.**	[cicpa]	'it tears'
f.	[sohsu]	'it cooked'	**l.**	[sospa]	'it cooks'

   i. What is the Zoque morpheme indicating the present tense?

   ii. For each verb, give the meaning and list the allomorphs of the stem.

   iii. Given any Zoque verb with two stem allomorphs, what morphological category determines the choice of stem? That is, how do you know which stem to use when?

   iv. Describe the relationship between the stem allomorphs in terms of phonological form.

   v. What is the Zoque morpheme meaning 'he' or 'it'?

41. Swedish

Swedish is a Germanic language with morphological marking of nouns similar to that of English, but with some significant differences. Consider the following forms (given in Standard Swedish spelling) of nouns and answer the questions.

a.	en lampa	'a lamp'	**l.**	en bil	'a car'
b.	stolen	'the chair'	**m.**	bilar	'cars'
c.	en tidning	'a newspaper'	**n.**	kattarna	'the cats'
d.	lampan	'the lamp'	**o.**	en katt	'a cat'
e.	bilen	'the car'	**p.**	soffor	'sofas'
f.	en stol	'a chair'	**q.**	tidningarna	'the newspapers'
g.	sofforna	'the sofas'	**r.**	bilarna	'the cars'
h.	katten	'the cat'	**s.**	lamporna	'the lamps'
i.	tidningen	'the newspaper'	**t.**	stolarna	'the chairs'
j.	kattar	'cats'	**u.**	en soffa	'a sofa'
k.	tidningar	'newspapers'	**v.**	soffan	'the sofa'
			w.	lampor	'lamps'

  i. What Swedish word corresponds to the English indefinite article ('a(n)')?
  ii. What are the allomorphs of the definite morpheme? Where do they appear?
  iii. How is the indefinite plural formed? The definite plural?
  iv. How would you say the forms of the following words?

		Definite	*Plural*	*Definite Plural*
en flicka	'a girl'	_____	_____	_____
en klänning	'a dress'	_____	_____	_____
en blomma	'a flower'	_____	_____	_____
en buss	'a bus'	_____	_____	_____

42. Hanunoo

Hanunoo is a language spoken in the Philippine Islands. Compare the data from this language horizontally (e.g., (a)-(h)-(o) go together), and answer the questions that follow.

a.	[ʔusa]	'one'	**h.**	[kasʔa]	'once'	**o.**	[ʔusahi]	'make it one'
b.	[duwa]	'two'	**i.**	[kadwa]	'twice'	**p.**	[duwahi]	'make it two'
c.	[tulu]	'three'	**j.**	[katlu]	'three times'	**q.**	[tuluhi]	'make it three'
d.	[ʔupat]	'four'	**k.**	[kapʔat]	'four times'	**r.**	[ʔupati]	'make it four'
e.	[lima]	'five'	**l.**	[kalima]	'five times'	**s.**	[limahi]	'make it five'
f.	[ʔunum]	'six'	**m.**	[kanʔum]	'six times'	**t.**	[ʔunumi]	'make it six'
g.	[pitu]	'seven'	**n.**	[kapitu]	'seven times'	**u.**	[pituhi]	'make it seven'

  i. Two affixes are illustrated in these data. Identify each of them, state what kind of affix each one is, and tell what information or change is associated with each affix.
  ii. Considering the horizontal sets of words, describe the phonological alternations in the stems in each set. (If you have already completed the phonology files, use the relevant terms for phonological processes in your descriptions.)

Advanced Exercises

43. Hungarian

Examine the Hungarian data below and answer the questions that follow. Note that [y] represents a high front rounded vowel.

		Singular	*Plural*
a.	'table'	[ɔstɔl]	[ɔstɔlok]
b.	'worker'	[munkaːʃ]	[munkaːʃok]
c.	'man'	[ɛmbɛr]	[ɛmbɛrɛk]
d.	'white'	[fɛheːr]	[fɛheːrɛk]
e.	'this'	[ɛz]	[ɛzɛk]
f.	'line'	[ʃoɾ]	[ʃoɾok]
g.	'eyeglasses'	[sɛmyvɛg]	[sɛmyvɛgɛk]
h.	'shirt'	[iŋ]	[iŋɛk]
i.	'head'	[fɛy]	[fɛyɛk]
j.	'box'	[doboz]	[dobozok]
k.	'drum'	[dob]	[dobok]
l.	'age'	[kor]	[korok]
m.	'coat'	[kɔbaːt]	[kɔbaːtok]
n.	'flower'	[viraːg]	[viraːgok]

    i. What are the allomorphs of the Hungarian plural marker?
    ii. State the conditioning environment for each allomorph.

44. Popoluca

Examine the following data from Popoluca, a language spoken in Mexico, and answer the questions that follow. (*Note:* 'you' is singular throughout this exercise.)

a. [ʔiŋkuʔtpa]	'you eat it'		**i.** [ʔinhokspa]	'you hoe it'
b. [ʔanhokspa]	'I hoe it'		**j.** [noːmi]	'boss'
c. [ʔikuʔt]	'he ate it'		**k.** [ʔanoːmi]	'my boss'
d. [ʔimoːja]	'his flower'		**l.** [ʔikaːma]	'his cornfield'
e. [moːja]	'flower'		**m.** [ʔiŋkaːma]	'your cornfield'
f. [ʔampetpa]	'I sweep it'		**n.** [ʔamoːja]	'my flower'
g. [ʔimpet]	'you swept it'		**o.** [ʔinoːmi]	'your boss'
h. [ʔantɛk]	'my house'			

    i. List all of the Popoluca allomorphs corresponding to the following translations:

       _____ 'cornfield'   _____ (past tense)
       _____ 'flower'   _____ (present tense)
       _____ 'boss'   _____ 'I/my'
       _____ 'house'   _____ 'you/your'
       _____ 'eat'   _____ 'he/his'
       _____ 'sweep'   _____ 'hoe'

    ii. For those morphemes with more than one allomorph, state the phonetic environments that determine the occurrence of each allomorph.

45. Mongolian

Examine the Mongolian data on the following page. Note that [y] represents a high front rounded vowel, [ø] represents a mid front rounded vowel, and [x] represents a voiceless velar fricative.

		Stem	*Future Imperative*
a.	'enter'	[or-]	[orːroɪ]
b.	'go'	[jav]	[javaːraɪ]
c.	'sit'	[suː-]	[suːgaːraɪ]
d.	'come'	[ir-]	[ireːreɪ]
e.	'do'	[xiː-]	[xiːgeːreɪ]
f.	'come out'	[gar-]	[garaːraɪ]
g.	'take'	[av-]	[avaːraɪ]
h.	'study'	[sur-]	[suraːraɪ]
i.	'finish'	[byteː-]	[byteːgeːreɪ]
j.	'drink'	[yː-]	[yːgøːrøɪ]
k.	'find out'	[ol-]	[oloːroɪ]
l.	'conquer'	[jal-]	[yalaːraɪ]
m.	'ask'	[asuː-]	[asuːgaːraɪ]
n.	'finish'	[tøgsg-]	[tøgsgøːrøɪ]
o.	'beat'	[dev-]	[deveːreɪ]
p.	'give'	[øg-]	[øgøːrøɪ]
q.	'say'	[xel-]	[xeleːreɪ]
r.	'meet'	[uːlz-]	[uːlzaːraɪ]
s.	'become'	[bol-]	[boloːroɪ]
t.	'write'	[bitʃ-]	[bitʃeːreɪ]
u.	'develop'	[xøgdʒ-]	[xøgdʒøːrøɪ]

    i. List all of the allomorphs of the Mongolian future imperative marker.

    ii. What environments condition the appearance of the different allomorphs?

46. Japanese

Consider the following inflected Japanese verb forms and answer the questions that follow. (X, Y, and Z are used as "dummy" pronouns in the glosses—they are not actually expressed morphologically in the data.)

a.	[tabeta]	'X ate Y'
b.	[aketa]	'X opened Y'
c.	[tabesaseta]	'X made Y eat Z'
d.	[akesaseta]	'X made Y open Z'
e.	[taberareta]	'X was eaten'
f.	[akerareta]	'X was opened'
g.	[tabesaserareta]	'X was made to eat Y'
h.	[akesaserareta]	'X was made to open Y'
i.	[tabesasenai]	'X doesn't/won't make Y eat Z'
j.	[tabenai]	'X doesn't/won't eat Y'
k.	[tabesaserareru]	'X is/will be made to eat Y'

    i. Give the Japanese morphemes for the following English translations:

        _____ 'open'

        _____ 'eat'

        _____ passive marker ('. . . be VERB-ed,' e.g., 'They were opened/eaten')

        _____ causative marker ('. . . make X VERB,' e.g., 'Robin makes Tracey laugh')

        _____ nonpast marker (present or future tense)

        _____ past marker

        _____ negative marker

(cont.)

ii. Suppose a Japanese verb form were to include the following sets of morphemes. For each set, indicate the order in which the morphemes would occur in a verb form.

- passive, root, past, causative
- causative, nonpast, root
- root, negative, causative

iii. Give the Japanese verb form that would be used for each of the following English translations. Remember that you don't need to worry about words like *she, him,* and *them*.

- '(She) will make (him) open (them).'
- (He) will be made to open (them).'

iv. In Japanese, [uketa] means '(She) took (a test).' Using this fact along with what you've observed above, how would you say the following in Japanese? Again, don't try to translate the items in parentheses.

- '(She) was made to take (a test).'
- '(She) makes (him) take (a test).'
- '(She) will not take (a test).'

CHAPTER
5

Syntax

FRANK & ERNEST: © Thaves/Dist. by Newspaper Enterprise Association, Inc.

FILE 5.0

What Is Syntax?

Words in a sentence are more than just a string of items that can be put together any which way. There are patterns and regularities to the ways in which they can be combined. **Syntax** studies the organization of words into phrases, and likewise the organization of phrases into sentences.

Linguists are interested in understanding the kinds of rules that govern phrase and sentence formation because they tell us something about what it means to use language, and moreover about what it means to be human. We find that although the rules for how words may be combined syntactically differ from language to language, there are many similarities as well. As we discussed in File 1.2, the rules for language use are stored in the human mind. Therefore, by understanding how rules of sentence formation work in various languages, we can understand something about how the human mind works: the sorts of structures that the human mind is able to process and store.

Contents

Basic Ideas of Syntax

5.1.1 Phrases, Sentences, and Structure

In this chapter we ask the question, "What determines whether a string of words in a language is a sentence or simply a string of **unrelated** words?" We emphasize **unrelated** because one of the key properties that makes a string of words a sentence is that the words are related to one another in particular ways. That is, a sentence is not just an arbitrary list of words. A sentence of a particular language is a sequence of words whose ordering with respect to one another follows certain rules. Of course, in order for speakers to be able to produce sentences according to these rules, the rules must be part of what speakers know about their language.

The study of syntax is the study of how words combine to form phrases and ultimately sentences in languages. Because it consists of phrases that are put together in a particular way, a sentence has a structure. The structure consists of the **way** in which the words are organized into phrases and the phrases are organized into larger phrases. Different languages structure sentences in different ways. For example, in Malagasy (an Austronesian language spoken in Madagascar), a sentence meaning 'The man washes clothes with the soap' is arranged with the verb corresponding to 'washes' at the beginning of the sentence and the subject corresponding to 'the man' at the end, as shown in (1).

(1) Manasa   lamba   amin'ny savony   ny lehilahy
    washes   *clothes*   *with the soap*   *the man*
    'The man washes clothes with the soap.'

Obviously, the rules for the syntax of Malagasy differ from those for the syntax of English.

As we proceed through this file and chapter, we will explore various aspects of these sorts of rules and their implications for language use. This file can stand alone as an essential introduction to syntax. The remaining files focus more closely on some, though not all, of the aspects of syntax introduced in this file.

5.1.2 Word Order

One of the most obvious aspects of syntax is word order. In (1) above, we saw how rules for word order can differ from language to language. That these rules must exist, though, is clear. If we translated the Malagasy sentence in (1) word for word into English, we would wind up with (2), which is certainly not a possible English sentence, even though that same word order was acceptable in Malagasy.

(2) *Washes clothes with the soap the man.

Thus, we see that not every string of words in a language is a sentence in that language.

As a further example, we can see by rearranging the words used in (3a) that some orders, such as (3b), are sentences, but most are unacceptable. They are not possible sentences of English.

(3) a.   The cat is on the mat.
     b.   The mat is on the cat.
     c.   *The is cat on the mat.
     d.   *Mat on is the cat the mat.
     e.   *The cat on is the mat.
     f.   *The cat on the is mat.
     g.   *The cat on the mat is.
     h.   *Mat the on is cat the.

Strings of words that form possible sentences of a language are said to be **grammatical.** They conform to the rules of that language. Sentences that are impossible either because the words are in the wrong order with respect to one another or for some other reason are said to be **ungrammatical.** We represent the ungrammaticality (impossibility) of particular word sequences with the symbol *.

We conclude from (2) and (3) that word order is an important part of determining grammaticality (at least for English and some large number of other languages) and therefore is an important element to consider when studying syntax.

5.1.3 Lexical Categories

A second critical component of syntax is the notion of **lexical categories,** also called **syntactic categories.** You have likely heard lexical categories referred to by the name "parts of speech." A lexical category is a group of words that can function in the same way in a sentence. A good way to determine whether or not two words are of the same lexical category is to see whether they can be substituted for one another in a grammatical sentence to yield another grammatical sentence. We have shown this test five times in (4).

(4) a.   I want to read a book.
     b.   *But want to read a book.
          You want to read a book.
     c.   *I purple to read a book.
          I hate to read a book.
     d.   *I want to sometimes a book.
          I want to acquire a book.
     e.   *I want to read never book.
          I want to read the book.
     f.   *I want to read a today.
          I want to read a magazine.

By comparing (4a) with (4b), we can conclude that *you* is the same lexical category as *I* but that *but* is a member of a different lexical category. We can draw similar conclusions from examining (4c) through (4f).

Not all languages have exactly the same kinds of lexical categories, but common lexical categories include nouns and verbs. More information about lexical categories can be found in File 5.3.

5.1.4 Agreement

One aspect of syntax that is related to the notion of lexical categories is that of **agreement.** Although we will not have much to say about agreement in this book, it is worth mentioning, since it is an aspect of grammar that is often covered in the sort of prescriptivist grammar class that you may have taken before, either about your own native language or about a second language. Agreement is the principle that says that certain words need to have a particular property (for example, a morphological marking) in order to work in a sentence with another word.

(5) a.   I read those articles.
    b.   *I read those article.

For example, in (5), the word *those* does not agree with the word *article* because *article* is singular and *those* is the sort of word that is allowed to be used only with a plural noun. Likewise, in many dialects of English, (6b) is ungrammatical because in those dialects, *eat* is the sort of word that can be used only if the subject is not third-person singular (e.g., he, she, it).

(6) a.   Joe eats pizza on Fridays.
    b.   *Joe eat pizza on Fridays.

Different languages (and different dialects of the same language) may differ in what types of features require agreement. For example, many languages require that adjectives and nouns agree with each other in gender, although English does not have such a feature for adjective agreement. Although specifications for how agreement works in various languages differ, agreement is an important element of syntax and of establishing grammaticality in many languages.

5.1.5   Constituency and Hierarchical Structure

We will now consider one final aspect of syntax. Consider the following sentence:

(7) We need more intelligent administrators.

This sentence is ambiguous—that is, it has more than one meaning. One meaning is 'We need administrators who are more intelligent.' The other meaning is 'We need a greater number of intelligent administrators.'

The type of ambiguity found in (7) is called **structural ambiguity.** The meaning of the sentence depends on how the words are put together, that is, the structure. Note that word order alone is not enough to tell us which meaning for the string of words in (7) is intended. The meaning comes out of the sequence in which words and groups of words were put together to create the string. In the first meaning of 'more intelligent administrators,' *more* is grouped with *intelligent* to form the phrase *more intelligent*. In the second meaning, *intelligent* is grouped with *administrators* to form the phrase *intelligent administrators*. One way to represent the difference in structure is to bracket together the words that form a **phrase,** as in (8).

(8) a.   meaning one: [more intelligent] administrators
    b.   meaning two: more [intelligent administrators]

Let us consider another case of structural ambiguity.

(9) Pat shot the soldier with the gun.

This sentence also has two meanings. In one meaning, the soldier whom Pat shot had a gun. In the other meaning, Pat used a gun to shoot the soldier. Again, we can represent the two structures for this single string of words by bracketing the words that go together. In the first meaning, *with the gun* is bracketed with *the soldier*. In the second meaning, *with the gun* is bracketed with *shot the soldier*.

(10) a. Pat shot [[the soldier][with the gun]]
      b. Pat [[shot the soldier][with the gun]]

What we are doing when we put words together in a set of brackets is saying that they form a **constituent**: a group of words that function together as a discrete unit in the sentence. Constituents may nest inside one another, thereby creating a **hierarchical structure** of constituents in a sentence.

Notice that sometimes a sentence that is potentially ambiguous lacks a possible meaning because it does not make sense from the perspective of how we understand the world. For example, let us take *gun* in (9) and replace it with *telescope*, which produces *Pat shot the soldier with a telescope*. In this case it is plausible that the soldier that Pat shot has a telescope, and it is much less plausible that Pat used a telescope to shoot the soldier. Of course, it is possible that in some imaginary world we could use telescopes to shoot people. But notice that we are not likely to seize on this as a possible meaning, because in our everyday world such a telescope is not familiar to us. But the sentence is ambiguous anyway. From the perspective of the language, it is perfectly possible for a completely grammatical sentence to mean something very improbable, or even something impossible or contradictory. This fact highlights the fact that form and meaning, while closely related, are distinct aspects of the expressions of the language.

Let us consider one more case of structural ambiguity.

(11) (That is) a large man's hat.

In one meaning, the hat is a hat that belongs to a large man. Hence we group *a large man's* as a phrase, as in (12a). In the other meaning, we are talking about a man's hat that is large. In this case, *man's hat* is a phrase, as shown by the bracketing in (12b).

(12) a. [a large man's] hat
      b. a large [man's hat]

The ambiguity of meaning of (7), (9), and (11) nicely indicates the fact that which words are bound together most closely in a sentence—the constituency—and how constituents are put together—the hierarchical structure—are both key parts of how sentences are created, and thereby key parts of syntax. More about these two ideas can be found in Files 5.4 and 5.5.

FILE **5.2**

How Sentences Express Ideas

5.2.1 The Relationship between Syntax and Meaning

As we have illustrated in File 5.1, principles of syntax aren't really about meaning. That is to say, both of the sentences in (1) below are grammatical sentences of English, even though (1a) is a very reasonable sentence and (1b) is entirely unreasonable. We have marked (1b) with an exclamation point rather than an asterisk because although it is semantically anomalous (its meaning is peculiar), it is not actually ungrammatical.

(1) a. The cat jumped on the table.
    b. !The flower jumped on the sound wave.

A more extreme and very oft cited sentence in the syntactic literature is the example in (2), which is an example due to Noam Chomsky.

(2) !Colorless green ideas sleep furiously.

These examples help to make an important point: syntax is not about meaning. Syntax is about the structure of phrases and sentences and about rules for how constituents (words and phrases) are allowed to be put together in any given language.

Nonetheless, there are times that we have to appeal to meaning in order to understand principles of how syntax is working. After all, when all is said and done, the point of language, and therefore the point of having syntactic structures at all, is to communicate some kind of meaning. This is why we had to appeal to meaning ambiguity in order to get at the idea of constituency and hierarchical structure in File 5.1. You will see other cases in the rest of Chapter 5 where we will also have to refer to meaning. Try to keep in mind, though, that considering meaning is only a tool to help us understand syntax. Meaning is not a part of syntax itself (at least not conventionally speaking).

Because the function of syntax is to put words together in ways that create meaning, though, it will be worthwhile to take some time to think explicitly about how that can happen before we take on any of the ideas presented in File 5.1 in greater detail.

5.2.2 Expressing Basic Roles

The job of a sentence in any language is to express an idea that has a basic structure: typically it is about one or more "things" (where we use the word *thing* very loosely for the moment) and expresses a property of that thing or a relationship between that thing and some other thing. Here are some examples:

(3) a. Robin trips and falls.
    b. Terry tripped Robin.
    c. Roses are red, violets are blue, nobody knows that I love you.

199

In the case of *Robin trips and falls*, the "thing" is the person Robin, and the properties involve actions of tripping and falling. In the case of *Terry tripped Robin*, the property expressed by the sentence is actually a relation between the "things" Terry and Robin. In the third sentence, *roses are red* expresses a property of roses, and *violets are blue* expresses a property of violets. *I love you* expresses a relationship between me and you. And *Nobody knows that I love you* expresses a very complicated relationship between people and the fact that I love you. You can see why we use the term *things* with caution. In fact, the relationships that we are considering can hold real or imaginary objects, substances, abstract qualities, facts, and much more.

Given this basic understanding of what a sentence does, we can make a rough sketch of the relationship between the words in the sentence and the meaning that the sentence expresses. For example, a sketch of *Robin trips and falls* is shown in (4). At the top is the actual sentence, the next line shows the basic meanings that are expressed, and the stick figures represent the events that the sentence is referring to. The circles and arrows are intended to show how there are two events, one involving the person 'Robin' and the action 'trips' and another involving the same person 'Robin' and the action 'falls.'

(4)
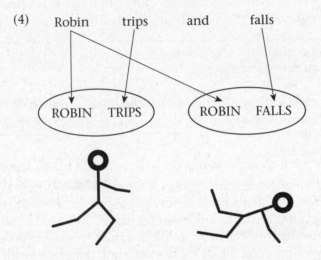

The basic idea is that some parts of the sentence correspond to things (in this case, Robin), and other parts correspond to properties, actions, or relationships (in this case, tripping and falling).

Of course, there are many ideas about things, properties, and relationships that we cannot draw pictures of, but these ideas do exist in our minds. We have already seen an example of one such idea in *Nobody knows that I love you*; here are some others:

(5) a. Space is infinite.
   b. You are very polite.
   c. Love conquers all.
   d. Are you going to vote in next year's election?

What these examples show is that a sentence really expresses ideas involving concepts that are in our minds; sometimes these concepts correspond to physical things, properties, and relationships, and sometimes they do not.

Given that the function of a sentence is to express ideas involving concepts, we must consider how a sentence does this. This is where structure comes in. The purpose of structure is to indicate which thing has which property.

(6) Pat shot the soldier with a gun.

If we group *soldier* with *with a gun*, then the sentence expresses a relation ('shot') between Pat and a particular soldier who has a gun. If we group *with a gun* with *shot the soldier*, then we are expressing a relationship between a gun and the action of shooting a soldier.

The function that something has in a relationship expressed by a sentence is called its **role.** In this file, we will use SMALL CAPS to indicate a role. The role of *a gun* in (6) is determined in part by the structure of the sentence. Since there are two possible structures, there are two possible roles that *gun* can play.

In English, roles are indicated most of the time by where a phrase is placed in the sentence, which is how the structure is expressed. Consider the sentence in (7).

(7) Robin ate the Cheerios with a spoon.

Here, Robin is the person doing the eating. We use the term AGENT to designate the individual that intentionally initiates some action. The Cheerios is what is acted upon; we call this the PATIENT. And the spoon, which in this case is the instrument that is used, is called the INSTRUMENT. These are shown in (8).

(8) Roles filled by the noun phrases in (7)

Phrase	Position	Role
Robin	immediately precedes *ate*	person who does the action (AGENT)
the Cheerios	immediately follows *ate*	thing that action happens to (PATIENT)
a spoon	immediately follows *with*	thing used for action (INSTRUMENT)

The phrase in the position immediately before the verb in most English sentences is called the **subject.** Most often the noun phrase in the position immediately after the verb (if there is one) is called the **object.** Knowing the meaning of a verb involves knowing what the role of its subject is and what the role of its object is, if there is one. For example, the verb *eat* has an agent for its subject and a patient for its object, but not all verbs assign these roles to their subject and object. In fact, many verbs don't take an object at all. Other roles are expressed by words such as *with*, *to*, *in*, etc. (the prepositions).

There are a number of roles that are commonly expressed by language, reflecting how it is that we humans conceptualize events and states. The roles have to do with those aspects of events and states that are most important to us, for example, who did it (the AGENT), what or who was affected (the PATIENT), what changed, and so on. There are many different roles, since there are many aspects of events and states that are relevant to us. We won't try to list and describe all of them here, but will focus just on the most commonly encountered ones. In addition to those we have already discussed, we will refer to THEME, EXPERIENCER, SOURCE, and RECIPIENT.

We use the role THEME for a thing that simply has a property that is being referred to or undergoes a movement or a change.

(9) a. Robin   fell.
       THEME
   b. Pat   is polite.
       THEME

EXPERIENCER is used for an animate being (person or animal) that has some kind of perceptual or mental experience, such as seeing, hearing, knowing, etc. The thing that is perceived, known, etc. is the THEME, as in (10).

(10) Terry   heard   the explosion.
     EXPERIENCER   THEME

The neutral term THEME is used here, rather than PATIENT, because when we see or know something, we do not act on the thing that we see or know; it is simply represented in our mind.

Suppose that a concept expressed in a sentence is change of possession. The individual that comes into possession of something (either something physical or something abstract) is the **RECIPIENT**. The **SOURCE** is where the thing starts out, that is, the former owner. The thing that is possessed is, again, the THEME.

(11) a. Lee   caught   a cold.
        RECIPIENT   THEME
     b. Terry   gave   a book to   Pat.
        AGENT/SOURCE   THEME   RECIPIENT

As we see in (11b), in some events we understand individuals as performing several roles simultaneously. In this example, Terry acts intentionally in giving a book to Pat, and also is the source of the book.

The major roles are summarized in (12).

(12) Major roles

Role	Definition
AGENT	person, animal, etc., that does the action
PATIENT	thing that the action happens to
INSTRUMENT	thing involved in performing the action (but not the agent)
THEME	thing that is in a state or location or undergoes change
EXPERIENCER	animate being (person or animal) that has some kind of perceptual or mental experience
SOURCE	where a change of possession begins
RECIPIENT	individual that comes into possession of something

There are two reasons that roles are important. First, the roles that are expressed by words and sentences correspond to those aspects of the world that are conceptually relevant to human beings, which languages are organized to express. Second, there can be several different ways of expressing the same roles by using different grammatical resources of a language. So it is possible to have sentences that mean the same thing but have different grammatical structure. It is therefore essential to distinguish between the meaning (which includes the roles expressed) and the structure.

For example, it is very important to note that there is a difference between subject/object and the roles. Every sentence in English has a subject, but the roles associated with this subject vary according to the verb. The examples that we have already seen illustrate this fact. Look at the examples in (7) and (9)–(11). As you can see, the role of the subject depends on what the verb is. The subject of catching a cold is not an AGENT, because an AGENT is someone who does an action. Catching a cold (unlike catching a baseball) is not an action.

We can see the difference between structure and function very clearly when we consider different sentences that have the same roles in different positions in the structure. Consider the examples in (13).

(13) a. Robin   frightens   me.
       SOURCE   EXPERIENCER
   b. I   fear   Robin.
       EXPERIENCER   SOURCE

In (13a), the SOURCE of the fear is the subject; in (13b) it is the object. The grammatical function of the fear is the object in (13a), and it is the subject in (13b). The roles are exactly the same, but clearly the structure is different.

Here is another example:

(14) a. Robin heard the explosion.
   b. The explosion was heard by Robin.

Sentence (14a) is said to have an "active" structure, while (14b) is said to have a "passive" structure. The structures are different, but again, the roles are the same.

5.2.3 Indicating Grammatical Function

Finally, we point out that every language has to do the same work of expressing function and roles, but different languages do it in different ways. In English, word order is used; in other languages, phrases are marked with different endings that indicate their function (subject, object, etc.) in the sentence. Here are some examples from Russian. (Here we use the Latin alphabet instead of the Cyrillic alphabet that is used in Russian. The symbol č is used for the sound [tʃ] in the standard transliteration of the Cyrillic alphabet into the Latin alphabet. (See File 2.3 for help on the pronunciation of the sound [tʃ], and Section 13.4.4 for the Cyrillic alphabet.)

(15) a. ja   čitaju   knigu
     I   *read*   *book*
     'I am reading the book.'
   b. ja   knigu   čitaju
     I   *book*   *read*
     'I am reading the book.'
   c. knigu   ja   čitaju
     book   *I*   *read*
     'I am reading the book.'
   d. kniga   byla   v komnate
     book   *was*   *in room*
     'The book was in the room.'

Notice that the position of the object can vary ((15)a–c). But no matter where *knigu* 'book' is in the sentence, it is the object of *čitaju* 'reading'; this is indicated by the fact that it ends in *-u*. When the form is *kniga* (ending in *-a*), that tells us that the book is the subject and not the object (again, regardless of the word order).

In terms of specifics (exactly which structures and word orders are allowed, exactly which prepositions and case markings are available, etc.), there are about as many ways of indicating roles and grammatical functions as there are languages. However, universally, all languages are able to accomplish the same communicative tasks by making use of some set of the aspects of syntax outlined in File 5.1.

Lexical Categories

5.3.1 The Nature of Lexical Categories

Recall from File 5.1 that lexical categories tell us something about the way that a word is allowed to function in a sentence. Different languages have different sets of lexical categories; herein we will consider those of English. The chief lexical categories of English are nouns, verbs, adjectives, and adverbs; and prepositions, pronouns, determiners, auxiliary verbs, and conjunctions.

As in morphology, where we distinguished between content morphemes and function morphemes, we will likewise divide lexical categories into two groups: **content words** and **function words**. Content words are those which contribute to the meaning of the sentence in some substantive way. (This definition is indeed vague, but it is hard to pin it down more precisely at this point in our investigation of syntax.) The categories of content words in English are nouns, verbs, adjectives, and adverbs. We also call these **open lexical categories.** They are "open" because new words can be (and are) added to them all the time. See Files 11.1 and 12.4 for more about how words come to be added to a lexicon.

Function words of English are prepositions, pronouns, determiners, auxiliary verbs, and conjunctions. These categories are **closed categories.** We call them "closed" because they do not allow new members (or, at least, it is very uncommon that a new member gets added to one of these categories).

5.3.2 The Open Lexical Categories of English

When we introduce the open lexical categories, we will have to provide you with criteria for identifying them; it would be impossible to list all of the members of any open lexical category, not only because we would run out of room in the book, but also because the set of members of these categories is always changing; that is why they are called "open"! Therefore, for each of the open lexical categories, we will give you some idea of how to recognize members based on meaning, based on morphology, and based on syntax.

Of course, you can also recognize whether a word is a member of some category by seeing whether you can "plug it in" to a sentence where you know that a word of that lexical category is allowed, as we did in Section 5.1.3. This is precisely because words of the same lexical category are able to function the same way in a sentence. You can use this fact to help you identify lexical categories.

a. Nouns (abbreviated N). Nouns can refer to real, imaginary, and abstract things, substances, people, places, actions, and events. Examples include *book, slug, unicorn, linguistics, sincerity, anger, water, dust, teacher, Joe, ocean, New York, cartwheel, thump, competition,* and *wedding.*

In English, there are a number of common characteristics of nouns that can be used to identify them. If they refer to things that can be counted, nouns can be identified morphologically because they can form a plural, often by adding -*s* as in *books, unicorns, teachers, slugs, cartwheels,* etc. (Note that sometimes plural forms may be marked in a different way,

204

such as in *feet, children, mice,* and *sheep,* but *foot, child, mouse,* and *sheep* are still nouns.) Although in other languages other lexical categories may take a plural marking, in English, nouns are the only open lexical category to do so.

We can also identify nouns syntactically: nouns can occur with the articles and demonstratives *the, this, that, these, those,* etc., as in *the book, this water, that unicorn,* etc. Another characteristic of nouns is that they can be modified with descriptive words (adjectives) like *funny, wet,* and *slippery: the funny book, that wet unicorn, these slippery slugs.* Any word that you can substitute for one of the underlined words in (1) is a noun.

(1) a. There is some spaghetti.
    b. There are some potatoes.
    c. There is a lemon.

b. Verbs (abbreviated V). Verbs refer to actions, events, processes, and states of being. They are words like *sing, walk, finish, formulate, grow, wish, enjoy, exist,* and *be.*

As with nouns, we can identify verbs based on the sort of morphological marking that they can take. In English, verbs express time and take particular forms corresponding to particular times; for example, regular verbs like *walk* express the past by adding *-ed;* irregular verbs express the past by using a special form like *sang, was,* etc. Verbs can also take other forms to indicate the manner of an event. For example, by adding *-ing* to a verb, we indicate an ongoing action (e.g., *I am singing*), and by adding *-en* or *-ed,* we can express a completed action (e.g., *I have written, I have walked*). For some verbs, the completed action uses a special form (e.g., *I have sung*).

Syntactically, we can identify verbs because they work with auxiliaries like *should* and *can,* so we find phrases like *should sing* and *can be.*

c. Adjectives (abbreviated Adj). Adjectives are words like *funny, wet, outrageous,* and *slippery* that can be used to describe the things, ideas, etc., that nouns refer to.

Adjectives can have comparative forms (indicated with *-er* or *more*) and superlative forms (indicated by *-est* or *most*), as in *funnier, wetter, more slippery* and *funniest, wettest, most slippery.*

One hallmark of adjectives is that they can be used in sentences with a form of the verb *to be,* as in *the book is funny, the unicorn is wet, these ideas are slippery,* etc. Another characteristic of adjectives is that they themselves can be modified by words like *very* and *too,* as in *very funny, too wet,* and *very slippery.*

d. Adverbs (abbreviated Adv). Adverbs are words like *quickly, obviously, unfortunately, often, maybe,* and *tomorrow* that are used to express manner (e.g., *quickly*), describe the attitude or judgment of the speaker (e.g., *unfortunately*), or indicate temporal frequency (e.g., *often*), among other relations.

A morphological fact about many adverbs is that they are formed with the suffix *-ly.* You have to be careful, though. First, there are a number of adverbs that do not end in *-ly,* like *very, quite, seldom,* etc. Second, there are words that do end in *-ly* that aren't adverbs, like *silly, friendly,* and *dally.* It is good to be aware that if a word does end in *-ly,* at least there's a good chance that it is an adverb, but you should always check to make sure that it really is an adverb.

Like adjectives, some adverbs can be modified by words like *very* (e.g., *very quickly*) and *too* (e.g., *too often*). In turn, adverbs can modify adjectives (e.g., *wonderfully nice*), verbs (e.g., *writes carefully*), and other adverbs (e.g., *very quickly*) as well as entire sentences (e.g., *Hopefully, the sun will come up tomorrow*).

5.3.3 The Closed Lexical Categories of English

When we introduce closed lexical categories, we will again give you some criteria for identifying each, but in this case we can also go a long way toward listing most of the members of each set. We won't actually list every member for any category, but we will show you a good representative sample!

a. Determiners (abbreviated Det). Determiners are words like *the, a, that, those, any, every, many, three, fifteen, some, his,* and *my.* These words are used to express definiteness (e.g., *the, those*), indefiniteness (e.g., *a*), possession (e.g., *our*), and quantity (e.g., *every, fifteen*), among other things.

You may at some point have been told that so-called possessive words like *his* and *my* were adjectives, but recall that when we identify lexical categories, what we are doing is looking to see how words function in a sentence. Possessives work in English the way that other determiners do; they do not function like adjectives. This point is illustrated in (2) and (3), where determiners are underlined. Notice that *my* behaves like the other determiners, not like the adjective *brown*.

(2) a. <u>The</u> dog is cute.
    b. <u>Some</u> dog is cute (even if mine isn't).
    c. <u>Every</u> dog is cute.
    d. *Brown dog is cute.
    e. <u>My</u> dog is cute.

(3) a. Do you have <u>a</u> brown dog?
    b. *Do you have <u>a</u> <u>the</u> dog?
    c. *Do you have <u>a</u> <u>my</u> dog?

The sentences in (2) and (3) also provide a nice example of how to test for the lexical category of a word that you are unsure of. By comparing the ways that the word whose lexical category you don't know can function with the functions of words whose lexical categories you do know, you can determine the lexical category of the unknown word.

Determiners always appear before nouns, as in the phrases *the book, a unicorn, every idea,* etc. (Sometimes, though, there may be one or more adjectives between the determiner and the noun: *my big brown dog.*)

b. Prepositions (abbreviated Prep). Prepositions are words like *with, in, on, into, for, of, before, without, over,* and *under* that are used to express a number of different roles, including instrument (e.g., *with,* as in *Mix the batter with the spoon*), possessor (e.g., *of,* as in *the leg of the table*), as well as various spatial and temporal relations (e.g., *in, on, before, during,* etc.).

Prepositions appear before noun phrases, as in the phrases *with a spoon, in the kitchen, on the first Tuesday of the month, for everyone,* and *before Sunday.*

c. Auxiliary Verbs (abbreviated Aux). Auxiliary verbs are words like *can, will, must, have, would,* and *do* that express notions of time, necessity, possibility, etc.

They are used in sentences along with other verbs, for example, in the sentences *I can sing, Carrie must write a paper,* and *Ben did go to the store.*

The words *be, have,* and *do* are sometimes main verbs but at other times are auxiliary verbs. (This can be confusing, since they therefore have verbal morphology like the verbs introduced above with the content verbs, e.g., *did* or *was* and *doing* or *being.*) You can tell whether or not these words are acting as auxiliaries in a particular sentence by looking to see whether or not they are working along with another verb.

d. Pronouns (abbreviated Pron). The following are some of the most common **pronouns** of English: *I, me, you, he, him, she, her, it, we, us, they,* and *them.* There are other pronouns as well, such as *some* in *Some like it hot.* Pronouns are used to refer to particular nouns or to noun phrases.

e. Conjunctions (abbreviated Conj). Conjunctions are words like *and, but, yet, so,* and *or* that are used to link together different elements within a phrase or sentence. For example, the phrases *run but not jump, soft yet uncomfortable, apples and oranges,* and *today or tomorrow* all use conjunctions to combine two constituents.

5.3.4 Some Final Comments about Lexical Categories

Some phonological words are members of more than one lexical category. (Note that in some of the examples below, the two uses of the word have similar meanings, and that in other cases they are unrelated.) In each of (4) through (12), there is a particular word that is used to perform two different functions in the (a) sentence and the (b) sentence. Thus, these are words that can be members of (at least) two different lexical categories.

(4) a. Does Joe love Rachel?
    b. Joe's love for Rachel will never fade.

(5) a. Joe likes to go for walks.
    b. Joe walks home from school every day.

(6) a. I bought a package of chewing gum.
    b. The teacher caught me chewing gum.

(7) a. I haven't been to a movie in so long.
    b. I should do my homework so I can go to a movie.

(8) a. January is a cold month.
    b. Joe can't go to school because he has a cold.

(9) a. I need some eggs; do you have any?
    b. Any sandwich is a good sandwich.

(10) a. A duck chased me at Mirror Lake.
    b. When the plane flies over head, you'd better duck.

(11) a. Bark protects the tree.
    b. Dogs often bark at the garbage collector.

(12) a. Michelle has a large library.
    b. Michelle has read fourteen books this summer.

We learn from examples like these that a word's lexical category can be identified only by looking to see how it is used in a sentence. Thus, while we endeavored to list exemplars from various lexical categories in Sections 5.3.2 and 5.3.3, doing so was rather misleading. Only a sentence's structure can reveal the lexical category of the words used in it.

As a final note, it is interesting that in English, many nouns can easily be turned into verbs without any morphological alteration at all. This is not necessarily true of all (or even of most) languages. Thus you must be extremely careful when assigning lexical categories to words: the best way to identify a word's lexical category is to look carefully at how it functions in a sentence.

Phrase Structure

5.4.1 An Introduction to How Phrases Are Constructed

In this file we look at how sentences of English are organized. There are five basic ideas:

- Every word is a member of a lexical category (e.g., noun, verb, etc.) that determines what kind of phrases it can form.
- A **phrase** is a string of words (one or more) that functions as a unit in a sentence.
- A phrase is built up around a single word, called its head.
- In a language, there is a set of specific ways in which phrases can be combined with one another to construct bigger phrases and sentences. We call these the phrase structure rules of the language.
- The way in which the phrases are combined in a sentence determines the phrase structure of the sentence.

Although we will only be considering English here, these five principles apply in one way or another to any language.

Because we have already spent some time examining lexical categories (in File 5.3), we will begin here by looking at how words in each of these categories can combine to form phrases. Like words, phrases can also be divided into various categories.

5.4.2 Phrasal Categories

Phrases in any given phrasal category are built up from a member of some particular lexical category (which becomes its **head**) and some number of other words, according to rules that are specified in the language's grammar. (Note that "some number of other words" could be zero, as in (1a).) In general, a phrase of a certain type has a head of the same type. For example, a noun phrase (NP) has a head noun in it, and possibly other things as well. Some examples of NPs are given in (1). The head of the NP is in boldface type.

(1) a. **Robin**
    b. the **book**
    c. an interesting **book**
    d. a **picture** of Robin
    e. a **picture** of the unicorn
    f. a nice **picture** of the unicorn
    g. a very nice **picture** of the white unicorn

Notice that it is possible to make a more complex NP by adding a prepositional phrase (PP), e.g., the PP *of the unicorn* in (1e) to the NP *a picture* (whose head is *picture*) in order to form the longer NP *a picture of the unicorn*. The prepositional phrase contains another NP, *the unicorn* (whose head is *unicorn*). It is this capacity of language to make bigger and bigger phrases by combining smaller phrases—its productivity—that gives it much of its expressive power. We will come back to this point shortly.

Just as a noun is the head of an NP, a verb functions as the head of a verb phrase (VP). A VP can consist of a verb alone, or a verb with other material, including NPs. Some examples are given in (2), where again the head is in boldface type.

(2) a. **fell**
   b. **fell** slowly
   c. **fell** into the pond
   d. **was** eating
   e. **was** eating the cake
   f. **was** eating the cake with a knife and fork
   g. **kicked** the ball
   h. **kicked** the ball to Peter

Each of the verb phrases in (2) describes an action, event, process, or state of being, without mentioning who is performing the action, engaging in the process, or experiencing the state of being. That is to say, a VP may include an object (as in (2g)), but it does not include a subject. When we combine a VP with an NP of the appropriate type (according to rules of agreement), we get a sentence, as shown in (3).

(3) a. Robin fell.
   b. Robin fell slowly.
   c. Robin fell into the pond.
   d. Terry was eating.
   e. Terry was eating the cake.
   f. Terry was eating the cake with a knife and fork.

Finally, as we have already seen, prepositions combine with noun phrases to form prepositional phrases (PPs). Examples appear in (4); the heads are in boldface type.

(4) a. **of** the white unicorn
   b. **after** forty days
   c. **in** the demilitarized zone
   d. **under** water
   e. **during** the soccer game

There are other sorts of phrasal constituents beyond those we have introduced here. These three will serve our purposes, however.

5.4.3 Phrase Structure Trees

As we have seen, there are several types of phrases in a language, and each type of phrase is composed of one or more words or phrases. It is convenient to visualize the structure of a phrase by using a "tree." Consider the phrase *the man,* which is of category NP. The word *the* is a member of the category determiner, which we abbreviate DET, and the word *man* is of the category noun, which we abbreviate N. The structure of this phrase can then be represented as shown in (5).

What this tree says is that the NP *the man* is composed of two elements; the first is the word *the,* of category DET, and the second is the word *man,* of category N. The labels are

(5)

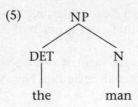

called **nodes**, and each label indicates the category of the word or group of words below it. The left-to-right order of words in the tree corresponds to the way that the words are ordered in speech. As the phrase becomes more complex (for an example of a rather complex NP, *the man that bought that used car from my brother's wife*), the complexity of the description in words would become unmanageable, but the tree simply grows more nodes and branches.

The verb phrase (VP) *fell slowly* can be represented in a similar way.

(6)

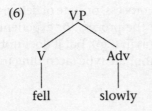

Since we know the structure of the NP and the VP, then if we put them together, we can show a complete tree structure for the sentence (which is of category S) as follows:

(7)

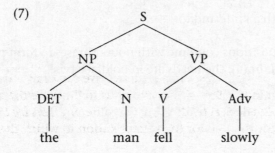

There are other types of structures that can be shown in tree structure diagrams as well. The tree in (8) shows that a prepositional phrase consists of a preposition followed by a noun phrase. We give some additional typical trees in (9)–(11).

(8)

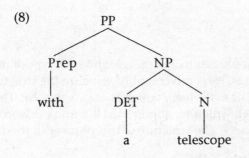

(9)

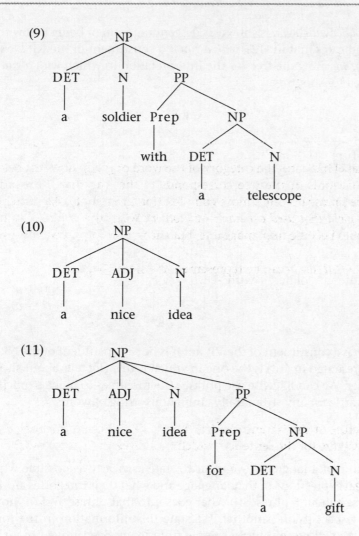

(10)

(11)

If we know the structure of all of the phrases in a sentence, we can draw a tree to visualize the entire sentence, as we did in (7). This ability allows us to illustrate the ambiguity of *Pat shot the soldier with a gun* (see File 5.1) by drawing two different trees for the same string of words. First, in (12), we show the tree for the interpretation in which the soldier has the gun.

(12)

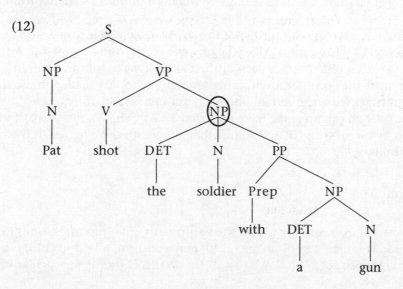

In (12), the phrase *the soldier with a gun* is shown as descending from or being below the NP node in the tree. This indicates that in (12), *with a gun* is a constituent of the NP *the soldier with a gun*. Next, in (13), we show the tree for the interpretation in which *with a gun* indicates the instrument used for shooting.

(13)

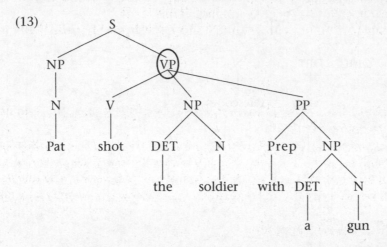

In (13), the PP *with a gun* is a constituent of the VP, but it is not a constituent of the NP. That is why the meaning represented in (13) is the one in which *with a gun* tells about shooting and not about the soldier. We can likewise use phrase structure trees to make explicit how two different meanings arise for any structurally ambiguous string of words.

5.4.4 Phrase Structure Rules

In describing the structure of a language, we want to state as clearly as possible what sequences of words are legal expressions in that language and what their categories are. There are two basic things to say about a phrase: (i) what goes into that phrase and (ii) how the parts are ordered with respect to one another. We state this information in the form of **phrase structure rules.** We will present just a sample from many descriptive phrase structure rules for English in this file.

The rules of a language are comparable to a menu. A menu tells us how to put together a complete meal from various parts (e.g., choose one: appetizer, soup, main course, dessert, etc.), arranged in a particular conventionalized order. Similarly, the rules of a language tell us how to put together individual phrases and eventually a complete sentence from various parts.

Developing this analogy a bit further, if the rules are like the instructions in a menu, an individual sentence is like a meal. All of the possible meals from a menu follow the rules of the menu, but each is different. For each distinct kind of meal, courses occur in a certain order. Similarly, all of the possible sentences of a language follow particular phrase structure rules. For each distinct sentence, certain phrases occur in a certain order.

Let us consider an example. We have seen that a VP in English may consist of a verb alone, or a verb followed by an NP, and some other possibilities. We represent the first two possibilities as follows:

(14) a. VP → V
      b. VP → V NP

The arrow, →, means 'may consist of,' and the left-to-right ordering corresponds to the ordering in time. So (14a) is a way of saying, 'A VP may consist of a V,' and (14b) is a way of saying, 'A VP may consist of a V followed by an NP.' Whether or not a particular verb may actually appear in a particular type of VP (that is, a VP formed according to a particular phrase structure rule) depends on various properties of the verb. For example, the verb *devour* requires an object, while the verb *fall* typically does not appear with an object. Thus, *devour* is more likely to appear in VPs constructed according to rule (14b), while *fall* is more likely to appear in VPs constructed according to rule (14a).

We can combine the two rules in (14) into a single rule by recognizing that V is common to both.

(15) VP → V (NP)

The parentheses around <NP> indicate that some VPs contain NPs and others do not, but when they do, the NP follows the verb.

Given this method for writing phrase structure rules, we can describe other types of phrases very easily and extend our description of VPs as well. Here is an extended rule describing ways that VPs are formed in English. Following the statement of the rule itself are examples of various ways you might find that rule being followed in everyday language use.

(16) VP → (Aux) V (NP) (Adv) (PP) (Adv)
    a. fell into the pond (V PP)
    b. pushed the poodle off the couch (V NP PP)
    c. ate the cake (V NP)
    d. fell slowly (V Adv)
    e. fell slowly into the pond (V Adv PP)
    f. fell into the pond slowly (V PP Adv)

As you can see, a relatively simple rule can describe a large number of possible structures, because of the possibility of including or leaving out optional parts of the phrase. But every VP must contain a V. Similarly, every NP must contain an N, as modeled in the rule and examples in (17).

(17) NP → (DET) (Adj) N (PP)
    a. Robin (N)
    b. the book (DET N)
    c. the book about unicorns (DET N PP)
    d. books about unicorns (N PP)
    e. expensive books (Adj N)
    f. expensive books about unicorns (Adj N PP)
    g. the expensive books about unicorns (DET Adj N PP)

As was the case with verbs and VP rules, there are some nouns that are better suited to appearing in structures based on some NP patterns, and other nouns that are better suited to other NP patterns. Look, for example at the data in (18).

(18) a.   a blue bird (DET Adj N)
    b. *a blue France
    c.   dogs with fleas (N PP)
    d. *dog with fleas

Such data show that the rules we are writing are actually too vague to be the actual rules that we have in our mental grammars. These rules merely describe various general patterns of how words combine into phrases and sentences.

Finally, let us look at some typical sentences of English, the examples in (3). We can see that all of these sentences have the same basic structure. All of the sentences in (3) begin with NPs, in this case simple ones like *Robin* and *Terry*, but in fact any NP can, in principle, appear in the position at the beginning of a sentence (in subject position). In addition to the sentences in (3), we can have examples like the following; the phrases are marked with square brackets.

(19) a. [The person that I was talking to] [fell slowly into the pond]
     b. [Terry's best friend] [fell]

In fact, any NP whatsoever can be combined with any VP whatsoever to make a sentence. We summarize this observation in the following rule. (An NP or a VP may need to be modified because of rules of agreement, but that is not a fact about phrase structure.)

(20) S → NP VP

Of course, many combinations of NP and VP will be nonsensical, like *!The picture of Pat ate the cake with a knife and blue jeans*. Examples such as these are grammatical sentences as far as structure is concerned (they obey all of the rules), but violate principles of meaning (see Chapter 6 on semantics).

Next, we note that in English (and in many other languages), there are special verbs, called *auxiliary verbs* (AUX), that express notions of time, necessity, possibility, and so on. In English, an auxiliary verb like *will, can,* or *have* appears between the subject NP and the VP. This rule is given in (21) and exemplified in (22).

(21) S → NP AUX VP

(22) Terry will fall into the pond.

If the word *not*, which is used to express negation, is used, it follows the auxiliary, which we represent as (23).

(23) S → NP AUX *not* VP

5.4.5 Conjunction

The last types of phrase structure rules that we will consider merit their own section, because they involve combining words and phrases of the same category. This sort of combination or conjoining, which is done with conjunctions such as *and* and *or,* forms larger phrases of the same category as the two words or phrases that were conjoined. These new larger phrases are called conjoined phrases; some examples are given in (24).

(24) a. Leslie and Robin make a good team. (conjoined NPs)
     b. It's time to fish or cut bait. (conjoined VPs)
     c. You can buy your tickets now or you can watch the game on TV. (conjoined Ss)

For each of the categories in the language, we could have a rule that says what the form of a conjoined phrase is. For example, we could have rule (25).

(25) NP → NP Conj NP

But notice that since conjunction is possible for many lexical categories and all phrasal categories, it is not necessary to state a separate rule for each category. All we have to do is define a special symbol, for example, X, to stand for 'any category.' Then we can state the rule for conjunction as follows:

(26) X → X Conj X

What this rule says is just what we have already noted, namely, that any category X can be made up of a conjunction of an X followed by a conjunction followed by another X.

5.4.6 Recursion

Here is a final note to tie together this discussion of phrase structure and phrase structure rules. You will see, if you look at the rules we have listed in this file, that the categories that appear on the left side of some rules also appear on the right side of other rules. Here are some rules that exemplify what we mean:

(27) NP → DET N PP

(28) PP → P NP

PP appears on the right side of rule (27) for the structure of NP, while NP appears on the right side of rule (28) for PP. What this means is that, in principle, we can keep on making larger and larger NPs, and hence larger and larger sentences; we can make them as large as we want, as long as we have the time and space. For example, starting with *the picture of* . . . , we can put a simple NP into the position of '. . .', and get something like *the picture of the house*, or we can put a more complex NP into that position.

(29) a. the picture of the house
     b. the picture of the house on the corner
     c. the picture of the house on the corner in the town
     d. the picture of the house on the corner in the town on the edge of the city near the river with the bridge over the path by the dock at . . .

   Remember when we said in File 1.4 that linguistic rules are productive? This is an excellent example of what we meant. By continuing to follow the rules, you can continue to generate more and more grammatical forms.

   The type of relationship between the categories of a language that we have just illustrated is called **recursion**. Recursion is a fundamental property of human language, and it is part of what gives language its capacity to express an unlimited number of ideas with limited resources: we can use the same structures over and over again and embed them inside one another to make long and complex but still interpretable sentences. The only limit on recursion is our capacity to keep track of the complexities in our memory. The communication systems of other species lack recursion. They therefore lack the infinite expressive power of human language. (See File 14.1.)

Tests for Structure and Constituency

5.5.1 Identifying Constituents

The claim that sentences have structure means that they are made up of discrete parts, which we call **constituents.** Each part is either an individual word or a phrase of a particular category, and, as we have seen, constituents must be arranged in a particular way in order to form a sentence. The identification of structure is an important aspect of modern linguistics. Another is that sentences are related to one another by virtue of the fact that they share certain properties of their structure. For example, consider the following two sentences.

(1) a. Robin was planning to see *the entire Lord of the Rings Trilogy* this coming Saturday.
    b. Lee was planning to see *it* too.

The first sentence expresses the object in the form of a noun phrase, while the second sentence expresses the object in the form of a pronoun, which refers to the same thing. The structure of the two sentences is otherwise essentially the same. The fact that we can let a single word carry out the same function in sentence (1b) that an entire phrase carries out in (1a) suggests that we are correct to treat *the entire Lord of the Rings Trilogy* as a discrete unit of (1a). Of course, our intuitions about the meaning may also tell us that *the entire Lord of the Rings Trilogy* is a phrase. But some people do not have strong intuitions about constituency, and even when we do, our intuitions do not always work. In those cases, we can gain some additional insight into the structure by performing various constituency tests.

    There are four types of tests for structure that we will introduce in this file.

5.5.2 Substitution

The first constituency test is **substitution,** which we have already seen in (1). In a substitution test, we take a single word or a simple phrase and substitute it for a longer phrase, thereby showing that the longer phrase is in fact a single unit. For NPs, a good substitute is a pronoun, like *he, she,* or *it.* For VPs expressing actions, a useful substitute is *do so.*

(2) a. Robin wants to visit Paris. I managed to do so last summer. (*do so* = 'visit Paris')
    b. We expect to run the Boston Marathon this year, although doing so will probably make us sick. (*doing so* = 'running the Boston Marathon')

In (2a) we conclude that *visit Paris* is a constituent, and in (2b) we conclude that *to run the Boston Marathon* is a constituent. However, we cannot replace elements that are not constituents with a pronoun or with a phrase like *do so.* An example of a case in which the test fails is given in (3).

(3) a. I looked for the key to the safe. Jane looked for it, too. (*it* = 'the key to the safe')
    b. I looked for the key to the safe. *Jane looked for it to the safe, too. (*it* = 'the key')

The data in (3) show that *the key* is not a constituent of *looked for the key to the safe,* although *the key to the safe* is a constituent.

5.5.3 Deletion

A second test for structure is **deletion,** in which we simply leave out a phrase. There are certain constructions that allow deletion; here is an example:

(4) Robin was planning to see the entire Lord of the Rings this coming Saturday, and Lee was, also.

What does *Lee was, also* mean? It means, in this case, that Lee was planning to see the entire Lord of the Rings this coming Saturday. What is missing is the VP *planning to see the entire Lord of the Rings this Saturday.* In general, a VP can be deleted when there is an identical VP in the discourse that can supply its meaning. We call this **ellipsis.**

Ellipsis can apply to a complex VP in a number of ways. Consider the examples in (5). We have represented the material deleted by ellipsis by drawing a line through it.

(5) Robin was planning to see the entire Lord of the Rings this coming Saturday, and
    a. Lee was ~~planning to see the entire Lord of the Rings this coming Saturday~~ also.
    b. Lee was planning to ~~see the entire Lord of the Rings this coming Saturday~~ also.
    c. Lee was planning to ~~see the entire Lord of the Rings~~ on Wednesday.

Since the original sentence contains several VPs, one inside the other, ellipsis can pick out any of these. We illustrate the structure with a tree as shown in (6); the VPs are circled. (We use *XP* for a phrasal category that we have not introduced.)

(6)

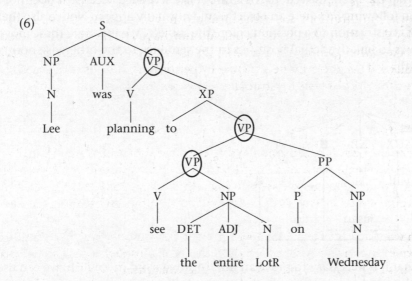

Notice that for any complete VP indicated in (5), we can find a way to delete that VP and be left with one of the grammatical sentences in (4). The same is not true for groups of words that are not constituents. For example, what would happen if we tried to ellipse only the group of words *planning to see?*

(7) *Lee was ~~planning to see~~ the entire Lord of the Rings this coming Saturday also.

The result, as seen in (7), would be considered ungrammatical by many; at the least, it is highly anomalous. We can therefore conclude that although the three words *planning, to,* and *see* are adjacent, they do not form a constituent.

5.5.4 Movement

The third type of test is **movement**. A good illustration of movement is given by the following two sentences:

(8) a. Susan will do *whatever she wants to do*.
    b. *Whatever she wants to do*, Susan will do.

The object of the first *do* is *whatever she wants to do*. Normally an object follows the verb in English, as in (8a). But under certain conditions of emphasis or other aspects of discourse,an object (and other constituents) may appear at the beginning of the sentence, as in (8b). We call the positioning of a constituent in a position other than where it would normally go movement. This particular type of movement is called 'topicalization.' The fact that we can move *whatever she wants to do* in (8) indicates that it is a constituent.

5.5.5 Answers to Questions

There are constructions in some languages where movement is required. Suppose we want to ask about the object of *do* in (6). We would use the interrogative word *what,* but we would not put the object *what* after the verb; we would move it to the front of the sentence.

(9) What will Susan do?

We say that *what* has been 'moved' to the front of the sentence because it does not appear in the position following *do* where an object would normally appear. Notice also that *will* is moved in this construction to a position before the subject. We illustrate these movements by using arrows to link the actual positions in the sentence to the otherwise normal positions, as in (10).

(10)

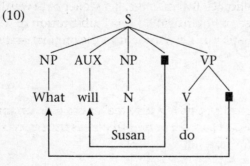

Given that it is necessary to move an interrogative word in English, we can use interrogative words to test for structure. First, we substitute an interrogative word for what we think is a constituent, and then we determine whether the movement of the interrogative word produces a good sentence. For any given sentence, there are a number of question word substitutions that will work: that is, substitutions that will produce grammatical questions. Examples are given in (11) and (12). For each, we go through the steps of performing the test one at a time. The section being replaced by the question word is underlined. In each case, we have also shown what the answer to the question would be, because it is important to see not only that the question seems grammatical on its own, but also that it is a question to which there is a grammatical answer. After all, the point of using questions in language is generally to receive answers, so this is something important to consider. Because of the nature of the test that we are performing, the answer to the question must be the constituent that we have replaced, because that is what the question is supposed to be asking about.

(11) a. Original S: Lee will send the children <u>home</u>.
     b. Substitute: Lee will send the children <u>where</u>.
     c. Move: Where will Lee send the children?
     d. Answer: Home.

(12) a. Original S: Lee will send <u>the children</u> home
     b. Substitute: Lee will send whom home
     c. Move: Whom will Lee send home?
     d. Answer: The children.

However, there are other substitution/movement processes that will not work: that is, ones that will not produce grammatical sentence/answer pairs.

(13) a. Original S: Lee will send <u>the children home</u>.
     b. Substitute: Lee will send <u>what</u>.
     c. Move: *What will Lee send?
     d. Answer: *The children home.

At a first glance, *What will Lee send?* in (13) may look like a perfectly good sentence. We can think of times that we might use that string of words as a question. For example, if everyone were planning on sending a piece of mail to Mrs. Lopez, someone could grammatically say, "Lucy will send a package. Lionel will send a letter. Layla will send a postcard. Leonard will send a bank statement. What will Lee send?" In that case, *What will Lee send?* is a well-structured sentence. However, the *What will Lee send?* in the context about Mrs. Lopez's mail has the wrong sort of meaning—because it has the wrong sort of structure—for the kind of substitution that we were trying to perform in (13). That is why it is also important to look at the answer to the question.

There is never a case where, in a conversation, someone could ask, "What will Lee send?" and another person could reply, "The children home" such that the second person would mean, 'Lee will send the children home.' By and large, if a sequence of words cannot be used as the answer to a question based on interrogative word substitution in some original sentence, then that group of words was not a constituent in the original sentence.

5.5.6 VP Topicalization

We will look at one final test for constituency; this test also makes use of a certain kind of movement. Consider the sentence *Robin will pass the exam*, which has the structure shown in (14).

(14)

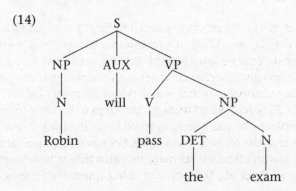

Under certain discourse circumstances, it is possible to move a VP to the front of a sentence, as illustrated by (15). The construction shown here is called **VP topicalization**.

(15) They said that Robin will pass the exam, and <u>pass the exam</u> Robin will.

The fact that the entire VP can appear in initial position confirms our intuition that it is a unit. Notice further that the same VP can be substituted for by *do so*, or it can be deleted by ellipsis, as shown in (16a, b).

(16) a. They said that Robin will pass the exam, and Robin will do so.
      b. They said that Robin will pass the exam, and Robin will ~~pass the exam~~.

If more than one test gives the same results, then we have strong confirmation that the structure is correct.

Word Order Typology

5.6.1 Subjects, Objects, and Verbs

The study of **typology** looks at ways in which the grammars of various languages are similar to and different from one another. In a declarative sentence in English (one that makes a statement by saying that a subject has some property or some relationship that it holds), the subject precedes the verb, and the object follows it, e.g., [[*the cat*] [*chased*] [*the mouse*]]. English is referred to as an SVO language (where S refers to subject, V to verb, and O to object). Only 35% of the world's languages display this same word order, however. Some place the verb at the beginning of the sentence, followed by the subject, then the object, and are thus labeled VSO languages. Irish, Arabic, and Welsh are among the 19% of the world's languages that have this word order. VOS languages, which place the verb first, followed by the object then the subject, also exist, although they are quite rare. (Only 2% of all languages are VOS types.) The most prevalent type of word order is SOV, where the subject precedes the object, but the verb is placed at the end of the sentence. Forty-four percent of the world's languages are SOV languages, including Russian and Turkish. A little quick addition will reveal that these numbers add up to 100. You may also notice that OSV and OVS haven't been discussed, and you may conclude that such languages don't exist. For a long time, that is what was believed. It turns out that there are object-first languages, but they are even rarer than VOS languages: there are only a couple of exemplars of each variety. In addition, there are languages, such as Dyirbal, an Australian aboriginal language, in which the normal order of subject, verb, and object is remarkably free. (Such "free word order" languages have been included in the statistics above according to their "preferred" word order.) Clearly there is no set of word order rules that is superior or that is valid for all languages.

5.6.2 Headedness

An interesting fact about word order typology is that, within phrasal categories, languages tend to place the head of the phrase either consistently before its modifiers and complements or after its modifiers and complements. The **head** of a phrase is the central, obligatory member of the phrase (e.g., an NP always has an N). Phrasal categories are typically named after their heads, so the head of an NP is N, the head of a PP is P, the head of an ADJP is ADJ, etc. (But note that although V is usually the head of VP, when AUX occurs in a VP, it is the head of the VP, which isn't contradictory, since AUXs are also a subtype of verb.) The other constituents in phrases are either modifiers, which serve to modify the meaning of the head, or complements, which are other constituents that typically occur with the head. Languages can be roughly classified as either **head-initial** or **head-final**. Some head-nonhead ordering combinations are given in (1).

There is a special term for a "preposition" that appears in a head-final language: *postposition*. Postpositions usually serve the same function as prepositions but appear after the noun phrase. So in (1c), the capital P can stand for either "preposition" or "postposition." In a language such as Japanese, which is generally SOV (and therefore head final since the

(1)

Type of Phrase	Head-Initial Languages		Head-Final Languages	
	Head	Nonhead	Nonhead	Head
a. VP	V_t[1]	(object) NP	(object) NP	V_t
b. VP	AUX	VP	VP	AUX
c. PP	P	NP	NP	P
d. NP	NP	relative clause	relative clause	NP
e. NP	N	possessive NP	possessive NP	N
f. NP	N	ADJP	ADJP	N

verb comes after its complement, the object), the grammatical relationship between words is often expressed using postpositions. See the exercises in File 5.7 for some examples of postpositions in Hindi and Japanese.

It is important to note that a particular language does not necessarily display the ordering relations of one of these types exclusively, even though the majority of the world's languages do exhibit consistent ordering relations across phrasal categories. English, for example, has mostly head-initial characteristics, but it also has some head-final characteristics. Specifically, English has the head-initial characteristics in (1a)–(1e) above, but it also possesses the head-final characteristics (1e) and (1f). Examples are given in (2).

(2)

Head-Initial Features	Head-Final Features
a. eat apples	
b. may go	
c. at home	
d. man who left	
e. cover of the book	e. the book's cover
	f. good food

A language is classified as head-initial or head-final according to the majority of its ordering relations with phrases. Once again, the distinction between head-initial and head-final languages is a significant one because most languages tend to lean strongly one way or the other.

---

[1]V_t designates a transitive verb, a verb that takes an object.

Practice

File 5.1—Basic Ideas of Syntax

Exercises

1. Refer to the *Frank and Ernest* cartoon at the beginning of the chapter and answer the following questions:

    i. Which of the following aspects of syntax is missing from the caveman's speech? (If you believe that more than one are missing, choose the one whose absence you think is most significant.) Defend your answer.

    - word order
    - lexical categories
    - agreement
    - hierarchical structure and constituency

    ii. Rewrite the caveman's utterance so that it is a grammatical sentence of English. Do your best to capture the idea that you think the comic's author is trying to convey. (Be sure that your rewrite uses all and only the words that are printed in the strip!)

    iii. How did you know how to rearrange the words? That is, what specific sorts of knowledge did you have to draw on from your mental grammar?

    iv. Consider the dash that is written in the middle of the utterance. What is its purpose? In speech we obviously don't have dashes (or periods, or any other punctuation) between sentences. Why is the dash necessary in this comic strip while it is not necessary in speech?

    v. There's an exclamation point with the second group of words. What if there had been a question mark instead? How would you have organized the words differently?

2. Each of the following sentences or phrases is ambiguous. State informally but as precisely as you can what the two meanings of each are. Then draw brackets showing how words group together in order to create each of the two meanings, showing a plausible structure corresponding to each meaning.

    a. sleepy men and boys
    b. the old women's shoes
    c. (Humor columnist Dave Barry wrote: "Toni Summers sent in a magazine advertisement for DiGiorno Brand pastas and sauces making this appetizing promise. You can enjoy a gourmet meal in your sweat pants.") You can enjoy a gourmet meal in your sweat pants.

3. Make up four more sentences that are ambiguous in the same way that *Pat shot the soldier with a gun* is, using such words as *to, from, under, without,* and *on.*

Discussion Questions

4. The caveman in the *Frank and Ernest* cartoon at the beginning of the chapter seems to be claiming that he speaks a language without any syntax. Why is it impractical to believe that this comic represents a stage of language development that might have actually existed?

Activities

5. Take the following twelve words:

A   Across   And   Boy   Down   Hall   Large   The   The   Threw   Skunk   Walked

   i. Use all of the words in this list. Put the words into an order to create a possible sentence of English. Then do it again. And again. And again. And again. You may find it helpful to write the words down on a sheet of paper and then cut them apart so that you can physically move them into new orders.

   ii. There are 239,500,800 possible ways that these words can be ordered. Are all of them sentences? How do you know? (*Note:* An editor of this book, along with her students, managed to create 240 possible grammatical sentences using all and only these words before growing bored and stopping.)

   iii. Now share your five results with the results of several of your classmates. Compare the orders that you and your classmates put the words in. Did you all group them in the same ways?

   iv. If there are differences, what do these differences tell you?

   v. What things are similar among all of your results? What do the similarities tell you?

   vi. Are there certain groups of words that tend to appear together, even in sentences that mean very different things? What are examples? What does this tell you?

   vii. Are there groups of words that seem never to appear together in a particular order? What are examples? What does this tell you?

   viii. Are there certain kinds of words that seem to fit into the same kinds of locations within the sentences? What does this tell you?

   ix. What does this activity tell you about the linguistic properties of discreteness and productivity? (See File 1.4.)

File 5.2—How Sentences Express Ideas

Exercises

6. Pick out all of the verbs in the following list whose subject is an AGENT. Explain your choices.

hit, buy, lose, see, trip, receive, hallucinate, rain, explode, destroy

7. Pick out all of the verbs in the following list whose object is a PATIENT. Explain your choices.

hit, buy, see, receive, destroy, discuss, paint, erase, enter, remember

8. Refer to the *Frank and Ernest* cartoon at the beginning of the chapter. Take just the second group of words, "should now invent we syntax."

   i. Write down all of the ways that you could arrange these words in order to make grammatical sentences of English.

   ii. Do all of the word orders you suggest create sentences that mean the same thing?

   iii. What does this tell you about the importance of word order in establishing roles in a language like English?

Discussion Questions

9. Consider the following four sentences:

- Marsha ate ice cream with a friend.
- Marsha ate ice cream with a cherry.
- Marsha ate ice cream with a spoon.
- Marsha ate ice cream with pleasure.

    i. These four sentences are very similar in many ways. However, it is likely that you interpret them very differently. Why do you get different kinds of interpretations for each? (That is, what is it about the noun phrases at the end of each sentence that tells you to interpret that sentence the way you do?)

    ii. Explain the differences in the interpretations that you assign to these sentences by appealing to the idea of roles.

    iii. What does your answer to part (ii) tell you about the word *with* and its relationship to role assignment?

    iv. Is there any one role assignment that you could assign to all four noun phrases to get a possible (if highly implausible) meaning for each sentence? Which role assignments come closest?

File 5.3—Lexical Categories

Exercises

10. Look at the example sentences in (4)–(12) in File 5.3. Identify the lexical category of each underlined word in both sentences that it is used in.

11. For each of the following sentences, identify the lexical category for each of the words in boldface. Remember that a word's lexical category should be identified based on how it is used in a sentence.

    a. The zoo owns some very funny **lions.** *[open noun]*

    b. The lion cubs are **fierce** for their age. *[Adj]*

    c. They broke the gate to their cage **from** its hinges. *[prep]*

    d. The cage was **empty.** *[Adj]*

    e. Can **you** guess where the lions went? *[pronoun]*

    f. They left the zoo **and** went into Central Park. *[conjunction]*

    g. The lions **eagerly** chased the pigeons. *[Adverb]*

    h. The pigeons flew **into** the trees. *[prep]*

    i. An angry lion never **chases** a pigeon. *[transitive verb]*

    j. The happy lions **love** to chase pigeons. *[verb ← transitive]*

    k. Their **love** of pigeons is greater than my love of peanut butter.

    l. No other love is greater than **my** love of peanut butter.

    m. The zookeepers **should** fix the lions' cage. *[modal aux]*

Discussion Questions

12. Consider the nature of what it means to be a function word and what it means to be a content word. Based on the natures of these two groups, why might you expect that content words are members of open lexical categories while function words are members of closed lexical categories?

File 5.4—Phrase Structure

Exercises

13. Refer to the *Frank and Ernest* cartoon at the beginning of the chapter. The caveman suggests that they need to invent syntax, but some of what he says reveals that he already has access to some word order rules. Which **single** word in his utterance reveals one of the rules of English word order? Which phrase structure rule or word ordering rule of English does this one word represent?

14. Refer to the sentences in Exercise 11. Copy the sentences and underline all of the noun phrases. We'll do one as an example. Remember that sometimes one noun phrase can be embedded inside another. So, in the example below, *the lions* is a noun phrase on its own, but *the habitat for the lions* is also a noun phrase.

    Example: The habitat for the lions needs to be repaired!

15. Draw a tree structure diagram for each of the following phrases:

    a. the dog
    b. under the bridge
    c. fell into the pond
    d. drifted slowly under the bridge
    e. this silly picture of Pat

16. Draw a tree structure diagram for each of the following sentences:

    a. Pat loves Robin passionately.
    b. Pat pushed the stubborn horse into the barn.
    c. Robin talked to the manager over the phone.
    d. Robin yelled angrily at the manager from Ohio.
    e. Lee bought a nice picture of the unicorn from Robin.

17. Translate each of the following statements into phrase structure rules:

    a. A verb phrase may consist of a verb followed by a sentence (as in *I think [that it is raining]* where *I* is an NP, *think* is a verb, and *that it is raining* is the sentence that joins with *think* to form the VP).
    b. An adjective phrase (AP) may consist of an adjective followed by a prepositional phrase (as in *angry [at the government]*).
    c. A verb phrase may consist of a verb followed by a noun phrase followed by *to* followed by a verb phrase (as in *expected Sandy to call*).

18. Draw the tree that expresses each of the following statements:

    a. *a tree* is a noun phrase composed of the determiner *a* followed by the noun *tree*.
    b. *two pictures of the dog* is a noun phrase. It is composed of a determiner followed by the noun *pictures*, followed by the prepositional phrase *of the dog*. This prepositional phrase is composed of the preposition *of* followed by the noun phrase *the dog*. The noun phrase *the dog* is composed of the determiner *the* followed by the noun *dog*.

19. Explain how the rule for coordination is another instance of recursion. Illustrate your explanation with a couple of examples.

20. Write examples of sentences that use conjunctions to conjoin each of the following:

    a. nouns
    b. NPs
    c. VPs   *on both sides*
    d. PPs
    e. Ss   *Same*
    f. Adjs
    g. Advs

File 5.5—Tests for Structure and Constituency

Exercises

21. Place brackets around all of the constituents (other than the individual words) in each of the following:

    a. Pat shot the soldier.
    b. with a gun
    c. Leslie said it rained.
    d. Kim looks angry about something.

22. List all of the NPs in the following sentence, and justify each of your answers by showing how that NP can be substituted for by an appropriate pronoun. (Be careful: there are some groups of words that look as though they could be NPs, but when you actually try to perform a substitution, you will discover that they are not.)

    • Joe and the large geese with striped feathers speedily raced the yellow duck for a shiny prize.

23. Using pronoun substitution, show that the underlined phrases in the following sentences are NPs:

    a. My neighbor's dog was barking all night at <u>the birds</u>.
    b. <u>My neighbor's dog</u> ate the groceries that my neighbor had put on <u>the kitchen table</u>.

24. Using substitution, deletion, and VP topicalization, construct examples that justify the three VPs in the structure in (6) from File 5.5.

25. Give the sentence that results when topicalization is applied to the underlined phrase in each of the following sentences:

    a. My neighbor always mows the lawn <u>right after it rains</u>.
    b. I would never give <u>a book like that</u> to my mother as a gift.
    c. I would never give a book like that <u>to my mother</u> as a gift.

File 5.6—Word Order Typology

Exercises

26. Following are some example phrases from Hindi (a language spoken in northern India), French, and Japanese. First examine the constituent structure of each sentence or phrase.

    i. What are the constituents of each sentence; what are the constituents of each phrase?

ii. How are the relationships between the words in a phrase indicated: by word order alone, or by pre- or postpositions?

iii. Determine whether the language is SVO, VSO, VOS, or SOV.

iv. Based on the sentences given, classify the three languages into the two language types, head-initial or head-final, with respect to each of the ordering relationships.

Hindi

a. [ram-ne   seb   kʰaːja]
Ram   apple   ate
'Ram ate an apple.'

b. [ram   angrezi   bol   səkta   hɛ]
Ram   English   speak   able   is
'Ram can speak English.'

c. [larke-ne   tʃari-se   kutte-ko   maːra]
boy   stick-with   dog   hit
'The boy hit the dog with a stick.'

d. [dʒis   larke-ne   kutte-ko   maːra   vo   mera   bhai   hɛ]
which   boy   dog   hit   he   my   brother   is
'The boy who hit the dog is my brother.'

e. [ram-ki   bahin]
Ram's   sister
'Ram's sister'

f. [safed   pʰul]
white   flower
'white flower'

French

g. Jean   a   mangé   une   pomme.
[ʒã   a   mãʒe   yn   pom]
Jean   has   eaten   an   apple
'Jean ate an apple.'

h. Jean   peut   parler   anglais.
[ʒã   pø   paʁle   ãŋgle]
Jean   can   speak   English
'Jean can speak English.'

i. Le   garçon   a   frappé   le   chien   avec   un   baton.
[lə   gaʁsõ   a   fʁape   lə   ʃjɛ̃   avɛk   ɔ̃   batõ]
the   boy   has   hit   the   dog   with   a   stick
'The boy hit the dog with a stick.'

j. Le   garçon   qui   a   frappé   le   chien   est   mon   frère.
[lə   gaʁsõ   ki   a   fʁape   lə   ʃjɛ̃   e   mõ   fʁɛʁ]
the   boy   who   has   hit   the   dog   is   my   brother
'The boy who hit the dog is my brother.'

k. la   soeur   de   Jean
[la   sœʁ   də   ʒã]
the   sister   of   Jean
'Jean's sister'

l. une   fleur   blanche
   [yn   fløʁ   blɑ̃ʃ]
   a   *flower*   *white*
   'a white flower'

Japanese

m. [Taroː-ga   ringo-o   tabeta]
    Taro   *apple*   *ate*
    'Taro ate an apple.'

n. [Taroː-wa   ɛigo-ga   hanaseru]
    Taro   *English*   *speak-can*
    'Taro can speak English.'

o. [sono   otokonoko-wa   boː-de   inu-o   butta]
    that   *boy*   *stick-with*   *dog*   *hit*
    'That boy hit the dog with a stick.'

p. [inu-o butta   otokonoko-wa   wataʃi-no   otoːto-da]
    dog   hit   *boy*   *my*   *brother-is*
    'The boy who hit the dog is my brother.'

q. [Taroː-no   imooto]
    Taro's   *sister*
    'Taro's sister'

r. [ʃiroi   hana]
    white   *flower*
    'white flower'

27. Tamil

Tamil is a language spoken in Southern India.

  a. The following are examples of word-by-word translations of Tamil PPs into English:

- *the tree on*   'on the tree'
- *the mountain from*   'from the mountain'

    i. If you had to guess the word order typology of this language using only these data, would you think it is head-final or head-initial? *Final*

    ii. Modify the phrase structure rule for English PPs to make them consistent with the structure of Tamil PPs. *PP→ NP P*

  b. The following are examples of word-by-word translations of Tamil VPs into English:

- *he is a fool that think* [*SOV*]   'think that he is a fool'
- *the earth is round that know* [*S O V*]   'know that the earth is round'

    i. Do these phrases show a head-final or a head-initial pattern? Is your answer here the same as it was in (a)i, or is it different? ~~Efnet~~ *Final   Same*

    ii. Modify the phrase structure rule for English VPs to make it consistent with the structure of the corresponding Tamil VPs. *VP→ NP V*

  c. Based on what you know about Tamil from the previous two problems, show what a word-by-word translation from Tamil to English phrases would look like for phrases meaning people from Boston and the mouse in the barn.

    ~~Bosto ppl from~~ *in the barn mouse*

    from boston ppl

Discussion Questions

28. Refer once again to the *Frank and Ernest* cartoon at the beginning of the chapter. So far, we have been assuming that the speaker has not been using any particular set of syntactic rules (partly because that is what he seems to be trying to say!). However, is it possible that he is merely using some other word order typology to organize the sentences he is uttering? Explain why you think so.

CHAPTER
6

Semantics

FILE 6.0

What Is Semantics?

In semantics, the focus of study is on meaning: the meaning of individual words as well as meanings of phrases and sentences. Semantics endeavors to answer such questions as the following: What are the components of word meanings? How do word meanings relate to one another? How do the meanings of discrete words combine to create more complex meanings (in phrases and sentences)? Why does one string of words mean one thing while a similar string of words may mean something very different? How can a single string of words mean more than one thing? When can two distinct sentences mean the same thing? Moreover, semantics asks, "What is meaning, anyway?"

Contents

==

An Overview of Semantics

6.1.1 Two Aspects of Linguistic Meaning

Semantics is the subfield of linguistics that studies meaning in language. Semantics deals with the meanings of words as well as the meanings of phrases and sentences; this chapter will address each of these types of meaning. Before we address either, though, it is important to consider what we mean by *meaning*. Meaning is a multifaceted phenomenon.

First, language communicates information about the world around us: we can refer to people, places, concrete objects, and abstract ideas (e.g., Queen Elizabeth, Alaska, bicycles, and love). We can also assert that these things have certain properties or stand in certain relationships to one another (such as the properties 'is purple' and 'is singing' or the relations 'is a brother of,' 'is located at,' and 'strongly dislikes'). By using sentences of a language, one person can expand another person's knowledge of the world—from simple facts, like who is sitting in the next chair, to complex facts about astrophysics. A language is thus a system of symbols that are used to represent objects and states of affairs in the world. One aspect of linguistic meaning, then, is the **information content** of language: what language tells us about the real world. In other words, one aspect of meaning is the relationship between the symbols that we use to refer to things and the actual things or states of affairs that we use these symbols to describe. We will term the relationship that holds between language and these things or states of affairs **reference.**

Second, meanings are things that are grasped, stored, and assembled in the minds of the speakers and hearers who use language. Recall from File 1.2 that linguistic meaning does not exist independently outside the minds that process language. Therefore, meaning is also a cognitive and psychological phenomenon. We will term the mental representation that we have of what a word or phrase means its **sense.**[1] Sense will tell us, among other things, about how the meanings of various words in our mental lexicons are related to each other.

These two aspects of meaning—information content and mental representation, i.e., reference and sense—are complementary. We need both. The ability to store linguistic constructs in our minds would be less useful if we couldn't use them to identify and talk about things in the world. By the same token, language would not be possible without the mental ability to abstract information about things in the world and integrate our perceptions of them with our other thoughts and observations. We will not have fully understood the phenomenon of meaning until we understand both of these two aspects. Therefore, we will need to take each into account as we proceed to examine the meanings of words, phrases, and sentences.

---

[1]Often this notion of a word's meaning is instead referred to by the term *intension,* in order to reserve *sense* for a somewhat different meaning; for the purposes of this text, however, we will adopt the word *sense.*

6.1.2 Lexical and Compositional Semantics

A major division in semantics, which cuts across the distinction drawn above, is between **lexical semantics,** the meanings of words, and **compositional semantics,** the way in which word meanings and syntactic structure combine to determine the meanings of phrases and sentences. This four-way split is illustrated in (1).

(1) Ways of studying meaning in language

Lexical Semantics and Reference	Compositional Semantics and Reference
Lexical Semantics and Sense	Compositional Semantics and Sense

Lexical semantics and compositional semantics are fundamentally different because the number of words in a language (the domain of lexical semantics) is finite, while the number of sentences (the domain of compositional semantics) is not. We tend to notice when we hear a new word for the first time, and we may or may not be able to guess what it means. But we generally don't notice when a sentence or its meaning is new to us. The reason is that we learn word meanings individually and independently, but we don't "learn" individual sentence meanings—we simply compute them unconsciously by compositional rules.

Various ways of thinking about both lexical and compositional semantics will be presented throughout the rest of this chapter. In each case, we will want to think about both reference and sense: about the information content as well as the cognitive reality that supports that content.

Lexical Semantics:
The Meanings of Words

6.2.1 Dictionary Definitions

When we think about the term *meaning,* we almost always think of word meanings. We are all familiar with looking words up in dictionaries, asking about the meaning of a word, and discussing or even arguing about exactly what a certain word means. The aim of this file is not to discuss what individual words mean, however. Rather, we will endeavor to pin down word meaning (lexical meaning) itself. That is, what exactly does it mean for a word to mean something?

We will look at several different approaches, but let's begin with a familiar one: using the dictionary to define word meanings. Most people tend to think of definitions in terms of dictionary entries. Dictionaries encapsulate words' definitions in terms of other words, making them easy to print in books, easy to access, and relatively easy to memorize.

Is it the case, though, that a word's meaning is just whatever a dictionary says it is? In our culture, where the use of dictionaries is widespread, many people accept dictionaries as authoritative sources for word meanings. Therefore, people may feel that the dictionary definition of a word more accurately represents the word's meaning than does an individual speaker's understanding of the word. But keep in mind that people who write dictionaries arrive at their definitions by studying the ways speakers of the language use words. A new word or definition could not be introduced into a language by way of being printed in a dictionary. Moreover, entries in dictionaries are not fixed and immutable; they change over time and from edition to edition as people come to use words differently. Dictionaries model usage: not the other way around. There simply is no higher authority on word meaning than the community of native speakers of a language.

Therefore, if we are to understand what words mean, we cannot rely on a dictionary. Rather, we must turn our attention to how words are used. In order to do this, we will consider both words' reference (the relationship that holds between words and the world) and words' sense (the notion of their meaning that we have in our minds).

6.2.2 Reference

As mentioned in File 6.1, language is used to talk about things in the world. Many words can be used to stand for or refer to actual objects or relations in the world. It therefore seems reasonable to consider the actual thing a word refers to—that is, its **referent**—to be one aspect of the word's meaning. According to this theory, a word like *Parthenon* will have as its meaning the specific thing in the world named by that word: in this case, a particular temple to the goddess Athena in Athens. It is relatively easy to discuss reference when we're talking about proper nouns. The referent of *White House* is that building in Washington, DC, where the president of the United States lives, and the referent of *Hawaii* is that group of islands in the Pacific Ocean that together compose the fiftieth state of the U.S.A. Therefore, if someone uses the word *White House,* it is a good bet that they **mean** the president's home, and if they use the word *Hawaii,* it is a good bet that they **mean** the island state. In

235

fact, it's hard to imagine a situation in which someone could use the word *Hawaii* and not intend to refer to the island state.

When it comes to common nouns, the notion of reference as meaning can be a bit more complex. Let's use the common noun *woman* as our example. Just as when we use the word *Hawaii*, when we use the word *woman*, we generally intend to refer to something in the world. In (1), for example, the referent of *woman* is that particular individual who was wearing the orange dress.

(1) On the bus yesterday, I met a woman in an orange dress named Judy.

Does that indicate that the meaning of *woman* in general is 'the person in an orange dress whom the speaker met on the bus'? Of course not. In this way, *woman* differs from *Hawaii*. The word *woman* can be used to refer to a great many individuals in the world. It has **variable reference**. For example, sentence (2) uses *woman* to refer to a completely different individual than (1) did. In (2), *woman* **refers** to Sally Ride, but we wouldn't want to say that *woman* **means** 'Sally Ride.'

(2) The first woman in outer space was Sally Ride.

Most everyone will agree that *woman* has the same meaning in (1) and (2), even though it is referring to a different individual in each case. It can be used to refer to many other women, too, because there are many women in the universe: Sally Ride and someone in an orange dress don't even begin to cover the spectrum of women. Think about it this way: there is some very large set of women in the universe, and the word *woman* has the ability to pick out some individual from that set to refer to. Critically, though, *woman* cannot pick out something that isn't in that set: you can't use *woman* to refer to a pine tree or a bicycle. According to the theory of reference, then, a common noun's meaning is determined by the set of all items that that word can be used to refer to. This idea is represented pictorially in (3): there are many things in the universe, but *woman* can be used to refer only to things in the circle, which is the set of women. Every common noun has its own set (its own circle) of things that it can refer to. (The same is true of many common noun phrases.)

In other words, if you know what a word means, then you know what things it can be used to refer to.[1] While there are thousands upon thousands of referents for the word *woman*, there are relatively fewer referents for *zebra* and even fewer still for the phrase *past president of the United States*. But, by knowing what these expressions mean, you know what they can and can't refer to.

So far we have considered reference only with regard to nouns; these cases are the most straightforward. It is possible, however, to talk about reference with respect to other kinds of words as well. For example, we could say that a verb like *jump* is a word that can refer to any individual in a set of objects as well: namely, the set of things that jump (that is, the set of things that spring off the ground under their own force, which happens to be the activity that we call "jumping"). Likewise we could say that an adjective like *purple* is a word that can refer to any individual in the set of objects that are purple (that is, the set of objects that reflect wavelengths of light between about 400–450 nanometers, which happens to be

---

[1]It is important to keep in mind that a referent must be one **particular** person, object, or whatever. Take the common noun *dog*. By knowing what *dog* means, you can identify any object as being a possible referent of *dog* or not being a possible referent of *dog*. So far so good. Now take it one step further. If you were asked to supply a referent for dog, you could not merely say, "golden retriever" or "poodle." These are not referents for *dog;* they are kinds of dog. Identifying a referent of *dog* would require picking out one particular individual dog, e.g., "the fox terrier with the blue collar that lives next door to my great aunt."

(3) A visual representation of the set identified by *woman,* relative to all things in the universe

the part of the spectrum that we call "purple"). We will come back to exploring reference with regard to adjectives and verbs in File 6.5.

Is a word's meaning summed up by its reference? For example, can *past president of the United States* be defined merely by listing all of the individuals who are members of that set? This isn't a bad idea. Generally, if someone uses that phrase, she is intending to refer to some individual who is a member of that set. It becomes a little more complicated with a case like *dog,* but one could still imagine a very long list of all the dogs in the world, such that whenever a person uses the word *dog,* you know that she must be referring to some individual on that list. This conception of meaning is tempting, then, because it allows us to tie words directly to the situations in the world that we are using language to describe.

6.2.3 Drawbacks to the Theory of Meaning as Reference: Why We Need Sense

It would be a mistake, though, to think of reference as all there is to word meaning. To do so would tie meaning too tightly to the real world. If meaning were defined as the actual thing an expression refers to, what would we do about words for things that don't exist? There is simply no actual thing that the words *Santa Claus* or *unicorn* refer to, yet obviously these words are not meaningless. Language can be used to talk about fiction, fantasy, or speculation in addition to the real world, and any complete explanation of meaning must take this fact into account.

But even some sentences that are about the real world appear to present problems for the idea that an expression's meaning is just its reference. First, sometimes we use words in ways that don't refer to objects in the world. Have a look at (4) and (5).

(4) No woman has become president of the United States.

(5) Is there a platypus in the bathtub?

What are the referents of the words *woman* and *platypus* in these sentences? There are none; in these sentences, *woman* and *platypus* don't have reference. In (4) the speaker is describing a state of affairs in which explicitly there is no woman being referred to; in (5) the speaker is not aware of whether there might be a particular platypus to refer to or not. Nonetheless, (4) and (5) are both perfectly well-formed and sensible sentences of English in which *woman* and *platypus* seem to have their conventional meanings. A good theory of word meaning must be able to account for such facts.

Also, if meaning were the same as reference, then if two expressions referred to the same thing, they would have to mean the same thing. For instance, since the name *Bill Clinton* and the phrase *the winner of the 1996 U.S. presidential election* both refer to the same individual, we would have to conclude that they meant the same thing. It would then follow that one could be substituted for the other in a sentence without changing the meaning of the sentence as a whole. The following two sentences should therefore mean the same thing:

(6) a. Bill Clinton is married to Hillary Rodham Clinton.
    b. The winner of the 1996 U.S. presidential election is married to Hillary Rodham Clinton.

And indeed the sentences in (6) do seem to describe the same state of affairs. But look now at a sentence like (7a):

(7) a. Robin wanted to know if Bill Clinton was the winner of the 1996 U.S. presidential election.
    b. Robin wanted to know if Bill Clinton was Bill Clinton.

Try substituting *Bill Clinton* for *the winner of the 1996 U.S. presidential election* as in (7b). You will immediately notice that (7a) and (7b) don't mean the same thing at all.

From examples like these, we learn that reference cannot be all that there is to meaning. Certainly reference is important, but if reference were the only aspect of lexical meaning, we would not be able to address the problems above. Furthermore, we would run into even more trouble if we tried to step outside the realm of nouns and noun phrases, considering such words as *nonexistent, sometimes, either,* and *the:* what real-world entities could these words possibly refer to?

Fortunately, however, our minds store all kinds of information about words and what they mean in ways that do not tie directly to reference. Clearly our minds do not store lists of referents. You know what *past presidents of the United States* means whether or not you can name all of the members of that set; you know what *dog* means, but there is certainly no way that you have come in contact with—let alone remembered—the identity of every single one in the universe. Instead, our minds must store information about word meanings in some other way distinct from the notion of reference.

It is now time to turn our attention to sense: the meanings that words have in our minds independent from any actual objects that they might refer to in the real world. Sense is useful precisely because it allows us to address the problems we have seen in this section. Although *Bill Clinton* and *the winner of the 1996 U.S. presidential* election do have the same reference, they do not have the same sense. We will now consider several kinds of ways that our minds could store lexical meanings. As we go through them, think about how each would avoid some of the problems involved in classifying a word's meaning as only its reference.

6.2.4 Dictionary-Style Definitions

We have already determined that what we have in our minds does not reflect what is printed in the dictionary. We don't want to turn authority for determining word meaning over to the publishers of dictionaries, but maybe we should think about dictionary-**style** definitions. Perhaps the nature of a word's meaning is similar to what we might find in some idealized dictionary: a dictionary-style definition that defines words in terms of other words, but that also reflects the way that speakers of a language really use that word. This idea seems much more promising. We can envision an imaginary idealized dictionary that changes with the times, lists all the words in a language at a given time, and provides a verbal definition of each according to speakers' use of that word. Would this be an appropriate way to conceptualize word meanings? The answer is that we would still run into problems.

If a word's meaning were a dictionary-style definition, then understanding this meaning would involve understanding the meanings of the words used in its definition. But understanding the meanings of these words would have to involve understanding the meanings of the words in their definitions. And understanding these definitions would have to involve understanding the words they use, which, of course, would have to involve understanding even more definitions. The process would be never ending. There would be no starting point: no way to build word meaning out of some more basic understanding. Moreover, circularities would inevitably arise. For instance, one English dictionary defines *divine* as 'being or having the nature of a deity,' but defines *deity* as 'divinity.' Another defines *pride* as 'the quality of state of being proud,' but defines *proud* as 'feeling or showing pride.' Examples like these are especially graphic, but essentially the same problem would hold sooner or later for any dictionary-style definition. Furthermore, don't forget that to understand a definition would require understanding not only the content words, but also such common function words as *the, of, to,* and so on.

We must conclude that dictionaries are written to be of practical aid to people who already speak a language and that they cannot make theoretical claims about the nature of meaning. A dictionary entry doesn't explain the meaning of a word or phrase in terms of something more basic—it just gives paraphrases (gives you one lexical item for another). People can and do learn the meanings of some words through dictionary definitions, so it would be unfair to say that such definitions are completely unable to characterize the meanings of words, but it should be clear that dictionary-style definitions can't be all there is to the meanings of the words in a language. In other words, it may be useful for us to define words in terms of other words, but that type of definition cannot be the only way in which meanings are stored in our heads.

6.2.5 Mental Image Definitions

What other options are there? One possibility is that a word's meaning is stored in our minds as a **mental image.** Words often do seem to conjure up particular mental images. Reading the words *Mona Lisa,* for example, may well cause an image of Leonardo da Vinci's painting to appear in your mind. You may find that many words have this sort of effect. Imagine that someone asked you, "What does fingernail mean?" You would very likely picture a fingernail in your mind while you tried to provide the definition. Your goal would likely be trying to get your conversational partner to wind up with a mental image similar to your own. In some ways, mental image definitions seem more promising than did dictionary definitions, because, as the fingernail example shows, mental images are things that we really do have in our heads and that we do use in some way to conceptualize reality.

However, a mental image can't be all there is to a word's meaning any more than a dictionary-style definition could be. One reason is that different people's mental images may be very different from each other without the words' meanings varying very much from individual to individual. For a student, the word *lecture* will probably be associated with an image of one person standing in front of a blackboard, and it may also include things like the backs of the heads of one's fellow students. The image associated with the word *lecture* in the mind of a teacher, however, is more likely to consist of an audience of students sitting in rows facing forward. A lecture as seen from a teacher's perspective is actually quite a bit different from a lecture as seen from a student's perspective. Even so, both the student and the teacher understand the word *lecture* as meaning more or less the same thing, despite the difference in mental images. Likewise, *food* might conjure a different mental image for a pet store owner, a gourmet chef, and your little brother, but presumably all three think that it has roughly the same meaning. It's hard to see how words like *lecture* and *food* could mean essentially the same thing for different people if meanings were just mental images without any other cognitive processing involved.

Consider a similar example: most people's mental image for *mother* is likely to be an image of their own mother—and, of course, different mothers look quite different from one another—but certainly we all mean the same thing when we use the word. This example raises a second concern, though. If you hear the word *mother* in isolation, you may well picture your own mother. But if you hear the word in some context, like "Mother Teresa" or "the elephant's mother," you almost certainly do not picture your own mother! This shows that the mental image you form when you hear *mother* out of the blue is far from being all that the word is able to mean to you. The same is true of almost any word.

Here is a third problem. The default mental image associated with a word tends to be of a typical or ideal example of the kind of thing the word represents: a **prototype.** Often, however, words can be used to signify a wide range of ideas, any one of which may or may not be typical of its kind. For example, try forming a mental image for the word *bird*. Make sure that the image is clear in your mind before reading on.

If you are like most people, your mental image was of a small bird that flies, not of an ostrich or a penguin. Yet ostriches and penguins are birds, and any analysis of the meaning of the word *bird* must take this into account. It may be that the meaning of *bird* should also include some indication of what a typical bird is like, but some provision must be made for atypical birds as well.

A fourth, and much more severe, problem with this theory is that many words, perhaps even most, simply have no clear mental images attached to them. What mental image is associated in your mind, for example, with the word *forget*? How about the word *the* or the word *aspect*? *Reciprocity*? *Useful*? Only certain words seem to have definite images, but no one would want to say that only these words have meanings.

We conclude that, as with dictionary definitions, mental image definitions have some merit, because mental images are associated in some way with the words stored in our heads. But, as with verbal dictionary-style definitions, mental image definitions cannot be all there is to how we store meaning in our minds.

6.2.6   Usage-Based Definitions

We have considered and rejected two possibilities for what constitutes the sense of a word, because neither was quite right for the task. In fact, defining the sense of a word is quite difficult. We know when two words (such as *groundhog* and *woodchuck*) have the same sense and when (such as in the case of *groundhog* and *platypus*) they have different senses, but it is difficult to know precisely what in our minds tells us this information. We could simply gloss over the entire issue by saying that sense is some sort of a mental concept, but *concept* itself is rather vague. However, we will leave it as an open question, at this point, as to exactly what lexical sense is: it is a question that linguists, philosophers, and psychologists must continue to investigate.

What we indisputably know when we know a word, though, is when it is suitable to use that word in order to convey a particular meaning or grammatical relationship. If I want to describe a large, soft piece of material draped across a bed for the purpose of keeping people warm while they sleep, I know that I can use the word *blanket*. That doesn't necessarily mean that *blanket* is stored in my mind with the particular set of words just used in the previous sentence ("large soft piece of material . . ."): just that something about a particular set of circumstances tells me whether it is suitable to use that word. Moreover, when somebody else uses a word, I know what the circumstances must be like for them to have used it. This is true for content words like *blanket, bird,* and *reciprocity* as well as for function words like *the, if,* and *to.*

Thus, whatever form our mental representation of word meaning takes, one of the functions it serves is to tell us when we may use these words. A part of that knowledge must be how meanings of words relate to one another. This is the topic that will be considered in the next file.

Lexical Semantics: Word Relations

6.3.1 Word Meanings in the Lexicon

Lexical semantics deals with a language's **lexicon,** or the collection of words in a language. Of the many ways that lexical semantics can be studied, we will discuss two in this file: (a) classifying the semantic relationships that word meanings have with one another, and (b) componential analysis, which is a way of analyzing word meanings by dividing them into smaller parts. Both of these processes involve word meanings relative only to other word meanings, without particular attention to their contribution to reference or to the way they are processed mentally, although these elements cannot be left completely behind in any discussion of meaning! Primarily, though, we will be interested in the properties of items in the lexicon itself.

While it may seem at first glance that a language's lexicon is little more than a mishmash of unrelated words thrown together into a big "soup," nothing could be further from the truth. The lexicon is an intricately structured system, with a dense web of relationships among its members.

6.3.2 Meaning Relationships

There are many ways for two words to be related. In previous chapters we have already seen a number of ways: they may be phonologically related (e.g., *night/knight,* which share the same pronunciation), they may be morphologically related (e.g., *lift/lifted,* which both share the same stem), or they may be syntactically related (e.g., *write/paint,* which are both transitive verbs). There is yet another way two words can be related, and that is semantically. For instance, the word *pot* is intuitively more closely related semantically to the word *pan* than it is to the word *floor.* The reason, clearly, is that both *pot* and *pan* have meanings that involve being containers used for cooking, while *floor* does not. (We will later reach the conclusion that *pot* and *pan* are sister terms.)

What kinds of semantic relationships are there? Before we answer that question, let's decide on how we are going to talk about meanings. For simplicity's sake, we will characterize words' meanings using the formal notion of **sets,** as we did when discussing reference in File 6.2. A set is simply a collection of items of any sort. Some examples of sets are the set of red bicycles in North America, the set of whole numbers from 1 to 7, and the rather peculiar set consisting of just George Washington's horse, the original manuscript of Shakespeare's *Hamlet,* Buckingham Palace, and the remains of the *Titanic.* So you see, a set can contain anything at all. We will say that the meaning of any noun is the set of entities in the world which the noun describes. So the meaning of *dog* determines the set of dogs in the world. Likewise, an adjective's meaning will be the set of entities of which it is true, so the meaning of *red* determines the set of things which are red. Once we have defined these words in terms of sets, it becomes quite easy to see when the sets bear certain relationships to one another. When we see particular relationships between sets, then we will be able to define relationships between the words that name those sets.

a. Hyponymy. The first kind of semantic relation we can talk about is **hyponymy.** We can say that word X is a hyponym of word Y if in all possible scenarios, X's set is always contained in (is always a subset of) Y's set. For example, consider the words *poodle* and *dog.* Suppose that the current set of poodles includes three individuals: Froofroo, Princess, and Miffy. The current set of dogs will then include at least these three dogs (Froofroo, Princess, and Miffy) and possibly others as well (such as Fido the Labrador retriever, Spot the fox terrier, and Butch the bulldog).

A visual representation of these sets, a Venn diagram, appears in (1). The names of the sets—words in the lexicon—are in capital letters and underlined. The individual referents referred to by those words appear inside the circles in normal type. Ideally what would be inside these circles is not the printed names of particular dogs but rather the dogs themselves. That is, the sequence of visual characters <Spot> is not a dog! However, for reasons of cost, liability, and the proper treatment of animals, it is not possible for us to put actual dogs in the book, so you will have to pretend. (Note that, for simplicity's sake, there are sets that have not been included in the diagram: that is, Spot should be contained in a subset circle of dogs labeled "<u>FOX TERRIERS</u>" and so on. But the current representation will serve our purposes.)

(1) Visual representation of the hyponymous relation between *poodle* and *dog*

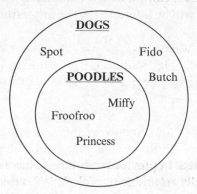

The set of poodles is contained within the set of dogs. It's clear from our knowledge of the meanings of these words that the same will be the case regardless of what particular dogs there are in the world: it is impossible to imagine a case in which there will be a poodle but there will not be any dogs. Hence we conclude that the word *poodle* is a hyponym of the word *dog.* Hyponymy can be viewed as the loss of specificity: when we say, "*poodle* is a hyponym of *dog,*" it involves moving from something more specific to something more general. In this case, we say that *poodle* is a **hyponym** and *dog* is a **hypernym.**

Hyponymous relationships stack very well. For example, *poodle* is a hyponym of *dog; dog* is a hyponym of *mammal; mammal* is a hyponym of *vertebrate; vertebrate* is a hyponym of *animal;* and so on. Any words that occur at the same level of any given hierarchy are called **sister terms.** For example, in the Venn diagram in (2), it is apparent that *sheep* and *cow* are sister terms. Note, however, that *cow* and *poodle* are not sister terms, since the set defined by *poodle* fits inside the set defined by *dog.*

b. Synonymy. A second kind of semantic relation, perhaps a more familiar one, is **synonymy.** Two words are synonymous if they have the same meaning. In the case of nouns and adjectives, two words are synonymous if the sets of entities they pick out are always the same. While it is difficult, perhaps impossible, to find pairs of words that are truly 100% interchangeable, pairs such as *couch/sofa, groundhog/woodchuck,* and *quick/rapid* come close. There is no entity that one would call a groundhog but not a woodchuck, and vice versa.

(2) Visual representation of sister terms and of nested hyponymous relations

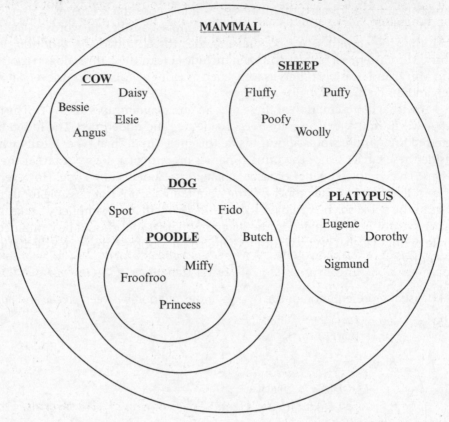

Similarly, for most people every couch is also a sofa, and every sofa is also a couch. Thus, identifying synonyms doesn't actually require finding words that are 100% interchangeable. We may choose to use one word over another for all kinds of reasons, including the speech community we are in (refer to File 10.1) and the exact connotation that we wish to convey. Rather, in identifying synonyms, we are looking for words with the same **extension:** words that can be used to refer only to members of the same set.

   c. Antonymy. A third kind of semantic relation is **antonymy.** The basic notion of antonymy is of being "opposite" in some sense. In order for two words to be antonyms of one another, they must have meanings that are related, yet these meanings must contrast with each other in some significant way.

   It turns out that the word *opposite* is fairly vague: there are actually several ways for a pair of words to be opposites, and each is distinct from the others. The most straightforward are **complementary** pairs. Given two words X and Y, if every entity in the world is either in X's set or in Y's set (or in neither) but not in both, and if saying "not X" generally implies Y, then X and Y form a complementary pair. In (3) are examples of complementary antonyms.

(3) Complementary antonyms
   a. married/unmarried
   b. existent/nonexistent
   c. alive/dead
   d. win/lose

For each of these pairs, everything is either one or the other, or else is neither. So, for example, a boulder is neither alive nor dead, but critically, it isn't both.

   Similar to complementary pairs of antonyms are **gradable** pairs. As with complementary pairs, in the case of gradable antonyms, everything must be one or the other or neither, but not both. However, in the case of gradable antonyms, saying "not X" does not imply "and therefore Y." For example, an individual may be rich, poor, or neither, but cannot be both. However, if you say of a person that he is not rich, it does not imply that he is poor. Examples of gradable antonyms appear in (4).

(4) Gradable antonyms
   a. wet/dry
   b. easy/hard
   c. old/young
   d. love/hate

Often you can identify gradable antonyms because there are words to describe states in between the two extremes; for example, *damp* means something like 'between being wet and being dry,' and *middle-aged* means something like 'between being old and being young.' Notice that there is no word that means 'between being married and being unmarried.' Also, it is possible to ask about the extent of a gradable antonym. Asking such questions with complementary antonyms is almost always semantically anomalous. Compare (5a) and (5b) with (5c) and (5d).

(5) a.   How old is he?
    b.   How hard was the test?
    c.   ! How alive is he?
    d.   ! How nonexistent is that unicorn?

The third kind of antonymy is seen in pairs of words called **reverses,** which are pairs such as those in (6).

(6) Reverses
   a. right/left
   b. inside/outside
   c. put together/take apart
   d. expand/contract
   e. ascent/descent

Reverses are pairs of words that suggest some kind of movement, where one word in the pair suggests movement that "undoes" the movement suggested by the other. For example, moving to the right undoes movement to the left, and putting something together undoes taking it apart.

Finally, there are **converses.** Converses have to do with two opposing points of view: for one member of the pair to have reference, the other must as well. Consider the examples in (7).

(7) Converses
   a. lend/borrow
   b. send/receive
   c. employer/employee
   d. over/under

In order for lending to take place, borrowing must take place as well. In order for there to be an employer, there must also necessarily be an employee. If an object is over something, then something must be under it. Note how the pairs in (7) thereby differ from the pairs in (6). It is possible, for example, for something to be inside a box without having anything outside the box.

6.3.3 Semantic Features

A second way of analyzing lexical meaning is to try to decompose word meanings into more basic parts. This process is called **lexical decomposition** or **componential analysis.** The idea is that most words have meanings that are "built up" out of simpler meanings. If we knew what basic meanings there were and which words incorporated which of those basic meanings into their own meanings, then we would be able to explain a number of intuitions we have about meaning. In doing such an analysis, we identify **semantic features** of words: conditions that must be met in order for a word to be appropriate to use.

For example, the words *mare, stallion, hen,* and *rooster* all have the common meaning of 'animal' in them. We could say that these four words share the common semantic feature ANIMAL. In addition, *mare* and *hen* share the common feature FEMALE, and similarly *stallion* and *rooster* share the feature MALE. One could add more features like HORSE and CHICKEN, so that the collection of features CHICKEN and MALE would constitute the semantic components of the word *rooster,* whereas the collection of features HORSE and FEMALE would constitute the semantic components of *mare.* Any time that we use a word yet deny some of the semantic features of that word, the sentence that we wind up with is semantically anomalous. Consider the cases in (8). What is anomalous in each case?

(8) a. ! That rooster by the fence is the nicest of the female chickens on the farm.
 b. ! The green glass bottles are completely colorless.
 c. ! I'm glad you finally got a chair for your new apartment; it's a shame you don't have any furniture yet, though!
 d. ! I never touched it! I have been poking it all afternoon, but I didn't touch it!

A rooster cannot be a female; something that is green must have color; if someone does not have any furniture, then he cannot have any chairs; in order to poke something, a person must touch it. All of these facts are true because of semantic features of the words *rooster, green, chair,* and *poke.*

Our second illustration of lexical decomposition is of causative verbs: verbs that denote actions involving a change in affairs in the world. Consider the following pairs of sentences, which use the intransitive verbs *boil, open, turn,* and *wake* in the sentences on the left and their transitive counterparts in the sentences on the right:

(9) a. The water boiled.   Robin boiled the water.
 b. The door opened.   Robin opened the door.
 c. The car turned.   Robin turned the car.
 d. Bill woke up.   Robin woke Bill.

We can analyze the meaning of the transitive verbs in terms of their intransitive counterparts: in *Robin boiled the water,* the transitive verb *boil* can be analyzed as X CAUSE Y to BOIL, where X and Y are noun phrases (in this case, X is *Robin* and Y is *the water*) and CAUSE and BOIL are the basic components of the meaning of the transitive verb *boil.* The other intransitive-transitive verb pairs can be similarly analyzed.

In the examples of causative constructions given above, the intransitive and transitive verb pairs are morphologically indistinguishable (they have the same phonological form), but this need not be the case. For example, most speakers of English would say that there is something contradictory about the sentence in (10).

(10) ! The sheriff killed Jesse, but Jesse is not dead.

Without looking closely at the meaning of *kill,* however, we cannot say explicitly what is wrong. As it turns out, *kill* might be best analyzed as 'X cause Y to become dead.' Since it is part of the meaning of *kill* that the killed individual is dead afterward, we can now explain why it is contradictory to say that Jesse was killed but not dead. Before decomposing the meaning of *kill,* we had no direct way to explain the clear contradiction in the sentence.

It turns out that investigating semantic features can also help uncover meaning relationships of the type mentioned above in Section 6.3.2. Hyponymy, especially, can be demonstrated in many cases by recourse to semantic features. For example, let us reconsider the pair of words *poodle* and *dog.* Above we reasoned that *poodle* must be a hyponym of (be more specific than) *dog,* because whenever we collect all available poodles and all available dogs, the set of poodles is always contained within the set of dogs. But we can also say that one of the semantic features of *poodle* is DOG. Whenever we use the word *poodle,* the meaning of *dog* is implicitly there. It is no wonder, then, that we can never find a poodle that is not a dog.

Thus, componential analysis provides us with yet one more tool for identifying relationships between lexical meanings and for describing lexical meanings themselves.

Compositional Semantics: The Meanings of Sentences

6.4.1 Truth Conditions

Thinking about what words mean is a critical part of semantics. Having a knowledge of lexical semantics, however, doesn't get us even halfway to being able to perform some of the complex communicative acts that we perform every day. If we could communicate only using individual words, then our language would lack the sort of productivity that allows us to communicate complex new ideas and that makes language uniquely human. Therefore, we must consider not only word meanings but phrase and sentence meanings as well. We will begin by exploring one theory for sentence meaning.

Recall from the discussion of reference in Files 6.1 and 6.2 that one aspect of meaning involves a relationship between language and the world. In this file, we will consider how a sentence relates to the world, rather than just how individual words relate to the world. That is, we will look at the relationship between a sentence and the situation that it describes.

Sentence meaning, even more than word meaning, may seem like a difficult concept to characterize; but perhaps it can be understood more clearly if we take an indirect approach and ask, "What do you know when you know what a sentence means?" Stop and think about this for a moment, using a particular example:

(1) Bill Clinton is asleep.

Obviously, to know what sentence (1) means is not the same as to know that Bill Clinton is asleep: any English-speaking person knows what the sentence means, but relatively few people know at any given time whether Bill Clinton is asleep or not. Rather, anyone who understands the sentence knows what the world would have to be like in order for it to be true. That is, anyone who knows a sentence's meaning knows the conditions under which it would be true; they know its **truth conditions**. You know, for example, that in order for the sentence *Bill Clinton is asleep* to be true, the individual designated by the words *Bill Clinton* must be in the condition designated by the words *is asleep*. Consider a second example.

(2) A unicorn named Charlie bought one dozen red roses.

Because you are a speaker of English, you also know the truth conditions of (2). Try to formulate them for yourself now.

The truth conditions of (2) are something like: a horse-like creature with a single horn growing out of its forehead that is called by a name, /tʃɑɹli/, purchased twelve (likely fragrant and thorned) flowers of a certain color denoted by the word *red*. In order for (2) to be true, these are the conditions that must obtain in the world. You know that (2) is false, because unicorns do not exist. Nonetheless, you know exactly what would have to have happened in order for (2) to be true: you know its truth conditions.

Thinking about truth conditions can tell us a lot about the way that we interpret sentence meanings; it can also help us to account for problems that we have run into in the past. Recall that in File 6.2, we had trouble accounting for why we could not simply replace one noun phrase with some other noun phrase that had the same referent. A modified version of the example sentences illustrating that problem appears below in (3).

(3) a. The winner of the 1996 U.S. presidential election was Bill Clinton.
   b. The winner of the 1996 U.S. presidential election was the winner of the 1996 U.S. presidential election.
   c. The winner of the 1996 U.S. presidential election was the man married to Hilary Rodham Clinton.

The sentence in (3a) is quite clear, and it is easy to state its truth conditions. However, in File 6.2 we were looking at meanings of noun phrases (like *the winner of the 1996 U.S. presidential election,* or *the man married to Hilary Rodham Clinton,* or *Bill Clinton*) only in terms of their referents. Since all three of the noun phrases in (3) have the same referent, we could not easily explain why (3a), (3b), and (3c) all had different meanings.

   Truth conditions give us the tool that we need to explain this difference. Since the conditions under which something qualifies as 'Bill Clinton' are different from the conditions under which something qualifies as 'the winner of the 1996 U.S. presidential election,' an explanation of meaning that includes the notion of truth conditions is also able to explain why the phrases *Bill Clinton* and *the winner of the 1996 U.S. presidential election* cannot be freely substituted for one another. Reference to the same individual is not enough to guarantee that two words or phrases have identical meanings. The name *Bill Clinton* directly picks out the individual Bill Clinton, once and for all. But *the winner of the 1996 U.S. presidential election* picks out whoever won in 1996; if the election had gone differently, it would pick out Bob Dole; if Ross Perot had run and been successful, it would pick out Perot; if one of the editors of this book had been eligible to run in that election and had done so and had been successful, then it would pick her out, and so on. Thus (3a) has different truth conditions than does (3b) because (3b) is necessarily true, whereas (3a) is true only because that happens to be the way that things worked out. Of course, the same is true for (3c). Had somebody different won the 1996 election, or had Hilary Rodham Clinton married somebody else, then (3c) would be false, but (3b) would still be true.

6.4.2 Possible Scenarios

When we think about ways the world could have been like but in fact isn't (e.g., the way the world would be if one of the editors of *Language Files* had won the 1996 presidential election), we are thinking about meaning in terms of "**possible scenarios.**" We have already seen how thinking somewhat loosely about possible scenarios can be helpful in thinking about what truth conditions are. We also need the idea of possible scenarios in order to describe the semantics of **counterfactual** sentences such as (4).

(4) If I had an apple, I would eat it right now.

Sentence (4) is analyzed as saying that in possible scenarios that are similar to the situation I am actually in, except that the proposition *I have an apple* is true, then *I will eat it right now* is true as well. In this case, the possible scenarios are implied to be incompatible with what is actually true (hence the term "counterfactual").

   With this idea, we could define the meaning (information content) of a sentence (i.e., its truth conditions) to be the collection or set of all those possible scenarios in which the sentence is true. Thus the meaning of the sentence *Bill Clinton is in Columbus* is conceived of in this theory as the set of all the possible scenarios that this sentence describes truthfully.

   What this boils down to in terms of a speaker's or hearer's knowledge is the idea that a person understands the meaning of *Bill Clinton is in Columbus* if and only if the person knows how to distinguish possible scenarios where Clinton is in Columbus from scenarios in which he is not—given an opportunity to make the relevant observations of things in each scenario. Thus in this theory the meaning of a sentence, a linguistic object, is explained in terms of nonlinguistic objects (scenarios). The information content of the sentence, when uttered, amounts to letting the hearer know that the actual world fits one or another of these scenarios. (We will get an idea of how this set of possible scenarios is determined from the words and syntax of the sentence in File 7.4.)

Another way in which possible scenarios can help us understand meaning is by augmenting the theory of reference in such a way that imaginary items and individuals can receive referents. We simply allow referents to exist in nonactual scenarios. So the name *Santa Claus* can in fact be given a referent, namely, the large man in the red suit who lives at the North Pole. The only difference is that this man exists only in nonactual scenarios. We can similarly give referents to such words as *unicorn, centaur,* and *Quidditch.* While the availability of extra referents in nonactual scenarios does not help for words such as *the* and *forget,* it does represent an improvement over the case in which the notion of possible scenarios was not available and a word like *unicorn* could have no reference.

6.4.3   Truth Values

If, in addition to knowing a sentence's truth conditions, you also know whether or not the sentence really is true, then you know another facet of the sentence's meaning, its **truth value.** Truth values are always either *true* or *false.*[1] As we pointed out above, knowing the truth conditions for a sentence doesn't necessarily mean that you know its truth value. Take the sentence *There are two lions at the Dallas zoo.* It is almost certain that every reader of this book knows the truth conditions of that sentence (prove this to yourself), but it is rather unlikely that you know its truth value unless you have recently been to the Dallas zoo.

We can also know a sentence's truth value without being able to precisely identify its truth conditions. For example, if you had a wool sweater, you would know that the truth value of *This sweater is made of nylon* would be false, but you might not know the exact truth conditions for *This sweater is made of nylon.* That is, you might not know exactly what chemical properties something must have in order for it to be nylon.

It is therefore clear that truth value is something quite different from truth conditions. We would never want to say that a sentence's truth value is all there is to its meaning. If we did, then we would have to conclude that *One plus one equals two* has the same meaning as *Either Elvis Presley is alive or else he is not alive,* since both are necessarily true. Of course, this is a conclusion that we do not want to reach!

Nonetheless, truth value is an important part of a sentence's meaning. After all, the point of describing a sentence's truth conditions is that it provides one mechanism for identifying its truth value. Since ultimately language is a way to share information with one another, when we actually use language, what we care about is whether sentences are true or false—not what we would have to know in order to figure out whether they were true or false!

---

[1]You may not actually know whether the truth value of a particular sentence is *true* or *false,* and in fact there are sentences for which nobody knows the truth value (such as a sentence claiming that there is life on other planets or a sentence telling exactly how many pigeons are in New York City at any given time) or for which the truth value is hotly debated (such as sentences that make claims about political or religious matters), but "I don't know" isn't a truth value! This isn't a statement of ideology, but rather of semantics. In terms of semantics, we will say that every declarative sentence has a truth value of *true* or *false,* whether or not you know what it is.

6.4.4 Meaning and Language Use

Identifying truth values or specifying truth conditions relative to possible scenarios effectively characterizes many important aspects of sentence meaning, especially for ordinary declarative sentences. But how could you determine the conditions under which a question is true? Or an order, a request, or an apology? In fact, many types of sentences do not seem to be true or false at all. It should be clear, then, that truth value and truth conditions are just two out of many aspects of sentence meaning.

   In addition to notions concerning truth, sentence meaning is probably also determined in part by the conditions under which a sentence may be used. Questions are used differently from assertions, orders are used differently from apologies, and so on. By specifying the kind of practical situation that must exist in order for a speaker to use a particular type of utterance, many facts about the meaning associated with that particular type of utterance may be made explicit. This is a goal of pragmatics (discussed in Chapter 7).

Compositional Semantics: Putting Words Together and Meaning Relationships

6.5.1 The Principle of Compositionality

Compositional semantics investigates how the meanings of individual words are combined to create larger units of meaning. Note first of all that we can't just add up all the word meanings to get the meaning of the whole. If semantics worked this way, we would expect the two sentences *The cat chased the dog* and *The dog chased the cat* to mean exactly the same thing, because they are formed from exactly the same words. By this simplistic principle, we would also expect to get the same meaning from the nonsensical string of words **The chased dog cat the*, yet that string has no meaning at all. We can therefore conclude that, at least in English, the order of words in a phrase helps determine the meaning of the phrase. But there is still more to determining a phrase's meaning. Although the sentences *The dog chased the cat* and *The cat was chased by the dog* are not composed of exactly the same set of words and do not have the same word order, they nevertheless have the same meaning. From these examples, we see that syntactic structure also plays a part in determining the meaning of a sentence. There must therefore be some grammatical principles governing how meanings of words combine in phrases and sentences.

How do we know that systematic principles are involved? Notice that, although we look up words fairly often, there are no dictionaries that we can refer to that list the meanings of sentences! Every day, every person hears and uses new sentences that she or he has never heard or used before, sentences that may never have been uttered before by anyone (see File 1.4). This is why there could never be a dictionary of all sentences. We understand the meanings of new sentences quite easily, and all speakers of English understand a novel sentence in the same way (though, again, they may differ in their interpretation of that meaning). This would hold true for the meaning of any grammatical and semantically well-formed sentence you could make up. The sentences in (1) are almost certainly ones you have never heard before, but you will have no difficulty interpreting them.

(1) a. I stuffed my apron full of cheese and frantically ran away from the dairy snatchers.
    b. It seems unlikely that this book will spontaneously combust while you are reading it, but nonetheless it is theoretically possible that that might happen.
    c. The platypus is enjoying a bubble bath.

Because all speakers of English can understand these sentences, we know that systematic principles exist that determine the meaning of any sentence from its syntactic structure along with the meanings of the individual words in it. The ways that these principles work can be remarkably varied as well as systematic.

This relationship between meaning and syntactic structure is often referred to as the **Principle of Compositionality:** the meaning of a sentence is determined by the meaning of its words in conjunction with the way they are put together syntactically.

That word meanings normally combine by regular principles that are dependent on syntactic structure can be seen vividly from the exceptional cases in which they do not.

Such cases are called idioms. The sentence *He kicked the bucket* can be used to mean 'he died.' We cannot determine this meaning by combining the meaning of *kick* and the meaning of *the bucket* in the normal way, but rather we must learn the special meaning of the whole phrase *kick the bucket* as if it were a new "word." Similarly, with *to pull someone's leg* or *a red herring*, we can't understand the meaning simply by combining *pull* with *leg* or *red* with *herring*. Idioms are cases where a sequence of words has a fixed meaning that is **not** composed of the literal meanings of its words by regular principles.

But just what are these regular principles? What does it mean to "combine" two meanings into a single new meaning? There are as many semantic rules for combining meanings as there are syntactic structures in a language, and clearly we cannot consider them all here. To get a sense of how meanings are built up, we will look at two classes of examples: combining subjects and predicates in simple sentences, and applying adjective meanings to modify nouns.

6.5.2 Sentential Meanings

Recall from Chapter 5 that simple declarative sentences in English normally consist of a noun phrase (NP) that serves as the subject followed by a verb phrase (VP) that serves as the predicate. As an example, consider the sentence *Sandy runs,* shown in (2). What would be the process of computing the meaning of the whole sentence from the meanings of these two syntactic parts?

(2)

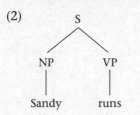

Before we answer this question, we need to decide what the meanings of the NP and the VP will be. For purposes of simplifying discussion, we will consider expressions only in terms of their reference (see File 6.2). Therefore, the NP *Sandy* has as its meaning the (real-life) individual Sandy. We will likewise say that a VP has as its meaning the set of individuals who "do" that VP.[1] For our example, then, the denotation of the word *runs* is the set of individuals who run in some particular scenario that we are considering.

As for the meaning of the sentence, we want to know two things: (i) whether it is in fact true or false given what we know about the world (its truth value) and (ii) the minimal conditions under which it would be true (its truth conditions). We get the first of these directly and the second indirectly. To compute the truth value, we simply check to see whether the individual that is the denotation of the NP is a member of the set that is the denotation of the VP. If it is, then the sentence is true. The sentence is false if the individual is not a member. In other words, we need to check out the set of runners and find out whether or not Sandy is a member of that set. For example, she is not a member of that set in the possible scenario shown in (3b), but she is a member of that set in (4b).

---

[1]This notion of verb phrase meaning may seem peculiar at a first glance. However, when we use a verb phrase as the predicate of a sentence, what we are really doing is simply telling a property of the sentence's subject: the property of running if the predicate is *runs,* or the property of writing a poem if the predicate is *writes a poem,* or the property of being afraid of giants if the predicate is *is afraid of giants*. And properties are the sorts of things that hold of individuals; they do not exist in and of themselves. (That is, there can't be any sort of running taking place unless there is an individual who is doing that running.) That is why even though 'run' is an action, we say that the denotation of *runs* is a set of individuals.

(3) a.   S: false (since Sandy is not a member of the set {Robin, Lee, Kim})

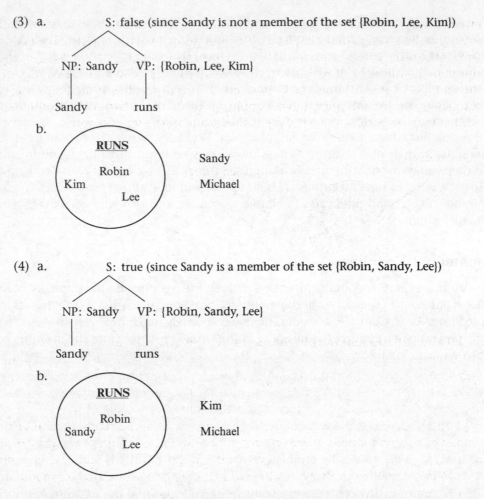

In the tree in (3a), the set of people who run does not include Sandy, and so the sentence *Sandy runs* is false. In the tree in (4a), Sandy is a member of the set of people who run, so *Sandy runs* is true.

Now we have a system for computing the truth value of a (simple declarative) sentence: simply check to see whether the meaning of the subject is a member of the set that is the predicate's meaning. But how do we arrive at the truth conditions? In effect, we already have: it was implicit in the way we computed the truth value. The truth conditions of the sentence *Sandy runs* can be stated in the following way: it must be the case that the individual Sandy is a member of the set of people who run. This seems like no more than a simple paraphrase, but it is, in fact, precisely the truth conditions of this sentence. While *Sandy runs* is a very simple sentence, it is possible to imagine, at least abstractly, how such a mechanism of using sets to identify truth conditions and truth values could be extended for much more complicated sentences, such as the one you are reading right now.

6.5.3 Adjective Meanings

Computing truth values for simple sentences was a fairly straightforward demonstration of semantic composition. We find a more complex sort of composition when we turn our attention to adjective-noun combinations. While there is presumably only one syntactic configuration for all three of the phrases *green sweater*, *good food*, and *fake money*, we shall see that each of these involves a different sort of semantic combination.

Which sort of semantic combination is used depends primarily on the particular adjective involved. We'll start out with the simplest form of adjectival combination, **pure**

intersection. In the phrase *green sweater*, we have two words, *green* and *sweater*, each of which can be given as denoting a set of entities (individuals or objects). The denotation of *green* is the set of green entities, and that of *sweater* is the set of entities that are sweaters. To compute the meaning of the phrase, then, we need only collect all the entities that are in the set both of green things and of sweaters. This is illustrated in the following Venn diagram; here, the intersection (the overlapping portions of the two circles) contains the set of entities that are both in the set of green things and in the set of sweaters.

(5)

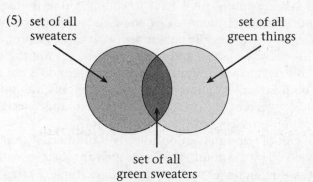

Other phrases that work in the same way are *healthy cow, blue suit,* and *working woman,* etc. Because they produce pure intersections, adjectives like *healthy, blue,* and *working* are called **intersective adjectives.** An important point about these cases of pure intersection is that the two sets can be identified independently. For example, we can decide what is green and what isn't before we even know that we're going to look for sweaters.

Other adjectives do not necessarily combine with nouns according to this pattern; examples of a second kind of intersection can be found in the phrases *big whale* or *good beer.* In the case of *big whale*, the problem is that it is not possible to identify a set of big things in absolute terms. Size is always relative: what is big for whales is tiny for mountains; what is big for mice is tiny for whales; what is short for a giraffe is tall for a chicken. While it is possible to find a set of whales independently, the set represented by the adjective *big* can't be just a set identified by the meaning 'big' but rather must be a set identified by 'big-for-a-whale.' Similarly, *tall giraffe* will involve a set of things that are tall-for-a-giraffe, and *loud explosion,* a set of things that are loud-for-an-explosion (compare this with *loud whisper,* which would use a completely different standard for loudness). Such cases we call **relative intersection,** since the members of the set denoted by the adjective are determined relative to the type of thing denoted by the noun. Examples are shown in (6).

(6)

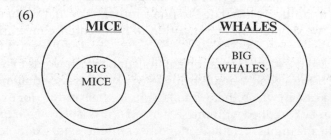

Here, the adjective *big* selects a subset of mice, a subset of whales, and likewise a subset for any other set that we might want to identify big elements of (big planets, big refrigerators, big feet, etc.). Therefore, they are called **subsective adjectives.**

Good beer is another case of relative intersection. But *good* is even more relative than *tall* or *loud. Tall,* for example, always refers to a scale of vertical distance, and *loud* refers to a scale of volume of sound. We might say that good refers to a scale of quality, but what kind of quality? A good beer is probably judged on its taste, but a good ladder on how sturdy and useful it is, and a good record on how pleasurable the music is. *Good beer* could even describe a beer that removes dirt well if we said *That's good beer to wash the walls with*. So *good* apparently refers to anything that fits our purposes well, and these purposes vary with the object and with how that object is used in a given case. In order to use and understand phrases of the form *good + common noun* correctly, we must have more knowledge about the context than in other cases of relative intersection.

Both types of intersection, pure and relative, have in common that these combinations actually refer to some of the objects denoted by the nouns themselves. For *green sweater, tall giraffe,* and *good beer,* we are necessarily talking about sweaters, giraffes, and beer, respectively. But in phrases like *possible solution* and *alleged thief,* this is not the case: *possible solution* does not necessarily refer to a real solution, and *alleged thief* does not necessarily refer to a thief. These are both examples of **non-intersection**. Logically, we can say that the use of intersection-type adjectives entails (or requires) reference to the objects denoted by the nouns, while the use of non-intersection adjectives does not.

Finally, there is a second type of non-intersection adjective (an adjective that does not require reference to objects denoted by the noun); the use of such an adjective with a noun in fact entails that the adjective does not refer to that noun. For example, a *fake Picasso* by definition cannot refer to a Picasso. Of course, a fake thing must have some characteristics of the real thing, or the word would not be used at all; in fact a good fake may be like the real thing in every respect except actually being genuine. Adjectives like *fake* we call **anti-intersection adjectives.**

Researchers in compositional semantics concern themselves, among other things, with discovering the sorts of differences examined here and with writing precise rules to describe exactly how different types of expressions combine. It becomes obvious that these rules must actually exist in our minds once one considers that there are an infinite number of sentences in any language and hence an infinite number of meanings to understand and produce. Just as the concepts of generativity and recursion (and hence rules) were crucial in explaining how we can process the syntax of sentences we have never heard before, they are also crucial in explaining how we can understand the meaning of those sentences.

6.5.4 Meaning Relationships between Sentences

Of course, there are many kinds of phrases besides the sort formed when simple subjects combine with simple predicates or when adjectives modify nouns, and it will not be possible to consider them all here. We should, however, consider sentence meaning one more time. In the same way that, after we discussed what individual words meant, we then turned our attention to how word meanings were related to one another, now that we have considered sentence meanings, we should turn our attention to how sentence meanings can relate to one another.

In File 6.3, we introduced the idea of semantic entailment between words in terms of lexical decomposition (e.g., being a poodle entails being a dog). There is also entailment between sentences. Consider a case in which there is a platypus in the bathtub, for example. This situation, of course, can be described with the sentence *There is a platypus in the bathtub*. That sentence entails the meanings of a number of other sentences: for example, *There is an animal in the bathtub* and *The bathtub is not empty*. As a speaker of English, you intuitively know the meaning relationships that hold between these sentences, but let's try to define exactly what it means for one sentence to entail another.

To do this, we must appeal again to truth conditions. Assume that there is a particular bathtub that we are talking about. What are the truth conditions of *The bathtub is not empty*? Well, there is only one: there must be something in the bathtub. What are the truth conditions of *There is a platypus in the bathtub?* Well, there has to be something in the bathtub; moreover, that thing must be an animal, and more specifically still, it must be a platypus. Thus, we see that the list of truth conditions for *There is a platypus in the bathtub* includes the (shorter) list of truth conditions for *The bathtub is not empty.*

This will be our definition for entailment: if the set of truth conditions for one sentence (X) includes all of the truth conditions for a second sentence (Y), then sentence X entails sentence Y. Another way of saying this is that the possible scenarios described by sentence X is a subset of the possible scenarios described by sentence Y. This relationship between sets of possible scenarios is shown in (7).

(7)

Y: The bathtub is not empty.

X: There is a platypus in the bathtub.

Put more succinctly, we will say that sentence X entails sentence Y if whenever X is true, Y must be true as well. Stated in yet a fourth way, if X entails Y, then there is no situation or possible scenario in which X is true and Y is false. If a speaker utters a sentence that has an entailment, then he commits equally to the truth of the sentence uttered and also to the truth of its entailment. That is, if you claim X, and X entails Y, then you are committed to claiming Y; you cannot simultaneously claim X and deny Y without contradicting yourself.

In each of the examples below, the X sentence entails the Y sentence. Take a minute to try to prove this to yourself.

(8)   X: Ian owns a Corvette.
      Y: Ian owns a car.

(9)   X: Ian eats a large breakfast every day.
      Y: Ian eats a large breakfast on Mondays.

(10) X: Ian has a wife and two children.
      Y: Ian is married.

(11) X: Ian killed the mosquito.
      Y: Ian caused the mosquito to die.

(12) X: Ian has visited Spain four times.
      Y_1: Ian has visited Spain more than once.
      Y_2: Ian has visited Europe.

Notice that entailment does not generally go both ways. In fact, in all five of the examples above, the Y sentences do not entail the X sentences. We can demonstrate this by citing a possible scenario in which the Y sentence would be true and the X sentence would be false: if Ian doesn't own a Corvette, but rather a Honda, then (8Y) is true and (8X) is false. The entailment relations here follow obviously from the meanings of the words *car* and

Corvette, since all Corvettes are cars, but not all cars are Corvettes. Now, take a minute to prove to yourself that, for each of the other examples above, the Y sentences do not entail the X sentences by describing a scenario in which the Y sentence is true and the X sentence isn't.

Other types of meaning relationship include implicature (File 7.3) and presupposition (File 7.5), but these two types of relationship are generally considered to fall within the realm of pragmatics (how meaning interacts with context), so they will be discussed in the next chapter.

Practice

File 6.1—An Overview of Semantics

Exercises

1. Identify each of the following statements as being either mostly about lexical semantics or mostly about compositional semantics:

   a. The phrase *purple books* describes a group of objects (books) that have a certain property (being purple).
   b. The words *couch* and *sofa* mean roughly the same thing.
   c. *Water under the bridge* means something different than *bridge under the water*.
   d. The sentence *John ate a bagel for breakfast* is true just in case an individual by the name of John consumed a round bread product with a hole in the middle for his morning meal.
   e. The opposite of *open* is *shut*.
   f. *Paris* is a word that refers to a particular city in France.
   g. If the sentence *Harold likes checkers and backgammon* is true, then the sentence *Harold likes backgammon* must be true as well.
   h. *Bird* means something like 'warm-blooded, egg-laying animal with feathers, wings, two legs, and a beak.'
   i. When most people hear the word *bird* out of the blue, they are more likely to think of a songbird than a penguin, flamingo, duck, or vulture; however, penguins, flamingos, ducks, and vultures are also kinds of bird.
   j. *Jelly beans that are lemon flavored* has the same meaning as *lemon-flavored jelly beans*.

Discussion Questions

2. In File 6.1, *sense* was defined as 'the mental representation that we have of what a word or phrase means.' Speculate about what kind of form this mental representation could take. Put another way, what sort of idea do you think you must have in your mind in order to know what a word means?

File 6.2—Lexical Semantics: The Meanings of Words

Exercises

3. **i.** Define the term *referent* in your own words.
   ii. Then give an example of a referent for each of the following. (*Note:* See footnote 1 in File 6.2.)

    a. past president of the United States   **e.** Muppet
    b. football team   **f.** country in Europe
    c. linguistics instructor   **g.** car
    d. pencil

4. As explained in File 6.2, what do dictionary definitions and dictionary-style definitions have in common? What distinguishes them from one another?

5. Consider the following four scenarios. In each case, pay particular attention to the phrase, *your right ear*. In each of these scenarios, does the phrase *your right ear* have the same sense? In each of these scenarios, does the phrase *your right ear* have the same referent? Briefly explain your answers to these two questions.

- A woman visits her physician and says that she isn't feeling well. After a brief examination, the physician tells her, "It looks like you have an infection in your right ear."
- A family goes to a park for a picnic. One of the children turns to his father and says with concern, "Daddy, you got some peanut butter on your right ear!"
- While playing a game of Simon Says, a kindergarten teacher says to her class, "Simon Says touch your right ear."
- Two heavy metal musicians are discussing what they will wear at an upcoming concert. One says to the other, "I think that the chain with the spikes would look better if you attached it to your right ear."

6. Assume that we are discussing the planet Earth in the year 2007. Consider the four phrases below. Do these phrases have the same sense? Do they have the same referent? Explain your answers.

- *The ocean that borders the California coast*
- *The ocean that contains the Hawaiian Islands*
- *The largest body of water on Earth*
- *The Pacific Ocean*

7. For each of the following, give an example of a possible prototype and a non-prototype.

Example: bird   Prototype: sparrow   Non-prototype: swan

    a. building   **c.** sport   **e.** tree
    b. fish   **d.** car

Discussion Questions

8. In his 1993 book *Words Fail Us,* author Bob Blackburn writes the following about dictionaries: "I keep two *big* and expensive U.S. dictionaries lying open on racks beside my desk. My personal attitude is that one (almost a half-century old) is to tell me what words mean, and the other (published in 1987) is to tell me what too many people *think* they mean."

    i. What attitudes is Blackburn expressing both about word meanings and about the nature of dictionaries?

    ii. Blackburn's older dictionary was presumably published in the 1940s. What do you suppose he would think about a dictionary from 1840?

    iii. What does Blackburn mean by the phrase, "what too many people *think*" words mean?

(cont.)

    iv. Speaking as a linguist and a descriptivist, how might you respond to Blackburn's claim that the only purpose served by his newer dictionary is to tell him "what too many people *think*" words mean?

9. In File 6.2, both dictionary-style definitions and mental image definitions are presented as possible ways that word meanings might be stored in our brains. Although neither turns out to be a completely acceptable answer, does one or the other seem to have more merit? Why do you think so?

10. Consider the following two scenarios:

- A man has lost his dog: a collie named Sadie. The man walks into his county dog shelter and says to the person at the reception desk, "Excuse me; I'm looking for a dog."
- A man who has never had a pet before decides that he would like to get a dog. He isn't sure what kind he wants, so he goes to his county dog shelter. He says to the person at the reception desk, "Excuse me; I'm looking for a dog."

The man in each scenario says exactly the same sentence, but one man intends the sense component of the meaning of *a dog*, whereas the other man intends the reference component of the meaning of *a dog*. Which is which? How do these two scenarios differ from one another?

Activities

11. Choose any word that you like. Look it up in the dictionary. Now look up some word in that word's definition. Then look up some word in THAT word's definition. Keep track of the list of words that you look up.

    i. What is the shortest chain that you can make such that the last word you look up contains the first word in its definition? Compare your results with those of one or more classmates.

    ii. Do you get longer chains when you begin with content words (nouns, adjectives, verbs, adverbs) or function words (determiners, conjunctions, prepositions, pronouns)? Why do you think that is?

File 6.3—Lexical Semantics: Word Relations

Exercises

12. In what way is each of the following pairs of words related? In cases of hyponymy, indicate which word is the hyponym and which word is the hypernym; in cases of antonymy, tell what kind of antonymy it is.

a.	shallow	deep
b.	mature	ripe
c.	suite	sweet
d.	table	furniture
e.	single	married
f.	study	studying
g.	move	run
h.	sofa	couch
i.	green	blue
j.	punch	touch

13. **i.** Propose a hypernym for each of the following words:

   a. hammer
   b. T-shirt
   c. pink
   d. fish

   ii. Propose a hyponym for each of the following words:

   e. appliance
   f. musical instrument
   g. furniture
   h. fish

14. Come up with your own hierarchical hyponymy relationship for some noun like the one given for *poodle* in File 6.4. It should have at least four hierarchical levels. (For an extra challenge, try to do this exercise with verbs as well!)

15. Refer to the *Tiger* cartoon at the beginning of this chapter. *Pretty* and *ugly* are both words used to describe the insect in the strip. Are these two words antonyms? If so, are they complementary antonyms, gradable antonyms, converses, or reverses? Justify your answer.

16. Classify the following pairs of antonyms as complementary, gradable, reverses, or converses:

   a. wide/narrow - gradeable
   b. smoking/nonsmoking Complementary
   c. inflate/deflate
   d. defeat/lose to
   e. good/bad gradable
   f. innocent/guilty Complementary
   g. in front/behind Reverse
   h. hot/cold gradable
   i. teacher/student Complementary
   j. grow/shrink

17. Consider the English prefix *un-* that attaches to verbs to form such verbs as the following:

   unwrap   *undress*   *untangle*
   unlock   *unwind*   *uncoil*

   Which type of antonym does *un-* create? Explain your answer.

18. Consider the English prefix *in-* that attaches to adjectives in order to form such adjectives as the following:

   intolerant   *inhospitable*   *incredible*   Complementary
   inelegant   *insincere*   *insecure*

   Which type of antonym does *in-* create? Explain your answer.

19. What semantic feature (if any) is shared by all six nouns in each set below? For each set, what semantic feature differentiates the three nouns on the left from the three nouns on the right?

   Example: niece, daughter, sister   vs.   nun, woman, girl

The six words niece, daughter, sister, nun, woman, and girl all share the semantic feature FEMALE. However, the ones on the left all have the semantic feature FAMILY RELATIONSHIP whereas the ones on the right do not.

    a. mailman, nephew, priest   vs.   gander, stag, bull
    b. pen, marker, crayon   vs.   staple, tape, paperclip
    c. table, chair, pencil   vs.   love, thought, idea
    d. table, chair, pencil   vs.   water, cream, juice
    e. sand, gravel, pebbles   vs.   rice, lentils, chickpeas

20. Refer to the *Tiger* cartoon at the beginning of this chapter to answer the following questions:

    a. The child on the left believes that there is a butterfly, while the child on the right believes that it is a moth. What semantic features are shared by *butterfly* and *moth*?

    b. Why does this sharing of semantic features make it plausible that the children would disagree over what they are looking at?

    c. When the boy on the left believes that the insect is a butterfly, he calls it "ugly," but when he believes that it is a moth, he says that it's "pretty." What does this tell you about semantic features that he applies to *butterfly* and *moth* that differ from one another? (Whether or not you agree with his assessment is irrelevant to your answer to this question.)

21. How would you describe what makes each of the following sentences odd, using semantic features?

    a. !The television drank my water.
    b. !Your dog writes poetry.
    c. !I ate a bowl of happiness for lunch with a plate of juice on the side.
    d. !Colorless green ideas sleep furiously.

22. Consider the following set of words:

    {angry, sad, happy, excited, depressed, afraid, worried, joyful, frightened, anxious, cheerful}

    i. Propose one semantic feature that is shared by all of these words.
    ii. Give two types of meaning relationship (e.g., hyponymy, synonymy, gradable antonymy, etc.) that you can identify for any pair of words from this set.

23. Consider this set of words:

    {uncertainty, donkey, pink, delicious}

    Can you propose a single semantic feature that is shared by all four of these words? What makes assigning a semantic feature to this set of words more challenging than assigning a semantic feature to the set of words given in Exercise 22?

File 6.4—Compositional Semantics: The Meanings of Sentences

Exercises

24. For each of the following sentences, state its truth conditions and its possible truth values:

    a. The moon is made of green cheese.
    b. The first president of the United States was George Washington.   *(cont.)*

    c. Some computers are able to synthesize human voices.

    d. Last week a monkey and an elephant escaped from the zoo, broke into the national gallery, and stole a valuable painting.

    e. Your linguistics instructor is currently wearing a sock with a hole in it.

    f. You are currently holding a copy of the 10th edition of *Language Files*.

25. For each of the following pairs of sentences, tell whether they have the same truth conditions or different truth conditions, and explain how you know.

    a. I ate turkey at Thanksgiving.
       I ate turkey at New Years.

    b. There's a sofa in the living room.
       There's a couch in the living room.

    c. The first president of the United States had dental trouble.
       George Washington had dental trouble.

    d. Susan closed the door.
       The door was closed by Susan.

    e. Penguins live in Antarctica.
       Penguins live on the coldest continent on Earth.

26. Revise your answer to Exercise 6 to include the ideas of truth conditions and possible scenarios.

27. Describe the truth conditions of the following sentences. (Be careful: some of these are tricky!)

    a. If I had a million dollars, I would buy you a green dress.

    b. If Barry could sing, he would join a choir.

    c. If it had been sunny yesterday, we would have gone to the beach.

    d. Bea will wash the dishes if Jay will dry them.

    e. If you wash your sheets with bleach, the stains will come out.

Discussion Questions

28. Based on your answers to Exercise 24, is it possible to know the truth conditions of a sentence without knowing its truth value? Is it possible to know the truth value of a sentence without knowing its truth conditions? Explain.

File 6.5—Compositional Semantics: Putting Words Together and Meaning Relationships

Exercises

29. Using the example of compositional analysis of the sentence *Sandy runs* as a guide, provide an analysis for the sentence *Kim sleeps*. Draw trees as in the example in the text, with one tree showing the case where the sentence's truth value is *true* and one tree showing a case where the sentence's truth value is *false*.

30. Refer to the *Tiger* cartoon at the beginning of this chapter to answer the following question: Are *pretty* and *ugly* intersective adjectives or subsective adjectives? Defend your answer using information from the cartoon and at least one additional example of your own.

31. Think about a sentence such as *Kim doesn't sleep*. What is the meaning of *doesn't*? (*Hint:* Consider the condition under which the sentence's truth value is "true.")

32. Which of the following are examples of relative intersection, and which are examples of pure intersection?

   a. lavender crayons
   b. huge TVs
   c. old temples
   d. square rugs
   e. fast trains
   f. empty bottles
   g. long streets
   h. sliding doors

33. Refer to (9)–(12) in File 6.5. For each, demonstrate that the Y sentence does not entail the X sentence as was done in the text for (8).

34. For each of the following, tell whether the X sentence entails the Y sentence; give evidence for how you know.

   a. X: Fifi is a poodle.
       Y: Fifi is a dog.
   b. X: My last name is Jones.
       Y: My father's last name was Jones.
   c. X: I live in Ohio.
       Y: I live in the U.S.A.
   d. X: I speak Russian.
       Y: I am from Russia.
   e. X: At least 30 people will come to the party.
       Y: At least 20 people will come to the party.
   f. X: If you go to the party, I'll go too.
       Y: If you don't go to the party, I won't go.

Discussion Questions

35. Why is lexical semantics alone not enough to interpret the meaning of a phrase or a sentence? On the other hand, could we work on compositional semantics without having information from the lexical side? Why or why not?

36. The discussion of adjectives given in File 6.5 reveals that there is quite a bit of complexity when it comes to understanding the meanings of adjectives. As if this were not complicated enough, there are many other types of Adjective + Noun combinations besides the four discussed in File 6.5. For example, the adjectives in *An occasional sailor walked by* and *I do a daily six-mile run* function very much like adverbs, as seen by the paraphrases *Occasionally, a sailor walked by* and *Every day I do a six-mile run*. These Adjective + Noun combinations do not follow the same rule of combination as the types discussed in File 6.5. Consider yet another case: in the phrase *a hot cup of coffee,* what is hot is the coffee and not necessarily the cup. Here, the adjective combines with cup, which comes to denote its contents.

Speculate about some of the ways that speakers of a language might go about trying to figure out what kind of intersection (if any) to use to interpret an adjective meaning when that adjective appears in some context.

Further Readings

Both of these are excellent and nontechnical introductory texts that presuppose no specialized knowledge of semantics or linguistics.

Hurford, J. R., & Heasley, B. (1983). *Semantics: A coursebook*. Cambridge: Cambridge University Press.

Lyons, J. (1995). *Linguistic semantics: An introduction*. Cambridge: Cambridge University Press.

CHAPTER

7

Pragmatics

GET FUZZY: © Darby Conley/Dist. by United Feature Syndicate, Inc.

FILE **7.0**

What Is Pragmatics?

In chapter 6, semantics was defined as the study of meaning. Given such a definition, it is tempting to suspect that once we understand the semantics of a language, we will automatically understand the meaning of any utterance in that language. In fact, however, identifying the semantic contribution of words and sentences gets us only partway to understanding what an utterance means. Why? The context in which a sentence is uttered may critically affect the meaning that the speaker intends!

Pragmatics is the study of the ways people use language in actual conversations. Pragmaticists study both how context helps to determine whether a particular utterance is appropriate or inappropriate as well as how changes to context alter sentences' meanings.

Contents

FILE 7.1

▰▰▰▰▰▰▰▰▰▰▰▰▰▰▰▰▰▰

Language in Context

7.1.1 The Importance of Context

We may often hear someone use a quotation—for example, in defense of a political opinion or a religious viewpoint—only to hear someone else counter, "But that's not really what he (the original speaker) meant! You've taken it completely out of context!" We also become frustrated when something we have said is taken out of context, feeling as though we have been misquoted. We know intrinsically that to ignore the original context of an utterance can misrepresent the speaker's intentions. Experiences like these tell us that context can affect an utterance's meaning. One of the jobs of pragmatics is to investigate the relationship between context and meaning.

7.1.2 Sentences and Utterances

In order to investigate this relationship, we need a way to talk about language in context. Pragmaticists therefore distinguish between sentences and utterances. A sentence is the group of words used to express some (complete) idea. Consider a sentence like *There is a platypus in the bathtub*. We know many things about this sentence: it is a sentence of English; it contains seven words; it has a certain syntactic structure; and so on. However, while we are able to describe such properties of a sentence, sentences are abstract entities.

Whenever a sentence is used, though—whenever a person speaks (or signs) it—there has been an **utterance** of the sentence. An utterance is not an abstraction. It is an event, something that happens. Read the sentence *There is a platypus in the bathtub* out loud. Now, ask the next person you see to do the same thing. If you have followed these instructions, then you have just heard two utterances, but there is only one sentence. Likewise, if a theater company puts on a play and performs it ten times, the play will open with the same sentence each time, but there will be ten different utterances.

The distinction between sentences and utterances is so important that it gets marked typographically. Anytime that you see a group of words that look like a sentence and are set in italics, what is being referred to is the sentence: the abstract entity. If you see the same words in quotations, then there is a particular utterance that is being discussed.

Utterances may be described as having many of the same properties as sentences (e.g., language and length). However, utterances have other properties as well: we may talk about the time of an utterance, the place of an utterance, the volume of an utterance, the speaker of an utterance, and so on. It does not make sense to talk about the time or the place of a sentence, though, because a sentence is only an abstract idea; it is not an event, and therefore it does not have a context.

7.1.3 How Context Affects Meaning

There are many ways in which context can affect the meaning of an utterance. Consider a simple sentence such as (1) at the top of the next page.

269

(1) He is there now.

The above sentence, heard or read out of context, is difficult to interpret, because it includes many **deictic** or "placeholder" words that don't inherently refer to something specific. These words' meanings are always determined by the context in which they are uttered. We know that *he* refers to a male and that *there* refers to a place and that *now* refers to a time, but these vague meanings alone don't give us the precise information that we need to figure out what would be meant by this sentence when uttered in some context. Considering this sentence in isolation, we don't know whom we are talking about, where he is, or when he is there. Sentence (1) could mean that George Bush is in Washington, DC, in June of 2007 or that he is in Texas in June of 1997; it could mean that Elvis Presley is in Las Vegas in the 1970s or that Santa Claus is at the North Pole on Christmas Eve. To determine which meaning was intended by the speaker, one would need to know when the sentence was uttered and what the speaker was talking about.

Deictic elements aren't the only reason that sentences are context dependent, though. Any sentence can take on a particular, novel, and distinct meaning relative to a particular context. Consider the example in (2).

(2) Can you take the trash out?

This sentence seems fairly straightforward, but in fact it could have a range of different meanings. Suppose that your roommate is running late one morning and calls, "Can you take the trash out?" over her shoulder as she leaves. She probably is requesting that you take the trash out. On the other hand, suppose that you have been in a crippling accident and that you are only just beginning to take on simple housework again. If your physical therapist asks you the question in (2), she is not making a request but rather inquiring about your ability to carry out a set of actions. Here's a third case: suppose that your younger sibling is pestering you while you are trying to have a conversation with a friend. Finally, in frustration, you turn to your sibling and say, "Don't you have anything else to do? Can you take the trash out?" Here you might not care whether your sibling takes the trash out at all. Rather, you just want to be left alone! Suppose, on the other hand, that in the same context, instead of saying (2) to your sibling, you have instead turned to your friend and, while pointing at your sibling, asked whether your friend can take the trash out. Now you are suggesting that your sibling **is** the trash, and you want your friend to carry your sibling out of the room! The same simple sentence can thus have at least four very different meanings. With a little creativity, you could come up with many more.

From both of these examples, it is plain to see that we cannot talk about what an utterance of a sentence means without knowing about the context in which it was uttered.

Some people may argue that there are certain default or "out-of-the-blue" interpretations for many sentences. Of course they are correct. For example, for most speakers, the default out-of-the-blue interpretation of (2) is that it is a request. What is important to recognize, however, is that out-of-the-blue is one particular kind of context that affects the meaning of an utterance as much as would any other kind of context.

7.1.4 Types of Context

An utterance's context can be broken up into several components. **Linguistic context** has to do with what preceded a particular utterance in a discourse. It refers to what others have said earlier in the conversation. So, for example, the answer "Yes" means something entirely different when it is an answer to "Do you like green beans?" than when it is an answer to "Is there a computer available in the computer lab?" or "Will you marry me?" The linguistic context of an utterance tells what speakers are talking about: green beans, a platypus,

Santa Claus, or whatever. The linguistic context is made up of all of the sentences that have been uttered in a discourse leading up to the utterance in question.

A second aspect of context is **situational context**. Not surprisingly, an utterance's situational context gives information about the situation in which it is uttered. Situational context allows us to refer to things in the world around us even if they have not been mentioned before in the discourse. If a goat suddenly walked into your classroom, you could say, "It smells," and everyone there would know that you were talking about the goat. No one would wonder whether you meant the fish you had for dinner or your grandmother's perfume. This is true even though no one had mentioned the goat's presence already in the discourse. Likewise, if a friend tells you, "The governor was on TV last night," your friend most likely means the governor of Rhode Island if you are in Rhode Island, the governor of Ohio if you are in Ohio, the governor of Arizona if you are in Arizona, and so on. We apply our situational knowledge to what we hear all the time.

As a third example, a sentence such as *Rachael is very tall* has a different meaning if the Rachael in question is a preschooler, a ten-year-old, or a professional basketball player. In the first case, the speaker might mean that Rachael is three and a half feet tall; in the second or third case, the speaker could not possibly mean this. Why? Because people know that preschoolers tend to be around three feet tall but that basketball players tend to be much taller. Consider a situation in which you are describing your three-year-old niece. If you say to your sister, who has not seen your niece since she was an infant, "Rachael is very tall," your sister will know that you do not mean that Rachael is seven feet tall—or anything resembling that height! This information does not need to have been previously mentioned in the discourse in order for the speakers to use it to understand what others mean. (Refer to File 6.5 for more information about subsective adjectives like *tall*.)

Finally, **social context** includes information about the relationships between the people who are speaking and what their roles are. Social context is what makes it okay for your football coach to tell you to run two laps around the field but makes it unacceptable for you to tell your coach the same thing. Social context lets us know when saying "yes ma'am" is a sign of respect and when it indicates sarcasm. We use social context to figure out whether the person who says to us, "Can you take out the trash?" means 'You must do so right now' or whether she means 'You don't have to, but I'd appreciate it if you did.' (For a more in-depth discussion of the way social context affects language use, refer to File 10.1 about speech style and register.)

Together, these three aspects of context—along with several others—provide critical information about what utterances mean.

7.1.5 Felicity: Appropriateness Relative to a Context

In addition to using context to figure out meaning, speakers also use context to figure out whether an utterance is appropriate in any given setting. Recall that when discussing syntax and other elements of grammar, we may refer to sentences as grammatical or ungrammatical. For example, in the sentences below, (3) is grammatical while (4) is ungrammatical.

(3) There is a platypus in the bathtub.
(4) *There is platypus a in bathtub the.

In the same way, when we discuss pragmatics, we refer to utterances as being **felicitous** or **infelicitous.** An utterance that is felicitous is one that is situationally appropriate, one that is appropriate relative to the context in which it is uttered. An utterance that is infelicitous is inappropriate in some way. For example, speaker B's answer in (5) is felicitous, but her responses in (6) and (7) are infelicitous. (Notice that a pound sign # is used to indicate infelicity, just as an asterisk is used to indicate ungrammaticality.)

(5) A: What do you do for a living?
     B: I'm a linguistics professor at Ohio State.

(6) A: What do you do for a living?
     B: #I have a job.

(7) A: What do you do for a living?
     B: #My favorite color is purple, too!

Look more carefully at (6) and (7). What seems to be wrong with these two conversations? In (6), the person answering the question isn't providing enough detail. In (7) she doesn't seem to give an answer that is at all related to the question. There are many different reasons why it might be infelicitous to utter a particular sentence in a particular context; the examples above show only two of these reasons.

It is also important to recognize that an utterance may be called felicitous or infelicitous only relative to a particular context. It is very easy to think of contexts in which the infelicitous sentences in (6) and (7) could be uttered quite acceptably. They aren't felicitous, however, in the context given.[1] In other words, felicity is a property of utterances, not a property of sentences.

In general, the speakers of a language know intuitively whether an utterance is felicitous or infelicitous, just as they know intuitively whether a sentence is grammatical or ungrammatical. Also, as with grammaticality, judgments of felicity may differ from one speaker to another. Nonetheless, there are general guidelines which utterances must follow in order to be deemed felicitous.

The rest of Chapter 7 will be concerned with how to determine whether utterances are felicitous and with how context helps us to figure out the meaning of felicitous utterances.

---

[1]In fact, one could imagine a context in which the entire exchange in (6) was felicitous relative to the rest of a discourse. Suppose, for example, that a thief is discussing his thievery with a business executive. The executive might remark that he thinks thievery is unethical. The thief could then respond that, in spite of the ethical side of things, "Stealing is an excellent way to make sure there's always enough money to go around. What do you do for a living?" At this, the executive could respond indignantly—and perfectly felicitously—"I have a job." However, supposing that a person were asked this question out of the blue, for example, by a seatmate on an airplane, then the answer would be under-informative. The point is that the more you know about the context of an utterance, the better able you are to determine whether or not it is felicitous.

FILE **7.2**

Rules of Conversation

7.2.1 Rules for Conversation

Most social enterprises are governed by rules. A family may have a rule that determines who will set the table on any given night; traffic rules govern who may go first at a four-way stop; board games and sports have rules that outline which plays may be made at any point during the game. The use of language, like other forms of social behavior, is also governed by social rules. Some of these rules are designed to protect people's feelings by showing respect or politeness (e.g., rules governing whether you can use a first name in addressing someone or must use a title and last name). Rather more essential are rules designed to protect the integrity of our communication: rules that allow our communication to work.

It is reasonably clear that if people were to decide to tell lies in some random way, so that listeners would have no way of determining when speakers were lying and when they were telling the truth, language would cease to be of any value to us. In response to this and other similar concerns, there is a set of conventions governing language use that preserve its integrity by requiring us, among other things, to be honest, to have evidence for what we say, and to make what we say relevant to the speech context. One thing that is interesting about these conventions is that they were never officially proposed and voted on by anybody but instead have emerged naturally.

The philosopher H. P. Grice (1913–88) formulated a **Cooperative Principle,** according to which we are instructed to make sure that what we say in a conversation furthers the purposes of the conversation. Obviously, the requirements of different types of conversations will be different. In a business meeting, one is normally expected to keep one's remarks confined to the topic at hand unless it is changed in some approved way. Some close friends having a few beers at a bar would not be governed by tight rules of this sort. Nevertheless, even in a casual conversation, the conversation will normally have one or more purposes, and each of the participants can be expected by the rest to behave in ways that further these purposes. Thus, even the most casual conversation is unlikely to consist of such random sentences as the following:

(1) Kim: How are you today?
    Sandy: Oh, Harrisburg is the capital of Pennsylvania.
    Kim: Really? I thought the weather would be warmer.
    Sandy: Well, in my opinion, the soup could use a little more salt.

Grice argued that in order to prevent such meaningless discourse, there are a number of conversational rules, or **maxims,** that regulate conversation and enforce compliance with the Cooperative Principle. Following these rules is yet one more way of ensuring that our utterances are felicitous. Of course, we may not follow all of the rules all of the time. Rather, the rules function as guidelines in order to help ensure effective communication. In general, felicitous utterances are ones that follow Grice's maxims.

273

7.2.2 Introducing Grice's Maxims

Grice divided his maxims into four categories, each of which focuses on a different aspect of the way that utterances should be used relative to a discourse. These categories are quality, relevance, quantity, and manner. Each category contains between one and four maxims.

a. The maxims of quality are those which solve the aforementioned problem that conversation would never work if we were to tell lies in some haphazard way. However, it makes stipulations more specific than merely disallowing haphazard lying. There are two maxims of quality:

- Do not say what you believe to be false.
- Do not say that for which you lack adequate evidence.

The first maxim of quality is self-evident. Without regular compliance with this maxim, language would be useless to us. The second maxim is more interesting, because it is only when we believe we have adequate evidence for some claim that we can have much confidence that we are not saying something false. That is, in order to follow the first maxim, we must also follow the second.

Nevertheless, people differ strikingly in what they think is good evidence for their views. It is also the case that in different contexts, there are different requirements for how much or what kind of evidence will qualify as "adequate." For example, consider a claim like the one made in (2).

(2) The venom of the purple-toothed spider isn't strong enough to kill people.

If a biologist specializing in human reactions to venomous bites uttered this at a scientific conference, she would need to have met a certain standard of evidence before she could felicitously incorporate this utterance into her talk. She would need some knowledge of the kinds of chemicals in the venom and human reactions to them; she would also presumably have to know about the history of people who had suffered purple-toothed spider bites and how they had fared. On the other hand, consider a person—not a biologist—who had been bitten by a purple-toothed spider: as a result, he got a painful swelling at the location of the bite but was otherwise unaffected. In chatting with his friends, he might legitimately be able to utter (2) without knowing anything more general about these spider bites; his evidence would be only his personal experience. Thus these two individuals speaking in different contexts have two distinct standards for quality of evidence. Of course, the second individual might be wrong: it might be the case that he was merely very lucky and didn't get very much venom in his body, but a worse bite (or perhaps a bite to a smaller or less healthy person) could cause death. Nonetheless, he has followed Grice's maxims by saying what he does not **believe** to be false and something for which he has adequate evidence based on the situation. If someone asked him, "Are you sure?" he might then consider explaining his evidence or weakening his claim: something like (3).

(3) Well, when I was bitten by a purple-toothed spider, I didn't die. So at least I know that the venom doesn't always kill people.

Meanwhile, the biologist could likely answer, "Yes; I'm sure," without further qualifications. Even though their levels of certainty differ, both of them would have equal claim to utter (2) given the appropriate context and their stated experience.

b. The maxim of relevance (also called the maxim of relation) is often perceived as being the most obvious. It is also the most simply stated.

- Be relevant.

This maxim has a central role in maintaining the organization of conversation by preventing random topic shifts like those found in (1). To avoid such discourse, we are expected to make contributions that pertain to the subject of the conversation. If someone asks you about your plans for dinner, you should give an answer about that topic rather than telling a story about your trip to the zoo.

In addition to maintaining the organization of a conversation, the maxim of relevance can also help us to figure out what others mean by a particular utterance. Our default assumption is that the people we are talking with are cooperative and that they are doing their best to make the conversation work. This assumption allows us to make **inferences**. Consider the following conversation:

(4) Alana: Is Jamie dating anyone these days?
     Sam: Well, she goes to Cleveland every weekend.

If she did not have rules for conversation as a part of her linguistic competence, Alana could take Sam's response to be completely unhelpful. However, Alana will assume that Sam knows his contribution must be relevant, so she will likely draw the inference that Jamie is dating someone, in particular, someone who lives in Cleveland. (For a more detailed explanation of inference and implicature, refer to the discussion in File 7.3.)

As with the first maxim of quality, the maxim of relevance seems perfectly obvious, but that doesn't mean that people don't violate it. Imagine that two roommates have just arrived back in their dorm on a Friday afternoon; the following is an excerpt from their conversation:

(5) Rachel: We should think of something fun to do this weekend!
     Sarah: Can we talk about something that happened to me in class instead? I want
              your advice about something.

In (5), Sarah knows she is supposed to stay on topic and be relevant—by discussing weekend plans—but she has something else on her mind. She uses the word *instead* to show Rachel that she knows this, and she asks for permission to break the rule. Of course, people don't always point out when they are about to violate the maxim of relevance. We have all had conversations in which we are trying to discuss some particular topic, only to have our conversational partner jump in with an unrelated fact or story. We may or may not be bothered—sometimes we do allow others to go off on tangents—but we are justified to object. We are justified to say, "Wait a minute! You're changing the subject." It is the maxim of relevance that gives us the authority to make that objection.

c. The maxims of quantity concern how much information it is appropriate for a speaker to give in a discourse. Of course, there are some situations in which more information is needed and others in which less is needed. Notice how the two maxims of quantity are phrased in order to make allowances for these differences.

- Make your contribution as informative as is required.
- Do not make your contribution more informative than is required.

The first of these maxims is intended to ensure that we give all of the information necessary for a given circumstance and also that we make as strong a claim as is warranted (see the second maxim of quality). The second is meant to ensure that we neither provide too much information nor make a stronger claim than is warranted. Some examples will help to illustrate.

Suppose that you are asked what you are going to do over the weekend. If your German professor asks you in a language conversation drill, it will likely be acceptable to mention only one or two things that you intend to do (and it would be both infelicitous and rude to subject your class to a complete schedule of everything you plan to do). However, if a classmate is trying to schedule a meeting with you, she likely needs to know specific times that you will be available. In this case, if you were to respond with the same short answer, it would be under-informative and therefore infelicitous.

Consider a second example. In this case, the degree of informativeness relates to specificity, or the "strength of the claim." Suppose that someone asks you where you grew up. One could imagine that any of the possible responses given in (6) could be true answers to the question (and thereby follow Grice's maxims of quality and relevance), but it is obvious that some of these answers would be appropriate in certain contexts and not in others. Each response could be too informative, not informative enough, or just right, depending on the circumstances. Try to think of an example of each kind of context.

(6) a. On the corner of Main Street and Minor Road
    b. In Dayton
    c. In Dayton, Ohio
    d. In Dayton, Ohio, on the corner of Main Street and Minor Road
    e. In Ohio
    f. In the Midwest
    g. In the United States

For more information about making claims with the appropriate strength and how the maxim of quantity is used to calculate certain implicatures, refer to File 7.3.

d. The maxims of manner differ critically from the other three sets of maxims. The maxims of quality, relevance, and quantity all instruct speakers about the information that they should or shouldn't give in a discourse. The maxims of manner, on the other hand, have nothing to do with the information itself; rather, these maxims instruct speakers in how they should go about giving that information.

- Avoid obscurity of expression. (That is, don't use words or phrases that are hard to understand.)
- Avoid ambiguity.
- Be brief.
- Be orderly.

The first maxim, "Avoid obscurity of expression," instructs us to avoid the use of **jargon** (terms restricted primarily to specialized areas of knowledge) or other terms that our listeners cannot reasonably be expected to know. It also instructs us to avoid needlessly complex sentence structures.

The second maxim requires us to avoid saying things that have more than one meaning (e.g., *He promised to phone at noon:* what happened at noon—the promise or the phone call?) unless our listeners can be expected to know which meaning was intended. Grice is not trying to tell us that we may never use a word or phrase that would be ambiguous out of context. If he were, then there would be a number of words that we would never be allowed to use. Rather, he is instructing us to use words and phrases whose meanings are clear given the context in which we utter them. He is telling us not to go out of our way to confuse the people whom we are speaking with.

The third maxim, "Be brief," tells us not to expound at length on a topic when a few words will do. Note that when Grice tells speakers to be brief, he does not mean the same thing as when he says, "Do not give too much information." Notice that the speakers in both (7B) and (8B) give exactly the same amount of information, but do so in different words. Thus, the speaker in (8B) violates a maxim of manner because he is being wordy, but he does not violate a maxim of quantity.

(7) A: What do you do for a living?

    B: I'm a linguistics instructor.

(8) A: What do you do for a living?

    B: #What I do is that I'm an instructor and the subject matter that I teach is linguistics.

The fourth maxim, "Be orderly," comes down to saying that we should organize what we say in some intelligent way. That is to say, among other things, that if you have information to convey about several different topics, you should convey all of the information on one topic first, followed by the next, rather than giving one sentence about each in alternation. Often speakers follow this maxim by giving general overview information first and then moving on to specifics. The injunction to be orderly also dictates that a story should be told in chronological order. For example, consider the strangeness of (9) and (10). The first merely sounds peculiar, while the second is actually hard to follow.

(9) #Leslie read fifty pages and opened her book.

(10) #My mother didn't really want my room to be painted purple. I was worried that I wouldn't get good grades at the new school. When I was a child, my favorite color was purple. I worked very hard in all of my classes to get good grades. My mother told me that if I got good grades, I could paint my room. When I was ten years old, I switched to a new school. I wanted to paint my bedroom a bright color.

Neither (9) nor (10) could be considered felicitous in almost any context: they are so unorderly as to be almost nonsensical.

Thus, we find that although the four maxims of manner do not provide any insight into what information a speaker should share, they are critical in regulating how intelligible the speaker's utterances are.

7.2.3 Flouting Maxims

So far, for the most part, we have considered cases in which speakers follow Grice's maxims. Of course, there are times in which people may violate the maxims: at some point everyone has told a lie, changed the subject, given too much information, or said something confusing! Sometimes people violate the maxims on purpose (e.g., lying in order to intentionally deceive someone) and other times by accident. Strictly speaking, these violations are infelicitous.

Sometimes, however, speakers may use the maxims in order to communicate indirectly. They are several reasons that one might choose to use the maxims in this way. We sometimes need to avoid saying something directly because doing so could hurt us or because doing so could hurt someone else. Grice gave an example of a professor who was asked to write a letter of recommendation for a recent Ph.D. graduate who was applying for a teaching position. Suppose that the letter went like this:

(11)

    Dear Colleague:

        Mr. John J. Jones has asked me to write a letter on his behalf. Let me say that Mr. Jones is unfailingly polite, is neatly dressed at all times, and is always on time for his classes.

        Sincerely yours,

        Harry H. Homer

Do you think Mr. Jones would get the job? Probably not! This is an example of **flouting** a maxim—in this case, the maxim of quantity. Professor Homer wanted to convey his negative impression of the candidate without actually saying anything negative about him. The recipient of this letter will assume that although Professor Homer has appeared to be violating the maxim of quantity, he is nevertheless not actually intending to be uncooperative; he has said all of the relevant positive things he could think of—which is the essence of "damning with faint praise."

The other maxims can also be flouted. For example, if you and a classmate are discussing your professor, and you see your professor rapidly approaching, you may suddenly change the subject by looking pointedly at your classmate and saying, "Oh, really? I didn't know that chocolate originated in Mexico!" In this case, you probably don't want to change the subject to the history of chocolate; rather, you are hoping to prevent your classmate from saying anything untoward! You expect that he will notice your abrupt change in subject and deduce that something is up. You have successfully flouted the maxim of relevance.

It is also possible to flout the maxim of quality. If someone says to you something that you don't believe, you may respond, "Right, and I'm Cookie Monster." You don't mean that you have blue fur and a home on Sesame Street; rather you mean something like, 'What you just said is as obviously false as it is that I'm Cookie Monster.' A sarcastic comment such as this may sound harsh, but it may be perceived (in some contexts) as less hurtful than coming right out and saying, "You're wrong." Flouting the maxim of quality can also allow us to insult people and (usually) get away with it. If someone does some bragging and another says, *I'm totally awed,* the first will probably take it as an insult, but not one that he can legitimately take exception to. This conversational inference arises out of the recognition that the insulter is violating the first maxim of quality—the recognition that the claim is too strong (see the maxims of quantity) for it to likely be true.

7.2.4   Grice's Maxims in a Wider Context

The needs of social harmony, politeness, and linguistic integrity are not always consistent with each other. We have already seen several cases in which politeness keeps us from following pragmatic rules. Recall that we said at the outset that the rules for conversation are **social** rules (i.e., they are not a part of a language's grammar). As such, they are in competition with social rules that come from other aspects of a society, and sometimes, for one reason or another, they lose.

It is said that there are societies in which the failure to answer a stranger's question is considered very impolite and therefore people in this society will give a stranger a wrong or intentionally imprecise answer to a question rather than give no answer. From this we learn that Grice's maxims, being conventions, are very different from natural laws. While their essence may be universal across languages and cultures, the way that they are implemented and the way that they interact with other societal rules will obviously vary between societies.

Drawing Conclusions

7.3.1 Drawing Conclusions: Entailment

A crucial part of understanding utterances is being able to draw conclusions from those utterances about the way the world is. However, the conclusions we draw can be based on different kinds of evidence or reasoning. The sorts of reasoning that we use depend largely on the context of the utterance that we are interpreting.

One kind of reasoning commonly used to draw conclusions is based on the concept of **entailment,** which was introduced in File 6.5. For any two sentences X and Y, sentence X entails sentence Y if whenever X is true, Y must be true as well. In the example in (1), the X sentence entails the Y sentence.

(1) X: Ian eats a large breakfast every day.
    Y: Ian eats a large breakfast on Mondays.

As explained in File 6.5, entailment indicates a commitment from the speaker's point of view. Entailment also does something for the hearer: from the hearer's point of view, entailment allows a conclusion to be drawn very confidently. If you hear and believe X, and X entails Y, then concluding Y is completely safe.

Entailment is a relationship based on literal meaning. Thus, entailments are conclusions that can be drawn irrespective of an utterance's context. But often, if you take only what is literally asserted and entailed by an utterance, that part of the meaning alone is not enough to account for hearers' understanding of the utterance. Speakers routinely intend to convey information in addition to what is entailed by the sentences they utter. Fortunately, hearers also routinely draw conclusions from the utterances they hear, even when the sentence uttered does not entail the conclusion drawn. That is to say, an utterance's context often helps us to draw conclusions—inferences—that were not entailed by the sentence that was spoken.

7.3.2 Drawing Conclusions: Inference, Implication, and Implicature

In File 7.2, we pointed out that people commonly draw inferences from what others say based on the assumption that speakers are adhering to the cooperative principle. It's time now to focus our attention on what is actually happening when a person draws such an inference.

First, consider a situation in which an inference is drawn that does not involve linguistic communication. A meeting between a supervisor and an employee is running longer than the allotted time. The employee doesn't want to say, "Our meeting is running longer than we'd scheduled," because the supervisor might find it rude. Instead, the employee glances at his watch. The employee is **implying** that the meeting is running long: sending the message without saying it directly. The supervisor, if he understands the message, infers that the employee wishes the meeting to end. An **inference** is a conclusion that a person is reasonably entitled to draw based on a set of circumstances.[1]

A person may draw an inference in cases when no one has tried to imply anything at all. If you walk outside and notice that the pavement is wet, you might infer that it had been raining, but you wouldn't want to say that the pavement had implied anything! (There must be someone trying to communicate an idea in order to say that any implying has happened.) In this file, however, we will be considering only inferences drawn when there is a person trying to send a message, and more specifically, we will consider only cases in which—unlike those above—the message is sent using language. When a speaker implies something using language, we say that her utterance contains an **implicature**. Implicatures are conclusions that are drawn about what people mean based on what we know about how conversation works. There are many different kinds of implicature, and we will consider only a few of them here, namely, those that arise via one of Grice's maxims for cooperative conversation. You should be familiar with Grice's maxims (introduced in File 7.2) before continuing.

7.3.3 Implicature Based on the Maxim of Relevance

If given a suitable context, any maxim can be responsible for helping to generate an implicature. Consider the following sample of discourse between two strangers at a bus stop:

(2) Speaker 1: I'd really like a cup of coffee.
    Speaker 2: There's a place around the corner called Joe's.

Here's a reasonable conclusion Y that we can draw from Speaker 2's statement of X:

(3) X: There's a place around the corner called Joe's.
    Y: Joe's sells coffee.

It is important to recognize that in (3), X does not entail Y: it is obviously possible for there to be a place around the corner called Joe's that doesn't sell coffee. Thus, the conclusion of Y is an inference: it is based on an implicature rather than an entailment.

How does the implicature arise? Speaker 1 is talking about coffee and looking for information about coffee. If Joe's were a bookstore that didn't serve coffee, then Speaker 2 would be changing the subject, which people usually don't do in the middle of a conversation. Speaker 1 is much more likely to assume that Speaker 2 is following Grice's maxim of relevance: if he wants to interpret Speaker 2's contribution as relevant, he has to "read something into it" that Speaker 2's utterance didn't entail, namely, that Joe's sells coffee. In order to justify conclusion Y, we had to think about pragmatic concepts: people and conversation in context. We say that X **implicates** Y in this situation.

Consider this second example.

(4) Alana: Is Jamie dating anyone these days?
    Sam: Well, she goes to Cleveland every weekend.

Recall this example from File 7.2. The implicature from Sam's utterance (again based on the assumption that his contribution is relevant) is that Jamie is dating someone in Cleveland.

---

[1]Increasingly, the words *imply* and *infer* are used interchangeably in casual conversation. For the purposes of engaging in linguistic analysis, however, it is important to distinguish between these two actions. Implying is what is done by the person sending the message; inferring is what is done by the person receiving the message.

Sam might instead have said *I believe she may be dating someone because she goes to Cleveland every weekend, and that's not her hometown, and she doesn't have a job there.* Given our set of maxims, though, Sam can say what he does and rely on the listener to figure out what he means without explicitly stating these other steps.

It is important to note that if Sam knew that Jamie went to Cleveland on the weekends to visit her grandmother, then his response would have been either very misleading (if he understood that his utterance had generated an implicature) or at least infelicitous (if he merely thought he was saying something unrelated to the topic at hand).

7.3.4 Implicature Based on the Maxim of Quantity

The conversation in (5) illustrates an implicature that might arise on the assumption that the speaker is obeying the first maxim of quantity: a speaker should give as much information as required.

(5) Mother: Have you done your homework for all of your classes yet?
    Son: I've finished my history homework.

Let us again consider the actual content of what is uttered compared with the conclusion that is likely to be drawn, shown in (6X) and (6Y), respectively.

(6) X: I've finished my history homework.
    Y: I have not finished my homework for my other classes.

Clearly, in this case X does not entail Y. It is very possible for a child to say truthfully that he has finished his history homework and to have also finished the work for his other classes. Rather, the mother is likely to infer Y because her question wasn't looking for information merely about the history homework but rather for information about work for all of her son's classes. She will assume that her son is giving as much of the information as possible that is required to give a complete answer to her question.

Numbers are a particularly common source for the generation of quantity implicatures. Consider the following discourse. What seems to be wrong with it?

(7) Gail: How far can you run without stopping?
    Kim: Ten miles.
    Gail: I guess you can't run a whole marathon without stopping, then.
    Kim: Nonsense, I've done it a number of times.

Notice that what Kim says first must be true if what she says next is true. Certainly, if Kim can run over twenty-six miles without stopping, then she can run ten miles without stopping. However, Gail quite naturally assumed that Kim was obeying the first maxim of quantity with her answer of "ten miles"; Gail therefore inferred that Kim meant 'exactly ten miles, and no more.' If you pay attention, you are likely to be surprised by how often numbers such as 47 are used to implicate 'exactly 47' when the entailed meaning is 'at least 47.'

7.3.5 Implicature Based on the Maxim of Manner

Recall that one of Grice's maxims of manner tells speakers to be orderly. Keeping this in mind, consider the two stories told in (8) and (9).

(8) Rebecca took the medication and had an allergic reaction.

(9) Rebecca had an allergic reaction and took the medication.

Both of these sentences provide exactly the same entailed meaning. However, someone who assumes that the speaker is being cooperative will assume that the speaker is telling the story in an orderly fashion. Thus, someone who hears (8) may infer that Rebecca had an allergic reaction to the medication, whereas someone who hears (9) is more likely to infer that Rebecca took the medication in order to counter her allergic reaction to something else.

Another one of the maxims of manner dictates that speakers be brief. Consider the following utterance:

(10) The man who lives with me is an electrician.

Upon hearing this sentence uttered by a person whom you don't know particularly well, you might infer that the speaker is talking about a house mate (or an apartment mate, or something similar). Of course, as far as entailment is concerned, the speaker could be talking about a husband, son, or brother—all of which might explain their living together—but because "my husband" is shorter than "the man who lives with me," it is likely that the speaker would have used the shorter phrase, were it true.[2] Thus, by using the lengthier expression, the speaker implicates that she does not have one of these other more specific kinds of relationships to the electrician.

7.3.6 Implicature Based on the Maxim of Quality

The second maxim of quality tells us that we can felicitously say only that for which we have adequate evidence. In File 7.2, we pointed out that people often differ in what they think is sufficient evidence for their views. Sometimes, we may draw inferences based on the assumption that we have the same standards for evidence as do our conversational partners. Consider the following conversation:

(11) Sandy: We need someone to make some sort of cake for the picnic.
       Tom: I can make my family's favorite chocolate cake.

Sandy might draw the inference that Tom has made his family's favorite chocolate cake before, because the best evidence that Tom can make this cake would be that he had indeed made it, as spelled out in (12).

(12) X: I can make my family's favorite chocolate cake.
       Y: I have succeeded in making this cake before.

However, this inference is not entailed by Tom's statement; it is only implicated. Tom could legitimately say that he could make the chocolate cake based on the fact that he had a recipe and had watched it being made many times and thought he knew all he needed to know to make it. Suppose Tom were to make the cake and it turned out very badly. Something like the following conversation might take place:

(13) Sandy: I thought you said you could make this cake!
       Tom: Well, I thought I could.

As Sandy's challenge—which sounds quite felicitous—illustrates, she is justified in being upset that Tom did not have a high enough standard of evidence for saying that he could

---

[2]Of course, the inference that the speaker is not related to the electrician could also be taken to arise from an implicature based on the maxim of quantity. Can you see why? It is important to recognize that the maxims work together with one another: thus we may infer the content of an implicature for more than one reason!

make the cake. Thus, the inference that she drew was well founded. Was Tom justified in saying that he could make the cake in the first place? This question is one whose answer will be open to differences of opinion. The point, though, is that we ought to be aware that people may often infer a stronger claim than what has been entailed, based on their assumption about the sort of evidence that might be required in order to felicitously express some proposition.

7.3.7 The Significance of Implicatures to Communication

The system of implicature that has been described in this file is a kind of side effect of Grice's maxims, maxims whose primary reason for being is to regulate conversation.

Implicatures are still very useful, however. They allow us to introduce ideas into a discourse with less commitment than we would have to express were we entailing the same propositions. In (4), why would Sam choose to give the answer that he gave instead of saying, "Yes; she's dating someone in Cleveland," or something similar? Whatever his reason, it is clear that he wants Alana to draw her own conclusions. Maybe he isn't certain about Jamie's dating practices and doesn't want to commit for that reason. Perhaps he wishes to be discrete and merely hint at Jamie's dating practices (so that she cannot later accuse him of revealing secrets about her). Implicature gives him a way to communicate the idea he has in mind while still protecting himself from committing to the truth of a proposition that he does not want to commit to.

On the other hand, implicature can serve a function much more fundamental to our conversations than merely protecting noncommittal speakers. One major reason for exploiting the maxims in this way is to make conversation easier. If we were forced to speak only in logically impeccable ways, making sure that what we said entailed every fact that we wanted our hearers to conclude, conversation would proceed at a very slow pace. That is assuming (counterfactually) that most of us have the logical capacity to do this. Communication would become very cumbersome if we could not rely on implicature. We use context and our knowledge about the universe to draw inferences from what we hear because it allows us to use language more effectively.

FILE **7.4**

Speech Acts

7.4.1 An Introduction to Speech Acts

Just as people can perform physical acts, such as hitting a baseball, they can also perform mental acts, such as imagining hitting a baseball. People can also perform another kind of act simply by using language; these are called **speech acts.**

We use language to do an extraordinarily wide range of activities. We use it to convey information, request information, give orders, make requests, make threats, give warnings, make bets, give advice, offer apologies, tell jokes, pay compliments, etc., as the following sentences suggest:

(1) John Jones has five dollars.
(2) Who ate my porridge?
(3) Shut up.
(4) Please scratch my nose.
(5) Do that again, and I'll punch your lights out.
(6) There is a mouse in the back seat of your car.
(7) Five bucks says that the Buckeyes will beat the Wolverines this year.
(8) You ought to go to class at least once a quarter.

There can be little doubt that it is our ability to do things with language—to perform speech acts—that makes language useful to us. In fact, with language we can do things that would otherwise be impossible. Consider (4), a request for a hearer to scratch the speaker's nose. If we did not have language, how would this request be made? We could imagine the speaker taking the hearer's hand and rubbing his nose with it, but would this action have the same force as a spoken request? Probably not. How would the hearer know that the speaker meant *scratch*, not *rub*? How would the hearer know that this action was a request and not an order? The action itself could not convey the politeness of the word *please*, a major difference between requests and orders. In (6), we could warn someone that a mouse is in the back seat of his car by pointing at it, but even then, only if we were near the car and the hearer were in a position to see us. How could we give the advice in (8) without words? It would certainly be difficult.

The following list contains some of the most common speech acts, which we will discuss in this file. Of course, language can be used for all sorts of purposes other than those listed, as well.

(9) Some common speech acts and their functions

Speech Act	Function
assertion	conveys information
question	elicits information
request	(more or less politely) elicits action or information
order	demands action

| promise | commits the speaker to an action |
| threat | commits the speaker to an action that the hearer does not want |

7.4.2 Felicity Conditions

In order to be felicitous, each of the kinds of speech acts listed in (9) must be uttered in a certain kind of context. As a rather silly example, consider how infelicitous it would be to request your garbage can to empty itself (assuming a typical garbage can in the early twenty-first century). For a request to be felicitous, it must be directed to a person (or animal or machine) that is capable of doing whatever action was requested. In fact, for any speech act, there is a set of conditions that must hold in order for that speech act to be felicitous. Fittingly, these conditions are called **felicity conditions.** Here are some examples of felicity conditions for two very common speech acts: requests and questions.

(10) Felicity conditions for requests
In order for a speaker to felicitously request a hearer to complete some action, it should be the case that . . .
a. The speaker believes that the action has not yet been done.
b. The speaker wants the action to be done (or thinks that the action should be done for some reason).
c. The speaker believes that the hearer is able to do the action.
d. The speaker believes that the hearer may be willing to do things of that sort for the speaker.

(11) Felicity conditions for questions
In order for a speaker to felicitously question a hearer about some state of affairs, it should be the case that . . .
a. The speaker does not know some piece of information about some state of affairs.
b. The speaker wants to know that information about the state of affairs.
c. The speaker believes that the hearer may be able to supply the information about the state of affairs that the speaker wants.

Look carefully at the case of requests in (10). The purpose of a request is to get a task accomplished. In light of that goal, these felicity conditions make sense. If any of these conditions were not met, then the goal could not be reached.

To understand when it is appropriate to make a request or to ask a question, then, we need to think about the felicity conditions associated with each of these speech acts. Clearly, the same holds true for other speech acts as well. In order for giving thanks to be felicitous, the thanker must (among other things) appreciate what the thankee has done; in order for an apology to be felicitous, the apologizer must (among other things) want the apologizee to believe that he is contrite; and so on.

When we introduced Grice's maxims in File 7.2, we said that utterances generally had to follow the maxims in order to be felicitous, but that there were exceptions (e.g., flouting). The same is true of felicity conditions: some of the felicity conditions for a speech act may be suspended in certain contexts. For example, in normal conversation we do not ask people questions that we already know the answers to, but there are exceptions: people playing trivia games, lawyers questioning witnesses, teachers giving exams. We recognize these situations to be socially exceptional in one way or another. Playing trivia violates (11b), because in trivia games people don't seriously want the information they seem to ask about; interrogating witnesses violates (11a), because a good lawyer tries to avoid surprises; and asking exam questions violates both (11a) and (11b), because the teacher does know the answers. Exam questions also possibly violate condition (11c) since the point of asking an exam question is to determine whether or not students can provide an answer. The fact is that we ask questions for a number of different purposes in different social contexts, and to reflect these differences, we can modify the particular felicity conditions. For trivia players we could eliminate felicity condition (11b); for lawyers we could eliminate condition (11a); for teachers we could eliminate all three. However, we have to be careful: for example, we wouldn't want to say that in the case of a teacher asking a question there were no felicity conditions at all; rather, there would be a modified set of felicity conditions including perhaps such items as 'The speaker wants to know whether the hearer is able to supply an answer.'

It will be useful, as we go through the discussion of speech acts in this chapter, to think about them in terms of their felicity conditions. For each type of speech act, think about what the speaker must believe and desire in order for it to be felicitous to use that type of speech act.

7.4.3 Performative Verbs and Performative Speech Acts

Any time that you open your mouth and utter a sentence, you perform a speech act. A special kind of speech act, known as a **performative speech act**, shows that we consider speech action just as legitimate as any other physical action. This is made clear by the large number of verbs called **performative verbs** that denote purely linguistic actions. Compare (12)–(19) with (1)–(8).

(12) I assert that John Jones has five dollars.
(13) I ask who ate my porridge.
(14) I order you to shut up.
(15) I request that you scratch my nose.
(16) I threaten you that if you do that again, I'll punch your lights out.
(17) I warn you that there is a mouse in the back of your car.
(18) I bet you five bucks that the Buckeyes will beat the Wolverines this year.
(19) I advise you to go to class at least once a quarter.

As these sentences illustrate, the speech acts performed by utterances of the sentences in (1)–(8) can also be performed by embedding these sentences as complements of verbs that state the speech act. In (14), for example, we have an order with the performative verb *order*, followed by a specific command.

Certain ceremonies require the use of performative words in order to tell what action is being performed; by reading examples (20) through (23), you can likely deduce the type of event in which each would be used.

(20) I hereby pronounce you husband and wife.
(21) I christen this ship the *U.S.S. Language*.
(22) I hereby dub you Sir Lancelot.
(23) We declare the defendant not guilty.

These examples contain a very specialized group of performative verbs in that, by using one, a speaker not only performs a speech act but also changes something about the world: the marriage between two people, the name of a ship, and so on. (Note that when you perform other speech acts, such as giving an order, you do not effect some change on the world: although you give the order, the other person may or may not do what you have said. In such a case, saying the words alone was not enough to effect a change.) The specialized performative verbs that alter the world often have additional felicity conditions associated with them having to do with the authority of the speaker. For example, if a dentist walked up to two patients in the waiting room and said, "I hereby pronounce you husband and wife," it would be infelicitous, because the dentist does not have the authority necessary to perform this speech act. Furthermore, the two dental patients would not be married as a result of the dentist's infelicitous pronouncement. When one of these specialized speech acts using a performative verb is used infelicitously, then not only is it infelicitous, but also there is no effect on the world (no marriage, christening, knighting, or whatever).

7.4.4 Identifying Performative Speech Acts

When identifying speech acts containing performative verbs, it can be tempting to conclude that the utterance is the action named by the verb. While our conclusion may be correct, we must look at more than the verb. Consider the following sentences:

(24) I promise to take him to a bar tonight.
(25) John promises to take me to a bar tonight.
(26) I will promise to take him to a bar tonight.

Although all of these sentences use the verb *promise,* only (24) uses it as a performative verb. Sentence (25) is an assumption about a promise, and (26) is a promise to make a promise sometime in the future, without actually using the verb *promise* performatively. Why? Sentence (25) is not a promise because the subject of the sentence is *John.* When we use a verb performatively, the subject must be *I* or *we,* since these speech acts concern the interaction between speakers and hearers. Sentence (26) is not a performative use of the verb *promise* because it is in the future tense. Performative speech acts, like all actions, take place in the present, so they must use the present tense. (Note that these grammatical constraints are constraints on performative speech acts, not speech acts in general. Sentence (25) is still an assertion, though it does not have a first-person singular subject, and (26) is a promise though it is not in the present tense.)

One test to see whether a verb is used performatively or not is the *hereby* test. We take the word *hereby* and insert it before the alleged performative verb:

(27)   I hereby promise to take him to a bar tonight.
(28) #John hereby promises to take me to a bar tonight.
(29) #I will hereby promise to take him to a bar tonight.

If the sentence sounds acceptable with *hereby,* then the verb is being used performatively. If the sentence sounds bad, then the verb is not being used performatively. (Sometimes, this test is difficult to use because many such sentences sound awkward. This awkwardness may arise because people tend not to utter speech acts using performative verbs or because *hereby* may sound somewhat archaic.) Note, however, the naturalness of using *hereby* in (20) and (22).

A further complication arises in identifying speech acts when a performative verb is used to perform a speech act other than the one it names. Consider (30).

(30) I promise to tell Mom if you touch my toys one more time.

Sentence (30)—though it has the verb *promise,* uses *I* as its subject, and is in the present tense—is not a promise. Instead it is a threat. When we make a promise, we commit to do something that we believe is beneficial to or desired by the hearer. When we make a threat, we commit to do something that the hearer will not like. Since 'telling Mom' is something that hearers generally do not appreciate, we must construe (30) as a threat. In identifying speech acts, then, we must consider what it means to perform a particular speech act, the actual words of the utterance we hear, and elements of the situational and social contexts. Felicity conditions can also help us in the task of identifying types of speech acts.

7.4.5 Direct and Indirect Speech Acts

The types of speech acts that we have been considering, including both performative speech acts and the examples in (1)–(8), are called **direct speech acts,** because they perform their functions in a direct and literal manner. That is, the function that the sentence performs in a discourse is evident from its literal meaning. Perhaps the most interesting single fact about speech acts, though, is that we very commonly perform them indirectly, especially when we are trying to be polite. So far, we have discussed direct speech acts that can be performed in two ways: (a) by making a direct, literal utterance, or (b) by using a performative verb that names the speech act. In addition to these direct speech acts, we can use the felicity conditions to make **indirect speech acts.** Consider the speech acts *question* and *request* once again.

(31) Questions
    A. Direct
        a. Did John marry Helen?
        b. I ask you whether or not John married Helen.

    B. Indirect
        a. I don't know if John married Helen. (cf. (11a))
        b. I would like to know if John married Helen. (cf. (11b))
        c. Do you know whether John married Helen? (cf. (11c))

(32) Requests
    A. Direct
        a. (Please) Take out the garbage.
        b. I request that you take out the garbage.

    B. Indirect
        a. The garbage hasn't been taken out yet. (cf. (10a))
        b. I would like for you to take out the garbage. (cf. 10b))
        c. Could you take out the garbage? (cf. (10c))
        d. Would you mind taking out the garbage? (cf. (10d))

There is something up-front about the (31A) questions and the (32A) requests. Sentence (31A.a) taken literally is a request for information about John's marrying Helen. The same is true of (31A.b). Notice, however, that (31B.a) taken literally would not be a question at all. It would be an assertion about the speaker's knowledge. Sentence (31B.b) would also be an assertion if taken literally. Sentence (31B.c), in contrast, is a question, but a question that literally asks whether the hearer knows something.

As the notes given in connection with sentences (31B) and (32B) suggest, indirect speech acts enjoy a very close connection with the felicity conditions on speech acts. That is, we can perform an indirect speech act in many cases by appealing to a particular one of its felicity conditions. At the same time they are often, although not always, indicative of politeness considerations on behalf of the speaker. So instead of assuming that felicity condition (10d) on requests holds, the speaker might ask if it does, as in *Would you mind taking me to work?* in order to make a polite request.

7.4.6 Identifying Indirect Speech Acts

In an indirect speech act, what the speaker actually means is different from what she or he literally says.

There are several ways to determine whether an utterance is an indirect speech act. First check to see whether there is a performative verb in the sentence, since only direct speech acts are accomplished using performative verbs. If the utterance uses a performative verb (in the present tense with the subject *I* or *we*), it must be a direct speech act. If it doesn't, the speech act might be indirect. For example, (31A.b) and (32A.b) both contain performative verbs, and therefore neither performs an indirect speech act.

We can also check to see whether any felicity conditions are violated for the sentence's literal meaning but not for its intended meaning. If there are violations for the literal but not the intended meaning, then the sentence must be an indirect speech act. For example, if taken literally (32B.c) would be a question asking whether or not the hearer is able to take out the garbage. For this sentence to be a felicitous question, felicity conditions (11a) through (11c) must be satisfied. But in many situations (e.g., assuming the hearer is not disabled), (11a) is violated because the speaker clearly knows the answer to this question. On the other hand, for the intended meaning of the speaker requesting the hearer to take out the garbage, felicity conditions (10a) through (10d) are all satisfied. Therefore, this sentence is not a direct speech act of questioning, but an indirect speech act of making a request.

Finally, we can imagine a context in which the utterance is used and consider the way people normally respond to it. Different speech acts arouse different responses. Listeners respond to an assertion by a signal of acknowledgment, such as a nod or a verbal response like *Oh, I see.* People respond to a question by a confirmation or denial, or by supplying the information being solicited. People respond to a request or command by either carrying out the action accordingly or refusing with some explanation. If the standard response to an utterance is different from what its literal meaning would arouse, then it is used to perform an indirect speech act. For example, the literal interpretation of (32B.c) would be a question. But compare it with something like *Could you lift 200 pounds?* You can respond to this question by simply saying *Yes, I could,* or *No, I couldn't,* but it is not appropriate, felicitous or polite to respond to (32B.c) this way. Instead, people normally respond to (32B.c) by actually carrying out the requested action—taking out the garbage. This shows that while *Could you lift 200 pounds?* is usually a direct speech act of questioning, (32B.c) is usually an indirect speech act of requesting: it has the same effect as (32A.a).

7.4.7 Sentence Forms and Their Relation to Speech Acts

It is time now to turn our attention to the relationship between speech acts and sentence forms (or, perhaps, the lack thereof). Remember that speech acts are identified by the speakers' goals. Thus there are many different ways to perform the same speech act, because there are many different sentences that will accomplish the same goal. Not only do we have the choice between speaking directly (with or without performative verbs) or indirectly, but we can also choose the **form** or structure of the sentence we utter.

Certain speech acts are so common that many languages have syntactic structures conventionally used to mark them. You will find some examples of different sentence forms for English in (33).

(33) *Form*   *Examples*
 Declarative   He is cooking the chicken.
 Interrogative   Is he cooking the chicken?
                  Who is cooking the chicken?
 Imperative   Cook the chicken.

On the surface, it may (and should!) seem as though each kind of sentence form is specifically designed for one of the speech acts that we have discussed above. It looks as though declarative sentences are perfect for making assertions, as though interrogative sentences are designed for asking questions, and as though imperative sentences are made for giving orders. This association is fairly typical and often holds. Don't confuse the names of the sentence forms (declarative, interrogative, and imperative) with the names of the speech acts (assertion, question, and request), though! This association does not always hold.

As with all things related to pragmatics, the key is context. Consider the sentences in table (34). All of these sentences are ones which, when taken in an out-of-the-blue context, might be interpreted as serving the function indicated in the table (depending on prosody or other factors). (Note, by the way, that in each column, the third sample declarative sentence is a direct speech act employing a performative verb.)

(34) Ways to use different sentence forms to complete various speech acts

| Form of Sentence | Type of Speech Act | | |
	Assertion	Question	Order/Request
Declarative	• Columbus is the capital of Ohio. • I'm telling you that Columbus is the capital of Ohio. • I hereby assert that the capital of Ohio is Columbus.	• I would like to know what the capital of Ohio is. • I've been wondering about which city is the capital of Ohio. • I ask you what the capital of Ohio is.	• It would make me very happy if you would take out the garbage. • I need you to take out the garbage. • I order you to take out the garbage.
Interrogative	• Did you know that Columbus is the capital of Ohio? • May I inform you that Columbus is the capital of Ohio?	• What is the capital of Ohio? • Can you tell me what the capital of Ohio is?	• Will you take out the garbage? • Would you mind terribly if I asked you to take out the garbage?
Imperative	• Remember that Columbus is the capital of Ohio. • Let me tell you that Columbus is the capital of Ohio.	• Tell me what the capital of Ohio is. • Let me ask you what the capital of Ohio is.	• Take out the garbage. • Don't forget to take out the garbage. • Allow me to request that you take out the garbage.

The sentences in table (34) show that any of the three sentence forms can be used to perform any of these three speech acts. It is often the case that when declarative sentences are used to make assertions, or when interrogative sentences are used to ask questions, or when imperative sentences are used to give orders, the resulting sentences are direct speech acts while other pairings between form and speech act yield indirect speech acts. This generalization does not hold all of the time, however. Note that often within one square of the grid, you may find both a direct and an indirect speech act using the same sentence form to perform the same type of speech act. For example, *Columbus is the capital of Ohio* is asserting something directly about Ohio, but *I'm telling you that Columbus is the capital of Ohio* is literally asserting something about what the speaker is saying and only indirectly asserting something about Ohio. Likewise, *Take out the garbage* is a direct request, whereas *Allow me to request that you take out the garbage* literally is a request that the speaker be permitted to make another request! It only indirectly asks the hearer to take out the garbage.

Regardless of how we perform our speech acts, though—directly or indirectly, and using whichever syntax and words that we choose—the take-home message is that there is much that we can accomplish by using language.

Presupposition

7.5.1 Presuppositions of Existence

(1) The Amazon River runs through northern Europe.

Most readers probably have a fairly strong reaction to sentence (1). Some of you may have thought, "Oh, yeah, I knew that," but presumably most of you responded by thinking something like, "No it doesn't! The Amazon River is in South America!" Regardless of which reaction you had, however, none of you responded by thinking, "But there's no such thing as the Amazon River," or wondering whether there's a place called Europe. If you were having a conversation with someone who asserted (1), you would do very well to disagree with that person, but you would be disagreeing about the location of the Amazon River, not its existence. Compare your reaction to (1) with the sort of reaction you might have to (2).

(2) The Bvryzax River runs through northern Europe.

Could you respond to (2) by saying, "No it doesn't!" Indeed, you could not. Why? Because (at least at the time of this publication) there is no river anywhere in the known universe by the name of Bvryzax. In order to say of a river that it does not run through northern Europe, you must believe that the river exists! If you wanted—very rightly—to object to someone's uttering (2), you would have to say something more along the lines of, "There's no such thing as the Bvryzax River." Similarly, if a child you know tells you that the monster under her bed has fangs, you would likely not want to say, "No, it doesn't." Responding in that way would merely corroborate the existence of the (perhaps fanged) monster. Rather, you would want to dispute the child's underlying assumption that a monster existed at all.

Both (1) and (2) would be infelicitous in almost any context that you can think of—other than perhaps a work of fiction—but they would be infelicitous for different reasons. An utterance of (1) would be infelicitous because of a violation of Grice's maxim of quality. An utterance of (2) would be infelicitous because it **presupposes** the existence of something that in fact does not exist. A **presupposition** is an underlying assumption that must be satisfied in order for an utterance to make sense or for it to be debatable. Presuppositions appear exceedingly often in the sentences that we hear uttered every day, and most of the time we don't notice their presence at all. However, when they are not satisfied, we are often left not knowing quite how to respond.

What does it mean for a presupposition to be **satisfied?** It means that the participants in the discourse must believe that the presupposed information is true (or at least that they behave as though they believe it) before the sentence containing the presupposition is uttered. Presuppositions can be satisfied either when the information that they contain is considered common knowledge—for example, that there is such a river as the Amazon—or when they contain information that has previously been asserted in the discourse. Either way, the speaker can reasonably assume that all of the participants are aware of it. If a sentence containing a presupposition is uttered in a context where the presupposition is not satisfied, most of the time that utterance is infelicitous.

For example, the claim "The monster under my bed has fangs" presupposes that there is a monster under the speaker's bed. If the presupposition is not satisfied (because not all of the speakers believe it is true), then there is something odd about the utterance: if no such monster exists, then it can neither have fangs nor not have fangs, and if the speakers don't believe the monster exists, they can't felicitously discuss whether or not it does. The new information being presented—the information about fangs—doesn't make sense until after the presupposition of the monster's existence has been dealt with.

One of the most common kinds of presupposition is the variety discussed so far: these are **existence presuppositions.** Whenever someone utters a sentence about a specific thing or person, then the speaker presupposes that that thing or person exists in order to be able to say something about it. (We may sometimes utter sentences that are about things we know don't exist, such as Santa Claus, but we have agreed as a society to continue to behave much of the time as though he did, and this allows us to felicitously make claims about his red suit, reindeer, etc.) To consider another case in which an existence presupposition has not been satisfied, imagine the following discourse between two co-workers who do not know each other very well yet:

(3) First co-worker: # I'm sorry that I was late to our meeting; I had to take my pet giraffe to the veterinarian.
Second co-worker: Wait a minute! You have a pet giraffe?

The second co-worker is right to object to the first co-worker's excuse for being late. Having a pet giraffe is not very common or likely, so the first co-worker really should not have assumed that she could discuss the giraffe in passing without first establishing that it existed. On the other hand, the second co-worker is put in a bit of a difficult situation, because he cannot simply disagree. If he retorts, "No, you didn't have to take your giraffe to the veterinarian," then he has done exactly what he did not want to do, which is to affirm the giraffe's existence. Instead, all he can do is sputter and say, "Wait a minute!" Such is the nature of what infelicity does to conversation. The conversation would have gone much better had the first co-worker said (4) instead.

(4) I'm sorry that I was late to our meeting. I have a pet giraffe, and it hasn't been feeling well, so I had to take it to the veterinarian.

In this case, the second co-worker might believe that the first co-worker is lying, but at least the first co-worker has done her job to establish the existence of something (her giraffe) before beginning to talk about it. Now there is a specific sentence in the first co-worker's utterance ("I have a pet giraffe") that the second co-worker can refute.

7.5.2 Presuppositions and Truth Values

We mentioned above that one of the problems that can arise with sentences containing unsatisfied presuppositions is that we don't seem to be able to tell whether they are true or false. The sentences in (5) presuppose that there is such a place as Disneyland.

(5) a. Yesterday, Disneyland had over 3,000 visitors.
    b. Yesterday, Disneyland did not have over 3,000 visitors.

Well, in fact there is such a place as Disneyland. Because that is common knowledge, it is almost certain that you, the reader, acknowledged the existence of Disneyland prior to reading (5a). Thus the presupposition was satisfied, and we can move on to answer another question: is (5a) true or false? It is probable that you do not know. (Of course, whether it is true or false will depend largely on which day is denoted by the deictic word *yesterday*.) Whichever day we are talking about, though, either Disneyland did have more than 3,000 visitors, or else it did not. That is, either (5a) is true, or else (5b) is. It is not possible for both (5a) and (5b) to be false.

Now, let's consider the Bvryzax River again. Of course, we see immediately that the sentences in (6) contain a presupposition that is not satisfied: there is no such river as the Bvryzax.

(6) a. #The Bvryzax River reaches a depth of 25 meters.
     b. #The Bvryzax River does not reach a depth of 25 meters.

Is (6a) true? No, it is not. Well, then, following the pattern we saw in (5), if (6a) is not true, then (6b) must be true, right? Well, no; that doesn't seem correct either. Under ordinary circumstances, if you negate a true sentence, then you are left with a false sentence, and if you negate a false sentence, then you are left with a true sentence. In the case of sentences with unsatisfied presuppositions, though, this generality seems to fall through.

This gives us one way of identifying an unsatisfied presupposition: if a sentence and its logical negation both seem equally untrue, then that sentence likely has an unsatisfied presupposition. There are a number of semantic and pragmatic theories that try to account for how to reconcile this puzzle; for our purposes, we will merely mention it as an intriguing facet of our use of language.

So far we have considered only presuppositions of existence, but there are also many other **presupposition triggers**: words or phrases whose use in a sentence often indicates the presence of a presupposition. We will provide only a small sample here. In each case, notice that if the presupposition is not satisfied, it is not clear whether the sentence containing the presupposition is true or false.

In (7), the presupposition trigger is the phrase *come back*. Think about what *come back* means. In order for a person to come back to a place, he must come to that place after having been there before at some time in the past. But *come back* doesn't mean 'be at a place, leave it, and then come to that place again.' It only has the meaning 'come to that place again.' The part about having been there before is presupposed.

(7) a. Linus <u>came back</u> to the pumpkin patch this October.
     b. Linus did not <u>come back</u> to the pumpkin patch this October.

Therefore, the sentences in (7) presuppose that Linus had previously been in the pumpkin patch. If Linus had never been in the pumpkin patch before, then we cannot felicitously say that he came back, nor can we felicitously say that he did not come back. If Linus had never been to the pumpkin patch before, then (7a) and (7b) would both seem untrue. Moreover, if the speakers in a discourse do not know whether Linus has been to the pumpkin patch before or not, then it would be infelicitous to utter either (7a) or (7b).

Now consider the trigger *stop* in (8) and the trigger *after* in (9). Try not to worry too much about why they these words are triggers. Just think about what must be true in order for a person to felicitously say one of the sentences in (8) or (9).

(8) a. Alan <u>stopped</u> falling asleep during meetings.
     b. Alan did not <u>stop</u> falling asleep during meetings.

(9) a. <u>After</u> the United States added a fifty-fourth state, the U.S. flag design was modified to contain 54 stars.
     b. <u>After</u> the United States added a fifty-fourth state, the U.S. flag design was not modified to contain 54 stars. (Instead, the decision was made to keep the old flag design.)

Could one of the sentences in (8) be uttered if Alan had never fallen asleep during meetings? No; in such a case (8a) and (8b) would both be equally inadequate descriptions of the state of affairs: both would seem untrue. Thus we can conclude that *stop* triggers a presupposition that a person had to previously do whatever it is that he is supposed to have stopped. Therefore, if it were not common knowledge among the participants in a conversation that Alan used to fall asleep in meetings, a speaker could not felicitously utter either (8a) or (8b).

What about the sentences in (9)? Based on what you know about the world, is (9a) true or false? It doesn't seem to be either true or false: we cannot assess what did or didn't happen after the addition of a fifty-fourth state because (as of 2007, at which time the United States has only fifty states), no such addition has taken place. Therefore, (9a) is infelicitous, and (9b) is infelicitous for the same reason.

7.5.3 Prosody as a Presupposition Trigger

We will consider one more kind of presupposition trigger. The prosodic structure of our utterances can also cause certain information to be presupposed. Recall from File 2.5 that we can use **pitch accents** on words in order to make some words more prominent than others. By our choices in where to put these pitch accents, we can force different information to be presupposed. (As in File 2.5, we will use the convention of capitalizing words that are prosodically prominent.)

A particularly clear way of seeing how prosody affects presupposition can be found in sentences containing certain additive words (words like *too, either, also,* and *as well*). Here's an example using *too:* (10a) is felicitous, while (10b) is infelicitous.

(10) a. Jessica went to Toledo. LAURA went to Toledo, too.
    b. #Laura went to Fort Wayne. LAURA went to Toledo, too.

The *too* in (10) triggers a presupposition that someone else went to Toledo in addition to Laura, because the prosodically prominent word is *Laura*. Thus its use in (10a) is perfectly acceptable, while it is infelicitous in (10b). The presupposition has not been satisfied: in (10b) we do not know of someone other than Laura who went to Toledo; therefore we aren't allowed to use *too*.

However, the content of the presupposition is dependent entirely on the prosodic structure of the sentence in which *too* appears. To prove this to yourself, consider the pair of sentences in (11).

(11) a. #Jessica went to Toledo. Laura went to TOLEDO, too.
    b. Laura went to Fort Wayne. Laura went to TOLEDO, too.

In (11), the presupposition is that Laura went somewhere other than Toledo, because the prosodically prominent word is *Toledo*. When uttered with this prosody, therefore, the sentence is felicitous in context (b), but not in context (a). The explanation for (11) is exactly the inverse of the explanation for (10).

7.5.4 Presupposition Accommodation

So far, we have assumed that the only way for a sentence containing a presupposition to be felicitous is if that presupposition is satisfied at the time that the sentence is uttered. In fact, people use sentences containing presuppositions all the time when the other participants in the conversation would have no way of knowing the presupposed information ahead of time. Consider again the woman who was late for a meeting in (3). She didn't get away with presupposing that she had a pet giraffe. But suppose instead she had said one of the sentences in (12).

(12) a. I'm sorry that I was late to our meeting; I had to take my pet cat to the veterinarian.
     b. I'm sorry that I was late to our meeting; my car broke down.

Both of these sentences also contain existence presuppositions: that the speaker has a pet cat in the first case and that she has a car in the second. Her co-worker is much less likely to object to these presuppositions, however, even if he did not previously know about the car or the cat. The reason is that it is much more plausible that a person might have a car or a cat. The second co-worker **accommodates** the presupposed information, behaving as though he had known it all along and not objecting to its being inserted like this. You can think of accommodation as being sort of like retroactive satisfaction.

Notice, however, that we accommodate only presuppositions that we find plausible. There is no hard-and-fast standard for what is or isn't plausible, but some things (like giraffe ownership) are almost certainly too implausible to pass by without an objection.

There is one more requirement for presupposition accommodation in addition to plausibility. To illustrate, imagine that your roommate (whom you have not seen all day) comes home and exclaims the following:

(13) Roommate: Guess what I did today!
     You: What?
     Roommate: #I also went to the LIBRARY.

In this case, your roommate's last utterance would be infelicitous because it presupposes that she went somewhere in addition to the library. However, because she hasn't told you where else she has gone, that information is not already common knowledge at the time of utterance. Although you can probably guess that she must have gone many other places during the day (to class, or the store, or a park, or wherever), rendering the presupposition plausible, you cannot access a specific other place that you are certain she went to. Thus the presupposition is inaccessible, so you cannot accommodate it.

These, then, are the two requirements for presupposition accommodation: plausibility and accessibility. By and large, if the content of a presupposition is both plausible and accessible, people will be willing to accommodate it. Suppose that you are sitting indoors in November in Ohio and have not looked out a window recently. If a child were to run up to you and proclaim (14), she would be telling you about her emotional state.

(14) I'm so happy that it's snowing!

Although her sentence is about her being happy, it presupposes that it is snowing, a fact that was not common knowledge before her utterance. Nonetheless, you would likely accommodate the presupposition that it was, indeed, snowing. The presupposition is readily accessible, because it was contained directly in the sentence that the child uttered, and it is plausible, because snow is fairly expected in November in Ohio.

It should not be surprising that this is the note we end on. As a general rule, in order for an utterance to be felicitous, any presuppositions it contains must be satisfied; however, very frequently presuppositions that were not satisfied before the utterance are accommodated afterwards based on elements of the context. Pragmatic rules, principles, and generalizations are all subject to factors that can be determined only from context.

Practice

File 7.1—Language in Context

Exercises

1. Below are descriptions of several possible contexts for the sentence *Do any of you have a watch?*

   i. For each context, paraphrase the message that the speaker seems to be trying to get across by uttering that sentence.

   ii. After doing part (i), write one or two sentences that explain how this exercise as a whole shows the way that context affects the meaning of sentences.

   a. A frantic-looking man runs up to a group of people standing at a bus stop, checks the bus schedule, and then says hurriedly, "Do any of you have a watch?"

   b. A jeweler who is renowned for the beautiful wristwatches that she makes sees a group of people walk into her shop and says to them, "Do any of you have a watch?"

   c. The security guard who works at the metal detector at an airport holds out a pile of trays into which people may put their possessions before placing them on the conveyor belt. He says to the people standing in line, "Do any of you have a watch?"

   d. A group of preteen girls is comparing jewelry. One girl says, "My jewelry is best, because I have the most." Another says, "Nope. Mine is the best because it all matches." This sort of thing goes on for a while. Finally the last girl pipes up that she thinks she has the best jewelry. "Oh yeah? What makes you so special?" She replies, "Just look at my wrist! Do any of you have a watch?"

   e. A mugger traps a group of people in a dark alley and waves a gun at them while screaming, "Do any of you have a watch?"

   f. Your linguistics instructor left his watch at home this morning, but he will need to monitor his time use in class. He wanders into the department lounge and says to his colleagues, "Do any of you have a watch?"

   g. A woman goes to a masquerade ball and falls in love with one of her dance partners. However, of course, she cannot see his face. She knows only that he wore a very ornate and easily recognizable wristwatch. Now, every time that she approaches a group of eligible-looking men, she begins her conversation with, "Do any of you have a watch?"

   h. A zookeeper is about to let a group of patrons try holding an exotic bird with a known tendency to peck at shiny objects. Before letting anybody hold her, the keeper says, "Do any of you have a watch?"

   i. A kindergarten student has just learned how to tell time. Very proud of her new skill and certain that others will be as well, she marches up to a group of grown-ups and eagerly says, "Do any of you have a watch?"

   (cont.)

j. A Martian has read all about Earth and is very interested in its time-telling devices. On its first trip to our planet, it exits its flying saucer and oozes up to the first group of people it sees. It says excitedly, "Do any of you have a watch?"

2. Identify each of the following as a property that can hold of both sentences and utterances or of utterances only:

a. volume	**d.** location	**g.** length	**j.** pitch
b. truth/falsity	**e.** language	**h.** time	**k.** syntactic structure
c. speaker	**f.** idea expressed	**i.** speed	**l.** number of morphemes

3. In File 7.1, we introduced four possible interpretations of the sentence *Can you take the trash out?* Now, come up with your own context for *Can you take the trash out?* that differs from all of those given so far and that thereby gives it a different meaning from all of those given so far. Describe the context, and then tell what the sentence would mean if uttered in that context.

Example: An author writes a short story and takes it to a publisher. The story contains scenes of a so-called adult nature that the publisher objects to. When the author asks the publisher whether she will publish it, she responds, "Can you take the trash out?" Here, she means 'If I agree to publish your story, will you remove the objectionable material from it?"

4. For each of the following sentences, construct two different contexts, such that the sentence would mean something different depending on which of the two contexts it was uttered in. (You may specify the situational context, the linguistic context, the social context, or all three.) Then paraphrase what the meaning of the sentence would be in each context that you write.

    a. I seem to have lost my pencil.
    b. There's always a police officer on duty.
    c. I'm supposed to write a five-page paper for my history class.

5. Tell whether each of the following sentences contains any deictic words. For the ones that do, list those words.

    a. They want to go to your concert to see your band perform.
    b. The Ohio State Buckeyes won the NCAA football championship in 2003.
    c. Many authors, such as Mark Twain and Carolyn Keene, chose to write under a pseudonym.
    d. That is so cool; let me see it!
    e. Although there will certainly be another major earthquake in California, no one can predict for sure whether the next big quake will happen tomorrow, next week, or a decade from now.
    f. Hippopotamuses are herbivores.
    g. Is it possible for a technician to come here to help fix the problem, or do I have to take my computer over there?

6. For each of the following questions, write one felicitous response and one infelicitous response. Explain what makes your infelicitous responses infelicitous. Try to have a different reason in each case. (*Hint:* Try answering this question once after reading File 7.1 and a second time after you have read the rest of Chapter 7. What new ways have you learned to make utterances infelicitous?)

> **a.** What did you do for your birthday?
> **b.** Which classes do you think you will take next spring?
> **c.** I'm going to the grocery store. Do you need me to pick anything up for you?

Discussion Questions

7. Think of experiences in which something that you or someone else said was reported out of context. How did this out-of-context report change the meaning of what was said? Why do people often choose to use quotations out of context? What is gained by this practice? What is lost?

8. How would language be different if we had no deictic elements? Could you still communicate as effectively? Could you still communicate as efficiently? Why, or why not?

9. Assuming that you have read File 6.4, discuss the difference between truth conditions and felicity conditions. Are there times that an utterance could be true but infelicitous? Are there times that an utterance could be felicitous but untrue?

Activities

10. Pay attention to the language around you.
> **i.** Transcribe one utterance that you hear today. Then write down the context of that utterance, being sure to note its linguistic, situational, and social contexts.
> **ii.** How did knowing the context help you interpret the meaning of that utterance?
> **iii.** What else might the sentence have meant had it been uttered in a different context?

11. Pay attention to the language being used around you.
> **i.** Find an example of somebody saying something infelicitous.
> **ii.** Tell what was said, and describe the context.
> **iii.** Explain what makes you believe that the utterance was infelicitous for that context.

File 7.2—Rules of Conversation

Exercises

12. Below are descriptions of four university professors. Hopefully you will never have an instructor like any of them, because they are not very pragmatically savvy. Each one is failing to follow one of Grice's maxims in particular. For each professor, tell which category of maxim is being violated.

> **a.** He's so well spoken that you can get lulled into thinking that you believe him. Then, after a while, you start to realize that most of what he's saying is just unfounded opinion. He never backs up his statements with anything factual.
> **b.** Her lectures are really hard to understand. I think that she knows what she's talking about, but she uses all this complicated vocabulary, and she never defines any of the words. Plus, every sentence is about a million words long, and by the time you figure out what it meant, she's giving you another sentence that's even more complicated!
> **c.** His classes are hard to follow because he goes off on so many tangents. We'll be talking about Russian politics one minute, and then he'll veer off to tell us something about democracy in Ancient Greece. Then he'll get back to the Russian politics only to interrupt himself with a story about what his son did at breakfast this morning.

d. I feel as though she never gives us thorough answers to our questions. For example, I asked her yesterday why we shiver when we're cold. All she said was "because you're warm-blooded," and then she went on with her lecture. I already knew that people are warm-blooded, but I don't know what that has to do with shivering.

13. In (6) in Section 7.2.2, the following possible answers are given to the question "Where did you grow up?" Suppose that they are all true answers and that the only difference between them is how informative they are. Write a one- or two-sentence linguistic context for each response in which that response would be felicitous.

   ✦ On the corner of Main Street and Minor Road
   a. In Dayton
   b. In Dayton, Ohio
   c. In Dayton, Ohio, on the corner of Main Street and Minor Road
   d. In Ohio
   e. In the Midwest
   f. In the United States

14. Instead of merely saying, "Be brief," Grice's actual statement of the third maxim of manner was "Be brief (avoid unnecessary prolixity)." By phrasing the maxim this way, which two of his maxims of manner did Grice violate?

15. In the discourse below, Sophie violates one of Grice's maxims. Tell which maxim she violates, and explain the violation. Be sure that your explanation takes the context into account.

   Josh: What did you do yesterday?
   Sophie: I went to the pet show at the elementary school. It was a lot of fun.
   Josh: What did you see?
   Sophie: I saw David and his dog, and I saw Robin and her cat. Oh, and Jessica was there. I saw her duck.
   Josh: Did it quack?
   Sophie: What? Oh. Jessica doesn't have a pet duck; she has a pony. But I saw her duck out of the way every time that it tried to bend over to chew on her hair!

16. Refer to the *Get Fuzzy* comic strip at the beginning of this chapter. In the strip, Rob is trying to make vacation arrangements for his cat, Bucky. Much of the humor in this strip refers to ways that the characters manipulate their use of Gricean maxims. Answer the following questions:
   i. When Bucky declares, "Wait, your Dad is bald . . ." which maxim is he accusing Rob's father of violating?
   ii. Why might Rob's father have chosen to give an excuse about a hair styling appointment instead of declaring outright that he didn't want to watch Bucky during Rob's vacation? What does this tell us about the ways in which we manipulate pragmatic rules?
   iii. In the final frame, Bucky asks whether Rob's father is still angry about "the chocolate pudding incident," which hadn't been previously mentioned in this discourse. Is Bucky violating the maxim of relevance when he asks this question? Justify your answer.

17. In eighth grade, Chris thought (mistakenly) that it would be funny to prank-call the fire department from a payphone on the wall of the school cafeteria. Based on the following dialogue, answer questions (i)–(iii).

Fire department operator: Where is the phone that you're calling from?
Chris: On the wall.

   i. In general, why would an operator at a fire department ask where a caller is calling from?

   ii. Based on the situation (the operator's goals), which maxim does Chris's answer violate?

   iii. Is Chris's answer true? Justify your answer relative to the maxim of quality.

18. Suppose that you ask a friend what he thought of a new movie, and he replies, "Well, the costumes were authentic." His answer does seem to be saying something positive about the movie. Nevertheless, he is guiding you to infer that he probably did not like the movie.

   i. Which maxim is he flouting in order to do this?

   ii. Why might he choose to convey his dislike by flouting that maxim instead of saying directly that he didn't like the movie?

Discussion Questions

19. In Section 7.2.1, we mentioned several components of society in which rules are important. What other social institutions can you think of for which there are preset rules? How is language similar to these institutions? How is it different?

20.   **i.** We are taught at a young age not to lie. Nevertheless, there are many times that someone might choose to break Grice's maxim of quality in order to serve a particular purpose. What are some reasons that one might have for doing so?

   ii. Considering how many reasons there are to say things that are untrue, and considering how often the maxim of quality must therefore be violated, what evidence do we have that it exists in the first place?

   iii. Is there a difference between breaking Grice's maxim of quality and lying? If so, what is the difference? If not, why not? (It is acceptable to argue on behalf of both sides, but be sure that your answer is clear and well justified.)

Activities

21. Pay attention to the conversation you hear around you. Find **two** cases of a person flouting or violating one of Grice's maxims. In each case, explain which maxim is at stake and what effect it has on the conversation when it is broken/flouted. *(If you like, you can intentionally break several maxims in your conversations and write about what happens, but neither the editors of this book nor your instructor can take any responsibility for any effect this activity may have on your social life!)*

22. Comic strips are often a great place to find violations of Grice's maxims.

   i. Locate a comic strip in which the joke or humor value comes from one of the characters violating one of Grice's maxims for cooperativity in conversation. Photocopy the comic, or staple or tape it to a full-sized sheet of paper.

   ii. Tell which maxim is being violated. (Be specific: for example, if it's a maxim of manner, be sure to tell which one is being violated.)

   iii. Explain why what the character says is a violation of that maxim.

   iv. Briefly describe why the violation leads to a humorous reading of the comic strip.

23. Construct your own example of a conversation in which one of Grice's maxims is flouted. Each speaker should have at least several turns in the dialogue in order to establish sufficient context to show the function of the flouting. After you have written your dialogue, tell which maxim is flouted, and to what end.

File 7.3—Drawing Conclusions

Exercises

24. Below is a discourse between Daniel and Amy. They are in the kitchen at their home. Following the discourse is a list of questions. None of the questions is directly answered in the discourse, but all of the answers are implicated by something that either Daniel or Amy says. Answer each question. Then tell which line of the discourse contains the implicature that answers the question and which Gricean maxim you had to appeal to in order to figure out the implicature.

a. Daniel: Would you like me to make chocolate chip cookies this afternoon?
b. Amy: Sure. That would be great! Do you have all of the ingredients?
c. Daniel: Well, I meant to go to the bank this morning, and then I was going to stop at the store on the way home, but I wasn't feeling well, so I didn't go.
d. Amy: That's too bad. What did you need to buy?
e. Daniel: Just a few things. Do you know whether we have any eggs?
f. Amy: After breakfast, there were two left.
g. Daniel: Then I guess I'll have to borrow some. Are the neighbors home?
h. Amy: (Looks out the window) I don't see their car out front.
i. Daniel: That's too bad. Maybe I should make cookies some other day.

  i. What kind of cookies is Daniel planning to make?
  ii. What kind of store had Daniel meant to go to this morning?
    A. shoe store   B. grocery store   C. book store
  iii. What did Amy eat for breakfast this morning?
  iv. How many eggs does Amy think there are in the house?
    A. fewer than two   B. exactly two   C. more than two
  v. How many eggs does the cookie recipe call for?
    A. fewer than two   B. exactly two   C. more than two
  vi. From where does Daniel hope to get eggs now?
  vii. Are Daniel and Amy's neighbors at home?
  viii. Why does Daniel decide not to make cookies today?
  ix. Which of these activities is Daniel most likely to have wanted to do at the bank?
    A. give blood   B. go fishing in the river   C. withdraw cash
  x. How was Daniel feeling this morning?
    A. healthy   B. a little sick   C. extremely ill

25. Refer to the *Get Fuzzy* comic strip at the beginning of this chapter. (The following questions serve as a follow-up to those asked in Exercise 16.)
  i. Once Bucky realizes that Rob's father has lied, he infers that Rob's father is angry about "the pudding incident." Who was responsible for this incident? How do you know? Which maxim did you have to appeal to in order to figure it out?
  ii. In the third cell, Bucky's thought bubble reads, "2+2= . . ." Does the author of the strip intend to show that Bucky is actually performing this arithmetic problem in his head? If not, then what message is the author trying to convey to you, the reader? Which maxim is the author using in order to convey this message?

26. Two basketball players are close friends. One is a very good player and makes every shot that he attempts. The other is not as good. Their coach has instructed them to try a new and very difficult drill. Both players try the new drill ten times. Of course, the first player puts the ball through the hoop all ten times. Afterwards, the friends get together to discuss how their practice went and have the following conversation:

1st Player: How did you do?
2nd Player: Well, I made it on my fifth try. I bet you did a lot better than me.
1st Player: Well, yeah, but don't feel too bad. I made it on my fourth shot.

    i. Of the ten tries, how many times did the first player make the shot?
    ii. What inference is the first player hoping that the second player will draw, counter to this fact, by saying, "I made it on my fourth shot"?
    iii. Which maxim is the first player using in order to create this implicature?
    iv. Why has the first player chosen to give this answer?
    v. Is the first player violating a maxim of **quality** by saying, "I made it on my fourth shot"?
    vi. Has the first player violated any other maxims? Justify your answer.

Discussion Questions

27.   **i.** In Section 7.3.2, the gesture of glancing at a watch is mentioned as a way to imply that a meeting is running late. What are other conventional nonlinguistic signals that are often sent in order to imply various messages? For each signal, what is the intended inference that should be drawn?
    ii. What is the purpose or benefit of having conventionalized these signals?

28. We tend to think of number words as naming exact values—of *forty-seven* meaning 'exactly forty-seven, no more and no less.' However, often we do not use them as though they had these meanings. If a friend asks you, "Do you have five bucks I can borrow?" your friend means, "Do you have at least five bucks I can borrow?" If you have ten dollars that you would be willing to lend your friend, but he asks about only five of them, you would still answer yes.
    i. In what sorts of contexts do we use the names of numbers to mean 'exactly that amount'?
    ii. In what sorts of contexts do we use the names of numbers to mean 'at least that amount'?
    iii. Can you think of examples of contexts in which the name of a number is used to mean 'at most that amount'?
    iv. When you hear a number word used, what sort of information do you consider in order to figure out whether it is being used with an 'at least,' 'at most,' or 'exactly' meaning?

Activities

29. Construct your own examples of discourse samples that make use of relevance, quantity, or manner implicatures. After writing the discourse, write a short analysis explaining what the implicatures are, why they are used by the speakers in your discourse, and from which maxim they derive.

File 7.4—Speech Acts

Exercises

30. Look at the contexts given for the sentence *Do any of you have a wrist watch?* in Exercise 1. In each case, which speech act is the speaker performing by uttering this sentence (e.g., request, threat, apology, etc.)?

31. Look at your answers to Exercise 4. (If you haven't yet done that exercise, do it now.) For each of your answers, tell whether it was a direct speech act or an indirect speech act.

32. Imagine that you have a child or a younger sibling who wants you to drive him/her to a friend's house.

    i. What speech act would this person need to perform in order to communicate this idea to you?

    ii. Write three sentences that s/he could use to get this point across: make one declarative, one imperative, and one interrogative. Label which is which. Also, label which are direct and which indirect.

33. Take the sentence *It's very warm outside.*

    i. What is the **form** of this sentence?

    ii. Write two contexts for this sentence in which it is used for different purposes.

    iii. In each case, tell the speaker's goal in uttering the sentence; in other words, what is the speech act in question?

    iv. Also, in each case, tell whether the speech act is being performed directly or indirectly.

34. Assume that a speaker wants another person to open the window. This speaker could try to communicate this idea by uttering any of the sentences in (a)–(g) below.

    i. What type of speech act corresponds with the speaker's goal?

    ii. Identify each sentence as a direct or an indirect speech act relative to that goal.

    iii. Identify the form of each sentence.

        a. I see that the window is not yet open.

        b. Can you open the window?

        c. I order you to open the window.

        d. I would appreciate it if you opened the window.

        e. I sure would love to have some fresh air in this room.

        f. Please open the window.

        g. Would you mind opening the window?

35. For each of the following speech acts, write three sentences. (That is, you will write a total of nine sentences: three for each kind of speech act.) First, write two direct speech acts, one with a performative verb and one without; then write an indirect speech act. Be sure to label which is which.

    a. question

    b. request

    c. promise

36. Refer to the table in (34) in Section 7.4.7. Assume that for each column, all of the sentences have the same communicative intention. Which are direct speech acts, and which are indirect speech acts?

37. The speech act of *promising* has the following felicity conditions:

- The speaker believes that the hearer wants something done.
- The speaker is able to do that thing.
- The speaker is willing to do it.
- It has not already been done (or it could be done again).

The speech act of threatening is very similar to promising. We should therefore expect their felicity conditions to be similar as well. Modify the felicity conditions for promises in order to create the felicity conditions for threats.

38. For each of the following scenarios, tell what kind of speech act seems to be being performed. Then tell whether the utterance is felicitous or infelicitous and why, appealing to the idea of felicity conditions.

- **a.** A woman sitting next to the ketchup and mustard containers at a table in a restaurant asks the man across the table from her to pass the ketchup.
- **b.** The bailiff in a courtroom approaches the judge and says, "I find the defendant guilty, your honor."
- **c.** A girl approaches the school librarian and says, "Excuse me; where can I find a book about butterflies?"
- **d.** A child who has just been punched by the school bully says, "Thank you so much for the wonderful gift."
- **e.** A woman who sees someone wearing a sweater that she admires says, "I really like your sweater."
- **f.** At the end of a business meeting, an employee says to his supervisor, "You may go now."
- **g.** A customer walks up to the cashier at a grocery store and says, "The canned vegetables are located in aisle five."
- **h.** On her way out the door, a woman says to her dog, "I'm going to be home late today. Would you please put dinner in the oven around 6:00?"
- **i.** A geography teacher says to her fifth-grade class, "The largest mountain range in the eastern half of the United States is the Appalachians."
- **j.** A boy, bundled up in all of his winter clothing, walks up to his parents and asks, "Where is my winter coat?"
- **k.** A man at a bus stop has his hands full of books. One slides off the pile onto the ground, and he says to the person next to him, "Excuse me; could you please pick up that book for me?"

39. Consider the following four scenarios. Each contains a warning, but the warning in each case is infelicitous.

- **a.** Someone warns an extremely careful and experienced carpenter that his saw is sharp and could cut him.
- **b.** Two children are taking a walk in the park; one says to the other, "Be careful! There's a daffodil growing by the side of the pavement!"
- **c.** A murderer lurking in the shadows yells to his next victim, "Watch out; there's someone here to kill you!" before lunging at her with his knife.
- **d.** A mother living with her child in a neighborhood in New England warns her child, "Be careful; there's an escaped madman running around Vienna!"

    - **i.** First, explain what makes each an infelicitous warning.
    - **ii.** Then, based on what you have observed about these infelicities, write a set of felicity conditions for warnings that would prevent such inappropriate utter-

ances. (For models of what felicity conditions look like, refer to Exercise 36 or to the examples given in Section 7.4.2.)

40. Which of the following sentences contain performative verbs? (*Hint:* Exactly five of the underlined verbs are performative.) Explain the difference between the five verbs you chose as performative verbs and the other five verbs that you did not choose.

   a. I <u>promise</u> to be there.
   b. I <u>suggest</u> that you leave.
   c. I <u>convince</u> you that I am right.
   d. I <u>warn</u> you not to come any closer.
   e. I <u>incite</u> you to be angry.
   f. I <u>forbid</u> you to enter this room.
   g. I <u>inspire</u> you to write beautiful music.
   h. I <u>amuse</u> you with my jokes.
   i. I <u>order</u> you to be quiet.
   j. I <u>provoke</u> you to punch me.

Activities

41. Choose a short section of a television show or a movie in which there is a lot of dialogue. (Your instructor will tell you how long a segment to choose. It would be best to choose a clip that you have a recording of so that you can watch it multiple times.) List all of the kinds of speech acts that you hear during the clip.

42. Pay attention to language use around you, and keep track of the various speech acts that you hear in various contexts. Choose between two and five kinds of contexts. (Your instructor will tell you how many to choose and how long to spend observing each.) For example, you might choose a conversation between a supervisor and an employee, a group of friends chatting over lunch, two people having an argument, someone explaining an assignment to a classmate, and so on. (It will be **much** easier to complete this activity if you choose conversations in which you are not a participant!)

Create a simple table like the one below that you can fill in. You will fill in the contexts in the left-hand column. Then use tick marks to note how many times you hear each speech act in a given conversation. Don't worry about who utters which; just keep track on a conversation-by-conversation basis. Remember that the form of an utterance doesn't always correspond to the type of speech act that it is! (If you hear an utterance and are not sure of how to categorize it, make a note in the margin of your paper.)

Write a short analysis of what you have observed. Do certain speech acts tend to appear more frequently or less frequently in particular contexts? Offer some hypotheses of why you think this may be so. (Keep in mind that you will be interested in **relative** frequency, that is, how often some kind of speech act appears relative to the other kinds: the actual tally count that you have doesn't give you useful information unless you know how it compares to the others.)

Compare your responses with those of classmates who observed similar kinds of discourse. Are your observations similar to theirs?

CONTEXT	assertion	question	request	order	promise	threat	apology	warning	advice
(fill in . . .)									
(fill in . . .)									

File 7.5—Presupposition

Exercises

43. A classic example of a question that a lawyer might unfairly ask a defendant in a court room is "Have you stopped beating your wife?" Explain, as precisely as possible, why this is a so-called unfair question.

44. List all of the existence presuppositions contained in the following sentences. (Of course, normally when we read nursery rhymes such as these, we are very willing to accommodate the presuppositions that they contain.)

    a. Old Mother Hubbard went to the cupboard to fetch her poor dog a bone.
    b. Little Boy Blue went to blow his horn on account of the sheep were in the meadow and the cows were in the corn.
    c. The black sheep had a bag of wool for his master, a bag of wool for his dame, and a bag of wool for the little boy who lived down the lane.
    d. Jack and Jill went up the hill because they wanted to test Jack's new high-tech anti-fall machine.

45. Pick a book—fiction or nonfiction—of your choosing. Copy out two sentences that contain existence presuppositions and one sentence that contains some other type of presupposition. Then explicitly state the presuppositions.

46. Consider the sentence *Andrea read a book about how ice cream is made, too.* How many different presuppositions could this sentence have if uttered with different prosodies? For each possibility, write a sentence that could go in a discourse before this sentence, and write the given sentence with the appropriate part marked for prosodic prominence. Finally, tell what the presupposition would be. (There are many possible responses for this exercise; try to come up with at least four.)

    Example: Andrea read a book about how pencils are made.
              Andrea read a book about how ICE CREAM is made, too.
              Presupposition: Andrea read a book about how something is made.

Discussion Questions

47. Is each of the following sentences true or false? Why do you think so? (Assume that they are spoken in the early twenty-first century about the present time, such that there is no monarchy in France.) Do you feel the same way about the truth value of all of them?

    a. The king of France has red hair.
    b. The king of France is bald.
    c. The king of France had lunch with me yesterday.
    d. I had lunch with the king of France yesterday.

48. Using sentences with presuppositions that have not been satisfied is a strategy often associated with gossips. For example, a gossip might say, "Are you surprised that Jack and Jill are getting married?" In this sentence, the words *surprised that* are a presupposition trigger, so the sentence presupposes that Jack and Jill are getting married without actually coming right out and saying it. Why might a gossip adopt this strategy? Do you believe that it is an effective strategy? Can you think of times that you have heard this strategy used? Describe them.

49. In File 7.5, we mentioned that there are many presupposition triggers other than the ones that we explicitly discussed. Consider the following examples. What are the presuppositions contained in each of the following sentences? What is the presupposition trigger in each case? (Be forewarned that the answers to these questions are not contained in the file; they are an opportunity for further thought and reflection on the topic of presupposition.)

   a. Please take me out to the ball game again.
   b. When we bought our new house, our pet platypus was delighted that it would have its very own bathtub.
   c. That her pet turtle ran away made Emily very sad.
   d. Eli wants more popcorn.
   e. If pigs had wings, where would they fly?
   f. I, too, often have a glass of milk at night.
   g. The elephant will continue to be endangered until we stop destroying its natural habitat.

Activities

50. In casual conversation with your friends, try using sentences that presuppose information that has not yet been asserted in the conversation. (Make sure that it's relevant to whatever you are talking about, though!) How do your friends react? What kinds of presuppositions can you get away with (i.e., which ones do they accommodate?)? What kinds of presuppositions do they call you on or give you weird looks about? Can you make any generalizations? *(As with Activity 21, neither the editors of this book nor your instructor can take any responsibility for any effect this activity may have on your social life!)* How, if at all, do you think your findings would differ if you did this experiment with a group of your professors or with your supervisor at work? Explain.

CHAPTER

8

Language Acquisition

"Lahwaah, buwha buwhaah, gullygah abawaa mey ayeeyaah. Is that normal?"

Cartoon by Mike Baldwin, available at www.CartoonStock.com

FILE **8.0**

What Is Language Acquisition?

Many people believe that language is what sets humans apart from other animals. Languages are highly complex and sophisticated systems. So how do we humans manage to learn such complicated systems? This chapter addresses that question. The predominant theory assumes that part of our ability to acquire language is innate and that children learn language by "inventing" the rules specific to their language.

When acquiring one or more native language(s), all children go through the same stages of language development: they start by babbling, then learn their first words, go through a so-called one-word stage (during which they can utter only one word at a time), enter the two-word stage, and finally learn the more complex structures of their language(s). Language acquisition is not limited to children; many people learn a second language later in life. However, second-language acquisition can differ from first-language acquisition in many respects.

Contents

Theories of Language Acquisition

8.1.1 About Language Acquisition

Humans are not born talking. Instead, we typically learn to understand language and to speak during the first few years of our lives, before we even enter kindergarten or grade school. Recall from File 1.2 that language is a communication system consisting of sounds, morphemes, words, and rules for combining all of these. The knowledge of these elements enables people to understand and produce sentences they may never have heard or uttered before. So how does a child acquire this knowledge? If knowing a language were simply a matter of knowing a lot of words, language acquisition would just be a process of figuring out what the words were and memorizing them. Instead, children must acquire a grammar with all its components and rules. How do children learn these rules? For instance, how do they learn that the morpheme *un-* (meaning 'not') attaches to adjectives to form other adjectives having the opposite meanings? How do they learn to compose a sentence from a noun phrase and a verb phrase? Rules, unlike words, are never explicitly stated, so the child cannot just memorize them: he must somehow figure the rules out on his own—a remarkable intellectual feat.

Various theories have arisen that attempt to account for how children acquire language. One theory that has found a lot of support throughout the years is that at least part of the human language ability is **innate.** In the sections that follow, we will first explore the **innateness hypothesis** and the evidence for it.

However, innateness alone does not answer all of the questions about how children acquire the specific language that is spoken around them. Again, there are a number of theories that have been proposed for how additional, more specific knowledge is acquired. We will briefly consider two early ones, **Imitation Theory** and **Reinforcement Theory,** which have been refuted but which remain part of popular belief. It is therefore important to point out why these theories are inadequate. We will then consider three more current theories of language acquisition: the most influential of them is the **Active Construction of a Grammar Theory.** This theory is the one that most linguists believe today. However, there are a number of influential competing theories. Of these, we will introduce **Connectionist Theories** and **Social Interaction Theory.**

8.1.2 The Innateness Hypothesis

The first theory of language acquisition that we will consider asserts that language ability is **innate** in humans. That is, humans are genetically predisposed to acquire and use language (though not any particular language, of course). This theory claims that babies are born with the knowledge that languages have patterns and with the ability to seek out and identify those patterns. Some theorists have even claimed that humans have innate knowledge of some core characteristics common to all languages, such as the concepts of 'noun' and 'verb.' These basic features shared by all languages are called **linguistic universals,** and the theoretically inborn set of structural characteristics shared by all languages is known as

311

universal grammar. No one knows exactly what the contents of universal grammar are, though this is currently an active area of research in linguistics.

The claim that linguistic ability is innate in humans is supported by, for example, the work of biologist Eric Lenneberg. He studied animal behavior and developed a list of characteristics that are typical of innately determined behaviors. Innate behaviors are present in all normal individuals of a species, whereas learned behaviors are not. Walking, for instance, is a behavior for which humans are genetically predisposed (that is, humans learn to walk as a natural part of development, without being explicitly taught), but playing the piano or riding a bicycle must be specifically taught. Is talking like walking, or is it like playing the piano?

To answer this, let's examine Lenneberg's characteristics of biologically controlled behaviors. If language acquisition has each of these characteristics, we can safely assume that it is a genetically triggered behavior.

(1) Lenneberg's characteristics of biologically controlled behaviors:[1]
     1. The behavior emerges before it is necessary.
     2. Its appearance is not the result of a conscious decision.
     3. Its emergence is not triggered by external events (though the surrounding environment must be sufficiently "rich" for it to develop adequately).
     4. Direct teaching and intensive practice have relatively little effect.
     5. There is a regular sequence of "milestones" as the behavior develops, and these can usually be correlated with age and other aspects of development.
     6. There is likely to be a "critical period" for the acquisition of the behavior.

Consider the first criterion. In what sense is language necessary? From a biological standpoint, language is a behavior that has encouraged the survival and predominance of the human species. Each individual needs the ability to use language in order to take care of other basic needs. But children ordinarily begin to speak a language between the ages of twelve and twenty-four months, long before their parents have stopped providing them with the necessities of life. So language is a behavior that, like walking, emerges well before children have to fend for themselves.

As for the second and third criteria, language is neither the result of a conscious decision nor triggered by external events. Children decide whether or not they want to learn to play baseball or checkers, but they do not make a conscious choice about acquiring a native language; it's just something that all children do. Also, language is not learned as a result of something special triggering the learning. It is not taught the way (for example) piano playing is taught. Think about this: if you grew up hearing brilliantly played piano music, would you automatically pick up that skill the way we all seem to have automatically picked up language? Clearly not. While it is true that a child has to be exposed to language— this is what is meant by the environment being "rich"—it is not the case that a child's caretakers need to make a special effort to teach the child to speak. Other than hearing normal conversation and being spoken to, the child needs no special external stimulus to begin the process of acquiring language.

But doesn't intensive teaching help children learn language? Surprisingly, it does not seem to have much of an effect. Children don't necessarily perceive (or correct!) their mistakes just because an adult points them out (see Section 8.1.4).

Language acquisition also exhibits Lenneberg's fifth characteristic of having a sequence of "milestones" or identifiable stages associated with its development. Specifically, children master linguistic skills in a certain order. You will read about these stages in more detail in subsequent files. Although there is some variability in the milestones and the ages

---

[1]From Aitchinson (1976), adapted from Lenneberg (1967).

at which children achieve them, there is a path of developmental stepping stones that all children follow.

Lenneberg further proposes that innate behaviors have a **critical period** associated with their emergence. The term *critical period* describes a period of time in an individual's life during which a behavior—in this case language—must be acquired; that is, the acquisition will fail if it is attempted either before or after the critical period.

The critical period for language acquisition is assumed to extend from birth to approximately the onset of puberty. During this time, a child needs exposure to language in order to develop the brain structures necessary for language acquisition. If a child is not exposed to language at all during this time, then the child will never acquire normal language skills and, in fact, may not acquire language skills at all. If a child has acquired a native language during the critical period and starts learning a second language before the age of twelve, the child will likely achieve native competence in this second language as well. However, if the second language is learned after about age twelve, the child is likely never to acquire complete native competence in the language.

How can we tell whether there really is a critical period for first-language acquisition? To prove this, we would have to show that language skills could not be acquired normally or even at all if the learning began after the critical period had ended. This could be accomplished by depriving a child of linguistic input for the early years of life, but obviously it would be highly unethical to submit a child to such treatment. However, there are least two sources of information available to linguists which support the claims that there is a critical period for first-language acquisition.

First, evidence for the critical period hypothesis comes from children who, owing to unfortunate circumstances, were exposed to little or no language during their early lives. These children were either neglected by their caretakers (**neglected children**) or grew up in the wild, often with animals (**feral children**). When these children were rescued or discovered, researchers attempted to help them acquire language. The success of these attempts depended largely on the age at which the children were discovered. We will consider two such cases, outlined in (2) and (3).

(2) Genie was found in 1970 when she was nearly fourteen years old. She had been abused and isolated since the age of twenty months. When first discovered, Genie was completely silent. Thereafter her language acquisition was extremely slow, and although she did learn to speak, her speech was abnormal. She was able to memorize many vocabulary items, but her expressions were formulaic, as in *what is X* and *give me X*. She never learned grammar.

(3) Isabelle was discovered in 1937 at the age of six and a half. Her mother was deaf and could not speak. Isabelle's grandfather had kept Isabelle and her mother isolated but had not otherwise mistreated them. Isabelle then began lessons at The Ohio State University, and although her progress was at first slow, it soon accelerated. In two years her intelligence and her language use were completely normal for a child her age.

At first sight, the cases of Genie and Isabelle seem to provide good evidence for the critical period hypothesis: Genie, discovered after the supposed critical period was over, never learned language; Isabelle, discovered before the end of the period, did. But evidence from feral or neglected children is problematic. Such children are usually traumatized or are not socialized before they are rescued or found. So it is possible that it is not the lack of exposure to language but rather a larger trauma that prevents them from acquiring language properly. For example, Genie had been beaten by her father for making noises, so her difficulty with language could have had multiple causes. The case of Isabelle is problematic for the opposite reason: prior to being found, she was locked in a room with her mother, and although her mother could not speak, they developed a rudimentary personal gesture system to communicate. Thus, Isabelle did have some exposure to a communication system during the early years of her life. It is possible that Isabelle acquired language not because she was discovered at an earlier age than Genie, but because she had access to a rudimentary communication system. Likewise, it is possible that Genie didn't learn language not because she was discovered at an older age than was Isabelle, but rather because she had been abused.

Stronger evidence supporting both the innateness of language and the critical period hypothesis for first-language acquisition can be found in instances of deaf children and adults who were initially raised in environments without access to signed language input. One particularly illustrative example is the case of the deaf population of Nicaragua in the late twentieth century. At the end of the 1970s, following Nicaragua's civil war, the country founded a new state school for the deaf. In the late 1970s and early 1980s, deaf children and adults were able to come together in a way that had not been possible earlier in the country's history. Most children and adults arrived at the schools with idiosyncratic and rudimentary **homesign** gesture systems. Homesign gestures are communicative gestures (a form associated with a meaning) that are invented by deaf children and the people with whom they routinely interact in cases where a signed language is not made available. Homesigns may represent the names of individuals such as family members and the names of common activities ('eat') or common objects ('house') that are often referred to. However, a homesign system is not a language: it is an extremely limited lexicon without a grammar. Thus the students arrived at the school with backgrounds that involved social interactions and communication and that were normal in every way except that they did not include exposure to language.

Soon, combining the homesigns that the students brought with them as well as some newly created signs, the children at the school created a pidgin (a type of simplified language—see File 11.3) to communicate with each other. After the pidgin was created by the first students at the school, younger children came and were exposed to the pidgin. Without instruction, and based only on their exposure to the pidgin used by their older peers, these younger children created Idioma de Signos Nicaragense (ISN), which is a full-fledged language with a complex system of grammatical rules.

The creation of ISN has been cited as evidence for the innateness of language, because within two or three generations of students, children created a new and complete language. Because they did not have exposure to any other linguistic system, all of the grammatical principles that were developed in ISN must have arisen through some innate ability in the children to create a complete grammatical system.

However, those students who first came to the school as older children, and who had not acquired any linguistic communication system prior to the time that they enrolled but had otherwise grown up in a caring environment, did not perfectly acquire this new language: in adulthood, their language use still resembles the pidgin, and there are inconsistencies in their use of phonological, morphological, and syntactic principles of the sort that one would not see in a native speaker of the language. This evidence supports the critical period hypothesis because the older children came from backgrounds similar to those of the younger children, yet they were unable to fully acquire language.

Support for a critical period for second-language acquisition involves comparing the acquisition of a second language by children and by teenagers and adults. Teenagers and adults have more difficulty learning languages than do children. People who have learned a language as an adult almost always have a foreign accent, indicating that they have not acquired the phonological rules of the second language perfectly. They may also find syntactic and other rules difficult to master completely. Children, however, can acquire a second (or third) language easily and completely as long as they have sufficient input from those languages. This ability tapers off around the age of puberty. However, the idea of a critical period for second-language acquisition is very controversial. Critics argue that there are (rare) cases of adults learning a second language perfectly. Furthermore, it is possible to learn a second language at any age. Rather than a critical period, there seems to be a steady decline in how well one can learn a second language. Finally, factors such as teaching methods, motivation, identity, dedication, utility, and so on, play a role in how successfully a second language is learned, and these factors may also change with age, confounding studies looking for critical period effects in second-language acquisition.

Another concern related to the critical period hypothesis is that different aspects of language acquisition may behave differently relative to the critical period. For example, many feral or neglected children gain the ability to learn vocabulary and to understand others' speech, but they are not able to learn to use syntax productively. Second-language learners are able to learn large amounts of vocabulary and frequently master the language's syntax, but they rarely master the phonological system. This suggests that a critical period may exist for certain aspects of language (syntax in first-language acquisition and phonology in second-language acquisition), but not for others.

Despite our lack of a complete understanding of the acquisition process, we can conclude that language acquisition shows characteristics of being an innate human behavior.

8.1.3 Imitation Theory

Moving on to how the specifics of language are acquired, we will first consider **Imitation Theory,** which claims that children learn language by listening to the speech around them and reproducing what they hear. According to this theory, language acquisition consists of memorizing the words and sentences of some language. The idea that acquiring a language is a process of learning to imitate the speech of others is at least partly true. Since the connection between the way a word sounds and what it means is largely arbitrary (see File 1.4), children cannot guess what the words of their target language are. They must hear the words used by other speakers and then reproduce or "imitate" them. This theory also helps explain the fact that children learn the language that is spoken around them by parents, caretakers, and others, regardless of what the language of their ancestors may have been. Thus a Korean child, for instance, will speak Korean if raised in a Korean-speaking environment, but Arabic if raised in an Arabic-speaking environment. In other words, a child's genetic makeup has nothing to do with which language the child will acquire.

Unfortunately, however, Imitation Theory explains little else of what we know about language acquisition. Children's speech differs from adult norms: it is full of "errors" of many types. A two-year-old might say *nana* for adult *banana,* a three-year-old might say *Mommy tie shoe,* and a four-year-old might say *hitted* or *goed* rather *hit* or *went.*

The last example clearly cannot be a case of imitation because children would not have heard an adult say *hitted* or *goed.* Rather, it seems that the child who says *hitted* has a rule in her internal grammar which adds -*ed* (pronounced as /d/, /t/ or /əd/) to a verb to make it past tense. The child has not mastered the fact that there are exceptions to this rule, such as the use of *hit* rather than *hitted* in the past tense. However, Imitation Theory fails to acknowledge that a child has any sort of internal mental grammar that includes rules for combining words and other elements in systematic ways, so it would incorrectly predict that a child would not produce words like *hitted.*

The most serious fault of Imitation Theory is that it cannot account for how children and adults are able to produce and understand new sentences. If children learned only by imitation, the only way they could understand a sentence is if they had heard it before. However, we know that there are an infinite number of possible sentences in any language, and speakers (even children) are able to understand and produce completely novel utterances.

8.1.4 Reinforcement Theory

Reinforcement Theory asserts that children learn to speak like adults because they are praised, rewarded, or otherwise reinforced when they use the right forms and are corrected when they use wrong forms. However, the claim that parents and other caretakers frequently correct their children's grammatical mistakes and praise their correct forms is unfounded. Such corrections seldom happen, for although parents often do correct their children, their corrections generally have more to do with the accuracy or truth of a statement than with its grammatical form. Thus, *The dog wants to eat* may receive the response *No, the dog doesn't want to eat* if the dog has just finished its dinner, whereas the sentence *Robin goed to school today* may receive the response *Yes, he did* if Robin did go to school that day.

Reinforcement Theory is also contradicted by the fact that even when adults do try to correct a child's grammar, the attempts usually fail entirely. Consider the following conversation:

(4) Child: Nobody don't like me.
    Mother: No, say "nobody likes me."
    Child: Nobody don't like me.
    (repeated 8 times)
    Mother (now exasperated):   Now listen carefully! Say, "Nobody likes me."
    Child: Oh! Nobody don't likes me.

Notice that although the child does not form negative sentences in the same way the adult does, the child's utterances follow a pattern just as the adult's do. The child's way of forming negative sentences involving *nobody* is completely regular: every such sentence contains *nobody* + a negative auxiliary verb, such as *Nobody can't spell that* or *Nobody won't listen*. If the child produces a variety of such sentences, then he or she must possess a rule that defines this pattern, but the rule is not the same as the one in the adult's grammar. Reinforcement Theory can explain neither where the child's rule came from nor why the child seems impervious to correction. (Incidentally, the conversation sample above is a good example of how direct teaching does not help children to acquire language—recall the criteria for innate behaviors in Section 8.1.2.)

8.1.5 Active Construction of a Grammar Theory

The **Active Construction of a Grammar Theory,** the most influential theory of language acquisition, holds that children actually invent the rules of grammar themselves. The theory assumes that the ability to develop rules is innate, but that the actual rules are based on the speech children hear around them; this is their input or data for analysis. Children listen to the language around them and analyze it to determine the patterns that exist. When they think they have discovered a pattern, they hypothesize a rule to account for it. They add this rule to their growing grammar and use it in constructing utterances. For example, a child's early hypothesis about how to form the past tense of verbs will be to add an allomorph of *-ed*. All past tense verbs would then be constructed with this rule, producing forms such as *holded* and *eated* alongside *needed* and *walked*. Notice that at this point the child would have already learned the rules of when the regular past tense ending is pronounced /d/, /t/, or /əd/. When children discover that there are forms in the language that do not match those produced by this rule, they modify the rule or add another one to produce the additional forms. Eventually, the child has created and edited his or her own grammar to the point where it matches an adult's grammar. At this point, there are no significant discrepancies between the forms produced by the child and those produced by the adults. Clearly, the child has a complete working grammar all along, even before it is essentially adultlike. The child uses this grammar to produce utterances; when those utterances differ from adult speech, they are reflecting the differences in the two grammars.

Within this framework, children's mistakes are expected to occur and to follow nonrandom patterns. This is because the child is forming utterances according to grammatical rules even though the rules are often different from those that adults use. It is important to note also that active reinforcement by adults about a child's mistakes is not enough to help the child "discover" what is wrong with his or her own utterances; the child must make the connection in his or her own time.

8.1.6 Connectionist Theories

Connectionist theories of language acquisition assume that children learn language by creating neural connections in the brain. A child develops such connections through exposure to language and by using language. Through these connections, the child learns associations between words, meanings, sound sequences, and so on. For example, a child may hear the word *bottle* in different circumstances and establish neural connections every time the word is heard. Such connections can be to the word itself, to the initial sound /b/, to the word *milk*, to what the bottle looks like, to the activity of drinking, and so on. Eventually, all of these connections become the child's mental representation of the meaning and the form of the word (see Section 1.4.7). Connections can have different strengths, and language acquisition involves adjusting the strengths of the connections appropriately. The strength of a connection is dependent on input frequency. For example, if a child hears the word *bottle* more frequently in connection with *milk* than with *water,* then the connection between *bottle* and *milk* will be stronger than that between *bottle* and *water.* Thus, instead of developing abstract **rules,** according to connectionist theories, children exploit statistical information from linguistic input. Such theories assume that the input children receive is indeed rich enough to learn language without an innate mechanism to invent linguistic rules (though note that the ability to make statistical generalizations must be innate).

To get a better feel for how this theory works and how it differs from other theories, let's look at the acquisition of the past tense of verbs again. The Active Construction of a Grammar Theory assumes that children produce words like *goed* or *growed* because they have formed a rule that tells them to add *-ed* to a verb to form the past tense. Connectionist models assume that the child merely exploits statistical information about forming past tenses. Thus, the child says *goed* and *growed* because the existence of forms like *showed, mowed, towed,* and *glowed* makes this pattern statistically likely.

Evidence for the exploitation of statistics as opposed to the development of abstract rules comes from experiments in which, for example, children create the past tense of nonsense verbs. For instance, when asked to complete the phrase "This man is fringing; Yesterday, he _____," many children create nonsense irregular forms such as *frang* or *frought* instead of the nonsense regular form *fringed.* Such data pose a problem for the Active Construction of a Grammar Theory, but the data can be explained in terms of a connectionist model. If children invent rules and then learn exceptions to the rules, they should produce *fringed* as the past tense of *fring* because it is not one of the learned exceptions. However, if children exploit statistical data, they would be expected to sometimes produce irregular forms because of their exposure to words like *sing, ring,* or *bring.*

Of course, it is possible that children both develop rules and also make use of statistical data. That is, it is possible that acquisition of grammatical rules proceeds according to a hybrid model and that children actively construct a grammar by establishing and exploiting neural connections.

8.1.7 Social Interaction Theory

Social Interaction Theory assumes that children acquire language through social interaction, with older children and adults in particular. This approach holds that children prompt their parents to supply them with the appropriate language experience they need. Thus, children and their language environment are seen as a dynamic system: children need their language environment to improve their social and linguistic communication skills, and the appropriate language environment exists because it is cued by the child. Like those who advocate the Active Construction of Grammar Theory, social interactionists believe that children must develop rules and that they have a predisposition to learn language. However, social interaction theorists place a great deal of emphasis on social interaction and the kind of input that children receive, instead of assuming that simply being exposed to language use will suffice. According to this approach, the ways in which older children and adults talk to infants play a crucial role in how a child acquires language. In many Western societies, speech to infants (so-called **child-directed speech**) is slow and high-pitched and contains many repetitions, simplified syntax, exaggerated intonation, and a simple and concrete vocabulary (see File 8.4). Consider the following examples from Berko Gleason and Bernstein Ratner (1998):

(5) See the birdie? Look at the birdie! What a pretty birdie!

(6) Has it come to your attention that one of our better-looking feathered friends is perched upon the windowsill?

When pointing out a bird on the windowsill to an infant, adults and older children are likely to say something like (5) in a slow, high-pitched voice with exaggerated intonation. In addition, they are likely to point at the bird. The social aspect of the interaction involves sharing an observation with the child. All of this helps the child to decode what the speech might mean. No adult would point out a bird to an infant by uttering something like (6). Social interactionists believe that the way adults speak to children and interact with children is crucial to acquiring language.

Of course, one of the problems with this theory is that children eventually do acquire the ability to utter and understand sentences like those in (6). While child-directed speech may be crucial early on, it is unclear how long a child must be exposed to it. Furthermore, the characteristics of child-directed speech vary from culture to culture, and we do not at this point know what specific aspects of such speech might, in fact, be crucial.

At the same time, this theory is also not completely incompatible with either of the two previous theories. That is, the types of social interactions that infants have may, in fact, be invaluable to language acquisition, which may develop through neural connections and involve the hypothesizing of particular grammatical rules on the part of the child.

First-Language Acquisition: The Acquisition of Speech Sounds and Phonology

8.2.1 Physiological Prerequisites of Sound Perception and Production

Before children can begin to speak a language, they must first master several tasks related to the form of language: they must be able to identify the sounds (phonemes) of the language they hear; they must learn how to produce each allophone of these phonemes—the variants of the phoneme that depend on the context in which it occurs (see File 3.1); they must decode the larger strings of sounds that they hear into syllables and words; and they must learn to combine the sounds into larger strings themselves. Below, we discuss the basics of how children learn to perceive and produce speech sounds, as well as some of the experimental techniques that researchers use to study child language acquisition.

a. Identifying Sounds. In order to produce spoken language, infants first need to be able to perceive it. In fact, they are able to perceive many distinctions in language much earlier than they are able to produce them. Since we cannot just ask babies about their perception and receive an answer, special methodologies are needed to determine what they can and cannot perceive. One of the most successful techniques used for studying the abilities of infants up to the age of six months is called **High Amplitude Sucking** (HAS). In this technique, infants are given a special pacifier that is connected to a sound-generating system. Each suck on the pacifier generates a noise, and infants learn quickly that their sucking produces the noise. At first, babies suck often because they are interested in hearing the noise. They lose interest, however, in hearing the same noise over again, and their sucking rate slows down. When this happens, the experimenter changes the sound that the pacifier generates. If the infant sucks faster after the change, we infer that he has recognized the change in sound and is sucking faster to hear the interesting new sound. If the infant does not suck faster, we infer that he could not discriminate between the two sounds.

Another important technique is the **Conditioned Head-Turn Procedure** (HT), usually used with infants between five and eighteen months. This procedure has two phases: conditioning and testing. The infant sits on a parent's lap, watching a display and listening to sounds. During the conditioning phase, the infant learns to associate a change in sound with the activation of visual reinforcers. At first, the visual reinforcers are presented at the same time as the change in sound. Then the visual reinforcers are presented shortly after the change. The infant will begin to anticipate the appearance of the visual reinforcers and look for them before they are activated. During the testing phase, if the infant looks to the visual reinforcers immediately after a change in sound, we infer that the infant has perceived the change in sound and can thus discriminate between the two sounds involved. If the infant does not look to the visual reinforcers, we infer that he did not perceive the change and thus cannot discriminate between the two sounds.

HAS and HT have been used in many studies on infants to determine what they can hear and how they process what they hear. DeCasper and Spence (1986), for example, used HAS to show that infants can hear speech in the womb. The researchers wanted to see whether infants whose mothers had read a Dr. Seuss story aloud during the final six months of pregnancy would recognize the story after they were born. Following birth, a group of

319

babies heard several stories, including the Dr. Seuss story. Only the babies who had heard the story in the womb modified their sucking rate when read the Dr. Seuss story. Infants who had not heard the story before birth showed no change in sucking rate. DeCasper and Spence concluded that the infants who modified their sucking rate recognized the story as a new stimulus (that is, they heard familiar sounds after hearing unfamiliar sounds). The babies who did not change their sucking rate heard unfamiliar sounds throughout the experiment.

Perception studies have also shown that by the age of four months infants can already distinguish between the production of vowels [ɑ] and [i]. In one experimental paradigm, infants are shown the mouths of two adult faces, one saying [ɑ], the other one saying [i]. Simultaneously, a tape plays one of the two sounds. When the infants hear an [ɑ], they show a preference by looking at the face saying [ɑ]; when they hear an [i], they show a preference by looking at the face producing the [i]. These findings suggest that infants of about four months of age are able not only to distinguish different vowel qualities but also to use visual cues to determine the kind of articulation involved in producing the sounds. In fact, the infants' own coos differ in these two contexts: they are more [ɑ]-like (or [i]-like, respectively), to match the sound heard and the mouth watched.

Not only are babies born with the ability to hear very slight differences between sounds; they can also hear distinctions between sounds that their parents cannot. For example, sounds that English-speaking adults perceive as a /b/ or a /p/ differ in their **voice onset time** (**VOT;** see **aspiration** in Section 2.6.5). English-speaking adults perceive bilabial stops with a VOT of 20 ms as a /b/, but those with a VOT of 40 ms as a /p/. Six-month-old infants can also perceive this difference. Studies using HAS or HT have shown, however, that the infants can also perceive the difference between a bilabial stop with a VOT of −60 ms (that is, voicing starts 60 ms before the consonant is released) and a VOT of −20 ms. English-speaking adults don't perceive this difference; rather, they hear both sounds as /b/. In contrast, six-month-old infants show an increase in sucking rate when a recording switches from the first to the second sound. Interestingly, however, by the time they are twelve months old, infants living in an English-speaking environment will have lost the ability to perceive the difference between a bilabial stop with a VOT of −60 ms and a VOT of −20 ms. Twelve-month-old infants born to Thai-speaking parents, on the other hand, are still able to differentiate between these sounds, as are Thai-speaking adults.

It seems, then, that at six months, infants are able to perceive phonetic distinctions that correspond to phonemes in many languages. Yet by twelve months they are able to distinguish only between sounds that are phonemic (contrastive) in their native language; that is, the particular sounds that can be used in the language to distinguish words. This means that a twelve-month-old with English-speaking parents can no longer differentiate between a bilabial stop with a VOT of −60 and a VOT of −20 because this ability is not important for distinguishing English words. On the other hand, a twelve-month-old child with Thai-speaking parents can tell these sounds apart because the sounds are important for understanding the meaning of words in Thai. It seems that once infants have figured out the important distinctions of their native language(s), they ignore distinctions that are not important.

In addition to being able to distinguish between phonemes of the language they are acquiring, children also need to figure out where one word ends and the next one begins. This is a difficult task because even in relatively slow speech, adults do not pause after every word. In fact, whole phrases or sentences are often uttered as one continuous stream of speech. Some researchers have suggested that children make use of intonational cues (see File 2.5) to help them segment speech. For example, many words in English are stressed on the first syllable. If children born to English-speaking parents take a stressed syllable to indicate the beginning of a word, they would be correct more often than not. A child using this strategy would segment the stream *What a pretty birdie* into *What-a, pretty* and *birdie*. However, this cannot be the only strategy a child uses because not all English words are stressed on the first syllable. Another approach to word segmentation assumes that children make use of statistical cues. For example, if a child hears sentences like *What a pretty birdie. Look! The birdie is flying,* he or she can use the fact that [bɹ] always seems to be followed by [di] to arrive at the conclusion that [bɹdi] is probably a word.

    b. Producing Sounds. A child's first vocalizations are present at the very beginning of life. (Everyone knows how adept babies are at crying!) Within a few weeks after birth a child begins to coo, producing sequences of vowel-like sounds. The child uses these cooing and gurgling noises to indicate contentment and pleasure, or at least this is how most adults interpret these sounds.

    Since an infant's tongue is relatively large compared to the size of its vocal tract, the front of the tongue easily makes contact with the roof of the mouth, and a baby is very likely to produce coos that sound vaguely palatal, like the adult phonemes /j/ or /ɲ/. From very early on, the baby "practices" sounds of various kinds. What the baby has to learn are the articulatory **gestures** involved in producing a particular sound (e.g., bringing both lips together to produce a bilabial sound), as well as the timing relationships between these gestures (i.e., starting vocal-fold vibration for voicing a sound, opening the mouth, lowering the velum to allow air passage through the nasal cavity, raising the tongue for an alveolar closure, etc.) (see Files 2.2–2.4). The young child has to practice the execution of the motor programs that underlie speech production. This might seem to be an easy task, but, by analogy, if you were to try patting your right hand on your left knee and rubbing your left hand in circles on your right knee, it would probably take a bit of practice to get the different movements coordinated. Learning to speak is just as hard or harder for infants, since they have to learn to gain control over the muscles in their speech organs and to coordinate the execution of articulatory movements. Therefore, a child's production of speech will generally be slower and more variable than that of an adult.

8.2.2 Babbling

At the age of four to six months or so, children in all cultures begin to **babble,** producing sequences of vowels and consonants if they are acquiring spoken language, or producing hand movements if they are acquiring signed language. Children acquiring signed languages babble by moving their fingers in repetitive rhythmic ways that are very similar to the hand motions that will be needed for making actual signs. Some linguists assume that babies babble to practice the muscle coordination needed to produce language. In the case of spoken languages, this involves the opening and closing movement of the jaw and manipulating other articulators; in the case of signed languages, it involves hand and finger coordination. The following discussion focuses on babbling by children acquiring spoken language. However, apart from the modality, there seems to be no cognitive difference between the babbling of children learning spoken and signed languages.

    As mentioned above, a baby's tongue is relatively large compared to the size of its oral cavity. Since the tongue is attached to the lower jaw, as the lower jaw moves up, the tongue moves up with it. For this reason, it is very likely that the infant will produce vaguely palatal sounds like [ɲ] or [j] as the tongue moves up near the hard palate. Since the lower lip is also attached to the jaw, labials such as [b] and [m] occur frequently, too. When the jaw goes down and the tongue lies on the jaw, the infant is very likely to produce the vowel sound [ɑ]. These are, of course, not the only sounds that an infant produces, but they are likely sounds in the very beginning. Also, keep in mind that babbling a certain sequence of sounds is not a conscious process. It is probably accidental if the infant produces a syllable like [ti], since the tongue tip has to contact the alveolar ridge while the mouth is open.

    Repeated or **canonical babbling** starts around the age of seven to ten months. The continual repetition of syllables helps the infant practice a sequence of consonant and vowel sounds. For example, a common canonical babble like [mɑmɑmɑmɑ] involves the sequence of a bilabial nasal consonant followed by a low vowel. Since babies breathe mostly through their noses, the velum is open already, and producing an [m] "just" involves closing the lips. However, practicing a sequence consisting of a nasal consonant and a non-nasal vowel also helps practice working on when the velum has to lower and open relative to when the mouth opens for the production of the vowel. Between about ten and twelve months of age, infants begin to produce a variety of speech sounds, even sounds that are not part of the language the child is acquiring natively. At this age, babbling is no longer canonical. Instead of repeating the same syllables as in [mɑmɑmɑmɑ], the infant strings together different syllables as in [bugɑbimo]. This is called **variegated babbling.**

Though babbling is far from being language, it resembles adult language in a number of important respects. For one thing, babbled sequences are not linked to immediate biological needs like food or physical comfort and are thus frequently uttered in isolation for sheer pleasure. Moreover, babbled sequences have many physical characteristics of adult speech. For example, syllables can be identified in a sequence like [gɔŋgɔŋ], and often there is a clear alternation between consonants and vowels. In longer sequences, intonation patterns that might be interpreted in some languages as questions can be discerned. However, the resemblance to adult speech stops here, since there is no evidence for the existence of more abstract structures like sentences or even single words. Only later does the child come to associate word meanings with vocal noises.

Although precisely how babbling relates to language development is not yet clearly understood, psychologists and linguists have suggested that babbling serves at least two functions: as practice for later speech and as a social reward. The first function is intuitively plausible, because the fine motor movements necessary for accurate articulation are exercised extensively during babbling. Indeed, babbling children of about one year of age produce a great variety of sounds, mainly practicing sequences of consonants and vowels.

The second possible function, that children babble for social reward, also seems plausible. Parents often encourage their babies to continue babbling by responding with smiles or speech or nonsense "babbling" of their own, giving the child important experience with the social aspects and rewards of speech. Evidence for the importance of the social factor in babbling comes from the study of severely neglected children, who may begin to babble at approximately the same age as children reared in normal settings but will stop if not encouraged by their parents or caretakers.

It remains to be explained why babbling occurs at more or less the same time in all children, since children receive encouragement for their efforts in unequal doses. According to one hypothesis, children babble because language development involves a process of biological maturation. Thus babbling occurs automatically when the relevant structures in the brain reach a critical level of development. If all children have brains that develop at comparable rates, the universality of babbling is no longer surprising.

Dramatic evidence for this hypothesis comes from some of the children studied by biologist Eric Lenneberg. These children had vocal passages that had become so narrow because of swelling caused by various diseases that they were in danger of choking to death. Breathing could be restored only by constructing an alternative route that bypassed the mouth; this was accomplished by inserting tubes in the trachea (air pipe) through an opening in the neck. Under such conditions, babbling and any other vocalizations are prevented, since air never reaches the vocal cords. Yet Lenneberg observed that when children of babbling age underwent this operation, they produced the babbling sounds typical of their age as soon as the tubing was removed. The behavior of these children demonstrates that babbling is possible when the brain is ready even if physical limitations prevent any real practice.

8.2.3 Phonological Acquisition

When an eighteen-month-old child attempts to pronounce the word *water,* he or she might say [wɑwɑ], a pronunciation that is quite different from the adult's model. A child's pronunciation of the word *that* may sound like [dæt]. Differences in pronunciations like these may persist for some time, despite drilling by the child's parents or caretakers and even despite the child's own realization that his or her pronunciation does not quite match the adults' pronunciation. All children, regardless of what language they are acquiring natively, make mistakes like these before they have mastered the phonological system of their native language. Yet such errors reveal that they have already learned a great deal, because the errors are systematic, that is, rule-governed, rather than random. In roughly two and a half more years, their speech will resemble that of their parents in all important respects.

It is important to keep in mind that adults analyze the speech of children with reference to their own adult system. Child speech is therefore analyzed as imperfect and full of errors according to the adult's model of grammar. If you listen to young children speak, you will notice that although they try to approximate the forms and pronunciations that they hear around them, many of the sounds they produce do not quite match the adult form. It takes a long time for a child to gain absolute control over the individual movements of the articulators and the timing of these gestures. For example, it is difficult for a young child to produce a consonant sequence like [dɹ] as it occurs in the word *drum.* The child may say something like [dwʌm], which sounds close enough to make an adult understand what is meant, especially if the child is pointing to a drum at the same time.

A major task in the acquisition of phonology involves understanding the word as a link between sound and meaning (see File 1.4). Around the age of eighteen months, children learn and ask for the names of objects in their environment. When children first acquire the concept of a word, their first attempts at production show tremendous variability in pronunciation. Some may be perfect productions; others may be so distorted that they are comprehensible only to the child's closest companions. Some children vary considerably in their pronunciations from one occasion to the next, while others consistently use a "wrong" sound relative to the adult speech model, saying, for example, [wɑɪt] for *right,* [wɛd] for *red,* or [əwɑʊnd] for *around.*

Children initially appear to regard an entire word as if it were a single sound (a sound that can vary somewhat). However, as their vocabulary expands between fifteen and twenty-one months of age, keeping track of a large store of independent sounds becomes very difficult for them to manage. So in order to learn more words, children must begin to break words into a smaller number of simpler units, which are sounds that can be used in different combinations to make up many other words. (Refer to **duality of patterning** in Section 1.4.8.) That is, they arrive at the idea of a word as a sequence of phonemes whose pronunciation is systematic and predictable. In the course of learning a language natively, children must acquire the complete set of phonemes as well as the set of phonological processes found in the language of the adults in their surroundings.

When children learn the phonemes of their native language, they first master sounds that differ maximally from one another. Thus it is no accident that the first meaningful word learned in many languages is often [mɑ] or [pɑ]. When a bilabial stop or nasal is pronounced, the passage of air in the mouth is completely blocked; but the vocal tract is wide open in the low back vowel [ɑ]. Thus, these two sounds are maximally different because one is a consonant (C) and one is a vowel (V). This kind of CV-syllable structure or template appears to be the preferred structure in young children's productions. Only later will they produce consonant clusters, such as [sp] in words like *spill* or [tɹ] as in *tree,* and syllable-final consonants, such as [t] in *cat.* Final consonants are often omitted in children's productions. It is even later before a child will learn to produce longer words or utterances that consist of more than one syllable. Very often, consonants like [l] and [ɹ], which share many properties of vowels and are thus difficult to distinguish from vowels, are mastered last.

Even though children master CV sequences early on, we often find that in longer words, some CV syllables are deleted. In the speech sample in (1), at least one syllable is omitted from every word.

(1) *banana* [___nænə]   *granola* [___owə]   *potato* [___deɪdoʊ]

We might wonder why children leave out the first syllable in these examples and whether this first syllable is in any way different from the other syllables in the word. An answer to this question is that since all of these first syllables are unstressed, they are not very perceptually prominent. In English there is usually one syllable (or vowel) within a word that is somewhat louder and more prominent in relation to the other vowels in that word. This is the vowel with primary stress (see File 2.5).

However, infants may also make use of the stress pattern of a stream of speech to determine where a word ends and the next one begins. This is a big problem for the infant to solve because the baby has only a very limited knowledge of the structure of the language's vocabulary. Babies and young children might begin to master the difficult task of finding the boundaries between words by looking for the most stressed syllable or the most prominent part of the word, since in English the first syllable of a word is often stressed. Such a strategy allows the infant to correctly determine word boundaries more often than not. However, this strategy does not always guarantee the correct result or the correct analysis of where one word begins and where it ends. Consider the word *banana*. This word consists of three syllables: [bə.næ.nə]. The first and the third syllables are not stressed, but the second one is. In this case, a child might unconsciously look for the most stressed syllable and believe it to be the beginning of a word. If the child has already learned that a word can consist of more than one syllable and generalizes that the most stressed syllable is the beginning of the word *banana*, then it makes sense that he or she will incorrectly think that the word is actually [næ.nə].

To summarize, when children acquire the phonological system of their native language, they must master the fine muscle coordination necessary for producing a rich variety of sounds, learn that combinations of sounds are associated with particular meanings, and eventually realize that their pronunciations of words must consistently match those of adults. Learning a language natively does not result from a conscious learning strategy spontaneously invented by children or from a teaching method devised by adults. Instead, it is a consequence of the human brain's innate capacity for learning language. Children of all backgrounds, provided they have enough input, will learn a language and master the phonological system of their native language. The acquisition of phonology appears to involve a process of biological maturation and is in many aspects like motor development: first the child babbles to practice for later speech, then the articulatory sequences become longer and more complex, and the child is able to pronounce "difficult" consonant clusters. Nevertheless, the adult phonological system is learned only when the child is given models to imitate as well as encouragement.

8.2.4   Language Development from Birth to Twelve Months

The table in (2), adapted from Lenneberg (1967), provides an overview of infants' language abilities from birth to twelve months of age.

(2) Infants' language abilities, birth to twelve months

Approximate Age at Onset of Behavior	Vocalizations and Language
12 weeks	• Cries markedly less than at 8 weeks • Smiles when talked to and nodded at, followed by making squealing-gurgling sounds (cooing) • Sustains cooing for 15 to 20 seconds • Produces vaguely palatal sounds like [j] and [ɲ]
16 weeks	• Responds to human sounds more definitely • Turns head and eyes, seems to search for speaker • Occasionally makes some chuckling sounds • Distinguishes between vowels [i] and [ɑ] and the corresponding adult mouth producing these sounds
20 weeks	• Begins to intersperse vowel-like cooing sounds with more consonantal sounds
6 months	• Changes from cooing to babbling that resembles one-syllable utterances • Most commonly produces utterances that sound somewhat like [mɑ], [mu], [dɑ], or [di][1]
8 months	• Frequently uses continuous repetitions of the same syllable • Begins to have distinct intonation patterns • Begins using utterances to signal emphasis and emotions
10 months	• Mixes vocalizations with sound-play such as gurgling or bubble blowing • Appears to wish to imitate sounds, but the imitations are never quite successful
12 months	• Replicates identical sound sequences with higher relative frequency of occurrence; words (*mamma* or *dadda*) are emerging • Shows definite signs of understanding some words and simple commands (*Show me your eyes*)

[1]Notice that these sounds are often similar to the words for *mother* and *father* in many languages. While many parents think it is a sign of their child's developing genius that they learn to produce *mommy* and *daddy* as their first words, it is quite likely that the form of these words is simply taken from the first sounds a child can recognizably make!

First-Language Acquisition: The Acquisition of Morphology, Syntax, and Word Meaning

8.3.1 The Acquisition of Morphology and Syntax

It is not until about the age of twelve months that a child will begin to consistently produce words of the language he or she is learning. It is at this stage that we can begin to examine the development of syntax and morphology in children's speech.

It is important to note, however, that there is much variation in the age range during which children acquire words, fundamental cognitive concepts, and so on. The fact that a child reaches certain stages more quickly or more slowly than average does not mean that the child is necessarily more or less intelligent or well-developed: it is normal for children to vary in this regard. The ages associated with the different "stages" of language acquisition are only averages. There is also variability in terms of children's behavior. While the term "stage" seems to imply that a child abruptly changes his or her behavior when moving from one stage to the next, this is not actually the case. A child can have behaviors associated with different stages at the same time. Finally, it's important to keep in mind that stages are not specific to children acquiring English: all children tend to go through the same stages no matter what language they are acquiring. The following sections describe some of these stages of language acquisition.

8.3.2 The One-Word Stage

The first stage of morphological acquisition usually involves the child's producing single words in isolation. These first words uttered by a one-year-old child typically name people, objects, pets, and other familiar and important parts of his or her environment. The child's vocabulary soon comes to include verbs and other useful words (including *no, gimme,* and *mine*). Often a phrase used by adults will become a single word in the speech of a child, such as *all-gone* and *whasat?* ('what's that?'). The single words produced at this stage are used as more than just labels for objects or events; they may be used for naming, commenting, requesting, inquiring, and so on. This level of development has been called the **holophrastic stage** (a **holophrase** being a one-word sentence). Children at this phase of linguistic development are limited to a word at a time in their production, but they understand and probably intend the meaning of more than a single word. Furthermore, the intonation children use on their one-word utterances may be that of a question, an ordinary or emphatic statement, or demand. If children do consistently use these adultlike sentence intonation patterns (and researchers disagree about whether they do or not), "holophrastic" would seem an especially appropriate name for this phase.

8.3.3 The Two-Word Stage

Between approximately eighteen and twenty-four months of age, children begin to use two-word utterances. At first the utterances may seem to be simply two one-word sentences produced one right after the other. There may be a pause between them, and each word may bear a separate intonation contour. Before long, however, the two words are produced without pausing and with a single intonational pattern.

    Children at this stage do not just produce any two words in any order; rather, they adopt a consistent set of word orders that convey an important part of the meaning of their utterances. At this level of development, the structure of utterances is determined by semantic roles and relationships, rather than adult syntactic ones. Word order is used to express these semantic relations; it is not until later that additional syntactic devices are added to the basic word-order rules. Most of the utterances produced by a child at this stage will express a semantic relation like one of the following:

(1) agent + action   baby sleep
    action + object   kick ball
    action + location   sit chair
    entity + location   teddy bed
    possessor + possession   Mommy book
    entity + attribute   block red
    demonstrative + entity   this shoe

Words such as *more* and *'nother* may be used as modifiers of nouns (*more juice*, *'nother cup*) to indicate or request recurrence. *Here* and *there* may be used as deictic terms (Section 8.3.5). Some children at this stage of development also use pronouns. For the most part, however, their speech lacks function morphemes and function words, that is, words like prepositions, auxiliary verbs, articles, and inflectional affixes (see Files 4.1 and 5.3).

    Because of the omission of function words (which continues even after the child begins to produce more than two words at a time), the speech of young children is often called **telegraphic.** When you send a telegram or run a classified ad, every word you include costs you money. Therefore, you put in only the words you really need, and not the ones that carry no new information. Children follow the same principle of economy. The words they use and the order in which they use them convey the relevant information; function morphemes are not, strictly speaking, necessary for the child to effectively communicate ideas. Eventually, children do acquire the full set of function morphemes of their language—the "syntactic devices" mentioned above that supplement the expression of semantic relations through word-order rules.

8.3.4   Later Stages of Development

Three-word utterances are initially formed by combining or expanding two-word utterances. Two two-word strings with a common element may be combined; for example, *Daddy cookie* and *eat cookie* may be combined to form *Daddy eat cookie*. A two-word utterance may also be expanded from within, when, for example, *throw ball* becomes *throw red ball*. That is, one of the elements of a two-term relation itself becomes a two-term relation.

    There is no clear-cut three-word stage of language acquisition, however. Once children are capable of combining more than two words into an utterance, they may use three, four, five, or even more words at a time. These longer utterances are syntactically organized; that is, they possess hierarchical syntactic structure (see File 5.4) rather than being flat sequences of words like those produced in the two-word stage.

    Children's speech at this stage is still telegraphic, including only morphemes and words that carry important semantic content. Gradually a child will begin to include function morphemes in his or her utterances, but these function morphemes are not acquired randomly. Instead, children acquire them in a remarkably consistent order. For example, in English, the present progressive verbal suffix *-ing* (*she walking*) appears in children's speech well before the past tense marker *-ed* (*she walked*), which in turn is acquired a little before the third-person present tense marker -*s* (*she walks*). Around the time -*ing* appears, so do the prepositions *in* and *on*. Three homophonous morphemes, all phonologically /-z/, are acquired at different times. First children use the plural morpheme -*s* (e.g., *shoes*); later they acquire the possessive -*'s* (*Mommy's*); and finally the third-person present tense morpheme mentioned above is added to verbs. Articles (*a* and *the*) are acquired fairly early, but forms of the (highly irregular) verb *to be* appear only at a relatively late stage.

a. Plurals. Recall that the plural morpheme -*s* is acquired quite early by children—in fact, it is usually one of the very first function morphemes to appear, along with *in*, *on*, and -*ing*. That does not mean, however, that very young children have complete mastery over the plural system of English.

At first, no plural marker is used at all. Nouns appear only in their singular forms (e.g., *man*). Next, irregular plural forms may appear for a while—that is, a child may say *men* instead of *man,* using the same form adults do. Then the child discovers the morpheme -*s* and suddenly applies it uniformly to all plural nouns. In some cases this involves **overgeneralization** of the rule of plural formation; for example, the plural of *man* becomes *mans*. During this stage the child often leaves nouns ending in sibilants (e.g., *nose, house, church,* etc.) in their singular forms. Once children discover the generalization about how the plurals of these nouns are formed, they may go through a brief period during which [-əz] is added to all nouns, giving not only *houses* but also *man-es* or even *mans-es*. This soon passes, however, and the child produces all plurals correctly, except for the irregular ones they haven't encountered yet, of course (such as *oxen* or *sheep* or *octopi*). These are learned gradually and may not be fully acquired by the time the child is five years old. When irregular plurals first appear in a young child's speech, they are simply isolated forms that fit into no pattern. Once they are learned, however, they are exceptions to the child's regular process of plural formation, just as they are for an adult.

b. Negatives. Children also go through a series of stages in learning to produce negative sentences. At first they simply put the word *no* in front of a sentence to negate it, for example, *no baby sleep* or *no I drink milk*. As a matter of fact, this word shows a fairly high occurrence in children's speech, even if children might not initially understand what the word means. Next, they insert a negative word, most often a word like *no, not, can't,* or *don't*, between the subject and the verb of a sentence, resulting in *baby no sleep* or *I no drink milk*. (It is interesting to note that at this stage, *can't, won't,* and *don't* are unanalyzed negative words; that is, the child doesn't parse them as containing two morphemes: an auxiliary verb and a consistent negative marker. The auxiliaries *can, will,* and *do* are not acquired until later; even three-year-olds still tend to have trouble with them.)

The child continues to develop a more adult system of negation, but for a while he or she will use words such as *something* and *somebody* in negated sentences, producing results such as *I don't see something*. Later these words are replaced by *nothing* and *nobody*. Finally, if the child's adult models use the forms *anything* and *anybody*, the child eventually acquires these words.

c. Interrogatives. Very young children can produce questions only by using a rising intonation, rather than by using a particular syntactic structure. The meaning of *Mommy cup?* or *more ride?* would be quite clear when produced with the same question intonation that adults use. Later, at around three years, children begin to use *can, will,* and other auxiliary verbs in yes-no questions, using the appropriate word order. That is, the auxiliary precedes the subject in these questions, as in, for example, *Are you sad?* At this point, however, children still fail to use adult word order in questions that use a *wh-* word (such as *what, who,* or *why*). They follow instead the question word with a sentence in normal declarative word order: *Why you are sad?* Eventually, of course, they learn to invert the subject and the verb in these constructions, as adult speakers do.

The fact that children produce words and sentences like *foots* or *I don't want something* or *Where he is going?* provides clear evidence that they are not merely imitating the adult speakers around them. What we as adults perceive and interpret as "mistakes" are not random but reflect the system of grammar that children are in the process of constructing for themselves.

8.3.5 The Acquisition of Word Meaning

When children hear a word for the first time, they don't know what makes the use of the word appropriate. Consider a preschooler whose teacher chose teams by dividing the class in half, and asked each team to sit on a blanket. At home later that day, the student got annoyed because her younger brother kept crawling onto her blanket while she was watching television. "He won't stay way from my team," she complained. With a single exposure to the word *team,* this child formed a definition something like 'a group of people on a blanket'—a reasonable, but incorrect, guess.

Though this trial-and-error process may seem laborious from an adult perspective, consider what every normal child is able to accomplish by using it: children produce their first words at age one, and by age six they have a vocabulary approaching 14,000 words. Simple arithmetic will reveal that children master an average of ten words a day starting from their first birthday. This feat might suggest that children learn the vocabulary of their native language in a more systematic fashion than is apparent from the above example. While it is not possible to speak of particular stages in the acquisition of word meaning like those identified in the acquisition of phonology, morphology, and syntax, linguists have determined that the acquisition of word meaning does follow certain patterns. First of all, the order in which words are learned reflects the intrinsic complexity of the concepts involved. Second, children's initial definitions of words do not deviate randomly from those of adults, but rather they are usually related to and progress toward adult definitions in systematic ways. For example, many nouns are used to denote sets of objects with something in common (e.g., the adult word *chair* is used appropriately with desk chairs, rocking chairs, easy chairs, and so on, because all of these things can be sat on), but sometimes children may select the wrong unifying characteristic(s), as happens in complexive concepts, overextensions, and underextensions.

a. Complexive Concepts. Sometimes, not only will a child associate a wrong or incomplete set of unifying characteristics with a word, but she will also seem to try out different characteristics each time she uses the word. For example, a child might learn that the word *doggie* refers to dogs and then use it to name other furry things, like soft slippers, and on later occasions, she may use *doggie* to refer to things that move by themselves, like birds, toads, and small toy cars. When a child associates different characteristics with the meaning of a word on successive uses, thereby creating a set of objects that do not have any particular unifying characteristic, we say that she has produced a **complexive concept.** The linguist William Labov reports another example of a complexive concept. His one-year-old son used *oo* to refer to the music produced by his brothers rock and roll band; on later occasions *oo* was applied to the group's jackets, their musical instruments, their cigarettes, and then other people's cigarettes. Note that successive uses of the word tend to pick out objects with similar properties, but the class of objects as a whole has little in common. Complexive concepts serve to form a loose bond between items associated in the child's experience and represent a primitive conception of word meaning.

b. Overextensions. When a child extends the range of a word's meaning beyond that typically used by adults, we say that he has produced an **overextension.** For example, one American-English-speaking child called specks of dirt, dust, small insects, and bread crumbs *fly;* another gave *moon* as the name for cakes, round marks, postmarks, and the letter <O>. A third child overextended the word *ticktock,* using it to refer to clocks, watches, parking meters, and a dial on a set of scales.

At first glance, the set of objects named in overextensions may look as varied and random as those in complexive concepts. In fact, children of age two or so frequently have overextensions and complexive concepts in their speech at the same time. But closer inspection reveals that the concept defined in an overextension does not shift from one occasion to the next. In the above examples, the child's definition of *moon* is applied consistently to pick out any round thing. Likewise, *fly* referred to any small, possibly mobile object. The concept underlying the use of *ticktock* was perhaps more complex, but all of the objects in the child's list contained a dial with small marks.

Usually, the common properties of objects included in the overextension of a word are perceptual features like shape, size, color, or taste. In this respect, the child's strategy for defining a word resembles that of adults, since adults also define words in terms of perceptual features. But if the child's strategy of defining words now resembles that of adults, what misunderstanding is responsible for the overextensions?

Linguist Eve Clark offers one plausible explanation. In her view, the child who uses overgeneralizations has only an incomplete definition of the adult word. The child who calls dogs, cats, slippers, fur coats, and rugs *doggie* has recognized the significance of being furry, but the adult definition mentions more properties; for example, dogs are four-legged. Once the child grasps this property as part of the definition of *dog,* it will no longer over-extend the word *doggie* to slippers, rugs, and fur coats. Eventually the child becomes aware of all properties in a definition, which enables her to narrow down the class of objects named by *doggie* to just those observed in adult usage.

c. Underextensions. An **underextension** is the application of a word to a smaller set of objects than is appropriate for mature adult speech. Careful study reveals that, although less commonly noticed than overextensions, underextensions are at least equally frequent in the language of children.

Underextensions also occur among older, school-aged children when they encounter category names like *fruit* or *mammal*. Since most people are unsure of the properties that constitute the definitions of these words, they prefer to think of them in terms of their most ordinary members; thus for many Americans, dogs are the most ordinary mammals and apples are the most ordinary fruits. Children are surprised to learn that whales are mammals, or that olives are fruits, because these deviate so profoundly from the ordinary members of their categories. As a result, children underextend the words *mammal* and *fruit,* failing to apply these labels to the unusual members.

Why do children's first definitions fall into the three classes that we have discussed? Each class represents a different strategy for seeking out the adult definition of a word. Complexive concepts are the most basic and are present in a child's speech for only a short period of time before being replaced by overextensions and underextensions. Psychologists have determined that a child who overgeneralizes a word tries to make the most out of a limited vocabulary. Accordingly, overgeneralizations decrease dramatically after age two, when children experience a rapid vocabulary expansion. The opposite strategy underlies the formation of underextensions: children attempt to be as conservative as possible in their use of language, with the result that they perceive restrictions on the use of words not imposed by adults. By systematically over- and underextending the range of a concept, the child eventually arrives at the adult definition.

The words discussed so far have been limited to those that denote the members of a set of objects. For example, the word *chair* is used correctly when it is applied to the set that includes objects as different as straight chairs, folding chairs, and rocking chairs. The same skill, identifying members of a set, is required for understanding some types of verbs. For example, all people walk differently, but native speakers of English use the word *walk* correctly when they realize that these minor differences are irrelevant.

But not all words in a language involve the identification of sets. In fact, the mastery of a working vocabulary in any human language requires a wide range of intellectual skills, some easier and some more difficult than those required for grasping the meaning of common nouns and verbs. As an example of a relatively easy concept, consider what is required for understanding **proper nouns:** one must simply point out a single individual and attach a label, like *John* or *Daddy.* Because it is easier to associate a label with a single individual than to name a set with common properties, children master the comprehension of proper nouns first, sometimes when they are as young as six to nine months old.

In contrast, a **relational term** like *large* or *small* constitutes a relatively complex concept. (Refer to Section 6.5.3.) The correct use of words like these requires that two things be kept in mind: the absolute size of the object in question and its position on a scale of similar objects. For example, an elephant that is six feet tall at the shoulders may be small as far as elephants go, but a dog of the same height would be huge. Five- and six-year-old children are often unable to make the shift in perspective necessary for using relational words appropriately. In one well-known experiment documenting this conclusion, children were engaged in a pretend tea party with dolls and an adult observer. The adult gave the child an ordinary juice glass and asked the child if it was large or small. Though all of the children in the study agreed that the glass was small from their own perspective, it appeared ridiculously large when placed on the toy table around which the dolls were seated. Nevertheless, the youngest children were still inclined to say that the glass was small when asked about its size with respect to its new context.

Another difficult concept underlies **deictic expressions,** which are words referring to personal, temporal, or spatial aspects of an utterance, and whose meaning depends on the context in which the word is used (refer to Section 7.1.3). For example, a speaker may use *here* or *this* to point out objects that may be close to him, while *there* and *that* are appropriate only when the objects are relatively far away. But since there are no absolute distances involved in the correct use of these deictic expressions, children have difficulty determining when the 'close' terms are to be preferred over the 'far' terms. As with relational terms, it is necessary to take into account the size of the object pointed to. Thus a thirty-story building six feet in front of us is close enough to be called *this building,* but an ant removed from us by the same distance is far enough away to be called *that ant.*

Many verbs are conceptually more complex than most nouns. For example, every time someone *gives* something, someone else *takes* it; and every time someone *buys* an item, somebody else *sells* that item. Thus, every event of *giving* or *buying* is also an event of *taking* or *selling,* respectively. However, speakers usually don't talk about such events using both verbs. For example, people will probably say a sentence such as *Peter bought the car from Mike* or *Mike sold the car to Peter,* but not both sentences. So children need to figure out that both sentences refer to the same action without ever hearing both sentences describing the action. Furthermore, many common verbs like *think* or *believe* are abstract, referring to events that cannot be observed. Some researchers believe that verbs' greater conceptual complexity is one of the reasons why verbs are learned later than nouns.

Common and proper nouns, relational terms, deictic expressions and verbs do not exhaust the range of concepts mastered by children, but they do illustrate the variety of tasks involved in acquiring the vocabulary of a first language. Linguists can examine the evidence from the acquisition of word meaning and find support for two fundamental hypotheses: that some concepts are more complex than others and that the acquisition of language requires a considerable exercise of intelligence.

8.3.6   Overview: Language Abilities from Eighteen Months to Four Years

The table in (2), adapted from Lenneberg (1967), provides an overview of infants' language abilities from eighteen months to four years of age.

(2) Infants' language abilities, eighteen months to four years

Approximate Age at Onset of Behavior	Vocalizations and Language
18 months	• Has definite repertoire of words—more than three, but fewer than fifty • Still engages in much babbling but now of several syllables, with intricate intonation pattern • Exhibits no frustration at not being understood • May include items such as *thank you* or *come here,* but has little ability to combine words into spontaneous two-item phrases • Progresses rapidly in understanding
24 months	• Has vocabulary of more than fifty items • Begins spontaneously joining vocabulary items into two-word phrases • Phrases appear to be own creations, not modeled on adult speech • Shows definite increase in communicative behavior and interest in language
30 months	• Shows fastest increase in vocabulary, with many new additions every day • No longer babbles • Becomes frustrated if not understood by adults • Produces utterances consisting of at least two words • Displays characteristic child grammar in sentences and phrases • Is generally not yet very intelligible (though there is great variation among children)
3 years	• Has vocabulary of about a thousand words • Produces utterances about 80% intelligible, even to strangers • Produces utterances with grammatical complexity comparable to that of colloquial adult language, although mistakes still occur
4 years	• Has well-established language • Tends to deviate from the adult norm more in style than in grammar

FILE **8.4**

How Adults Talk to Young Children

8.4.1 Talking to Children

When people talk to one another, their general goal is to get listeners to understand what they are saying, as was illustrated by the communication chain in File 1.2. This goal applies just as much when listeners are young children as when they are adults. The problem is that young children know very little about the structure and function of the language adults use to communicate with each other. As a result, adult speakers often modify their speech to help children understand them. Speech directed at children is called **infant-directed speech** or **child-directed speech.**

How adults talk to children is influenced by three things. First, adults have to make sure that children realize that an utterance is being addressed to them and not to someone else. To do this, adults can use a name, speak in a special tone of voice, or even touch the child to get his attention. Second, once they have the child's attention, they must choose concepts that maximize the child's chances of understanding what is being said. For example, adults are unlikely to discuss philosophy but very likely to talk about what the child is doing, looking at, or playing with at that moment. Third, adults choose a particular style of speaking that they think will be most beneficial to the child. They can talk quickly or slowly, use short sentences or long ones, and so on. Children are thus presented with a specially tailored model of language use, adjusted to fit, as far as possible, what they appear to understand. Each of these three factors will be addressed in turn below.

8.4.2 How Adults Get Children to Pay Attention

Speakers depend on their listeners being cooperative and listening when they are spoken to. But when the listeners are children, adult speakers normally have to work a bit harder to ensure that this happens. They use **attention getters** to tell children which utterances are addressed to them rather than to someone else, and hence which utterances they ought to be listening to. And they use **attention holders** whenever they have more than one thing to say, for example, when telling a story.

Attention getters and attention holders fall into two broad classes. The first consists of names and exclamations. For example, adults often use the child's name at the beginning of an utterance, as in *Ned, there's a car.* Even four-year-olds know that this is an effective way to get a two-year-old's attention. Or, instead of the child's name, adults use exclamations like *Look!* or *Hey!* as a preface to an utterance that they want the child to pay attention to. The second class of attention getters consists of modulations that adults use to distinguish utterances addressed to young children from utterances addressed to other listeners. One of the most noticeable is the high-pitched voice adults use for talking to small children. When the linguist Olga Garnica compared recordings of English-speaking adults talking to two-year-olds, five-year-olds, and adults in the same setting (1977), she found that when talking to children, adults use a wider pitch range: the range of the adults' voices was widest with the youngest children, next widest with the five-year-olds, and narrowest with other

333

adults. These results are consistent with the findings of the psychologist Anne Fernald (1992), who found that in various cultures, speech directed to children is usually higher pitched and shows more pitch excursion (variation) compared to speech addressing adults.

Another modulation adults use is whispering. If children are sitting on their laps or standing right next to them, adults will speak directly into their ears so it is clear they are intended to listen. Garnica observed that all the mothers in her study on occasion whispered to two-year-olds, a few whispered to five-year-olds, but none whispered to adults.

Not all attention getters and attention holders are linguistic. Speakers often rely on gestures as well and may touch a child's shoulder or cheek, for example, as they begin talking. They also use gestures to hold a child's attention and frequently look at and point to objects they name or describe.

8.4.3 What Adults Say to Young Children

Adults both observe and impose the cooperative principle (see File 7.2) when they talk to young children. They make what they say relevant, talking about the "here and now" of the child's world. They encourage children to take their turns and contribute to the conversation. And they make sure that children make their contributions truthful by correcting them, if necessary.

a. The "Here and Now." Adults talk to young children mainly about the "here and now." They make running commentaries on what children do, either anticipating their actions—for example, *Build me a tower now,* said just as a child picks up a box of building blocks—or describing what has just happened: *That's right, pick up the blocks,* said just after a child has done so. Adults talk about the objects children show interest in. They name them (*That's a puppy*), describe their properties (*He's very soft and furry*), and talk about relations between objects (*The puppy's in the basket*). In talking about the "here and now," usually whatever is directly under the child's eyes, adults are very selective about the words they use. They seem to be guided by the following assumptions:

(1) • Some words are easier for children to pronounce than others.
     • Some words are more useful for children than others.
     • Some words are hard to understand and best avoided.

Most languages contain "baby talk," words that are considered appropriate in talking only to very young children. For example, adult speakers of English often replace the word for an animal with the word for the sound it makes, as in *meow* and *woofwoof* instead of *cat* and *dog,* or with a diminutive form of the adult word, like *kitty*(*-cat*) or *doggie.* As one would expect, not all types of words have equivalent baby-talk words; instead the domains in which baby-talk words are found overlap considerably with the domains young children first talk about. They include kinship terms and nicknames (such as *mommy, daddy*); the child's bodily functions and routines (*wee-wee, night-night*); names of animals; games and toys (*peek-a-boo, choo-choo*); and a few general qualities (such as *uh-oh!* for disapproval). Adults appear to use baby-talk words because they seem to be easier for children to pronounce. This assumption may well have some basis in fact, since in many languages, baby-talk words seem to be modeled on the sounds and combinations of sounds that young children tend to produce when trying their first words. At the same time, baby-talk words provide yet another signal that a particular utterance is addressed to a child rather than someone else.

Psychologist Roger Brown (1925–98) has argued that the words parents use in speaking to young children anticipate the nature of the child's world. This seems to be true not only of baby-talk words but also of the other words used in speaking to young children. Adults select the words that seem to have the most immediate relevance to what their children might want to talk about. For instance, they supply words for different kinds of fruit the child might eat, such as *apple* or *orange,* but not the more abstract word *fruit*. They likewise supply the names of animals, but not the word *animal*. In other domains, though, they provide more general words like *tree* rather than the more specific words for different kinds of tree like *oak, ash,* or *birch*. Similarly, they are not likely to point to an Irish wolfhound and say to a one- or two-year-old *That's an Irish wolfhound*. They would be much more likely to say *That's a dog*. Some of the words adults select are very frequent in adult-to-adult speech; others are not. The criterion adults seem to use can be characterized by what Brown called "level of utility": the judgment that one word is more likely to be useful than another in the child's own utterances.

Adults are selective in another way too: they seem to leave out function words and word endings because they think this simplifies what they are saying. (In fact, they do the same thing when talking to non-native speakers.) For example, instead of using pronouns like *he, she,* or *they,* adults often repeat the antecedent noun phrase instead, as in *The boy was running, The boy climbed the tree,* where the second instance of *the boy* would normally be changed to *he*. Where *I* and *you* would be used in adult-to-adult speech, adults often use names instead, as in *Mommy's going to lift Tommy up* for *I'm going to lift you up,* or *Daddy wants to tie Julie's shoe* for *I want to tie your shoe*. Adults often use names in questions addressed to children too, for example, *Does Jenny want to play in the sand today?* addressed to Jenny herself. Adults seem to realize that pronouns are complicated for young children, so they try to avoid them.

b. Taking Turns. From very early on, adults encourage children to take their turns as speaker and listener in conversation. Even when adults talk to very young infants, they thrust **conversational turns** upon them. Adults respond to infants during their very first months of life as though their burps, yawns, and blinks count as turns in conversations. This is illustrated in the following dialogue between a mother and her three-month-old daughter Ann (taken from Snow 1977):

(2) Ann: [smiles]
   Mom: Oh, what a nice little smile! Yes, isn't that nice? There. There's a nice little smile.
   Ann: [burps]
   Mom: What a nice wind as well! Yes, that's better, isn't it? Yes.
   Ann: [vocalizes]
   Mom: Yes! There's a nice noise.

Whatever the infant does is treated as a conversational turn, even though at this stage the adult carries the entire conversation alone. As infants develop, adults become more demanding about what "counts" as a turn. Yawning or stretching may be enough at three months, but by eight months babbling is what really counts. And by the age of one year or so, only words will do.

Once children begin to use one- and two-word utterances, adults begin to provide both implicit and explicit information about conversational turns. For example, they may provide model dialogues in which the same speaker asks a question and then supplies a possible answer to it.

(3) Adult: Where's the ball?
              [picks up ball] THERE'S the ball.

   Adult: [looking at picture book with child]
              What's the little boy doing?
              He's CLIMBING up the TREE.

On other occasions, adults expand on whatever topic the child introduces.

(4) Child: Dere rabbit.
    Adult: The rabbit likes eating lettuce.
           Do you want to give him some?

By ending with a question, the adult offers the child another turn and in this way deliberately prolongs the conversation. In fact, when necessary, adults also use "prompt" questions to get the child to make a contribution and to take his or her turn as speaker.

(5) Adult: What did you see?
    Child: [silence]
    Adult: You saw WHAT?

Prompt questions like *You saw what?* or *He went where?* are often more successful in eliciting speech from a child than questions with normal interrogative word order.

    c. Making Corrections. Adults seldom correct what children have to say (see File 8.1), but when they do, they seem to do it mostly to make sure that the child's contribution is true rather than grammatically correct. They may correct children explicitly, as in examples (6) and (7) below, or implicitly, as in (8). In example (9), the child is being corrected with regard to the truth value of the utterances, but the adult also uses the correct form of the verb.

(6) Child: [points] doggie.
    Adult: No, that's a HORSIE.

(7) Child: That's the animal farmhouse.
    Adult: No, that's the LIGHTHOUSE.

(8) Child: [pointing to a picture of bird on nest] Bird house.
    Adult: Yes, the bird's sitting on a NEST.

(9) Child: Robin goed to school yesterday.
    Adult: No, Robin went to a BIRTHDAY PARTY yesterday.

In each instance, the adult speaker is concerned with the truth of what the child has said, that is, with whether she has used the right words for her listener to be able to work out what she is talking about.

    The other type of correction adults make is of a child's pronunciation. If a child's version of a word sounds quite different from the adult version, a listener may have a hard time understanding what the child is trying to say. Getting children to pronounce recognizable words is a prerequisite for carrying on conversations. What is striking, though, is that adults do not consistently and persistently correct any other "mistakes" that children make when they talk. Grammatical errors tend to go uncorrected as long as what the child says is true and pronounced intelligibly. In correcting children's language, adults seem to be concerned primarily with the ability to communicate with a listener.

8.4.4   How Adults Talk to Children

Just as adults select what they say to young children by restricting it largely to the "here and now," so too do they alter the **way** they say what they say when talking to children. They do this in four ways: they slow down; they use short, simple sentences; they use a higher pitch of voice; and they repeat themselves frequently. Each of these modifications seems to be geared to making sure young children attend to and understand what adults say.

    Speech addressed to two-year-olds is only half the speed of speech addressed to adults. When adults talk to children aged four to six, they go a little faster than with two-year-olds but still speak more slowly than they do to adults. To achieve this slower rate, adults put in more pauses between words, rather than stretch out each word. The higher pitch combined with exaggerated falls and rises in the intonation contour may be acoustically appealing to the infant (Goodluck 1991).

Adults also use very short sentences when talking to young children. Psychologist J. Phillips found that adult utterances to two-year-olds averaged fewer than four words each, while adult utterances to other adults averaged over eight words. These short sentences are generally very simple ones.

There is also a great deal of repetition in adult speech to children. One reason for this repetition is the adults' use of sentence frames like those in the left-hand column in (10).

$$(10) \quad \left\{ \begin{array}{l} \text{Where's} \\ \text{Let's play with} \\ \text{Look at} \\ \text{Here's} \\ \text{That's (a)} \\ \text{Here comes} \end{array} \right\} \quad + \quad \left\{ \begin{array}{l} \text{Mommy} \\ \text{Daddy} \\ \text{(the) birdie} \\ \dots \\ \dots \\ \text{etc.} \end{array} \right\}$$

These frames mark off the beginnings of words like those in the right-hand column by placing them in familiar slots within a sentence, and one of their main uses besides getting attention seems to be to introduce new vocabulary. Often, these kinds of sentence frames are used by the children too, and we might hear utterances like *Mommy tie shoe* or *Robin want cookie,* where we have a subject followed by a verb followed by an object. Adults also repeat themselves when giving instructions. Repetitions like those in (11) are three times more frequent in speech to two-year-olds than in speech to ten-year-olds:

(11) Adult: Pick up the red one. Find the red one. Not the GREEN one. I want the RED one. Can you find the red one?

These repetitions provide structural information about the kinds of frame the repeated unit (here *the red one*) can be used in. Also, these contrasts are often highlighted by emphasizing the difference in color (indicated by the capitalization). Repetitions also allow children more time to interpret adult utterances, because they don't have to try to remember the whole sentence.

When all of these modifications are put together, it is clear that adults adjust what they say and modify how they say it to make themselves better understood. They first get children to attend; then they select the appropriate words and the way to say them. This suggests that young children are able to best understand short sentences and need to have the beginnings and ends of sentences clearly identified. In addition, the sentences used are about the "here and now," since children rely heavily on the context to guess whenever they don't understand. But as children begin to show signs of understanding more, adults modify the way they talk less and less. The shortest sentences and the slowest rate are reserved for the youngest children; both sentence length and rate of speech increase when adults talk to older children.

8.4.5 How Necessary Is Child-Directed Speech?

The fact that adults systematically modify the speech they address to very young children forces us to ask two questions. First, are the modifications adults make necessary for acquisition? Second, even if they are not necessary, are they at least helpful? It seems that child-directed speech can help children acquire certain aspects of language earlier. For example, Newport and her colleagues (1977) found that mothers who used more yes-no questions in their speech had children who acquired auxiliaries earlier. But is child-directed speech actually **necessary** for language acquisition? Some exposure to language is obviously necessary before children can start to acquire it. But it is quite possible that any kind of spoken language might do. We need to know, for example, whether children could learn language if their only input came from speech they overheard between adults, or from what they heard on the radio or television. If they could, it would be clear that child-directed speech is not necessary, even though it might be helpful. On the other hand, if children could not learn from these other sources of information, it would be clear that some child-directed speech is not only helpful but necessary.

Experiments on these topics are difficult if not impossible to devise since it is unethical to deprive children of potentially useful input, but occasionally a real-life situation presents itself in a way that provides a glimpse of the answers to these questions. For example, the hearing children of deaf parents who use only sign language sometimes have little spoken language addressed to them by adults until they enter nursery school. The parents' solution for teaching their children to speak rather than use sign language is to turn on the radio or television as much as possible. Psychologists Jacqueline Sachs and Mary Johnson reported on one such child in 1972. When Jim was approximately three and a half years old, he had only a small spoken language vocabulary, which he had probably picked up from playmates, plus a few words from television jingles. His language was far behind that of other children his age. Although he had overheard a great deal of adult-to-adult speech on television, no adults had spoken to him directly on any regular basis. Once Jim was exposed to an adult who talked to him, his language improved rapidly. Sachs and Johnson concluded that exposure to adult speech intended for other adults does not necessarily help children acquire language.

Exposure to a second language on television constitutes another naturalistic situation in which children regularly hear adults talking to each other. However, psychologist Catherine Snow and her colleagues in the mid-1970s reported that young Dutch children who watched German television every day did not acquire any German. There are probably at least two reasons why children seem not to acquire language from radio or television. First, none of the speech on the radio can be matched to a situation visible to the child, and even on television people rarely talk about things immediately accessible to view for the audience. Children therefore receive no clues about how to map their own ideas onto words and sentences. Second, the stream of speech must be very hard to segment: they hear rapid speech that cannot easily be linked to familiar situations.

While such evidence may suggest that child-directed speech is necessary for language acquisition, that turns out not to be the case. There are cultures in which adults do not use child-directed speech to talk to infants and children. There are even cultures, for example, the Kaluli of Papua, New Guinea, in which adults do not talk to children at all until they have reached a certain age. Instead the Kaluli "show" their children culturally and socially appropriate language use by having them watch everyday communication routines.

The difference between these cultures, in which children do successfully acquire language, and studies like those of Sachs and Johnson, in which they did not, seems to be related to how immediate the language use is: television and radio speech is too remote to be of any real help to a child. This suggests that one ingredient that might prove necessary for acquisition is the "here and now" nature of the speech children are exposed to, be it through child-directed speech or by being "shown" how to use language in a context that somehow involves the child, even if the child is not being directly addressed.

Bilingual Language Acquisition

8.5.1 Scenarios of Bilingual Language Acquisition

In a country like the United States, where the vast majority of people would consider themselves to be monolingual, it may come as a surprise that the majority of people in the world are **bilingual** (speakers of two languages) or **multilingual** (speakers of more than two languages). But when exactly can a person be called bilingual? Definitions of bilingualism are very diverse, ranging from having native-like control of two languages (Bloomfield 1933) to being a fluent speaker of one language and also being able to read a little in another language (Macnamara 1969). Neither of these extreme definitions is satisfactory. We certainly wouldn't want to call a person who speaks English and can read a little French a *bilingual*. One reason is that while spoken or signed language is primary, written language is secondary (see File 1.3). Thus, a bilingual should be a person who is able to speak or sign two languages, not just read them. The main problem, however, with both definitions mentioned above bears on the central issue: how well does someone need to know two languages to be called bilingual? Bloomfield's definition excludes too many people: for example, second-language learners who are fluent in their second language, but speak with a foreign accent. Macnamara's definition, on the other hand, includes too many people. A better definition lies somewhere in between. For the purposes of this file, we will define being bilingual as being able to hold a conversation with monolingual speakers of two different languages.

There are different ways that a person may become bilingual. Some people learn more than one language from birth (**simultaneous bilingualism**) or begin learning their second language as young children (**sequential bilingualism**). Some children grow up with two or more languages from birth because their parents speak two different languages at home or because their parents speak a language at home that is different from the local language. This is often the case for children when one or two parents are immigrants. Children may also grow up bilingually from birth or early childhood because they grow up in a bilingual or multilingual society, for example, in parts of Belgium or Switzerland, where multiple languages are commonly heard and controlled by most speakers. Finally, children may become bilingual because the language used at school is not their native language. This is the case in many countries where many languages are spoken. Instead of offering instructions in all the languages natively spoken, a neutral language or one that is perceived to be advantageous is chosen as the language of instruction (refer to File 13.2). This is frequently the case in African and Asian countries.

Another way of becoming bilingual is to learn a second language not as a young child but rather later in life. This is called **second-language acquisition** and is the process used, for example, by immigrants who come to a new country as adults and have to learn the local language. Other late learners are often people who learned a second, third, etc., language through formal education and/or travel.

These different ways of becoming bilingual tend to have different characteristics and results; we will discuss each of them in turn below.

8.5.2 Bilingual First-Language Acquisition

When children acquire two languages from birth or from young childhood, we usually talk of bilingual first-language acquisition. Any child who receives sufficient input from two languages will grow up fully bilingual in the sense that Bloomfield meant of having native control over two languages. Research by Barbara Pearson and her colleagues in 1997 suggests that children will become competent speakers of a language only if at least 25% of their input is in that language. In addition, not just any input will do, as was discussed in File 8.4. Children learn language by interacting with speakers of that language. It's not enough, for example, to sit a child in front of a Spanish television program and expect him to learn Spanish. The child will learn Spanish only if interacted with in Spanish.

One typical feature of bilingual children's speech is **language mixing** or **code-switching**: using more than one language in a conversation or even within a phrase. Mario, a boy who grew up mostly in the United States and whose parents spoke Spanish to him, frequently used both English and Spanish in the same sentence, as in the following examples (Fantini 1985):

(1) *Sabes mi* school bus *no tiene un* stop sign.
"You know, my school bus does not have a stop sign."

Hoy, yo era line leader *en mi escuela.*
"Today, I was line leader at school."

Ponemos cranberries *y* marshmallows *y despues se pone el* glitter *con* glue.
"Let's put cranberries and marshmallows and then we put the glitter on with glue."

The fact that bilingual children mix their languages has led some early researchers to believe that they speak neither of their languages really well. It has even been suggested that mixing in young children shows that their languages are fused into one system. That is, children have not yet figured out that they are using two different languages. However, more recent research has shown that bilingual children can differentiate their languages by the time they are four months old—long before they utter their first words. Laura Bosch and Nuria Sebastián-Gallés (2001) found that four-month-old Spanish-Catalan bilingual infants could distinguish between even these rhythmically similar languages. Since infants can differentiate two rhythmically similar languages like Spanish and Catalan, it is reasonable to hypothesize that four-month-old bilingual infants would also be able to differentiate languages that are rhythmically different (because this would be an easier task). However, more research in this area is needed to confirm this hypothesis.

If bilingual children can differentiate their languages well before they utter their first word, why do they mix languages? Let's take a closer look at Mario's utterances in (1). We can see that Mario does not just randomly mix English and Spanish. Instead, he seems to use some English nouns in what are basically Spanish sentences. Furthermore, all of the English nouns he uses are related either to his school experience in the United States (*school bus, line leader,* etc.) or to typically American items (*cranberries, marshmallows,* etc.). It's then possible that he knows these words only in English or that he uses them more frequently in English. Even if we assume that Mario does not know these words in Spanish, we certainly can't conclude that he's unable to differentiate between Spanish and English.

Alternatively, Mario may mix his languages in the examples above because he knows that the people he is talking to understand both languages. Children are very sensitive to which languages their listeners can understand. If they believe that their listeners speak, say, only Spanish, they would try to stick to Spanish. But if they believe that their listeners know, for instance, English and Spanish, there is no reason for them to make an effort to stick to one language in particular, since many bilingual children grow up in an environment in which adults also frequently code-switch.

Finally, children's language mixing can be a strategy to avoid words that are difficult to pronounce. For example, Werner Leopold (1947) observed that his German-English bilingual daughter Hildegard preferred to use the German *da* [dɑ] instead of English *there* [ðɛɹ], but the English *high* [hɑɪ] over *hoch* [hox] because they were easier for her to pronounce.

8.5.3 Bilingual vs. Monolingual First-Language Acquisition

Let's go back to the idea that Mario may not know words like *stop sign* or *school bus* in Spanish. Does this mean that his language acquisition is lagging behind monolingual children of his age? Some early researchers have suggested that learning two languages from birth would exceed the limitations of the child's brain. They assumed that bilingual children would lag behind their monolingual peers, and, indeed, studies from that time indicate that bilingual children's language skills are inferior to those of monolingual children.

During the 1980s, however, researchers began reevaluating the earlier studies and found that many of them were methodologically flawed. For example, some studies compared monolinguals' language skills with bilinguals' skills in their non-dominant language. The studies conducted in the 1980s suggested that, on the contrary, growing up bilingually is advantageous. In particular, studies found that bilingual children develop some metalinguistic skills, such as understanding arbitrariness (see File 1.4), earlier than monolingual children.

Current studies on bilingual language acquisition display a more balanced view. On the one hand, bilingual children may lag behind their monolingual peers in certain specific areas, like the vocabulary of one of their two languages (after all, they have to learn twice as much), but they have usually caught up by the time they reach puberty. This doesn't mean that they can't communicate their ideas; instead, it usually just means that there are some concepts that are easier to express in one language than the other. On the other hand, growing up bilingually may have some cognitive advantages, as mentioned above; and, of course, the end result is the ability to communicate fluently in two different languages. Other than that, bilingual children go through the same stages of language acquisition as monolingual children of each of the languages.

It should be mentioned that there are cases of problematic bilingual language acquisition. Sometimes children who grow up bilingually do not become functional bilinguals, usually because they are confronted with a bad attitude toward bilingualism, or one of their languages is not valued in their community and its use is discouraged. Thus, it is not the limitations of a child's brain or capabilities that cause problems in bilingual language acquisition, but rather a negative social environment: any child exposed to two languages in a positive social environment can grow up to be fully bilingual.

8.5.4 Second-Language Acquisition

As mentioned above, not every bilingual speaker acquired both languages during childhood. Many people become bilingual later in life, after already acquiring their native language. This is called **second-language acquisition.** While children exposed to two languages from birth or early childhood will usually grow up mastering both languages as do monolingual native speakers of those languages, people learning a language later in life usually attain different levels of competence. Some people achieve native-like competence in a second language, but the vast majority of second-language learners do not. Speakers may learn the syntax and vocabulary of a second language perfectly (although even this is rare), but few learn the phonological system that well. Thus, most second-language speakers speak with a **foreign accent** (refer to the discussion in Section 3.3.3; also see **accent** in File 10.1). It seems that non-native forms, as part of either the morpho-syntax or pronunciation, can become fixed and not change, even after years of instruction. This is called **fossilization.**

There are a number of individual differences that contribute to how well a learner learns a second language. First, the learner's native language plays an important role. A Dutch speaker will have an easier time learning English than, for example, a Chinese speaker, because Dutch and English are closely related languages with similar grammatical and phonological systems, while Chinese and English are not. By the same token, a Burmese speaker will have a much easier time learning Chinese than a Dutch speaker. A speaker's native language also plays a role in second-language acquisition because having learned one language influences the subsequent learning of another language. This is called **transfer.** Transfer can be positive or negative, depending on whether it facilitates or inhibits the learning of the second language. For example, having a native language, regardless of which language it is, facilitates the learning of a second language because we already know much about how language works. In fact, evidence from feral children and deaf children suggests that it's not possible to learn a language later in life without having already learned a native language earlier (see File 8.1).

But a learner's native language can also inhibit learning the second language. For example, we learn the phonological system of our native language early in life. In fact, by the time we are twelve months old, we perceive speech in terms of the phonemic categories of our native language (see File 8.2). This specialization for the sounds of our native language can interfere with learning the phonological system of a second language and is one of the reasons why second-language learners usually have a foreign accent. Let's consider the sounds [p] and [pʰ]. In English, aspirated [pʰ] occurs only syllable-initially (e.g., in *pin, pot,* etc.), whereas unaspirated [p] occurs only after [s] (e.g., in *spin, spot,* etc., as was discussed in File 3.1). Most native speakers of English are not even aware they are using two "different kinds" of /p/ in their speech. In Thai, on the other hand, [p] and [pʰ] are allophones of different phonemes, namely, of the phonemes /p/ and /pʰ/. That is, [p] and [pʰ] are not restricted in their distribution as they are in English. Instead, both [p] and [pʰ] can occur syllable-initially in Thai, as in the words [pai] *to go* and [pʰai] *danger,* for example. Negative transfer occurs when native English speakers learning Thai apply English phonological rules to the Thai words and incorrectly pronounce both *to go* and *danger* as [pʰai]. Negative transfer is not limited to pronunciation; it may affect all levels of second-language acquisition.

A number of other factors influence how successfully a learner will learn a second language. They include the learner's age, working memory, motivation, and context. Motivation plays a particularly large role in the level of fluency second-language learners will achieve. Some learners are perfectly content speaking a second language with a foreign accent and making an occasional mistake here and there. A study by Theo Bongaerts and his colleagues (1997) found that Dutch second-language learners of English who had achieved native competence in English were highly motivated learners and considered not having a foreign accent to be one of their goals.

Finally, the context in which speakers learn a second language and the amount of exposure to the second language also play a role. For example, the highly competent learners in Bongaerts and colleagues' study all learned English in an immersion setting where English was the language of instruction and learners were constantly exposed to native speakers of English. Trying to learn a second language later in life in a situation where you receive forty-five minutes of instruction a day, five days a week, may not result in the same high degree of native-like fluency.

FILE **8.6**

Practice

File 8.1—Theories of Language Acquisition

Exercises

1. Suppose a friend of yours has a son, George, who is three years old. Your friend has been explaining to you that George has a problem with forming the past tense of verbs, for example, George says "Yesterday I go to the park" and "Last week I swim in the pool." But your friend has a plan: he is going to spend one hour each day with George, having the child imitate the past tense forms of the verbs, and he will give George a piece of candy for each correct imitation.

   i. Which theory/theories of language acquisition does your friend assume?

   ii. Will your friend's plan work? Explain why or why not.

   iii. What suggestions would you give your friend? Explain why, using a relevant theory.

2. For each pair of statements below, indicate which one is true and which one is false. For the true statement, say which theory of language acquisition best accounts for it as well as which theory is the least suited to explain the statement. Explain your answers.

   a. • A Chinese child adopted soon after birth by a Danish family will learn Danish just like other children growing up in Denmark with Danish parents.
   • A Chinese child adopted soon after birth by a Danish family will learn Danish more slowly than other children growing up in Denmark with Danish parents because the child is genetically predisposed to learn Chinese.

   b. • Children say things like *foots* and *both mans* before they master the correct forms *feet* and *both men* because they overuse the rule for regular plural formation.
   • Children never say things like *foots* and *both mans*, because they imitate what adults say and no adult would say this.

3. Consider the following examples of children's speech taken from Clark (1995), and answer the questions:

   [playing with a toy lawnmower] "I'm lawning."
   [pretending to be superman] "I'm supermanning."
   [realizing his father was joking] "Daddy, you joked me."
   [of food on his plate] "I'm gonna fork this."

   i. Explain what the children are doing with language. How are these utterances different from the adult norm? What do the children not know about the English language yet? On the other hand, what do the children already demonstrate knowing about English in order to use it so creatively?

   ii. Which theory of language acquisition best accounts for these data? Why?

343

4. Consider the following exchange taken from Braine (1971). Discuss the effectiveness of the father's strategy in teaching the child. Also think about what the father's and child's respective objectives are. Which theory of language acquisition does this example refute?

Child: Want other one spoon, Daddy.
Father: You mean, you want the other spoon.
Child: Yes, I want other one spoon, please Daddy.
Father: Can you say "the other spoon"?
Child: Other . . . one . . . spoon.
Father: Say "other."
Child: Other.
Father: "Spoon."
Child: Spoon.
Father: "Other spoon."
Child: Other . . . spoon. Now give me other one spoon.

5. Read the following description of a feral child named Victor, and answer the questions below:

Victor was found in France in 1797 when he was twelve or thirteen years old. He had no speech when he was found. However, his hearing was normal and he made some noises. A man named Jean Marc Gaspard-Itard spent five years trying to teach Victor language. When Victor was sixteen, he could name objects. However, he would never use the words to request the objects. He also applied each word to only one object. That is, he would call only a certain shoe a *shoe,* but not other shoes. Victor developed no grammar.

   i. Does Victor's case support the critical period hypothesis? Why or why not?
   ii. What factors other than a critical period could be responsible for Victor's not acquiring normal language skills?

Activities

6. Interview a highly proficient non-native speaker of your native language. How would you rate his or her language skills at each of the following levels of linguistic structure, and how does your non-native speaker rate his or her own skills at these levels? Relate your ratings to the critical period hypothesis for second-language acquisition. You may want to ask the speaker when he or she started to learn the second language.

   a. pronunciation (phonetics and phonology)
   b. grammar (syntax and morphology)
   c. word choice (lexicon)
   d. intonation (phonetics and phonology)
   e. appropriateness (pragmatics)
   f. general comprehension

File 8.2—First-Language Acquisition:
The Acquisition of Speech Sounds and Phonology

Exercises

7. For this exercise, refer to the comic at the beginning of this chapter and answer the following questions:

i. What stage of language acquisition is the infant in? In particular, what kind of babbling does he or she produce? Based on this, how old could the infant be?

ii. How old would you have guessed the child is, based on the drawing? Does the child's physical development seem to match his language development; in other words, is his development "normal"?

iii. What is anomalous about having the child end his speech with "Is that normal?"

iv. Given the syllable structures of his babbled speech, how do you think he would actually produce the words *Is that normal*?

8. The data below are from a child named Paul at the age of two. They were collected by his father, Timothy Shopen. Consider each set of examples, and answer the questions at the end of each section.

A.

	Adult Word	Paul		Adult Word	Paul
a.	sun	[sʌn]	**d.**	snake	[neɪk]
b.	see	[si]	**e.**	sky	[kɑɪ]
c.	spoon	[pun]	**f.**	stop	[tɑp]

i. State a principle that describes Paul's pronunciation of these words. That is, how does Paul's pronunciation systematically differ from the adult pronunciation?

B.

	Adult Word	Paul		Adult Word	Paul
g.	bed	[bɛt]	**m.**	bus	[bʌs]
h.	wet	[wɛt]	**n.**	buzz	[bʌs]
i.	egg	[ɛk]	**o.**	man	[mæn]
j.	rake	[ɹeɪk]	**p.**	door	[dɔɹ]
k.	tub	[tʌp]	**q.**	some	[sʌm]
l.	soap	[soʊp]	**r.**	boy	[bɔɪ]

ii. State another principle describing Paul's pronunciations here. Be sure to word your statement in a way that reflects the fact that (o)–(r) are not affected.

C.

	Adult Word	Paul
s.	laugh	[læp]
t.	off	[ɔp]
u.	coffee	[kɔfi]

iii. State a third principle describing Paul's pronunciation in this section. Based on the principles you have seen so far, suggest how Paul would pronounce the word *love*.

D.

	Adult Word	Paul		Adult Word	Paul
v.	truck	[tʌk]	**aa.**	clay	[keɪ]
w.	brownie	[baʊni]	**bb.**	cute	[kut]
x.	plane	[peɪn]	**cc.**	beautiful	[butəpəl]
y.	broken	[boʊkən]	**dd.**	twig	[tɪk]
z.	crack	[kæk]			

iv. State a fourth principle describing the new aspects of Paul's pronunciation in these examples.

E.

	Adult Word	Paul
ee.	quick	[kwɪk]
ff.	quack	[kwæk]

v. Do these two words illustrate an exception to the fourth principle? If so, how?

9. The data below are taken from Fasold and Connor-Linton (2006). The data show words pronounced by different children at about the same age. Are there any sounds or sound sequences that seem to be particularly difficult? What patterns are evident in the children's pronunciations?

	Adult Word	Child		Adult Word	Child
a.	bottle	[bɑbɑ]	**h.**	key	[ti]
b.	butterfly	[bʌfɑɪ]	**i.**	duck	[gʌk]
c.	tub	[bʌb]	**j.**	water	[wɑwɑ]
d.	baby	[bibi]	**k.**	stop	[tɔp]
e.	tree	[ti]	**l.**	blanket	[bæki]
f.	candy	[kæki]	**m.**	doggie	[gɔgi]
g.	banana	[nænə]	**n.**	this	[dɪs]

10. Consider the data below taken from Berko Gleason (2005), and determine how each child will most likely pronounce the six words that follow the data.

Child A:

	Adult Word	Child		Adult Word	Child
a.	pot	[bat]	**d.**	back	[bæk]
b.	top	[dap]	**e.**	day	[deɪ]
c.	cat	[gæt]	**f.**	game	[geɪm]

Child B:

	Adult Word	Child		Adult Word	Child
a.	pot	[bat]	**d.**	back	[bæt]
b.	top	[dap]	**e.**	day	[deɪ]
c.	cat	[tæt]	**f.**	game	[deɪm]

- pull
- tummy
- go
- pay
- gate
- kiss

File 8.3—First-Language Acquisition: The Acquisition of Morphology, Syntax, and Word Meaning

Exercises

11. For this exercise, refer to the comic at the beginning of this chapter and answer the following questions:
    i. The infant in the comic is preverbal: he babbles. However, after babbling for a while, he asks, "Is that normal?" Of course, infants that can only babble could not produce this question. Which stages of language acquisition would an infant have to go through to get from babbling to producing yes-no questions correctly?
    ii. Which "stages" do children normally go through during the acquisition of the interrogative? Illustrate the "stages" using the question *Is that normal?* (that is, how would younger children ask, 'Is that normal?').

12. Consider the examples from children's speech below. Using the linguistic terminology you have learned so far, explain what mistakes the children make. Be as specific as pos-

sible. The examples are taken from Jay (2003), Carroll (2004), Fasold and Connor-Linton (2006), and Yule (1996).

a. Patrick: Where are you going?
Tim: I have to go back to Miami.
Patrick: [to his mother] Mom, where's Tim's "ami"?

b. Child: I camed here.

c. Child: I'll clean it up because I was the one who mested it up.

d. Child calls leaves, grass, moss, green carpet, green towels, spinach, lettuce, and avocado a *leaf*.

e. Child: No the sun shining.

f. Child: Why you waking me up?

13. Read the description of the feral child Victor given in Exercise 5. What mistake does Victor make regarding object names? Do children who were exposed to language from birth make the same mistake? Do children eventually learn the correct referents for these object names? Which stage of the acquisition of lexical items does Victor seem to be stuck in?

14. Each pair of utterances below comes from children at different ages. For each pair, which utterance was most likely said by the older child? Explain your answers. Some of the examples are taken from Berko Gleason (2005).

a. I'm not sad now.
I no like it.
b. Where Daddy go?
What she is playing?
c. I no want book.
No Mommy do it.
d. Daddy go.
Whasat?
e. I see men.
I see manses.

15. For each word below, explain what a child has to learn about the word in order to use it correctly.

a. cold
b. Susan
c. you
d. bird
e. this

Activities

16. This activity is adapted from Yule (1996). Show the following list of expressions to some friends and ask them to guess the meaning:

a. a snow-car
a running-stick
a water-cake
a finger-brush
a pony-kid

(cont.)

Now compare your friends' versions with those of a two-year-old child below (from Clark 1993). What do the examples suggest about the nature of vocabulary acquisition?

b. [talking about a toy car completely painted white]
Child: This is a snow-car.
Parent: Why is this a snow-car?
Child: 'Cause it's got lots of snow on it. I can't see the windows.

Child: This is a running stick.
Parent: A running-stick?
Child: Yes, because I run with it.

Child: [in the bath] It's a water-cake.
Parent: Why do you call it a water-cake?
Child: I made it in the water.

Child: I bought you a toothbrush and a finger-brush.
Parent: What's a finger-brush?
Child: It's for cleaning your nails.

Child: [wearing a sun hat] I look like a pony-kid.
Parent: What's a pony-kid?
Child: A kid who rides ponies.

File 8.4—How Adults Talk to Young Children

Exercises

17. Read the following "conversations" between three-month-old Ann and her mother (from Snow 1977). Which aspects of how adults talk to young children and what they say to young children can you identify in each "conversation"?

   a. Mom: Oh you are a funny little one, aren't you, hmm?
                     [pause]
                     Aren't you a funny little one?
                     [pause]
                     Hmm?

   b. Ann: abaabaa
             Mom: Baba.
                     Yes, that's you, what you are.

18. For each pair of sentences, which of the two would an adult most likely say to a young child? Justify your answer.

   a. Timmy, see the bird?
         Do you see the bird?
   b. You are taking a bath now.
         Timmy is taking a bath now.
   c. Look, the girl is eating. And now she is playing with the ball.
         Look, the girl is eating. And now the girl is playing with the ball.
   d. That's a birdie.
         That's a robin.
   e. No, that's a kitty, not a doggy.
         No, say *went*, not *goed*.

Discussion Questions

19. Many adults use child-directed speech to speak to children, and they seem to be able to use child-directed speech in ways that are helpful to the child. How do you think adults know what to do to be most helpful?

Activities

20. Make a list of all the aspects of how adults talk to children and what they say to children that are discussed in this file. Then observe adults interacting with two children of different ages. Which of the aspects on your list do the adults use? Write down examples. How does the child's age influence the adult speech?

File 8.5—Bilingual Language Acquisition
Discussion Questions

21. Why do you think motivation plays such a big role in the success of second-language acquisition?

22. Do you have any experience trying to learn a second language? How proficient are you? How do you think the factors mentioned in this file affected your proficiency?

Activities

23. Interview a proficient non-native speaker of your language. Find out where and when your speaker learned your native language. Also ask your speaker how motivated he or she was in learning the language. Then listen carefully to your speaker: do you find features in his or her speech that could be attributed to transfer? Think about pronunciation (phonology), grammar (syntax and morphology), word choice (lexicon), intonation, and appropriateness. Does your speaker speak your language at a level that you would expect, considering his or her language-learning background? Why or why not?

Further Reading

Senghas, Ann & Coppola, Marie. "Children Creating Language." *Psychological Science* 2001: 12 (4), 323–28.

9

Language Storage and Processing

RHYMES WITH ORANGE   **BY HILARY B. PRICE**

© HILARY B. PRICE. KING FEATURES SYNDICATE

How Do We Store and Process Language?

Psycholinguists and neurolinguists study language storage and processing. **Psycholinguistics** is the study of language and the mind; **neurolinguistics** is the study of language and the physical brain. Psycholinguists study what people know about language and how they use that knowledge to produce and understand it. Our collected experiences with our native language(s) structure our memory for language, which contains precise details about every aspect of language. One goal of psycholinguistics is to explain how all this unconscious and usually effortless marshalling of so much remembered experience works for all language users on an everyday basis.

To discover where and how the brain stores and processes language, we need to know where the language centers of the brain are and how we perceive and produce language. Our knowledge of language storage and processing comes mainly from experiments and studies of patients with (partial) language loss due to brain injury.

Contents

352

9.7   Experimental Methods in Psycholinguistics
       Provides general information regarding experimental work and gives examples of some common
       experimental methods.

9.8   Practice
       Provides exercises, discussion questions, and activities related to language storage and processing.

Language and the Brain

9.1.1 Why Study the Brain?

Linguists analyze the structure of language and propose models that can account for the linguistic phenomena they observe—sets of phonemes, collections of phonological or morphological rules, guidelines for building syntactic structures, and so on. However, this level of linguistic pursuit is quite abstract and often removed from considerations of the physiology of language: how is language actually stored in and processed by the brain? By learning about how the brain acquires, stores, and processes language, we can investigate whether the models that linguists propose to account for certain linguistic phenomena are plausible or even possible models. The areas of linguistics that deal with questions about the brain are **neurolinguistics,** the study of the neural and electrochemical bases of language development and use; and **psycholinguistics,** the study of the acquisition, storage, comprehension, and production of language. Chapter 8 covered language acquisition; the focus of this chapter is language storage and processing, from both a neurolinguistic and a psycholinguistic point of view.

The human brain is somewhat like the CPU (central processing unit) of a computer: it governs all human activities, including the ability to understand and produce language. This file will introduce you to some of the regions and properties of the human brain that are thought to be essential for understanding and using language. Keep in mind as you read that the human brain is an extremely complex organ, and our knowledge of its inner workings is still very limited. There are many aspects of brain function that are understood only poorly and others that we do not understand at all. We present you here with facts that have been reliably established at this point and time, facts discovered through numerous elaborate psychological studies and linguistic experiments.

9.1.2 Physical Features of the Brain

The brain is divided into two nearly symmetrical halves, the right and left **hemispheres,** each of which is responsible for processing certain kinds of information concerning the world around us. Each hemisphere is further divided into four areas of the brain called **lobes.** The **temporal lobe** is associated with the perception and recognition of auditory stimuli; the **frontal lobe** is concerned with higher thinking and language production; and the **occipital lobe** is associated with many aspects of vision. The **parietal lobe** is least involved in language perception and production.

The two hemispheres are connected by a bundle of nerve fibers called the **corpus callosum.** This bundle of about 200 million nerve fibers makes it possible for the two hemispheres to communicate with each other and build a single, coherent picture of our environment from the many different kinds of stimuli—visual, tactile, oral, auditory, and olfactory—that we receive.

The brain is covered by a one-quarter-inch thick membrane called the **cortex.** It has been suggested that it is this membrane that makes human beings capable of higher cogni-

(1) The left hemisphere of the human brain

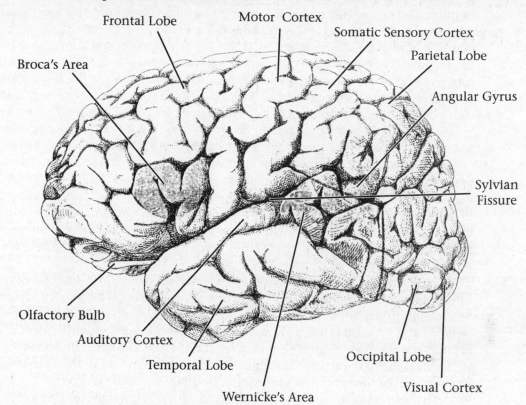

Frontal Lobe

Motor Cortex

Somatic Sensory Cortex

Broca's Area

Parietal Lobe

Angular Gyrus

Sylvian Fissure

Olfactory Bulb

Auditory Cortex

Temporal Lobe

Occipital Lobe

Visual Cortex

Wernicke's Area

"Map of the Human Cortex," figure by Carol Donner from "Specializations of the Human Brain," by Norman Geschwind. Copyright © 1979 by Scientific American, Inc. All rights reserved.

tive functions, such as the ability to do math or use language, and that its development was one of the primary evolutionary changes that separated us from other animals. In fact, most of the language centers of the brain that we will be discussing later in this file are contained in the cortex. This is why even minor damage to the surface of the brain, for example, that caused by a strong blow to the head, can result in language impairment.

As you can see from the drawing in (1), the cortex is not flat but covered with bumps and indentations. The bumps on the surface of the brain are called **gyri** (singular *gyrus*), and the depressions are called **fissures.** Scientists use certain fissures to demarcate the lobes of the brain. One of the most prominent of these is the **Sylvian Fissure,** the large horizontal fold located in the middle of each hemisphere separating the temporal lobe from the frontal lobe of the brain.

Several portions of the cortex are specialized to perform particular functions that play a role in language use. The first that we will introduce is the **auditory cortex,** located in the temporal lobe next to the Sylvian Fissure. The auditory cortex is responsible for receiving and identifying auditory signals and converting them into a form that can be interpreted by other areas of the brain. Another specialized area is the **visual cortex,** located in the occipital lobe in the lower back of each hemisphere. This area receives and interprets visual stimuli and is thought to be the storage site for pictorial images. A third is the **motor cortex,** which is found in the frontal lobe in the upper middle of each hemisphere, perpendicular to the Sylvian Fissure. This part of the brain is responsible for sending signals to your muscles, including those of your face, jaw, and tongue.

The brain also contains so-called **language centers**—parts of the cortex that, as far as we know, are used only for the production and comprehension of language. In contrast to the other areas we have introduced here, which are found in both hemispheres, these centers are usually found only in the hemisphere that is specialized for language: for over 90% of right-handed people (who make up about 90% of the population) and approximately 70% of left-handed people, this is the **left hemisphere.** For such people, the opposing hemisphere does not have these language centers. In the remaining right- and left-handed people, language centers are either found only in the **right hemisphere** or divided between both hemispheres. Studies have suggested that women and illiterate people are more likely to have language centers in both hemispheres. Furthermore, left-hemisphere-dominant multilinguals use the right hemisphere more for languages learned later in life that are not regularly heard.

The first of these language centers is **Broca's area.** Located at the base of the motor cortex, this language center appears to be responsible for organizing the articulatory patterns of language and directing the motor cortex when we want to talk. This involves the face, jaw, and tongue in the case of spoken language, and the hands, arms, face, and body in the case of signed language. Broca's area also seems to control the use of inflectional morphemes, like the plural and past tense markers, as well as function words, like determiners and prepositions (see File 4.1), which both have important functions with respect to the formation of words and sentences. Thus, Broca's area is mainly responsible for language production.

Another language center is **Wernicke's area.** Located near the back section of the auditory cortex, this area of the brain is involved in the comprehension of words and sentences and the selection of words from the mental lexicon (see File 9.4) when producing sentences. As opposed to Broca's area, Wernicke's area is largely responsible for language perception and comprehension. Wernicke's area and Broca's area are connected by a bundle of nerve fibers called the **arcuate fasciculus.** Like the corpus callosum, these nerve fibers allow the two areas of the brain that they connect to share information.

The final language center we will introduce is the **angular gyrus.** This area, located between Wernicke's area and the visual cortex, converts visual stimuli into auditory stimuli (and vice versa), allowing us to match the spoken form of a word with the object it describes, as well as with the written form of the word. This ability is crucial to the human capacity to read and write.

9.1.3   The Flow of Linguistic Information

Now that we have identified the relevant physical areas of the brain, let's turn to the question of how these areas of the brain work together to process language. The answer to this question depends on what type of stimulus (auditory, visual, etc.) and what type of linguistic result (speaking, reading, understanding, etc.) are involved. For example, to produce a spoken word (see (2)), a person first chooses a word from the mental lexicon. The process of accessing the lexicon activates Wernicke's area, which then interprets the lexical entry, identifying the meaning of the word, how to pronounce it, and so on. The phonetic information for the entry (how to pronounce it) is sent via the arcuate fasciculus to Broca's area. Then Broca's area determines what combination of the various articulators is necessary to produce each sound in the word and instructs the motor cortex which muscles to move. You may find it useful to compare this process to the steps in the communication chain described in File 1.2.

(2)   Producing a spoken word

Wernicke's area	activated when accessing the lexicon; interprets lexical entry
Arcuate fasciculus	phonetic information sent from Wernicke's area to Broca's area
Broca's area	interprets information received from arcuate fasciculus; transmits articulatory information to motor cortex
Motor cortex	directs movement of muscles for articulation

You can reverse this process to hear and understand a word that has been said to you. First, as shown in (3), the stimulus is brought into the auditory cortex through the ears (or into the visual cortex through the eyes, if you speak a signed language). Wernicke's area is activated as that auditory stimulus is matched to a word in your mental lexicon. If you have an image or a written form associated with the word, the angular gyrus will activate the visual cortex, and you will have a picture of the item and its spelling available to you.

(3) Hearing a word

Auditory cortex	processes information perceived by ears
Wernicke's area	interprets auditory stimulus and matches information to a lexical entry

Before reading ahead, can you figure out how you understand a word that you read?

When you are reading a word, the visual information taken in by your eyes is first sent to the visual cortex (see (4)). The angular gyrus then associates the written form of the word with an entry in the mental lexicon, which releases information about the word into Wernicke's area. Wernicke's area then interprets the entry and gives you the meaning of the word.

(4) Reading a word

Visual cortex	processes information perceived by eyes
Angular gyrus	associates written form of word with lexical entry
Wernicke's area	activated during lexical access; makes available the meaning and pronunciation of word

9.1.4 Lateralization and Contralateralization

As mentioned earlier, each of the brain's hemispheres is responsible for different cognitive functions. This specialization is referred to as **lateralization** (*lateral* means "of or related to the side"). For most individuals, the left hemisphere is dominant in the areas of analytic reasoning, temporal ordering, arithmetic, and language processing. The right hemisphere is in charge of processing music, perceiving nonlinguistic sounds, and performing tasks that require visual and spatial skills or pattern recognition. Lateralization happens in early childhood and can be reversed in its initial stages if there is damage to a part of the brain that is crucially involved in an important function. For example, if a very young child whose brain was originally lateralized so that language functions were in the left hemisphere receives severe damage to the language centers, the right hemisphere can develop language centers to compensate for the loss. After a certain period, however, lateralization is permanent and cannot be reversed.

There are a number of ways to study the effects of lateralization. Most of them rely on the fact that the connections between the brain and the body are almost completely **contralateral** (*contra* means "opposite," and thus *contralateral* means "on the opposite side"). This means that the right side of the body is controlled by the left hemisphere, while the left side of the body is controlled by the right hemisphere. It is also important to realize that this contralateral connection means that sensory information from the right side of the body is received by the left hemisphere, while sensory information from the left side of the body is received by the right hemisphere. Sensory information can be any data one gathers through hearing, seeing, touching, tasting, or smelling. Many different experiments have provided evidence for contralateralization. One example of this type of experiment, which is rather intrusive, is the anesthetizing of one hemisphere. An anesthetic is injected into the artery of the patient leading to one side of the brain or the other. The patient is then asked to stand with both arms stretched forward from the shoulders. The arm opposite the anesthetized hemisphere slowly goes down as the anesthesia takes effect, providing evidence for contralateralization. If the language hemisphere is anesthetized, the patient also cannot speak at all for a few minutes after the injection, and in the next few minutes after that, the patient appears to be aphasic (unable to perceive or produce fluent language; see File 9.2), providing evidence that the patient's language centers are in that hemisphere.

One experiment that relies on the existence of contralateralization and is designed to test the location of language processing centers is the **dichotic listening task.** The diagram in (5) is a schematic representation of how this kind of task is designed. In this test, two sounds are presented at the same time to a person with normal hearing—one sound in the left ear and one in the right. The sounds may be linguistic (e.g., a person saying a word) or nonlinguistic (e.g., a door slamming). The subject is asked what sound he or she heard in one ear or another. These tests show that responses to the right-ear stimuli are quicker and more accurate when the stimuli are verbal, while responses to the left-ear stimuli are quicker and more accurate when the stimuli are nonverbal. To understand why this is so, recall that the theory of contralateralization predicts that a linguistic signal presented to the left ear will go first to the right hemisphere. Before it can be perceived as language, the signal must cross the corpus callosum to the left hemisphere, where the language centers are for most people. On the other hand, a linguistic signal presented to the right ear goes directly to the left hemisphere. We find just the opposite effect with nonlinguistic sounds, where a stimulus presented to the left ear is recognized faster and better than one presented to the right ear. This is because the right hemisphere processes nonverbal sounds. If a nonverbal stimulus is presented to the right ear, the signal goes to the left hemisphere, and then it must cross the corpus callosum to the right hemisphere in order to be processed. A nonverbal stimulus presented to the left ear goes directly to the right hemisphere, where it can be processed immediately.

(5) A schematic representation of a dichotic listening task

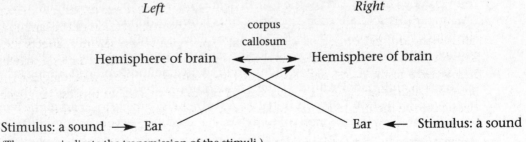

(The arrows indicate the transmission of the stimuli.)

Further evidence for the locations of the language processing centers comes from so-called **split-brain patients.** Normally, the two hemispheres are connected by the corpus callosum, but for certain kinds of severe epilepsy, the corpus callosum used to be surgically severed, preventing the two hemispheres from transmitting information to each other. Since epileptic seizures are caused in part by a patient's motor cortices "overloading" on information sent back and forth between the two hemispheres, this procedure greatly reduced the number and danger of such seizures. This kind of treatment was used in the 1940s and the 1950s, but it is no longer used because medications have been developed for managing severe epilepsy.

Since the connections from the brain to the rest of the body are contralateral, various experiments can be performed on these split-brain patients in order to identify the cognitive characteristics of the two hemispheres. In one experiment, split-brain patients are blindfolded and an object is placed in one of their hands. The patients are then asked to name the object. The representation in (6) illustrates how this kind of naming task is designed. If an object is placed in a patient's left hand, the patient usually cannot identify the object verbally. If, however, the object is placed in the patient's right hand, he or she usually can name the object. Can you explain why? When the object is in the patient's left hand, sensory information from holding the object, which in this case is tactile information, reaches the right hemisphere. Since the corpus callosum is severed, the information cannot be transferred to the left hemisphere; because the patient is then unable to name the object despite being able to feel what it is, we conclude that the language centers must be in the left hemisphere. When the object is in the patient's right hand, however, sensory information from holding the object reaches the left hemisphere. In this case, the patient is able to name the object; therefore, the language centers must be in the left hemisphere. The information can be transferred to the language centers because it does not have to cross the corpus callosum to get there. Once it reaches the language centers, the patient can say what the object is.

(6) A schematic representation of an object-naming task

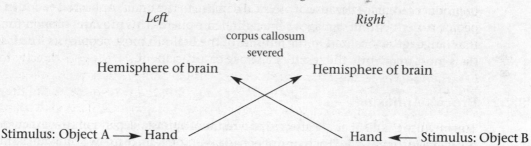

Result: The patient can name object B, but not object A. Therefore, this patient's language centers must be located in the left hemisphere.
(The arrows indicate the transmission of the stimuli.)

Hemispherectomy, an operation in which one hemisphere or part of one hemisphere is removed from the brain, also provides evidence for the location of the language centers. This operation, performed on people who experience severe seizures, affects the patient's behavior and ability to think. It has been found that hemispherectomies involving the left hemisphere result in aphasia much more frequently than those involving the right hemisphere. This indicates that the left side of the brain is used to process language in most people, while the right side has much less to do with language processing.

Much of the evidence for the lateralization of the areas of the brain that deal with language processing presented in this file comes from psycholinguistic experiments (e.g., dichotic listening task) and from patients whose brain was damaged as a result of an operation (e.g., hemispherectomies, split-brain patients). However, much of the evidence regarding the exact locations of language centers, such as Broca's and Wernicke's areas, within the left hemisphere comes from patients who received brain damage as the result of a stroke or an accident. Such cases are discussed in File 9.2.

FILE 9.2

Aphasia

9.2.1 Language Disorders

In the 1860s, physician Paul Broca observed that damage to the left side of the brain resulted in impaired language ability, while damage to the right side of the brain did not. Since that time, researchers have observed that approximately 70% of people with damage to the left hemisphere of the brain experience **aphasia,** an inability to perceive, process, or produce language because of physical damage to the brain. Aphasia is found in very few people suffering from damage to the right hemisphere. This provides support for the view that language is localized in the left side of the brain in most people (see File 9.1). Aphasia is most frequently the result of a stroke or an accident.

9.2.2 Broca's Aphasia

The linguistic skills that are affected as a result of aphasia depend on the exact location of the damage to the brain. Each case of aphasia is unique, since no two individuals have damage to the exact same parts of the brain. However, patients with damage to similar regions of the brain show similar symptoms. Individuals with **Broca's aphasia**, a result of damage to Broca's area—the language center that is responsible for speech **production**—suffer from an inability to plan the motor sequences used in speech or sign. When they attempt to produce language, they speak or sign haltingly and have a difficult time forming complete words. They also tend to use telegraphic speech. For English, for example, this means that their speech lacks morphological inflection and function words like *to* and *the*. For ASL, this means that their language contains no inflections or classifiers. The examples in (1) and (2) illustrate the speech of two Broca's aphasics, speakers of English and of ASL, respectively.

(1) Speech produced by a Broca's aphasic

    Examiner: Tell me, what did you do before you retired?
    Aphasic: Uh, uh, uh, pub, par, partender, no.
    Examiner: Carpenter?
    Aphasic: [nodding] Carpenter, tuh, tuh, tenty year.

(2) Sign produced by a Broca's aphasic. Examiner's signs are translated into English; aphasic's signs are in CAPITALS; finger-spelled words are hyphenated (from Lane et al. 1996).

    Examiner: What else happened?
    Aphasic: CAR . . . DRIVE . . . BROTHER . . . DRIVE . . . I . . . S-T-A-D . . . [attempts to gesture stand up]
    Examiner: You stood up?
    Aphasic: YES . . . I . . . DRIVE . . . [attempts to gesture goodbye]
    Examiner: Wave goodbye?
    Aphasic: YES . . . BROTHER . . . DRIVE . . . DUNNO . . . [attempts to wave goodbye]

Examiner:	Your brother was driving?
Aphasic:	YES . . . BACK . . . DRIVE . . . BROTHER . . . MAN . . . MAMA . . . STAY . . . BROTHER . . . DRIVE.
Examiner:	Were you in the car?
Aphasic:	YES.
Examiner:	Or outside?
Aphasic:	NO.
Examiner:	In the car.
Aphasic:	YES.
Examiner:	You were standing up with your mother?
Aphasic:	NO . . . BROTHER . . . DRIVE . . . [points in back] DEAF BROTHER . . . I . . .
Examiner:	Your brother didn't know you were in the car?
Aphasic:	YES.
Examiner:	Your brother was driving and saw you in the back seat?
Aphasic:	YES, YES. [laughs]

Broca's aphasia seems to result in primarily expressive disorders: it is very difficult for Broca's aphasics to produce speech. The aphasic in (1), for example, produces the word *carpenter* correctly only after several attempts. The aphasic in (2) pauses after almost every word, as indicated by the ellipses. For the most part, Broca's aphasics do not have a problem understanding the speech of others, although they may have some difficulty matching the correct semantic interpretation to the syntactic order of the sentence. For instance, comprehension is likely to break down when the order of words in a sentence is extremely important to the understanding of the message, as in reversible passives such as *The lion was killed by the tiger*. A Broca's aphasic is quite likely to understand this as identical to the active sentence *The lion killed the tiger*.

9.2.3 Wernicke's Aphasia

Wernicke's aphasia, a result of damage to Wernicke's area—the language center responsible for speech **comprehension**—results in primarily receptive disorders; it is very difficult for a patient with this problem to understand the speech of others. This often results in the Wernicke's aphasic misinterpreting what others say and responding in an unexpected way. Moreover, because Wernicke's patients have trouble interpreting words from their mental lexicon, they have a tendency to produce semantically incoherent speech. These two effects result in the type of speech you see in (3).

(3) A sample of speech produced by a patient with Wernicke's aphasia

Examiner:	Do you like it here in Kansas City?
Aphasic:	Yes, I am.
Examiner:	I'd like to have you tell me something about your problem.
Aphasic:	Yes, I, ugh, can't hill all of my way. I can't talk all of the things I do, and part of the part I can go all right, but I can't tell from the other people. I usually most of my things. I know what can I talk and know what they are, but I can't always come back even though I know they should be in, and I know should something eely I should know what I'm doing. . . .

Wernicke's patients also often speak in **circumlocutions**, or round-about descriptions that people use when they are unable to name the word they want. For example, the patient may say *what you drink* for *water* and *what we smell with* for *nose*. The syntactic order of words is also altered. *I know I can say* may become *I know can I say*. That patients with Wernicke's aphasia are unable to comprehend the speech of others is demonstrated by the fact that they often cannot follow simple instructions, such as "stand up," "turn to your right," and so on. Wernicke's aphasics are the most likely of the aphasic types to experience **anosognosia,** the unawareness of the disturbances in their own language. Patients with anosognosia often seem to believe that their speech is interpretable by others when in fact it is not.

9.2.4　Conduction Aphasia

A third type of language disorder, called **conduction aphasia,** results from damage to the arcuate fasciculus, the bundle of nerve fibers that connects Broca's and Wernicke's areas. A patient suffering from conduction aphasia sounds something like a Wernicke's aphasic (fluent but meaningless speech) but shows signs of being able to comprehend the speech of others. Like a Broca's aphasic, the patient will be able to understand utterances but will not be able to repeat them. This pattern of symptoms makes sense if you consider what the arcuate fasciculus does: it transmits information from Wernicke's area to Broca's area. If these two language centers are unable to communicate, the patient with damage to the arcuate fasciculus may be able to understand speech and correctly interpret words from the mental lexicon (since Wernicke's area is not damaged) but will not be able to transmit information to Broca's area so that words can be articulated (though Broca's area may be intact, it receives incomplete information).

9.2.5　Other Language Disorders

The last two language disorders we will mention are **alexia** and **agraphia,** which are both caused by damage to the angular gyrus, the part of the brain that converts visual stimuli to auditory stimuli, and vice versa. Alexia is defined as the inability to read and comprehend written words. This occurs when the angular gyrus cannot accurately match the visual form of a word with a phonetic form interpretable by Wernicke's area. Occasionally, this problem is accompanied by the inability to write words, known as agraphia. This disorder is often attributed to the inability of the angular gyrus to relate the phonetic form of a stimulus with a written form in the visual cortex. Note that alexia is not the same thing as dyslexia. Alexia is the result of damage to the angular gyrus caused by an accident, stroke, or lesion; dyslexia, as current research indicates, is caused by a structural difference in a portion of the brain called the temporal lobe. People with dyslexia can almost always read and write normally with special training; someone with alexia cannot regain his or her previous reading skill.

9.2.6　Aphasia in Signers

In Section 9.2.2 you saw that aphasia can occur in users of both spoken and signed languages. You further saw that both the speaker in (1) and the signer in (2) have damage to the same region of the brain (Broca's area) and display similar symptoms (both have trouble producing words). These similarities were an important finding, because researchers had previously been unsure about whether signed languages were processed in the same areas of the brain as spoken languages (Broca's area and Wernicke's area, both usually found in the left hemisphere). It had been thought that signed languages were processed in the right hemisphere of the brain because the right hemisphere is responsible for motor control functions in most people, and producing ASL uses the same muscles as, say, picking up a cup. However, this is not the case: users of signed languages with aphasia show damage to the same regions in the left hemisphere of the brain and have the same symptoms as users of spoken languages. A signer with damage to Wernicke's area, for example, would display fluent but meaningless speech, similar to the aphasic in (3).

In hindsight, it makes a lot of sense that signed languages are also processed in the language centers of the brain; after all, they exhibit all the other characteristics of human languages. The idea that they could be processed in the right hemisphere of the brain was possibly guided by a lingering doubt that signed languages were real languages. However, of course, we know that spoken languages are not controlled by the motor control centers of the right hemisphere of the brain, even though the same muscles used to make speech sounds are also used for eating and chewing. Thus, regardless of whether a language user speaks or signs, the muscles he or she uses to do this are controlled by language centers in the left hemisphere of the brain, even though the very same muscles are controlled by the motor control centers of the right hemisphere if he or she is involved in a nonlinguistic motor task.

David Corina and his colleagues (1999) report some interesting data from two signers with brain damage that illustrate the point made above. We all have different facial expressions: we can convey sadness, happiness, anger, fear, surprise, and so on, on our face. These are called **affective facial expressions.** Signed languages, such as ASL, also have particular facial expressions with grammatical functions in the language (see Section 2.7.7). These facial expressions, called **linguistic facial expressions,** differ from affective facial expressions in that they do not have to express something about the speaker's emotions, they have a rapid onset and offset, and they may involve the use of individual muscles which generally are not used in affective facial expressions. ASL, for example, requires the use of particular facial expressions in relative clauses, conditionals, some adverbials, and so on. If a relative clause or conditional is signed without the appropriate linguistic facial expression, it is ungrammatical.

Corina and his colleagues investigated the signing of two native ASL speakers with brain damage. Gail had damage to Broca's area, and Sarah had damage to the right hemisphere of the brain, the area responsible for motor control. Examples of how these two women signed are given in (4), (5), and (6) and are discussed below. Signs are given in CAPITAL letters, finger-spelled words are hyphenated, and linguistic facial expressions are given above the signs.

(4) Sign produced by Gail

    ASL: *DIANE, HEARING AUNT, WAIT, PHONE[Iterative]
    English translation: 'Diane, hearing aunt, waited for a long time and phoned again and again.'

                                            rel
                                        ———————
    Correct ASL: DIANE, HEARING AUNT, WAIT, PHONE[Iterative]
    English translation: 'Diane, who is my hearing aunt, waited for a long time and phoned again and again.'

(5) Sign produced by Sarah

                                                  th
                                          ————————
    ASL: WOMAN WASH WATER OVERFLOW STUPID
                          'The woman washed (the dishes), the water flows and she didn't notice it. That's stupid, she's really stupid.'

(6) Sign produced by Sarah

    ASL: SOMETIMES[Habitual] DEPRESS[Intense], CRY, WHEN I UPSET, FIRST STROKE, I CRIED.
    English translation: 'Sometimes I got depressed and I cried. When I first had my stroke, I became very upset about it and cried.

Gail, who has damage to Broca's area, is not able to use linguistic facial expressions. The example in (4) illustrates this. The sentence requires the linguistic facial expression for a relative clause, indicated by the *rel* above the sign *AUNT* in the correct version of the sentence. However, Gail omits the *rel* facial marker, and her sentence is ungrammatical. Despite this, Gail is still able to use affective facial expressions. In fact, she uses more affective facial expressions than many people when she speaks.

Sarah, on the other hand, uses linguistic facial expressions perfectly. An example of this is given in (5), where she correctly uses the linguistic facial expression *th* (which means 'carelessly'). However, she talks about her depression when she first had her stroke (in (6)) without a single affective facial expression. Her face is blank while she tells the story, even though the story is sad and we would expect it to be accompanied by a "sad face," especially because affective facial expressions are particularly prevalent in Deaf culture in the United States. The cases of Gail and Sarah illustrate nicely how the same set of muscles can work for one task but not for another if the tasks are controlled by different parts of the brain. They also provide evidence that linguistic facial expressions are not just muscle movements—they are part of language.

Speech Production

9.3.1 From Thought to Utterance

As described in File 1.2, the communication chain involves both the sending and the receiving of messages. When we send messages using language—that is, when we speak or sign—the brain is involved in planning what we want to say and in instructing the muscles used for speaking or signing. This process of sending messages is called **speech production** and is the focus of this file.

A fair amount of planning is involved in producing an utterance. Refer to the diagram in (1) in File 1.2: steps 1–4 all illustrate the planning stages. First, we need to know what we want to say before we can decide how to say it. That is, we first have an idea or a thought which we then translate into an utterance. However, the nature of our thoughts is different from the nature of our utterances. Our thought process is global or holistic: we think of the complete idea simultaneously. But producing an utterance is linear: we cannot produce all parts of our idea at once. Instead, we produce a sentence one word at a time and, within each word, one sound at a time. (This is true at least of spoken languages. In signed languages, various linguistic elements can be expressed simultaneously. See Files 2.7 and 3.2 for simultaneous aspects of signed language phonetics and morphology; there are also simultaneous elements of the syntax of signed languages. However, even in signed languages, only some elements are produced simultaneously: there is a linear ordering of various components in any given utterance.)

Imagine that you wanted to express to a friend that you are tired. The idea of being tired is in your thoughts as a whole, in its totality. But when you actually tell your friend that you are tired, that is, when you translate the thought into an utterance, you cannot convey the complete idea simultaneously. Instead, you need to translate your thought into a linear order of words. Suppose that you said to your friend, *I am tired*. In this case, you first convey the information that the message pertains to you, then you express that the message concerns your state of being, and finally you express that this state of being is feeling tired. You cannot convey all the parts of the message at the same time. Note that this linearity is true also at the phonetic level: you don't express the word *tired* in one action; instead, you start with the [t] and then move on to the vowel [ɑɪ] and so on.

9.3.2 Models of Speech Production

Many steps are involved in translating a message from a thought into an utterance. The example above hinted at two of them: when planning an utterance, we need to choose appropriate words and put them in an appropriate order. But much more is involved in producing an utterance. The diagram of the communication chain that was presented in File 1.2 includes some of the other steps, such as putting sounds together with those words. This diagram, however, was an oversimplification of one view of how the chain of events in speech production works. Two of the most prominent models of speech production are discussed below.

Let's first look at Fromkin's model of speech production (1971), one of the earliest models proposing planning stages for speech production.

(1) Fromkin's model of speech production
    1. Meaning is identified.
    2. Syntactic structure is selected.
    3. Intonation contour is generated.
    4. Content words are inserted.
    5. Function words and affixes are inserted.
    6. Phonetic segments are specified.

Fromkin's model suggests that utterance planning progresses from meaning to the selection of a syntactic frame, into which morphemes are inserted, to the choice of allophones. Let's look at an example. To convey *Peter walked down the stairs,* the planning would go through the following stages:

(2) 1. The meaning of the idea of 'Peter walking down the stairs sometime in the past' is identified.
    2. The frame _____ (NP) _____ (V) _____ (Prep) _____ (Det) _____ (NP) is chosen.
    3. An intonation contour appropriate for a statement is chosen.
    4. The content words are inserted into the frame: *Peter* (NP) *walk* (V) _____ (Prep) _____ (Det) *stair* (NP)
    5. Function words and affixes are added to the frame: *Peter* (NP) *walk-ed* (V) *down* (Prep) *the* (Det) *stair-s* (NP)
    6. Phonological rules are applied: for example, the *-ed* in *walked* is pronounced as [t], and the *-s* in *stairs* is pronounced as [z].

Fromkin's model assumes that utterance planning goes through the proposed stages in the order given. Such a model is called **serial** because the different stages of the model form a series or succession. However, other models assume that the different stages involved in planning are all processed simultaneously and influence each other. Such models are called **parallel.**

The model proposed by Levelt (1989) is one of the most influential parallel models. According to this model, three major levels are involved in speech production. The level that corresponds to Fromkin's first stage is called *conceptualization*. Here the concepts of what a speaker wants to express are generated. The second level is called *formulation*. At this level the concepts to be expressed are mapped onto a linguistic form. The formulation level has two sublevels: *grammatical encoding* and *phonological encoding*. At the grammatical encoding level, a syntactic structure and lexical items are selected. Thus, this corresponds to Fromkin's stages 2, 4, and 5. At the phonological encoding level, the phonetic form is specified. This corresponds to Fromkin's stages 3 and 6. The third level is the process of *articulation,* which involves two steps corresponding to grammatical encoding and phonological encoding. Levelt's model is summarized in (3).

(3) Levelt's model of speech production
    • Conceptualization
    • Formulation:
        • Grammatical encoding (selection of syntactic frame and lexical items)
        • Phonological encoding (specification of phonetic form)
    • Articulation

Levelt's model is different from Fromkin's model mainly in that it allows positive feedback to occur in both directions. In other words, later stages of processing can influence earlier stages. This is not possible in Fromkin's model. Slips of the tongue, discussed in the next section, are one source of evidence both for and against each of these kinds of models.

9.3.3 Production Errors: Slips of the Tongue

The previous sections illustrate how much is involved in planning and producing even a simple utterance. This complexity has made speech production difficult to study, especially when you remember that all of these steps occur in the mind, before any actual production has occurred. To learn about the stages involved in speech production, it has proven useful to investigate what happens when something in the production process goes wrong, that is, when we make a **production error** or "slip of the tongue." By production error we mean any **inadvertent** flaws in a speaker's use of his or her language. It is important to note that production errors are unintentional: we say something that we did not intend to say. For example, if we say *distactful* because we incorrectly believe that it is an English word, then this error relates to our linguistic competence and our knowledge of English, not to the production process. However, if we say *distactful* even though we meant to say *untactful*, then this error relates to the production process, not to our knowledge of English. This is why only inadvertent errors can tell us something about speech production.

Production errors can tell us a lot about the process of speech production because they are very systematic: entire units are moved, added, or omitted during a speech error. These units may be features, sounds, morphemes, and words. The fact that virtually all production errors involve these units provides evidence for the psychological reality of the units and suggests that speakers do indeed organize the speech wave in terms of these units.

a. Types of Production Errors. This section will introduce you to some basic types of speech errors. Examples of all error types are given in (4). **Anticipations** occur when a later unit is substituted for an earlier unit or when a later unit is added earlier in an utterance (4a). **Perseverations** can be seen as the opposite of anticipations: they occur when an earlier unit is substituted for a later unit or when an earlier unit is added later in an utterance (4b). **Addition** and **deletion** errors involve the addition of extra units (out of the blue, so to speak) and the omission of units, respectively ((4c) and (4d)). **Metathesis** is the switching of two units, each taking the place of the other (4e). When a metathesis involves the first sounds of two separate words, the error is called a **spoonerism** (4f) (named after the Reverend Spooner, a renowned chronic sufferer of this type of slip of the tongue). **Shifts** occur when a unit is moved from one location to another (4g). **Substitutions** happen when one unit is replaced with another (4h), while **blends** occur when two words "fuse" into a single item (4i).

(4)

	Intended Utterance	*Actual Utterance*	*Error Type*
a.	splicing from one tape	splacing from one tape	anticipation
b.	splicing from one tape	splicing from one type	perseveration
c.	spic and span	spic and splan	addition
d.	his immortal soul	his immoral soul	deletion
e.	fill the pool	fool the pill	metathesis
f.	dear old queen	queer old dean	spoonerism
g.	she decides to hit it	she decide to hits it	shift
h.	it's hot in here	it's cold in here	substitution
i.	grizzly/ghastly	grastly	blend

b. What Production Errors Can Tell Us about Speech Production. In most of the examples in (4), the unit involved in the production error is a phone. However, the shift in (4g) and the substitution of *distactful* for *untactful* in the previous section involve moving or replacing a morpheme, and the substitution in (4h) involves replacing one word with another. Examples like these provide evidence for the psychological reality of phones, morphemes, and words. That is, phones, morphemes, and words are part of our mental organization of the speech wave. Let's think about how these examples show this: in order to substitute, add, move, or delete a phone, the speaker must think of it as a discrete unit. So the speaker is imposing a structure on the speech signal in his mind, even though this structure does not exist physically. (Remember that we do not produce sounds as discrete units. Rather, in a continuous stream of speech, adjacent sounds are coarticulated, and it is difficult to say where one sound ends and the next one starts.) Because these units can be inadvertently separated by the speaker, we say that the sound unit is psychologically real.

But we can go further than this: production errors also provide evidence that phonetic features (the subparts of sound structure, such as the voicing, place, and manner of articulation of consonants; see File 2.2) are psychologically real and not just a descriptive construct made up by linguists. Consider the production errors in (5), where phonetic features, not whole sounds, are being exchanged.

(5) **Intended Utterance**   **Actual Utterance**   **Error Type**
    a. clear blue sky   glear plue sky   spoonerism
    b. Cedars of Lebanon   Cedars of Lemadon   metathesis

In (5a), the [k] in *clear* is mistakenly voiced, whereas the [b] in *blue* is mistakenly not voiced. Thus, this is a case of spoonerism involving the feature of voicing. In the second example, air is allowed to resonate in the nasal cavity during the [b] rather than during the [n], resulting in *Lemadon* rather than *Lebanon*. That is, the [b] in *Lebanon* is mistakenly nasalized, whereas the [n] in *Lebanon* is mistakenly not nasalized. The fact that individual articulatory movements can be involved in production errors shows that they too are psychologically real units to the speaker, that is, speakers do mentally organize sounds as being made up of a set of articulatory movements.

Language, of course, involves more than just units of speech. In particular, linguists maintain that there is a complex set of rules which the language user follows when making use of these units. One type of rule whose psychological reality can be confirmed by studying speech errors are **phonotactic constraints.** These constraints tell us which sequences of sounds are possible in a given language. For example, the sequence of sounds [sɹ] doesn't occur at the beginning of a word in English. That speakers of English follow this rule is clear from the slip in (6). Notice that the error looks similar to metatheses of [l] and [ɹ]. But the [s] of *slip* has also been converted to [ʃ]. Since [sɹ], which would be the result of simple metathesis, does not occur word-initially in English (see File 3.3 for more on phonotactic constraints), a further change was made to avoid violating this phonotactic rule. Thus, speakers unconsciously follow these rules, even when making mistakes.

(6) **Intended Utterance**   **Actual Utterance**   **Error Type**
    Freudian slip   fleudian shrip   metathesis + phonotactics

The rules that tell us how morphemes are to be pronounced are also obeyed when making speech errors. For example, recall that the morpheme that is used most often to indicate past tense has three different pronunciations, [d], [t], and [ad], depending on the nature of the preceding sound. The reality of the rule governing the distribution of these pronunciations is indicated by the fact that it is followed even when the past tense morpheme is attached to a different word as the result of a production error. Since these rules are always followed, they must be part of our mental organization of the language.

(7) **Intended Utterance**   **Actual Utterance**   **Error Type**
    a. cooked a roast ([t])   roasted a cook ([ad])   metathesis
    b. his team rested ([ad])   his rest teamed ([d])   metathesis

These examples also demonstrate the reality of the rules for combining morphemes, since even during a speech error we find only past tense morphemes combined with verbs, plural morphemes combined with nouns, and so on. Because we rarely get nonsensical combinations like "noun + past tense," the rules which tell us how words are built must also be part of our mental organization of language.

Furthermore, speech errors can also give us insights into the organization of words in the **mental lexicon** (see Files 1.2 and 9.5). For example, many errors in the production of speech involve the substitution of one word for another because of some semantic relationship between the words. The errors in (8), and many more like them, reveal that the intended word and the substituted word often share some common semantic feature, and that the retrieval process mistakes one word for another. Thus, these semantic similarities must be recognized and the lexical entries in the brain organized accordingly.

(8) *Intended Utterance*   *Actual Utterance*   *Error Type*

	Intended Utterance	*Actual Utterance*	*Error Type*
a.	My thesis is too <u>long</u>	My thesis is too <u>short</u>	substitution
b.	before the place <u>opens</u>	before the place <u>closes</u>	substitution
c.	He got hot under the <u>collar</u>	He got hot under the <u>belt</u>	substitution

A similar type of speech error involves a substitution of one word for another based on phonological, rather than semantic, similarities. Examples of this are given in (9). What happens in these cases is that the speaker's retrieval process inadvertently pulls out a word that sounds like the one they intended to use but that is semantically distinct. Thus, evidence from speech errors suggests that the mental lexicon is organized in terms of sound as well as meaning.

	Intended Utterance	*Actual Utterance*	*Error Type*
a.	spreading like <u>wildfire</u>	spreading like <u>wildflowers</u>	malapropism
b.	<u>equivalent</u>	equivocal	malapropism
c.	<u>marinade</u>	serenade	malapropism
d.	I'm a <u>contortionist</u>!	I'm an <u>extortionist</u>!	malapropism

This type of error, called a **malapropism,** must be distinguished from cases where the word the speaker used is the one she intended to use even though it is semantically incorrect (unbeknownst to the speaker). This latter type of mistake, called a **classical malapropism,** does not involve a performance error per se, since the speakers are saying what they meant to say; rather, it is a competence error since the speakers have incorrect beliefs about the meaning of a particular word. Mrs. Malaprop (after whom this kind of error is named) was a character from Richard B. Sheridan's eighteenth-century play *The Rivals* and was particularly prone to this kind of error, as was the television character Archie Bunker in *All in the Family.* Classical malapropisms reveal more about how words are learned than how they are organized, because the retrieval process is functioning perfectly in these cases. Some examples of classical malapropisms are given in (10).

	Intended Meaning	*Actual Utterance*
a.	<u>obscure</u>	obtuse
b.	I hereby <u>deputize</u> you	I hereby <u>jeopardize</u> you
c.	express <u>appreciation</u>	express <u>depreciation</u>

Production errors can provide evidence for or against different models of speech production. For example, the error in (11a) suggests that Fromkin's stage 5 (insertion of function words and affixes) does indeed come before her proposed stage 6 (specification of phonetic segments). Notice that the error in the example occurred during stage 4: When the content words were inserted, *minister* and *church* were switched. Next, the function words and affixes were added, and *church* received the plural suffix that was intended for *minister*. If the phonetic form of the suffix had already been specified at this point, then the speaker would have pronounced *churches* as [tʃɹtʃ] + [z] because the phonetic form of the plural suffix for *minister* (the intended recipient of the plural suffix) is [z]. Notice that even though this example provides evidence for Fromkin's model, it is not incompatible with Levelt's model.

(11) ***Intended Utterance***   ***Actual Utterance***
  a. <u>minister</u>s [mɪnɪstɹz] in our <u>church</u>   <u>church</u>es [tʃɹtʃəz] in our <u>minister</u>
  b. <u>s</u>peech <u>pr</u>oduction   <u>pr</u>each <u>s</u>eduction

Let's consider an example that provides evidence for Levelt's parallel model. At first sight, the example in (11b) looks like a type of spoonerism. However, if that were the case, the speaker should have said *preach spoduction,* exchanging [pɹ] with [sp]. The fact that the speaker said *preach seduction* can be explained by the **lexical bias effect**, which refers to the fact that phonological errors give rise to real words more often than chance would predict. Fromkin's model cannot explain this effect since the specification of phonetic segments, the stage at which the error occurred, is the last stage of the model. To explain the error, the content word *seduction* would have to replace *spoduction* after specification of the phonetic segments. However, Fromkin proposes that content words are always inserted **before** phonetic segments are specified. Levelt's model, which allows feedback in both directions, can explain the lexical bias effect: after the phonetic form is specified, feedback from the phonological encoding level to the grammatical encoding level causes the selection of the real word *seduction*.

Many of the examples above illustrate that the speech wave, despite its physical continuity, is mentally organized into discrete units and that these units follow specific rules and patterns of formation. We also saw that constraints are never violated, not even by mistake, showing that they are an intrinsic part of language itself; that is, they define for us what language is like. Thus, by studying cases in which an individual's linguistic performance is less than perfect, we can gain more insight into the nature of linguistic **competence,** the unconscious knowledge that speakers of a language possess. Linguists can then formulate hypotheses about the mental constructs that represent this knowledge. We have seen such hypotheses in the form of two models of speech production.

9.3.4   Production Errors: Slips of the Hands

So far we have talked only about production errors in spoken languages. But the same phenomena exist in signed languages. In analogy to slips of the tongue, such errors are called "slips of the hands." As in spoken languages, signed production errors are systematic. They include all the types of speech errors that we introduced in Section 9.2.3a, thus giving more evidence for the fact that signed languages, like spoken languages, have all of the same levels of structure. Just as we have had to make some allowances for the different modalities of signed and spoken languages with respect to the notions of phonetics and phonology, however, we must understand that the units involved in slips of the hands are different from those in slips of the tongue. Where spoken language errors may involve units of sound like phones and features, comparable signed production errors involve the **parameters** that constitute a sign. These parameters (introduced in File 2.7) include place of articulation, movement, handshape, and hand orientation, as well as considerations such as whether one or two hands are used to produce the sign.

The pictures in (12)–(15) illustrate slips of the hands. Both (12) and (13) are instances of metathesis. In (12), the exchange involves the handshape parameter: the particular shape of the hands in MUST and SEE are exchanged. In (13), there is movement metathesis: TASTE is articulated with the movement for GOOD, and vice versa.

(12) a. Correctly signed phrase:

MUST   SEE

b. Error:

error   error

(13) a. Correctly signed phrase:

TASTE   GOOD

b. Error:

error   error

The error in (14) involves whether the sign is produced with just the dominant hand or with both hands. The error in (14) is an anticipation: the two-handedness of TRY is anticipated, and MUST is inadvertently produced with two hands.

(14) a. Correctly signed phrase:

MUST   TRY

b. Error:

error   TRY

Finally, (15) is a case of perseveration of place of articulation: the sign GIRL is accidentally produced at the forehead, the place of articulation for FATHER.

(15) a. Correctly signed phrase:

FATHER   GIRL

b. Error:

FATHER   error

As in spoken languages, the existence of such systematicity in errors provides evidence that the parameters proposed to describe the phonetics of signed languages are psychologically real. Furthermore, Klima and Bellugi (1979) remark that the overwhelming majority of production errors they observed resulted in possible signs (as opposed to gestures that could not be grammatical signs). This suggests that sign language constraints that are analogous to phonotactic constraints are also psychologically real.

Speech Perception

9.4.1 Receiving Messages

As described in both File 1.2 and File 9.2, the language communication chain involves both sending and receiving messages. This file and the following two files are concerned with how we receive messages, that is, how we perceive and interpret spoken and written language.[1] The process of receiving and interpreting messages is called **speech perception.** Speech perception can be seen as the reverse of speech production: in speech production, we have an idea that we turn into an utterance, whereas in speech perception, we hear or see an utterance and decode the idea it carries.

Our ability to understand linguistic messages is quite remarkable. In a matter of milliseconds, we identify sounds, match them with words in our mental lexicon (see File 9.5), and apply syntactic rules to understand the meaning of the message (see File 9.6). We can do this even in a crowded and noisy bar. We can pick out relevant acoustic information (what someone is telling us) in the presence of other noises such as the person at the next table telling a joke, the waiter dropping a glass of beer, and the music playing in the background.

This file deals with the process of identifying the sounds of speech. This is a difficult task because no sound is ever produced exactly the same way twice. For example, if a person utters the word *bee* ten times, neither the [b] nor the [i] in each production will be physically identical. So how do we match, for example, a [b] with the category /b/ in our head if no [b] is physically the same as another? This is called the **lack-of-invariance** problem. This file introduces a number of speech perception phenomena that help explain how we deal with the lack-of-invariance problem and manage to match highly variable phones to phonological categories in our heads.

9.4.2 Categorical Perception

One phenomenon that helps explain how we deal with lack of invariance is **categorical perception,** which occurs when equal-sized physical differences are not equal-sized psychologically, that is, when we do not perceive a continuum as a continuum. Rather, differences **within** categories are compressed, and differences **across** categories are expanded. People come to perceive entities differently after they learn to categorize them. In particular, members of the same category are perceived to be more alike than members of different categories, even if they are equally different. For example, two different kinds of yellow are perceived to be more similar than a yellow and a red, even if the differences in wavelength between the colors in each pair are identical. This is a case of categorical perception.

Categorical perception also occurs in language, particularly in consonant perception. Let's look at an example. The sounds [b] and [p] differ only in voicing: [b] is voiced, but [p] is voiceless (see File 2.2). Consider the syllables [bɑ] and [pɑ]. Physically, these sounds dif-

---

[1]The perception of signed language will not be considered here.

fer in their **voice onset time** (VOT), the time between the opening of the lips at the end of the stop and the beginning of vocal-fold vibration or voicing in the following vowel. In English, a bilabial stop with a 0-millisecond VOT would always be perceived as /b/. In this case, the voicing starts as soon as the stop is released (hence a value of 0 ms for the VOT). However, a bilabial stop with a 60-millisecond VOT would always be perceived in English as a /p/. Here the voicing for the /ɑ/ starts 60 milliseconds after the stop is released.

But what about a bilabial stop with a 10-, 20-, 30-, 40-, or 50-millisecond VOT? Would it be perceived as a /b/, as a /p/, or as something in between? The answer to this question can be determined by synthesizing bilabial stops with varying VOTs followed by the same vowel, for example, [ɑ], and asking people whether they heard /bɑ/ or /pɑ/. That is, we have a series of syllables of the form [bilabial stop]+[ɑ]; each bilabial stop has a different VOT value, ranging from 0 to 60 ms. If people listening to this continuum of VOT values were to perceive it as a continuum between /bɑ/ and /pɑ/, we would expect the results of such a task to look like the graph in (1). The larger the VOT, the more /p/-like the sounds would be perceived; we would see a gradual decline in /b/-identification and a gradual increase in /p/-identification as the VOT increases. But if /b/ and /p/ are perceived categorically, we would expect a graph like the one in (2). Sounds within one category (either the /b/ category or the /p/ category) would be perceived as similar or the same, but sounds across category boundaries would be heard as different. In this case we would expect to see a sharp drop in /b/-identifications at the category boundary.

(1) Schema of continuous perception in an identification task

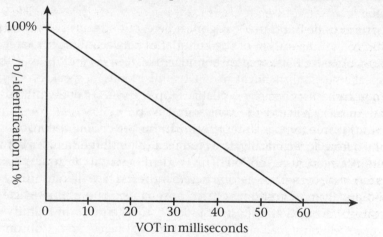

(2) Schema of categorical perception in an identification task

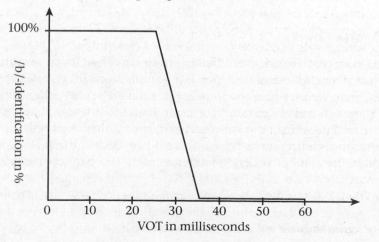

As already mentioned, consonants are perceived categorically, so (2) and not (1) shows how bilabial stops with continuously varying VOTs are perceived. The category boundary for speakers of English is at about 30 milliseconds, as shown in (2).

The identification task just described is not enough, however, to prove that consonants are perceived categorically. It is possible that we do perceive the synthesized bilabial stops as a continuum, but since we have names only for the sounds /b/ and /p/, we pick the sound name that is closest to what we heard: 'b' for everything that sounds similar to a /b/ and 'p' for everything that sounds similar to a /p/. To prove that within-category members are really perceived as the same sound and across-category members as different sounds, we need a second task: a discrimination task. Only if speakers of English cannot discriminate two bilabial stops from the same category (for example, two stops that were identified as /b/), but can discriminate two bilabial stops from different categories, can we claim that bilabial stops are perceived categorically. And this is indeed what discrimination experiments have shown.

Categorical perception occurs as a result of exposure to one's native language. Six-month-old infants of English-speaking parents perceive the difference between two bilabial stops with 0 and 20 milliseconds of VOT, something that English-speaking adults cannot do (since they hear them both as members of the /b/ category). By the time the infants are twelve months old, they no longer perceive this difference, and they display the same discrimination behavior as English-speaking adults. That is, by the age of twelve months, their perception of consonants is categorical. This means that exposure to our native language changes the way we perceive consonants in a way that allows us to deal with the lack-of-invariance problem.

It is important to mention that categorical perception seems to be found in all languages, but that the exact location of the boundaries between different categories differs from language to language. The category boundary between /b/ and /p/ is at about 30 milliseconds for speakers of English, but at around 0 milliseconds for speakers of Spanish.[2] This means that Spanish speakers perceive a bilabial stop with a VOT of 20 milliseconds as /p/, whereas English speakers perceive the same sound as /b/.

The previous discussion has dealt only with the perception of consonants, because vowels are not perceived categorically. How can we explain this difference between vowels and consonants if categorical perception helps us identify sound categories? It has been suggested that categorical perception is not necessary for vowels because they are usually longer and perceptually more prominent than consonants. Thus, when we hear a vowel, we get enough acoustic information, even in fast speech, to determine the identity of the vowel without having to rely on a mechanism like categorical perception. Consonants, on the other hand, do not always provide enough acoustic information to determine their identity, and we have to rely on categorical perception.

9.4.3 Context and Rate Effects

Knowing now that we perceive consonants categorically may lead us to conclude that making out individual sounds in a stream of speech is a straightforward task despite variability in the acoustic signal. We may hear the sounds [k], [æ], and [t] and understand *cat,* or we may hear [k], [u], and [l] and understand *cool,* both thanks to categorical perception. However, notice that in the previous section we considered bilabial stops only preceding the vowel [ɑ]. A further complication arises with the [k] in *cat* and the [k] in *cool:* they are acoustically rather different not because of differences in VOT but because the [k] in *cat* is

---

[2]This means that speakers of Spanish perceive bilabial stops with VOTs greater than 0 milliseconds as /p/, and bilabial stops with VOTs smaller than 0 milliseconds, such as –40 milliseconds, as /b/. A VOT of –40 milliseconds means that the voicing starts 40 milliseconds before the stop is released.

produced farther forward in the mouth than the [k] in *cool*. This presents a different kind of variance that the listener needs to deal with. Luckily, our perceptual system can also handle this: we are able to correctly identify both sounds as the phoneme /k/ by taking the following vowel into account.

Let's look at an example in more detail. The sounds [ʃ] and [s] are both voiceless fricatives. They differ only in their place of articulation: [ʃ] is palatal and [s] is alveolar (see File 2.2). Acoustically, [ʃ] has a lower frequency concentration than [s] (see File 2.6). This means that [s] and [ʃ] can be considered to be two ends of a frequency continuum. We can take a recording of someone producing the sound [s] in isolation and manipulate it to sound like [ʃ] using a computer program. All we need to do is move the frequency concentration up. But what happens if we take recordings of someone producing [s] and [ʃ] and we synthesize a sound that has its frequency concentration in the middle of the two sounds? Will it sound like [s] or [ʃ]? The answer is that this depends on the context, that is, on the following vowel. If the following vowel is [u], most people will hear our synthesized sound as [s]; if it is followed by [ɑ], most people will hear it as [ʃ]. This means that how we identify an individual sound depends on its context, that is, which sounds occur before and after it. The problem of contextual variation is handled by our perceptual system, but it is one of the major difficulties facing speech synthesis (see File 15.3).

Not only the context, but also the rate of speech, affects the acoustic properties of a sound. For example, in faster speech, bilabial stops have shorter VOTs. This means that a [pɑ] produced twice as fast as another [pɑ] will have a VOT that's approximately half the size as that of the slower production. So if the slower [pɑ] has a VOT of about 40 milliseconds, the faster [pɑ] will have a VOT of about 20 milliseconds. In the previous section we said that a speaker of English will perceive a bilabial stop with a VOT of 20 milliseconds as a /b/. So how can we tell whether a bilabial stop with a VOT of 20 milliseconds is a /b/ that is produced comparatively more slowly or a /p/ that is produced faster? The answer is that we are able to take the rate of speech into account when making this decision: listeners adjust to a person's speaking rate incredibly fast, often within several hundred milliseconds. Decisions about sound categories are then based on this rate adjustment.

9.4.4 The McGurk Effect

The **McGurk effect** (McGurk and MacDonald 1976) is another piece in the puzzle of how we deal with variability. It illustrates that we rely not only on the highly variable acoustic signal but also on visual information to perceive sounds.

The McGurk effect occurs when a video showing a person producing one sound is dubbed with a sound-recording of a different sound. As surprising at it may seem, if you watch a video showing a person producing the syllable [gɑ] with the sounds [bɑ] dubbed over it, you will actually hear [dɑ]!

Why would this be the case? The answer is that visual information is integrated with auditory information in the processing of speech. Of particular relevance to our example just above is the fact that [g], [b], and [d] are all voiced stops, differing only in their place of articulation. In addition, [gɑ] and [dɑ] are difficult to distinguish visually because both syllables start with the lips slightly open. Therefore, the visual information is consistent with both [dɑ] and [gɑ], while the auditory information is most consistent with [dɑ] and [bɑ]. One reason why the listener perceives [dɑ] then is that these sounds are most consistent with all the information they are receiving. Notice also that the place of articulation for [dɑ] is at the alveolar ridge, so it is in between the places of articulation for [gɑ] and [bɑ], which are produced with the tongue touching the velum in the case of [gɑ] and with both lips for [bɑ] (see File 2.2). This means that the conflicting visual and auditory information is resolved by a compromise: we hear the sound "in between" the one that is visually presented and the one that is auditorily presented.

As the McGurk effect illustrates, despite considerable variability in the acoustic signal, we are able to draw on both acoustic properties and visual information to identify speech sounds.

9.4.5 Other Factors Involved in Speech Perception

The previous sections showed that we are able to identify phonological categories despite high variability in the speech signal because our perceptual systems can accommodate many of the contributing factors. There are a number of additional factors that help us categorize sounds, such as our knowledge of phonotactic constraints, the words in our mental lexicon, and the context of an utterance.

As discussed in File 3.3, listeners have unconscious knowledge of the phonotactic constraints of their language. One source of evidence for this knowledge comes from perception errors, also called slips of the ear. Specifically, errors of this type always result in possible (though not always actual) words. For example, if we hear the beginning of a word and are not sure whether we heard the sequence [ʃk] or [sk], we can conclude that it was [sk] since English does not allow the consonant cluster [ʃk]. Listeners know what to expect in the way of sequences of sounds; if they did not have this knowledge, we would expect listeners to mistakenly hear words made up of sounds sequences that are impossible in their language.

The words in our mental lexicon can also help us identify individual sounds. For example, if we are not sure whether a sound we heard was an /m/ or an /n/, we can determine that it probably was an /m/ if it was preceded by the phones [kɹi] since *cream* is a word of English, but *crean* is not. On the other hand, if the sound was preceded by [kli], we can determine that it was probably an [n] since *clean* is a word of English, but *cleam* is not. Finally, the linguistic context of an utterance can help us identify sounds. For example, the word *heel* is more likely to appear in the context of shoes, whereas the word *peel* is more likely to occur in the context of oranges.

An effect called **phonemic restoration** illustrates how strongly both of these factors influence speech perception. In an experiment by Warren and Warren (1970), participants were played one of the sentences in (3). The * indicates that a sound was replaced with a cough. Interestingly, participants heard **eel* as *wheel, heel, peel,* or *meal,* depending on the context that followed. For example, for (3a), they heard *wheel,* while for (3d), they heard *meal.* This means that participants "heard" a sound that was actually not present in the acoustic signal because it fit into the context of the utterance. Furthermore, when they were told that a sound was missing from the utterance and were asked to guess which one it was, listeners were unable to identify the missing sound.

(3) a. It was found that the *eel was on the axle.
     b. It was found that the *eel was on the shoe.
     c. It was found that the *eel was on the orange.
     d. It was found that the *eel was on the table.

Lexical Processing

9.5.1 What Is Lexical Processing?

Lexical processing refers to the way that words are recognized. People can recognize words extremely quickly, even though the average college-educated adult knows between 40,000 and 60,000 words to select from (Miller 1996). In fact, it takes only about 250 milliseconds to "find" a word in the **mental lexicon**. This is remarkably fast since the task of finding a word is harder than it seems: many of the 40,000 to 60,000 words are similar given that they are constructed from a relatively small number of phonemes. For example, *state, snake, stack, stay, ache,* and *take* all sound similar to *steak*.

This file discusses how words are stored in the mental lexicon, the process of word recognition, and what word recognition reveals about the organization of the mental lexicon.

9.5.2 The Mental Lexicon

Think of the mental lexicon as a dictionary located in the brain, containing all the words an individual knows, including what each word means, how it is used in conjunction with other words, and how it is pronounced. Keep in mind, however, that this dictionary is not a tangible object but rather some abstract network of information in the brain. We cannot point to it, but we have strong reasons to believe that it exists.

We have just said that the mental lexicon contains all the words an individual knows. But given the productive nature of language, some linguists have questioned whether this is, in fact, the case. For example, they wonder whether complex words like *internationalization, generalization, visualization, globalization,* and *liberalization* are stored as whole words or are broken up into morphemes.

It seems reasonable to assume that the fastest way to access such complex words would be if they were all stored as separate, individual entries. This is called the **full listing hypothesis** (Butterworth 1983). In this case, *internationalization, generalization, visualization, globalization,* and *liberalization* would each be stored as a separate entry, as would the words *nation, national, international, nationalize, internationalize, nationalization, general, generalize, visual, visualize, globe, global, globalize, liberal,* and *liberalize.* However, storing every word individually, while allowing for fast access, takes up a lot of storage space; it also seems to miss the generalization that these words are in some way related to each other.

Alternatively, complex words could be broken down into morphemes, with each morpheme stored individually in the lexicon (see File 4.1). This is called the **affix-stripping hypothesis** (Taft and Forsters 1975). According to the affix-stripping hypothesis, complex words are built from the morphemes listed in the lexicon. For example, the words *internationalization, generalization, visualization, globalization,* and *liberalization* would be built from the entries *nation, general, visual, global, liberal, inter-, -al, -ize,* and *-ation.* Storing only morphemes would greatly reduce the number of entries in the lexicon. For example, if each of our 5 complex words and the 15 related words from the previous paragraph were listed separately, we would need 20 different entries. In contrast, we would need only 9 entries if only the individual morphemes were listed. This would not only reduce storage space, but it would also highlight the nature of the relationship between these words. Yet it would slow down lexical access since words would be constantly decomposed into and rebuilt from individual morphemes during comprehension and production.

Most recent models propose that the truth lies somewhere in between. That is, some complex words may be stored as whole units, while others may be stored partially decomposed or even fully decomposed. In most models, the degree of decomposition depends on the kinds of affixes a complex word contains. Some affixes are very transparent: attaching them to a root does not change the way the root is pronounced, and the meaning of the complex word is completely compositional. An example of such an affix is -*less* [ləs] 'without,' which can be attached to, for example, *hope* [houp] and *clue* [klu] to create the words *hopeless* [houp + ləs] 'without hope' and *clueless* [klu + ləs] 'without a clue.' Other affixes are not as easily decomposed since attaching them to a root frequently changes the way the root is pronounced. For example, when we attach -*ity* [ɪɾi] to *severe* [səvɪɹ], the pronunciation of the second root vowel changes from [i] to [ɛ], giving *severity* [səvɛɹ + ɪɾi]. Decomposing words with such affixes is not straightforward since the meaning is not always obvious from the parts. It is thus possible that a word such as *severity* is stored as in its entirety, whereas *clueless* is decomposed and stored as two elements: *clue* and -*less*. While there is experimental evidence supporting this intermediary hypothesis (see, for example, Vannest and Boland 1999), more research is needed to understand which affixes are listed separately in the mental lexicon and which ones are not.

Whether complex words are stored as a whole or are decomposed into individual morphemes may also depend on language and, in particular, on how many morphologically complex words a language has and how complex they are. Many analytic languages, such as Mandarin, have relatively few morphologically complex words. Thus, all the words of Mandarin could probably be stored in the lexicon as a whole without taking up too much storage space. However, agglutinating languages such as Turkish have many morphologically complex words. An example of how complex words in Turkish are formed is given in (1) (Hankamer 1989).

(1) göz   =   "eye"
    gözlük   =   "glasses"
    gözlükçü   =   "seller of glasses (oculist)"
    gözlükçülük   =   "the occupation of oculists"
    gözlükçülükçü   =   "a lobbyist for the oculist profession"
    gözlükçülükçülük =   "the occupation of being a lobbyist for the oculist profession"

Thus, for languages like Turkish, storing morphologically complex words as a whole could require more storage space than reasonably could be allotted to the mental lexicon. Hankamer (1989) even suggests that storing all the words of Turkish in their full form would require more storage space than the human brain has.

There are three major areas of study in the domain of psycholinguistics; so far we have considered how language is represented in the brain and how language is acquired. But another major area is how people use their knowledge of language. How do they understand what they hear? How do they produce messages that others can understand in turn?

We have already begun to answer these questions with regard to speech production (File 9.3) and speech perception (File 9.4). Much of the research on adult normal processes of the last twenty or thirty years, however, has focused on three areas: word recognition, syntactic analysis, and interpretation. This file will introduce the first of these, word recognition, and File 9.6 will deal with syntactic analysis and interpretation.

9.5.3 Word Recognition

An important step in understanding any linguistic message is being able to recognize the meaning of words. As seen in File 5.2, the meaning of a sentence is determined in part from the meanings of the words it contains. Identifying a word also tells us what syntactic category it belongs to, thus determining the range of phrase structures it can occur in (see Files 5.3 and 5.4). A word also provides information about the syntactic structure of the rest of the sentence. When we recognize a verb like *put,* for example, we expect certain types of information to follow. In particular, we expect to hear the object of the 'putting' (e.g., *the plate*) followed by where the object is being put (e.g., *on the table*). When we hear the verb *arrive,* we know that it does not take an object (we do not 'arrive someone' or 'arrive something'), but that it may take a prepositional phrase, as in *arrive at the hotel.* This kind of information is made available to us when we recognize a word and access the information pertaining to it in our memory.

Identifying words is such an effortless task under most conditions that we typically don't realize how difficult it really is; designing a computer system to accomplish this task, for instance, has proven very difficult. One reason for the difficulty is the sheer number of words that any given person knows: the average six-year-old already knows about 14,000 words, while a college-educated adult, as mentioned above, knows between 40,000 and 60,000 words. A second reason is the large amount of other linguistic information that is accessed during word recognition and stored along with each word, as illustrated just above.

9.5.4 The Cohort Model

One of the essential parts of understanding words is recognizing them as they come at us in a stream of speech. How do we go about recognizing words? One common-sense view that receives a lot of support from experimental evidence is that as soon as people hear speech, they start narrowing down the possible words that they may be hearing. If the first sound that they hear is /s/, all words beginning with any other sound are eliminated, but words like *summer, spring, stone, sister,* and *spine* remain on the "list of possible words." If the next sound is /p/, many other possible words are ruled out, including *summer, stone,* and *sister.* A word is identified as soon as there is only one possibility left. This is called the **uniqueness point** of a word, and we refer to this model of word recognition as the **cohort model** of lexical access. The word **cohort** refers to all the words that remain on the "list of possible words" as the auditory input progresses. The words that are activated as the first sound of a word is perceived are called the **initial cohort.** The cohort model hypothesizes that auditory word recognition begins with the formation of a group of words at the perception of the initial sound and proceeds sound by sound with the cohort of possible words decreasing as more sounds are perceived.

Several experiments have supported this view of word recognition. For example, one obvious prediction of this model is that if the beginning sound of a word is missing, recognition will be much more difficult, perhaps even impossible. As early as 1900, experiments showed that word recognition is impaired much more when the initial sound of a word is mispronounced than when the final sound is mispronounced. This supports the cohort theory: if the end of the word is missing, it can be predicted based on the initial portion, while it is much more difficult to use the end to predict the early part of the word.

Although this model makes a lot of intuitive sense and has some experimental support, it leaves several questions unanswered. One problem is that in listening to running speech, people can't always identify where a word starts. In written English, boundaries are fairly clearly marked, but this is not the case for spoken language: there is usually no pause between one word and the next. So, for example, when someone hears the sequence [pɑpəpoʊzd], it is not at all obvious whether the utterance should be understood as *Papa posed* or as *Pop opposed*. If people need to know a word's first sound in order to identify it, *opposed* might not even be part of the "list of possible words." This is because [ə] could be interpreted as the last sound of [pɑpə], rather than the first sound of [əpoʊzd]. More examples of this type of ambiguity relating to word boundaries are shown in (2). If you say these phrases aloud at a normal conversational speaking rate and without context, you may have difficulty identifying where the word boundaries are.

(2) the sky   this guy
     a name   an aim
     an ice man   a nice man
     I scream   ice cream
     see Mabel   seem able

Some other problems for the cohort model are described in the following section; each suggests additional aspects of word recognition that need to be addressed for a theory of word recognition to be correct.

9.5.5   Frequency, Recency, and Context Effects

One of the most important factors that affect word recognition is how frequently a word is encountered in a language. This **frequency effect** describes the additional ease with which a word is recognized because of its more frequent usage in the language. For example, some words (such as *better* or *TV*) occur more often than others (such as *debtor* or *mortgage*), and words that occur more frequently are easier to access. This effect is not easy to explain assuming the beginning-to-end word recognition approach sketched out above. One possible explanation of the frequency effect is that the lexicon is partially organized by frequency and that in addition to being accessed from beginning to end, more-frequent words are "at the top of the list" of cohorts.

People also recognize a word faster when they have just heard it or read it than when they have not recently encountered it; this phenomenon is known as the **recency effect.** Recency effects describe the additional ease with which a word is accessed because of its recent occurrence in the discourse or context. Note that frequent words are likely to have been encountered more recently than infrequent words, so it may be possible to explain the frequency effect as a recency phenomenon, thus reducing the number of separate effects that have to be explained.

Another factor that is involved in word recognition is **context.** People recognize a word more readily when the preceding words provide an appropriate context for it. For example, in the sentence *This is the aorta,* people are not given any context that helps identify the word *aorta.* But in the sentence *The heart surgeon carefully cut into the wall of the right aorta,* many people would find that the cue of the *heart surgeon* helps them identify the word more quickly. One mechanism that has been proposed to account for this kind of **context effect** is a **semantic association network** (see (3)). This network represents the relationships between various semantically related words. Word recognition is thought to be faster when other members of the association network are provided in the discourse. It is obvious that the meaning of a word is tied to our understanding and general knowledge of the concept to which it refers. Thus, it is not unreasonable to suppose that hearing the words *heart surgeon* not only activates the direct meaning of the words *heart surgeon* but also makes a number of associated concepts more available to the hearer, such as those involved in the physiology of the heart, modern surgical procedures, and so on. These concepts are in turn linked to the words that are used to refer to them, making these words also more available.

(3) Example of part of a semantic association network

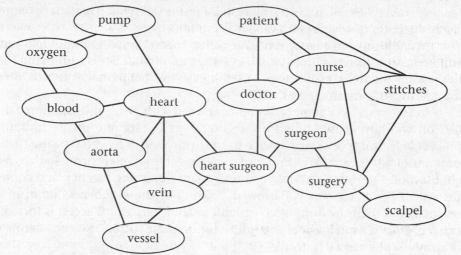

9.5.6 Lexical Ambiguity

Much research has centered on how ambiguous words are understood. How, for example, does a listener know whether *bug* refers to 'an insect' or 'a listening device'? This kind of ambiguity is called **lexical ambiguity,** meaning that a single lexical item—that is, a word—can have more than one meaning.

There are two main theories of how lexical ambiguity is resolved by listeners. The first claims that all the meanings associated with the word are accessed, with the correct meaning eventually being winnowed out (similar to the idea of the cohort model for word recognition). The second claims that only one meaning is accessed initially and that the listener holds on to this meaning until finding evidence that contradicts this first assumption. Support for the first position comes from experiments such as the following. When people are asked to finish a sentence, they take longer when the fragment to be finished contains an ambiguous word than when the ambiguous word is replaced by an unambiguous term, as in the sentences in (4).

(4) After taking the right turn at the intersection . . . (*right* is ambiguous: 'correct' vs. 'rightward')

   After taking the left turn at the intersection . . . (*left* is unambiguous)

This delay suggests that all meanings of ambiguous words are accessed and that time has to be taken to decide among them; if only one meaning were accessed, we would not expect a difference in timing between ambiguous and unambiguous words.

However, other experiments suggest that under some circumstances, only one meaning is initially accessed. The frequency effect mentioned above has been shown to be important here. If a word has more than one meaning and one of the meanings is more frequent than the other, people tend to assign the more frequent meaning to the word. *Chair,* for example, has at least two meanings: 'an object to sit on' and 'the head of a department or committee.' The former meaning occurs much more often in speech than the latter, and, as a result, when people hear the word *chair,* they tend to associate it with the more frequent meaning and in fact may be slower at processing the sentence if the less frequent meaning was intended. This seems to suggest that only one meaning is initially considered, at least for words whose meanings differ markedly in frequency of occurrence. Similarly, if the conversation has centered on one particular meaning of an ambiguous word (e.g., if the conversation is about how the committee chairman lost his temper at a meeting), then a listener may access only the less frequent meaning of *chair* in the sentence: . . . *and then the chair was reprimanded by the supervisor.* This is an example of the recency effect influencing word ambiguity resolution.

In addition to frequency, semantic context also plays a significant role in determining which meaning is relevant. For instance, when a word like *bug* is seen in the context of *spy,* it is reliably identified as meaning 'a listening device,' but in the context of *flies and roaches,* it is identified as meaning 'an insect.'

In summary, lexical processing is concerned with how words are stored in the mental lexicon and how those words are accessed. There is a lot of evidence indicating that the process of lexical access starts as soon as the first sound of a word is heard; that is, we don't wait until we've heard the entire word to retrieve it from our lexicon. Rather, much like the cohort model suggests—but taking into account frequency, recency, and context effects—the list of possible words is narrowed down until the uniqueness point of the word is reached, and then the word is recognized. In addition, lexical access is incredibly fast: we can recognize a word in about 250 milliseconds, a remarkable feat considering the number of words in our mental lexicon.

FILE **9.6**

Sentence Processing

9.6.1 How Do We Put Words Together?

The previous file described how we access words in our mental lexicon and some of the factors that can influence this lexical access. But language is not only about words; it is also about putting words together to form sentences. File 5.4 introduced many of the rules that we follow when we form sentences from words. However, for any given sentence that we utter or hear, most of us could not explain which rules we use to correctly form the sentence. That is, language users know how to build sentences in their native language(s), but they are not necessarily conscious of the rules that underlie these cognitive processes. Recall that these rules are part of our linguistic **competence** (see File 1.2).

Just as the word recognition process starts as soon as we hear the first sound of a word (see File 9.4), there is good evidence that we start building a syntactic structure as soon as possible. Let's take the sentence *The jealous woman went away* as an example. As soon as we hear the word *the,* which can only be a determiner, we expect the next word to be a noun (e.g., *the woman, the platypus,* etc.), an adjective (e.g., *the jealous woman, the angry platypus,* etc.), or an adverb (e.g., *the incredibly jealous woman, the vaguely angry platypus,* etc.). We also expect *the* to be part of a noun phrase and part of the subject of the sentence. Upon hearing *jealous,* we update our expectations concerning what comes next (e.g., *the jealous woman, the jealous platypus,* etc.). That is, as we hear a sentence unfold, we assign words to lexical categories (File 5.3) and build a syntactic structure that is updated as a new word comes in. This reconstruction of the syntactic structure of a sentence that is heard or read is called **syntactic parsing**.

9.6.2 Structural Ambiguity

If all words were unambiguous and had only one possible lexical category, processing sentences would be a relatively easy task. However, this is not the case. Both **lexical ambiguity** (when a word has more than one meaning; see Section 9.5.6) and **structural ambiguity** are constantly present during sentence processing. Structural ambiguity, first introduced in File 5.4, occurs when a sentence has two different possible parses resulting from different possible syntactic structures. Below, we consider several different types of structural ambiguity and the problems they cause for sentence processing.

a. Temporary Ambiguity. Let's have a closer look at the example above. We said that the word *the* is unambiguously a determiner. So far, so good. But as soon as we hit the word *jealous,* we encounter our first ambiguity. *Jealous* can be an adjective, as in *the jealous woman,* or a noun, as in *the jealous are troublesome.* Thus, the ambiguity is due to the ambiguous category of *jealous.* Once we hear *woman,* we can easily determine that *jealous* is used here as an adjective. However, now *woman* is ambiguous between being a noun, as in *The jealous woman went away,* or an adjective, as in *The jealous woman plumber went away.* The ambiguity is finally resolved once we hear *went:* we now know that *woman* is a noun, and *went* is not ambiguous. This means that the sentence *The jealous woman went away* is ambiguous only temporarily, namely, up until we hear the word *went*. **Temporary ambiguity** is constantly present in everyday conversations. For example, the vast majority of sentences that start with *the* followed by an adjective or noun (e.g., *the good, the tea, the bad, the dream, the small, the dog, the educated, the paper, the slow, the party, the old,* etc.) are temporarily ambiguous in English because most adjectives can also be nouns and most English nouns can also be adjectives.

b. The Garden Path Effect. As listeners comprehend temporarily ambiguous sentences, they sometimes momentarily recover a meaning that was not intended by the speaker. These mistakes in syntactic parsing are called **garden path effects** because the syntax of the sentence has led the comprehender "down the garden path" (to a spot where they can go no further and must retrace their steps). Garden path sentences are temporarily ambiguous and initially interpreted to have a different syntactic structure than they turn out to have. Let's look at an easy example, given in (1).

(1) a. While Mary was mending the sock fell off her lap.
   b. While Mary was mending the sock it fell off her lap.

When we first read *the sock* in (1a), we are likely to interpret it as the direct object of the verb *mending*. That is, we interpret the fragment to mean that Mary was mending the sock. However, at the verb *fell*, we notice that this parse could not have been correct (because then *fell* would have no subject), and we have to go back and reanalyze the sentence. In this case, we come to the conclusion that *the sock* is not the direct object of *mending*, but the subject of the main clause *the sock fell off her lap*. Such garden path sentences fool us into temporarily interpreting the wrong syntactic structure.

But why are we led down the garden path? The explanation depends on both the syntactic structure of the sentence and the particular lexical items it contains. In (1) we are led down the garden path because the verb *mending* can be (and often is) transitive; that is, it takes a direct object: we can mend something, as in (1b), where Mary is actually mending the sock. The problem, however, is that *mending* can also be intransitive (stand alone without a direct object), as in the sentence *Mary fell asleep while she was mending*. In (1a), the initial assumption is that *mending* is transitive and that *the sock* is its direct object; it is only when we come to the verb *fell* that we realize this initial assumption is wrong. This sentence is then a garden path sentence because of this particular property of the verb *mending*. Compare this to the sentence *While Mary was sneezing the sock fell off her lap*. Even though the sentence has the same structure as (1a), we are not led down the garden path because people usually don't sneeze socks; rather, people just sneeze.

Not all garden path sentences are as easy to recover from as the one above. In fact, for some sentences it can take quite a long time to figure out another structure if our first choice turns out to be incorrect. Some difficult garden path sentences remain **unparsable** for some people. That is, some garden path sentences are so difficult that some people never figure out the correct interpretation. To them the sentence remains ungrammatical. A famous example of a difficult garden path sentence is given in (2).

(2) The horse raced past the barn fell.

If we interpret the sentence as being about the horse racing past the barn, the sentence seems ungrammatical. This kind of sentence contains a reduced relative clause (that is, a relative clause that lacks the word *that* together with a form of the verb *to be*), in this case, *that was*. Thus, *raced* is not the action of the main clause but the verb of the reduced relative clause, and the sentence means *The horse **that was** raced past the barn fell*. Notice that this nonreduced version of (2) is easier to parse. However, both sentences are grammatical and convey the idea of a horse falling while someone was racing it past a barn. To help you understand that *The horse raced past the barn fell* is indeed grammatical, consider the sentence in (3).

(3) The woman driven to the hospital fainted.

This sentence also contains a reduced relative clause and has exactly the same syntactic structure as our difficult garden path sentence. However, people have no trouble identifying (3) as grammatical. If both (2) and (3) have the same syntactic structure and if (3) is grammatical, then our garden path sentence must also be grammatical. Then why is (2) so much harder to parse than (3)? The answer again lies in the lexical items, in this case the words *raced* and *driven*. First, notice that as a stand-alone sentence, *the horse raced* by itself is fine, but *the woman driven* is ungrammatical. Now consider the simple past and the past participle forms of *race* and *drive* given in (4).

(4) | *Infinitive* | *Simple Past Tense* | *Past Participle* |
|---|---|---|
| drive | drove | driven |
| race | raced | raced |

Notice that the simple past and past participle forms of *race* are identical. This conspires with the fact that a sentence-initial noun phrase such as *the horse* is much more likely to be followed by the verb of the main clause (e.g., *raced* or *drove*) than by a reduced relative clause (e.g., *raced* or *driven*). In conjunction, these facts mean that in the case of (2), we interpret *raced* as the verb of the main clause because this is not only a possible parse but also the more frequently encountered option. In the case of (3), however, we cannot interpret *driven* as the verb of the main clause. This would be ungrammatical and explains why we have little trouble interpreting *driven* as the verb of a reduced relative clause instead: unlike *raced*, it cannot be the verb of the main clause.

   c. Globally Ambiguous Sentences. Not all ambiguous sentences are only temporarily ambiguous. There are also sentences that are **globally ambiguous**, that is, sentences in which the ambiguity is not resolved by the end of the sentence. Without additional context (such as intonation or preceding/following sentences), there is no way to determine which structure and meaning the sentence has. A typical example of a globally ambiguous sentence is given in (5).

(5) The cop saw the spy with the binoculars.

The ambiguity lies in how the prepositional phrase *with the binoculars* fits into the rest of the sentence. It could modify the verb phrase *saw the spy,* in which case the sentence means that the cop used binoculars in order to see the spy. This interpretation corresponds to the syntactic structure given in (6a). Intuitively, this structure fits well with the interpretation that the binoculars are used to see the spy. Alternatively, *with the binoculars* could modify the noun phrase *the spy,* in which case it specifies that the spy has binoculars. This is shown in (6b). Sentences that are globally ambiguous always have two or more possible syntactic structures, one corresponding to each interpretation.

(6) Syntactic representation of the two meanings of the same sentence

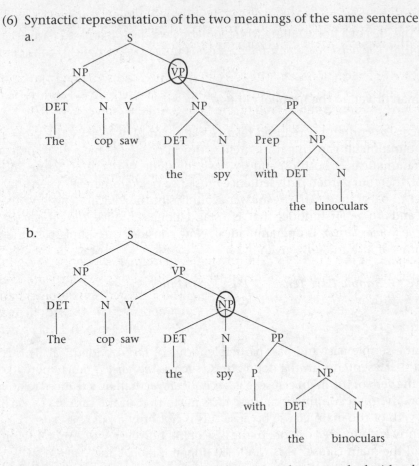

a.

b.

An important question in sentence processing is how people decide which structure a glob-ally ambiguous sentence has. As with lexical ambiguity, people could consider all possibil-ities and then decide which one is best, or they could use some strategy to decide which interpretation to consider first and then reconsider if that interpretation does not work out.

The garden path phenomenon introduced above suggests that people try one analy-sis first and consider other possibilities only when the initial analysis does not work out. If people initially considered all the possibilities, they would not be led down the garden path. But what strategies could people use to decide which structure to consider first? One influ-ential syntactic parsing strategy that has been proposed is called **late closure.** It suggests that incoming material is incorporated into the clause or phrase currently being processed if pos-sible. In other words, people attach material to the closest clause or phrase, as long as such attachment is possible. In our example, *The cop saw the spy with the binoculars,* this means that *with the binoculars* should be preferentially attached to modify *the spy* rather than *saw.* If you look at the syntactic trees in (6), you can see that the noun phrase *the spy* is "closer" to the prepositional phrase *with the binoculars* than is the verb phrase *saw the spy.* What late closure suggests then is that, all else being equal, people would interpret the sentence in (5) to mean that the spy has the binoculars.

However, many other factors contribute to how we interpret globally ambiguous sen-tences. Obvious factors are the choice of lexical items and the preceding context. If we change the sentence in (5) to *The cop saw the squirrel with the binoculars,* we would be more likely to interpret it to mean that the cop used the binoculars to see the squirrel than that the squirrel had the binoculars, given that squirrels usually don't have binoculars. On the other hand, if the sentence was preceded by the context in (7), we would probably interpret the sentence to mean that the squirrel had the binoculars, despite that fact that this is an unlikely occurrence.

(7) An unusually large squirrel stole a movie star's million-dollar binoculars. The star called the police to report the incident, and a cop was assigned to look for the stolen item. After an hour, the cop saw the squirrel with the binoculars.

Both the choice of lexical items and the preceding context can so strongly favor one interpretation over the other that we may not even notice that a sentence is ambiguous. In fact, naturally occurring conversation is full of ambiguities that are never detected.

Another factor that influences ambiguity resolution is **intonation**. Many spoken ambiguous sentences can be disambiguated through intonation (and punctuation can be used to disambiguate an otherwise ambiguous written sentence). The sentence in (8a), for example, is ambiguous. It can mean either that Jack and Paul will be invited or else that Mary will be. Alternatively, it can mean that Jack will be invited, and so will either Paul or Mary, but not both of them. Depending on how the sentence is pronounced, listeners will favor one interpretation over the other. In particular, the sentence can be said with a **prosodic break** (see File 2.5) after *Paul,* as illustrated in (8b). To see how this works, say the sentence aloud and pause after the word *Paul.* This intonation pattern corresponds to the first interpretation listed above. If people hear the sentence produced this way, they are likely to interpret it to mean that either Jack and Paul, or Mary, will be invited. On the other hand, if the sentence is produced with a prosodic break after Jack, as illustrated in (8c), listeners are more likely to interpret the sentence to mean that Jack and either Paul or Mary will be invited.

(8) a. I will invite Jack and Paul or Mary.
　　b. [I will invite Jack and Paul] [or Mary.]
　　c. [I will invite Jack] [and Paul or Mary.]

The influence of intonation on ambiguity resolution helps explain why we rarely notice ambiguities even though they occur all the time in conversations. This is not only the case for global ambiguities. Sentences that might be garden path sentences if they were written do not frequently lead people down the garden path when they are spoken, because a speaker's intonation influences the listener's syntactic parsing process, determining the interpretation that will be chosen before he or she can be misled. For example, if a speaker said the sentence *While Mary was mending the sock fell off her lap* with a prosodic break after *mending,* as in *[While Mary was mending] [the sock fell off her lap],* the listener would choose the correct parse to begin with and would not be led down the garden path.

However, it should be mentioned that not all ambiguous sentences can be disambiguated through intonation. For example, there are no consistent intonation patterns corresponding to the two interpretations of the sentence *Flying planes can be dangerous,* which can mean 'Planes that are flying can be dangerous' or 'The action of flying a plane can be dangerous.'

In this file we saw that one of the major issues arising in sentence processing is structural ambiguity. Temporary structural ambiguity is constantly present in everyday discourse. Yet we deal with it effortlessly and usually don't even notice the ambiguity. Even when we are led down the garden path, we can usually recover the correct parse of a sentence rather easily. Globally ambiguous sentences aren't any different: we frequently don't notice the ambiguity and are able to decide on a syntactic parse seemingly effortlessly. This is possible because the context of a sentence, common sense, and intonation can help determine the correct parse of an ambiguous sentence.

Experimental Methods in Psycholinguistics

9.7.1 Some General Issues

Other than phonetics, psycholinguistics is probably the area in linguistics that is most experimentally oriented. Files 2.2, 2.3, and 2.6 introduced some of the methods used in experimental phonetics. In this file we introduce selected experimental methods used in the area of psycholinguistics. In particular, we describe some common techniques that are used to investigate particular linguistic phenomena. Both fMRI and ERP, introduced below in Section 9.7.2, directly measure brain activity. The methods introduced in later sections are less direct: they allow us to draw conclusions about processing activity by studying participants' behavior: measuring their response times, response types, and so on.

Before talking about methods, however, we should discuss some general issues that arise in experimental research. First, an experiment needs to be well thought through: a researcher needs to find a task or experimental protocol that will actually address her research question. After selecting a task, the researcher needs to assemble appropriate materials, which, in psycholinguistics, usually consist of words, sentences, and/or pictures presented to subjects either visually or auditorily. In many experiments the materials are designed to trigger some sort of linguistic response in the participants, or the participants are asked to perform a particular task upon being presented with the materials. Two kinds of materials are required. In addition to the experimental stimuli (those words, sentences, and/or pictures that the researcher is interested in), filler items are needed. These are other materials interspersed with the experimental stimuli, used to prevent participants from guessing which aspect of the stimuli the researcher is interested in. Finally, in order to be able to generalize findings, an experimenter should have gathered a large enough number of participants to generate statistically significant data—it's impossible, for example, to draw conclusions about "what speakers of English do" if only three people have been tested.

9.7.2 Measuring Activity in the Brain: ERP and fMRI

Two common methods used to study activity in the brain are **ERP** (event-related potentials) and **fMRI** (functional magnetic resonance imaging).

fMRI is a technique for determining which physical sensations or activities activate which parts of the brain. Brain activity is investigated by scanning the brain every 1 to 5 seconds. The scan maps areas of increased blood flow in the brain, which can be related to increased brain activity because active nerve cells consume oxygen, in turn increasing the blood flow to that region. Participants in an fMRI experiment cannot move, so the tasks of an fMRI study are somewhat restricted. However, participants can be played auditory stimuli, shown visual stimuli, or told to think about something. For example, bilingual participants can be told to think in one of their languages and then in the other to determine whether the same areas of the brain are used for both languages.

ERP is a technique that uses electrodes placed on the scalp to detect electrical signals in the brain. Unlike fMRI, ERP can be used to study the time course of an event, because it detects changes in electrical activity in the brain at the millisecond level. ERP analysis refers to certain patterns of electrical activity, usually a positive or a negative peak. For example, many studies have found a negative peak around 400 milliseconds after the presentation of an unexpected linguistic stimulus. This is called an N400. Since it occurs after sentences containing unexpected words, it is interpreted as the participant trying to integrate the unexpected word into the sentence context.

9.7.3 Offline Tasks

An **offline task** measures the final result of a process, rather than what happens during the process. The following paragraphs introduce some offline tasks that are often used to study language processing.

a. Lexical Processing. Some common tasks used in the study of lexical processing are **lexical decision tasks** and naming tasks. In lexical decision experiments, a participant is asked to identify stimuli as words or nonwords, and the time that it takes the participant to make a decision is measured. Lexical decision experiments have found, for example, that more-frequent words are recognized faster than are less-frequent words. **Naming tasks** are similar to lexical decision tasks, but instead of deciding whether a stimulus is a word or not, the participant responds by saying the stimulus aloud. A frequency effect is also found in naming tasks: more-frequent words are produced more quickly than are less-frequent words.

Both tasks are often combined with techniques such as **priming.** In priming tasks, participants are presented with a stimulus, the **prime**, right before the stimulus of interest, the **target.** Priming is often used to study the structure of the mental lexicon. For example, studies have shown that participants are faster to confirm that a stimulus is a word when the prime is semantically related to the target. This means that participants will be faster at confirming that *nurse* is a word when the prime is the semantically related word *doctor* than when the prime is the unrelated word *butter.* From this we can infer that the mental lexicon is partially organized by semantic relatedness. The idea then is that the prime *doctor* partially activated words semantically related to it, such that *nurse* was already partially activated when the target word appeared.

b. Sentence Processing. One common task used in the study of sentence processing is an end-of-sentence comprehension task, used to study globally ambiguous sentences. The procedure is very easy: participants read ambiguous sentences and answer a comprehension question after they have read the sentence. For example, to address a question that we addressed in Section 9.6.2, participants might be asked to read the sentence *The cop saw the spy with the binoculars* and answer the comprehension question *Who had the binoculars?* The answer to this question can tell the researcher how participants interpreted the ambiguous sentence.

9.7.4 Online Tasks

An **online task** is designed to uncover what happens during a process and when during the process it happens. Both fMRI and ERP, introduced above, are considered online tasks. The following paragraphs introduce some online tasks commonly used to study language processing indirectly.

a. Lexical Processing. One recent development in the study of online lexical processing is **eye-tracking.** In eye-tracking experiments, an infrared light is reflected off the participants' eyes and used to record all eye movements the participants make during an experiment: by tracking participants' eye movements, the researcher is able to determine what they were looking at at any point during the experiment. So, for example, the participants could be looking at an array of pictures including a caterpillar, a ham, a hamster, a hamburger, a bone, and a bobcat. Participants then hear an auditory stimulus saying, "Now look at the _____," for example, "Now look at the hamster." The eye-tracking device records when during the auditory stimulus the subject looks to the correct object, providing clues about how quickly words are processed as they come into their brains. For example, how quickly can the participant distinguish *ham* from *hamster* from *hamburger*? Do they have to wait until the end of the word, or can they begin to decide what the word must be from phonetic cues that appear much earlier in the word?

b. Sentence Processing. The end-of-sentence comprehension task described above gives us information only about how a person ends up interpreting an ambiguous sentence. But participants are often given as much time as they need to answer a comprehension question. As a result, while conscious decision making may be involved in answering the question, that approach cannot tell us what happened during the actual reading and processing of the sentence. Recall our earlier example sentence: *The cop saw the spy with the binoculars.* If, in response to the question *Who had the binoculars?*, a participant answered that the cop had the binoculars, we would not know whether this was the participant's initial interpretation or whether he had originally considered more options before settling on this meaning. It's possible that a participant initially used parsing strategies such as late closure while reading, but later decided that cops are more likely to have binoculars and therefore changed his interpretation. To find out what happened during reading itself, a task called **self-paced reading** can be used. In self-paced reading, participants read a sentence in small chunks, usually one word at a time. Whenever they have read and understood a word, they push a button to move on to the next word.

For this task, temporarily ambiguous sentences are used. Compare the sentences in (1).

(1) a. Someone shot the servants of the actress who was standing on the balcony.
     b. Someone shot the servants of the actress who were standing on the balcony.

In (1a), it is the actress who is standing on the balcony, while in (1b), the servants are standing on the balcony. For these two sentences, there is temporary ambiguity up until the point at which participants read *who,* because whatever follows *who* could modify the servants (i.e., *the servants who did something*) or the actress (i.e., *the actress who did something*). The choice of *was* or *were* as the next word disambiguates the sentence: it tells us what *who* modifies because rules about verb agreement say that *was* must go with *actress* and *were* must go with *servants.* What we are interested in is how long it takes participants to read the word *was* versus the word *were,* because this will tell us something about how much processing is required in order to get whichever interpretation the participant is presented with. To get this information, we measure the time it takes a participant to read each word (the time between button pushes). If participants thought that *who* modified the **servants** while they were reading the word *who,* they should take longer to read a following *was* than a following *were.* On the other hand, if participants thought that *who* modified the **actress** while they were reading the word *who,* they should take longer to read a following *were* than a following *was.* The reason is that participants would have to change their analysis if their initial interpretation of what *who* modifies turned out to be incorrect, and changing the analysis takes time. Thus, unlike the end-of-sentence comprehension task, self-paced reading allows us to see what happens during the reading of a sentence. Clearly, however, both types of task are needed to give us a more complete picture of sentence processing.

F I L E **9.8**

Practice

File 9.1—Language and the Brain

Exercises

1. Modify each blank diagram of the left hemisphere according to the instructions:

   i. Shade and label Broca's area, Wernicke's area, the arcuate fasciculus, and the angular gyrus.

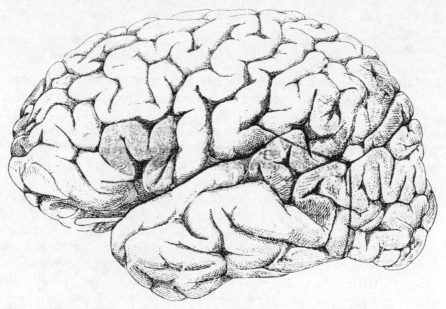

Adapted from figure by Carol Donner from "Specializations of the Human Brain," by Norman Geschwind. Copyright © 1979 by Scientific American, Inc. All rights reserved.

ii. Shade and label the three areas of the cortex involved in the production and comprehension of language.

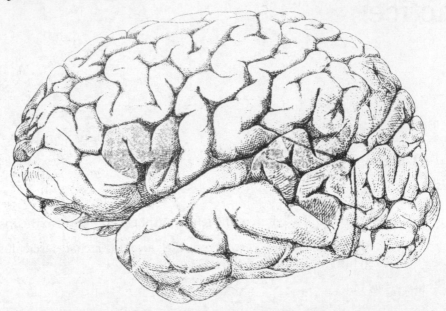

Adapted from figure by Carol Donner from "Specializations of the Human Brain," by Norman Geschwind. Copyright © 1979 by Scientific American, Inc. All rights reserved.

iii. Using arrows, show the flow of linguistic information when one is reading a word. Label all of the areas of the brain that are directly involved in this activity.

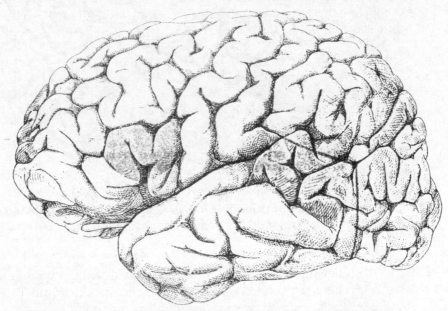

Adapted from figure by Carol Donner from "Specializations of the Human Brain," by Norman Geschwind. Copyright © 1979 by Scientific American, Inc. All rights reserved.

iv. Do the same as in (iii), but show what happens if you then say the word you just read out loud. Describe how and why (iii) and (iv) are different.

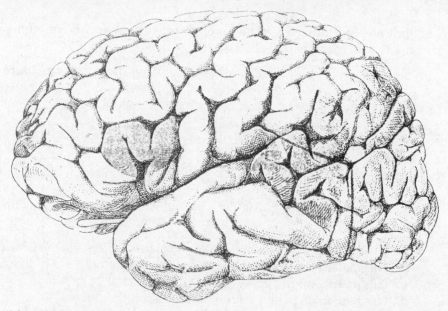

Adapted from figure by Carol Donner from "Specializations of the Human Brain," by Norman Geschwind. Copyright © 1979 by Scientific American, Inc. All rights reserved.

2. Assume that your brain functions are lateralized in the way that most people's are. Assume you are a subject in a dichotic listening test where you are presented with the following combinations of stimuli. For each pair, which stimulus would you most likely hear more clearly? Explain why you think so.

   a. Left ear: a man saying *cat*
   Right ear: a man saying *dog*
   b. Left ear: a woman coughing
   Right ear: a woman sneezing
   c. Left ear: a door hinge squeaking
   Right ear: a woman saying *horse*

3. A split-brain patient is blindfolded, and a common object is placed in his left hand. Will he be able to say the name of the object? Why or why not? Your answer should include a description of the flow of sensory information from the hand through the brain.

Activities

4. Go to the following Web site and do the dichotic listening experiments: http://www .linguistics.ucla.edu/people/schuh/lx001/Dichotic/dichotic.html. Based on your responses in the experiment, answer the following questions:
   i. Did the task work for you? In other words, did you hear the word presented either consistently to your right ear or consistently to your left ear?
   ii. Based on your answer, do you think that you process language in the left hemisphere, the right hemisphere, or both hemispheres of the brain? Explain why you think so.

File 9.2—Aphasia

Exercises

5. Indicate, by putting an "X" on the appropriate lines, which symptoms are found in patients with each type of aphasia.

	Expressive Disorder	Receptive Disorder	Articulatory Problems
Broca's aphasia	_____	_____	_____
Wernicke's aphasia	_____	_____	_____
Conduction aphasia	_____	_____	_____
Alexia	_____	_____	_____
Agraphia	_____	_____	_____

6. Identify which language disorder a patient with each of the following symptoms may have:

    a. This patient cannot follow simple verbal instructions, like *Sit down* or *Close the door*.
    b. This patient has slow and inaccurate pronunciation.
    c. This patient cannot understand written material.
    d. This patient often says *what we hear with* for *ear*.
    e. This patient frequently responds to linguistic input in an unexpected way.
    f. This patient often says *Go store* for *Go to the store*.
    g. This patient interprets *The cat was chased by the dog* as *The cat chased the dog*.
    h. This patient's speech does not make any sense.
    i. This patient can understand utterances but cannot repeat them.

7. A signer with Broca's aphasia has difficulty producing signs. However, the same signer can pick up a cup and even draw pictures. A hearing person, after suffering from a rare virus, lost all motor ability and could not even pick up a cup. However, he was still able to speak fluently. What conclusions do you draw from this for the neurological basis of signs, speech, and general motor control? Explain why.

8. Identify which kind of aphasia the following patients may have. Explain your answers.[1]

    a. Patient: Uh, well this is the . . . the [dodou] of this. This and this and this and this. These things going in there like that. This is [sen] things here. This one here, these two things here. And the other one here, back in this one, this one [gos] look at this one.
          Examiner: Yeah, what's happening there?
          Patient: I can't tell you what that is, but I know what it is, but I don't know where it is. But I don't know what's under. I know it's you couldn't say it's . . . I couldn't say what it is. I couldn't say what that is. This shu- that should be right in here. That's very bad in there. Anyway, this one here, and that, and that's it. This is the getting in here and that's the getting around here, and that, and that's it. This is getting in here and that's the getting around here, this one and one with this one. And this one, and that's it, isn't it? I don't know what else you'd want.

    b. Patient: Wife is dry dishes. Water down! Oh boy! Okay awright. Okay . . . cookie is down . . . fall, and girl, okay, girl . . . boy . . . um . . .

---

[1]Part (b) from Avrutin 2001; parts (c) and (d) adapted from Gardner 1975.

Examiner: What is the boy doing?
Patient: Cookie is . . . um . . . catch
Examiner: Who is getting the cookies?
Patient: Girl, girl
Examiner: Who is about to fall down?
Patient: Boy . . . fall down!

c. Examiner: Were you in the Coast Guard?
Patient: No, er, yes, yes . . . ship . . . Massachu . . . chusetts . . . Coast Guard . . .
          years [raises hands twice with fingers indicating "19"]
Examiner: Oh, you were in the Coast Guard 19 years?
Patient: Oh . . . boy . . . right . . . right.
Examiner: Why are you in the hospital?
Patient: [points to paralyzed arm] Arm no good. [points to mouth] Speech . . .
          can't say . . . talk, you see.
Examiner: What happened to make you lose your speech?
Patient: Head, fall, Jesus Christ, me no good, str, str . . . oh Jesus . . . stroke.
Examiner: Could you tell me what you've been doing in the hospital?
Patient: Yes sure. Me go, er, uh, P.T. nine o'cot, speech . . . two times. . . . read . . .
          wr . . . ripe, er, rike, er, write . . . practice.

d. Patient: Boy, I'm sweating. I'm awful nervous, you know, once in a while I get
             caught up. I can't mention the tarripoi, a month ago, quite a little. I've
             done a lot well. I impose a lot, while, on the other hand, you know what
             I mean. I have to run around, looked it over, trebin and all that sort of
             stuff.

e. Patient: Well this is . . . mother is away here working out o'here to get her better,
             but when she's working, the two boys looking in the other part. One
             their small tile into her time here. She's working another time because
             she's getting, too.

f. Examiner: What kind of work have you done?
Patient: We, the kids, all of us, and I, we were working for a long time in the . . .
          you know . . . it's kind of space, I mean place rear to the spedwan . . .

g. Examiner: What kind of work have you done?
Patient: Me . . . building . . . chairs, no, no cab-in-nets. One, saw . . . then cut-
          ting wood . . . working

File 9.3—Speech Production

Exercises

9. Here is a list of speech errors given in the form *intended production → error*. For each
   speech error, state what type of error it is (insertion, metathesis, shift, etc.) and which
   linguistic unit is involved in the error (e.g., phone, morpheme, word, etc.). Is there anything else going on in the error (e.g., phonotactics)? What does each error tell us about
   the processes involved in speech production?

   a. we have many ministers in our church → we have many churches in our minister
   b. brake fluid → blake fruid
   c. an eating marathon → a meeting marathon
   d. speech production → preach seduction
   e. phonological rule → phonological fool

(cont.)

f. untactful → distactful

g. big and fat → pig and vat

h. It's too damn hot in here → It's too damn cold in here

i. his immortal soul → his immoral soul

j. what that adds up to → what that add ups to

k. Where's the fire extinguisher? → Where's the fire distinguisher?

l. thin sheets → shin sheets

m. a no go zone → a no gone [goʊn] zone

n. also share → alsho share

o. There's a draft/breeze blowing through the room→ There's a dreeze blowing through the room

10. Here is a list of production errors made by signers of ASL. For each speech error, state what type of error it is (e.g., insertion, metathesis, shift, etc.) and which parameter is involved in the error (e.g., place of articulation, movement, hand shape, etc.). What does each error tell us about the processes involved in the production of signed languages?

    a. Correctly signed phrase:

RECENT   EAT

Error:

error   error

b. Correctly signed phrase:

FEEL   THAT

Error:

error   THAT

c. Correctly signed phrase:

PLEASE   HELP

Error:

PLEASE   error

Discussion Questions

11. Suppose you have been paralyzed in an auto accident. Your only way to communicate is to manipulate a pencil-like instrument with your mouth, which pushes buttons on an apparatus that produces humanlike sounds. How might this type of communication system influence your production of language?

Activities

12. Studies of speech errors may involve collecting naturally occurring speech errors or inducing speech errors in an experimental setting. One way to induce speech errors is to have people produce tongue twisters. Start by reading through the tongue twisters in (a) and (b), and answer the questions in (i). Then have a friend read the tongue twisters below out loud. Tell your friend to read them as fast as she can, and record your friend's errors on a piece of paper. Then answer the questions in (ii).

    a. Peter Piper picked a peck of pickled peppers.
       Did Peter Piper pick a peck of pickled peppers?
       If Peter Piper picked a peck of pickled peppers, where's the peck of pickled peppers Peter Piper picked?
    b. One smart fellow; he felt smart.
       Two smart fellows; they felt smart.
       Three smart fellows; they all felt smart.

    i. How do these tongue twisters induce speech errors? Which errors would you expect people to make? Why?
    ii. Which errors did your friend actually make? What type of error are they (e.g., anticipation)? Did you expect this type of error? Why or why not?

13. Another way to induce speech errors is to have people read lists of words such as the following aloud. Start by reading through the lists, and answer the questions in (i). Then have at least five of your friends read the lists out loud as fast as they can. Record any mistakes that they make, and answer the questions in (ii).

    a. ball doze   b. big dutch
       bash door   bang doll
       bean deck   bill deal
       bell dark   bark dog
       darn bore   dart board

    i. What kinds of mistakes would you expect your friends to make? Why?
    ii. Which list of words induced the most errors in the last line? Why do you think this is the case? How are the last lines different in the two lists?

File 9.4—Speech Perception

Exercise

14. Consider the list of perception errors (slips of the ear) below. Explain each error. If possible, make reference to the type of error (e.g., insertion, metathesis, shift, etc.) and the linguistic unit involved in the error (e.g., phone, morpheme, word, etc.). Otherwise, describe the error in your own words. What does each error tell us about the processes involved in speech perception?

Said	*Heard as*
a. death in Venice	deaf in Venice
b. what are those sticks?	what are those ticks?
c. give them an ice bucket	give them a nice bucket
d. of thee I sing	of the icing
e. the stuffy nose	the stuff he knows
f. the biggest hurdle	the biggest turtle
g. some others	some mothers
h. a Coke and a danish	a coconut danish

Activities

15. In this activity you will create your own McGurk effect and then answer the questions below. To demonstrate the McGurk effect, you need two other people. The first person will demonstrate the McGurk effect with you. That person should stand behind you and repeatedly produce the syllable [mɑ] while you silently mouth [kɑ]. You may want to practice coordinating your [mɑ]s and [kɑ]s. The second person should watch you, but should not be able to see the person standing behind you.

   i. What do you expect the person watching you to hear? Explain why.

   ii. What does the person watching you actually hear? What does he or she hear with closed eyes? How would you explain this?

   iii. Demonstrate the effect again, this time silently mouthing [mɑ] while the person behind you says [kɑ]. Does the effect still work? Why or why not?

   iv. Test the McGurk effect on two other pairs of consonants. Choose a pair of similar consonants and a pair of rather different consonants. For each pair, does the effect still work? Did you expect this? Why or why not?

File 9.5—Lexical Processing

Exercises

16. Study the cartoon at the beginning of this chapter. Explain how the cohort model relates to the cartoon by answering the following questions:

   i. What do the man and the woman think the word in the window will be?

   ii. Explain the cohort model using the example of the cartoon: what is the initial cohort? Why do the man and the woman think of two different words (i.e., which point has not been reached)? What will happen when the next letter is put up?

   iii. The cohort model, as we described it in File 9.5, explains lexical access of spoken language only. To also cover written language, it needs to be modified. The reason for this is the way we read words, which is different from the way we hear words: even though our eyes seem to move from letter to letter, our eyes actually land on a spot on the page and take in about 15 to 20 letters simultaneously before moving on to the next spot about 12 to 18 letters further along in the text. Higher-level brain processing is responsible for giving us the impression that our eyes move along from letter to letter. But in reality, we take in whole words at the same time. Compare this with how we hear words, and explain how the scene depicted in the comic makes the "word-in-progress" in the window imitate the way we hear, not read, words.

17. Say the following sentences out loud at normal speaking rate (that is, relatively fast). What problem do the sentences pose for the cohort model of lexical access?

- This guy looks interesting.
- The sky looks interesting.

Discussion Question

18. Do you think that a fluent bilingual would have two mental lexicons, one for each language? Or would there be a single lexicon? Explain your decision. Think about both storage and access of lexical items.

File 9.6—Sentence Processing

Exercises

19. Draw a semantic network for the following words:

cow, horse, pig, chicken, owl, zebra, buffalo, bison, ostrich, turkey, rooster, hen, sparrow, deer, elk, bull, pony, dog, cat, wolf, lion, coyote, hawk, eagle, bobcat, cheetah, tiger, panther, parakeet, canary, falcon, goat, sheep

20. Each of the following sentences is ambiguous. For each, indicate whether the ambiguity is lexical or structural (draw phrase structure trees if helpful). Paraphrase the two meanings of each sentence.

   a. The player knew that the ball would be attended by the prince.
   b. The clown caught the thief with the umbrella.
   c. Jill looked for the documents that Julie hid under the table.
   d. We will dispense water to anyone in a sterile plastic bottle.
   e. Tom said that Bill went on a date yesterday.
   f. The mysterious stranger tricked the man with the mask.
   g. Jason mentioned that Susan wanted to go to the movies yesterday.

The following are adapted from news headlines:
   h. We will sell gasoline to anyone in a glass container.
   i. Two sisters reunited after 18 years in checkout counter.
   j. Red tape holds up the new bridge.
   k. Lansing residents can drop off trees.
   l. Stolen painting found by tree.
   m. Enraged cow injures farmer with ax.
   n. Two cars were reported stolen by the Groveton Police.
   o. Kids make nutritious snacks.

21. Each of the following sentences is a garden path sentence. For each sentence, explain how people are led down the garden path. In other words, explain how the sentence is initially parsed and how it needs to be reanalyzed to be parsed correctly. Explain why these sentences lead people down the garden path.

   a. The boat floated downstream sank.
   b. The cotton clothing is made from grows in Mississippi.
   c. The daughter of the king's son admires himself.
   d. The florist sent the flowers was pleased.
   e. They told the boy that the girl met the story.

22. Consider the two sentences given below. The first sentence is ungrammatical but easily parsable, whereas the second sentence is difficult to parse (and for some people even unparsable) but grammatical.

Ungrammatical sentence: *The dog ate a bone big.*
Sentence that is difficult to parse: *The boat floated down the river sank.*

i. Explain why the first sentence is ungrammatical. For your explanation, you may want to refer to the phrase structure rules for English given in File 5.4.
ii. Explain why the second sentence is difficult to parse. Explain how the reader initially tries to parse the sentence and why this does not work. What is this kind of sentence called?
iii. Which of the sentences is harder to understand? Why is it beneficial that we can relatively easily understand at least some ungrammatical sentences in our native language?

File 9.7—Experimental Methods in Psycholinguistics
Exercises

23. Assume that your grandfather has had a stroke and is greatly limited in his ability to articulate meaningful speech. How might you determine his comprehension skills? Explain what task you would use and what you could conclude from different potential responses.

24. After completing the activity in Exercise 4, look at the list of reasons the experiment designers say might make the results "messy." (This should appear after you click on "See discussion of experiment.") Explain why each of the points they make might have an effect on your ability to draw conclusions from the experiment.

CHAPTER
10

Language Variation

What Is Language Variation?

Most people are aware of the fact that systematic differences exist among languages—for example, that English is different from Spanish, which is different from Arabic, which is different from Russian, and so on. However, many people are probably not aware of the extent to which systematic differences exist **within** languages. **Internal variation** refers to the property of languages of having different ways of expressing the same meaning. This property is inherent to all human languages and to all speakers of a language. Thus, no two speakers of a language speak exactly the same way; nor does any individual speaker speak the same way all the time.

The purpose of this chapter is to introduce the ways in which languages vary internally and the factors that contribute to language variation. For purposes of familiarity, these files will focus primarily on variation in English, but you should keep in mind that variation exists in all languages.

Contents

Language Varieties

10.1.1 Languages, Dialects, Slang, Jargons, and Idiolects

The term **language variety** is used by linguists as a cover term to refer to many different types of language variation; a language variety may be thought of as any form of language characterized by systematic features. The term may be used in reference to a distinct language, such as French or Italian, or in reference to a particular form of a language spoken by a specific group of people, such as Appalachian English or New York English, or even in reference to the speech of a single person. In addition to this cover term, there are more specific terms that are used to talk about these different types of language varieties. **Sociolinguistics** is the study of the interrelationships of language varieties and social structure.

When a group of speakers of a particular language differs noticeably in its speech from another group, we say that they are speaking different **dialects.** In English, the term *dialect* sometimes carries negative connotations associated with nonstandard varieties. Linguistically speaking, however, a dialect is any variety of a language spoken by a group of people that is characterized by systematic differences from other varieties of the same language in terms of structural or lexical features. In this sense, every person speaks a dialect of his or her native language. The term *dialect* is also misused by laypeople to refer strictly to differences in pronunciation or sometimes to refer to slang usage. Such mistakes are easy to understand since differences in pronunciation or vocabulary are usually accompanied by variation in other areas of the grammar as well and thus do correspond to dialectal differences. However, the appropriate term for systematic phonological variation (see more in File 10.2) is **accent.** In layperson's terminology, *accent* is often used in reference to "foreign accents" or regionally defined accents such as southern or northern accents. However, here again it must be noted that every person speaks with an accent. This point may be easier to see if you think about accents on a larger scale, such as an "American accent" or an "English accent." Every speaker of English speaks with an accent of some sort.

Also, as mentioned above, there is variation from speaker to speaker within any given language. The form of a language spoken by one person is known as an **idiolect.**

Slang, on the other hand, has to do more with stylistic choices in vocabulary than with systematic lexical differences between dialects; often words that are considered slang are less formal than other equivalent words. There are two basic types of slang. The nearly neutral everyday language that is just a little too informal for letters of application and the like is known as **common slang.** It includes words like *fridge* for *refrigerator* or *TV* for *television.* The more specialized, "slangier" slang of a particular group at a particular time is known as **in-group slang.** In-group slang can be used to keep insiders together and to exclude outsiders. Learning the appropriate slang can thus be a key to entrance into a particular group. In order for the group to preserve its closed status, however, there is often a fairly high turnover and renewal of slang expressions. Some slang is very short-lived, like *twenty-three skidoo!,* but some lasts long enough to become accepted in the stuffiest circles. *Fan* appeared as a slangy shortening of *fanatic* in the late sixteenth century, and today we have *fan* *letters, fan clubs, fan magazines,* and *fan (Web)sites* for all kinds of things from baseball stars to rock groups. Similarly, the fact that slang often injects a bit of color into otherwise ordinary language means that as the color fades, so to speak, new expressions will be needed. In this way, we see that slang in a sense is the linguistic counterpart of fad behavior: just as hula hoops came and went (and perhaps are coming back again), certain slang expressions have come and gone over the years, some to return again, but others not.

Slang responds to a need in people to be creative in their language use and to show group membership (often unconsciously) through their language use. These observations liken slang to some feature in the nature of being human and of interacting with humans. For these reasons, slang is found in all languages and has been found at all times (even in Ancient Greek of 2,500 years ago, for instance). Slang is thus a legitimate sociolinguistic phenomenon and is studied by linguists as such.

Another difference in vocabulary choice comes into play when we talk about technical language, or **jargon.** Many of us are more or less fluent in a number of different jargons. Every job and every field of study has some technical terms of its own, as does every hobby and sport. Within its own area, technical jargon is clear, expressive, and economical; for outsiders, much of it usually remains incomprehensible. Professional jargons are often used to impress people outside the profession. *Rhinitis* sounds a great deal more impressive than *runny nose. Rhinoplasty* sounds a lot more complicated and serious than *nose job.* When the dermatologist says you have *dermatitis,* it sounds like a real diagnosis by an expert; if he calls it *a rash,* you might not be so sure that he knows more about it than you do. Occasionally a word or expression that has a jargonistic origin escapes from that context into general use. In recent years we have seen this happen with *bottom line* (originally a technical term used in reference to business reports), with *hardware, software,* and *system* (all from computer usage), and less recently with words like *cool* (originally used to refer to a type of jazz). The space program has given us *countdown, A-OK,* and *blast off,* and even people with no interest in baseball know how it feels to *strike out.*

While these terms may seem simple and convenient, when we consider actual languages, it becomes immediately obvious how difficult it is to make certain distinctions. How do we know, for example, whether two or more language varieties are, say, different dialects of the same language or whether, in fact, they are separate, distinct languages? One criterion used to distinguish dialects from languages is **mutual intelligibility.** If speakers of one language variety can understand speakers of another language variety, and vice versa, we say that these varieties are mutually intelligible and therefore dialects of the same language. Suppose you are a native of Brooklyn, New York, and you go to visit some friends in Beaumont, Texas. You may notice some differences in the speech of your Beaumont friends (and they in yours), but essentially you will be able to understand each other. Your variety of speech and theirs are mutually intelligible but differ systematically; they are therefore dialects of the same language.

It is not always this easy, however, to decide whether two language varieties are different dialects of the same language or different languages just on the basis of mutual intelligibility. Other factors, such as cultural, political, geographical, or historical considerations, may cloud the issue. In China, for example, Mandarin is spoken in the northern provinces and Cantonese in the southern province of Guangdong. Even though in spoken form these language varieties are not mutually intelligible, they are considered by the speakers of these varieties themselves to be dialects of the same language. Why? One reason is that the varieties share a common writing system and are thus mutually intelligible in written form.

The opposite situation exists in the American Southwest between Papago and Pima, two Native American languages. These two language varieties are indeed mutually intelligible, having less linguistic difference between them than exists between Standard American English and Standard British English. However, because the two tribes regard themselves as politically and culturally distinct, they consider their respective languages to be distinct as well. Similarly, Serbo-Croatian has now split because of political and other reasons into at least three distinct, yet mutually intelligible, so-called languages in the Balkans: Croatian, Serbian, and Bosnian.

Another complication for the criterion of mutual intelligibility is found in a phenomenon known as a **dialect continuum.** This is a situation where, in a large number of contiguous dialects, each dialect is closely related to the next, but the dialects at either end of the continuum (scale) are mutually unintelligible. Thus, dialect A is intelligible to dialect B, which is intelligible to dialect C, which is intelligible to dialect D; but D and A are not mutually intelligible. A situation such as this is found near the border between Holland and Germany, where the dialects on either side of the national border are mutually intelligible, but dialects of Dutch and German that aren't near the border—including the standard dialects of the two languages—are not mutually intelligible.

At what point is the line between dialects and languages drawn? Clearly, the criterion of mutual intelligibility does not account for all the facts. Indeed, there may be no clear-cut, black-and-white answer to such a question in every case. In File 12.2, related languages are discussed in terms of what is known as the Family Tree Model. According to this model, a parent language may split and form daughter languages—for example, Germanic split off into English, Dutch, and German (among others). This type of split may also occur when dialect differences become so great that the dialects are no longer mutually intelligible to the speakers of these language varieties.

10.1.2 Speech Communities

A group of people speaking the same dialect is known as a **speech community.** Speech communities may be defined in terms of a number of **extralinguistic factors** (*extra-* in the sense of 'outside of,' i.e., factors not based in linguistic structure), including region, socioeconomic status, age, gender, and ethnicity, as will be discussed in more detail in Files 10.3 and 10.4. However, it is rarely, if ever, the case that there exists a speech community in which a "pure" dialect—that is, purely regional, purely ethnic, and so on—is spoken, because the identification of any speech variety as a pure dialect requires the assumption of **communicative isolation.** Communicative isolation results when a group of speakers forms a coherent speech community relatively isolated from speakers outside that community. This type of isolation was perhaps once a possibility but is becoming increasingly rare these days owing to social and geographic mobility, mass media, and so on. What is more likely the case today is that a particular dialect of a speech community is influenced by regional, social, and cultural factors. Thus, in most instances the varieties spoken among members of a speech community are not pure dialects but instead are influenced by the interaction of many different factors.

10.1.3 Style and Register

In Chapter 7 on pragmatics, we talked about the notion of sentences being infelicitous, or inappropriate in a certain situation. One particular reason that an utterance may be infelicitous is that even though it gives the right kind of information, it is inappropriate for the social context. For example, if you were to meet the President of the United States or the Queen of England, you would be ill-advised to say something along the lines of "Oh, hey. How's it going?" This might be a very acceptable way to start a conversation with someone you have just met at a college party, but it isn't acceptable for greeting a country's leader.

Some languages have complex markings in their grammar in order to reflect the social context of a discourse. For instance, some languages have one word for 'you' that is used for formal address and another used for informal, casual, or intimate situations, for example, *tú* (informal) and *Usted* (formal) in Spanish or *du* (informal) and *Sie* (formal) in German. Other languages, such as Japanese, have even more complex systems, with more than two levels of address and with formality markings on many other words as well. Even in English, though, which does not have such formality markers built explicitly into the lexicon, speakers nonetheless distinguish between different **speech styles.** Speech styles may be thought of as variations in speech based on factors such as topic, setting, and addressee, and they are normally described in terms of degrees of formality. Thus, a speech style may be described as "formal" or "informal," "casual" or "careful." Sometimes, these different levels of speech formality are called **registers**—for example, it is appropriate to use a formal register of speech when speaking to the President of the United States.

While we may be aware of making a special effort to produce our best language along with our best manners for certain people or in certain situations, the changes that we make are usually performed effortlessly. If you think about it, you will realize that you probably don't speak to your grandmother exactly the same way as you do to your neighbor's two-year-old; nor do you speak to your minister or rabbi as you do to your roommate—but you usually don't need to plan your speech styles in advance. Automatically adjusting from one speech style to another is known as **style shifting.**

Many people deny even having different speech styles, on the grounds that it would be insincere, a form of play acting, to speak differently to different people. However, "putting on airs" is not the only way to change speech style. It isn't even one of the most common. In reality, adapting one's spoken style to one's audience is like choosing the right tool for a particular task. You can't eat bouillon with a fork or sirloin steak with a spoon. If you were questioned by your four-year-old cousin about why your begonia needs light, you probably wouldn't explain it in terms of photosynthesis. On the other hand, you probably would include that word in your answer to the same sort of question on a botany exam. You may tell your mechanic that one of the wires seems to have come loose from "that funny-looking black thing," and he may respect the depths of your ignorance by replying to you in similar terms. However, if mechanics talk that way to each other, you may begin to doubt their competence. Thus, common sense makes you choose simple words to speak to a small child, and appropriate technical words, if you know them, to speak to an expert about her field.

10.1.4 Notions of Prestige

The popular attitude persists that every language consists of one "correct" dialect from which all other "inferior" or "substandard" dialects emerge. This misconception has arisen from social stereotypes and biases. It is not a linguistic fact. It is important to realize that a person's use of any particular dialect is not a reflection of his or her intelligence or judgment. **Linguistically speaking, no one dialect or language is better, more correct, more systematic, or more logical than any other.** Rather, every language variety is a rule-governed system and an effective means of communication.

The notion of **standard dialect** is really a complex one and in many ways an idealization. Descriptively speaking, the standard dialect is the variety used by political leaders, the media, and speakers from higher socioeconomic classes. It is also generally the variety taught in schools and to non-native speakers in language classes. Every language has at least one standard dialect, which serves as the primary means of communication across dialects. Other dialects can be called **nonstandard dialects** but should not be considered inferior.

In actuality, there is no one standard dialect, but instead there are many different varieties of what people consider to be the standard. What ties these different notions together is **prestige.** Socially speaking, the standard dialect is the dialect of prestige and power. However, the prestige of any speech variety is wholly dependent upon the prestige of the speakers who use it. In the United States, the prestige group usually corresponds to those in society who enjoy positions of power, wealth, and education. It is the speech of this group, therefore, that becomes the standard, but there is nothing about the variety itself that makes it prestigious.

For evidence of this claim, consider a case in which the status of a particular linguistic feature has changed over time from standard to nonstandard. Recall from the discussion of prescriptive versus descriptive rules of grammar (File 1.3) that multiple negatives were once commonly used by speakers of standard Old English and Middle English. Take, for example, the multiple-negative construction in (1), from Geoffrey Chaucer's description of the Knight in the General Prologue to the *Canterbury Tales* (from Millward 1989: 158), meaning roughly "he has never in all his life said anything villainous to any creature."

(1) He nevere yet no vileynye ne sayde
     He never yet no villainy not said
     In al his lyf unto no maner wight
     In all his life to no kind of creature

Today, however, speakers who most commonly employ multiple-negative constructions are not members of the higher socioeconomic (i.e., prestige) group. Such constructions are rarely used in public spheres by political leaders or media spokespeople, and English grammar instructors discourage use of these forms in writing or in speech. Thus, multiple negation is today considered a nonstandard feature. This example illustrates a change over time in the **prescriptive standard,** the standard by which we make judgments of "right" and "wrong." It shows that such judgments are not linguistically founded but are instead governed by societal opinion, and most often by societal evaluation of speakers.

To consider another example of how linguistically arbitrary notions of the standard are, let's look at the following case. Few Standard English speakers use object pronouns in subject position, as in (2).

(2) Kim and me went to the store.

Yet media spokespeople, political leaders, and others of higher socioeconomic status are more and more frequently observed using subject pronouns in object position as in (3) and (4).

(3) This is a matter between Kim and I.
(4) Give the books to Kim and I.

According to the prescriptive standard, sentences (2), (3), and (4) should all be "corrected" as follows:

(5) Kim and I went to the mall.
(6) This is a matter between Kim and me.
(7) Give the money to Kim and me.

However, not only would many standard English speakers not recognize (3) and (4) as violations of a prescriptive rule, but many would argue that intuitively sentences (3) and (4) seem "correct" while (6) and (7) seem "incorrect." This is known as **hypercorrection,** the act of producing nonstandard forms by way of false analogy. This example shows us that even violations of a prescriptive rule (such as sentences (3) and (4) above) can be perceived as standard if they are used by members of the prestige group.

The standard dialect in the United States is called **Standard American English** (**SAE**). As with any standard dialect, SAE is not a well-defined variety but rather an idealization, which even now defies definition because agreement on what exactly constitutes this variety is lacking. SAE is not a single, unitary, homogeneous dialect but instead comprises a number of varieties. When we speak of SAE, we usually have in mind features of grammar rather than pronunciation. In the United States, where class consciousness is minimal, pronunciation is not terribly important. Thus, there are varieties of SAE that are spoken with northern accents, southern accents, coastal New England accents, and so on, but that are still considered standard. This is not to say that we do not make evaluations of speech based on accent, because we do. But we seem to be far more "tolerant" of variation in accent than we are of grammatical variation. Compare, for example, the varieties of English spoken by John Kerry, who grew up in Massachusetts, and George W. Bush, who grew up in Texas, in the 2004 presidential debates. Most would agree that both are speakers of SAE, yet they speak with distinctly different accents.

In Britain, on the other hand, where class divisions are more clearly defined and social mobility is more restricted, standard pronunciation or Received Pronunciation (RP), also known as BBC English or the Queen's English, takes on the importance of standard grammar and vocabulary. Thus, in Britain both pronunciation and grammar are markers of social status.

All dialects that are not perceived as varieties of the standard are called nonstandard. It is important to understand that nonstandard does not mean "substandard" or "inferior," although this is the perception held by many. Just as standard dialects are associated with the language of the "powerful" and "prestigious," nonstandard dialects are usually associated with the language of the lower socioeconomic classes.

Most nonstandard varieties are stigmatized in the wider community as illogical and unsystematic. It is on this basis that many justify labeling nonstandard varieties as "bad" or "improper" ways of speaking, as opposed to standard varieties, which are said to be "good" or "proper." Again, it must be emphasized that such evaluations are linguistically unfounded. Consider the paradigms in (8) illustrating the use of reflexive pronouns in two varieties of English—one standard, the other nonstandard.

(8) **Standard**   **Nonstandard**
    I like myself   I like myself
    You like yourself   You like yourself
    He likes himself   He likes hisself
    She likes herself   She likes herself
    We like ourselves   We like ourselves
    You like yourselves   You like yourselves
    They like themselves   They like theirselves

Given these two paradigms, we can develop descriptive rules (see (9)) for the construction of reflexives in these two varieties.

(9) Standard: Add the reflexive suffix -self to possessive determiners in the first- and second-person singular, and -selves to possessive determiners in the first- and second-person plural.

                     Add the reflexive suffix -self to object pronouns in the third-person singular, and -selves to object pronouns in the third-person plural.

    Nonstandard: Add the reflexive suffix -self to possessive determiners in the first-, second-, and third-person singular, and -selves to possessive determiners in the first-, second-, and third-person plural.

Given these rules, what about the nonstandard variety makes it any less systematic or less logical than the standard variety? Nothing. Both varieties are systematic, and both are logically constructed. In fact, some may argue that in this instance, the nonstandard variety is more systematic than the standard variety because it consistently uses the same form, the possessive, as the stem for forming the reflexive paradigm. This system, consequently, would be much easier to teach to non-native speakers of English or children learning a first language than the standard system which must stipulate two separate conditions.

Often, speakers who do not adapt to the standard are considered "lazy," "uneducated," and "unambitious." Speakers of nonstandard varieties are told that the varieties they speak are "wrong" and "inferior" and that they must learn to speak the varieties taught in school in order to become successful. As a result, children who come from homes where nonstandard varieties are spoken are at an immediate disadvantage in school, where they are forced to make adjustments from the language of their home communities to the standard varieties of the schools (an adjustment unnecessary for children from homes where standard varieties are spoken). Some make these adjustments and become **bidialectal** speakers, having a mastery of two dialects—one a standard variety, the other a nonstandard variety. Others become only marginally fluent in the standard but retain a mastery of the nonstandard dialect. And still others master the standard and reject the nonstandard dialect altogether.

Which adjustments are made depends on a number of different factors. One factor returns us to the notion of **prestige,** specifically to the distinction between **overt prestige** and **covert prestige.** Overt prestige is the type of prestige discussed above as the "standard dialect." This is the prestige that is attached to a particular variety by the community at large and that defines how people should speak in order to gain status in the wider community. But there is another type of prestige that exists among members of nonstandard-speaking communities and that defines how people should speak in order to be considered members of those particular communities—covert prestige. The desire to "belong" to a particular group often becomes the overriding factor. For example, if you are hanging out with a bunch of old high school friends from back home, you might not want to use the prescriptive standard (which is overtly prestigious) because it does not fit in with how "the guys" are talking and might make you the subject of ridicule ("Listen to so-and-so's educated talk!"). Thus, in many ways, nonstandard varieties persist, despite their stigmatized status, because of covert prestige. In this sense, language becomes a marker of group identification. These ideas will be discussed in more detail in File 13.1, "Language and Identity," and File 13.2, "Language and Power."

Variation at Different Levels of Linguistic Structure

10.2.1 Introduction

While we are probably most consciously aware of differences in vocabulary choice or pronunciation, internal variation exists at all the levels of linguistic structure we have discussed in this book: phonetics, phonology, morphology, syntax, and semantics. If we compare any two language varieties (be they different languages, different dialects, different styles, etc.), we may find differences at any of these levels. In this file, we take each of these levels in turn and look at a few examples of how they may differ between varieties.

10.2.2 Phonetic Variation

Recall from Chapter 2 that phonetics is the study of how sounds are physically produced, the acoustics of sound waves, and the perception of sounds by the brain. Hence, differences at the phonetic level tend to be those where a sound that **functions** the same in the linguistic systems of two varieties has some difference in its physical characteristics. For example, all varieties of American English use the phonemes /t, d, n, s, z/; that is, we can find minimal pairs that make use of these sounds in American English. But the phonetics of these sounds are not always the same: some New York City dialects produce these sounds as dental, where the tongue tip touches the top teeth, while most other American English dialects produce them as alveolar, with the tongue touching the alveolar ridge.

Similarly, most dialects of English have a phoneme that functions as an /r/, in words like *really* or *right*. But, not all /r/s are the same: some English and Scottish dialects have a trilled [r], while most American dialects have a retroflex or bunched [ɹ].

Another source of phonetic variation is simply the fact that every utterance produced is somewhat different. Even if the same person says the same sentence twice in a row, trying to make them as similar as possible, there will be slight phonetic differences in the pronunciations of words, the duration of segments, the tone of voice, and so on. And, of course, these differences are magnified when the utterances are produced by different people. For example, the sign YEAR in Taiwan Sign Language consists of three basic units: two units in which the hands are either in motion or in the process of changing configuration, and then one unit in which the hands remain constant in a particular place of articulation. The durations of these units may vary from signer to signer, however; for example, Wayne Smith found in a 1989 study that one speaker's signed units were 667 ms, 100 ms, and 400 ms, respectively, while another's were 433 ms, 67 ms, and 400 ms. Thus, these two speakers were producing the same sign (the same form with the same meaning), but they showed differences in the details of articulation.

We can also find phonetic variation in different styles or registers of speech. For example, you may have been told to "enunciate" clearly when you are speaking in a formal situation like a job interview or when you are speaking to someone who may be hard of hearing. In such situations, you aren't changing the system of sounds you are using (your phonology), but rather you are changing how you pronounce the particular sounds in question (your phonetics). For instance, instead of pronouncing the word *little* with a flap and a syllabic [l] as in [lɪɾl̩], which is common in casual American speech, you might pronounce it with a [t] and a schwa, as in [lɪtʰəl], to make it "clearer" which phoneme you mean. Similarly, in ASL, the sign for KNOW (shown in (1)) is typically signed in informal situations with the fingers touching the cheekbone. But the "official" version of this sign, the one you might learn in the classroom or use in careful speech, for example, has the fingers touching the temple.

(1) a. ASL: KNOW (informal)   b. ASL: KNOW (formal)

© 2006, William Vicars, www.Lifeprint.com. Adapted by permission.

10.2.3 Phonological Variation

Phonology, unlike phonetics, deals with the inventory of sounds in a language and the way that those sounds are distributed, as was discussed in Chapter 3. So, to see whether two language varieties have differences in their phonologies, we could to look for words that actually make use of different phonemes in words that are semantically and historically the "same" words. For instance, we mentioned in Section 2.3.2 that many American dialects have the vowel [ɔ] in the words *caught, dawn,* and *hawk,* which is different from the vowel [ɑ] found in the words *cot, Don,* and *hock.* For these speakers, then, these words are minimal pairs that show the difference between the phonemes [ɔ] and [ɑ]. But in some dialects, all six of these words have the same vowel (usually a vowel closer to [ɑ] than to [ɔ]), so that the words *caught* and *cot* are homophonous. Thus, the distribution of the phonemes in the two dialects is different: they have different phonological systems.

Similarly, in dialects of southern England, words like *flood, but,* and *cup* have the vowel [ʌ], whereas words like *full, good,* and *put* have the vowel [ʊ]. In northern English dialects, however, both sets of words have the vowel [ʊ].

Another way in which language varieties may differ in their phonologies is in terms of what sequences of sounds they allow. For example, Spanish does not allow the sequences /sp/, /st/, or /sk/ to occur at the beginning of a word, while English does (this is why native Spanish speakers often pronounce English words like *student* with an initial vowel, [ɛstudɛnt]—see Section 3.3.2). Standard British English, like Bostonian English, does not permit sequences of vowel-/r/-consonant or vowel-/r/-word boundary; most other American English dialects do permit such sequences. So while a person from Oregon might say the phrase *park the car* as [pʰɑɹk ðə kʰɑɹ], a person from Boston or London might say [pʰɑːk ðɛ kʰɑː]. Similarly, some African-American English dialects do not permit sequences of consonant-/r/ or consonant-/l/, especially in unstressed syllables, so that the word *profession* is pronounced [pʰʌfɛʃn̩].

10.2.4 Morphological Variation

As discussed in Chapter 4, morphemes are the smallest unit of sound-meaning pairs in a language. While we would classify different pronunciations of the same morpheme as phonetic variation, we can talk about morphological variation by looking at the distribution of morphemes in two varieties or the use of completely different morphemes for the same function in two varieties.

As an example of the distribution of morphemes, consider the use of the possessive morpheme in English. In Standard American English, this morpheme is used whenever one person possesses something else, for example, *my life, his dog, Tom's car, the old lady's purse.* In some rural British English dialects, however, the possessive morpheme is used only with pronouns, and not with nouns: *my life, his dog,* but *Tom car* and *the old lady purse.*

In terms of using completely different morphemes for the same function, consider the example from File 10.1 of reflexive pronouns. Standard English uses the reflexive pronouns *myself, yourself, himself, ourselves, yourselves,* and *themselves.* Notice that in the first and second person, these pronouns make use of the possessive determiner plus *self* or *selves,* while in the third person, these pronouns are a combination of the object pronoun plus *self* or *selves.* Many dialects of English have made this set of reflexive pronouns more regular by using the possessive determiner in all of them, using *hisself* and *theirselves* instead of *himself* and *themselves.*

Another example of using different morphemes for the same purpose in two different varieties can be seen in the past tense of certain verbs in Appalachian English versus Standard American English. For example, the past tenses of the verbs *climb, eat,* and *heat* in Appalachian English are [klʌm], [ɛt], and [hɛt], respectively, while Standard American English has [klɑɪmd], [eɪt], and [hirəd].

Morphological variation also exists across styles and registers. For example, there are many languages that are called "pro-drop" languages, where pronouns can be "dropped" from speech. In Spanish, for instance, it is possible to say either *hablo español* or *yo hablo español* to mean 'I speak Spanish': the latter includes the subject pronoun *yo,* meaning 'I,' while the former does not. The choice to use a pronoun or not may depend on the context of the conversation or other stylistic considerations (e.g., how easy it is to infer what the "missing" pronoun is). Other pro-drop languages include Italian, American Sign Language, Japanese, Mandarin, and Polish. Spanish and Italian are sometimes considered only partial pro-drop languages because they allow only the subject pronoun to be dropped.

10.2.5 Syntactic Variation

Syntax has to do both with the types of categories certain words belong to and with how words are put together to form sentences (see Chapter 5). We can see variation in both of these properties across language varieties.

For example, in many southern American English dialects, *done* can function as an auxiliary verb, as in *she done already told you,* where Standard American English uses *has: she has already told you.* Similarly, in many Appalachian English dialects, *right* can function adverbially, as in *a right good meal,* where Standard American English would use *very: a very good meal.* Of course, Standard American English also has the morphemes *done* and *right,* but they function predominantly as a main verb and as an adjective, respectively: for example, *he has done it* or *the right answer.*

In terms of how words are combined, we can again compare many southern American English dialects to Standard American English. In many southern dialects, combinations of auxiliaries, such as *might could, might would, may can,* and *useta could* are permitted and form a single constituent; such combinations are impossible in Standard English, where the same ideas are expressed (more or less, though the exact meanings are somewhat nuanced) with combinations like *might be able to, might perhaps, may be able to,* and *used to be able to.*

Another difference in syntactic combination can be seen in the use by many midwestern Americans of constructions such as *the crops need watered* or *the cat wants petted* as a variant of standard American English *the crops need to be watered* or *the cat wants to be petted.*

10.2.6 Lexical Variation

Semantics has to do with meaning, from the meaning of particular words to the way sentences are meaningful because they are built up compositionally from their parts (see Chapter 6). While semantic variation in both of these areas does exist, the latter is decidedly more complicated and is closely interconnected with syntactic and pragmatic variation. Therefore, we will focus here on lexical variation, that is, differences in the words people use to mean the same thing or to refer to the same object, or differences in what the same word means or refers to.

For example, words for sweet carbonated beverages differ from place to place: *soda* is common in the northeastern and western parts of the United States, while *pop* is common in the midwest and northwest, and *coke* is common in the south. And, of course, there are other terms like *soft drink, soda pop, fizzy drinks,* or even *juice* that are used elsewhere.[1]

Another example comes from different varieties of French: in European French, the word for the verb 'to mail' is *poster,* while the Québécois French word is *maller.* Similarly, in Taiwan Sign Language, speakers from Taipei sign the word SHOE as shown in (2), while speakers from Tainan sign the same word by touching the fronts of the wrists together, with the hands crossed and in fists.

(2) TSL: SHOE (Taipei)

On the other hand, the same word can also be used to mean different things in different language varieties. For example, *knock up* means 'rouse from sleep by knocking' in British English but 'make pregnant' in American English. Similarly, *to be pissed* is 'to be drunk' in British English but 'to be mad' in American or Canadian English.

Lexical variation is very common in different styles: the choice of words you use often depends on the register you are speaking. So, for example, you might say "I fell on my butt" to a friend but "I fell on my backside" to your grandmother. We also have different words for things like *man* depending on the context: *gentleman* is more formal; *guy* is less formal. Likewise, in French, the standard word for 'man' is *homme;* the more formal word is *monsieur* or *gentilhomme;* and the more casual word is *mec* or *type.*

---

[1]See http://www.popvssoda.com/countystats/total-county.html for a detailed, county-by-county map of the United States showing the most common terms used, compiled by Matthew T. Campbell of East Central University in Oklahoma.

Factors Influencing Variation: Regional and Geographic Factors

10.3.1 Why Does Language Vary?

In the previous two files, we have seen that language variation is rampant: language varieties can range in differences from being two different languages to being two registers of the same dialect spoken by the same person. We have seen examples of the kinds of differences that language varieties can have: phonetic, phonological, morphological, syntactic, and lexical. But, so far, we have not discussed *why* languages vary.

Just as there are many types of variation, so are there many factors that influence variation, and although we can isolate out several factors that tend to be particularly influential, it is important to remember that **all** of the factors that will be discussed in the next two files play a role in determining the language variety used by any given person at any given time. For example, think of what you might expect for the language variety of a 13-year-old, African-American, middle-class female from Alabama, talking amongst her school friends. Change any one of those factors, and you might expect to hear something else: What does she sound like on the phone to her grandmother? What does her mother sound like? Her cousin from New York? Her white 85-year-old neighbor originally from Minnesota? Thinking about these variations should help you see how multiple factors work together to determine a language variety.

To begin the discussion of these factors, we turn first to the regional and geographic factors that influence variation. These factors typify **regional dialect** variation. A second set, which is equally important, includes attributes such as social class, age, gender, and ethnicity. These factors, which typify **social dialect** variation, are discussed in File 10.4.

10.3.2 Regional and Geographic Variation

One the most apparent reasons for the existence of different language varieties is that languages are spoken in different geographical locations that are separate from each other. This type of variation based on geographical boundaries, known as **regional variation**, is responsible, for example, for the differences between American English and British English, or the Portuguese spoken in Portugal versus that spoken in Brazil. It is also the type of variation that we associate with, say, New York English versus Texan English, or the English spoken in New York City versus that spoken in Saratoga Springs. An example of regional variation in the United States is shown in (1), where two different ASL signs for *football* are illustrated. The sign on the left is used throughout most of the United States, while the sign on the right is found specifically in Ohio; you can see that it is a completely different sign.

Why does geography play such a large role in determining a dialect? First, language varieties tend to be most influenced by the people you are in face-to-face communication with, so people who live close to each other will have considerably more influence on each other's dialects than people who live farther apart; that is, living in close proximity to a group of Scots-Irish will have more of an impact on your speech than living 100 miles from a group of Germans. So it is often really the patterns of settlement that people fall into,

(1) FOOTBALL (widespread) and FOOTBALL (Ohio)

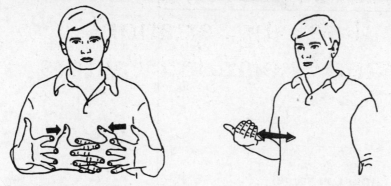

Reproduced by permission of Gallaudet College Press, from Shroyer and Shroyer, *Signs across America* (1984), pp. 96, 97.

rather than the geography of the region itself, that matters. This means, for example, that there is nothing inherent about southeastern Pennsylvania that makes people who live there more likely to use words like [jɑ] and [neɪ] instead of [jɛs] and [noʊ]; instead, this is because of the large population of German speakers who settled in the area.

This is not to say that physical geography cannot play any role in regional dialects, because dialects are often influenced by isolation. That is, being isolated from other speakers tends to allow a dialect to develop in its own way, through its own innovations that are different from those of other dialects. Regional dialect boundaries therefore often coincide with natural barriers such as rivers, mountains, or swamps. Tangier Island off the coast of Virginia has preserved a very distinctive variety of English owing in part to its geographic isolation, as have speakers of Gullah along the Sea Islands of South Carolina. And the distinctive dialect known as Appalachian English can be attributed at least in part to the isolation imposed by the Appalachian mountain range.

People who study regional dialects, known as **dialectologists,** often rely on fieldwork to determine dialect regions. For example, they may come up with a list of particular characteristics that they know typically vary in the part of a country they are interested in; then they go out and directly ask people in those areas how they say things.

The boundaries of areas where a particular linguistic form is used are marked by lines called **isoglosses.** When many isoglosses surround the same region or separate the same group of speakers, there is said to be a **bundle of isoglosses,** which indicates that the speech of a particular group is different in a number of ways from that of other groups around it—it may, then, correspond to a dialect boundary.

An example of this is shown in (2), where you can see a map of the northeastern United States. The three lines running through northern Pennsylvania represent three isoglosses. The dotted line represents variation between the terms *darning needle* and *dragonfly* to refer to the same insect: speakers north of the line tend to use *darning needle,* while speakers south of the line tend to use *dragonfly.* Similarly, the solid line represents the isogloss between people who say *whiffletree* (to the north) and people who say *swingletree* (to the south),[1] and the dashed line represents the dividing line between those who say *pail* (to the north) and those who say *bucket* (to the south). Although they do not exactly coincide, taken together, this bundle of isoglosses can be used to mark the dialect boundary between the northern dialect area (to the north) and the midland dialect area (to the south).

---

[1]A *whiffletree* (or *swingletree*) is, according to Merriam Webster, "the pivoted swinging bar to which the traces of a harness are fastened and by which a vehicle or implement is drawn."

(2) Bundling of three northern isoglosses

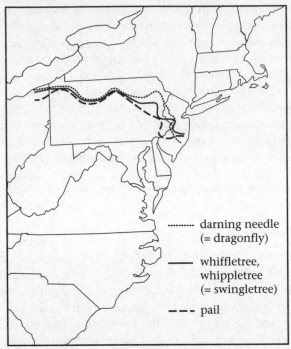

.... darning needle
          (= dragonfly)

———   whiffletree,
        whippletree
        (= swingletree)

– – –   pail

Reproduced by permission from the University of Michigan Press from Carver, *American Regional Dialects* (1987), p. 12 (original source *A Word Geography of the Eastern United States,* 1949, fig. 5a).

10.3.3 A Case Study in Regional Variation: The United States

The formation of U.S. regional dialects had its beginnings partly in England, as speakers from various regions of England journeyed across the Atlantic and settled the Eastern seaboard of the United States. Dialectal boundaries still present today are reflected in these earliest settlement patterns. Settlers from the eastern regions of central and southern England settled in eastern New England and the Virginia Tidewater area. From northern and western parts of England settlers came to the New Jersey and Delaware areas. And Scots-Irish from Ulster settled in parts of western New England, New York, and Appalachia. In time, certain colonial cities such as Boston, Philadelphia, and Charleston acquired prestige as centers of trade and culture. As a result, the dialects spoken in these cities became prestigious as well and began to exert influence on nearby settlements.

Migration westward to a large extent reflected the settlement patterns of the Atlantic states. Yankees from western New England and upstate New York, in moving west, fanned out, settling chiefly in the Great Lakes area; settlers from the Middle Atlantic region (primarily Pennsylvania and Maryland) journeyed west to Ohio, West Virginia, and the Mississippi Valley. Influence from the southern Atlantic colonies was felt as speakers from this area settled in the Gulf states. The lines are never clearly drawn, however, because the streams of migration often mingled. Sometimes, New Englanders and speakers from the Middle Atlantic region would form compact communities outside their usual area of settlement—for example, the Yankee enclave of Worthington, Ohio, or the North Carolina Quaker settlement of Richmond, Indiana. The spread of migration continued to the Rocky Mountain states, essentially following previously established patterns but with greater mingling, and finally reached the West Coast, resulting in even greater crossing of dialect lines.

These patterns of Anglo settlement and migration tell only part of the story, however. Contact between English and Native American languages in the seventeenth century contributed significantly to the development of North American English and the dialect regions of the United States. Furthermore, the arrival of other European immigrants resulted in some very distinct regional dialect areas in the United States, including the major influences of French in New Orleans, German in southern Pennsylvania, and Spanish in the southwest. The arrival of African slaves along the southeast Atlantic seaboard contributed significantly to the development of southern varieties of English. And the later migration of African Americans from rural areas such as Mississippi, Alabama, Georgia, and South Carolina to northern cities such as Chicago, Detroit, New York, Philadelphia, and Washington, DC, also had a major impact on the development of American English dialects.

Figure (3) shows the approximate boundaries of the major dialect regions in the United States. The boundary lines on this map represent not sharp demarcations but rather compromises between bundles of isoglosses that roughly come together along these lines.

(3) Approximate dialect regions of the United States

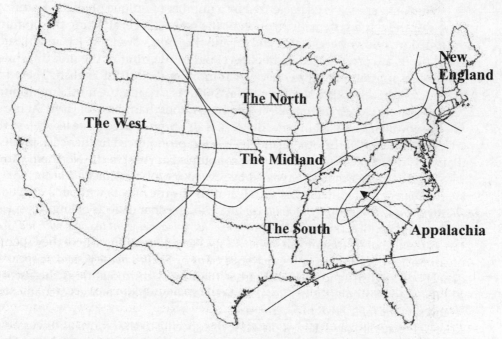

The present-day regional dialect areas for the most part continue to reflect the initial patterns of dialect formation discussed in the previous paragraphs. This fact may seem surprising, as you might expect that the impact of television, radio, and other forms of broadcast media on United States English over the past half-century would lead to more homogeneity among dialects rather than continuing heterogeneity. While it is true that middle-class Euro-American speech across the States is showing some signs of becoming more homogeneous, working-class speech shows little movement in this regard (Kretschmar 1997; Labov et al. 2005).

Although a number of explanations have been considered for why this is the case, the most likely reason is that the settlement of the East Coast, which led to the formation of the initial dialects of the United States, happened considerably earlier than settlement in other parts of the country. The time lag between initial settlement and later waves of westward migration among settlers led to the formation of strong dialect patterns in original areas, so much so that later immigration groups would have been under considerable pressure to conform to these initial patterns rather than establish different patterns when learning English as a second language. As time went on, this pattern of enculturation became entrenched, so that relatively stable patterns continued to be developed, a process known as the **founder principle.**

In the sections that follow, each of the present-day supra-regional dialect areas of the

United States will be briefly discussed.[2] These areas, shown in (3), include the North, New England, the South, Appalachia, the Midland, and the West. Throughout this discussion, it is important to note that the described patterns of speech reflect, for the most part, those of Euro-Americans because of their historical prominence as the majority speech group in the United States. Varieties of other ethnic groups populating these areas, such as African-Americans and Hispanic/Latino Americans, are discussed in more detail in Section 10.4.5.

10.3.4 The North

The North is defined in modern-day dialect studies as the portion of the country that includes western Massachusetts; the northern portions of New York, Pennsylvania, Ohio, Indiana, Illinois, Iowa, and South Dakota; and the entire states of Minnesota, Michigan, Wisconsin, and North Dakota.

Northern speech is characterized by a number of unique phonetic features. The most salient of these is a systematic rotation of the vowel space, affecting the pronunciation of the long low/mid vowels [æ], [ɑ], and [ɔ] and the short vowels [ʌ], [ɛ], and [ɪ], such that the long vowels are pronounced higher and closer to the front of the mouth, while the short vowels are pronounced further back than in other dialects of English. These patterns are known collectively as the **Northern Cities Shift.** As a result, the northern pronunciation of *bag* or *bat* more closely resembles [bɛg] or [bɛt] rather than [bæg] or [bæt]. At the same time, /ɑ/, the vowel in *lock* or *lot* in other dialects, is also pronounced more like [æ], so these words are [læk] or [læt]. On the other hand, [ɛ] is often pronounced further back in the mouth, so that *bet* is more like [bʌt], while *bus* is pronounced as [bɔs] in the Northern Cities.

Northern speech is also typified by several morpho-syntactic features that differentiate the dialect from others. One such feature is the use of *with* without a direct object, as in *Do you want to come with?* or *John is coming with.* In other dialects of English, speakers prefer to end this type of sentence with a pronoun, as in *Do you want to come with me?* Another feature is the use of *by* in sentences where a speaker is describing where they spent their time on an earlier occasion, as in the sentence *I was by Sarah's house yesterday;* speakers of other dialects of English tend to use *at* rather than *by.* A third feature is the use of the *needs VERB+ing* construction, as in *The table needs cleaning,* where speakers of many other dialects would say *The table needs to be cleaned.*

There are also a variety of dialect terms specific to the North, as discussed in the Harvard Dialect Survey. For example, the strip of grass that is found in someone's front yard between the sidewalk and the road is often referred to either as a *parkway* or a *tree lawn,* while the most common term for the gray creature that rolls up into a ball when touched is *roly poly.* In addition, for many speakers, the generic term for an athletic shoe is *sneaker* (as opposed to *tennis shoe,* which is widely used in other areas), while the most commonly used generic term for a sweetened carbonated beverage is *pop.*

10.3.5 New England

The New England dialect area is defined as the area including western New York (except New York City, which is a distinct speech island), eastern Massachusetts, Connecticut, Vermont, New Hampshire, Rhode Island, and Maine. An interesting fact to note is that New England and Northern speakers historically share many similar dialect traits, leading to a high degree of overlap of features generally between the areas. However, in the present day, there are also some notable differences, which are outlined below.

---

[2]Much of the description of these dialect areas comes from the *Atlas of North American English* by Labov, Ash, and Boberg (2005); from *American English* by Wolfram and Schilling-Estes (2005); or from papers in *American Voices: How Dialects Differ from Coast to Coast* by Wolfram and Ward (2006). Other references will be cited in the text.

Turning first to pronunciation, although the characteristics of New England are quite similar to those of the North, there are two exceptions. The first is the pronunciation of [ɑ], the vowel in words such as *cot, pot,* and *hock,* and [ɔ], the vowel in words such as *caught, thought, hawk,* as the same, so that these words are homophones (see Section 2.3.2). The second is that most areas within Eastern New England are /r/-less. That is, in words where an /r/ precedes a consonant, either within a word or at the end of the word, it is not pronounced. Thus, the sentence *park your car* is pronounced [pʰɑkjʌkʰɑ]. /r/-less pronunciation is discussed in more detail in File 10.4.

Beyond these phonetic differences, there are also differences in the use of morphological features in New England. For instance, speakers typically use *on line* to describe a situation where Northern speakers would use *in line,* as in the sentence *We were waiting on line for tickets.* Also, speakers throughout much of the area use *so don't I* as a way of showing agreement with another person, whereas other dialects use *so do I* to mean the same thing.

Many of the lexical items used in the New England area also differ. For example, *berm* or *verge* is used for the generic words that name the strip of grass found in someone's yard, while *pill bug* is used to name the little gray creatures that roll up into balls. Furthermore, many speakers in Eastern New England use *bubbler* as the generic synonym for what Northern speakers would call a *drinking* or *water fountain,* and the generic term usually used for a carbonated beverage is *soda* rather than *pop.*

10.3.6 The South

The Southern dialect area is roughly defined as the area of the country including much of Texas, Louisiana, Arkansas, Mississippi, Alabama, Georgia, Tennessee, Kentucky, much of West Virginia, Virginia, and most of North and South Carolina. (Note that it excludes Florida, which is considered a separate speech island.)

Just as the Northern Cities Shift leads to a series of systematic pronunciation differences in the North, there is another pattern—known as the **Southern Shift**—that leads to distinctions in the South. However, the Southern Shift is markedly different from the Northern Cities Shift, as the Southern pattern involves the nuclei of the back vowel diphthongs becoming fronted, while the short front vowels take on the characteristics of diphthongs. As a result, one of the features of Southern speech is the pronunciation of [ɛ] as [ɛɪ], so that *led* is pronounced [lɛɪd] and *net* is pronounced [nɛɪt]. Another difference involving [ɛ] is that it is pronounced as [ɪ] when [n] follows, a phenomenon also known as the "pin/pen merger." Hence, *pen,* which is typically pronounced [pɛn] in other dialects, is pronounced as [pɪn]. Another notable characteristic is the pronunciation of /aʊ/ as [æʊ], resulting in *house* as [hæʊs] and *out* as [æʊt] (Thomas 2001). A third characteristic is that /aɪ/ is often realized as the monophthong [ɑː], so that *wide* or *my* are pronounced more like [wɑːd] or [mɑː] rather than [waɪd] or [maɪ].

Beyond these pronunciation differences, two syntactic features distinguish the unique character of Southern speech. The first of these is the use of the phrase *fixin' to,* as in *I'm fixin' to clean the gutters,* to signal the intention of completing an action at some point in the near future, where speakers of other dialects would use *getting ready to.* The second is the use of two modals in a verb phrase, also known as a **double modal,** to indicate that a plan has a high degree of tentativeness, as in the sentence *I might could help you clean your house tomorrow.* In other dialects of English, speakers would likely say *I might be able to help you clean your house tomorrow (if something else doesn't come up)* to mean the same thing. Southern speakers appear to use the double modal as a politeness strategy when expressing that the plans are tentative, as it indicates more deference than its SAE equivalent. Although *might could* is the most frequently used double modal, others, such as *might should, might would,* and *useta' could,* are also quite common throughout the South.

As discussed in the Harvard Dialect survey, dialect terms that are common in the South include *roly poly* as the most widespread term for the gray creature that rolls up into a ball when touched (making it similar to the North), while the strip of grass found in someone's front yard between the sidewalk and the road is often referred to either as a *curb strip* or a *devil's strip*. In addition, a widely used term for a cart into which one places groceries is *buggy*, while the most commonly used generic term for a carbonated beverage is *coke*.

10.3.7 Appalachia

Appalachia is the area of the country including the southern Appalachian mountain range, which spans the mid and southern regions of West Virginia, western North Carolina and Virginia, and eastern Tennessee and Kentucky. Settlers to this region included English, Scots-Irish, Pennsylvania Dutch, and French Huguenots, who all contributed to the language varieties that developed in this area. Because of the mountainous barriers, speakers in these areas were for many years severely restricted in their travel outside the Appalachian region. From this isolation developed a culture and a language that today are still noticeably distinct from those of its surrounding areas and that appear to have preserved several linguistic features that no longer exist in surrounding dialects. While linguists disagree on the extent to which the varieties spoken in Appalachia can be considered a single dialect, it is clear that the varieties all share a set of common features that set them apart from other dialects of American English.

Among the most notable phonetic characteristics of Appalachian speech are the pronunciation words such as *fish* and *push*. In other dialects of English, these words are pronounced with [ɪ] and [ʊ], while in Appalachia, they are pronounced with [i] and [u], so that *fish* is pronounced [fiʃ] and *push* is pronounced [puʃ] (Brandes and Brewer 1977). In other cases, the [ɪ] sound is lowered and pronounced more like [æ], so that *think* is pronounced [θæŋk] (Wolfram and Christian 1976). A third salient difference is how Appalachian speech deals with primary stress. In many cases, primary stress (indicated by [́]) is placed on the first syllable of a multisyllabic word, even in cases where most other dialects place the stress elsewhere. Thus, *cigar* is pronounced *cígar* rather than *cigár*, *November* is pronounced *Nóvember* as opposed to *Novémber*, and *insurance* is pronounced *ínsurance* rather than *insúrance* (Brandes and Brewer 1977).

Several morpho-syntactic features also mark Appalachian speech as distinctive. First, there is the process known as **a-prefixing.** Appalachian English has preserved the prefix *a-* (which was used commonly in English from the twelfth to seventeenth centuries) in certain verbal constructions, such as *He come a-running to tell me the news* or *The dog was a-cryin' and a-hollerin' when he saw the deer* (Mallinson et al. 2006). Second, Appalachian speech preserves certain irregular verb conjugations in constructing the past tense, where other dialects now use the regular past tense suffix *-ed*. For example, speakers use *clumb* as opposed to *climbed* as the past tense form of *climb*, *het* rather than *heated* as the past tense of *heat*, and *ruck* as opposed to *raked* as the past tense of *rake* (Wolfram and Christian 1976). Third, there is the use of **multiple negation,** a process by which multiple markers are used to negate a sentence, so, for example, a sentence such as *I had some lunch* is negated as *I didn't have no lunch*. In many other dialects of English, *I had some lunch* can be negated only as either *I didn't have any lunch* or *I had no lunch* (Brandes and Brewer 1977).[3]

Lexical variation is also quite abundant in Appalachia. Dialect terms that typify Appalachian speech include *jasper*, which is used to describe an outsider or a stranger, and *sigogglin*, which is used to describe something that leans at an angle or is crooked or tilted. Other interesting words that distinguish the area are *poke*, a term used to describe what is usually called a *bag* or *sack* in other dialects of English, and *holler*, a word used to describe a

---

[3]It should be noted that although multiple negation is a salient feature of Appalachian English, it is not exclusive to this dialect. It is also found in African-American English (to be discussed in File 11.4) and in many working-class varieties of English across the United States.

valley surrounded by mountains, while *dope* is used as the generic term for carbonated beverages (Montgomery and Hall 2003).

10.3.8 The Midland

In present-day dialect studies, the Midland is defined as the section of the country stretching from the Pittsburgh area in western Pennsylvania to roughly the western edge of Kansas and Oklahoma, although it excludes a large pocket of land surrounding St. Louis (which is considered part of the North instead, since the speech features of the area are more Northern in character). In the map in (5), we have included eastern Pennsylvania and New Jersey in the Midland area, rather than putting them in a separate dialect group called the Mid-Atlantic, as is sometimes considered appropriate.

Although there has been a commonly held popular view that there is "nothing special" about language use in the Midland, research has shown that this stereotype is untrue. Probably one of the most salient characteristics is the pronunciation of /oʊ/ as [ɵʊ], with the nucleus of the vowel produced closer to the front of the mouth and more rounded than is standard. Thus, Midland speakers produce *boat* as [bɵʊt] and *mow* as [mɵʊ] (Thomas 2001). Another common feature of Midland pronunciation is the tendency to pronounce [1] at the end of a syllable as a vowel or glide, rather than as a consonant with tongue-tip contact on the roof of the mouth: this is known as /l/-**vocalization.** Hence, *belt* is often pronounced as [bɛwt] rather than [bɛlt], and *hill* is often pronounced [hɪw] rather than [hɪl] (Dodsworth 2005). A third feature of the Midland dialect is the pronunciation of the diphthong /aʊ/, the vowel in *now, down,* or *town,* with a reduced or deleted offglide, so that it is pronounced more like [aː], particularly before a nasal or at the end of a word. Consequently, *now* is often pronounced as [naː], while *down* is pronounced [daːn]. This pronunciation is especially salient in Pittsburgh (Johnstone et al. 2002), and it has also been observed in Central Ohio in recent years (Durian and Smith 2005).

In terms of syntactic features, many historically Scots-Irish speech patterns are prevalent in the Midland dialect. For example, Midland speakers can use the phrase *all the further* (or *farther*) where other dialects of American English would use *as far as,* as in the sentence *Johnstown was all the further I could drive* (Thomas 1993). Speakers also can use *anymore* without a preceding marker of negation, to mean 'these days,' as in the sentence *Anymore, I leave early on Fridays* (Murray 1993). A third feature with Scots roots used by many Midland speakers is the *needs VERB+ed* construction, as in *The table needs washed,* where speakers of many other dialects would say *The table needs to be washed* (Murray et al. 1996).

In regard to lexical variation, the Midland is characterized by a variety of dialect terms specific to the area, as described in part by the Harvard Dialect Survey. For instance, the strip of grass that is found in someone's front yard between the sidewalk and the road is typically referred to either as an *easement* or a *tree lawn,* while the most common term for the gray creature that rolls up into a ball when touched is *potato bug.* Sweetened carbonated beverages are typically referred to as *pop.* In addition, many speakers use *sweeper* as a generic synonym for *vacuum cleaner,* while a sweet green pepper is often referred to as a *mango,* particularly among older speakers.

10.3.9 The West

The West as a dialect area is defined as an area stretching from roughly the western sections of Kansas and Nebraska at its eastern-most perimeter, to the Western Coast of the United States. Geographically, this area includes New Mexico, Colorado, Arizona, Utah, Nevada, Idaho, California, Oregon, and Washington, as well as the western portions of South Dakota and Nebraska. Unlike the other regional dialects, Western speech among Anglo-Americans is less distinctive, in that there are fewer features that can be specifically discussed as occurring primarily in the West. The reason is that the West was the last dialect area to be extensively settled in the United States, and by the time settlers colonized the area, dialect patterns had become fairly solidified in other areas. Consequently, Western speech can perhaps be best thought in many ways as a hybrid of the other regional dialects of English.

Generally, Western pronunciation closely resembles that of the Midland patterns previously discussed, with a few notable exceptions. First, the nucleus of /u/ is typically pronounced closer to the front of the mouth than in the Midland (or other dialect areas for that matter), particularly after alveolar consonants like [t] and [d]. Consequently, where speakers of other dialects produce [u] in words such as *dude* or *new,* Western speakers produce [ʉ], resulting in *dude* as [dʉd] and *new* as [nʉ] (Ash 2003). However, although /u/ is extensively fronted, /oʊ/ is not, unlike in Midland speech. Also, [ɑ], the vowel in words such as *cot, pot,* and *hock,* and [ɔ], the vowels in words such as *caught, thought, hawk,* are produced as homophones, as in New England speech, rather than near-homophones, as in the Midland. A final difference is the Western pronunciation of /ɪ/. When it occurs in words before [ŋ], speakers tend to pronounce /ɪ/ as [i], so that *thing* is pronounced [θiŋ]. In other contexts, [ɪ] is pronounced as [ɛ], so that *hid* is pronounced [hɛd] rather than [hɪd]. These pronunciation patterns are especially salient in Northern California speech (Eckert 2004).

Syntactic variation, on the other hand, tends to most closely resemble the patterns previously discussed for the North, although California youth culture has been responsible for introducing a feature which is now becoming more pervasive throughout United States (and even global) English: the use of the discourse marker *I'm like.* This marker is used to introduce quoted speech, as in the sentence *I'm like, "No I don't have a crush on Kim."* A related marker is *I'm/(he's)/(she's) all,* which also traces its roots to California speech and serves a similar function, as in *I'm all "No he didn't,"* or *He's all "Shut your mouth"* (Eckert and Mendoza-Denton 2006).

Dialect terms specific to the West include *lookie lou* to describe a traffic jam caused by drivers slowing down to view an accident and *firefly* as the most common term for the flying bug found in the summertime that lights up at night, according to the Harvard Dialect Survey. As well, *granola* is often used to describe people who live healthy lifestyles, rather than a name for a breakfast item, as is the common use in other dialect areas. The most widely used generic term for a carbonated beverage is *soda,* making the West akin to Eastern New England (McConchie 2002).

Factors Influencing Variation: Social Factors

10.4.1 Social Influences on Language Variation

In File 10.3, we explored the regional and geographic factors that lead to language variation. As that file demonstrated, these factors play an important role in the formation of the dialects of a language, as they lead to the formation of regional dialects. However, regional variation only explains only half of the story. Although different regional dialects are particularly salient, there are plenty of language varieties that co-occur within any given regional dialect; to further our understanding, we need to explore the factors that lead to this linguistic differentiation within regional dialects. These additional factors refer to attributes such as socioeconomic class, age, gender, and ethnicity—speaker characteristics that result from the social groups to which speakers belong and that reflect what are known as **social dialects** of a language. Each of these social factors is briefly explored below. We will return to the issue of language as a social phenomenon in File 13.1, where we consider the role language plays in marking certain social characteristics. Here, however, we focus on which particular factors often influence differences among language varieties and examine particular examples of this type of variation.

10.4.2 Socioeconomic Variation

One of the lines along which language varieties often split is socioeconomic class. We mentioned some issues related to socioeconomic class in File 10.1, when we discussed the notion of "prestige" and the role it plays in deciding which dialect is considered standard: the dialect(s) spoken by people with higher prestige—generally those of a higher socioeconomic status—are considered the standard.

Socioeconomic status affects language varieties for a number of reasons. To a certain extent, people often want to be associated with a particular socioeconomic group (e.g., to express solidarity with those of the same group or to show distance from those of a different group), and language is one way to achieve this (see also File 13.1 on language and identity). Furthermore, socioeconomic status may be associated with particular levels or types of education that will subsequently affect language use.

One famous study on the way socioeconomic status is correlated with language variety is a study done by William Labov in 1972 in New York City. In New York City speech, /ɹ/-lessness is a common phonological phenomenon: /ɹ/s at the ends of syllables, such as in *four, card, paper, here, there,* and so on, are often not pronounced. The use of /ɹ/ was associated with high prestige, while the lack of /ɹ/ was associated with low prestige. Labov tested this claim using salespeople in three department stores also associated with different levels of prestige: Saks (high prestige), Macy's (moderate prestige), and S. Klein (low prestige). He went into the stores and asked salesclerks (who didn't know they were being tested!) a question that would elicit the answer *fourth floor*. This first elicitation represented casual speech; the interviewer then, pretending not to have heard the answer, would lean forward and ask the clerk to repeat the answer. The clerk repeated the answer, but this time in careful speech under emphatic stress.

The results of the study, summarized in (1), showed a clear stratification of /ɹ/-lessness among the salespeople according to socioeconomic status, as predicted.

(1) Percentage of [ɹ] in *floor*

	Casual	Careful
Saks	63	64
Macy's	44	61
S. Klein	8	18

The lowest-prestige/lowest-socioeconomic-class store, S. Klein, had the highest percentage of /ɹ/-lessness, while the highest-prestige/highest-socioeconomic-class store, Saks, had the lowest percentage of /ɹ/-lessness. We can also see that careful speech (when salesclerks switched to a higher register of speech) is similarly associated with a lower percentage of /ɹ/-lessness.

10.4.3 Age Variation

Another way in which language varieties differ has to do with age: younger speakers may not speak the same way as older speakers. Many times, older speakers will comment on the "degradation" of language, or the "desecration" of language, by the younger generation. From a linguistic point of view, however, the differences between older and younger speech are not "good" or "bad"; they are simply changes that occur naturally, just like any other differences between language varieties.

Some relatively recent changes in English include the use of the word *hopefully* as a sentential adverb (to modify the entire sentence as opposed to just modifying a particular action), as in "hopefully it won't rain tomorrow"; the use of high-rising intonation at the ends of even declarative sentences; the use of *like* as an interjection (*I, like, didn't know what to do*) or as a quotative (*he was like "well, I don't know either"*); the introduction of new words such as *download;* and the loss of older words such as *dungarees* to refer to *jeans.*

While it is certainly the case that some innovations are adopted by older speakers as well as younger speakers (almost everyone these days uses *hopefully* in the way described above), it is also true that younger speakers often sound distinctly different from the older speakers in their communities.

10.4.4 Gender Variation

In addition to region, socioeconomic class, and age, another factor that influences language variation is gender. Research in language and gender often tries to explain the role of language in defining, constructing, and reproducing gendered identities, as well as the role of gender in the perception and production of language.

While there certainly are differences in language varieties that are based on biological sexual differences between males and females (e.g., women's voices on average are of a higher pitch than men's because of differences in the average shape and length of the larynx and vocal folds), these are not the types of differences we mean when we talk about language and gender. Gender is not a dichotomous category, divided into males versus females, but rather a **practice** of a cultural pattern. Gender can be thought of as a set of ongoing behaviors, so that we are in a sense always "doing gender." To quote Candace West and Don

Zimmerman, "'Doing gender' involves a complex of socially guided perceptual, interactional, and micropolitical activities that cast particular pursuits as expressions of masculine and feminine natures" (1991: 13–14).

The linking of cultural norms for behavior—including linguistic behavior—with gender is usually arbitrary. This is evidenced by the fact that stereotypes involving language use (e.g., talkativeness, loudness, and silence) are, in different cultures, associated with different genders. For instance, in Malagasy culture (located on Madagascar and other islands in the Indian Ocean), indirect, deferential speech is valued. Malagasy men are often silent in public confrontations, while Malagasy women express anger and criticism through direct, confrontational speech, often to the benefit of their husbands or other male family members (Keenan 1974: 137–39). But there is clearly no direct link between silence and maleness in all cultures. Many western cultures value direct, public speech. A number of studies of conversation (see Coates 1993: 115 for a brief overview) have shown that in western societies, public speech tends to be dominated by men. Although the speech behaviors typical of Malagasy males and females are very different from those of much of western society, note that in both instances it is the male norms that are more highly valued by the community.

One pattern that has repeatedly been found, at least in studies of western cultures, is that women tend to use more prestige (standard) variants than men, and listeners even expect female speech to be more like that of the middle class and male speech to be more like that of the working class. For example, a study in Norwich, England (Trudgill 1974), showed that members of the middle class and women were more likely to use standard verb forms like *running* (with word-final [ŋ]), as opposed to nonstandard forms like *runnin'* (with word-final [ɪn]). This is not to say that the use of forms like *running* was limited only to women or only to the middle class, but rather that Norwich women, on average, used these forms more frequently than men. A similar pattern occurred in the speech of working-class adolescents in Sydney, Australia. Boys were more likely than girls to use nonstandard syntactic features such as multiple negation, for example, *they don't say nothing,* and nonstandard past tense forms, for example, *he woke up an' seen something* (Eisikovits 1988: 37–40).

John Edwards (1979) demonstrated the role of gender in perception in a study conducted in Dublin, Ireland, in which adults were asked to listen to recordings of preadolescent children, some of whom were from working-class families and some of whom were from middle-class families. The adults were then asked to identify the gender of each child. The adults had few problems identifying the working-class boys as boys and the middle-class girls as girls, but they did much worse identifying the middle-class boys and the working-class girls, more than doubling their number of errors. To these listeners, the speech of middle-class boys was perceived as girl-like, and the speech of working-class girls was perceived as boy-like.

A number of different hypotheses have been proposed to explain why this correlation between females and standard language should exist. Most explanations are again tied not to anything inherent about being male or female, but rather to the social roles that women and men play. For example, because women are often considered inferior to men in terms of social status, women may make more of an effort to imitate the prestigious and more standardized language of the social classes above them, in order to become more prestigious themselves. In addition, it has been suggested that women, being the primary caretakers for children in many societies, may try to expose their children to prestige dialects in order to improve the children's chances of success. And, of course, the social roles that women have can influence how the other factors we have mentioned affect their speech. For example, a study by Patricia Nichols (1983) of an African-American community in Georgetown County, South Carolina, looked at the variable use of Standard American English, African-American English, and a local English Creole known as Gullah. An analysis of the **social networks** of the island residents helped to explain their linguistic behavior. The men, both young and old, generally take construction jobs, which require little education but pay well. On the job the men interact a great deal with each other—their co-workers are their friends, family, and neighbors—and this reinforces both Gullah language norms and their group identity as Gullah speakers. Older women have primarily worked as farm day laborers or maids, jobs in which interaction is also primarily with co-workers. The younger women, on the other hand, are taking up less lucrative, service-related jobs associated with the tourist industry. As sales clerks, mail carriers, and elementary school teachers, young women need to have a higher level of education, and they have a great deal of interaction with speakers of standard English. So the end result made it look as if there were clear effects of gender and age (men and older women using more nonstandard forms, younger women using more standard forms), but these effects are clearly the combined result of the economic opportunities afforded to women versus men.

It is difficult to precisely determine the roles of prestige, economics, age, and so on, in shaping the language of women and men. Eckert and McConnell-Ginet (1992) suggest that limiting the scope of inquiry to isolated factors like these will prove unfruitful. They propose centering language and gender research on **communities of practice.** By their definition, a community of practice is "an aggregate of people who come together around mutual engagement in an endeavor" (p. 464). So a community of practice may be a softball team, a family sharing a meal, participants in a linguistics classroom, an election campaign team, the office staff in a workplace, and so on. An individual belongs to any number of overlapping communities of practice, and in each of them she or he will construct a gendered identity differently. For example, an outspoken leader of the local labor union may be quite docile as a student in night school. Focusing on local communities of practice may allow researchers to better understand the complex nature of gender as it is continually being redefined by individual and group behaviors. This, in turn, can enlighten our understanding of the role of gender in the construction of language in the community and the role of language in the construction of gender in the community.

10.4.5 Ethnic Variation

The last factor that we are going to talk about here is ethnicity, a factor that influences variation in multi-ethnic communities. Part of the reason for this is that ethnic groups are often associated with particular languages that represent the group's heritage and culture; pronunciations, words, and constructions from such a language may influence how the group speaks the standard language variety of the country or region they live in. Compounded with this is again the factor of language and identity, which will be discussed more extensively in File 13.1: an ethnic group may want to particularly associate themselves with an ethnicity or with the group, or distance themselves from other ethnicities and groups through their use of language. As with any language varieties, however, it is important to remember that no variety can be linguistically superior or inferior to any other.

It is also important to realize that just as there is nothing inherent about southeastern Pennsylvania that makes speakers in the region use German-influenced language, there is nothing inherent about any ethnic group that causes members of the group to speak one way as opposed to another. There are plenty of people who belong to a particular ethnic group who do not speak a dialect associated with that ethnicity, and there are plenty of people who are not associated with a particular ethnicity who nonetheless speak a dialect associated with it. As discussed in the files on language acquisition (Chapter 8), the language a person speaks is not in any way predestined but is instead determined by the language that she is exposed to. In addition, the other factors discussed in this file, as well as regional factors, can lead to further differentiation within ethnic varieties, such that, for example, a younger working-class female Pennsylvania German speaker may use somewhat different phonological and lexical features when her speech is compared to that of an older male middle-class speaker of the same ethnic group. Furthermore, no individual speaker of an ethnic variety speaks the same way all the time. Rather, we all vary our speech depending on style and context.

a. African-American English (AAE). There are several varieties of English that have been particularly influenced by ethnicity in the United States and that have been the subject of much linguistic study. One of these is African-American English (AAE), which is really itself a cover term used by linguists to refer to a continuum of varieties, spoken primarily by and among African Americans, whose features may be very similar to or very different from Standard American English (depending on which end of the continuum you consider). AAE comes from a variety of different sources; although it is clearly a dialect of American English, many of its features seem to come from southern dialects and from many different West African languages, because of the origins of AAE as being spoken by West Africans brought to the southern United States as part of the slave trade.

In terms of phonological features, there are several which distinguish AAE from SAE. First, there is the process by which diphthongs get reduced to monophthongs word-finally or before voiced consonants. Through this process, known as monophthongization, words such as *now* and *side,* which are typically pronounced as [naʊ] and [saɪd] in SAE, are pronounced as [nɑː] and [sɑːd] in AAE, while other words such as *time* (pronounced as [tʰaɪm] in SAE) are pronounced as [tʰaːm] in AAE. Monophthongization before voiceless consonants, such as *kite* pronounced as [kʰɑːt] or *like* as [lɑːk] also occurs in AAE, but is found less frequently. These patterns of monophthongization provide some evidence demonstrating the dialectal roots of AAE, as they are also found in some varieties of Southern speech (see Section 10.3.6) (Wolfram and Schilling-Estes 2005).

A second process that is quite prevalent in AAE is word-final consonant cluster reduction, when the following word begins with a consonant. This same process is found in some varieties of SAE. Via this process, words such as *cold cuts* [kʰoʊld kʰʌts] and *best kind* [bɛst kʰaɪnd] are pronounced as [kʰoʊl kʰʌts] and [bɛs kʰaɪnd]. AAE differs from SAE here, however, in that it is also possible to reduce word-final consonant clusters when the following word begins with a vowel. For instance, phrases such as *cold eggs* [kʰoʊld ɛgz] and *best arm* [bɛst ɑɪm] are often pronounced [kʰoʊl ɛgz] and [bɛs ɑɪm] in AAE. In SAE, the past tense is formed by the addition of a suffix, [t], [d], or [əd], depending on the final sound of the verb base. If the base ends in a consonant, the addition of the past tense suffix may create a consonant cluster. Word-final consonant clusters that are created by the addition of the past tense suffix are also subject to deletion in AAE. Thus, *burned my hand* [bɹ̩nd maɪ hænd] in SAE becomes [bɹ̩n maɪ hæn] in AAE, while *messed up* [mɛst ʌp] in SAE is pronounced [mɛs ʌp] in AAE. The fact that word-final past tense suffixes can be deleted in these environments may give AAE the appearance of lacking a past tense suffix. However, past tense suffixes that do not form consonant clusters are not deleted by this phonological process. Thus, words such as *hated* and *shouted* are pronounced [heɪɾəd] and [ʃaʊɾəd] in AAE, just as they are in SAE (Green 2004).

Besides these phonological processes, AAE is typified by several morpho-syntactic processes that distinguish it from SAE. One is the absence of the third-person singular suffix -*s,* as in *He need to get a book from the shelf,* or *She want us to pass the papers to the front* (Rickford 1998). Another is **multiple negation,** which is also found in Appalachian speech (as discussed in Section 10.3.7) and is another process providing evidence for AAE's dialectal roots (Wolfram and Schilling-Estes 2005). A third is **copula absence**—the absence of inflected present tense forms of *to be* in sentences where other varieties of English would use an inflected form, as in the sentence *John going to the store.* In SAE, the equivalent sentence is *John is going to the store* (Rickford 1998). Copula absence is possible with all pronominal cases except first-person singular, such that **I going to store* is ungrammatical. Copula absence is a feature of some West African languages, so here we have a feature providing some evidence of AAE's West African roots. A fourth feature that differentiates AAE from SAE morpho-syntactically is the use of **habitual** *be.* Where SAE varieties use adverbials such as *always* or *usually* to express habituality, AAE can employ an uninflected form of *be* to communicate that a state or activity is habitual or repeatable, and the use of *be* is all that is needed to indicate this property. Thus, in AAE, a speaker can say *The coffee be cold,* whereas in SAE, a speaker would say *The coffee is always cold* (Green 2004).

   b. Chicano English. Another prevalent ethnic dialect in the United States is Chicano English. Chicano English is a cover term for those varieties of English often spoken by second- or third-generation speakers of Mexican descent in the United States. As with AAE, Chicano English is considered a dialect of English, as most speakers are native speakers of English. In fact, in many cases, these speakers actually have little or no fluency in Spanish (Fought 2006). On occasions when Spanish words or phrases are used by these speakers, they are used to symbolically reference Latino and Hispanic cultural heritage and identity. This process is also known as **emblematic language** use. Thus, Chicano English is different from Spanglish (literally, Spanish-English), the mixed-language variety spoken by first- or second-generation speakers of Latino or Hispanic descent who use a mixture of Spanish and English, switching their use between languages in daily speech (Silvia-Corvalán 2004).

   Historically, Chicano English traces its roots to varieties of Spanish spoken by immigrant groups from Mexico. Thus, most of the phonological, syntactic, and lexical features that distinguish Chicano English from other dialects of English trace their roots initially to Spanish (Fought 2006). One feature is that /oʊ/ is typically pronounced as the monophthong [o] rather than as the diphthong [oʊ], as in most varieties of SAE, although this is not universally true for all varieties of Chicano English (Thomas 2001). Another feature showing the Spanish influence is that /ɪ/, when it precedes [ŋ], as in *going* or *walking,* is pronounced [i], rather than [ɪ] as in SAE (Fought 2006). A third feature which demonstrates the influence of Spanish is that [ɑ] and [ɔ] are usually pronounced as homophones, making the Chicano English pronunciation similar to those found in the New England and Western dialects of English (Thomas 2001). All of these vowel patterns are influenced by the fact that Spanish has only five vowels, [i e a o u], none of which are diphthongs.

   Syntactically, Chicano English is typified by several features that also serve to distinguish it as a unique dialect of English. One feature is the use of past participle verb forms in contexts where SAE speakers would use simple past tense forms, particularly in cases where *have* is normally contracted in SAE. Thus, in Chicano English, a speaker might say *I seen Ramon talking to Sally in her yard,* where speakers of SAE would say *I've seen Ramon talking to Sally in her yard* (Penfield and Ornstein-Galicia 1985). Another feature is the use of embedded question inversion involving *wh-* forms, as in the sentence *I ask myself what would I do without Lucy's help.* In SAE, a speaker would say *I ask myself what I would do* to mean the same thing (Duchnowski 1999). A third feature is the placement of noun phrases that typically occur in the object position of a sentence, but are also the topic of that sentence, at the beginning of the sentence, a process known as **topicalization.** Thus, in Chicano English, a speaker might say *To talk about myself; it's easy for me,* whereas a speaker of SAE would say *It's easy for me to talk about myself.* The use of topicalization appears to be Spanish influenced, as this is the preferred syntactic structure for these types of sentences in Standard Mexican Spanish (Penfield and Ornstein-Galicia 1985).

   In terms of lexical variation, Chicano English makes use of a variety of words found in Standard Mexican Spanish. However, as discussed above, the use of these words is often limited to symbolic contexts, either to reflect cultural heritage or to signify cultural identity. For example, many speakers may generically refer to their grandfather as *abuelo,* while *ándale* might be used to communicate that someone should move more quickly (Fought 2006). In addition, Chicano English youth in California have been reported to use taboo Spanish words and slang as a way of signaling "toughness" or being "street savvy" (Mendoza-Denton 1997; Public Broadcasting System 2005).

c. Lumbee English. A third ethnically distinct dialect of American English is that of the Lumbee Indians, the largest Native American group east of the Mississippi River. Although members of the Lumbee tribe live throughout the United States, today the largest concentration lives in Robeson County, North Carolina (Wolfram 2006). The historical origins of the Lumbee are not known, as records pertaining to their ancestors were never kept, and several major families of Native American tribes, including the Algonquian, Iroquoian, and Siouan, each of which speak distinct languages, have populated the area in colonial times. Most scholars believe that the Lumbee descend from an amalgam of these tribes, and as the Lumbee were reported to be speaking English by the early 1700s, there are no linguistic records by which to trace a historical Lumbee language (Wolfram et al. 2002).

Although the Lumbee have had difficulty tracing their historical roots, they are unified by a common dialect, which is typified by a unique set of linguistic features that, when considered together, mark their speech as distinctive from other varieties of English. One phonetic characteristic of Lumbee speech is the pronunciation of /aɪ/, pronounced as [aɪ] in SAE, as [ɔɪ]. Hence, *ride* is pronounced [ɹɔɪd] as opposed to [ɹaɪd], as in SAE, while *time* is pronounced [tʰɔɪm] as opposed to [tʰaɪm] (Wolfram and Dannenberg, 1999). Another characteristic is the pronunciation of *tobacco* as *baccer* and *potato* as *tater,* with a word-final [ɪ] as well as having only two (instead of three) syllables, two features that trace their origins to Appalachian speech (Wolfram 2006).

In regard to morphology and syntax, Lumbee speech is also marked by features unique to the dialect. One is the use of *weren't* as the first-person past tense form of the verb *to be,* as in the sentence *I weren't over there last night,* where speakers of SAE would use *wasn't* (Wolfram and Dannenberg 1999). Another salient feature of Lumbee English is the use of finite *be* with an -*s* inflection in contexts where speakers of SAE would use *is* or *are,* as in the sentences *John bes playing right now* or *the cats bes playing in the yard.* Like the use of habitual *be* in AAE, *bes* can also be used to indicate a habitual or recurring activity, as in *John bes tired after work* or *The cats usually bes playing in the yard.* In these sentences, speakers of SAE would use *is* or *are* and the adverbial *usually* or *always,* as in *John is usually tired after work* or *The cats usually are playing in the yard* to mean the same thing (Wolfram 2006).

Beyond these phonetic and syntactic features, Lumbee English is also typified by unique lexical items. For example, the word *ellick* is used as the term to describe what other dialects would call *coffee with cream and sugar,* while *yerker* is used as the term to describe a mischievous child (Wolfram et al. 2002). Other unique terms include *brickhouse* to describe someone who is of high social status, *buddyrow* as a commonly used word for 'friend,' and *toten* as a synonym for the word *ghost* (Wolfram 2006).

Practice

File 10.1—Language Varieties

Exercises

1. Suppose that you have a very close relationship with someone whom you plan to marry. How would you introduce your fiancé(e) to the following people under the following circumstances?

    a. your grandmother, at a family dinner
    b. your best friend from high school, at a picnic
    c. the dean of your college, at a reception for a visiting scholar
    d. a group of eight-year-olds in a Saturday morning class you've been working with

    See how many differences you can find in the forms of introduction you can come up with. Then compare your list with a friend's to determine if they differ significantly.

2. The following are some popular myths about slang. See if you can explain what about them is misconceived, especially from the viewpoint established in the discussion on slang in File 10.1.

    a. Slang is bad and degrades the user and the language itself.
    b. Only young people use slang.
    c. There are languages that have no slang.

3. Refer to the *For Better or For Worse* cartoon at the beginning of this chapter. Do you think that April would use the words *foob* and *prag* in a school essay? Why or why not?

4. To give you an idea of the richness and variety of slang, we give below a collection of terms for getting or being inebriated. As you look through this list, compare your own current slang usage with that reported here. Which terms are new to you? Can you see how they may have originated? Are there terms here that you know as meaning something else? If so, which ones are they and what do they mean? Why do you suppose there are so many different terms for this activity?

get wasted	loose
get stiff	fried
snockered	zoned
crocked	ripped
slushed	buzzed
stoned	tanked
shit-faced	lubered
plowed	rimmed

    (cont.)

hazed	aced
z'd	pound a few
blasted	catch a cold
plastered	pissed
loaded	toasted

Discussion Questions

5. An American was hitch-hiking in Italy and got picked up by an Italian truck driver. The American spoke no Italian but was fluent in Spanish. He and the truck driver (who spoke no English or Spanish) had a lively conversation for two hours: the American was speaking Spanish, and the truck driver was speaking Italian. At the end of the trip, the truck driver asked the American which dialect of Italian he was speaking. What does this tell you about the difference between the dialects of Spanish and Italian spoken by these two people as language varieties?

6. Consider the following:

At the turn of the century, the form *ain't* was prestigious among many upper middle class English speakers in southern England. Today, however, its use is considered non-standard or at best appropriate only for casual conversation.

In the United States "dropped *r*'s" in words like *car, father,* and *bark* are perceived as features of nonstandard speech. In Britain, however, "dropped *r*'s" are characteristic of Received Pronunciation and are thus considered part of the prestige dialect.

What do these two examples tell us about standard and nonstandard features? Are they defined on linguistic or social grounds? Explain your answer.

7. What is the significance of having a standard dialect in every language?

8. How might evaluations we make about language as "good" or "bad" help to preserve and perpetuate social stereotypes and biases?

Activities

9. Make up your own list of jargon by examining the terms and expressions that are associated with your major (or hobby or whatever). Compare your list with that of someone else in your major (or hobby or whatever) and with someone not in that group. Does the in-group/out-group designation applied to slang hold here?

File 10.2—Variation at Different Levels of Linguistic Structure
Exercises

10. Refer to the *For Better or For Worse* cartoon at the beginning of this chapter. What level of linguistic structure does April's use of the words *foob* and *prag* fall under? Explain your answer.

11. Look at the pictures below of two different variants of the ASL word *about*. What type of variation do these pictures illustrate; that is, what level of linguistic structure is relevant here? Explain your answer.

ABOUT variants in ASL:

Reproduced by permission of Gallaudet College Press, from Shroyer and Shroyer, *Signs across America* (1984), p. 3.

12. For each example below, identify the level of linguistic structure at which the variation exists.

P = Phonetic
Ph = Phonological
M = Morphological
S = Syntactic
Sm = Semantic

_____ Some Caribbean English dialects do not have the sounds [θ] or [ð]; instead the sounds [t] and [d], respectively, are substituted, for example, *both* [bout], *there* [dɛr].

_____ Many dialects of English have multiple negation, as in *I didn't see nobody take no pictures.*

_____ Many American dialects have the mid back lax vowel [ɔ]. However, this vowel is produced very differently in different dialects—some are more rounded, some less so; some are higher or lower than others.

_____ Names differ from place to place to refer to an insect that glows in the dark, including *firefly, lightning bug, glowworm,* and *fire bug.*

_____ Some African-American English dialects do not mark the third-person singular present tense with a suffix, for example, *he kiss, she see, it jump.*

_____ In some southern and midwestern dialects of American English, there is no distinction between [ɪ] and [ɛ] before nasals; only [ɪ] occurs. So for the words *pen* and *pin,* which are pronounced [pɛn] and [pɪn], respectively, in many other American English dialects, the pronunciation is [pɪn] for both words.

13. Pronunciation

Following is a list of words that have different pronunciations in different dialects. Circle the letter corresponding to the pronunciation you use in **relaxed, casual conversation.** If you use more than one, circle all the appropriate letters. If you use an entirely different pronunciation, indicate your pronunciation in the blank at the right. Finally, if you think there is a distinction among the choices between a standard and a nonstandard pronunciation, X out the letter corresponding to the one you consider to be standard.

a. *nucleus:* (a) [nukjələs] (b) [nukliəs]   a   b   _____

b. *washing:* (a) [wɔɹʃɪŋ] (b) [waʃɪŋ]   a   b   _____

c. *fire:* the vowel is (a) [aɪ] (b) [a]   a   b   _____

d. *tomato:* the second vowel is (a) [eɪ] (b) [a]   a   b   _____

e. *where:* begins with (a) [ʍ] (b) [w]   a   b   _____

f. *often:* (a) [afn̩] (b) [aftn̩]   a   b   _____

g. *greasy:* (a) [gɹisi] (b) [gɹizi]   a   b   _____

h. *either:* (a) [iðɹ̩] (b) [aɪðɹ̩]   a   b   _____

i. *Columbus:* (a) [kələʌmbəs] (b) [klʌmbəs]   a   b   _____

j. *police:* stressed on (a) 1st syllable (b) 2nd syllable   a   b   _____

14. Syntax

The sentences below, based on a questionnaire used by William Labov, were all produced by some speaker of English. Go through the list of sentences and check, for each sentence, whether you think it is:

- natural for you to use in casual conversation;
- something that some people would use but others wouldn't;
- something that only a nonnative speaker would say.

This exercise is intended to be **descriptive**, not **prescriptive**. The point is not whether you think the sentences are "correct" or "incorrect," "good" or "bad."

	Natural	Some	Non-native
a. The dog is falled asleep.	_____	_____	_____
b. Everyone opened their books.	_____	_____	_____
c. My shirt needs cleaned.	_____	_____	_____
d. Ever since he lost his job, he be sleepin' all day long.	_____	_____	_____
e. You shouldn't ought to put salt in your coffee.	_____	_____	_____
f. You usually go to the one you want, but me never.	_____	_____	_____
g. You can see the cops like they're grabbing kids left and right.	_____	_____	_____
h. He didn't have no book.	_____	_____	_____
i. I want for you to go home.	_____	_____	_____
j. Me and Sally played all afternoon.	_____	_____	_____
k. Noodles, I can't stand in chicken soup.	_____	_____	_____
l. There's nobody can beat her at telling stories.	_____	_____	_____
m. Of whom are you speaking?	_____	_____	_____
n. Them tomato plants won't live.	_____	_____	_____
o. So don't I.	_____	_____	_____

15. Vocabulary

Here are some sentences containing words and idioms that differ from dialect to dialect. Circle the letter corresponding to the expression you use. If you ordinarily use more than one, circle all the appropriate letters. If you use an entirely different word or idiom, write it in the blank at the right.

a. A large open metal container for water is a (a) bucket (b) pail. _____

b. To carry groceries, you put them in a paper (a) bag (b) sack (c) poke. _____

c. Window coverings on rollers are (a) blinds (b) shades (c) roller shades (d) window shades (e) curtains. _____

d. Pepsi-Cola, Coca-Cola, and Seven-Up are all kinds of (a) soda (b) pop (c) coke (d) soft drinks (e) soda pop (f) tonic. _____

e. On summer nights when we were kids, we used to try to catch (a) fireflies (b) lightning bugs (c) fire bugs (d) glow worms. _____

f. If you go to a popular film, you may have to stand (a) on line (b) in line. _____

g. If your living room is messy, before company comes you (a) straighten it up (b) red it up (c) ret it up (d) clean it up. _____

h. If you're talking to a group of friends, you call them (a) you guys (b) you all (c) y'all (d) youse guys (e) you'ns. _____

i. It's now (a) a quarter of 5 (b) a quarter to 5 (c) a quarter 'til 5. _____

j. The lifeguard (a) dove (b) dived into the swimming pool. _____

Discussion Questions

16. Compare your responses in Exercises 13, 14, and 15 with others in the class. What are some of the factors that may influence the choice of one form over another? (For example, *My shirt needs cleaned* is more typical of midwestern speech. It is, therefore, influenced by region.)

Activities

17. Take Exercises 13, 14, and 15 and make photocopies of them. Survey a broad group of people (friends, family, neighbors, co-workers), and collect their answers to these same questions. Can you find any patterns to the responses, based on any of the factors discussed in Files 10.3 and 10.4?

File 10.3—Factors Influencing Variation: Regional and Geographic Factors

Exercises

18. i. Consider the following data illustrating the *pin/pen* merger common in Southern speech patterns. Notice that [ɪ] and [ɛ] are not merged to [ɪ] in all contexts. Identify the phonetic environment that conditions the merger.

Word	Southern English	Standard English
pin	[pɪn]	[pɪn]
pen	[pɪn]	[pɛn]
lit	[lɪt]	[lɪt]
let	[lɛt]	[lɛt]
Nick	[nɪk]	[nɪk]
neck	[nɛk]	[nɛk]
tin	[tɪn]	[tɪn]
ten	[tɪn]	[tɛn]

(cont.)

ii. Based on your analysis in (i), indicate whether each of the following words would be pronounced with [ɪ] or with [ɛ] in these dialects: *lid, led, kin, Ken, pick, peck, bin, Ben*.

Discussion Questions

19. If you live in the United States, which dialect area does your community fall into? Are the descriptions given for that area accurate for the dialect you hear around you? Which things are inaccurate? Remember, these are rather broad generalizations, and every individual has his own idiolect.

20. If your dialect area was not described in the description of the United States, try to describe it. Although it may be hard to identify characteristics unique to your dialect if you are not familiar with other dialects for comparison purposes, use the descriptions here as a starting point. For example, what do people in your area call a sweetened carbonated beverage? Can you use the morpho-syntactic constructions listed for the various dialect areas? Do your pronunciations match the ones given?

Activities

21. Go to the Harvard Dialect Survey maps for the words *merry, marry,* and *Mary* by going to the Web site http://cfprod01.imt.uwm.edu/Dept/FLL/linguistics/dialect/maps.html and clicking on question 15. Where do you see the most variation in pronunciation? Why do you think this would be a region of high variation? Explore other maps—do you see similar amounts of high variation for this same area for other questions?

22. Investigate English dialects as spoken in England by going to the Web site http://www.collectbritain.co.uk/collections/dialects/ and clicking on one of the samples. Identify as many features (phonetic, morpho-syntactic, or lexical) as you can that differ from your own dialect.

23. Go to the activity "Where is the speaker from?" (designed by Cynthia Clopper and David Pisoni) on the "Do you speak American?" Web site at http://www.pbs.org/speak/seatosea/americanvarieties/map/map.html. Listen to the speech samples and try to place them in the correct regions. How accurate are you? Which samples are easiest to identify? Which are hardest? Why do you think this is? Compare your answers with those of other people in your class. Do all of you have trouble with the same speakers? How does your personal background influence your ability to categorize each sample?

File 10.4—Factors Influencing Variation: Social Factors

Exercises

24. Refer to the *For Better or For Worse* cartoon at the beginning of this chapter. Why do you think April's mother doesn't know the words *foob* and *prag?* Why do you think April's social group has words that her mother's group doesn't know? In addition to these words, what other linguistic elements does April use in the strip that might be associated with her group and not with her mother's?

25. In Columbus, Ohio, there are two variants of the pronunciation of /stɹ/ clusters at the beginnings of words like *street:* [stɹ] and [ʃtɹ]. David Durian conducted a study in 2004 about the distribution of the two pronunciations, and found the following results:

	Gender			Age (in 15-year groupings)		
	Male	**Female**		**15–30**	**35–50**	**55–70**
[stɹ]	84%	68%	[stɹ]	61%	71%	91%
[ʃtɹ]	16%	32%	[ʃtɹ]	39%	29%	9%

Based on the data above, when both gender and age are considered together as social factors affecting the use of the vernacular pronunciation [ʃtɹ], which gender/age group uses this pronunciation the most? Which gender/age group uses it the least? Based on the explanations provided for age and gender in this file, why do you think these were the patterns of language use Durian observed?

26. As in many dialects of English, there is variation in Norwich, England, in the pronunciation of the ending *–ing*. Some speakers say [ɪŋ] while others say [ɪn]. In 1974, Peter Trudgill studied this variation and how it was linked to both gender and speech style, collecting the following data:

	Gender			Speech Style		
	Male	**Female**		**Formal**	**Informal**	**Casual**
[ɪŋ]	39%	51%	[ɪŋ]	71%	45%	33%
[ɪn]	61%	49%	[ɪn]	29%	55%	67%

Based on the data above, when both gender and speech style are considered together as social and linguistic factors affecting the use of the vernacular pronunciation [ɪn], what are the speech style and gender of the speakers who use this pronunciation the most? What are the speech style and the gender of the speakers who use this pronunciation the least? Based on the explanations provided for gender in File 10.4, as well as speech style in File 10.1, why do you think these were the patterns of language use Trudgill observed?

27. In a study on /ɹ/-lessness (see discussion in File 10.4) among African-American speakers in Detroit, Michigan, in 1969, Walt Wolfram collected the following data:

	Socioeconomic Class			
	Upper-Middle	**Lower-Middle**	**Upper-Working**	**Lower-Working**
no [ɹ]	21%	39%	61%	71%
with [ɹ]	79%	61%	39%	29%

Based on the data above, which socioeconomic class group used the "no [ɹ]" pronunciation most often? Which group used it least often? Based on what you learned about overt and covert prestige (Section 10.1.4), speaker orientations to standard and nonstandard speech (Section 10.1.4), and variation based on socioeconomic class (Section 10.2.2), hypothesize a reasonable explanation for why these were the patterns of pronunciation that Wolfram found.

Discussion Questions

28. **i.** In Section 10.4.4, the concept of "communities of practice" is discussed in relationship to issues involving language variation and gender. However, the concept is one that can be applied to all manner of social behavior and the linguistic behavior of particular groups. Using the discussion of gender as a starting point, think of other groups whose linguistic behavior sets them apart as a community of practice.

    ii. Now, choose one of these groups and answer the following questions: What are the social and linguistic characteristics of the group? How does the language use of the group members signal their membership in the group? Are there other social practices which the members of the group engage in that mark their identity as members of the group? What are these practices, and how do they mark membership in the group?

29. What other ethnic groups, besides the ones discussed in Section 10.4.5, can you think of whose use of English may be marked as distinctive, along the lines of the ones discussed in this section? Choose one of these groups and try to determine two or three phonological and lexical features that distinguish the speech of this group. Are there any syntactic features you can think of that mark this group as distinctive? Once you have determined these linguistic factors, try to think of a social or historical explanation that might help us to determine why these linguistic features are particular to this group.

Activities

30. In many regional and social dialects of English, the consonant cluster /stɹ/, as in the words *street, straight,* or *strip,* undergoes a form of allophonic variation in which the cluster-initial /s/ can be pronounced in two different ways, either as [s] or as [ʃ]. Hence, in these dialects, *strip* can be pronounced either with the standard variant, as [stɹɪp], or with the vernacular variant, as [ʃtɹɪp].

    However, the story of /stɹ/ is more complicated than this, being sensitive to social variation, such that its use can be affected by each of the social factors discussed in this file (as we saw in Exercise 24). For this activity, your goal is to determine how /stɹ/-cluster variation differs by two of these social factors. For example, you may wish to investigate how people from different parts of the country differ in their use of these variants, as well as how younger speakers versus older speakers vary their use.

    In order to collect data, you will need to develop a question that you can use to obtain different /stɹ/ pronunciations from speakers. For example, to get a speaker to say the word *street,* you could ask them for directions to a nearby store that is located on a roadway that contains the word *street* as a part of its name (for instance, *Johnson Street*).

    To collect enough data to make meaningful conclusions regarding /stɹ/, we recommend that you collect data from at least ten people, dividing up your informants so that you obtain data from an equal number of people in each of your groups. Then share your data with three other students in your class, so that, combined, you can look at the language use patterns of 40 speakers. Finally, ask yourself the following questions: How does each groups use of /stɹ/ differ from each other? How are the patterns of use the same? Why do you think the patterns of use you observed turned out the way they did?

Further Readings

Bonvillain, N. (1997). Cross-cultural studies of language and gender. In *Language, culture, and communication: The meaning of messages* (pp. 194–216). Upper Saddle River, NJ: Prentice Hall.

Penfield, J., & Ornstein-Galicia, J. (1985). *Chicano English: An ethnic contact dialect.* Amsterdam: John Benjamins.

Rickford, J. (1998). *African-American Vernacular English.* Oxford: Blackwell.

Shroyer, E. H., & Shroyer, S. P. (1984). *Signs across America: A look at regional differences in American Sign Language.* Washington, DC: Gallaudet College Press.

Thorne, B., Kramarae, C., & Henley, N. (Eds.). (1983). *Language, gender, and society.* Rowley, MA: Newbury House.

Wolfram, W., & Schilling-Estes, N. (2005). *American English* (2nd ed.). Oxford: Blackwell.

Wolfram, W., & Ward, B. (Eds.). (2006). *American voices: How dialects differ from coast to coast.* Oxford: Blackwell.

CHAPTER

11

Language Contact

FILE 11.0

What Is Language Contact?

In **language contact** situations, two or more distinct languages or dialects come in to contact with each other either through direct social interaction of the speakers or indirectly through education or literature. Language contact situations differ in the intensity of contact, the kind of contact, and the outcomes of the contact, and such situations often result in changes to one or both of the languages involved. The major types of contact-induced change include **borrowing** and **native language** (L1) **interference,** also known as **transfer** and **substrate influence.** Borrowing usually involves the transfer of lexical items or even structural properties from one language to another. Other outcomes of contact include **language convergence** (where languages in contact become more alike), **language shift** (where one language has fewer and fewer speakers due to pressure from a dominant language), **language death** (where a language has no more speakers left), **code-switching** between the two languages, and the creation of contact languages such as **bilingual mixed languages, pidgins,** and **creoles.** The prestige and power relationships between speakers of the languages involved in contact situations affect the direction of influence and the outcome of the contact situation.

Contents

minority language; gives reasons why and how languages become endangered; and addresses whether dead languages can be revived.

11.7   Case Studies in Language Contact
Presents case studies of the contact situations in the Indian village of Kupwar and of Deitsch (Pennsylvania German), spoken in the Midwestern United States.

11.8   Practice
Provides exercises, discussion questions, and activities related to language contact.

Language Contact

11.1.1 Languages in Contact

Language contact involves the contact of two or more distinct languages either indirectly through the written form and other media, or directly through social contact between speakers. An example of the former is the contact between modern English and many other languages around the world: English is learned as a second language all over the world, frequently without there being any social contact between native speakers of English and the second-language learners. This kind of language contact is becoming more common due to globalization. The more usual type of contact historically, however, involves direct social contact between speakers, since languages and their speakers do not exist in isolation but rather in social settings. Thus, when we talk about language contact we are not actually talking about the contact of languages, but rather the contact of people who speak the languages.

Languages are continually coming into contact with other languages, creating a variety of contact situations, each with a potentially different result. Such contact may be caused by trade, conquest, migration, or other factors. Two thousand years ago, the expansion of the Roman Empire throughout Europe led to contact between Latin and a variety of local languages, many of which did not survive the contact—that is, they were replaced by Latin, and, as a result, people no longer spoke the local languages. Over one thousand years ago, the version of Latin spoken in the Iberian Peninsula (which was developing into what we now call Spanish and Portuguese) came into contact with Arabic during Arabic rule. In this case, Spanish, Portuguese, and Arabic all survived, but we can identify many influences that they had on each other. In the past century, the arrival of immigrants from Mexico, Cuba, and other Latin American countries to the United States has resulted in close contact between Spanish and American English; we will have to wait and see what the outcome of this contact situation will be.

Contact situations can be described in terms of their influence on the linguistic systems (i.e., the grammars), the social relationships of the speakers in contact, and the linguistic outcome of the contact. We will consider each of these in turn below.

11.1.2 Levels of Borrowing

In language contact situations, the linguistic systems involved are often influenced by **borrowing,** the adoption by one language of linguistic elements from another language. Borrowing can be **lexical** (i.e., the borrowing of words and phrases) or **structural** (i.e., the borrowing of phonological, morphological, or syntactic structures).

Lexical borrowing is the adoption of individual words into one language from another language. These words are commonly referred to as **loans** or **loanwords.** Examples in American English include the words *ballet* and *chaise* from French, *macho* and *taco* from Spanish, *pizza* and *spaghetti* from Italian, *zeitgeist* and *sauerkraut* from German, and *skunk* and *wigwam* from Algonquian. The pronunciation of such borrowings is adapted to English phonology, illustrating the fact that the effects of borrowing rarely enter the domain of phonological structure. For example, most English speakers pronounce the word *burrito* as [bɹiɾoʊ] (adapted to English phonology) instead of the typical Spanish pronunciation [burito].

Interestingly, there are certain types of words that do not tend to get borrowed between languages. These fall into two main categories: "core" vocabulary and grammatical function words. Core vocabulary consists of the words for basic items that most societies have words for: things like body parts (*head, arm, leg*), familial relations (*mother, sister, uncle*), or basic environmental entities (*sun, moon, water*). These tend not to be borrowed because there is usually no need: if a language exists, it usually already has these words because they are so universal in nature, and there is no reason it would need to adopt equivalent words from another language. On the other hand, words for new kinds of foods or animals (*squash, bratwurst, tequila, vodka, chipmunk, opossum*, etc.), cultural items (*sacrament, sombrero, pajama, mosque, karaoke*, etc.), or political terms (*bailiff, lieutenant, propaganda, democracy, czar*, etc.) are often borrowed because one language had no need for the terms until they were introduced by the other language's culture and society. Similarly, grammatical function words like *a, the, one, my, you, in, through, by, is*, and so on, do not tend to get borrowed from one language to another because most languages already have such words. Although both core vocabulary and function words are occasionally borrowed, in most cases, the trend is for languages to borrow only words for things they do not have, as opposed to replace words they already have.

In addition to single lexical items, whole phrases and idiomatic expressions can be borrowed. Examples include English *it goes without saying* from French *il va sans dire*, German *Kettenraucher* from English *chain smoker*, and English *worldview* from German *Weltanschauung*. Phrases such as these, acquired through a word-for-word translation into native morphemes, are called **loan translations** or **calques**. More on English borrowings will be discussed in File 11.2.

Phonological borrowing occurs when a language adopts new sounds or phonological rules from a language with which it is in contact. In many cases, this comes about through the borrowing of words. For example, [ʒ] was introduced into English from French via French loanwords like *rouge, leisure, measure*, and *prestige*. Similarly, educated Muslim speakers of Urdu have borrowed the Arabic sounds [z] and [ʔ]. Phonological borrowing is not limited to sounds, however; for example, phonological rules that convert root-final [k] to [s] in word pairs like *electric/electricity* and [t] to [ʃ] in word pairs like *nominate/nomination* were borrowed into English from French.

Morphological borrowing is the adoption of morphological elements by one language under the influence of another language. Words are often borrowed along with an attached affix, which then may become part of the morphological system of the language that borrowed it. For example, for many of the words English has borrowed from Latin, the Latin plural form has been maintained. For example, the plural of *colloquium* is *colloquia* for most speakers, not *colloquiums*. Similarly, Albanian has maintained the Turkish form of the plural of words that it has borrowed from Turkish. In some cases, the morpheme becomes productive and is able to be attached to other words. For example, English adopted derivational suffixes *-able/-ible* from French via the borrowing of words such as *incredible*. This affix then became productive and attached to non-French roots, as in words such as *writeable* and *drinkable*.

In syntactic borrowing, ordering requirements of surface elements in one language may be borrowed into another language, replacing the native word order. For example, Romansch, a Romance language spoken in Switzerland, replaced its original noun-before-adjective ordering with an adjective-before-noun ordering under the influence of German. Syntactic borrowing also occurs in Wutun (which belongs to the Chinese language family) from Tibetan. Wutun has borrowed rigid verb-final word order from Tibetan, as well as the use of postpositions instead of prepositions. And Greek as spoken in Turkey (originally subject-verb-object) has adopted subject-object-verb word order under the influence of Turkish.

11.1.3 Contact Situations

Contact-induced change is related to certain nonlinguistic characteristics such as **intensity of contact,** which is determined by the duration of the linguistic contact as well as by the level of interaction among the speakers. Intensity of contact is best seen as a continuum ranging from high intensity to low intensity. Long-term contact with a high level of social interaction is considered to be an intense contact situation, whereas contact that has not existed for a long time and that can be described as allowing only limited social interaction of the speakers in contact is characterized as a low-intensity contact situation.

The degree of intensity of the contact is directly related to the nature and degree of contact-induced change. Lexical borrowing requires only a low-intensity contact situation, since single words can be adopted without an in-depth knowledge of the grammatical system of the donor language. However, the adoption of structural elements or rules embedded in the phonology, morphology, or syntax of one language into another requires the existence of at least some speakers who are knowledgeable about both languages. In other words, structural borrowing requires the existence of **bilingualism,** which requires a relatively intense degree of contact between the groups in order to develop.

Another social factor that influences the effect of contact on the linguistic systems is the **prestige** (or **power**) of the speakers. If the speakers in the contact situation are equally prestigious, their respective languages are said to be in an **adstratal** relationship. For example, English and Norse in contact in early England were **adstratum languages.** If the speakers are unequal in terms of prestige, the language of the dominant group is called the **superstratum language,** while the language of the less dominant group is called the **substratum language.** In the contact between English and Native American languages, English is the superstratum language and Native American languages are the substratum languages, because of an imbalance in power and prestige. In Germany, the various languages of foreign workers (e.g., Turkish, Serbo-Croatian, Greek, and Italian) are considered to be substratum languages, and German is considered to be the superstratum language. It is important to keep in mind that these classifications of different strata are based only on cultural factors, not on linguistic ones: for example, while Greek may be a substratum language in Germany, it is a superstratum language in Greece.

In both adstratal and substratal/superstratal contact situations, lexical borrowing usually occurs first. However, the direction of the borrowing process usually differs. Adstratum languages function as donor and recipient at the same time and borrowing takes place in both directions. However, in a situation of unequal prestige or power, the superstratum language is typically the donor language and accepts only a few loanwords from the substratum language(s). To put it simply, adstratal borrowing is primarily bidirectional, while substratal/superstratal borrowing is unidirectional.

Especially in contact situations that result from immigration, **native language** (L1) **interference** plays an important role in shaping the result of language contact. Many adult immigrants learn the language of their new home (their second language, or L2) through interaction with native speakers, rather than in a school setting. This can be referred to as **second-language acquisition** in a "natural" setting. In this case, the immigrants' native language influences that way that the second language is learned. This is also called **transfer** or **substrate influence,** since immigrant languages are frequently substratum languages. For example, many Turkish immigrants in Germany do not use locative prepositions in their German. An immigrant may say *Ich gehe Doktor* ('I go doctor') instead of the standard German *Ich gehe zum Doktor* ('I am going to the doctor'). This is a case of L1 interference since

Turkish does not have any locative prepositions. Instead, Turkish has a locative case (which German does not have) as shown in (1).

(1) The Turkish locative case
     doktor-a   gid-iyor-um
     doctor-LOC   go-PROG-I
     'I am going to the doctor'

11.1.4 Results of Language Contact

If speakers of different adstratal languages enter into an extensive, long-term contact situation, **language convergence** may result. Convergence is the development of mutual agreement of the language systems in contact. File 11.7 discusses two cases of language convergence in more detail. When several languages enter into such a linguistic alliance, they form a so-called Sprachbund, a German word meaning 'union of languages.' An example is the Balkan Sprachbund of southeastern Europe where Albanian, Macedonian, Greek, Romanian, Bulgarian, and Serbo-Croatian show signs of linguistic convergence as a result of a long-standing linguistic contact.

If there is extensive, long-term contact between languages that have an unequal prestige relationship, **language shift** may result. This is defined as the shift by a group of speakers toward another language, while abandoning the native language. If the shifting group is the only group of speakers who used their original language, that language will no longer be spoken once the shift is completed. This is called **language death.** Many Native American languages in the United States have undergone the process of language death through language shift. In Oberwart, a village at the border between Austria and Hungary, language shift can be observed. After the Second World War, German came to be associated with the prestigious industrial economy, while Hungarian was felt to represent unprestigious "peasantness." The long-standing bilingualism of German and Hungarian, therefore, is giving way to a preference for German monolingualism, especially in the younger generation of Oberwart. Once the shift has been completed, Hungarian will no longer be used in Oberwart. However, this is not a case of language death as Hungarian, of course, is still widely used in Hungary. Language shift and death will be discussed in greater detail in File 11.6.

Finally, three distinct outcomes of language contact are the creation of **pidgin languages** (File 11.3), **creole languages** (File 11.4), and **bilingual mixed languages (intertwined languages)**. A pidgin language typically arises in a setting where two or more peoples come together for the purposes of trade. If the traders do not share a common language for communication, they might create a simplified yet distinct language, a pidgin, to facilitate trading. An example of such a trade pidgin is Chinook Jargon, a pidgin spoken by Native American, British, and French traders in the Pacific Northwest in the nineteenth century.

Whereas pidgins are not the primary languages of their users, creole languages arise in situations where the speakers in contact are in need of a common, primary means of communication. This situation characterized plantation settings in the Caribbean and parts of the southern United States in the seventeenth to nineteenth centuries. Here, a large number of Africans speaking a multitude of mutually unintelligible native languages came together with a small number of Europeans. This situation created the need for a common means of communication among the Africans as well as between the Africans and the Europeans. Because the common language that was created was used for a wide range of communicative purposes, not just for the facilitation of trade as in the case of pidgins, and for a prolonged period of time, this contact situation led to the development of creole languages. Examples of creoles include English-based Jamaican Creole, Guyanese Creole,

Gullah (a creole spoken in the coastal and island regions of South Carolina and Georgia), French-based Haitian Creole, and the Spanish/Portuguese-based creoles Papiamentu and Palenquero.

Bilingual mixed languages occur in contact situations with a high degree of bilingualism among speakers. Examples of intertwined languages are Media Lengua, spoken in Salcedo, Ecuador, by about 1,000 Native American people; as well as Michif spoken in Canada and in the Turtle Mountain Reservation in North Dakota by about 1,000 people altogether. Media Lengua combines Spanish vocabulary (adapted to Quechua phonology) with Quechua grammar, including Quechua morphology. Michif combines Plains Cree and Canadian French, with some borrowing from other languages. Plains Cree contributes the phonology, lexicon, morphology, and syntax of verb phrases (including their polysynthetic structure, see File 4.3), while Canadian French contributes the phonology, lexicon, morphology, and syntax of noun phrases (including lexical gender and adjective agreement).

Borrowings into English

11.2.1 Lexical Borrowing

A survey of the 1,000 most frequently used words in English found that only 61.7% had Old English (Germanic) origins. The other 38.3% were **lexical borrowings** from a variety of other languages: 30.9% French, 2.9% Latin, 1.7% Scandinavian, 1.3% mixed, and 0.3% Low German and Dutch. This massive amount of lexical borrowing is the direct result of the vast number of languages with which speakers of English have come into contact over the course of the language's history. Observing the external history of a language can show us why words were borrowed, as well as explain why certain types of words were borrowed.

Languages are always coming into contact with one another, and thus, a single word can be borrowed from one language to another through several intermediate sources. Therefore, it is necessary to distinguish between the **immediate source** of a borrowed word and the **ultimate source** of the word. For example, the Greek word πρόβλημα was borrowed into Latin and evolved naturally into the French word *problème*. Centuries later, the French word was borrowed into English as *problem*. While the word did enter English via French, its origins lie in Greek. The histories of other words can be even more complicated. For example, the English word *sugar* was borrowed from French, but it earlier passed through Latin and Arabic, and likely Greek, Persian, and Sanskrit as well. What follows is a brief sketch of the major periods of lexical borrowings (and thus history) of the English language.

11.2.2 Sources of English Words

The languages of the inhabitants of the British Isles were predominantly Celtic upon the withdrawal of Roman troops in the early fifth century CE, despite four centuries of Roman domination. Shortly thereafter, Germanic tribes entered, defeated the Celts, and took control not only politically, but linguistically as well. The arrival of the Angles, Saxons, and Jutes signified the arrival of Germanic languages (the name *English* comes from the tribe of people the Angles), which pushed the Celtic languages out of the center of Great Britain and into the periphery (Wales, Scotland), where they remain today.

Many words of Scandinavian origin entered the English language during the Norse invasions that took place between the ninth and eleventh centuries CE. Included in this set are the pronouns *they, them,* and *their,* words that are normally rather resistant to borrowing. Other examples of English words that were borrowed from Scandinavian languages are listed in (1).

(1) Borrowings from Scandinavian languages
anger, blight, clumsy, doze, eggs, garden, gate, geyser, law, ski, window

As mentioned above, the majority of words borrowed into English are of French origin. The Normans invaded England from Northern France and took control at the Battle of Hastings in 1066 CE. While Normandy and England were united for less than 200 years, the

451

mark Norman French left on the English vocabulary is immense. Some of the many words of French origin in English are listed in (2).

(2) Borrowings from French
     art, beauty, butcher, carpenter, cartoon, catch, cattle, cell, charity, chase, color, company, corpse, county, court, design, dinner, dress, enemy, fork, format, govern, grace, grocer, jail, judge, jury, lease, mercy, minister, miracle, napkin, painter, paradise, passion, plate, porch, power, reign, saint, soldier, suit, supper, table, tailor, troops

In later centuries a number of Parisian French words entered the English language. Some words were even borrowed twice, first from Norman French and later from Parisian French. For example, *chef* and *chief* were both borrowed from French *chef*. Many recent French borrowings can be easily identified as such, for example, *brassiere, fiancé(e), résumé,* or *hors d'oeuvres*. But others, especially the earlier borrowings, look and sound surprisingly English, as the list in (2) shows.

     Although England was part of the Roman Empire for over 400 years, English was not strongly influenced by Latin until after the fall of the Empire. Latin words like the ones in (3) entered English during two major periods: accompanying Christianity into England (ca. 600 CE) and during the Renaissance (sixteenth through seventeenth centuries).

(3) Borrowings from Latin
     abbot, agenda, alibi, animal, bonus, circulate, clerk, colloquium, data, deficit, diet, exit, extra, indicate, item, maximum, memento, nominate, penicillin, pope, priest, propaganda, radium, spectrum, sponsor, veto, via

     Latin was not the only classical language to affect English during the Renaissance. Many words of Greek origin were borrowed as well. Many of the English words of Greek origin listed in (4) passed through Latin due to substantial Greek-Latin contact prior to and during the Roman Empire (e.g., Eng. *stadium* < Lat. *stadium* < Gr. στάδιον).

(4) Borrowings from Greek
     analysis, angel, bacteriology, botany, catastrophe, climax, comedy, democracy, dialect, dialogue, episode, pediatrics, physiology, physics, philosophy, pneumonia, psychiatry, scene, system, theater, tyrant, zoology

     As the British began to colonize lands outside of Europe, English came into contact with a greater variety of languages. Many borrowings from Native American languages are plant terms, animal terms, and terms for other items that were new to New World immigrants, as shown in (5).

(5) Borrowings from Native American languages
     caucus, chipmunk, hickory, igloo, kayak, moccasin, moose, muskrat, opossum, pecan, raccoon, sequoia, skunk, teepee, tomahawk, totem, wigwam

     English and Spanish did not come into intensive contact in their homelands, but rather in America. It is worth noting that many of the Spanish words listed in (6) actually have their origins in Native American languages. The words passed through Spanish before entering English. For example, *condor* was borrowed from Spanish, but it is originally from Quechua, an indigenous language spoken in South America.

(6) Borrowings from Spanish
     adobe, alligator, armada, cafeteria, canyon, cargo, cockroach, coyote, guerilla, matador, mosquito, mustang, plaza, poncho, potato, renegade, rodeo, sombrero, tornado

Names for items that people consume (be it foods, drinks, or drugs) are frequently borrowed along with the introduction of the item. Examples are *cigar, marijuana, tequila,* and *vanilla* from Spanish; *bratwurst, frankfurter, pretzel,* and *sauerkraut* from German; *chutney* and *basmati* from Hindi; *bagel* and *lox* from Yiddish; *hashish* and *kabob* from Arabic; *yogurt* from Turkish; *sake, sushi,* and *wasabi* from Japanese; *vodka* from Russian; and *whiskey* from Irish. The following are borrowings from a variety of languages. Many of the words entered the English language because the item, idea, or concept they represent was imported as well.

(7) a. Borrowings from Celtic languages (Irish, Welsh, etc.)
    bog, clan, glen, leprechaun, penguin, slogan, shamrock
  b. Borrowings from German
    angst, delicatessen, kindergarten, lager, poke, pumpernickel, noodle, schnitzel
  c. Borrowings from Dutch
    bow, commodore, cruise, dock, freight, leak, lighter, pump, scour, scum, stripe, yacht
  d. Borrowings from Yiddish
    klutz, oy vey, schlep, schmuck
  e. Borrowings from Italian
    alto, attitude, balcony, fiasco, fresco, opera, pasta, piano, replica, soprano, spaghetti, studio, torso, umbrella
  f. Borrowings from South Asian Languages (Sanskrit, Hindi, Tamil, etc.)
    bandanna, bungalow, calico, curry, guru, indigo, jungle, loot, pajama, pundit, thug
  g. Borrowings from Arabic
    emir, gazelle, ghoul, giraffe, harem, lute, minaret, mosque, sultan
  h. Borrowings from Japanese
    anime, bonsai, futon, karaoke, kimono, tempura, typhoon

English is not alone, or even particularly rare, in having a substantial proportion of its lexicon of foreign origin. Any language whose history contains a series of periods of contact with other languages is going to have numerous borrowings.

Pidgin Languages

11.3.1 The Development of Pidgin Languages

Speakers of mutually unintelligible languages who are brought together (perhaps by social, economic, or political forces), and need to communicate with one another, develop various ways of overcoming the barriers to communication. One type of solution is to create **pidgin languages.** These are languages that typically come into being in trading centers or in areas under industrialization, where the opportunities for trade and work attract large numbers of people with different native tongues. Thus, the etymology of *pidgin* should come as no surprise: the word *pidgin* is actually a pidginized form of the English word *business*. Pidgin languages develop whenever speakers of different languages do not share a language in common, but need to communicate.

Before describing some features of pidgins, we should mention that pidgins are not "grammarless" or "broken" versions of other languages, as is sometimes believed. They do, however, grow and develop over time. In the initial stage of pidgin formation, often called the **prepidgin jargon** stage, there is little or no consistent grammar and rampant speaker-to-speaker variation. For this reason pidginists (people who study pidgin languages) talk about pidgins becoming **crystallized,** or establishing grammatical conventions. This is an essential characteristic of pidgins—if there is no established grammar, there is no pidgin.

After crystallizing from a prepidgin jargon, pidgins can develop in different ways. **Prototypical pidgins** are pidgins that emerged rather abruptly in situations where the contact is limited to certain social settings (such as trade). Prototypical pidgins have reduced grammar and vocabulary. Furthermore, they are nobody's native language. **Expanded pidgins,** on the other hand, are not limited to certain social settings. They have larger lexical and structural resources than prototypical pidgins, and they are as linguistically complex as any other language. A pidgin can evolve from a pre-pidgin jargon to a prototypical pidgin to an expanded pidgin.

11.3.2 Sources of Pidgin Lexicon and Grammar

Pidgin languages are usually made up of mixtures of elements from all of the languages in contact. In many cases, the vocabulary of pidgin languages is derived from the socially and/or economically dominant language in the contact situation (called the **superstrate** language), though other languages can also supply some of the lexicon. The language that provides most of the vocabulary of a pidgin is also called the **lexifier.** The word order (SVO, SOV, etc.) of pidgins is also frequently derived from the dominant language. The phonology of a pidgin, however, usually reflects the phonological systems of the languages of the other groups in contact and frequently has a strong influence from the socially and/or economically non-dominant language (called the **substrate** language). Pidgin syntax is frequently reduced, making it hard to determine which language it is based on. Finally, while pidgins usually have some derivational morphology, they usually do not have any productive inflectional morphology (see File 4.1).

To summarize, pidgin languages usually resemble their substratal inputs in phonology and their superstratal inputs in vocabulary and word order. Both grammar and lexicon are reduced in prototypical pidgins, often because they emerge so quickly and there is neither adequate instruction nor adequate time for complete mastery of any of the languages involved in the contact situation. We will look at a few examples from diverse pidgin languages to illustrate some typical characteristics of pidgins.

a. Chinook Jargon. Chinook Jargon was a prototypical pidgin that developed during the second half of the nineteenth century in Canada and the northwestern United States. It was used as a trade language among several Native American groups and was also learned by Europeans who began to settle in the Northwest. It is presumed that Chinook Jargon predates European settlement as it shows little early European influence. Its main source of vocabulary was Lower Chinook, and many of the features of Chinook Jargon grammar are derived from other Native American languages that played a role in its formation. Later, vocabulary items from Canadian French and English were borrowed into the language. Today, Chinook Jargon is an expanded pidgin. However, it is an endangered language with fewer than one hundred speakers. Examples of Chinook Jargon vocabulary can be seen in (1).

(1) | *Chinook Jargon* | *Source* | *Gloss* |
|---|---|---|
| ikt | ixt (Chinook) | 'one' |
| mokst | môkst (Chinook) | 'two' |
| man | man (English) | 'man' |
| chuck | ča'úk (Nootka) | 'water' |

One of the most interesting aspects of Chinook Jargon is its rich and complex consonant inventory, a feature found frequently among the input languages, but rarely among the languages of the world and not at all in other pidgins. Examples of the complexity of Chinook Jargon phonology include its numerous secondary articulations, such as glottalized stops and labialized back consonants; its clusters consisting of two stop consonants; and its rare phonemes, such as lateral obstruents, a velar and post-velar series of stops, and a glottal stop phoneme (see File 2.1.). The word *ikt* 'one,' for example, shows a consonant cluster consisting of two stops.

b. Tok Pisin. Tok Pisin is an expanded pidgin spoken in Papua New Guinea. Most of the words of Tok Pisin are clearly derived from English, as can be seen in (2), illustrating the point that much of the vocabulary of a pidgin is usually derived from the superstrate language.

(2) | *Tok Pisin* | *English Source* | *Gloss* |
|---|---|---|
| dok | dog | 'dog' |
| pik | pig | 'pig' |
| fis | fish | 'fish' |
| pen | paint | 'to paint' |
| penim | paint | 'to paint something/someone' |
| painim | find | 'to find' |
| lukim | look | 'to look at something/someone' |
| hukim | hook | 'to hook' |
| nogut | no good | 'bad' |
| man | man | 'man' |
| baimbai | by and by | 'soon' |
| sekan | shake hands | 'to make peace' |

Notice that most of the words in the above list are not exactly like their English counterparts. They have undergone some phonological and morphological changes from

English to Tok Pisin. For example, the word for 'to find' shows [f] changing to [p], and the [d] is deleted in the consonant cluster [nd], both examples of phonological changes. The suffix *-im* [im] found in *penim, painim, lukim,* and *hukim* is a morphological marker that indicates that the verb is transitive. Compare this to the intransitive verb *pen.* Semantic changes are also evident, as in the extension of *shake hands* to the much more general meaning 'to make peace.' These changes from English to Tok Pisin are due at least in part to contributions from the grammar(s) of the substrate language(s). Even though the vocabulary of Tok Pisin derives mostly from English, it shows a significant substrate influence, mainly from Oceanic languages. This is typical for expanded pidgins: they usually begin as prototypical pidgins and then expand their vocabulary and grammar to meet the increasing demands of everyday communication. In this process, speakers draw more and more on the resources of their native languages.

   c. Solomon Islands Pidgin. From the perspective of the linguist, it is not always easy to tell which language contributed which words or grammatical features found in a pidgin. While it's true that many words found in a pidgin derive from the superstrate language, and many grammatical features in an expanded pidgin derive from the speakers' native languages, we cannot conclude that a feature is derived from, say, English just because it looks similar to English. As an illustration of this, let's consider Solomon Islands Pidgin, an expanded pidgin spoken on the Solomon Islands and a close relative of Tok Pisin. The superstrate language that gave Solomon Islands Pidgin its vocabulary was English, while the grammatical rules of Solomon Islands Pidgin come from the Oceanic substrate languages. One of the most interesting examples of a substrate-derived construction is the transitive marker *-im* that is suffixed to verbal stems, and that we have already seen in Tok Pisin. At first sight it looks as if this marker is derived from the English words *him* or *them.* This makes sense, especially if one looks at the sorts of places where *-im* occurs:

(3) | **Solomon Islands Pidgin** | **Gloss** |
|---|---|
| luk | 'look' |
| luk-im | 'see something' |
| | |
| hamar | 'pound, hammer' |
| hamar-im | 'pound, hammer something' |
| | |
| sut | 'shoot' |
| sut-im | 'shoot something' |

As a speaker of English, one might easily imagine that a sentence like *mi hamar-im* ('I pounded it/him/them') is based on English *I hammered (h)im* or *I hammered (th)em.* This analysis may be partially correct, but the facts are actually more complex. If we look at Kwaio (an Oceanic language that served as a substrate language to Solomon Islands Pidgin) and compare some transitive and intransitive verbs, such as *look* and *see,* we notice an interesting similarity to the pidgin data:

(4) | **Kwaio** | **Gloss** |
|---|---|
| aga | 'look' |
| aga-si | 'see something' |
| gumu | 'pound, hammer' |
| gumu-ri | 'pound, hammer something' |
| fana | 'shoot' |
| fana-si | 'shoot something' |

These data are strikingly similar to the Solomon Islands Pidgin examples above: both languages have intransitive verbs that become transitive by adding a transitive suffix (TRS).

This suffix is *-im* in the case of Tok Pisin and Solomon Islands Pidgin and *-si* in the case of Kwaio. There are numerous reasons to believe that this grammatical rule derives from Oceanic substrate languages rather than from English. First of all, we can see immediately that Solomon Islands Pidgin does not exactly follow English in every use of *-im*. In English one can either *look at 'em* or *see 'em*, but never *look 'em*. In Solomon Islands Pidgin, however, one can *luk-im* someone or something. Second, in English it is ungrammatical to use both an object pronoun (*(h)im* or *(th)em*) and another explicit object. For example, one can say, *I shot the burglar* or *I shot 'im*, but not **I shot 'im the burglar*. In Solomon Islands Pidgin it is not only possible to use *-im* if there is an object present but necessary to do so, just as it is in Kwaio.

(5) Mi no luk-im pikipiki bulong iu
   I   *not* *see*-TRS *pig*   *belong* *you*
   'I didn't see your pig(s)'

Without *-im* the sentence in (5) is ungrammatical: **mi no luk pikipiki bulong iu*. Third, and perhaps most persuasive, researchers have noted that very few European speakers of Solomon Islands Pidgin ever master this detail of the grammar. Had this grammatical feature come from English, one would expect English speakers to have no trouble in mastering it. It seems reasonable, therefore, that the substrate languages have contributed this rule of grammar to Solomon Islands Pidgin.

11.3.3 Common Features of Pidgins

Many pidgin languages, regardless of their source languages, share certain characteristics. The similarities of pidgin languages (even ones that have formed entirely independently of each other) are sometimes so striking that some researchers have suggested that universal strategies of second-language learning play a role in their formation. Currently debated by researchers is the question of whether the errors people make when learning a foreign language are a result of the strategies adults use in learning second languages or of some innate language learning device. It seems likely that a full account of pidgin formation will have to include an appeal to some sort of language universals.

Some typical features of pidgins are described in the following paragraphs. If you look back at the examples given in the sections above, you will also find some of these features. The examples here are taken from Cameroonian Pidgin, an expanded pidgin spoken in (yes, you guessed it) Cameroon, in West Africa. English supplied much of the vocabulary of this pidgin. For reference, an excerpt from Loreto Todd's *Some Day Been Dey*, a folktale about a tortoise and a hawk told in Cameroonian Pidgin, is given below, with a loose translation into English.

We join the tale after the hawk meets the tortoise, explains that she needs food for her children, and invites the tortoise to visit them.

(6) An excerpt from *Some Day Been Dey* by Loreto Todd
    a. [a datwan go gud pas mak, trɔki. ju go kam, e]
       "Oh, that would be great, tortoise. You will come, won't you?

    b. [a go glad dat deɪ we ju go kam fɔ ma haʊs]
       "I'll be glad the day when you come to my house."

    c. [i tɔk so, i tɔn i bak, i go]
       She said this, turned her back, and left.

    d. [i di laf fɔ i bele. i tɔk seɪ:]
       She was laughing inside. And said:

e. [ha! so trɔki tiŋk seɪ i tu fit go flaɪ ɔp stik. i go si]
"Ha! So Tortoise thinks he too can fly up trees. We'll see."

[The tortoise notices the hawk's disdain and tricks her into carrying him to her nest, where he eats the hawk's young. She tries to kill him by dropping him from the sky.]

f. [bɔt trɔki gɛt trɔŋ nkanda. nɔtiŋ no fit du i.]
But the tortoise has strong skin. Nothing could hurt him.

g. [i wikɔp, i ʃek i skin, muf ɔl dɔs fɔ i skin,]
He got up, shook himself, removed all the dust from his body,

h. [i go, i seɪ: a! a dɔn du ju wɛl]
and left, saying: "Oh! I have taught you a good lesson!"

i. [ɔl dis pipul we dem di praʊd]
"All these people who are proud!

j. [dem tiŋk seɪ fɔseka seɪ]
"They think that because

k. [a no gɛt wiŋ, a no fit du as dem tu di du]
"I don't have wings, I can't do as they do.

l. [a no fit flaɪ, bɔt mi a dɔn ʃo ju seɪ sens pas ɔl.]
"I can't fly, but I've shown you that intelligence beats everything."

a. Phonology. Consonant clusters are usually reduced in pidgins (see 'strong' [trɔŋ] in (6f) and 'dust' [dɔs] in (6g)). Consonant cluster reduction is an indication that pidgins have a preference for syllable types closer to the CV type.

b. Morphology. A common feature of pidgin morphology is the absence of affixes. Notice from the Cameroonian example in (6) that 'wings' is [wiŋ] (see (6k)), 'thinks' is [tiŋk] (see 6(e)), and 'passes' is [pas] (see (6l)). However, the examples from Tok Pisin and Solomon Islands Pidgin given in (2) and (3) show that this does not mean that pidgins never have affixes; expanded pidgins can have rather complex morphology.

Note also that [i] is the only third-person pronoun in Cameroonian Pidgin, replacing English *he* and *she* (subjective), *him* and *her* (objective), and *his* and *her* (possessive). This simplification avoids the use of case and gender marking.

One other common morphological feature in pidgin languages that is not demonstrated in (6) is the use of reduplication as a simple word formation process. For example, in Korean Bamboo English (a pidgin developed in among Koreans and Americans during the Korean war), reduplication is used (a) to avoid homonymy, as in [san] 'sun' versus [sansan] 'sand,' and (b) for emphasis, as in [takitaki] 'very talkative.'

c. Syntax. The basic word order for pidgins tends to be subject-verb-object (SVO). Like other SVO languages (such as English), pidgins generally use prepositions rather than postpositions (*in the house* rather than **the house in*), auxiliaries are usually ordered before main verbs (*must go* rather than **go must*), and nouns before relative clauses (*the man who snores* rather than **who snores the man*). Pidgins show a preference for coordinated sentences (sentences connected by conjunctions such as *and, or,* etc.) over subordinate clauses (sentences connected by conjunctions such as *if, although,* etc.), though subordinate structures do sometimes exist. Articles are generally not used in pidgins, as illustrated by [ɔl dɔs] 'all the dust,' in line (6g). Aspectual distinctions (loosely: the manner of an action) are often marked by auxiliaries in pidgins. Cameroonian Pidgin, for example, classifies actions as to whether they are ongoing, completed, or repeated, as shown in (7).

(7) Verb aspect in Cameroonian Pidgin

Type of Action	Auxiliary	Example	Gloss	Reference
ongoing:	di	[di laf]	'was laughing'	(6d)
completed:	dɔn	[dɔn du]	'have done'	(6h)
repeated:	di	[di du]	'do (always)'	(6k)

d. Semantics. Pidgins, especially prototypical pidgins, usually have comparatively small vocabularies. To compensate for the lack of variety, however, meanings are extended. Thus [stik] means not only 'stick' but also 'tree' (see (6e)), and [wikɔp] means not only 'wake up' but also 'get up' (see (6g)). Because there are not many words in the vocabulary of the typical pidgin, compounds are more frequent. For example, compounds such as *dog baby* and *cow baby* could be used for 'puppy' and 'calf.'

FILE 11.4

Creole Languages

11.4.1 Social Contexts of Creole Formation

Imagine yourself as the son or daughter of first-generation slaves in the New World. Your parents and others like them were kidnapped from their homes, corralled together with other slaves, shipped across vast oceans under inhumane conditions, and forced to work and live in a strange country surrounded by people who didn't speak their language. Your owners divided their slaves into linguistically diverse groups so that you are not with many other slaves who speak the same language. This tactic means that it is difficult for you to organize any sort of resistance. In order to communicate with either the slaveholders or the other slaves, you will have to adopt some new form of communication. It is in plantation settings of this sort that **creole languages** came into being.

Traditionally, creole languages were defined as pidgin languages that had been adopted as the first, or native, language of a group of speakers (for example, by you and the other children of slaves in the hypothetical scenario above). There is an element of truth in this definition, but recent research has suggested it is not entirely accurate in all situations. The kernel of truth in the traditional definition of creolization is that all creoles seem to be languages that were initially non-native to any group of speakers and were adopted as first languages by some speech community. This is called **nativization** and occurs when a variety of speech that was no one's native language is learned by children in a speech community as their first language. The problem with the traditional definition is that it presumes a predecessor pidgin language for every creole language. However, in many cases it is not clear whether the input was in fact a pidgin language or a prepidgin (or rather, precreole) jargon.

Various researchers have suggested that the social context found in multilingual plantation settings is unique in human history. On many plantations there was a radical break in linguistic tradition, more severe than simply the coming together of speakers of different languages that typifies the situation in the development of pidgins. Because of this absolute inability to use their native languages to communicate, many adults developed very simplified jargons, as this was the best means of communicating with people from such varied linguistic backgrounds. Children rarely learned the native language of their parents (even when they were allowed to remain with their parents) because it was of little or no value to them on the plantation. The only accessible variety of language of significant usefulness in plantation settings was the jargon that their parents used. Thus, these jargons became the primary language of the adult slaves and eventually the native language of their children. Because of the innate capacity to develop language (see Chapter 8), these children then turned the jargon into a full-fledged new language, known as a creole. So, while some creoles may develop from pidgin languages, others develop straight from precreole jargons.

Another typical feature of creoles is that the formation of many creoles involves repeated second-language acquisition, that is, second-language acquisition by successive groups of people. For example, the early contact variety of what is now Haitian Creole was much closer to French dialects than is Haitian Creole itself. The subsequent divergence from French is the result of repeated second-language acquisition of the available contact variety by successive waves of African immigrants. This led to greater substrate influence as well as to drastic changes in the structure of Haitian Creole.

11.4.2 Shared Features

The linguistic structure of a creole depends on the varieties that came into contact to form it. In the case that the precreole language was a crystallized or expanded pidgin, the creole bears many of the same features as its predecessor language. For example, the Tok Pisin pidgin introduced in File 11.3 has been nativized into a creole. The differences between nativized (creole) and non-nativized (pidgin) varieties of Tok Pisin are quite subtle. Often, native speakers of Tok Pisin creole will employ the same grammatical devices as second-language speakers of Tok Pisin pidgin, but on a more frequent or consistent basis. Also, native speakers of Tok Pisin creole reduce various phonological elements (e.g., syllables) more than speakers of Tok Pisin pidgin do. On the whole, though, the differences between nativized and non-nativized Tok Pisin are rather small.

However, if the precreole language was a jargon, or in cases of repeated second-language acquisition, the creole tends to bear less structural resemblance to the input varieties. Instead, such creoles seem to develop based on more universal principles (be they linguistic, social, or cognitive), as evidenced by the striking structural similarities between creoles that developed from a rather diverse set of input varieties. Derek Bickerton and other scholars have catalogued many of the similarities among such creoles. One of the most striking of these similarities is the inflectional tense, mood, and aspect (TMA) system used with verbs. Bickerton gives the table shown in (1), slightly modified in its presentation, which illustrates the similarities in TMA systems among these creoles. Note: *anterior* refers to (past) tense, *nonpunctual* refers to aspect (ongoing or habitual action), and *irrealis* refers to mood (future, conditional, and subjunctive).

(1) Comparing tense, mood, and aspect in three creoles

	Hawaiian Creole	**Haitian Creole**	**Sranan**
BASE FORM 'he walked/s'	He walk	Li maché	A waka
ANT(ERIOR) 'he had walked'	He bin walk	Li té maché	A ben waka
IRR(EALIS) 'he would/will walk'	He go walk	L'av(a) maché	A sa waka
NON(PUNCTUAL) 'he is/was walking'	He stay walk	L'ap maché	A e waka
ANT + IRR 'he would have walked'	He bin go walk	Li t'av(a) maché	A ben sa waka
ANT + NON 'he was/had been walking'	He bin stay walk	Li t'ap maché	A ben e waka
IRR + NON 'he will/would be walking'	He go stay walk	L'av ap maché	A sa e waka
ANT + IRR + NON 'he would've been walking'	He bin go stay walk	Li t'av ap maché	A ben sa e waka

The examples in (1) include two English-based creoles (Hawaiian Creole and Sranan) and one French-based creole (Haitian Creole). The substrate languages that contributed to the three languages represented in table (1) are quite different. In Sranan (spoken in Surinam) and Haitian Creole, the substrate was composed of West African languages. In Hawaiian Creole the substrate was composed of languages such as Portuguese and Chinese. But the patterns of TMA marking are the same in all three creoles. Note that in each of them, the anterior element always precedes the irrealis and nonpunctual elements, and the irrealis element always precedes the nonpunctual element.

What is the source of these shared features among creoles with such diverse backgrounds? Bickerton attributes the similarities to innate properties of the human mind. He claims that the similarities among widely scattered creoles provide support for the claim that human beings are linguistically preprogrammed. Bickerton would say that the shared TMA pattern shown in (1) follows from a very specific "bioprogram" in the human mind. Part of this bioprogram includes the TMA categories that human beings will always use automatically unless the patterns of whatever language they are learning are different.

According to Bickerton, in the relevant plantation contexts, only a relatively grammarless jargon is available as the input for children who are trying to acquire a native language. Hence, children have to appeal to their innate bioprogram to create a new grammar. This, according to Bickerton and his followers, is the primary mechanism of creolization, and it accounts for all of the similarities among the creoles shown in (1).

It should be noted, however, that many creolists do not accept the bioprogram hypothesis and have suggested other explanations to account for the similarities, including the common social context of creolization, universal strategies of language learning, universal strategies for reducing language in contact situations, and structural similarities among the substrate and/or superstrate languages that were historically present in these creole contact situations. Most creolists nowadays propose that the similarities among creoles emerged as a result of a special form of second-language acquisition.

FILE 11.5

=============================

Societal Multilingualism

11.5.1 Societal Multilingualism

When hearing the term **bilingualism** or **multilingualism,** most people think of an individual's ability to speak two or more languages or dialects (see File 8.5). (We will use the terms *multilingualism* and *multilingual* here for people who speak two, three, four, or more languages or dialects.) However, whole communities or societies can also be multilingual. This is called **societal bilingualism** or **multilingualism** and is particularly common in Africa and Asia, although it occurs in other parts of the world as well.

Societal multilingualism usually refers to a situation in which communities of speakers share two or more languages and use them in everyday life. In India, for example, many people speak their regional language as well as Hindi, the most widely spoken of the country's indigenous official languages. Most educated speakers also speak English, which is also an official language of India. In Kenya, educated people usually speak at least three languages: their tribal (regional) language, Swahili (the national language), and English (the language used in education throughout the country). In many African countries, the language of the former colonizer, mostly French or English, is still used either in the government or in education, making the vast majority of educated speakers multilingual. Finally, in the Al-Sayyid Bedouin tribe, most members speak both Al-Sayyid Bedouin Sign Language and Arabic, making this community bimodally multilingual

Societal multilingualism is also common among immigrant communities, for example, in Europe and the United States. In these cases, minority-language speakers maintain their language, while using their variety of the host language for interaction with its speakers.

Societal multilingualism is sometimes used in a broader sense to refer to the use of two or more languages within the same country. If we equate society with country, we have to conclude that almost all countries in the world, if not all, are multilingual. This is the case even for countries we usually associate with only one language, for example France, where the regional dialects and languages Provençal, Breton, Alsatian, Corsican, Catalan, Basque, and Flemish are spoken in certain regions of the country. In addition, many other languages, such as Armenian, Turkish, and different dialects of Arabic are spoken mainly in bigger cities by various immigrant groups. When we think about the languages spoken in the United States, English and Spanish come to mind. However, Ethnologue lists 162 living languages that are spoken in the United States. For example, there are over 300,000 Russian speakers, over 1 million Armenian speakers, over 1 million French speakers, over 1.2 million Yiddish speakers, over 1.4 million Czech speakers, and over 3.3 million Polish speakers in the United States. A number of the languages listed on Ethnologue, however, have fewer than 10 speakers left. This is the case for many indigenous (Native American) languages, which are considered **endangered languages** (see File 11.6).

However, equating society with country is problematic: even though there are 162 languages spoken in the United States, the majority of Americans are actually monolingual (making them a minority since the majority of people in the world are multilingual).

463

11.5.2 Code-Switching and Diglossia

In multilingual communities, two common though distinct linguistic phenomena are code-switching and diglossia. **Code-switching** refers to the use of two languages or dialects within a single utterance or within a single conversation. Consider the example in (1) and (2), from an interview of a nurse in Nairobi (Myers-Scotton 1990). The languages she uses are Swahili (in normal type), English (in italics), and Lwidakho (in bold). The translation is given in (2).

(1) Interviewer: Unapenda kufanya kazi yako lini? Mchanaau usiku?
    Nurse: *As I told you, I like my job.* Sina ubaguzi wo wote kuhusu wakati ninapo-fanya kazi. *I enjoy working either during the day* au usiku yote ni sawa kwangu. Hata *family members* w-angu wamezoea mtindo huu. *There is no quarrel at all.* **Obubi bubulaho.** Saa zengine kazi huwa nyingi sana na *there are other times when we just have light duty.* **Valwale vanji,** *more work;* **valwale vadi,** hazi kidogo.

(2) Interviewer: When do you like to work? Days or nights?
    Nurse: *As I told you, I like my job.* I have no difficulty at all regarding when I do work. *I enjoy working either during the day* or at night, all is OK as far as I'm concerned. Even my *family members* have gotten used to this plan. *There is no quarrel at all.* **There is no badness.** Sometimes there is a lot of work and *there are other times when we just have light duty.* **More patients,** *more work;* **fewer patients,** little work.

The reason the nurse can code-switch extensively in the interview is that she knows that her interviewer also speaks Swahili, English, and Lwidakho. However, she could have chosen to just speak in one language with the interviewer. Such choices are frequently politically, socially, or personally motivated. For example, multilinguals may be more comfortable with one of their languages or insist on speaking only one language to express their cultural identity. However, in the example above, the nurse leaves the **language choice** open.

Sometimes the choice of language is determined by the social setting. The situation where different languages or dialects are used for different functions is called **diglossia**. Traditionally, diglossia referred to a situation where a standard or regional dialect was used in ordinary conversation, but a variety learned by formal education was used for most written communication. An example of this is the use of standard Arabic in literature and other writings and the use of local varieties of Arabic in ordinary conversation in the various countries where Arabic is spoken. More recently, diglossia has been expanded to refer to any situation where two distinct languages or dialects are used for different functions within one society. Frequently, diglossic situations involve one language that is spoken at home or in informal situations and another language that is used for official purposes or in (higher) education. For example, in many African countries, the language of education and instruction is English or French. However, the languages spoken in everyday life, depending on the country and region, are various African languages.

Many of the examples above show that societal multilingualism frequently arises when speakers of different languages are in contact, as in the cases of immigration and colonization. Societal multilingualism is often an outcome of contact if a group of people retain their cultural and language heritage, but also learn the language that is dominant in some area of society.

Language Endangerment and Language Death

11.6.1 Minority Language Status

Material in other files makes it clear that there are many, many languages around today. Even with the difficulties involved in distinguishing languages from dialects (see File 10.1) and even with our imperfect knowledge of the range of speech forms found in some parts of the world (e.g., Papua New Guinea or various regions in South America), a figure of some 6,000 languages is widely cited and generally accepted as a rough estimate of how many languages there are in the world today. This number is in accord, for instance, with what is known about global ethnic diversity (even if it draws on an overly simplistic equation of language with ethnicity, a not uncontroversial issue) and with the array of nations, virtually all of which are home to many languages.

A basic fact about these 6,000 or so languages is that not all are equally robust in terms of the number of speakers each one has. In fact, the number of speakers differs greatly from language to language: there are some with millions of speakers, some with thousands, some with hundreds, some with tens, and some with just one. Moreover, the number of languages with a small number of speakers is far greater than the number with millions of speakers. In fact, a total of less than 10% of the known languages accounts for more than 90% of the speakers. It follows from these numbers that a good many, even most, languages are minority languages within their larger societal context.

The fact that a given language may not just have a small number of speakers, but is in fact often in a minority status compared to some other language or languages that it shares territory with, is a key to understanding the phenomena of **language endangerment** and ultimate **language death**: the death of a language is taken to occur when it no longer has any speakers actively using it.

Minority speakers, especially when they are an overt minority immediately and directly confronted by a dominant culture, face particular sorts of pressures that often lead them to give up their language in favor of a language of the majority, or at least of a politically, economically, and socially more dominant group. Among these pressures are the following, some of which are also discussed in File 13.2:

- problems of access to mainstream economic opportunities (e.g., if jobs require skills in the dominant language)
- potential for ridicule, overt discrimination, and prejudice for being different (e.g., being forbidden by law or regulation to speak one's own language)
- lack of instruction in their native language (with the possibility that schools will force the majority language on minority-language-speaking children)
- limited "scope" for using the language (what can be referred to as its "domains of usage")

There are, of course, some positive aspects to maintaining one's language even if it is a minority language. Among these benefits are:

- potential to maintain one's culture and prevent a sense of rootlessness (to the extent that aspects of the minority culture are tied up with language)

- enhanced pride and self-esteem
- a well-developed self-identity and group membership that allows access to a different culture (see File 13.1)
- cognitive advantages through bilingualism (e.g., added expressiveness, new perspectives afforded by a different worldview, etc.)

11.6.2 From Minority Status to Endangerment

For many minority language speakers, the more concrete pressures of access to jobs and stigmatization override the less tangible benefits, and as a result they move toward linguistic assimilation with the more dominant language. In such cases, there is typically a three-generational "drop-off," with the last fully fluent generation giving way as assimilation sets in, to a transitional generation, which in turn spawns a generation often more at home—linguistically and culturally—with the dominant setting than the traditional one. At that point, especially if this scenario is replicated across all the pockets of minority language use, or if such minority communities are small to start with, the viability of the minority language as a whole is threatened, and in such a case, we talk of the language being endangered, on its way to extinction, and, we might say, death.

This sort of scenario is being instantiated in all corners of the earth, with different dominant languages and cultures being the "heavy," the "killer language," as it were. While many of the European colonial languages, such as English in the United States, Spanish in much of Latin America, or Portuguese in Brazil, have become the dominant language that threatens the viability of indigenous languages in various areas, other languages play the same role elsewhere, including Arabic in northern Africa, varieties of Chinese in parts of China, Thai in northern Thailand, and so on.

Endangerment is really a locally determined phenomenon. For instance, Greek has been a minority language of immigrants within the last century in the United States and Australia but is increasingly losing ground to the more dominant English in each country. However, in Greece itself, where Greek is the socially more powerful language, the Albanian dialect known as Arvanitika is nearing extinction due to pressures on its speakers to function in Greek. In fact, a few of the widespread "killer languages" ("serial killers," some linguists have called them) are themselves threatened in some places. Spanish is giving way to English in parts of the United States, and it is even the case that English is an endangered language in the Bonin Islands, off of Japan, where despite being spoken by Westerners for over 100 years it is yielding to the local dominant language, Japanese. What cases like these mean is that there is nothing inherent about a particular language itself that makes it a dominant language, nothing intrinsic to English or Spanish, for instance; rather, endangerment is determined by the particular social circumstances that guide the interaction between two speech communities occupying roughly the same geographical space but differing as to their population numbers and dominance relations as measured by utility in the economic marketplace, cultural dominance, and the like. (Languages can, of course, happily co-exist without one threatening the viability of the other; sees Files 11.1 and 11.7 for some discussion of the long-term, more or less peaceful coexistence of languages.)

This process of language loss through language endangerment and language death is quite widespread today, to the point that many scholars are seriously worried about the survival of the rich linguistic diversity that the world has known for millennia, of the particular (and often unique) viewpoints on representing and structuring knowledge about the world that different languages provide, and of the variety of linguistic structure offered by the range of languages that currently exists. It is certainly the case that language endangerment and language death have taken place in the past; one need only see the many names of tribes recorded in ancient histories, for example, that of the fifth-century BCE Greek historian Herodotus, to get a sense of how many peoples were assimilated, linguistically and culturally, in times long past. But the pace at which language extinction is proceeding seems to have accelerated in recent decades, giving a sense of urgency to the current situation.

Many analysts talk about language death when there are no longer any fluent speakers. At such a point, there may well be speakers with some command of the targeted language but not full fluency; such speakers can be referred to as **semi-speakers,** though the more chilling designation *terminal speakers* has also been used. Fluency in a language is a scalar phenomenon, with different degrees possible, and in a language endangerment situation, one finds differing levels of competence with the language on the part of its remaining speakers. Some might have very limited abilities and essentially just barely "pass" as speakers by knowing a few formulaic phrases and appropriate utterances. If all the more fluent speakers die off—they tend to be the elders in such communities—sometimes all that are left are some speakers who remember a few words and phrases but have no active command of the language. When there are only such *rememberers,* the language is effectively dead, though *moribund* might be a fairer characterization.

11.6.3 Can Dying/Dead Languages Be Revived?

Some linguists prefer the term **dormant** language to **dead** or **extinct language,** their thinking being that under the right conditions, languages can be "reawakened" and revived. Although the collective will needed to effect such a revival can be daunting and does not happen often, there are some success stories to point to. The revival of a form of Biblical Hebrew in the nineteenth and twentieth centuries in what has become the state of Israel is perhaps the most famous case, with modern Israeli Hebrew being a testament to what dedication to a cause can do. Similarly, dedication is evident in the way that the indigenous New Zealand language Maori has been staging a comeback, as the institution of *te kohanga reo* 'language nests,' a language-immersion experience for young Maori children, has proven to be a successful revival strategy. And, in Ohio, the tireless efforts of one member of the Miami Tribe, Daryl Baldwin, in learning the dormant Miami language as an adult, speaking it with his children, and promoting its use in summer language camps, has created an awareness of the language that would not have seemed possible even a decade ago.

It must be admitted, however, that the road to renewed viability for any given endangered language is not an easy one. The pressures on speakers referred to above can be overwhelming, and one often finds that speakers "vote with their mouths," as it were, and abandon their heritage language in favor of the locally dominant language.

11.6.4 What Happens to a Language as It Loses Speakers and Dies?

Typically, endangered languages show massive influx of vocabulary and even syntactic structures from the dominant language, but such is not always the case. Languages can die with their native lexicon and native grammatical apparatus more or less intact. Moreover, borrowing, as seen in Files 11.1 and 11.2, is a phenomenon that even healthy and robust languages engage in. Thus, it is hard to generalize about what a language will look like in an endangered state, but vocabulary loss, loss of some phonological contrasts (e.g., semi-speakers of Arvanitika generally do not distinguish between the trilled /r/ and the tap /ɾ/ found in other healthier dialects), and the decline of native word orders or syntactic combinations are not at all uncommon in seriously threatened languages. Interestingly, new elements can also enter the language at this point, often in the form of sounds from the dominant language that come in with the loanwords (as with the voiced velar fricative [ɣ] found in recent Greek loanwords into Arvanitika).

11.6.5 A Final Word (Or Two)

Two final points are worth making. First, even though the discussion above talks about **language** endangerment and death, the same considerations apply just as readily at the level of **dialect.** That is, there can be endangered dialects just as there are endangered languages. Some of the once-distinctive dialects of English heard on the Sea Islands on the Atlantic coast of South Carolina and Georgia, for example, have been giving way to more Standard English forms in recent years, for instance. Second, even with the loss of languages on a large scale worldwide, there is some replenishing of the stock of the world's languages occurring, through ongoing and continual dialect differentiation as well as processes of creolization (see File 11.4). Still, the creation of new languages seems not to be occurring at the same rate as the loss of existing languages. This situation has led many linguists to action with regard to the documentation of poorly described languages that may not survive many more years and to revival efforts such as those described above.

FILE **11.7**

Case Studies in Language Contact

11.7.1 Introduction

The following two case studies illustrate some of the different effects that can arise when two or more languages are used regularly in the same locality. In language contact, both linguistic factors and sociohistorical factors can influence the outcomes in particular multilingual communities. Recall the different contact effects mentioned in File 11.1, and note any examples of those effects that you find in the following discussion.

11.7.2 Kupwar

The village of Kupwar, India, with a population of approximately 3,000, is located in the southern Indian district of Maharashtra. This village represents a rather complex example of language contact (Gumperz and Wilson 1971). The residents of this village speak three main languages: Marathi and Urdu, members of the Indo-European language family, and Kannada, a Dravidian language. In this village, sociolinguistic factors have contributed to an intricate language contact situation (see File 10.4 for an introduction to some of these factors).

The inhabitants of Kupwar are divided into distinct social groups, according to profession, religion, and a strict caste system. A specific language is associated with each social group. Kannada-speaking Jains are the larger of two landowning social classes. Urdu-speaking Muslims constitute the other. Two other social groups pertinent to this discussion are a large Kannada-speaking craftsman class and a class of Marathi-speaking "untouchables." Speakers of both Kannada and Marathi have been in contact in the area for around 600 years, and speakers of Urdu have been in the area for around 400 years. Family interactions are generally monolingual in the native language of that family's social group. Neighborhoods are generally arranged according to language group. Most men in the village are (at least) bilingual, but communication between members of different social groups is customarily carried out in Marathi. Because it is neither the home language of the majority of inhabitants nor the language of either of the socially dominant language groups, Marathi has come to be perceived as a socially neutral language. Rules of social interaction require the use of Marathi in mixed social group settings, even by members of the upper social classes, neither of which use it natively. If a Kannada-speaking landowner were to converse in Kannada with a Marathi-speaking farmhand, the landowner would be implicitly including the farmhand in the landowner's higher social group. The strict caste system forbids such acts. This system of social separation leads the languages spoken in Kupwar to maintain a high degree of autonomy: for example, each of these languages retains its own distinct vocabulary. Owing to the pervasive bilingualism and the intensive and long-standing social contact among the various members of the Kupwar community, however, many other linguistic features have been transferred between the languages. The following examples illustrate both of these features of language contact in Kupwar.

a. Possessive Pronouns and Adjectives. The example in (1) demonstrates how Kupwar Kannada follows a Kupwar Marathi pattern. Kannada spoken outside Kupwar has a distinction in form between the words that mean 'yours' and 'your,' *nim-də* and *nim,* respectively. Kannada as spoken in Kupwar has come to follow the pattern seen in Marathi, which has no distinction in form between the words (Urdu follows a pattern similar to that of Marathi). The underlined words in the example in (1) show this pattern.

(1) Non-Kupwar Kannada: ii   məne   <u>nim-də</u>   i-du   <u>nim</u>   məne
     Kupwar Kannada: id   məni   <u>nim-d</u> eti   id   <u>nim-d</u>   məni eti
     Kupwar Marathi: he   ghər   <u>tumc-ə</u> haɪ   he   <u>tumc-ə</u>   ghər haɪ
     Gloss: *this-one house yours   is*   *this-one your   house is*
                          'This house is yours.'   'This is your house.'

This example also shows another difference between Kupwar and non-Kupwar varieties of Kannada. Kupwar Kannada follows the Marathi pattern of requiring an explicitly expressed form of the verb 'to be,' *eti* 'is,' while non-Kupwar Kannada permits the lack of an explicit form of 'is,' that is, the empty space that corresponds to 'is' in the non-Kupwar Kannada sentence above.

b. Verb Formations. In example (2), we see that Kupwar Urdu follows the Kupwar Kannada pattern. Compare the Kupwar and non-Kupwar varieties of Urdu. The forms that mean 'having VERB-ed' represent a verb form called the *past non-finite,* which occurs in both Kannada and Marathi and is similar to an English past participle. Notice the differences between the Kupwar and non-Kupwar Urdu words for 'having cut' and 'having taken.' Non-Kupwar Urdu uses a different form for each verb, while Kupwar Urdu follows the pattern of using the same form for each verb, transferred from Kupwar Kannada.

(2) Non-Kupwar Urdu: pala   jəra   <u>kat-kər</u>   <u>le</u>   a-ɪa
     Kupwar Urdu: pala   jəra   <u>kat-kə</u>   <u>le-kə</u>   a-ɪa
     Kupwar Kannada: təpla jəra   <u>khod-i</u>   <u>təgond-i</u>   bə-ɪn
     Gloss: *greens some   having cut   having taken   (I) came*
                       'I cut some greens and brought them.'

From these examples, we can see that two distinct phenomena are occurring. In one respect, these languages are becoming more alike, as patterns of language use are transferred between languages. At the same time, the languages are being kept distinct from each other, in that Kannada uses Kannada words, Urdu uses Urdu words, and so on. The fact that we see both of these patterns happening concurrently is what makes Kupwar a case of such linguistic interest, especially in light of the fact (mentioned in File 11.1) that languages in contact tend to first share lexical items and only later share structural properties.

11.7.3 Deitsch

Also known as Pennsylvania German or Pennsylvania Dutch, Deitsch has a long history of both dialect and language contact. Deitsch emerged in Pennsylvania in the early 1700s as the result of contact between speakers of western varieties of both middle and upper German dialects. There are currently several hundred thousand Deitsch speakers in North America. Most live in the midwestern states, and the vast majority belong to separatist Anabaptist groups, that is, the Amish and the Old Order Mennonites, which are the only groups among whom children still acquire Deitsch as a first language. All Deitsch speakers are fluent Deitsch-English bilinguals. Schooling is entirely in English, and thus English is the language of literacy, though most speakers also achieve rudimentary literacy in standard German. In spite of their tradition of separation from mainstream society, these groups have always been in contact with English speakers, and the effects on the Deitsch language are unmistakable.

a. Lexicon. The amount of borrowing of vocabulary from English varies from community to community and is sometimes exaggerated by native speakers. Actual estimates of the percentage of vocabulary borrowed from English range from 8% (Buffington and Barba 1965) to 14% (Enninger and Raith 1988). This percentage appears to be increasing, however, as speakers replace function words, such as *weil* ('because') and even relatively "basic" rural vocabulary, such as *Sai* ('pigs') and *Bauerei* ('farm'), with their English counterparts.

English borrowings are often incorporated into Deitsch morphology as example (3) shows. In this case, the word *bark* is borrowed from English, but it appears with Deitsch infinitive marking. Sometimes, however, English morphology is borrowed along with the word, as example (4) shows. Here, *switch, kick,* and *pressure* as well as the suffix *-s* are borrowed from English. Notice also that *pressure* is given masculine grammatical gender through the use of the masculine definite article *der*. Thus, the borrowed word is integrated into the grammatical gender system of Deitsch.

(3) And de Hund wa   an <u>bark-e</u>
    And the dog   was on to-bark
    'and the dog was barking . . .'   (Fuller 1999)

(4) Sel dat   <u>switch</u> <u>kick-s</u> nei venn   der <u>pressure</u> so veit drop . . .
    That there switch   kicks   in   when/if the pressure   so far   drops . . .
    'That switch kicks in when/if the pressure drops so far . . .'   (Keiser 1999)

b. Lexical Semantics. A number of Deitsch words have changed or extended their meanings so that they match the semantics of the equivalent word in English. Louden (1997) notes that this often occurs as a result of calquing (see File 11.1), in this case word-for-word translations of English phrases into Deitsch, and appears particularly strong with respect to Deitsch prepositions that are acquiring English idiomatic meanings, and in some cases English compound structure. Examples are shown in (5) and (6)

(5) Mir kenne sie   net <u>nei-schwetze</u> fer gehe.
    We   can   them not into-talk   for to-go
    'We can't talk them into going'   (Louden 1997)

(6) Er hot si   <u>raus-gechecked</u>
    He has them out-checked
    'He checked them out' (i.e., 'he ogled them')   (Keiser 1999)

c. Phonetics. The sound system of Deitsch remains largely unaffected by contact with English, although some new sounds (e.g., /æ/, /t/, and /tʃ/) occur primarily in English loanwords, and in some Pennsylvania communities the trilled or tapped [r] is being replaced by the American retroflex [ɹ].

d. Syntax. The tense and aspect system of Deitsch is based on German. However, due to contact with English, Deitsch has developed a progressive tense, which is not found in German but is found in English. Compare the data in table (7).

The Deitsch progressive tense is modeled on the (Standard) German forms *ich war am Schreiben* ('I was writing') and *ich bin am Schreiben* ('I am writing'). These forms are very similar to a progressive tense since they have the same meaning as that expressed by a progressive tense. However, the Standard German forms are nominalizations. Thus, Deitsch developed a progressive tense in order to better match the English tense/aspect system, but

(7) Comparison of Deitsch, Standard German, and English tense/aspect systems

Tense/Aspect	Deitsch	Standard German	English
Past	*ich hab tschriwwe*	*ich schrieb*	'I wrote'
Present perfect	*ich hab tschriwwe ghatt*	*ich habe geschrieben*	'I have written'
Past progressive	*ich war an schreiwe*	—	'I was writing'
Present	*ich schreib*	*ich schreibe*	'I write'
Present progressive	*ich bin an schreiwe*	—	'I am writing'
Future	*ich zell/figger schreiwe*	*ich werde schreiben*	'I will/am going to write'
Future perfect	*ich zell/figger tschriwwe hawwe*	*ich werde geschrieben haben*	'I will/am going to have written'

the specific content of the progressive tense is based on German. Many of the changes that Deitsch has undergone in contact with English are changes that make it easier for speakers to switch back and forth between Deitsch and English.

11.7.4 Conclusion

The Kupwar and Deitsch cases show how language varieties can **converge** on similar patterns of meaning and structure when they remain in contact for an extended period. This can result in particular regional varieties (dialects) which are in some ways more like the neighboring variety of a different language than they are like other varieties of the same language. The development of convergent varieties allows speakers to switch from one language to another more directly, and it may be that the similarity of expression also allows children to acquire the multiple local languages more readily than they might learn two totally different (non-convergent) language varieties.

FILE **11.8**

Practice

File 11.1—Language Contact

Exercises

1. Find ten words that English has recently borrowed from another language. One way to find lists of words that have recently been created or borrowed is by Googling the word *neologisms*. What language(s) were the words you found borrowed from? Why do you think these words were borrowed? Do you think the words are just a fad, or do you think they will become widely used? Why do you think so? Was it easy to find ten borrowed words? What does your answer tell you about the use of borrowings in English?

2. Pick a language from the list below and find ten words that were recently borrowed from English into that language. Why do you think these words were borrowed? What topic do the words relate to?

    German: http://www.sfs.uni-tuebingen.de/~lothar/nw/Projekt/index.html#Kandidat (click on a year on the left)
    Dutch: http://www.nlterm.org/neoterm/lijst.htm
    Spanish: http://cvc.cervantes.es/obref/banco_neologismos/listado_neologismos.asp
    Catalan: http://cvc.cervantes.es/obref/banco_neologismos/listado_neologismos.asp ?idioma=Catalan
    Italian: http://www.neologismi.it/?ordine=alfabetico

3. For this exercise, refer to the *Zits* comic at the beginning of this chapter and answer the following questions:

    i. If English borrowed *über* from German, what kind of borrowing would this be an example of?
    ii. In German, *über* is pronounced [ybɐ]. How do you think English speakers would pronounce the word? Why?

Discussion Questions

4. What languages are in contact in the area or in the country where you live? Are they in an adstratal or a substratal/superstratal relationship? Is there evidence of borrowing between the languages? How intense is the language contact? Are there bilingual speakers? What do you predict for the future development of the languages in contact?

File 11.2—Borrowings into English

Exercises

5. The following is from the *Oxford English Dictionary*'s etymological entry for *chocolate*:

> [a. F. *chocolat*, Sp. *chocolate*, ad. Mexican *chocolatl* 'an article of food made of equal parts of the seeds of cacao and those of the tree called pochotl' [*Bombax ceiba*] Siméon *Dict. de langue Nahuatl*.]

Dissect this rather densely worded definition. Show the history of this word, from its origins to the point in which it was borrowed into English. State the language of origin, as well as any intermediate languages.

6. The following is the *Oxford English Dictionary*'s etymological entry for *apricot*:

> [orig. ad. Pg. *albricoque* or Sp. *albaricoque*, but subseq. assimilated to the cognate F. *abricot* (*t* mute). Cf. also It. *albercocca*, *albicocca*, OSp. *albarcoque*, a. Sp. Arab. *al-borcoq*(*ue* (P. de Alcala) for Arab. *al-burqūq*, *-birqūq*, i.e. *al* the + *birqūq*, ad. Gr.πραικόκιον (Dioscorides, *c* 100; later Gr.πρεκόκκια and βερικόκκια pl.), prob. ad. L. *præcoquum*, variant of *præcox*, pl. *præcocia*, 'early-ripe, ripe in summer,' an epithet and, in later writers, appellation of this fruit, orig. called *prūnum* or *mālum Armeniacum*. Thus Pallad. (*c* 350): 'armenia vel præcoqua.' The change in Eng. from *abr-* to *apr-* was perhaps due to false etymol.; Minsheu 1617 explained the name, quasi, 'in *aprīco coctus*' ripened in a sunny place: cf. the spelling *abricoct*.]

Dissect this rather densely worded definition. Show the history of this word, from its origins to the point in which it was borrowed into English. State the language of origin, as well as any intermediate languages.

Discussion Questions

7. Many speakers of languages that borrow freely from English feel that their language is threatened by this "infiltration" of English words. The French even have an agency, the Académie Française, which tries to limit the borrowing of foreign words and promote the use of French words. Do you think that extensive borrowing is a threat to a language? Why or why not?

Activities

8. Using the *Oxford English Dictionary* (in print or online at http://www.oed.com), list the language that English **most recently borrowed** each of the following words from. (*Hint*: Look for the first language listed after a./ad., which stands for 'adapted from.')

a. brandy	**d.** dinner	**g.** jaguar	**j.** sauna
b. elephant	**e.** jungle	**h.** tycoon	**k.** squash
c. yam	**f.** ballot	**i.** robot	**l.** shampoo

9. Using the *Oxford English Dictionary* (in print or online at http://www.oed.com), list the language that each of the following words **originally** descends from. (In this case, you will have to read the whole entry.)

a. tea	**c.** hurricane
b. coach	**d.** admiral

10. Using the *Oxford English Dictionary* (in print or online at http://www.oed.com), answer the following questions about the English word *hippopotamus:*

    i. The word *hippopotamus* was adopted from Latin, but its origins lie in another language. What language does this word originally come from?

    ii. The OED entry shows how this word can be broken down into constituent parts. What morphological process is responsible for the formation of this word? What are the parts that this word can be broken down into? What do these words mean in English? (To answer these questions, you may want to refer to File 4.2.)

11. English has established itself as the current international language of commerce and scholarship. Many languages are currently borrowing words from English, especially in the areas of technology, computers, telecommunications, sports, and business. Pick two of these areas and write down ten words related to each. Then pick two foreign languages and find an online dictionary. A good way to find online dictionaries is to Google, for example, "English-Zulu translation" for an English-Zulu online dictionary. Now translate your words into your chosen languages and answer the following questions:

    i. Which of the words translated into each language seem to be borrowings from English? How, if at all, do they differ from the original English words (e.g., spelling and structure)?

    ii. Which of the languages you chose seems to borrow more from English? Which words of which topic are more widely borrowed?

    iii. Do some of the English words have more than one equivalent in the foreign languages you picked? Do all the translations seem to be borrowings, or do some seem to be native? Do you think speakers would prefer a native word or a borrowed word? Why?

File 11.3—Pidgin Languages

Exercises

12. The following data are taken from Tok Pisin, an English-based expanded pidgin. Which of the common features of pidgins mentioned in File 11.3 are found in these examples? Consider phonology, morphology, syntax, and semantics.

    a. [kapa   biloŋ   pinga   i waitpela]
        lid/cap   belong   finger   white
        'The fingernail is white / The fingernails are white'

    b. [jumi   save   tok   pisin]
        we   can   talk   pidgin
        'We can speak Tok Pisin"

    c. [mi laik   baim   sampela   pis]
        I   like   buy   some   fish
        'I want/would like to buy some fish'

    d. [mi dringim   liklik   hap   wara]
        I   drink-*trans*   little   bit   water
        'I drink a little water'

13. The following words are from Tok Pisin, an English-based expanded pidgin. Which English words are the Tok Pisin words derived from? In other words, how would they be translated literally into English? (*Hint:* Try saying the Tok Pisin words aloud.)

Tok Pisin	*English Translation*
a. taim bilong kol	'winter'
b. taim bilong san	'summer'
c. man bilong wokim gaden	'farmer'
d. kamup	'arrive'
e. tasol	'only'
f. haus sik	'hospital'
g. haus moni	'bank'
h. olgeta	'all'
i. sapos	'if'
j. solwara	'ocean'
k. kukim long paia	'barbeque'
l. handet yia	'century'
m. Hamas krismas yu gat?	'How old are you?'
n. hangre long dring	'thirsty'
o. pinga bilong fut	'toe'

14. Consider the Russenorsk, Norwegian, and Russian data below and answer the questions. Russenorsk is a pidgin derived through contact of Norwegian and Russian. (Data are adapted from Jahr 1996 and Broch and Jahr 1984.)

   i. Based on the example sentences given, which Russenorsk elements do you think derive from Russian and which from Norwegian?

   ii. Why do you think the Russenorsk phrase for *I shall die soon* is *I'll sleep on the church soon*?

   iii. Why do you think the Russenorsk word for *captain* is *principal*?

   a. Russenorsk: Moja kopom fiska
       Norwegian: jeg kjøper fish
       Russian: Ja pokupaju rybu
       Translation: 'I buy fish'

   b. Russenorsk: stari gammel, snart på kjæka slipom
       Norwegian: jeg er gammel, jeg skal dør snart
       Russian: Ja staryj. Ja skoro umru
       Translation: 'I'm old, I shall die soon'
               (literally: 'I'm old, I'll sleep on the church soon')

   c. Russenorsk: Moja vil spraek på principal
       Norwegian: Jeg vil taler med kapteinen
       Russian: Jaču pogovorit's kapitanom
       Translation: 'I want to speak with the captain.'

15. Consider the following Melanesian Pidgin text from Tanna in the New Hebrides (Clark 1983). The text is from 1859. Which aspects of the text are similar to and which are different from today's English? How much of the text can you understand?

You see . . . no good missionary stop Tanna. Suppose missionary stop here, by and by he speak, "Very good, all Tanna man make a work." You see that no good: Tanna man he no too much like work. By–and–by missionary speak, "No good woman make a work; very good, all man he only get one woman." You see Tanna man no like that:

he speak, "Very good plenty woman; very good woman make all work." Tanna man no savé work . . . he too much lazy; he too much gentleman!

File 11.4—Creole Languages

Exercises

16. Consider the Belize Creole text below. It is the beginning of a story involving Anansi and Tiger. Which aspects of the text are similar to and which are different from English? How much of the text can you understand? (*Hint:* Try to read the text as if it were written in IPA.)

> Wans apan a taim dier waz bra hanasi an bra taiga. So nou, ina kriol yu want a tel yu? Ina kriol? So nou de . . . wa maami tri mi de klos di haus. So nou . . . wan de . . . bra hanansi, yu no hou him triki aredi . . . i tel bra taiga mek dem go pik . . . maami. So nou bra taiga se "oke den les go," so . . . den gaan.

17. Consider the text Hawaiian Creole English below (*Hawai'i Tribune Herald* 1946). Which aspects of the text are similar to and which are different from English? How much of the text can you understand?

> Hukilepo, get many peoples on dees islan who stay tink me I outa be een som pupule hospeetal. But me I goin tell you something . . . One keiki been tell da udder one fo go buy ice cream fo dey eat up on top da bus. Den da udder one newa like go so he been say, "Poho money." Wasamala wid heem, he no can say "Me I stay broke?"

Discussion Questions

18. Discuss Bickerton's claim that the similarities found in the TMA marking of many creoles is due to a "bioprogram" in the human mind. Is his argument convincing? Why or why not?

File 11.5—Societal Multilingualism

Exercises

19. Consider the following dialogue that took place in Quebec (Heller 1982). French is marked by *italics*. What do you think is going on in the dialogue? What does this tell you about language choice or language abilities?

Man:	Could you tell me where the French test is?
Receptionist:	*Pardon?* (Pardon?)
Man:	Could you tell me where the French test is?
Receptionist:	*En français?* (In French?)
Man:	I have the right to be addressed in English by the government of Quebec.
Receptionist:	*Qu'est-ce qu'il dit?* (What's he saying?)

20. Consider the following dialogue in Spanish and Galician (adapted from Auer 1995). Spanish is marked by *italics*. What do you think is going on in the dialogue? What does this tell you about language choice or language abilities?

A:	*Y, qué tal el bivel de la Universidad? Es alto no?*
R:	Si.
A:	*Y qué qué haces? Filología inglesa? O . . .*

R: Nom, e, lingüística . . . pero estou interessado no galego.

A: Ai, no galego. *Bueno y fuiste becado, becado para allá? O, o . . .*

R: Eh? Si, bueno ali estou tamém trabalhando na universidade e . . . despois derom-me umha beca pra vor aqui a Galiza.

R: Ai, pra vir a Galícia.

English Translation:

A: *And what about the standards of the universities? They are high, aren't they?*

R: Yes.

A: *And what what are you studying? English Philology? Or . . .*

R: No, uh, linguistics . . . but I'm interested in Galician.

A: Oh, in Galician. *So you went there with a scholarship? Or, or . . .*

R: Uh? Yes, well, there I'm also working at the university and . . . later they gave me a grant to come here to Galiza.

R: Oh, to come to Galicia.

File 11.6—Language Endangerment and Language Death

Discussion Questions

21. Files 11.1 and 11.6 mention that many Native American languages in the United States have undergone the process of language death—that is, they are no longer spoken. In many regions of the world, there is an effort to prevent endangered languages from dying out or even to revive dormant languages. Do you think this is a worthwhile effort? Why? For your discussion, consider the following comments from people of the Miami tribe:

Person: Rosa Boington Beck (1969)

Comment: But they never allowed them to talk Indian. They couldn't talk their Indian language out there. Everything had to be English. And sometimes I think that was kind of bad because it got them away from their Indian language, their own tongue you know. I think we ought to kind of had some of that left to us. But they didn't. They took it away from us.

Person: Daryl Baldwin (2003)

Comment: Because the language reflects traditional beliefs and values, it begins to bring many community elements back together. The language is truly the glue that holds us together in our thoughts and in our hearts.

Person: Scott Shoemaker (Harrison, 1999)

Comment: The language is part of who we are. When you speak Miami, you think Miami. By learning the language, you learn about our ancestors' views of the world and their place in it.

Person: A writer for the tribal newspaper (2002)

Comment: Sometimes we [the Oklahoma tribal community] question, "Does anyone speak Miami?" Then we all point with confidence, at Daryl Baldwin, his family and those members who return year after year to the summer language program, and say 'Yes—we have members who speak Miami.'

22. Consider a minority language or minority dialect that is spoken in the area where you live. Do you think this language or dialect is endangered? Why? For your answer, think about the number of speakers the minority language or dialect has, what the prestige and the power situation are, how much pressure to assimilate to the majority language exists, and so on.

File 11.7—Case Studies in Language Contact
Discussion Questions

23. Both of the case studies given in this file had characteristics that are atypical of language contact situations (e.g., the lack of lexical borrowing among the languages in Kupwar, the borrowing of English basic vocabulary and morphology into Deitsch). Explain why these are atypical, and then give reasons why they might be happening in these particular contact situations.

Activities

24. Interview someone who speaks a language at home other than the majority language. Find out the following information from your language informant:

i. How well do your informant and his or her family speak the minority and majority languages? This may differ for different members of the family.

ii. Do you think the languages of your informant are in an adstratal or a substratal/superstratal relationship? Why do you think so?

iii. Is the way your informant and his or her family speak the majority language affected by the language of the home? Consider pronunciation, grammar, vocabulary, and usage. How can you explain these effects? Consider the speakers' proficiency and the contact situation (adstratal versus substratal/superstratal).

iv. Is the way your informant and his or her family speak the language of the home affected by the majority language? Again, consider pronunciation, grammar, vocabulary, and usage. How can you explain these effects? Consider the speakers' proficiency and the contact situation (adstratal versus substratal/superstratal).

CHAPTER

12

Language Change

FILE 12.0

What Is Language Change?

All languages change through time, but how they change, what drives these changes, and what kinds of changes we can expect may not be obvious. By comparing different languages, different dialects of the same language, or different historical stages of the same language, we can discover the history of languages and language groups or **families.** We can make hypotheses about the grammar, vocabulary, and pronunciation of a language long dead. This chapter considers the ways in which languages change and some of the factors that influence those changes.

Contents

FILE 12.1

Introducing Language Change

12.1.1 Synchronic vs. Diachronic Linguistics

One of the biggest successes of linguistics has been the scientific investigation and understanding of language change for what it really is: an inescapable fact about natural human languages and not the result of moral corruption or intellectual deterioration of communities of speakers, as traditionally thought by many language "authorities." All languages change except for the ones that do not have any native speakers left (i.e., dead languages) such as Latin, Sanskrit, and Attic Greek—and when these languages did have native speakers, they changed, too. When linguists describe the current phonological processes of a particular language, isolate that language's morphemes, or discover that language's syntactic rules, they analyze that language **synchronically;** that is, they analyze that language at a particular point in time. Languages, however, are not static; they are constantly changing entities. For example, consider the English word *know*. Why is it spelled with a <k> at the beginning? Was this letter ever pronounced? If it was pronounced at some earlier stage of the language, when and why was it "dropped"? The <k> in English words like *know* is a linguistic fossil reflecting in its spelling an earlier stage of the pronunciation of the language, as we will see in the following files. Although most of what has been presented in this book so far has been synchronic linguistics, linguists can also study language development through time, providing **diachronic** ('across-time') analyses. It may seem odd that languages would change, but if you consider the ways in which languages are tied to other social factors, it may begin to make more sense. For example, think about the numerous types of variation that were discussed in Chapter 10: a single language may have different varieties tied to the regions, ages, genders, ethnicities, or social classes of its speakers. This variation contributes to language change in at least two ways. First, if any of those external factors changes, the language may change in tandem. Second, the large amount of variation present in a language means that there are more choices, as it were, for speakers to select from in forming an utterance. Speakers and hearers thus may not use or encounter the same linguistic structures every time they use language. This variation gives language more capacity for change, since its users must be flexible anyway.

Historical linguistics is concerned with language change. It is interested in what kinds of changes occur and why, and equally important, what kinds of changes don't occur and why not. Historical linguists attempt to determine the changes that have occurred in a language's history, and how languages relate to one another historically.

12.1.2 An Example of Language Change

To see how English has changed over time, compare the following versions in ((1) through (4)) of the Lord's Prayer from the three major periods in the history of English. A contemporary version is also included. These passages are written in the standard spelling of the times they come from. While we know (see File 2.1) that spelling is not necessarily a good transcription system, the writings here do give a fairly accurate sense of some of the changes that have occurred in English. *Note:* The symbol <þ>, called *thorn,* is an Old English symbol for the voiceless interdental fricative [θ], as in <u>th</u>ree; <ð>, called *edh* (or *eth*), is the more familiar symbol for the voiced interdental fricative [ð], as in <u>th</u>en.)

(1) *Old English* (text ca. 1100)
Fæder ure þu þe eart on heofonum, si þin nama gehalgod. Tobecume þin rice. Gewurþe þin willa on eorðan swa swa on heofonum. Urne gedœghwamlican hlaf syle us to dæg. And forgyf us ure gyltas, swa swa we forgyfað urum gyltedum. And ne gelæd þu us on costnungen ac alys us of yfele. Soþlice.

(2) *Middle English* (text ca. 1400)
Oure fadir that art in heuenes halowid be thi name, thi kyngdom come to, be thi wille don in erthe es in heuene, yeue to us this day oure bread ouir other substance, & foryeue to us oure dettis, as we forgeuen to oure dettouris, & lede us not in to temptacion: but delyuer us from yuel, amen.

(3) *Early Modern English* (text 1611)
Our father which art in heaven, hallowed be thy Name. Thy kingdome come. Thy will be done, in earth, as it is in heaven. Giue vs this day our dayly bread. And forgiue vs our debts, as we forgiue our debters. And leade vs not into temptation, but deliuer vs from euill: For thine is the kingdome, and the power, and the glory, for euer, Amen.

(4) *Contemporary English*
Our Father, who is in heaven, may your name be kept holy. May your kingdom come into being. May your will be followed on earth, just as it is in heaven. Give us this day our food for the day. And forgive us our offenses, just as we forgive those who have offended us. And do not bring us to the test, but free us from evil. For the kingdom, the power, and the glory are yours forever. Amen.

Languages change in all aspects of the grammar: the phonology, morphology, syntax, and semantics, as these passages illustrate. Subsequent files will describe the various types of language change in detail.

12.1.3 Explaining Language Change

Historical linguistics as we know it began in the late eighteenth century, when Western European scholars began to notice some shared similar linguistic characteristics among ancient European and Asian languages, such as Latin, Greek, Gothic, Old Persian, and Sanskrit. These similarities led linguists to believe that these languages, and their modern descendants, must have evolved from a single ancestor, or "mother," language called **Proto-Indo-European** (PIE). Thus, these languages form a language family. Since then, we have discovered many other language families (see File 12.2).

If these languages did in fact share a common ancestor, a reasonable question to ask is, why are they different languages? One of the causes for language change is loss of homogeneity due to geographical division. No two people speak exactly the same way, let alone two groups of people. This intrinsic variation between speakers is compounded by other external factors such as geographical or social barriers. As groups of people spread out through Europe, they lost communication with each other, so that the language of each group went its own way, underwent its own changes, and thus came to differ from the others. Another major cause of language change is language contact (see Chapter 11), with the effect that languages in contact with each other begin to show similarities. American English has borrowed many Spanish words from Spanish-speaking communities in California and the Southwest, for example, as well as from contact with Mexican and Cuban immigrants. Language contact does not, of course, explain why Proto-Indo-European sub-divided as it did, but it does help to explain a number of shared characteristics—especially lexical items—among the world's languages. Language contact, like any other explanation for language change, does not provide a complete explanation, only a partial one. At times, linguists cannot find any particular cause that would motivate a language to change in a particular direction. Language change, then, may simply just happen.

12.1.4 Is Language Change Bad?

Often people view such change as a bad thing, so they try to resist it. Jonathan Swift, the late-seventeenth-century satirist who wrote *Gulliver's Travels*, felt that if the language changed, people would no longer be able to read his essays, so he supported the movement among English grammarians to stipulate prescriptive rules that would have the effect of reg-ulating current language usage as well as change. These grammarians based their rules on classical Latin from the first century B.C., viewing it as the perfect, model language, since it did not change. Even today, when we don't look to a language such as Latin as a model, some people consciously resist linguistic change. Consider the word *comprise.* Traditionally, the whole comprises, that is, 'takes in' or 'encompasses,' its parts as in:

(5) A chess set comprises thirty-two pieces.

Increasingly, however, people say:

(6) A chess set is comprised of thirty-two pieces.

in which the parts now comprise, that is, 'make up' or 'constitute,' the whole. Strict pre-scriptive grammarians regard this second utterance as ungrammatical. Despite these social views toward change, linguists regard change as neither good nor bad; descriptively speak-ing, it is simply a fact of language.

Language Relatedness

12.2.1 Similarities across Languages

If you look at two different languages, you often find similarities between them in addition to the numerous differences. Why might this be the case? As it turns out, there are a number of reasons for two languages to have certain elements in common.

One reason is so basic that it seems rather obvious: languages are spoken by humans, and humans are anatomically similar. So, the fact that lots of languages around the world make use of many of the same sounds in their phonological inventories is at least in part due to the similarity of the apparatus we all use to make those sounds. The sounds [p] and [a] occur in most languages of the world because they are some of the most basic sounds a human can make. The fact that these sounds recur does not tell us anything about the history of the languages with respect to each other (but see File 3.4 for more on implicational hierarchies in the sound systems of the world's languages).

Another reason two languages might look similar is that they have completely coincidentally hit upon similar ways of expressing the same meaning. In File 1.4, we said that language is arbitrary: that is, the sounds or gestures used to express particular thoughts are independent of the meanings of those thoughts. Though it is therefore quite rare that two languages would independently end up with words for the same concept that are similar phonetically, it does occasionally happen. For example, the Modern Greek word for *eye* is [mati], and the Malay word for *eye* is [mata]. These similarities are purely coincidental: the two languages in each pair are not related to each other in any way.

Yet another reason for two languages to have similar words for the same concepts is that occasionally, language is **not** arbitrary: that is, there is an iconic connection between the form of the word and the meaning. This is the case with many onomatopoeic words: for example, the words in English, Arabic, and Mandarin for a clock ticking are [tɪktɑk], [tɪktɪk], and [tiʔtaʔ], respectively (see File 1.4). This is not coincidence; it is a consequence of the fact that clocks make a particular sound when they tick, and this sound is mimicked by speakers of the language.

There are two other main reasons why languages might be similar to each other. The first, which was discussed in some detail in File 11.1, is language borrowing. When two languages are in contact with each other, it is quite common for one language to borrow words from the other language. So, for example, Spanish has borrowed the words *alcalde* 'mayor' and *naranja* 'orange' from Arabic, and Taiwan Sign Language borrowed the "thumbs-up" sign meaning 'good' from British Sign Language. Again, Spanish and Arabic are not related; nor are Taiwan and British Sign Languages. These languages simply share some of the same vocabulary because they were in contact with each other.

The final main reason that languages can be similar to each other is that they may in fact be what linguists refer to as "genetically related" to each other.[1] That is, at one point,

---

[1] Note that this is not "genetically related" in the biological sense, but rather in the sense of "having to do with common origins."

the two languages may have been the same language—but over time, the language split into two different varieties, and each variety underwent enough changes that they can now be considered separate languages.

It is important to realize, however, that there are many reasons that languages might be similar to each other, and you should never assume that just because two languages share some similar form-meaning mappings, they must be related.

How, then, might we determine whether two languages are in fact related or simply similar for other reasons? First, we would want to see that there are a large number of correlations between form and meaning across the two languages (these correlations often involve similarities, but they need not). When the correlations are not confined to a few words, and occur across the entire vocabulary, we minimize the chances of coincidence or onomatopoeia misleading our thinking. For example, if we looked at the Latin and the Basque words for 'peace,' shown in (1), we might think that they are similar.

(1) Latin: [pakem]
    Basque: [bake]
               'peace'

Both words start with a bilabial stop, followed by the vowel [a] and a voiceless velar stop, and they mean the same thing. Also, there is not any obvious use of onomatopoeia here: what is the sound of 'peace,' after all? Could the languages be related?

To find out, we would first try to gather other words in the two languages to see whether these similarities are widespread. What do the data in (2) tell you?

(2) Latin: [uːnus]   [treːs]   [auris]   [soror]
    Basque: [bat]   [iru]   [belari]   [aispa]
               'one'   'three'   'ear'   'sister'

Based on the words in (2), we would not be tempted to think that Latin and Basque are related. As it turns out, there are far more words that seem to be dissimilar than similar in the two languages, which indicates that they are not genetically related—the similarity between the two words for 'peace' in (1) must be due either to borrowing or to coincidence.

Another good indicator of whether or not two languages are related is the type of words that correlate across the two languages. That is, finding a lot of words that seem to have similar form-meaning mappings still doesn't mean that the two languages are necessarily related. Sometimes, one language borrows so heavily from another language that their vocabularies overlap to a high degree.

Fortunately for linguists, not all words tend to get borrowed, as was discussed in File 11.1 on language contact. In that file, we explained how both core vocabulary items and grammatical function words are not usually borrowed, because they tend to already exist in a language, and so there is no need to borrow terms from another language. So, even though core vocabulary or function words can sometimes be borrowed, most borrowings are of words for things that a culture does not already have.

This fact about borrowings is useful for linguists because it can help tease apart languages that are actually related from languages that have simply been in contact with each other. When two languages share many form-meaning mappings across their vocabularies, particularly in the areas of core vocabulary and grammatical function words, it is generally the case that the two languages are genetically related to each other—that is, derived from a common source. The rest of this file discusses some of the ways that language relatedness can be modeled, given what linguists have discovered about the language families of the world. More about discovering **how** languages are related is presented in File 12.7.

12.2.2 Models of Language Relatedness

The notion that similar languages are related and descended from an earlier, common language (a **protolanguage**) goes back to the late eighteenth century when Sir William Jones suggested that the linguistic similarities of Sanskrit (an important ancient language of India) to Ancient Greek and Latin could best be accounted for by assuming that all three were descended from a common ancestral language. This language was called Proto-Indo-European.

Jones's suggestion was developed in the nineteenth century and gradually came under the influence of Darwin's theory of the evolution of species. Scholars at the time considered language and linguistic development to be analogous in many ways to biological phenomena. Thus, it was suggested that languages, like other living organisms, had "family trees" and "ancestors." A sample "genealogical tree" for the Indo-European (I-E) family of languages appears in (3).

(3) Indo-European family tree

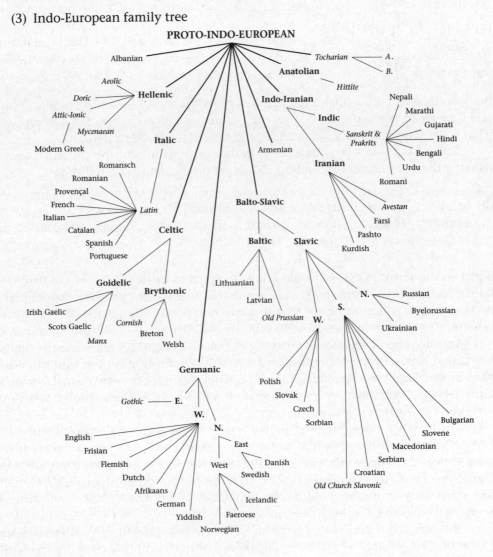

Languages that are no longer spoken are italicized (*Cornish*), and significant subbranches are in boldface (**Baltic**). Indo-European Family Tree adapted from Jeffers and Lehiste, *Principles and Methods for Historical Linguistics* (1979), p. 302. © 1979 MIT Press. All rights reserved.

The **family tree theory,** as formulated by August Schleicher in 1871, assumes that speech sounds change in regular, recognizable ways (the **regularity hypothesis**) and that because of this, phonological similarities among languages may be due to a genetic relationship among those languages (the **relatedness hypothesis**). In order to fill in the particulars of such a relationship, it is necessary to **reconstruct** the hypothetical parent from which the related languages are derived. The principal technique for reconstructing the common ancestor (the protolanguage) of related languages is known as the **comparative method** (discussed in detail in File 12.7).

In keeping with the analogy of language relationships to human families, the theory makes use of the terms mother (or parent), daughter, and sister languages. In the family tree of I-E, for example, French and Spanish are sisters, and both are daughters of Latin; Germanic is the mother of English; and so on. The model clearly shows the direction of change and the relations among languages, the older stages of the languages being located fewer nodes from the top of the tree and direct descendants being linked to their ancestors through the straight lines or "branches."

Of course, family tree models can be created for any group of related languages, not just Indo-European languages. Current linguistic research has traced most of the world's languages back to a certain number of language families that are essentially independent of each other. According to SIL International's publication Ethnologue,[2] there are 100 language families (e.g., Indo-European, Sino-Tibetan, Niger-Congo, etc.) along with 121 signed languages, 86 creoles, 18 pidgins, 21 mixed languages, 40 language "isolates" that do not seem to be related to any other languages, and 78 unclassified languages. As you can see in the tree model for Indo-European in (3), most families can be broken down into smaller sub-branches of even more closely related languages. These relationships may be somewhat familiar to you because we have made reference to them throughout the book when presenting data from various languages. For example, in the phonology exercises, we might tell you that Russian is an Indo-European language (the major family) of the Slavic branch (the smaller branch of the main family), or that Bukusu is a Niger-Congo language of the Bantu branch. To illustrate another group of language families, (4) gives the family tree of the Uralic family. Most of the Uralic languages are spoken in northern and eastern Europe, in Finland, Sweden, Estonia, Russia, and Hungary. Although many are in close contact with Indo-European languages such as Swedish or Russian, the Uralic languages seem to be unrelated to the Indo-European languages.

However, a disadvantage exists in that the structure of the family tree may lead people to develop faulty views of two aspects of language change: (1) that each language forms a uniform speech community without internal variation and without contact with its neighbor languages, so that all speakers of Latin, for example, are assumed to have spoken exactly the same way at the time French and Spanish split off; and (2) that the split of a parent language into its daughter languages is a sudden or abrupt occurrence, happening without intermediate stages.

These two views are not supported by the linguistic evidence we have from modern languages, however. No language is uniform or isolated from others, but rather is always made up of dialects that are still recognized as belonging to the same language (see Chapter 10 on language variation), and a language always shares similarities with other languages in its family, even those belonging to a different subgroup. Furthermore, studies of modern language change have shown that languages do not split apart abruptly, but rather drift apart very gradually, starting as dialects and ending up as separate languages only after years of accumulated change. In fact, the dividing point between two "dialects" and two "languages" is often impossible to locate exactly and is often obscured by nonlinguistic (e.g., political, social, or geographic) factors. Thus, there are a number of changes that can

---

[2]See http://www.ethnologue.com.

(4) Uralic family tree

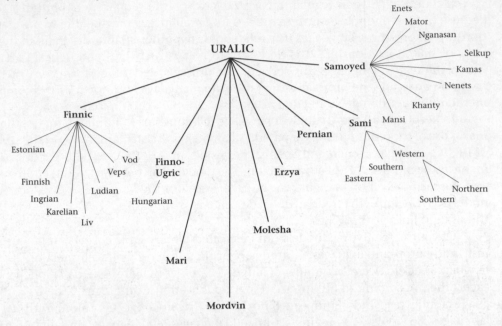

Adapted from descriptions in Gordon, Raymond G., Jr. (ed.), 2005. Ethnologue: Languages of the World, Fifteenth edition. Dallas, Tex.: SIL International. Online version: http://www.ethnologue.com/.

spread across the branches depicted in tree diagrams, or that don't map neatly onto single, separate lines.

To supplement the family tree model and help overcome these difficulties by representing language relationships in a different manner, Johannes Schmidt proposed the **wave theory** in 1872. This theory recognizes the gradual spread of change throughout a dialect, language, or group of languages, much as a wave expands on the surface of a pond from the point where a pebble (representing the source of the sound change) has been tossed in. Dialects are formed by the spread of different changes from different starting points and at different rates; some changes reinforce each other while others only partially overlap or affect only a certain area, much as the waves formed by a scattering of pebbles thrown into a pond may partially overlap. These changes can either bring branches of language families closer together or push them farther apart.

The diagram in (5) illustrates how part of the same Indo-European family shown in the tree diagram in (3) might be modeled in wave theory. In (5), traditional genetic subgroups of languages that you might find on a tree diagram are enclosed in solid lines, while "diffusion" groups (those that have become more similar over time through the sharing of particular historical changes, despite being considered separate genetic subgroups at the time of their mutual influences), are enclosed in dashed lines, thus cutting across the traditional categories of the family tree. By looking at ever-smaller linguistic changes, one can also show the languages within each group and the dialects within each language, indicating clearly how variable languages can be. In this way, the wave diagram avoids the two faults of the family tree model, though it in turn suffers from disadvantages relating to problems in analyzing the genetic history of the languages involved.

(5) Indo-European wave diagram

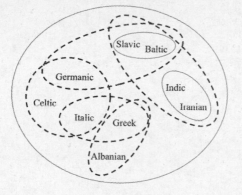

In fact, neither the family tree model nor the wave model presents entirely adequate or accurate accounts of language change or the relatedness of languages. For example, it is now known that languages can show linguistic similarities without necessarily being related. The similarities may be the result of borrowing in situations of language contact, language drift (i.e., independent but identical changes in distinct dialects or languages), similarities in types of morphological structures, syntactic similarities, or other reasons. Nonetheless, the family tree model and wave model do provide useful frameworks for the discussion of language change—both accurately represent certain aspects of language relatedness.

Sound Change

12.3.1 What Is Sound Change?

Sound change is the most widely studied aspect of language change. There are a number of reasons why this is so. First, the study of how the sounds of languages change has a long tradition behind it, more so than any other area of historical linguistics. As a result we are more informed about this particular area of language change than other areas. Second, it is often impossible to understand changes in other areas of the language system without studying sound change, because sound change does not affect just the system of sounds of a language but may also affect a language's morphology, and it can be involved in changes in syntax and semantics.[1] Third, the study of sound change has provided a basis for the study of language relationships and the reconstruction of parent (proto-) languages. Finally, sound change provides a very good introduction to the basic aims and goals of those who study language change: to describe the types of changes possible in language systems and to determine the causes of those changes.

Sound change is an alteration in the phonetics (Chapter 2) of a sound as a result of a phonological process (Chapter 3). If a phonological process is introduced into a language where it did not formerly occur, it may result in a sound change. For example, at an early period in the history of English the voiceless velar stop [k] occurred before the long front vowel [iː] in words like 'chide' *cidan* [kiːdan]. Later in the Old English period the velar consonant [k] was palatalized to [tʃ] before the front vowel [iː]. The introduction of the phonological process of palatalization resulted in the sound change k > tʃ before [iː] in Old English. The phonetic shape of [k] (the voiceless velar stop) was altered to [tʃ] (a voiceless palatal affricate) as a result of the phonological process of palatalization.

At this point, it is necessary to make the distinction between the introduction of a phonological process and sound change clearly understood. The introduction of a phonological process into a language alone cannot be considered sound change. While it is a necessary first step in the process of sound change, the introduction of a phonological process at first changes the structure of a word in certain specific speech contexts. For example, the basic pronunciation of the word *interesting* is [ɪntəɹɛstɪŋ], and this pronunciation occurs most often in formal speech situations, for example, when talking with business associates. When we speak with close friends in a casual situation, however, we may allow the

---

[1]For example, nouns in Latin were phonologically marked to indicate their grammatical roles (subject, object, etc.). This marking allowed Latin to have relatively free word order, because each word's role was marked, regardless of where it appeared in the sentence. However, many of the markers of grammatical roles eventually disappeared through sound changes. As a result, the nouns themselves did not have any overt indication of their grammatical roles anymore. This meant that Latin had to develop another way of indicating the roles; instead of having morphemes marking them, word order was used. So, for example, the subject always came first, the verb second, and the object third, an order that had not been required before. In this way, sound changes led to morphological and then syntactic changes!

phonological process that deletes schwa [ə] before the liquids [ɹ] and [l] to apply and pronounce the word [ɪntɹɛstɪŋ]. But we cannot assume that there has been a sound change of ə > Ø before liquids on the basis that a phonological process has been applied in casual speech. For sound change to occur, the basic form of a word must be permanently altered in all contexts. In the example above, speakers would have to choose the variant pronunciation of interesting [ɪntɹɛstɪŋ] in all speech situations and abandon the pronunciation [ɪntəɹɛstɪŋ] altogether.

Obviously this has not happened (yet!) in the case of *interesting*, though it did happen in the Old English example discussed above. Recall that the introduction of palatalization resulted in alternate pronunciations for the word 'chide' *cidan* [kiːdan] and [tʃiːdan]. When the pronunciation [tʃiːdan] was first introduced into Old English, it was no doubt tied to certain speech situations, much as the pronunciation [ɪntɹɛstɪŋ] is in Modern English. Gradually, however, over a considerable period of time, the pronunciation [tʃiːdan] was adopted by Old English speakers and the pronunciation [kiːdan] was abandoned. In this way the basic form of the word was permanently altered in Old English to [tʃiːdan]. Thus the introduction of the palatalization process resulted ultimately in the sound change k > tʃ before [iː]. *Note*: As you may have already noticed, when writing sound change rules, it is traditional to use a 'greater than' sign, >, pointing from the earlier sound to its later outcome.

12.3.2 The Regularity of Sound Change

One of the most fascinating aspects of sound change that emerges after studying a particular change over a long enough period of time is that it will always turn out to be completely regular; that is, every instance of the sound in question will undergo the change. Thus, in our Old English example we would say that the sound change k > tʃ before [iː] is **regular** because in every Old English word that contained [k] before [iː] it changed to [tʃ]; the change was not isolated to the word for 'chide.' Sound change does not spread to all possible words instantaneously, nor does every speaker in a community pick up a sound change overnight. The acceptance of sound change in a community is a gradual process, spreading, often rapidly, from word to word, or word-class to word-class, and from one speaker to the next until all possible words and speakers are affected. You may recall, from the language variation files in Chapter 10, that a particular pronunciation may be associated with one or another segment of a speech community, and that this may be correlated with region, social class, age, ethnicity, and so on. One way to conceive of the dynamic spread of sound change is as spread across socially based varieties.

Though sound change spreads gradually, the ultimate regularity of sound change can be verified quite easily. In Old English, for example, the ancestor of our Modern English word *house* was spelled *hus* and pronounced [huːs]. If we compare these two words, we observe a change in the quality of the vowel. In Old English, the vowel was the long high back rounded vowel [uː], while in Modern English the vowel is a diphthong, [aʊ]. What is important is that this is not the only example of the sound change uː > aʊ in the history of English. In fact we can find any number of Old English words with [uː] that are pronounced with the diphthong [aʊ] in Modern English, for example, Old English *mus* [muːs] > Modern English *mouse* [maʊs]; Old English *lus* [luːs] > Modern English *louse* [laʊs]; Old English *ut* [uːt] > Modern English *out* [aʊt]; and so on.

12.3.3 Types of Sound Change

The development of Old English [uː] is an example of **unconditioned sound change**. That is, every instance of [uː], no matter where it occurred in a word or what sounds were next to it, became [ɑʊ]. More often than not, however, it is the case that sounds are influenced by the sounds that occur around them. When a sound changes because of the influence of a neighboring sound, the change is called a **conditioned sound change.** We have already considered a good example of a conditioned sound change from the history of English, namely, the palatalization of [k] before the front vowel [iː]. Notice that the only voiceless velar stops that were palatalized were those occurring before the vowel [iː]; all other velar stops remain nonpalatal. Evidence of this is Old English *ku* [kuː], corresponding to Modern English *cow* [kɑʊ]. It is important to focus on the phonetics here, rather than the spelling, because even though the spelling happens to have changed from <k> to <c>, this in itself does not necessarily imply a change in pronunciation.

One of the ways to determine whether a sound change is conditioned or not is to see if it applies only when a sound appears in particular environments (conditioned) or if it applies wherever that sound appears (unconditioned). For example, if you can write a rule to describe the sound change in the form that we saw in File 3.2 on phonological rules, X → Y / C __ D, then the sound change must be conditioned: X becomes Y only when it comes after C and before D. If, on the other hand, your rule simply looks like X → Y, then you have an unconditioned sound change.

Below we discuss several types of sound changes that are particularly common in the world's languages. For each type, we give an example or two of changes that have happened in English. Note that the first two, assimilation and dissimilation, are by definition conditioned sound changes: they both involve sounds becoming more like or less like the sounds that are near them. The other changes can occur as either conditioned changes or unconditioned changes; for each example we give, we indicate whether it is conditioned or not. (Some of the terms may be familiar from Chapter 3, "Phonology"; see File 3.2 in particular.)

a. Assimilation refers to a situation in which one sound becomes more like another sound. In Old English, voiceless fricatives became voiced when they occurred between voiced sounds, for example, the Old English word for 'wolves,' *wulfas* [wulfas] came to be pronounced [wulvas] in Middle English. This is how modern English comes to have an alternation between [f] and [v] in the singular *wolf* versus the plural *wolves.*

b. Dissimilation refers to a situation in which two similar sounds become less like one another. The English word *fifth* [fɪfθ], which ends with two consecutive voiceless fricatives [f] and [θ], has undergone a dissimilating sound change in some varieties whereby the second fricative has been replaced by a voiceless stop [t], giving the pronunciation [fɪft].

It is interesting (and important) to observe that in varieties where this change occurred, we talk about a **diachronic** sound change (θ > t / f__#), but if we compare a changed variety to a variety of English which has not undergone this change, we can see **synchronic** variation within English ([fɪfθ] in some varieties, [fɪft] in others). Consider this distinction with respect to the other examples as well.

c. Deletion occurs when a sound is no longer pronounced. At the end of the Middle English period unstressed word-final [ə] was deleted, for example, Middle English *nose* [nɔːzə] > Modern English *nose* [noʊz]. In this case, spelling has remained the same, yet a sound change has taken place. This is an example of a conditioned sound change because only word-final [ə] was deleted, not [ə] in all environments.

d. Insertion is the opposite of deletion and occurs when a sound is added to the pronunciation of a word. In a considerable number of Modern English varieties the basic form of the word *athlete* is pronounced [æθəlit]. In this word a sound change has taken place, inserting [ə] between consonants of a cluster that was perceived to be difficult to pronounce. The older form of the word, still common in varieties which have not undergone this change, is [æθlit]. This, too, is an example of a conditioned sound change: [ə] is inserted only between[θ] and [l], not in between every two segments!

e. Monophthongization refers to a change from a **diphthong** (a complex vowel sound consisting of two vowel sounds) to a simple vowel sound, a **monophthong.** A good example of unconditioned monophthongization occurred at the beginning of the Modern English period. In Middle English the diphthong [ɪʊ] occurred in words such as *rude* [rɪʊdə], *rule* [rɪʊlə], *new* [nɪʊə], *due* [dɪʊə], and so forth. In Modern English this diphthong became a simple vowel [u]; this change is apparent in the modern pronunciations for these words: *rude* [ɹud], *rule* [ɹul], *new* [nu], *due* [du]. This is an unconditioned change because *all* instances of [ɪʊ] have changed to [u], at least in some dialects.

f. Diphthongization is the opposite of monophthongization, and refers to a change from a simple vowel sound to a complex one. In the Middle English period the long high front vowel [iː] became a diphthong [aɪ], for example, Middle English *is* [iːs] became Modern English *ice* [aɪs]. This is parallel in many ways to the diphthongizing change discussed earlier of uː > aʊ, seen in Old English *hus* [huːs] > Modern English *house* [haʊs]. This, too, was an unconditioned sound change, as all instances of [iː] were affected.

g. Metathesis refers to a change in the order of sounds. For example, the Old English words *hros, frist, thridde,* and *bridd* are Modern English *horse, first, third,* and *bird,* respectively: in these words, a consonant-/r/-vowel-consonant sequence changed to a consonant-vowel-/r/-consonant sequence, with the vowel and /r/ sounds switching places. This is a conditioned sound change; it is not just any /r/-vowel sequence that metathesized, but rather only ones both preceded and followed by another consonant. So, for example, *rude* and *brew* did not undergo this change.

h. Raising and **lowering** refer to changes in the height of the tongue in the production of sounds. At the beginning of the Middle English period the word *noon* was pronounced [noːn], with a long mid, back, round vowel. By the end of the Middle English period, however, the word was pronounced [nuːn], the tongue height being raised from mid to high. Thus the sound change oː > uː is called raising. Though raising is often conditioned by surrounding segments, such as neighboring higher or lower vowels, this particular change was unconditioned in English.

i. Backing and **fronting** refer to alterations in the frontness or backness of the tongue in the production of sounds. At the beginning of the Modern English period there was an unconditioned sound change whereby the back vowel [ɑ] became the front vowel [æ], for example in words like *calf, path, glass, past, ask.*

12.3.4 Phonetic vs. Phonemic Change

When we speak of sound change, it is possible to make a distinction between **phonetic** and **phonemic** change. Phonetic change refers to a change in pronunciation of allophones that has no effect on the phonemic system of the language. For example, over the course of time the English phoneme /r/ has undergone several changes. Early in the history of English the unrestricted ("elsewhere") allophone of the phoneme /r/ was pronounced as a trill, [r] (as it still is in Scottish English). At present, however, in American English at least, the unrestricted allophone of /r/ is pronounced as an alveolar retroflex liquid [ɹ]. This is a phonetic change because it affects only the **pronunciation** of words with /r/: all of them still have the phoneme /r/ in the same phonological distribution. That is, it is not the case that one dialect has developed a phonemic contrast between, for example, /ɹ/ and /r/; all of the dialects have the same phonemes but with different phonetic realizations.

Similarly, in the Middle English period voiceless stops were not aspirated in initial position. There was only one allophone for each of the three stop phonemes: /p/-[p], /t/-[t], /k/-[k]. Then these sounds underwent a sound change whereby stop consonants became aspirated initially before a stressed vowel. This sound change altered the pronunciation of the stop phonemes by adding one allophone to each phoneme: /p/-[p] and [pʰ], /t/-[t] and [tʰ], /k/-[k] and [kʰ]. Still, the phonemic system of English has remained unaffected, that is, the number of voiceless stop phonemes neither increased nor decreased subsequent to the introduction of the aspirated allophones. This, then, was a phonetic change. Phonetic changes do not affect the phonemic system at all but rather add or delete an allophone of a phoneme, or substitute one allophone for another.

Phonemic change, on the other hand, refers to sound change that changes the phonemic system of a language in some way, usually by the addition or loss of a phoneme. In Old English the phoneme /f/ had one allophone, [f], until about CE 700, and there was no separate phoneme /v/. Then a change occurred whereby [f] was voiced when it occurred between voiced sounds, for example, Old English *wives* [wiːvas]. At this time the sound change had no effect on the phonemic system; it merely created an additional allophone for the phoneme /f/, namely, [v]. Later borrowings from French into English, however, created situations in which the two sounds came into contrast with one another, e.g., *safe* [seɪf] and *save* [seɪv]. As a result, we must now consider these two sounds members of separate phonemes—/f/-[f] and /v/-[v], respectively. Thus, the originally phonetic sound change f > v ultimately led to a phonemic change, since it resulted in the creation of a new phoneme, /v/.

Morphological Change

12.4.1 Proportional Analogy and Paradigm Leveling

As a first example of morphological change, which will serve to introduce the topic, let us consider the early Modern English past tense of the verb *climb*. As recently as several hundred years ago, the usual past tense of this verb was *clomb* (/klom/). In Modern English, on the other hand, the past tense is *climbed* (/klaɪmd/). Thus, over the course of the past few centuries *climbed* has replaced *clomb* as the past tense of *climb*.

It should not have escaped your notice that in this example the new form of the past tense of *climb* is exactly what would be expected as the regular past tense of an English verb, that is, [-d] after a voiced consonant (compare *rhyme* [ɹaɪm] : *rhymed* [ɹaɪm-d]). In terms of the formation of the past tense, *clomb* is an irregularity because past tense in English is not generally formed by altering the vowel of the base. Thus, it appears that the irregular past tense form (*clomb*) has given way to a past tense form made with the productive, regular past tense morpheme, *-ed*. In a sense, then, we can talk about the change as being one that brought *climb* more in line with a majority of verbs of English, and that these verbs—and in particular the productive pattern of forming the past tense with these verbs—exerted some influence on *climb*. This led to the replacement of *clomb* by the more expected and usual (by the rules of English past tense formation) *climbed*.

This account also provides us with some insight into the nature of morphological change: it often involves the influence of one form or group of forms over another. In the case of *clomb* → *climbed,* the influence of the regular past tense forms led to the change; this type of morphological change can often be schematized as a four-part proportion, as in (1).

(1) a   :   b   ::   c   :   X
   Read: "*a*   is to   *b*   as   *c*   is to   *X*"

The proportion is complete when you "solve for X" and find something that bears the same relationship to *c* that *b* bears to *a*. This four-part proportion applied to the past tense of *climb* gives the following:

(2) rhyme   :   rhym + ed   ::   climb   :   X = climb + ed

You don't have to be a mathematician to solve for X and get *climbed*. The word *rhyme* was chosen here only as an example; it is perhaps more accurate to state the proportion in terms of a general pattern that is extended to another verb, i.e.,

(3) VERB   :   VERB + ed   ::   climb   :   climb + ed
   (present)   (past)   (present)   (past)

Since this type of morphological change can be schematized as a four-part proportion, it is generally known as **proportional analogy.**

In general, morphological change involving the influence of one form or set of forms over another is called **analogy** (or **analogical change**). As with *clomb* → *climbed,* analogical change generally introduces regularity into a system. For example, in the early stages of Latin, the **paradigm** (a set of inflectionally related forms) for the word for 'honor' was included in the following forms:

(4) Nominative   honos
    Genitive   honos-is
    Accusative   honos-em

This paradigm was perfectly regular in that there was just a single form of the stem *honos-* to which the inflectional endings were added. Somewhat later in the development of Latin, a sound change took place by which [s] became [r] between vowels (intervocalic position); this was quite general and affected all instances of intervocalic [s] in that language. The effect on the paradigm of the word for 'honor' was to create two different forms of the stem: *honos-* in the nominative and *honor-* in the other cases (because the [s] was intervocalic in them but final in the nominative):

(5) Nominative   honos
    Genitive   honor-is
    Accusative   honor-em

The resulting paradigm was thus irregular in its having two stem shapes. Later on in Latin, a further change took place creating a regular paradigm once more: the nominative took the form *honor,* giving:

(6) Nominative   honor
    Genitive   honor-is
    Accusative   honor-em

This last change was not a widespread one, and there are many instances of final [s] in Latin that did not change to [r] (e.g., *genus* 'kind,' *navis* 'ship,' etc.). This change is therefore different from sound change; only one word paradigm was affected.

Note that this morphological change has a result similar to that in the first example, namely, introducing regularity. This change introduced regularity into a paradigm that had been disturbed by the workings of sound change. This type of analogical change that takes place within a paradigm is often called **paradigm leveling**; the motivation, though, is the same as with the form-class type of analogy (proportional analogy) seen with *clomb* → *climbed,* that is, it eliminates irregularity among morphologically related forms.

The two analogical changes discussed above involve the elimination of irregularities in the morphological subsystem of a language. While regularity is perhaps the most notable result of analogical change, regularity is not, however, the only outcome. There are other analogical changes that have little if anything to do with regularization. We turn now to a brief discussion of these changes.

12.4.2 Back Formation and Folk Etymology

The process of **back formation** can be illustrated by the following examples:

(7) a. work + er   :   work   ::   burglar   :   X = burgle
     (agent noun)   (verb)   (agent noun)   (verb)

    b. operat + ion   :   operate   ::   orientation   :   X = orientate
        (noun)   (verb)   (noun)   (verb)

As you may have noticed, the process of back formation appears to be similar to the process of proportional analogy. However, the fundamental difference becomes apparent upon closer inspection. Back formation involves the creation of a new base form (e.g., *burgle*), whereas proportional analogy involves the creation of a new inflected form.

One of the more important differences between back formation and proportional analogy has to do with the fact that back formation is often preceded by misanalysis. The first example of back formation cited above is a case in point. English speakers borrowed *burglar* from Norman French speakers as a monomorphemic word; at this time there was no word *burgle* in English. But *burglar* was misanalyzed by English speakers as consisting of a verb *burgle* plus an affix *-er* because its phonological structure and its meaning resembled the set of English words that had been formed by such a process, for example, *worker, runner,* and so on. As a result, the identification of *burglar* with this pattern of word formation, namely, verb + *-er* → agent noun, has resulted in the creation of a new verb, *burgle*.

As we saw from the preceding discussion, the primary motivation for the back formation of *burgle* from *burglar* was the common derivational process verb + *-er* → agent noun. Interestingly, the influence of productive inflectional processes can also result in back formations. Consider the case of Modern English *cherry—cherries*. This word was borrowed from Norman French *cherise*. Note, however, that this word was a singular, not a plural, noun for French speakers. But to English speakers this noun sounded like a plural since it appeared to follow the regular pattern for the formation of plural nouns. As a result, the word *cherise* was misanalyzed as a plural, and a new singular noun was back-formed, namely, *cherry*.

As a final example of analogical change we consider the process known as **folk etymology.** As we saw from the example of back formation discussed above, misanalysis played an important role as a motivating factor for the creation of the verb *burgle*. Similarly, the driving force behind the process of folk etymology is also misanalysis. In the case of folk etymology, however, obscure morphemes are misanalyzed in terms of more familiar morphemes. As an example of folk etymology consider the following case taken from an article in a university student newspaper. In this article the author referred to a variety of snake known as the garter snake as a "garden snake." In this example, the word *garden* has been substituted for the word *garter*. There were probably a number of reasons for the misanalysis of *garter* as *garden*. Foremost among them was undoubtedly the fact that the two words are very similar phonologically, differing significantly only in the point and manner of articulation of the final consonant. Moreover, from the point of view of semantics it is not very clear to most English speakers why the word *garter* should be used to describe the stripes that are found on most varieties of garter snakes, particularly since the noun *garter* refers most commonly to an elasticized band worn around the leg to support hose. The final factor contributing to this misanalysis was undoubtedly the fact that, at least in urban areas, garter snakes are commonly found in and around gardens.

The case of folk etymology just discussed illustrates an important point about this analogical process: it occurs most often in cases where the morphological makeup of a word is obscure to speakers. There are a variety of reasons for morphological obscurity. One variety is illustrated by the Old English word *brydeguma*, Modern English *bridegroom*. The morphological makeup of this word ('bride-man' in Old English) was obscured by the fact that *guma* 'man' ceased to exist as an independent word in English. In order to make this word more accessible in terms of its structure, English speakers substituted the word *groom*. Note again that, as was the case with the substitution of *garden* for *garter*, the substitution of *groom* is motivated by phonological similarity (*guma* and *groom* sound a lot alike) and a semantic relationship (a *groom* is also a man, more specifically a serving-man or a man who attends to others). Some other examples of folk etymology are given in (8).

(8) **Folk Etymology**   **Source Phrase or Word**
   sick-as-hell anemia   <   sickle-cell anemia
   old-timer's disease   <   Alzheimer's Disease
   nephew-tism   <   nepotism
   sparrow-grass   <   asparagus
   chaise lounge   <   chaise longue

12.4.3 Adding New Words to a Language

One other way that languages can change morphologically is by the addition of new words to their vocabularies. Of course, words are often borrowed from other languages (see File 11.2 for borrowings in English), but there are also other ways in which new words come into a language, and many of these processes occur not only in English but in many of the world's languages. Here we will look at some of the other types of new-word formation processes. Processes of derivational morphology discussed in Chapter 4 are also relevant here.

a. Acronyms are formed by taking the initial sounds (or letters) of the words of a phrase and uniting them into a combination that is itself pronounceable as a separate word. Thus *NATO* is an acronym for **N**orth **A**tlantic **T**reaty **O**rganization, *laser* for **l**ight **a**mplification *through the* **s**timulated **e**mission *of* **r**adiation, and *radar* for **r**adio **d**etection **a**nd **r**anging. Notice that the initials used are not always one per word, and function words are often skipped altogether in the creation of acronyms.

b. Blends are combinations of the parts of two words, usually (but not necessarily) the beginning of one word and the end of another: *smog* from *smoke* and *fog*, *brunch* from *breakfast* and *lunch*, and *chortle* from *chuckle* and *snort*. (Lewis Carroll invented this last blend, and his poem "Jabberwocky" contains several other examples of interesting blends.) An important point here is that neither piece used in the formation of a blend should be a morpheme in its own right; for example, given that the pieces of *brunch* are *br-* + *-unch*, neither piece is meaningful on its own otherwise in English.

c. Clipping is a way of shortening words without paying attention to the derivational morphology of the word (or related words). *Exam* has been clipped from *examination*, *dorm* from *dormitory*, and both *taxi* and *cab* from *taxi cab* (itself a clipping from *taximeter cabriolet*). Be careful to distinguish clipping from the pieces used in blending.

d. Coinages are words that are created without using any of the methods described above and without employing any other word or word parts already in existence; that is, they are created out of thin air. Such brand names as *Kodak* and *Exxon* were made up without reference to any other existing word or morpheme, as were the words *pooch* and *snob*.

e. Conversions are new words created simply by shifting the part of speech of a word to another part without changing the form of the word. *Laugh, run, buy*, and *steal* started out as verbs but can now also be used as nouns, while *position, process*, and *contrast* are nouns from which verbs have been formed. This process is sometimes also called **functional shift**.

f. Eponyms are words (often places, inventions, activities, etc.) that are named for persons somehow connected with them; for instance, *Washington, DC* (for *George Washington*, and *District of Columbia* for *Christopher Columbus*), German *Kaiser* and Russian *tsar* (for *Julius Caesar*), and the units of measurement *ohm* and *watt* (for *George Simon Ohm* and *James Watt*, respectively).

12.4.4 Summary

Proportional analogy and paradigm leveling are characterized by the elimination of irregularities from the morphological subsystem of a language. Back formation and folk etymology do not involve the elimination of irregularities per se. Rather, they involve the misanalysis of unfamiliar morphemes in ways that make them more accessible to speakers. Nevertheless, the four varieties of analogical change that we have discussed are characterized by the fact that they involve the influence of one particular form or set of forms over another.

As with sound change, the new forms introduced by morphological changes and new word-formation processes do not necessarily take hold instantaneously. Most often, there is a period of competition between the old form and the new one. This helps to explain some of the fluctuation evident in Modern English past tense formations, for example, in which some people say *fit* and others say *fitted,* or some say *lit* and others say *lighted,* and so on. Thus the processes of morphological change are often at the heart of synchronic variation, which is evident in all languages.

Unlike sound change, however, morphological change does not necessarily apply regularly in the system: changes can apply to individual words or end up not being accepted by speakers. One particularly interesting aspect of word formation is that it is sometimes rather analogous to fads and fashion, in that new items are introduced in particular groups or communities, and these may or may not spread and become popular in the wider population of consumers (in this case, language users). For example, there was a time in recent American popular usage when the suffix *-age* (as in established lexical items like *mileage* and *roughage*) was applied productively to roots from several part-of-speech classes to form new nouns meaning 'some unspecified amount of (root),' for example, *beerage* 'some amount of beer,' *spoilage* 'some amount of spoiled material,' *tun(e)age* 'some amount of music (tunes),' and so on. These words are/were acceptable on a socially and perhaps regionally limited basis; that is, they are not equally known to or used by all speakers of English.

Syntactic Change

12.5.1 Defining Syntactic Change

As noted in File 12.1, linguistic change is not restricted to one particular component of a language. Thus, in the same way that the sounds and words and meanings of a language are subject to change, so too are the patterns into which meaningful elements—words and morphemes—fit in order to form sentences. That is to say, change can be found in the syntactic component of a language, that domain of a grammar concerned with the organization of words and morphemes into phrases and sentences.

In syntactic change, therefore, the primary data that historical linguists deal with are changes in the variety of elements that go into the syntactic structuring of a sentence. These include (but are not restricted to) changes in word order, changes in the use of morphemes that indicate relations among words in a sentence (e.g., agreement markings on a verb caused by the occurrence of a particular noun or on an adjective caused by the noun it modifies), and changes in the type of elements that one word "selects" as being able to occur with it (e.g., the adjective *worthy* requires the preposition *of,* as in *worthy of consideration;* the verb *believe* can occur with a *that*-clause following it; etc.). All of these aspects of sentence structure are subject to change through time (diachronically).

12.5.2 Examples of Syntactic Change

One example of syntactic change is that, in earlier stages of English, it was quite usual (though not obligatory) for a possessive determiner to follow the noun it modified, in the opposite order from what the rule is today. Thus, where currently we say *our father,* in Old English the phrase was usually *fæder ure.* One way of describing this change is to say that the generalization about the placement of words in such a noun phrase has changed. Thus whereas one of the two possible structures for a noun phrase in Old English was

(1) NP → N + DET$_{poss}$

(where DET$_{poss}$ is the subcategory of DET(erminers) that includes the possessives), that structure is not a part of the grammar of Modern English; instead, the modern phrase structure rule for a noun phrase has (2) as one of its possibilities.

(2) NP → DET$_{poss}$ + N

Similarly, in earlier stages of English, in an imperative (command) sentence, the pronoun *you,* if expressed at all, could appear either before or after the verb, while today, such a pronoun regularly precedes the verb (so that *You go!* is acceptable while **Go you!* is not).

The change of *fæder ure* to *our father* shows another type of syntactic change in addition to the change in word order. In Modern English, a noun phrase such as *our father* has the same form regardless of whether it is a subject or an object, as in (3).

502

(3) (subject)   Our father drinks a lot of coffee.
    (object)   We love our father.

In Old English, however, such a difference in grammatical function of a noun phrase was signaled by changes in the form of a noun phrase:

(4) (subject)   fæder ure
    (object)   fæder urne

Thus the passage from Old English to Modern English has seen a change in the way that grammatical function—a matter of sentence structure—is marked (from a "case-marking" morphological system to a syntactic system based on word order).

Similarly, adjectives in Old English regularly agreed with the noun they modified in gender (masculine/feminine/neuter), number (singular/plural), and case (e.g., subject/object, etc.); in Modern English, the only remnants of Old English number agreement with adjectives are to be found with the modern determiners *this/that* (with singular nouns) and *these/those* (with plural nouns).

Another very dramatic syntactic change in English has been the positioning of main verbs in questions and negative statements. In Modern English, if a statement lacks an auxiliary verb (a verb such as *will, can,* or *have*), then the word *do* must be used. Compare (5) and (6) with (7).

(5) Statement: she   will   go
    Question: **will** she   go?
    Negative: she   will   **not**   go.

(6) Statement: he   has   gone.
    Question: **has** he   gone?
    Negative: he   has   **not**   gone.

(7) Statement: they   went.
    Question: **did** they   go?
    Negative: they   did   **not**   go.

There is no *did* in *they went;* it is inserted in the question and the negative.

But as the examples in (8) from Shakespeare's *Othello* show, in Early Modern English the main verb appears before the subject of the sentence in the question, and before *not* in the negative.

(8) a. O heaven! **How got she out?** O treason of the blood! (Act 1, Scene 1)
       cf. How did she get out?

    b. Fathers, from hence **trust not your daughters' minds**
       By what you see them act. (Act 1, Scene 1)
       cf. Do not trust your daughters' minds.

    c. But though **they jump not** on a just account,—
       (Act 1, Scene 3)
       cf. They do not jump.

Finally, as an example of a syntactic change involving selectional facts, we can consider the adjective *worthy.* In earlier stages of English, this adjective regularly occurred with a *that*-clause following it, as in:

(9) ic ne   eom   wyrðe   þæt ic   þin   sunu beo   genemned
   I *not* *am*   *worthy* *that* *I*   *your* *son*   *be*   *called*

which literally is 'I am not worthy that I be called your son'; the Modern English equivalent of this sentence, though, is *I am not worthy to be called your son,* indicating that the selection properties of *worthy* have changed from permitting a following *that*-clause to requiring only infinitival clauses (clauses with *to* plus a verb).

The examples given here have been drawn from the history of English, but they can be taken as illustrative of change in the syntactic component of any language. Moreover, they are representative of the nature of syntactic change in general and show ways in which syntactic change differs from sound change (discussed in File 12.3), for example. Perhaps the most striking characteristic of sound change is that it is regular, in that it affects all possible candidates for a particular change; for example, all instances of Old English [uː] became Modern (American) English [ɑʊ], and no examples of the older pronunciation remain. With syntactic change, however, while new patterns are produced that the language generally adheres to, exceptions nonetheless can occur; for example, even though word order in commands changed, the interjectional commands *mind you* and *believe you me* retain the older order with the pronoun after the verb, and so does the (consciously) archaic expression *hear ye, hear ye.* Also, as noted above, number agreement is still found, but only with the demonstrative determiners. Moreover, unlike sound change and more like morphological change, syntactic changes are often specific to the syntactic properties of particular words; thus the change in the syntax of a clause following *worthy* mentioned above is one that is specific to that word, and not, for instance, generally true for all adjectives that occur in such a construction (e.g., *hopeful* can still occur with a *that*-clause).

A few words on the causes of syntactic change are in order. As with all other language change, there is both a language-internal and a language-external dimension to the causation of change. Thus, word-order changes in specific constructions, for example, the noun + possessive determiner construction, are often linked (correlated) with other changes in word order (e.g., involving the placement of an object with respect to the verb, a relative clause with respect to the noun it modifies, a noun with respect to a prepositional element, etc.). That is, there is often a system-wide change in the ordering of elements that is realized in different ways in different constructions (see Chapter 5). At the same time, though, such system-internal factors are only one side of the story. Innovative syntactic patterns often compete with older patterns for some time, and external, that is, social, factors often play a role in deciding the competition. An example is the case-marking distinction involving *who* versus *whom* in Modern English, where the use of one as opposed to the other in a sentence such as *Tell me who/whom you saw yesterday* is tied to such socially relevant factors as speakers' educational level, their attitudes toward education, the impression they wish to convey, and the like. On the matter of causation, then, syntactic change follows much the same pattern as other types of linguistic change.

Semantic Change

12.6.1 Changing the Meanings of Words

The semantic system of a language (see Chapter 6), like all other aspects of its grammar, is subject to change over time. As a result, the meanings of words do not always remain constant from one stage of the language to the next. If we think of the meaning of a word as being determined by the set of contexts in which the word can be used, we can characterize semantic change as a shift in the set of appropriate contexts for that word's use. Alternatively, we could view semantic change as a change in the set of **referents** for a word, that is, as a change in the set of objects the word refers to. Since these views are simply two aspects of what we call meaning, these two characterizations of semantic change are more or less equivalent.

The motivating factors behind semantic change are not well understood. Such changes sometimes result from language contact or accompany technological innovations or migrations to new geographic regions. In each of these cases the introduction of a new object or concept into the culture may initiate a change in the meaning of a word for a related object or concept, though this does not always occur. Semantic changes can also result from changes in the relative status of the set referred to by the word; that is, the word will take on new aspects of meaning to reflect this difference in social status. Sometimes changes result from a change in the status of the word itself, as is often the case with taboo words. It is, however, frequently the case that the sources of particular changes are not at all obvious; they appear to be spontaneous and unmotivated (though this may simply be due to our own lack of understanding).

Whatever the underlying source, only certain types of changes seem to occur with any frequency. Some of the most common types include extensions, reductions, elevations, and degradations.

12.6.2 Semantic Extensions

Extensions in meaning occur when the set of appropriate contexts or referents for a word increases. Extensions are frequently the result of generalizing from the specific case to the class of which the specific case is a member. An example of this type would be the change in meaning undergone by the Old English (OE) word *docga,* modern-day *dog.* In OE *docga* referred to a particular breed of dog, while in modern usage it refers to the class of dogs as a whole. Thus the set of contexts in which the word may be used has been extended from the specific case (a particular breed of dog) to the general class (all dogs, dogs in general). A similar type of change has affected modern English *bird.* Though it once referred to a particular species of bird, it now is used for the general class.

A contemporary example of this type of change would be the shift in meaning undergone by the recently formed verb *nuke.* This verb was based on the noun *nuke,* a shortening (clipping; see Section 12.4.3) of *nuclear weapon* (as in "no nukes"), and originally meant 'to drop a nuclear bomb on something.' In the speech of some, this verb has been

505

extended to mean simply 'to damage' or 'to destroy,' as in *Robin nuked his Porsche last night.* Thus the meaning of *nuke,* for these speakers at least, has gone from referring to a particular type of damage or destruction to damage or destruction in general. Semantic extensions are particularly common with proper names and brand names. Thus the name *Benedict Arnold* has come to be synonymous with the word *traitor.* Similarly, the name of the fictional character *Scrooge* can be used to refer to anyone with miserly traits. Examples of the semantic extension of brand names are equally easy to find: *Jell-O* is often used to refer to any flavored gelatin, regardless of brand. *Kleenex* is used for any facial tissue and *Xerox* for any photocopy. In some parts of the United States *Coke* can be used for any carbonated beverage, not just one particular brand (as a sign of its generality, it may even appear without the capital <C>, as <coke>). In each of these cases the meaning of the word has been generalized to include related items in its set of referents.

In the examples discussed thus far, the relationship between the original meaning of the word and the extended meaning of the word has been quite straightforward: the name of a particular traitor has been generalized to any traitor, the name of a particular type of photocopy has been generalized to any photocopy, and so on. This needn't always be the case, however. The meanings of words often become less narrow as a result of what is referred to as **metaphorical extension.** Thus, the meaning of a word is extended to include an object or a concept that is like the original referent in some metaphorical sense rather than a literal sense. A classic example of this type is the word *broadcast,* which originally meant 'to scatter seed over a field.' In its most common present-day usage, however, *broadcast* refers to the diffusion of radio waves through space—a metaphorical extension of its original sense. Another classic example of metaphorical extension is the application of preexisting nautical terms (such as *ship, navigate, dock, hull, hatch, crew,* etc.) to the relatively new realm of space exploration. Again, notice that space exploration is not like ocean navigation in a literal sense, since very different actions and physical properties are involved. Rather, the comparison between the two realms is a metaphorical one. Another example that we've seen in this text is the use of *phoneme* to apply to a minimal unit of form in signed languages. When the term was first used, it was clearly related to minimal units of sound, but because the linguistic concept of the phoneme is present in signed languages, the term has been extended.

We can also find cases of metaphorical extension in progress in the language around us, particularly if we consider creative uses of slang terms. For example, the dictionary definition of the noun *load* is something like 'unit or quantity that can be carried' or 'burden of responsibility.' In some circles the meaning of this word has been extended to refer to people who are lazy or unproductive, presumably because these people do not do their fair share and therefore place a burden on others. Literally speaking, however, it is not people themselves who are the burden; rather it is the result of their actions that is the burden. Thus this use of the word is an abstraction from its original sense, that is, a metaphorical extension. Another example of this type of change in progress is the use of the verb *nuke,* discussed above, to refer to microwave cooking. In this case, the metaphor hinges on the idea that microwave radiation is released during nuclear explosions. Thus, a parallel is being drawn between cooking in a microwave and bombing your food, though literally the two actions are quite different. Notice that these uses of *load* and *nuke* are not accepted by all speakers. However, if enough people adopt these meanings, we may eventually have a full-fledged semantic change in the language.

12.6.3 Semantic Reductions

Reductions occur when the set of appropriate contexts or referents for a word decreases. Historically speaking, this is relatively less common than extensions of meaning, though it still occurs fairly frequently. An example of a semantic reduction would be the Old

English word *hund,* modern-day *hound.* While this word originally referred to dogs in general, its meaning has now been restricted, for the most part, to a few particular breeds of dog. Thus its usage has become less general over time. Similarly, the word *worm* once was used for any crawling creature but is now restricted to a particular type of crawling creature.

Additional examples of this type of change include the Modern English words *skyline* and *girl. Skyline* originally referred to the horizon in general. It has since been restricted to particular types of horizons—ones in which the outlines of hills, buildings, or other structures appear. In Middle English the word corresponding to modern-day *girl* referred to young people of either sex. A semantic reduction has resulted in its current, more specific meaning.

12.6.4 Semantic Elevations

Semantic **elevations** occur when a word takes on somewhat grander connotations over time. For example, the word *knight* (OE *cniht* or *cneoht*) originally meant 'youth' or 'military follower'—relatively powerless and unimportant people. The meaning of *knight* has since been elevated to refer to people of a somewhat more romantic and impressive status. Similarly, the word *chivalrous* was at one time synonymous with *warlike;* it now refers to more refined properties such as fairness, generosity, and honor. A particularly good example of this type is the shift in meaning undergone by the word *squire.* The Middle English (ME) equivalent of *squire* was used to refer to a knight's attendant, the person who held his shield and armor for him. In Modern English, however, a squire is a country gentleman or large landowner. Thus the meaning of *squire* has changed rather drastically over time, acquiring a socially more positive meaning.

12.6.5 Semantic Degradations

Semantic **degradations** are the opposite of semantic elevations; they occur when a word acquires a more pejorative meaning over time. Examples of words whose meanings have been degraded include *lust, wench,* and *silly.* In OE *lust* simply meant 'pleasure,' making its current association with sinfulness a degradation of the original meaning. Similarly, the ME word *wenche(l)* meant 'female child' and later 'female servant.' It then came to mean 'lewd female' or 'woman of a low social class.' The word *silly* is a particularly interesting example of semantic degradation because the social force of the word has almost completely reversed. Whereas in ME *silly* meant something akin to 'happy, blessed, innocent,' it now is more on a par with 'foolish, inane, absurd.' Thus the connotations of *silly* have gone from strongly positive to strongly negative in a matter of a few centuries.

12.6.6 Discussion

In conclusion, it is interesting to note that semantic changes in one word of a language are often accompanied by (or result in) semantic changes in another word. Note, for instance, the opposite changes undergone by OE *hund* and *docga,* discussed above. As *hund* became more specific in meaning, *docga* became more general. Thus, the semantic system as a whole remains in balance despite changes to individual elements within the system.

A somewhat more elaborate example of the same principle involves the OE words *mete, flæsc,* and *foda.* In OE, *mete,* modern-day *meat,* referred to food in general while *flæsc,* now *flesh,* referred to any type of animal tissue. Since then, the meaning of *meat* has been restricted to the flesh of animals and the meaning of *flesh* largely to human tissue. *Foda,* which was the OE word for 'animal fodder,' became modern-day *food,* and its meaning was generalized to include all forms of nourishment. Thus the semantic hole left by the change in referent for *meat* has been filled by the word *food.*

FILE 12.7

Reconstruction: Internal Reconstruction vs. Comparative Reconstruction

12.7.1 Reconstruction

One of the goals of historical linguistics is to document and examine how languages change over time. In order to do this, linguists must know both what languages today look like and how they used to look. Unfortunately, of course, we do not have a time machine that would allow us to go back in time to study earlier states of languages directly. Therefore, linguists have come up with a number of ways of looking at older states of language.

The most useful tools for a historical linguist are direct samples of older language: recordings of speakers from the late nineteenth century, for example, or transcripts of speech from eras before sound recording was possible. In the absence of such transcripts, other early written descriptions of a language, or documents in the language, can help linguists see how a given language used to be. But even when few (or no) written sources exist, linguists can often determine both how a single language used to look and how several languages might have derived from a common source historically. These tasks are accomplished using methods of **reconstruction**. Internal reconstruction involves the analysis of data from a single language in order to make hypotheses about that language's history. Comparative reconstruction involves the systematic comparison of multiple related languages in order to make hypotheses about the common protolanguage they descended from. We will consider each in turn in the sections that follow.

12.7.2 Internal Reconstruction

As we have seen from our survey of sound changes that have occurred in the history of English, one of the effects of conditioned sound change is the creation of alternate pronunciations for the same morpheme, what is usually called morphological **alternation.** For example, early in the history of English, fricatives became voiced intervocalically. As a result, the plural form of the word *wife* changed from [wiːfas] to [wiːvas]. In the singular form [wiːf], however, the fricative [f] did not become voiced because it did not occur before a vowel. The net result of this sound change was to create alternate pronunciations for the different forms of the word 'wife,' [wiːf] in the singular but with a stem [wiːv] in the plural. The alternation is still evident in Modern English today, as is evident in the forms *wife/wives*.

When morphological alternations are created by sound change, we can often examine the phonetic context of the alternate pronunciations and infer what sound change(s) caused the alternations in the first place. This type of analysis, whereby the linguist examines data available from one language and one language only and makes hypotheses about that language's history, is what we mean by **internal reconstruction.** Using the internal reconstruction method, a linguist may learn much about a language's history, even if for some reason there are no known related languages to compare it with.

English can provide us with a very straightforward example of the recovery of an earlier sound change via morphological alternation. In English the voiced velar stop [g] is not pronounced when it precedes a word-final nasal, for example, *sign* [saɪn], but it is pronounced in related words if this nasal is not word-final, for example, *signal* [sɪgnəl]. As a result, morphological alternations occur between morphemes with and without the voiced velar stop, for example, *dignity* [dɪgnəti], *deign* [deɪn]; *paradigmatic* [pɛɹədɪgmæɾɪk], *paradigm* [pɛɹədaɪm]. On the basis of these alternations we can make some inferences about the history of English. Specifically, we can assume that at an earlier period the morphological alternation did not exist—that there was only one pronunciation for morphemes that had the sound sequence [gn] or [gm], and that at some point there was a sound change whereby voiced velar stops were lost when they occurred before a word-final nasal.

Sometimes, however, it is impossible to detect the sound change(s) that have created the morphological alternations which exist in a language. This is usually the case when later sound changes take place which obscure the original cause of the alternate pronunciations. Consider the following example from the history of English. At present in English the past tense of the verb *sleep* is [slɛpt] and not [slipt] as we might expect. It is only natural to wonder why the word *sleep* has forms with alternate pronunciations [slɛp] and [slip]. Unfortunately we can arrive at no satisfactory answer just by considering the evidence that exists in Modern English. We cannot say that the alternation is due to the fact that the vowel is followed by two consonants in the past tense form, because other verbs that form the past tense in a similar manner do not have alternate pronunciations, for example, *freak* [fɹik], *freaked* [fɹikt] and *peak* [pik], *peaked* [pikt]. Since we have words that form the past tense regularly and words that have an alternate pronunciation in the past tense and we can determine nothing from the phonetic contexts, it is impossible to attempt internal reconstruction in the way we did with *sign* and *signal*. In cases such as this we must consider evidence from the Middle English period in the form of written records to find out how the alternate pronunciation came into existence.

12.7.3 Comparative Reconstruction

Unlike internal reconstruction, comparative reconstruction relies on the existence of multiple related languages; these are compared in order to establish what language the related languages descended from and how closely related they are.

In order to use the **comparative method** of reconstruction, you must start out with related languages, using the techniques discussed in File 12.2 on language relatedness. Otherwise, you would be "reconstructing" a system that would not represent any actually occurring language. By working with related languages, you know that you can at least theoretically reconstruct an actual source language from which the languages you are working with have descended.

Another key to using the comparative method successfully is the assumption (discussed in File 12.3) that sound change is regular; that is, all the sounds in a given environment will undergo the same change, and when a language undergoes a certain sound change, that change will (eventually) be reflected systematically throughout the vocabulary of that language. For example, a language might undergo an unconditioned sound change of [p] to [f], in which every [p] in every word is replaced by [f]. Or, for example, a language might undergo a conditioned sound change of [p] to [f] in some specific phonetic environment, such as between vowels, in which case every word with a [p] between two vowels would acquire an [f] in place of the intervocalic [p]. A sound change may be conditioned by phonetic environment (e.g., it occurs only when the sound in question is between two vowels, or before a certain other sound, or after a certain sound, or at the beginning of a word, or at the end of a word, etc.), but nothing other than the phonetic environment ever limits a sound change. A sound change never randomly affects some words but not other phonetically similar words, never occurs just in words with a certain kind of meaning, and so on. That is what is meant by the regularity of sound change.

These then are the two tendencies that make it possible for linguists to establish language relationships. The arbitrary relationship between a word's form and meaning is important because it makes it highly unlikely that unrelated languages will share large numbers of words of similar form and meaning. The regularity of sound change is important because it means that two (or more) languages that are related will show regular **sound correspondences**. Let us consider an example to illustrate what we mean. Consider the forms in (1).

(1) | *English* | *German* | *Dutch* | *Swedish* | *Gloss* |
|---|---|---|---|---|
| [mæn] | [man] | [man] | [man] | 'man' |
| [hænd] | [hant] | [hant] | [hand] | 'hand' |

If we compare the vowel sounds in all four languages, we can establish the following sound correspondence in the word meaning 'man': [æ] in English corresponds to [a] in German, Swedish, and Dutch. In order for this sound correspondence to be regular, it must occur in other words that have form-meaning pairings that are similar across languages. And, of course, it does, as a comparison of the words meaning 'hand' confirms.[1] Note that since this correspondence (æ—a—a—a) occurs regularly (is not unique to the word for 'man'), we have eliminated the possibility of being misled by chance similarity between words with similar form and meaning in unrelated languages.

The task of the comparative linguist does not end with the discussion of correspondences between languages or with the assumption that these correspondences indicate that the languages in question are related. The linguist is also interested in discovering how languages that are related developed from the protolanguage into their present forms; in other words, the linguist is interested in linguistic history.

In order to discover how languages have developed from a protolanguage, the protolanguage itself must be recoverable. And in some cases it is. For the Romance languages (French, Spanish, Portuguese, Romanian, etc.) the protolanguage (Vulgar Latin) is attested by numerous written records, for example, manuscripts, public inscriptions, funerary inscriptions, graffiti, and so on. As a result it is possible to trace the development of the various Romance languages from their parent with considerable accuracy.

In other cases, however, written records for the protolanguage do not exist. But this does not mean that we cannot gather any information about the protolanguage; in these cases it is possible to infer what the protolanguage looked like by comparing the forms and grammars of the related languages. For example, some words in Proto-Indo-European can be reconstructed on the basis of words in the daughter languages. The lists in (2) and (3) contain sets of words having the same meaning from six Indo-European languages. The asterisk (*) means that the word is a **reconstructed form**, or a **protoform**, not one that we have ever seen attested by people who spoke the language.[2]

(2) | | *'father'* | *'mother'* | *'brother'* |
|---|---|---|---|
| Proto-Indo-European | *[pəteːr] | *[maːteːr] | *[bʰraːteːr] |
| English | [faðɹ̩] | [mʌðɹ̩] | [bɹʌðɹ̩] |
| Greek | [pateːr] | [mɛːteːr] | [pʰraːtɛːr] |
| Latin | [patɛr] | [maːtɛr] | [fraːtɛr] |
| Old Church Slavonic | —[3] | [mati] | [bratrə] |
| Old Irish | [aθɪr] | [maːθɪr] | [braːθɪr] |
| Sanskrit | [pɪtər-] | [maːtər-] | [bʰraːtər-] |

---

[1]Actually, we would want to see more than just two words with the same correspondences, but these serve as an example.
[2]Note that this is the same symbol that we use for marking ungrammaticality. Generally you can tell from context which meaning is intended.
[3]There was an OCS word for 'father' [otətsə], but it derives from a different root.

(3)		*'mead'*	*'is'*	*'I bear'*
	Proto-Indo-European	*[medʰu]	*[esti]	*[bʰer-]
	English	[mid]	[ɪz]	[bɛɹ]
	Greek	[mɛtʰu]	[ɛsti]	[pʰɛrɔː]
	Latin	—	[ɛst]	[fɛroː]
	Old Church Slavonic	[mɛdə]	[jɛstə]	[bɛrõ]
	Old Irish	[mið]	[is]	[biru]
	Sanskrit	[mədʰu]	[əstɪ]	[bʰraːmɪ]

Since inferences are made by comparing words of similar form and meaning in the languages we assume to be related, the method is called the comparative method. Note that the comparative method is itself possible because of the regularity of sound change. If two or more languages show regular correspondences between themselves in words where the meanings are the same or similar, it means that these words have descended from a common source.

As a small preliminary example of how the comparative method works, let us return to our English-German-Dutch-Swedish example from (1). We note that the first consonant in the first word is an [m] and that the final consonant is an [n] in all four languages. Thus we can safely assume that the protolanguage had an initial *[m] and a final *[n] in the word meaning 'man,' so that at this point we can reconstruct *[m_n] in our protolanguage. With respect to the vowel sound there is some uncertainty because there is variation in the sound: English has [æ], while German, Dutch, and Swedish have [a]. However, since there are more [a] outcomes in the daughter languages than [æ] outcomes, assuming that [a] is the sound that the protolanguage possessed and that English alone has changed *[a] to [æ] allows for a simpler solution overall, with fewer changes needing to be posited. Thus we reconstruct the protoform for 'man' as *[man], and the sound change *a > æ ("*[a] changes to [æ]") for English.

12.7.4 Comparative Method Procedure

The goal of the comparative method is to reconstruct the protoforms of the protolanguage from the comparison of languages that are assumed to be related. Once the protolanguage forms have been reconstructed, it is possible to determine the changes by which the daughter languages have become distinct by comparing the protoforms with the forms present in the daughter languages.

a. Compile Cognate Sets, Eliminating Borrowings. The first step is to gather and organize data from the languages in question, forming **cognate sets.** A **cognate** of a word is another word that has descended from the same source; consequently, cognates are very similar in form and are usually identical or similar in meaning. As an example of a cognate set, imagine three languages, A, B, and C, and the word meaning 'strawberry' pronounced as follows in each:

(4) *A*	*B*	*C*	*Gloss*
[siza]	[sesa]	[siza]	'strawberry'

Because of their semantic identity and phonetic similarity, these three words form a cognate set.

While gathering cognates you should make sure that "suspicious-looking" forms are eliminated. Sometimes among the cognate sets you are compiling for some group of languages, there will be a cognate set with an "oddball," a form that is phonetically so different from the other members of the cognate set that it is improbable that it derived from the same source. The "oddball" may have been borrowed from some other possibly genetically unrelated language. The original form, which fit the cognate set, was probably dropped in favor of the borrowed form. When you come across one of these borrowed forms, simply ignore it for the purposes of the comparative method.

    b. Determine Sound Correspondences. Next determine the sound correspondences that exist between sounds in the same positions in the words in each cognate set. The sound correspondences for our cognate set in step (a) are given in (5).

(5) | *Position* | *A* | *B* | *C* |
|---|---|---|---|
| 1. | [s] | [s] | [s] |
| 2. | [i] | [e] | [i] |
| 3. | [z] | [s] | [z] |
| 4. | [a] | [a] | [a] |

    c. Reconstruct a Sound for Each Position. Given these sound correspondences, you must try to determine the earlier protoform from which the cognates have descended, following these steps **in this order:**

    (i) *Total Correspondence.* If all the languages exhibit the same sound in some position in a cognate set, reconstruct that sound. In our example, in positions 1 and 4, each of the languages has the same sound, so we can reconstruct [s] for position 1 and [a] for position 4. Leaving blanks for positions 2 and 3, we can collapse and write this information as *[s__a].

    (ii) *Most Natural Development.* For each of the remaining positions, if possible, reconstruct the sound that would have undergone the most **natural** sound change. Years of study in phonetics and historical linguistics have shown that certain types of sound changes are very common, while others almost never happen. For example, in a position between vowels, the change of a stop to a fricative at the same point of articulation is a very common change, while the reverse is much less common. Thus, if one cognate contains a stop between vowels and the other contains a fricative, the stop should be reconstructed. For each of the common sound changes listed below, it should be understood that the reverse direction of change is rare, or "unnatural."

(6) Common sound changes
- Voiceless sounds become voiced between vowels and before voiced consonants.
- Stops become fricatives between vowels.
- Consonants become palatalized before front vowels.
- Consonants become voiceless at the ends of words.
- Difficult consonant clusters are simplified.
- Difficult consonants are made easier (for example, voiced aspirated stops might become plain voiced stops).
- Oral vowels become nasalized before nasals.
- Fricatives other than [h] become [h].
- [h] deletes between vowels.
- Clusters of vowels are broken up by consonants.

    In our example, in position 2 we have a choice between [i] and [e]. Neither direction of change is favored by our list of common sound changes, so we cannot make a choice for position 2 at this point.

    In position 3, which is a position between vowels, we have a choice between [s] and [z]. Because we know that "voiceless sounds often become voiced between vowels," we reconstruct [s] (so that *[s] becomes [z] in B and C; *[z] becoming [s] in A would be unnatural). At this point we have reconstructed *[s_sa] for our cognate set.

(iii) *Occam's Razor.* This technical term refers to a guideline for evaluating competing analyses: given any pair of possible analyses, prefer the one which is simpler overall. In the case of historical linguistics, this translates into preferring a solution which requires the positing of fewer changes over one which covers the same facts but requires more changes to do so. (*Occam's Razor* is named for the medieval English philosopher William of Occam, who proposed the principle, and "razor" refers here to the way the guideline encourages the "cutting out" of extra complications.) We have already applied this principle in the English-German-Dutch-Swedish example above when it was suggested that a single change *a > æ for English was a simpler solution than having three instances of a change *æ > a.

So for position 2 in our example, we reconstruct *[i], since this would involve a single change *i > e, occurring in language B only. To do the reverse would require us to posit two instances of the change *e > i, separately in languages A and C. Using the comparative method, then, we have determined that the pronunciation of the word meaning 'strawberry' in the protolanguage from which A, B, and C descended was most probably *[sisa].

d. Check for Regularity of Sound Change. Although the procedure outlined in steps (a) through (c) can be used to reconstruct a protoform for each cognate set individually, you must check to see whether your results are consistent across the whole collection of cognate sets. We know that sound change is regular, and therefore we should be able to give for each daughter language (A, B, and C in our example) a list of sound changes that applied regularly to all words in the protolanguage, resulting in the respective daughter languages. If you cannot formulate the sound changes, you must minimally modify the choices you made in step (c) so that your results conform to the regularity hypothesis.

In order to demonstrate this situation, we need to add another cognate set to our data as shown in (7).

(7)

A	B	C	Gloss	Protolanguage
[siza]	[sesa]	[siza]	'strawberry'	*[sisa]
[sizu]	[sisu]	[sizu]	'pitchfork'	*[sisu]

Confirm that steps (a) through (c) produce *[sisu] for the word meaning 'pitchfork.' We will see now that we run into trouble in formulating the sound change for the [e] that occurs in position 2 for the word meaning 'strawberry' in language B. If we posit the sound change *i > e for language B, then we predict that the *[i] in *[sisu] should also have become [e] in B. And because both instances of *[i] occur in identical phonetic environments (between *[s] and *[s]), adding a condition to the rule—that is, limiting the environments in which the sound change applies—does not help.

The solution to this problem is to reverse the decision we made in step ((c)iii) for the 'strawberry' cognate set, making our reconstruction for 'strawberry' *[sesa]. Now, the sound changes listed in (8) can apply regularly to both reconstructed forms, giving the correct results in A, B, and C.

(8) Derivation of 'strawberry'

	A	B	C
Protoform	*[sesa]	*[sesa]	*[sesa]
Sound changes	*s > z / V___V	none	*s > z / V___V
	*e > i		*e > i
Cognate set	[siza]	[sesa]	[siza]

Note that the condition "between vowels" (V___V) on the rule *s > z in A and C is necessary to avoid the prediction that the word-initial *[s]s also would have become [z]s. See for yourself whether this analysis gives the correct daughter-language cognates from the hypothetical protoform for 'pitchfork,' *[sisu].

Another clue that you may find helpful in doing comparative reconstruction is to find a pair of words that is the same (homophonous) in language A but different in language B. When such a situation arises, you may be fairly confident in reconstructing the protoforms as they appear in B (or at least as being different from one another, unlike in A). This reconstruction follows from the fact that, if you were to reconstruct both the forms as they appear in A (i.e., as identical to each other), there would be no way that they would subsequently differentiate themselves in B: no sound change can apply to only one of two homophones. This is illustrated by the data in (9).

(9) ***A***   ***B***   ***Gloss***
    [uti]   [uti]   'frog'
    [uti]   [oti]   'snake'

Given the data in (9), we would have to reconstruct the protoforms *[uti] 'frog' and *[oti] 'snake,' and assume a sound change of the form [o] → [u] in language A. If we had instead reconstructed both forms as *[uti], as they appear in language A, it would be impossible, given the regularity of sound change, to write a rule that makes one of them (but not the other) into [oti] in language B.

The flowchart in (10) should help you work through a set of data to reconstruct earlier forms of words that are related in several languages. The rectangular boxes ask you to do something or give you some information that your working through the flowchart has revealed. The diamond-shaped boxes pose a question. Try reading through the flowchart before you attempt to solve a reconstruction problem like those found in File 12.8; it may help you understand how the whole process works.

(10) Flowchart for reconstructing word formation using the comparative method

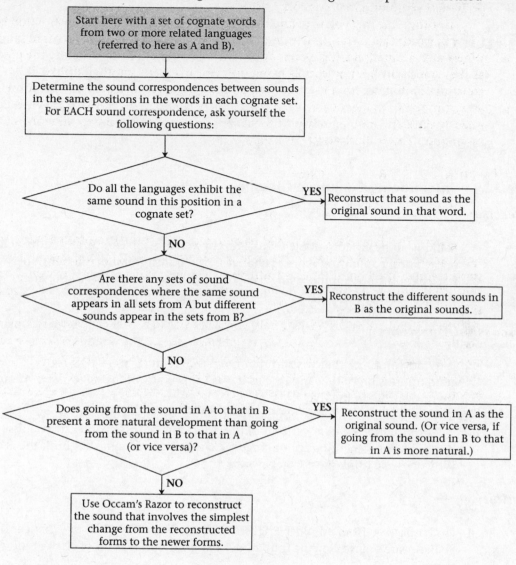

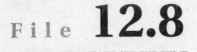

Practice

File 12.1—Introducing Language Change

Exercise

1. Looking at the versions of the Lord's Prayer given in (1) in File 12.1, identify at least one of each of the following types of change in the transformation of English between Old English and Contemporary English: sound change, morphological change, syntactic change, semantic change.

Discussion Questions

2. Why do you think that we said that the passages in (1) in File 12.1 give a reasonably good impression of the language as it was spoken at various stages, even though they are not written in the IPA?

3. Refer to the *Non Sequitur* cartoon at the beginning of this chapter. If you assume that Danae knows something about language change, why might she think she is cursing? Why does she think she can get away with it?

Activity

4. Find a passage from an older English text like *Canterbury Tales* by Chaucer or one of Shakespeare's plays. Rewrite it in modern English. What kinds of changes do you have to make?

File 12.2—Language Relatedness

Exercises

5. For each of the following Indo-European branches, list two modern languages that are members of that branch:

   a. Celtic
   b. Baltic
   c. Indic
   d. Iranian

6. Look at the following data:

Language A	Language B	Language C	Language D	Gloss
due	bi	dó	doi	'two'
naso	sudur	srón	nas	'nose'
fratello	anaia	bráthair	frate	'brother'
padre	aita	athair	tată	'father'
sette	zazpi	seacht	sapte	'seven'
orecchio	belarri	cluas	ureche	'ear'
dieci	hamar	deich	zece	'ten'

i. Which two languages seem to be very closely related? How can you tell?

ii. Of the two remaining languages, which seems to be (at least distantly) related to the two languages you identified in (i)? How can you tell?

iii. Which language is not related to the others? How can you tell?

Discussion Questions

7. If you look at the "Language Family Index" at http://www.ethnologue.org, you will see that there are languages that do not have a familial classification. Why do you think researchers have not been able to affiliate these languages with other groups? (There may be multiple reasons!) Do you think we are likely to be able to determine their affiliations in the future? Why or why not?

8. The words meaning 'city' in Hungarian (*varós*) and Romanian (*oraş*) are related. Given **only** this information, can we assume that Hungarian and Romanian are closely genetically related? Could there be other reasons for this similarity? What do you think caused this similarity?

Activities

9. Look up a language family under the "Language Family Index" at http://www.ethnologue.org. Draw a family tree model to show how the languages in that family are related.

10. Investigate the relatedness of Taiwan Sign Language and Japanese Sign Language. Given the criteria for language relatedness described in File 12.2, do you think these languages are related or not? Justify your conclusion based on what you have learned.

File 12.3—Sound Change

Exercises

11. **i.** Based **only** on the data below, what seems to be the outcome of word-initial Latin [k] in Italian?

Latin		Italian	Gloss
[keno]	>	[tʃeno]	'I dine'
[kentum]	>	[tʃɛnto]	'hundred'
[kirkus]	>	[tʃirko]	'circus'
[kivilis]	>	[tʃivile]	'civil'

(cont.)

ii. Now look at the additional data below. Do these data make you revise your answer? Why? According to these two sets of data, what are the outcomes of word-initial Latin [k] in Italian? Explain your answer and be as specific as possible: describe the different environments required for each outcome.

Latin		Italian	Gloss
[kampus]	>	[kampo]	'field'
[kontra]	>	[kontra]	'against'
[kuriositas]	>	[kuriosita]	'curiosity'
[kredo]	>	[kredo]	'I know'

12. Why do we spell the words *knife* and *knight* with a <k> when they are pronounced with an initial alveolar nasal?

13. For each word specify the sound change(s) between Proto-Quechua and one of its daughter languages, Tena. Then, after considering all the data, say whether each sound change is conditioned or unconditioned and, further, what type of conditioned or unconditioned change each sound change is.

Proto-Quechua	Tena	Gloss
[tʃumpi]	[tʃumbi]	'belt'
[timpu]	[timbu]	'boil'
[nutku]	[nuktu]	'brains'
[akla]	[agla]	'choose'
[wakli]	[wagli]	'damage'
[utka]	[ukta]	'fast'
[kunka]	[kunga]	'neck'
[ljantu]	[ljandu]	'shade'
[mutki]	[mukti]	'smell'
[pukju]	[pugju]	'spring'
[inti]	[indi]	'sun'
[sanku]	[sangu]	'thick'
[hampatu]	[hambatu]	'toad'

14. Specify the changes between Proto-Slavic and one of its daughter languages, Bulgarian. Classify the changes as conditioned or unconditioned. Then say what type of conditioned or unconditioned change each sound change is. Finally, note that the order of the changes is important, that is, if the changes occurred in different orders, they would have given different results. The order of changes which gives exactly the results we see in Bulgarian is the best hypothesis about the actual relative chronological ordering of the changes, that is, how they unfolded in time with respect to one another. Give the correct order of the changes you have identified, and point out at least one wrong result that a different order of changes would produce.

Proto-Slavic	Bulgarian	Gloss
[gladuka]	[glatkə]	'smooth'
[kratuka]	[kratkə]	'short'
[blizuka]	[bliskə]	'near'
[ʒeʒika]	[ʒeʃkə]	'scorching'
[lovuka]	[lofkə]	'adroit'

15. Determine the sound changes that took place in the development of the Marathi from Old Indic. Classify the sound changes as conditioned or unconditioned. Then specify what type of conditioned or unconditioned change each sound change is.

Old Indic	Marathi	Gloss
[aŋka]	[aŋka]	'hook'
[arka]	[akka]	'sun'
[bʰakti]	[bʰatti]	'devotion'
[catwaːri]	[cattaːri]	'four'
[kalpa]	[kappa]	'rule'
[kardama]	[kaddama]	'mud'
[kaʈaka]	[kaɖaː]	'bracelet'
[kaʈaka]	[kaɖaː]	'crow'
[mudgara]	[muggara]	'mallet'
[pitaː]	[piaː]	'father'
[rudra]	[rudda]	'terrible'
[sapatniː]	[savattiː]	'co-wife'
[supta]	[sutta]	'asleep'
[ʃabda]	[sadda]	'sound'
[ʃata]	[saː]	'hundred'
[utkaɳʈaː]	[ukkaɳʈa]	'desire'
[vikrama]	[vikkama]	'strength'
[viʈapa]	[viʈava]	'branch'

([bʰ] represents a murmured (breathy voiced) bilabial stop; [ʈ, ɖ, ɳ] represent retroflex stops.)

Discussion Questions

16. Based on what you know about the outcome of sound change, do you think it is possible for two homonyms (like *pair* and *pear*) to be pronounced differently in the future just because of a sound change? Why or why not?

17. Just as signed languages can metaphorically be thought of as having phonetics and phonology, so too can they metaphorically undergo sound change—and, in fact, they can undergo both phonetic and phonemic change.

One example of sound change in American Sign Language is the tendency for signs that were originally made with both hands in the same shape, making the same motion on either side of the signer, to now be signed with just one hand. Many signs for the names of animals are like this: DEER, RABBIT, COW, and so on, as illustrated in (a).

a. ASL: COW (older) and COW (newer)

From *Signing: How to Speak with Your Hands* by Elaine Costello. Copyright 1983 by Elaine Costello. Used by permission of Bantam Books, a division of Bantam Doubleday Dell Publishing Group, Inc., p. 29.

Another example of a sound change is shown in (b). In this case, the difference in the signs is which handshape is being used. The older sign for DECIDE used an F-handshape, while the newer one uses a D-handshape.

b. ASL: DECIDE (older) and DECIDE (newer)

Based on this information, answer the following questions for each picture ((a) and (b)):
    i. Why is this change considered to be analogous to sound change (as opposed to, for example, morphological change or semantic change)?
    ii. What type of sound change is this an example of, given the list in Section 12.3.3? Why? If you don't think that the sound change type is given on the list, explain why, tell what kind of change you think it is, and say which type of change you think it is most analogous to.
    iii. Would you consider this to be a phonetic or a phonemic change? Why?

File 12.4—Morphological Change

Exercises

18. Refer to the *For Better or For Worse* cartoon at the beginning of Chapter 10 on language variation. Using your knowledge of morphological change, through what process was the word *foob* created?

19. Historically, the past tense of the verb *dive* is formed by the regular pattern of past tense word formation, that is, verb + *-ed* → [past tense] (*dived*). However, in a number of American English dialects *dived* has been replaced by *dove* [doʊv]. It is normally assumed that *dove* replaced *dived* as the result of the pattern *drive* [present tense] : *drove* [past tense]. Would you consider the replacement of *dived* by *dove* to be an example of proportional analogy? What does this tell us about the notions of *productivity/regularity* and analogical change?

20. Try to come up with other aspects of English morphology that currently show some degree of fluctuation and variation (e.g., *saw* versus *seen* as the past tense form of *see*). To what extent are analogical processes at work in causing these fluctuations?

Discussion Questions

21. Refer to the *For Better or For Worse* cartoon at the beginning of Chapter 10 on language variation. What do you think the word *prag* means? How do you think it was created?

22. We have seen that natural phonological processes were at the heart of most sound changes. As a result, when an "unnatural" change is encountered, for example, the addition of final [-d] as part of the change of *clomb* to *climbed*, we should suspect that morphological change is at work. What is the unnatural aspect of the change of final [s] to [r] that we saw in the Latin example of paradigm leveling? We have a good indication from the lack of regularity of this change that it is the result of morphological change, but is there any phonetic reason for being suspicious of this as a sound change?

23. Consider the statement (sometimes called "Sturtevant's Paradox") that "sound change is regular but produces irregularity; analogy is irregular but produces regularity." What do you think this means? Do you think it's true? Why or why not?

File 12.5—Syntactic Change

Exercises

24. Here are a few lines from Geoffrey Chaucer's *Canterbury Tales,* written in Middle English (translation from http://icg.fas.harvard.edu/~chaucer/teachslf/gp-par.htm). Identify and discuss the difference(s) between the Middle English syntax and the Modern English syntax, and give a brief description.

   a. Whan that Aprill with his shoures soote
   When April with its sweet-smelling showers

   b. Thanne longen folk to goon on pilgrimages,
   Then folk long to go on pilgrimages,

   c. The hooly blisful martir for to seke,
   To seek the holy blessed martyr,

25. How would the following sentences of Shakespeare appear in Modern English? Explain what the difference is in each case (from *All's Well That Ends Well,* Act 1, Scene 1).

   a. How called you the man you speak of, madam?
   b. Virginity being blown down, man will quicklier be blown up.
   c. I will return perfect courtier; in the which, my instruction shall serve to naturalize thee . . .

File 12.6—Semantic Change

Exercises

26. Refer to the *Non Sequitur* cartoon at the beginning of this chapter. What type of semantic change have the words *balderdash* and *poppycock* gone through?

27. Refer to the *Non Sequitur* cartoon at the beginning of this chapter. Why do you think curse words often lose their "taboo" status after time?

28. Refer to the *Non Sequitur* cartoon at the beginning of this chapter. Using the *Oxford English Dictionary* or some other etymological reference, find out what the original meanings of *balderdash* and *poppycock* were. Do we have modern curse words that refer to similar things? Why were these curse words?

Discussion Questions

29. Think about terms you use to talk about computers and actions on computers (e.g., *surf the net*). How many of these are old words that have been put to new use, and how many are totally new words? Why do you think this would be the case?

30. In ASL, many signs have become less iconic over time; that is, the signs are less transparently related to what they mean. This is especially the case for a number of compound words. For example, the sign for HOME at one point was a compound of the signs for EAT (an O-hand at the mouth) and BED (a flat hand against the cheek); now it is a series of two touches of the O-handshape on the cheek. Do you think this change in form has affected the meaning of the word in any way? Why? What design feature of language (see File 1.4) is this evidence for?

Activities

31. Particularly interesting cases of semantic change are ones in which the meaning of a word appears to have been reversed through time. For example, the English word *black* is closely related to Slavic words meaning 'white.' *Black* is actually derived from a Germanic past participle meaning 'to have blazed' or 'to have burned.' Given these facts, can you think of a plausible explanation for the present-day meaning of *black*? Using a good etymological dictionary (such as the *Oxford English Dictionary* [*OED*]) for reference, list some Modern English words that are related to *black*. Try to determine the types of semantic change these words must have undergone to arrive at their present-day meanings.

32. Refer to the *Non Sequitur* cartoon at the beginning of this chapter. Do some research to find other words that used to be curse words but that have lost their taboo nature.

33. Refer to the *Non Sequitur* cartoon at the beginning of this chapter. Using the *Oxford English Dictionary* or some other etymological reference, find out what the original two words that composed *poppycock* were. What two modern words do we have that are cognates of these? What types of sound changes have they undergone?

34. The following paragraph is logically incoherent if all the words are understood in their current meanings. But, if we take each of the italicized words in a sense it once had at an earlier stage of English, the paragraph has no inconsistencies at all.

   i. Your job is to determine an earlier meaning for each of the italicized words that will remove the logical contradictions created by the current meaning. The earlier meanings need not be contemporary with one another. They can be found in the *Oxford English Dictionary* or in a comparably complete dictionary. For each word, determine the type of semantic change it has been through.

      He was a happy and *sad girl* who lived in a *town* 40 miles from the closest neighbor. His unmarried sister, a *wife* who was a vegetarian member of the Women's Christian Temperance Union, ate *meat* and drank *liquor* three times a day. She was so fond of oatmeal bread made from *corn* her brother grew, that one night, when it was dark and *wan* out, she *starved* from overeating. He fed nuts to the *deer* who lived in the branches of an *apple* tree that bore pears. He was a *silly* and wise *boor,* a *knave* and a *villain,* and everyone liked him. Moreover, he was a *lewd* man whom the general *censure* held to be a model of chastity.[1]

   ii. What type of semantic change is illustrated in each case? Give examples for each type.

---

[1]Adapted from T. Pyles and J. Algeo, *English: An Introduction to Language.* New York: Harcourt Brace, 1970.

File 12.7—Reconstruction: Internal Reconstruction vs. Comparative Reconstruction

Exercises

The following directions pertain to all of the reconstruction exercises contained in this file:
   i. Set up the sound correspondences for each cognate set, and reconstruct the earlier form for the word from which the cognates have descended.
   ii. Establish the sound changes that have affected each language.

35. 🔊 **Middle Chinese**
   For this exercise, we have simplified the Chinese data somewhat.

Mandarin (Beijing)	*Hakka (Huizhou)*	*Gloss*
a. [tɕin]	[kim]	'zither'
b. [la]	[lat]	'spicy hot'
c. [mɔ]	[mɔk]	'lonesome'
d. [lan]	[lam]	'basket'
e. [tɕi]	[gip]	'worry'
f. [lan]	[lan]	'lazy'
g. [pa]	[pa]	'fear'

36. Proto-Peninsular Spanish

Castilian	*Andalusian*	*Gloss*
a. [majo]	[majo]	'May'
b. [kaʎe]	[kaje]	'street'
c. [poʎo]	[pojo]	'chicken'
d. [pojo]	[pojo]	'stone bench'
e. [dos]	[dos]	'two'
f. [dieθ]	[dies]	'ten'
g. [θiŋko]	[siŋko]	'five'
h. [si]	[si]	'yes'
i. [kasa]	[kasa]	'house'
j. [kaθa]	[kasa]	'a hunt'
k. [θiβiliθaθion]	[siβilisasion]	'civilization'

   [ʎ] represents a palatal lateral.
   [β] represents a voiced bilabial fricative.

37. Proto-Numic

Yerington Paviotso	*Northfork Monachi*	*Gloss*
a. [mupi]	[mupi]	'nose'
b. [tama]	[tawa]	'tooth'
c. [piwɪ]	[piwɪ]	'heart'
d. [soŋo]	[sono]	'lungs'
e. [sawaʔpono]	[sawaʔpono]	'proper name (fem.)'
f. [nɪwɪ]	[nɪwɪ]	'liver'
g. [tamano]	[tawano]	'springtime'
h. [pahwa]	[pahwa]	'aunt'
i. [kuma]	[kuwa]	'husband'
j. [wowaʔa]	[wowaʔa]	'Indians to the West'
k. [mɪhɪ]	[mɪhɪ]	'porcupine'

(cont.)

l.	[noto]	[noto]	'throat'
m.	[tapa]	[tape]	'sun'
n.	[ʔatapɪ]	[ʔatapɪ]	'jaw'
o.	[papiʔi]	[papiʔi]	'older brother'
p.	[patɪ]	[petɪ]	'daughter'
q.	[nana]	[nana]	'man'
r.	[ʔati]	[ʔeti]	'bow, gun'

38. Proto-Uto-Aztecan

	Shoshone	*Ute*	*Northern Paiute*	*Gloss*
a.	[tuhu]	[tuu]	[tuhu]	'black'
b.	[nika]	[nɪka]	[nika]	'dance'
c.	[kasa]	[kąsi]	[kasa]	'feather'
d.	[tuku]	[tʉku]	[tuku]	'flesh'
e.	[juhu]	[juu]	[juhu]	'grease'
f.	[pida]	[pida]	[pita]	'arm'
g.	[kadi]	[kadi]	[kati]	'sit'
h.	[kwasi]	[kwąsi]	[kwasi]	'tail'
i.	[kwida]	—	[kwita]	'excrement'

39. Proto-Western Turkic

	Turkish	*Azerbaijani*	*Crimean Tartar*	*Kazan Tartar*	*Gloss*
a.	[burun]	[burun]	[burun]	[bɪrɪn]	'nose'
b.	[kabuk]	[gabɪx]	—	[kabɪk]	'bark'
c.	[bojun]	[bojun]	[mojun]	[mujɪn]	'neck'
d.	[toprak]	[torpax]	[toprak]	[tufrak]	'earth'
e.	[kujruk]	[gujruk]	[kujruk]	[kɪjrɪk]	'tail'
f.	[japrak]	[jarpak]	[dʒaprak]	[jafrak]	'leaf'

Discussion Question

40. We have seen that the regularity of sound change provides one of the bases for the comparative method. How might the workings of analogical change pose problems for the comparative method?

CHAPTER
13

Language and Culture

'NAH! HE'S NOT MY TYPE.'

Cartoon by Gordon Gurvan, available at www.CartoonStock.com

What Is the Study of "Language and Culture"?

While the focus of much of this textbook has been on the systematic internal structure of language, language is also inextricably tied to human culture—our identities, our relationships between one another, our expression of language, our thoughts, and so on. **Anthropological linguistics** is the study of the relationship between language and culture; **sociolinguistics** is the study of the relationship between language and human society. Language is one of the key characteristics that separates humans from other living creatures; it has shaped our societies into what they are today. In this chapter, we briefly survey some of the ways in which language can both reflect and influence humanity, society, and culture.

Contents

Language and Identity

13.1.1 Using Language to Mark Identity

Up to this point in the book, we have focused on discussing language as though it were an independent object that can be studied in isolation, thinking about the internal structure of language. In reality, of course, this is not the only way to look at language: language exists only because people have created it and use it on a daily basis to communicate. Language is therefore a social phenomenon, and **sociolinguistics** is the study of language as it relates to society. As was introduced in Chapter 1, and as will be further elaborated in Chapter 14 on animal communication, language is a strictly human phenomenon: no other creatures use language as humans do—yet all humans, in all societies, have used language. Language therefore sets us apart from the rest of the world and unifies us: it is an indicator of the unique place humans have in the world, a marker of our identity as humans.

At the same time, given the diversity of human languages (some of which was discussed in Chapter 10 on language variation), language has often also been used as a marker of identity **within** the greater human society, and this use of language is the focus of this file. Because every typically-developing human acquires language, and acquiring language depends on the ambient language varieties surrounding the learner (see Chapter 8), language is readily available as a way to show which social groups a person identifies with or dissociates from.

In Files 10.3 and 10.4, we described some of the lines along which languages vary: nationality, ethnicity, age, gender, socioeconomic class, and so on. Throughout those files, we pointed out that there is not usually anything **inherent** about one particular group or another that might condition the members of that group to speak one way as opposed to some other way. That is, for example, there's nothing about being younger in itself that makes some younger English speakers use more rising intonation than older English speakers—one can easily imagine a world in which the older speakers use more rising intonation and the younger speakers use less, or a world in which older and younger speakers' language is differentiated in some other way entirely. What matters here is that age is one factor that differentiates groups of speakers who identify with each other in some manner, and once these groups are formed, the members of the group may develop particular language characteristics that distinguish their group from other groups. These characteristics are often not consciously developed; they simply happen naturally in the course of language use and are then picked up and propagated by new acquirers of each language variety.

13.1.2 Defining "Identity"

The notion of "identity" is obviously a complex one. Most people have more than one group that they may identify with. For example, you may identify yourself in the classroom as a student but at the camp you work at in the summer as an instructor. Or you may identify yourself broadly as an American, but more specifically as someone from northwest Ohio rather than some other part of the country or the state.

To a large degree, your "identity" at any given moment actually depends on the circumstances of the situation—where you are, whom you are talking with, what you are talking about, how you want to be perceived, what you hope to accomplish, who else is present, and so on. Most scholars agree that identity is not a static thing that anyone "possesses" but rather is a dynamic construct that emerges from social interactions. It revolves around establishing the relationship between one individual and the rest of society.

One of the focuses of sociolinguistic research has been to determine both what elements define a person's identity and how identity is established in linguistic interactions. Clearly, identity is not expressed solely through language use—other actions, practices, and characteristics also create a person's identity. At the same time, however, it is common to use language to establish or indicate the identity of yourself or of others.

It is important to remember that this use of language is not always conscious or intentional, or even within your control as the speaker. You may use particular lexical items that mark you as coming from a particular region, without even realizing that people from other regions might use different terms. Or the person you are talking to may have ideas about what your pronunciation of a particular word signifies that you do not intend—for example, not pronouncing your /ɹ/s at the ends of syllables, such as in *four, card, paper,* and so on, might be taken as a sign of your low prestige by a listener from New York but as a sign of your high prestige by a listener from London. The perception of your identity by those listening to you is arguably just as important as **your** perception of it, as identity is rather meaningless in isolation. While you can certainly use your own knowledge of society's associations between particular linguistic phenomena and elements of identity to bolster, downplay, or separate yourself from certain types of identities, you do not have complete control over your linguistic identity.

13.1.3 Signaling Identity

How exactly can particular aspects of identity be signaled through language? You will probably not be surprised to learn that identity can be indicated at every level of linguistic structure, from phonetics to pragmatics.

The most obvious use of language to signal identity is when people overtly state affiliation with or dissociation from a particular group (e.g., *I'm from Ireland,* or *Oh, no, you shouldn't think I'm British*).

Another overt use of language to establish identity that is slightly more subtle than simply stating it is the use of forms that mark particular identity. For example, when there are different words for male and female versions of the same profession, the use of one or the other signals the speaker's association with a particular gender (*I'm an actor/actress*). And, in a language such as French where adjectives must agree in gender-marking with the noun they modify, this association is even stronger (*je suis une actrice sportive* 'I am an (fem.) athletic (fem.) actress'). Other speakers also signal their views of someone's identity this way—for example, using the pronoun *he* or *she* indicates that a speaker assumes that the person they are referring to is of a particular gender.

More obliquely, identity can be signaled by making use of linguistic characteristics that society associates with particular social groups.[1] For example, using monophthongal [ɑː] instead of diphthongal [ɑɪ] in words such as *tide* or *I* is associated with the southeast

---

[1]An interesting twist on this is the use of identity to affect language perception. Elizabeth Strand found in a 1999 study that listeners will actually classify phonemes (see File 3.1) differently depending on whether they think they are hearing a man or a woman. Strand synthesized a continuum of fricatives from [s] to [ʃ] and had people categorize each sound on the continuum as one or the other. The listeners heard the sounds while looking at either a male face or a female face—and the categorization of the continuum was different depending on the face!

United States. Using *like* as an interjection (*I was, like, going to the store*) is associated with younger speakers. Using *be* to mark habitual action, as in *I always be late to school*, is associated with African-American English. So, using such forms can be taken as a sign of belonging to the associated group.

Related to the above examples, people also use even more oblique associations to indicate a particular identity. For example, using the word *partner* as opposed to *boyfriend, girlfriend, husband,* or *wife,* which are all marked for gender, often carries with it the pragmatic implicature that the partner is of the same gender as the speaker—that is, that they are a gay couple. Of course, there is nothing overt in the gender of the word *partner* that indicates this, but it is rather the lack of overt gender that carries this association.

On a broader level, in societies where multiple languages are used, the choice of one language over another can be used to indicate a certain affiliation or identity. For example, in Canada, both French and English are official languages at the federal level (see File 13.2 for more on official languages). However, most provinces are almost exclusively anglophone (English-speaking), while Quebec is francophone (French-speaking)—New Brunswick is the only official bilingual province in Canada. Because of various political tensions between Quebec and anglophone Canada (e.g., there has long been an independence movement to separate Quebec from the rest of Canada), the choice of language can sometimes be seen as making a political statement. In 1978, Soma Day told of an encounter she had: "I stopped in a garage and struggled to explain that my windshield wipers were *congellé* [frozen over] and I wanted to make them *fonctionner* [function]. The man listened in mild amusement and then said, 'You don't have to speak French to me, Madame. I'm not a separatist'" (reported in Fraser 2006: 144–45). While it has become more socially acceptable for anglophones to speak French in Quebec, the choice of which language to speak when two bilinguals encounter each other is still influenced by a number of factors: "the language the relationship was established in, where the conversation happens, the presence of other people, the nature of the relationship, and a whole series of other factors that can involve shadings of power ('I'll pick the language here'), one-upmanship ('I speak your language better than you speak mine'), exclusion ('I speak my language only with my people—and you're not one of them'), complicity ('We speak this language and they don't'), solidarity ('I'm one of you' or 'You're one of us')—or simply convenience" (Fraser 2006: 144).

It is interesting to note in the above discussion that identity can be marked either by showing the inclusion of the speaker in a particular group or by showing the dissociation of the speaker from a different group. That is, sometimes, the usage of linguistic forms directly marks a particular identity (e.g., using habitual *be* might mark the speaker as being African-American). But sometimes, the usage indicates identity by showing that the speaker is choosing **not** to speak in some other way that might be expected. For example, Elaine Chun did a study in 2001 that showed that some Korean-American men use characteristics of African-American English, not to show that they are African-American, but instead to show that they are not Euro-American.

Finally, we should point out that signaling identity through language can have various consequences. There are plenty of social stereotypes that accompany ideas of identity, so your language use may cause listeners to form ideas about you, your personality, your abilities, and so on. For example, in the United States, British dialects are often considered to be a mark of a more educated person, while southern U.S. dialects are considered uneducated. Of course, these associations are usually unfounded—someone from Alabama may be more highly educated than someone from Oxford—but they do have consequences for communication. Thomas Purnell, William Idsardi, and John Baugh did a study in 1999 that showed discrimination by landlords based on the perceived ethnicity of a potential renter, as determined through a telephone conversation. John Baugh, who has fluent command of Standard American English, African-American English, and Chicano English (see Section 10.4.5), called various landlords who had advertised housing for rent. In housing districts that were largely Euro-American in population, when he spoke using either the African-American or the Chicano English dialects, he was often told that the housing was unavailable—and then, using the Standard American English dialect within 30 minutes of the other calls, he was told that it was. This kind of dialect discrimination (which is illegal in the United States) is an unfortunate consequence of the use of language to mark identity; fortunately, John Baugh and his colleagues are working with the U.S. government to fight against it.[2]

13.1.4 Studying Identity

In the early days of sociolinguistic research, scholars often tried to isolate "essential" elements of speakers' identities. They would determine certain sociological factors that could be defined relatively easily (such as region, age, gender, etc.) and then pick a particular linguistic variable (such as /ɹ/-lessness, use of *pop* versus *soda,* use of the *needs washed* construction, etc.). Next they would see how the two were correlated (e.g., whether younger speakers use more /ɹ/s at the end of syllables than older speakers do). These studies were extremely valuable at establishing broad characteristics of different types of speech, and the studies formed the foundation of modern sociolinguistic methodology. They are easily replicable and are well suited to doing statistical analysis. Most of the discussion of sociolinguistics that we have presented has been based on such studies.

At the same time, these studies are somewhat limited in determining a person's sociolinguistic identity. First, they make use of sociological factors that are predetermined by the researcher and may or may not have any actual relevance for a particular speaker's identity. Second, they are rather tied to the sociological variables that are salient in a society; it is therefore difficult to do meaningful comparative studies across societies. Third, some of these variables are difficult to isolate or establish for a particular person—for example, what do you do about someone who has moved around several times? Someone who is of mixed ethnicity? Someone who grew up with wealthy parents but has since rejected that lifestyle?

While the factors used in such studies clearly do play a role in identity formation (and establishing particular correlations can help determine a person's identity based on her speech patterns), they do not tell the whole story. More recently, researchers have expanded their studies to try to include factors that speakers themselves may identify as being more relevant. For example, does a speaker feel that her involvement in the service organization Habitat for Humanity has created for herself a particular community with which she identifies? Do people involved in Habitat for Humanity have unique speech patterns—for example, the use of certain home-building jargon? Similar groups can be identified for all sorts of communities. One obvious location of such groups is schools—high schoolers often form cliques that distinguish themselves linguistically. Although two speakers could both be seventeen-year-old, Euro-American, female, middle-class students at the same high school, they may belong to radically different social groups and have different speech patterns that mark those groups. Rachelle Waksler did a study in 2001 showing that one such student, who self-identified as a non-conformist, nerdy type, tended to use *go* or *be like* to introduce quoted speech (e.g., *she went, 'uh-oh,' and he was like, 'oh wow'*), whereas another such student, who self-identified as a trendy, popular type, tended to use the even more innovative form *be all* (e.g., *he was all, 'oh wow'*). While both of these constructions might be identified with younger female speech, these two girls have distinctly different usage patterns that reflect their different social groups within a fairly narrowly defined environment.

One problem with many sociolinguistic studies of identity is known as the "observer's paradox." Often, it is impossible to get an accurate picture of what speakers do "naturally"

---

[2]To find out more about this study, and to hear recordings of John Baugh, you can visit his Web site at http://www.stanford.edu/~jbaugh/baugh.fft.

amongst themselves precisely because observing them makes them change their speech. Knowing that they are being watched, recorded, or studied may make speakers self-conscious, and many will try to speak the way they think the researcher wants them to, rather than how they would normally speak. The perceived identity of the researcher may also play a role in determining the speech of a person being studied: John Rickford and Faye McNair-Knox found in a 1994 study that the same African-American participant talked markedly differently when being interviewed by a Euro-American researcher than when being interviewed by an African-American researcher. This type of differing language use also points out the ever-changing notion of identity: clearly, the participant was the same person in both situations, but projected a different identity each time.

One way of at least partially avoiding the observer's paradox is to use larger databases of speech that have been recorded for other purposes or in such large quantities that speakers seem to forget that they are being recorded. These data can be used for subsequent analysis using techniques known as **discourse analysis** or **conversational analysis** to see how particular identities are established in the course of a conversation. In discourse analysis, the researcher breaks down a conversation between two or more people into its various component parts (e.g., the types of turns that are taken by the participants, the information conveyed, and the linguistic forms at all levels in which it is conveyed). Of course, this kind of study often does not give the researcher the same sort of flexibility as doing a direct interview with someone, because the researcher is reliant on whatever the speakers happened to be talking about.

No matter what technique a researcher uses, there will be advantages and disadvantages. These days, a more complete picture of sociolinguistic identity can be obtained by doing multiple types of studies that complement each other and each bring out a different aspect: for example, starting with a broad ethnographic study of a community and using surveys to begin to study language patterns that naturally occur, and then narrowing down the research with one-on-one interviews and using techniques of discourse analysis that pinpoint particular phenomena.

13.1.5 Martha's Vineyard: A Case Study in Language and Identity

In 1961, William Labov conducted a sociolinguistic study on the island of Martha's Vineyard in Dukes County, Massachusetts, to investigate the impact of social patterns on linguistic variation and change. The linguistic feature chosen for analysis was **centralization** of the diphthongs /aɪ/ and /aʊ/, as in *why* and *wow,* to [əɪ] and [əʊ], respectively. In a preliminary investigation, Labov discovered that after all phonetic, prosodic, and stylistic motivation had been accounted for, there was still variation in speakers' use of centralized diphthongs. His subsequent study was designed to investigate the motivation underlying this residual variation. Toward this end, Labov set out to test a number of different variables, many of which were introduced in Files 10.3 and 10.4 on factors that affect linguistic variation.

Was centralization related to **geography?** The island was, by universal consensus, divided into up-island (strictly rural) and down-island (consisting of the three small towns where 75% of the population lived). United States Census reports were consulted for information on the population distribution of the island.

Was **ethnic group** a factor in centralization? Native Vineyarders fell into four ethnic groups: (1) descendants of old English families, (2) descendants of Portuguese immigrants, (3) a small Native American population, and (4) a miscellaneous group from a number of origins. Another group, not considered in the study, was the summer population.

Was the **economic background** and current economic situation of the island in any way correlated with linguistic behavior? In comparison to the rest of the state, the Vineyard had higher unemployment, lower average income, and no industry, and thus was heavily dependent on the summer tourist trade. This heavy reliance on tourism was viewed by some islanders as a threat to independence. As a result many islanders displayed resistance to the summer visitors and took pride in being different from the tourists, the greatest resistance being felt in the rural up-island areas.

The results of the study revealed that, first of all, centralization was a linguistic feature of Martha's Vineyard and thus **regional** in character. That is, residents of the island pronounced /aɪ/ and /aʊ/ as [əɪ] and [əʊ], while summer tourists and mainland residents did not centralize the diphthongs. But within the island population, some residents centralized, while some did not.

Analysis of centralization by **age** indicated an increase of centralized diphthong use with age, peaking between thirty-one and forty-five years and then decreasing. It was also interesting to note the economic situation of this particular group. Members of this age group seemed to suffer the greatest degree of economic pressure, having chosen to remain on the island while supporting their families, even though employment opportunities were not abundant. Additionally, high-school students planning to go to college and then return to the island exhibited greater centralization than those going to college but not planning to return to the island.

With respect to ethnic group, the Portuguese population, which for years had been attempting to enter the mainstream of island life, showed a high degree of centralization. And those of Native American descent, having battled discrimination from the other groups for more than 150 years and also desiring acceptance, also displayed a high incidence of centralization.

Although it is clear that each of the regional and social factors that we might expect to influence linguistic variation does play a role, we can reach a deeper understanding of the effects at work here by thinking about language and identity. Specifically, we can summarize the effects of these different factors on centralization in terms of **group identification.** How closely speakers identified with the island, wanted to remain, wanted to enter into the mainstream, saw themselves as Vineyarders and were proud of it, was positively correlated with degree of centralization. Keep in mind that use of centralization was not necessarily conscious on the part of these speakers; centralization was, however, associated with being an integral part of being a Martha's Vineyard native, so those who felt especially close to the island tended to increase their use of this linguistic variable.

Language and Power

13.2.1 The Role of Language in Power Relationships

The idea that words have "power" is not a new one: for example, there are countless ancient legends that revolve around the act of naming someone or something in order to gain power over that person or thing, or the uttering of spells whose words alone have the power to work magic. In the modern world, we can think of the power of words to hold audiences spellbound, to persuade voters to vote a certain way, to educate students in how to become skilled professionals, to convince consumers to purchase particular products, to talk parents into letting their children stay up late, to wound a person's feelings, to calm a child's distress, or to win over a sweetheart's love, among many other extraordinary tasks.

How does language accomplish all this? As with the old question "If a tree should fall in the forest with no one there to hear it, would it make a sound?" one can ask, "If words were uttered and no one was there to hear them, would they have any power?" Unless magical spells really do exist, the answer to the latter question is no. The interpretation of words, and of which aspects of language can be used to indicate power, is socially determined. Language may have an effect on other humans, and thus it may seem to be powerful, but of course it is really humans' use and interpretation of language that is powerful.

There are many levels at which the use of language can have power. In any given conversation, there are various linguistic cues that those engaged in the conversation may use or perceive as indicators of power relations: is one speaker more dominant or subservient? Is one more conciliatory or aggressive? Is one asserting knowledge or ignorance? In Section 13.2.2, we will discuss some of the specific ways in which elements of linguistic structure have been used to indicate these different roles.

On the opposite end of the spectrum, language can be used to exert power over entire communities or societies. For example, in countries where multiple languages are spoken, the choice of one or two particular languages as the "official" language of politics, government, education, healthcare, and so on, can empower some citizens while excluding or minimizing others; this type of power is discussed in Section 13.2.3.

13.2.2 Power in Conversations

Of course, one of the most obvious ways to use language to express power or subservience is to make a direct statement. By saying, for example, "I am king of the castle," the speaker has asserted that he is in charge and in a superior position to those around him. But there is more to establishing power or lack thereof than simply the literal meaning of the words spoken: a servant who says clearly and firmly, "I bow to your lordship's wishes," may indeed seem more powerful than the lord who responds meekly "Uh, well, yes, um, thank you. . . ."

Just as the association of particular linguistic characteristics with certain social groups is arbitrary, the association of particular linguistic characteristics with the designation of power is also arbitrary. The power relationships expressed by language are defined by those who use language rather than by any inherent properties of the language. In different cultures, stereotypes about various aspects of language use (e.g., talkativeness, loudness, or silence) are associated with different values.

For instance, in Malagasy culture (on Madagascar and other islands in the Indian Ocean), indirect, deferential speech is valued. Men, who are dominant in Malagasy culture, are the ones who are chiefly associated with this sort of indirect speech. Malagasy men are stereotypically silent in public confrontations, while it is more socially acceptable for Malagasy women to express anger and criticism through direct, confrontational speech, often to the advantage of their husbands or other male family members (Keenan 1974: 137–39). But there is clearly no direct link between silence and higher worth in all cultures. Many western cultures value direct, public speech. A number of studies of conversation (see Coates 1993: 115 for a brief overview) have shown that in western societies, public speech tends to be dominated by men, where again, it is male norms that are more highly valued by the community. Thus, two different cultures use entirely opposite strategies in order to indicate the relative power of men in the society.

An interesting study, however, has demonstrated that silence can also be interpreted as a measure of power in conversation in western cultures. In an analysis of the October 1991 congressional hearings of Supreme Court nominee Clarence Thomas, Norma Mendoza-Denton (1995) paid special attention to the contexts in which silence was used in the testimony of Thomas as opposed to that of Anita Hill, who accused Thomas of sexual harassment. The average length of the silent gaps following statements by Thomas was 33% longer than the average length of the silent gaps following statements by Hill. According to Mendoza-Denton's analysis, this difference produced the effect of giving more weight and credibility to Thomas's statements.

Power in a society is related to a number of different sociological factors (many of which we have discussed previously in Chapter 10 on language variation and File 13.2 on language and identity). For example, William O'Barr and Bowman Atkins found in a 1980 study of speech in a North Carolina courtroom that people who had relatively little power in the courtroom tended to use similar linguistic constructions. "Powerless" language was marked by the use of hedges (e.g., *It's sort of hot; I'd kind of like to go*), polite or complimentary speech (e.g., *would you please close the door?* vs. *close the door*), more indirect statements, and so on. Thus, there are particular linguistic characteristics that tend to be used to indicate relative power in particular social settings. It is important to remember, however, that these particular markers of subservience are those found in American courtrooms and cannot be taken to be universal markers of subservience or powerlessness.

Power relationships can be established through means that make use of every level of linguistic structure. For example, at the phonetic and phonological levels, a speaker's prosody and volume can influence whether or not he is perceived as powerful in a certain situation. Use of certain morpho-syntactic structures (e.g., whether the speaker uses more declarative or interrogative sentence forms, whether the speaker uses more active sentences or more passive sentences, etc.) can likewise signify power or subservience. Word choice and the way that lexical items are used can also play a role. (For example, a speaker's use of technical jargon that her audience is unfamiliar with can, in some circumstances, indicate the speaker's attempt to show power relative to a certain topic. As a second example, consider whether, in your speech community, the use of profanity correlates with speakers who have more power or less power in a given situation.) Finally, pragmatic factors are involved in the marking of power relationships: for example, whether the speaker uses more direct or more indirect speech acts. And, of course, the message conveyed by the use of any of these strategies will vary between societies and speech communities. The same strategy that establishes dominance in one community may be used to indicate subservience in another.

13.2.3 Power in Society

In the previous section, we saw various ways that individuals' language use can both establish and enforce power differences between individuals. Language is also a powerful tool for establishing more global power relationships, though: power relationships that are established not between individuals, but rather within and between entire communities. Strategies used to establish these more global sorts of power relationships are based not on particular individual uses of language (e.g., whether a direct or an indirect speech act is used in one instance) but rather on prescriptions of how language may be used at all, or which languages may be used. A rather profound example is found in the fact that the United States (among other countries) guarantees freedom of speech. Under some governments, such liberties may not be guaranteed: thus a government can establish its power over the people it governs by determining when and how they may use language.

Another common (though less extreme) way in which language is used to create power relationships within a society on a large scale is through "official" languages adopted by the governments of particular nations. When a country declares an official language, all official government business must be done in that language.

There are many reasons for nations to declare an official language. For instance, many nations have so many languages spoken within their borders that the government must pick one or two to be the official language to avoid the practical difficulties of trying to deal with five, ten, or more languages on an official level. Some countries declare an indigenous language to be official in order to preserve the language's heritage. In Ireland, for example, the indigenous language is Irish, but it is in the process of being replaced by English in general society. Declaring Irish an official language of the country is a way of recognizing the place and importance of this language in the country's past. On the other hand, a "world language" such as French or English, used over wide areas of the globe, is often chosen as an official language (especially of developing countries), even though it may not be the native language of any speakers in that country. Making a world language official in a country makes it easier for that country to participate in the world economy.

Moves like these can clearly have social ramifications, both positive and negative. While declaring one language official may help those who speak it natively or who learn to speak it proficiently to succeed in the worlds of politics and economics, it can seriously hurt those who are not proficient speakers. Citizens who are not comfortable with the official language may be prevented from participating in the political process if ballots are printed only in the official language; they may be physically at risk if public safety messages are monolingual; they may be economically subjugated if they cannot hold jobs without speaking the official language. Sometimes, individuals who dislike a group that does not happen to speak the official language feel that the legality of the "official language" validates their feelings, thus allowing them to be more open in their contempt for such groups. When a world language like English is chosen over indigenous languages, it can send a message of indigenous inferiority and American or British supremacy, fueling resentment or conflict within a nation.

Issues of multilingualism, nationhood, and language planning are extremely complicated and the subject of much study, debate, and politics. Because language is tied to so many social factors and to people's very identity, these topics often spark strong feelings and opinions. It is therefore important to be well informed of as many aspects of the issues at hand as possible.

13.2.4 A Case Study: Language and Power Relative to a Particular Community

A particularly interesting (and unfortunate) case of how language and choice of language has been used to subjugate a community can be found in the case of how various institutions have instituted policies about the use of signed languages. Recall, from Chapter 8, that although all children can acquire language naturally, they will do so only if they have adequate exposure to some particular language. Thus, deaf children will acquire language naturally only if they have exposure to a signed language (because they cannot perceive and interpret spoken language—e.g., through lip reading—without explicit instruction). In and of itself, this fact does not create any problem at all. However, during the course of the history of deaf education in the United States (and in many other countries as well), educators and politicians have used this fact to create a linguistic power differential between deaf and hearing individuals, even within Deaf institutions. As a result, although ASL is one of the most widely used non-English languages in the United States, most hearing people do not perceive the Deaf community as comprising a large part of the overall community. Let's look at the some of the history through which this state of affairs came to be.

In 1880, the International Congress of Instructors for the Deaf was held in Milan, Italy. At this conference were 164 participants (only one of whom was deaf) who voted on whether it was preferable to educate deaf children using signed language or whether it was preferable to instruct them to communicate orally: teaching them to read lips, to vocalize, and to speak. Of the 164 who voted, only six voted for instruction in sign language. (An interesting side note is that, of those six, five were American—and this, in fact, represented the entire American delegation.) The others voted that an **oralist education** was preferable. There are many reasons that this may have been the predominant opinion. Among these reasons are that at the time there was a poor understanding of the linguistic properties that signed languages have; that the instructors themselves were often not well enough versed in any signed language to use it as a language of instruction (and were not eager to learn); that many of the educators genuinely believed that it would not be possible for deaf individuals to become gainfully employed and fully participant members of society without the ability to use the predominant spoken languages of their countries of residence; and that the educators did not appreciate that using a sign language as a naturally acquired first language in order to teach a spoken language as a second language was a viable possibility. Whatever the reasons, this vote had a profound affect on Deaf culture in the United States that continues to this day.

In spite of the fact that several Americans voted against the oralist method at the conference in Milan, the oralist approach to Deaf education was adopted in most schools for the Deaf in America for close to the next century. It was only in the 1970s that a return to sign language once again began to appear in the classroom. During the intervening years, use of sign language was often considered a punishable offence at schools for the Deaf—not only in classrooms where English was being used, but also during students' free time. Today, older signers may remember the harsh treatment and punishment that they received for using ASL to communicate at school. The message that those enforcing these rules sent was that use of ASL was bad, that it would detract from the Deaf children's ability to communicate, and that their use of ASL was part of establishing a community that the hearing instructors and administrators did not want established. Thus, the educators' goal was not only to make sure that English was the official language of communication (as may be the goal for some countries choosing an official language) but also to make sure that ASL was not used at all.

This case is particularly extreme. Whereas a country that declares an official language may require that its citizens use the official language in court or to vote or participate in other official activities, it does not (usually) forbid use of some other language by families around the dinner table! The goal of at least some of the educators who taught using oralist methods, however, was to completely subjugate the culture that went along with signing. This is not to suggest that these people were necessarily uncaring or that they did not value their pupils: rather they had an educational philosophy that intrinsically required the rejection of signed languages being used. Regardless of their personal beliefs, however, the effect was to send the message that ASL, and, by extension, users of ASL, were somehow inferior to English and, by extension, users of English.

Of course, ASL did not die out in response to these pressures; ASL and Deaf culture both flourish today, and both were propagated throughout the twentieth century in the very schools where their use was forbidden. However, ramifications of the ideology espoused by oralist schools for much of the last century (that ASL is inferior to spoken languages in some way) still exist in our society today: there is still an underlying belief among many people that Deaf individuals are somehow less able to function in society or that they cannot communicate as effectively as can hearing individuals who use spoken language. This model is one that considers deafness to be pathological—that considers it a disease. Members of the Deaf community, on the other hand, consider Deafness to be a cultural phenomenon: as such it does not inhibit their participation in society at all but rather increases solidarity within the Deaf community.

Once again, we are witnessing an arbitrary association of a particular aspect of language use—in this case modality—with a particular role. There is nothing intrinsically more or less powerful about visual-gestural languages or about auditory-vocal languages, but in some communities those who use one modality are seen as more powerful, whereas in other communities those who use the other are seen as more powerful. There is no evidence whatsoever suggesting that use of a signed language is any more or less linguistically valid, efficient, or effective than use of a spoken language.

It is the case that in order for successful linguistic communication to take place between individuals, the individuals need to have some language in common. Thus, it stands to reason that a country, an international alliance, an organization, a school, or some other group might choose some particular official language. The choice to recognize a language as official is not, in and of itself, a bad thing. However, any language at all (e.g., ASL or Irish) has particular import, cultural value, and communicative significance for the communities of speakers who use it. Thus, recognizing or not recognizing a language as official will inevitably lead to perceptions of how that language does or does not connote power within the society.

Language and Thought

13.3.1 Developing the Principle of Linguistic Relativity

One of the most prominent debates in linguistics in the past century has been the issue of how language, thought, and culture are interrelated. Does language simply reflect culture, giving us a way of expressing our thoughts? Or can language actually influence a society's worldview? If it can have such an influence, how strong is that influence—does the language we speak completely determine our outlook on the world, or does it simply help to shape it?

The association of language with thought and culture is not new, but the modern discussion of it can be traced to American anthropological linguists starting with Franz Boas in the early twentieth century. Boas noted that language is used to classify our experiences with the world. For example, if you see several small-ish furry creatures that meow, with long tails and whiskers, you might classify them all under the category *cat*. Because languages have different ways of classifying the world, different people will classify the world differently, based on the languages they speak. In Boas' view, language could be used to describe or enunciate how a person saw the world, but it would not constrain it: "presumably the language alone would not prevent a people from advancing to more generalized forms of thinking if the general state of their culture should require expression of such a thought" (Boas 1966 [1911]: 63). Boas' ideas were shaped by his extensive study of North American languages, which showed him that there is much more linguistic diversity in the world than had been commonly thought by those who study primarily Indo-European languages.

One of Boas' students, Edward Sapir, took this basic idea and expanded it, with the idea that linguistic classification is actually the **way** in which people think. That is, his belief was that our thoughts themselves are channeled by our language: all of our thoughts are "done" in language, so the language we speak can shape our thoughts. This theory then meant that people will have different ways not just of classifying but of actually thinking about the world. At the same time, Sapir did not try to extend this line of reasoning to say that language would actually influence culture: "Culture may be defined as *what* a society does and thinks. Language is a particular *how* of thought" (Sapir 1949 [1921]: 218).

The person most associated with the idea that language can influence both thought and culture is Benjamin Lee Whorf, an associate of Sapir's. Professionally, Whorf was neither an anthropologist nor a linguist; he worked as a fire prevention expert for the Hartford Fire Insurance Company. He found himself drawn, however, to questions of linguistics through his interests in biblical interpretation and from his own observations about people's use of language and how it seemed to influence their thoughts and behaviors. For example, on the job he noticed that workers tended to be careful around full gasoline drums but might smoke or throw cigarette stubs around apparently "empty" gasoline drums. By classifying the drums as "empty," that is, having been emptied of the original contents, the workers then assumed that the drums were in fact "empty," that is, that they did not in fact contain anything. The apparently empty drums, however, could be full of highly explosive vapors or inflammable gasoline residue, making the workers' actions highly dangerous. The mental classification of the drums using a particular meaning of the word influenced the workers' actual perception of the world and then their actions.

Intrigued by such patterns, Whorf delved deeply into the study of linguistics and language diversity, both through his association with Sapir and through his own linguistic study of several Native American languages, including Hopi. Based on these studies, Whorf developed a principle that he called **linguistic relativity** (sometimes called the **Whorf Hypothesis**), which he defined as follows: "users of markedly different grammars are pointed by the grammars toward different types of observations and different evaluations of externally similar acts of observation, and hence are not equivalent as observers but must arrive at somewhat different views of the world" (1956, 58). Essentially, this meant that the language someone speaks affects how she perceives the world.

13.3.2 Whorf's Evidence for Linguistic Relativity

Whorf's evidence for this principle came from many of the comparisons he made between English (and other "Standard Average European" languages, as he termed them) and Hopi or other Native American languages. For instance, Whorf saw that English tends to classify concepts and experiences into objects more than Hopi does. In English, for example, we apply plurality and cardinal numbers to both spatial and temporal entities. We say *ten men* and *ten days;* but physically, they are quite different. It is possible to place ten men in an objective group, but not ten days, ten steps forward, or ten strokes on a bell. Physically, such events are cyclical rather than spatial, but English treats them all as countable nouns, predisposing English speakers to place them in an imaginary mental group.

According to Whorf's studies of Hopi, on the other hand, time is not divided up into units that are used as count nouns; time is expressed adverbially. Rather than saying something like *they stayed for ten days* as an English speaker might, Whorf claimed that a Hopi speaker would express the same idea as something like *they left after the tenth day*. He said that in Hopi, ten days is not viewed as a collection of different days but as successive appearances of the same day.

These kinds of differences are present throughout the systems of the languages. The attitude in Standard Average European languages that time is linear and segmentable is reinforced by tense systems in which past, present, and future are obligatory categories. We think of ourselves as on a point, the present, moving along the line of time, which extends indefinitely into the past and the future. The past is irrevocably behind us, whether an event occurred ten minutes ago or ten million years ago. Hopi verbs, on the other hand, lack the tense system so common in such European languages. The primary distinction indicated by Hopi verbs instead concerns whether the action takes place in the Objective (Manifested) Realm or the Subjective (Unmanifest) Realm.

Based on his analysis of the Hopi system, Whorf made the claim that language influences thought, which may in turn influence culture. For example, western society tends to be very concerned with exact dates and records, keeping calendars and diaries that mark time into sequential units. The Hopi that Whorf described seemed to be unconcerned with this sort of timekeeping; whatever had happened still was, but in an altered form. According to Whorf, the Hopi believed that the present should not be recorded but rather treated as "preparing," and he claimed that there is much emphasize on preparation in their culture.

It should be noted, however, that Whorf's studies of the Hopi and their language and culture have been disputed (see, for example, Ekkehart Malotki's 1983 book). First, some scholars have questioned Whorf's analysis of the Hopi worldview of space and time, suggesting that Whorf was simply projecting his ideas about their culture from what he understood of the Hopi grammatical structure, which would make his arguments circular. Second, while the Hopi may not express time on verbs using tenses, this does not mean that they do not have ways of locating particular events in time, just as English does. There are certainly other languages that are also tenseless (i.e., they do not express time on verbs), but this fact is not actually incompatible with the conceptualization of time progressing in a linear fashion. Third, even Whorf's descriptions of how the Hopi linguistic system categorizes time do not seem to have been completely accurate: for example, time in Hopi can be expressed using nouns, and there are such nouns for words like *day, night, month,* and *year.* Does this mean that the principle of linguistic relativity is wrong? Not necessarily, but it does mean that we need stronger evidence than Whorf was able to provide. The next two sections will outline some of the further investigations of this principle.

13.3.3 Beyond Relativity: Linguistic Determinism and Cultural Anthropology

Since Whorf first made these claims, they have been interpreted in many different forms. Some have claimed that Whorf said that language actually **determines** thought and culture: that people are in some way confined by their language to only be able to understand or think about concepts that their language can describe. This view is called **linguistic determinism** and is not actually attributable to Whorf. Recently, it has been claimed that evidence for linguistic determinism has been found in the inability of adult speakers of Pirahã, an indigenous language of Brazil, to learn cardinal numbers as we know them in western languages (as reported in studies by Peter Gordon (2004) and Daniel Everett (2005)). While Pirahã speakers could accurately respond to tasks in which they had to count up to two or three objects, and could at least partially count up to ten, their performance with counting numbers larger than these was extremely low. Despite efforts to teach the Pirahã cardinal numbers, and the apparent willingness of the Pirahã to learn, very little success has been seen. This has been attributed to their language's lack of numbers or other quantificational markers. For example, they have no words for 'all,' 'each,' 'every,' 'most,' and so on; there is no word for 'one,' but rather only a word that means 'roughly one' or 'small'; there are not separate words for 'he' as opposed to 'they'; and so on. If it is, in fact, the case that the Pirahã cannot learn to count (some scientists have questioned the validity of the training techniques or elicitation methods used), then it could support the idea that the continued use of a particular language system can, in fact, determine one's ability to categorize the world.[1]

Proponents of linguistic determinism might claim that one's worldview is almost totally dependent upon language, and that it is possible to greatly modify public attitudes by forcing changes in language. That language can, in fact, be changed at all in some ways undermines this entire idea: clearly, introducing new concepts (and subsequently words for them) is quite possible at least in some cases (see Chapter 12 on language change), meaning that our worldview is not entirely determined by language. At the same time, simply substituting one word for another will not necessarily change one's worldview, as becomes apparent when one examines the results of past substitutions, such as *underprivileged* or *disadvantaged* for *poor,* or *retarded* for *dull* or *stupid.* In time, the substitutions acquire most of the unpleasant connotations of the original term.

Another extension of linguistic relativity that sometimes reveals itself is the idea that, if you assume that language influences thought, which influences culture, it is possible to interpret a culture simply by looking at the language a people speaks. Occasionally, anthropologists have tried to describe a culture's worldview by analyzing their language and not looking more deeply for additional behavioral, cultural, or cognitive evidence (see Lucy 1992). While most scientists today realize the futility of such attempts, they have certainly added to the debate and confusion about what linguistic relativity is and whether it should be accepted as a principle or not.

---

[1] It should be noted that Everett himself believes that linguistic determinism is not quite the right explanation here, and he prefers to appeal to some larger cultural constraint: see Everett (2005).

At this point, however, it seems relatively uncontroversial that language does have some influence on how we think about the world: if you speak a foreign language, you have probably noticed times when the classification of the world is different in one language than in another. Dan Slobin has expressed the idea that perhaps we should not be concerned with "language and thought" but rather "thinking and speaking" (1996). That is, we should accept the fact that in order to speak a particular language, a speaker must make use of particular language-specific classifications and therefore perhaps take note of different aspects of the world around her. For example, a speaker of English must mark the tense on the verb in a sentence such as *The platypus was in the bathtub,* signifying that the platypus was in the bathtub at some point in the past, but may not be at the time of speaking. On the other hand, a speaker of Mandarin would not have to specify when the event happened. Thus, the speaker of English **must** notice (i.e., think about) when the event happened because her language requires her to specify this when she speaks about the event; a speaker of Mandarin would not **have** to think about this (although he could if he wanted to), because his language does not require this to be specified. Thus, Slobin says that we have to learn to "think for speech"—the things we need to think about are influenced by the language we speak, essentially a soft view of linguistic relativity.

One important point to make, however, is that these different ways of thinking about the world are not "better" or "worse" than one another. Much of the debate about the plausibility of linguistic relativity seems to have come from fears that one worldview might be superior to or more "correct" than another. But Whorf himself made the point that "alternative views of the world encapsulated in language categories are functionally equivalent" (Lucy 1992: 33). Not only is it possible for languages to have different but equally valid outlooks on life, but, except according to a strong linguistic determinism hypothesis, then one's worldview can, in fact, change to incorporate other ideas if you are exposed to them. For example, if your language does not distinguish between 'misleading with malicious intent' versus 'misleading accidentally,' then you might not usually think about the distinction. But if a new word were introduced to your language (let's say it's *misle,* to mean 'mislead with malicious intent'), then you might begin to wonder whether someone was misle-ing you or simply misleading you (accidentally), a distinction you might not have even noticed until you had different words available.

13.3.4 Further Investigation of Linguistic Relativity

As the discussion above highlights, the validity of the principle of linguistic relativity does remain very much in question, especially if one wants to pin down exactly how much influence language has or can have on thought and culture.

The Whorf Hypothesis can be difficult to test, because it can be difficult to identify tasks that really are language- and culture-neutral (features that are desirable if you are trying to isolate the effects of language and culture on each other). Many of the experiments that have been carried out to examine it have been based on the classification of colors, as reflected by color terms in different languages. These studies are based on the idea that there is a physical universal color continuum, but that different languages have different ways of dividing this continuum into discrete categories. Although it is usually acknowledged that languages may have numerous descriptive terms for many different subtle color gradations (e.g., *brick red* versus *fire engine red* versus *scarlet . . .*), such studies generally focus on the "basic" color terms of a language. Basic color words (like *black, white, red, green, yellow, blue, brown, purple, pink, orange,* and *gray* in English) are words that every speaker knows and that have essentially the same reference for all speakers. Such words tend to be offered at the beginning of lists of color terms; they are not used only for certain objects (as English *blond* is); they are not included in the range of another color word (as English *magenta* is); and they do not have meanings predictable from the meanings of their parts (as English *bluish* does). Basic color terms differ across languages, being used to refer to different sub-groupings of colors.

There are many variations on experimental techniques designed to test the linguistic relativity hypothesis with regard to color classification. The most straightforward are studies in which speakers of different languages are asked to sort or identify chips of colors that fall along a continuum; there are generally many more chips than basic color terms in any known language. The idea is that if speakers consistently divide the colors along the divisions that their language makes, then those linguistic divisions have influenced how they perceive the color categories (i.e., the linguistic relativity hypothesis is supported); if they are inconsistent, or if they use divisions different from those in their language, then this is seen as evidence against the linguistic relativity hypothesis.

Even with such an oversimplified view of the Whorf Hypothesis and of the scientific method (the hypothesis cannot be proven or disproven simply by one test of color terms!), the evidence has been mixed. In one study from 1956, Eric Lenneberg and John Roberts describe an experiment in which groups of English speakers and a group of monolingual Zuñi speakers were presented with diverse colors ranging between yellow and orange. The English speakers, who have two basic color terms for this range (namely, *yellow* and *orange*), were highly consistent in naming the colors, whereas the Zuñi, who have a single term encompassing yellow and orange, made no consistent choice. These results seem to support the Whorf Hypothesis. A similar experiment by Andre von Wattenwyl and Heinrich Zollinger in 1978, with Quechi subjects on the blue–green area of the spectrum (for which Quechi has a single term), showed that speakers tended to perform groupings based on criteria apart from their lexicon, separating out blue chips from green chips despite not having terms for these categories. These findings would seem to counter the Whorf Hypothesis.

An interesting related study was done in 1969 by Brent Berlin and Paul Kay in order to establish a baseline of color terminology across languages. For each of twenty languages, they listed the basic color words. Then they gave speakers of each language a chart of 329 chips of different colors and asked them to perform two tasks: (a) for each basic color word, to circle all of those chips that could be called by that word, and (b) for each basic color word, to select the best, most typical example of that color. They then calculated the focus of each color word in each language—the best and most central chips for each color.

Berlin and Kay found that:

- About 70% of the chips did not fall within the range of any color word in any language.
- The foci of the color terms for different languages were quite close.
- Universally, every language has at least two color words: black (covering also most dark hues) and white (covering also most light hues).
- If a language has more than two basic color terms, then it follows a hierarchy of color terms:
  - Languages with three color terms have 'black,' 'white,' and 'red' (the latter having its focus close to English 'red');
  - Languages with four terms have 'black,' 'white,' 'red,' and either 'green' or 'yellow';
  - Languages with five terms have 'black,' 'white,' 'red,' and both 'green' and 'yellow';
  - Language with six terms have these five plus 'blue';
  - Languages with seven terms have these six plus 'brown';
  - Languages with more than seven terms have these seven plus some of 'purple,' 'pink,' 'orange,' or 'gray.'

English, according to Berlin and Kay, is an eleven-term language, as are Japanese and Hebrew. Hungarian and Russian have twelve basic terms—Hungarian has the standard eleven with a distinction between *vörös* 'dark red' and *piros* 'light red,' while Russian has the standard eleven with a distinction between *siniy* 'dark blue' and *goluboy* 'light blue.' Shona (a Niger-Congo language of Zimbabwe) is a typical three-term language: *citema* covers 'black,' *cicena* 'white,' and *cipswuka* 'red.' Bassa (a Niger-Congo language of Liberia) is a typical two-term language in the Berlin-Kay color scheme.

Though somewhat controversial (it has been claimed, for example, that the Pirahã of Brazil do not have any color terms—see Everett (2005)), the Berlin-Kay findings provide a relatively clear case in which similar physical stimuli are categorized differently by speakers of different languages. Whether or not there is a causal relationship between the linguistic categorization and the categorization by speakers of colors in particular tasks, or the directionality of such a relationship if it exists, is still debated.

Another arena in which the principle of linguistic relativity has been debated is the study of spatial relationships and the categorization of space in different languages. Some languages, like English, use relative terms such as *left, right, front,* and *back* to indicate the spatial orientation of one object to another: *the chair is to the left of the table,* and so on. Not all languages have such terms, however; for example, Tenejapan Tzeltal (a Mayan language spoken in Mexico) uses absolute terms similar to *north, south, east,* and *west* instead. That is, they make use of a fixed point of reference to locate particular objects (e.g., *the chair is to the north of the table*) rather than using relative reference points that may change based on the location of the speaker.

Various aspects of culture seem to reflect such differences in spatial categorization: for example, in Tzeltal, time "is conceived of as stretching up to the south" (Levinson 1996b: 376), whereas in English, time tends to be conceived of as stretching either from left (past) to right (future) or from behind (past) to in front (future). Perhaps most tellingly, Tzeltal and English speakers respond very differently in experimental tasks that require them to describe objects they see in the world. For example, consider the diagram shown in (1), which sketches the experimental setup used by Stephen Levinson and Penelope Brown to explore the Tzeltal system of spatial reference (see, for example, Levinson 1996b, and Brown and Levinson 1993).

(1) Comparing relative and absolute frames of reference

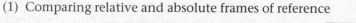
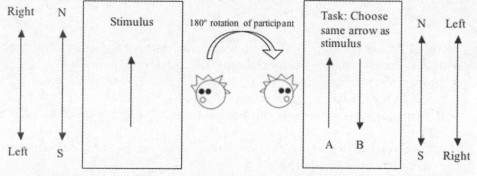

In experiments like this, a participant is first seated at a table as shown on the left side of the diagram; an arrow on the table acts as a stimulus. The participant is asked to look at the arrow and remember which direction it points. The participant is then turned 180°, so that she is facing the opposite direction, as is shown on the right side of the diagram. Two arrows are shown, A and B, pointing in opposite directions. The participant is then asked which one matches the arrow she saw earlier (the stimulus arrow).

Speakers of a language with a relative frame of reference, such as English, consistently choose arrow B, while speakers of a language with an absolute frame of reference, such as Tzeltal, consistently choose arrow A! Levinson and Brown hypothesize that this consistent difference between the groups of speakers is based on the way the languages categorize directions. For English speakers, the stimulus arrow goes from their left to their right; when they are turned around, they still pick an arrow that goes from their left to their right (arrow B). For Tzeltal speakers, on the other hand, the stimulus arrow points from south to north, regardless of which way they are facing; when they are turned around, they still pick an arrow that goes from south to north (arrow A).

This result is particularly compelling given that the tasks can be carried out nonlinguistically; that is, the speakers don't have to say anything in the course of looking at the stimulus, turning around, and indicating which arrow matches the stimulus. Thus, Levinson and Brown have found evidence that the linguistic categories available in a speaker's language can directly affect the speaker's nonlinguistic perception of spatial relationships. Once again, however, while studies like these support the basic principle of linguistic relativity (i.e., that speakers of different languages may have different views of the world), it is difficult to draw any stronger conclusions (e.g., either that the language we speak determines the way we see the world, or that the way we see the world determines aspects of the language that we speak).

FILE **13.4**

Writing Systems

13.4.1 Writing: What Is It?

We made the point in Chapter 1 that the primary form of linguistic expression is either vocal or manual (spoken or signed) rather than written. Knowing a language requires knowing how to speak it, but not how to read or write it: in fact, most of the languages that exist today or have existed in the past have not had a writing system. The majority of this book therefore has focused exclusively on the structure of spoken language itself and not on how it is written. (Ironically, of course, we have had to rely on written language in order to create this book!)

At the same time, however, writing is an interesting topic, and it is clearly related to the study of language: even though language does not depend on writing, writing does depend on language. While the actual noun *writing* may refer to various things (e.g., a person's style of handwriting, or an author's technique of composition), the type of **writing** we are referring to here is "the use of graphic marks to represent specific linguistic utterances" (Rogers 2005: 2). Hence, writing is a system that is used to record language.

Writing has had a profound impact on human culture. Spoken language encodes thought into a physically transmittable form, while writing, in turn, encodes spoken language into a physically preservable form. Writing allows us to encode thoughts in a way that can be preserved over space and time and therefore shared with many more people than spoken language alone. It allows much more complex calculation than could be done just using spoken language and memory, and it is much more suited to revision and refinement: that is, you can go back and change or edit a written document before it is shared in a way that you can't go back and change utterances that have been spoken. Spoken language is, on the one hand, more fleeting than writing (once an utterance has been said, we rely on memory alone to preserve it) but on the other is less changeable (once you have said something, you can't "take it back").

All this is not to say that languages that are only spoken are in any way inferior to ones that have a writing system. Indeed, when writing systems (and, later, printing) were introduced, many people worried about their potentially negative impact on the human mind (much as people today worry about the influence of calculators and computers on our ability to think for ourselves). Walter Ong, in his book comparing oral and literate cultures, describes some of the complaints against writing systems:

> Writing, Plato has Socrates say in the *Phaedrus,* is inhuman, pretending to establish outside the mind what in reality can only be in the mind. It is a thing, a manufactured product. . . . Secondly, Plato's Socrates urges, writing destroys memory. Those who use writing will become forgetful, relying on an external resource for what they lack in internal resources. Writing weakens the mind. . . . Thirdly, a written text is basically unresponsive. If you ask a person to explain his or her statement, you can get an explanation; if you ask a text, you get back

nothing except the same, often stupid, words which called for your question in the first place. (1982: 79)

So, while writing has indubitably caused a massive transformation in the structure of human communication and culture, it is clear that this transformation can be seen in both positive and negative lights. There have been many discussions on the effect of writing systems on culture (it has been called "one of the most significant cultural accomplishments of human beings" (Rogers 2005: 1)), some of which are listed in File 13.5 under "Further Readings." In the rest of this file, however, we are going to focus on some of the different types of writing systems that humans have developed, for as you are probably aware, there are many different ways to put language into graphic form.

13.4.2 Types of Writing Systems

Since writing represents language, and spoken language consists of arbitrary matchings between particular sounds (or gestures[1]) and particular meanings, there are at least three angles from which a particular writing system may approach the language it represents: from the *meaning* side, the *sound* side, or simultaneously from both the meaning and the sound sides. (1) helps you visualize the (somewhat simplified) relationship between the spoken language and its writing system. In (1a), we illustrate how English writes the word *box* with symbols that represent only the sounds of the language, without any regard to the meaning. In (1b), we illustrate how Mandarin Chinese writes the word *box* with symbols that represent both the sound and the meaning of the word. Finally, in (1c), we illustrate how Cantonese (a southern dialect of Chinese) writes the word *angry* with symbols that represent only the meaning of the word, without any regard to the sound.

(1) Visualizing the relationship between the spoken language and its writing system
   a. English

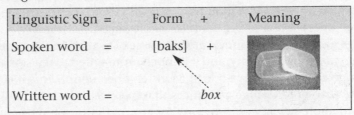

   b. Mandarin Chinese

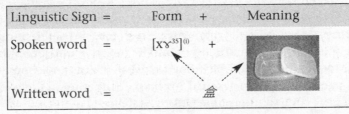

---

[1]We should note that most signed languages do not have their own writing systems, instead often relying on the writing system and language used by the dominant spoken language in a country. Most dictionaries and references represent signed languages pictorially, with pictures of the hands and arrows representing movement, as we have done throughout this book. There are some writing systems for sign languages, which often represent the various phonetic components of the signs (e.g., handshape, orientation, and movement) (see, for example, Martin 2000). Because of the current limited use of written forms of signed languages, we will not go into any detail about them here.

c. Cantonese Chinese

Linguistic Sign	=	Form	+	Meaning
Spoken word	=	[nɐu⁵⁵]	+	'angry'
Written word	=	嬲		

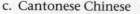

- - - - ➤ indicates the written form's approximation of form and/or meaning.

(i) The numbers after the segments are so-called Chao-type tone numbers, with '5' denoting the highest pitch in the pitch range, and '1' the lowest (see Section 2.5.4).

In English, we use the letters <box> to represent the sounds [bɑks], which is how we pronounce the word *box*. These sounds and letters have nothing to do with the meaning of the word as a type of 'container'—for example, the same set of sounds could (and in fact is!) used to mean 'to spar with someone using fists.' In Mandarin Chinese, the written word 盒 represents both the sound and the meaning of the word. The upper half of the written form, pronounced as [xɤ³⁵], indicates the pronunciation; the lower half indicates that the meaning of the word is 'container.' In Cantonese, the written word does not give any indication as to the pronunciation: instead, it is a combination of two characters for 'man' (男, [naːm²¹]) and the character for 'woman' (女, [nθy²³]), which together make 'angry' (because two men are likely to be fighting over a single woman: note that the sign for 'woman' must be in the middle of the two for 'men').

In English, all of our standard writing is based on sound correspondences only (although you do sometimes see writing incorporated with images representing meaning in advertising or illustrations, as in (2)). In Chinese, both Mandarin and Cantonese (as well as other dialects), the writing system is a combination of sound- and meaning-based representations. Some written forms, like the Mandarin word for *box* above, represent both in the same word; others may represent either the sound in isolation or the meaning in isolation.

(2) Example of symbols representing both sound and meaning in English

We can classify writing systems along the lines above. Systems that rely predominantly on the representation of sound can be considered **phonographic** systems, where the *phono-* prefix relates to the notion of speech sounds. These systems may be either like English, where each symbol approximately represents a single sound (so-called **alphabetic** or **phonemic** writing systems), or like Cherokee, where each symbol approximately represents a consonant plus vowel combination (so-called **syllabic** or **moraic** writing systems). Systems that rely predominantly on the representation of meaning or sound-meaning pairs, on the other hand, can be considered **morphographic** systems, where the *morpho-* prefix relates to the notion of the *morpheme*. Such systems are sometimes referred to as **logographic**, where the prefix *logo-* means 'word,' but since we know that words may be made up of smaller sound-meaning pairs (see Chapter 4), and such writing systems usually represent these smaller units, it is more accurate to call these systems morphographic (see Rogers 2005).

When you look at a written text, you may also see symbols on the page that do not (at least directly) represent either sound or meaning: these symbols include spaces between words, indentation at the start of paragraphs, and commas, periods, exclamation points, and other punctuation. Such symbols are used to visually mark the structure of the written language and may or may not correspond to aspects of the spoken language. For example, when we speak, we do not usually pause between words: adding spaces between written words gives the reader an aid in word segmentation that a listener does not have (see Files 9.3 and 9.4). On the other hand, we do often place commas at natural spoken intonation breaks, and question marks may correspond to a particular type of question intonation (see Section 2.5.3). Different writing systems have different conventions for what elements are marked: for example, most Chinese texts do not mark the boundaries between words, while in Tibetan, every syllable boundary is marked with a raised dot.

It is important to remember that writing systems are largely arbitrary, just as spoken language is (see Section 1.4.7 for the meaning of *arbitrary* with respect to language), and that they are used successfully only because of social conventions. Any language could be written using some other writing system, and there is no inherent correspondence between **graphemes** (symbols used for writing) and their associated sound or meaning. This arbitrariness is particularly clear when you consider the case of Cherokee, an Iroquois language spoken in North Carolina and Oklahoma. A man named Sequoyah developed a phonographic writing system for Cherokee in the nineteenth century, making use of both Roman letters he had seen in English texts as well as new characters of his own design. Interestingly, however, the system he developed was syllabic, so each character represented a consonant-vowel sequence, and because he was illiterate in English, the Roman letters do not represent anything remotely like the sounds they represent in English! For example, the symbol <K> represents the sounds [tso] and [tsʰo], while the symbol <J> represents the sounds [ku] and [kʰu]. The point is simply that there is a convention mapping the written grapheme to the spoken word: the mapping itself must be learned explicitly for each language. Note that this arbitrariness also applies to the arrangement of characters on the page: writing can go horizontally (as in English and Hebrew) or vertically (as in Akkadian and Chinese); it can also proceed from left to right (as in English and Akkadian), or right to left (as in Hebrew and Chinese[2]).

In the next few sections, we will take a closer look at both morphographic and phonographic writing systems and then briefly discuss the historical evolution of writing systems.

13.4.3 Morphographic Writing Systems

As mentioned above, morphographic writing systems rely on a correspondence between a written grapheme and a particular morpheme. The symbols themselves may or may not tell the reader anything about how the morpheme is pronounced: the reader just has to know. While this may at first seem a bit strange to someone who only reads a language like English, which uses a phonographic writing system, it may be easier to understand once you realize that we do, in fact, have some morphographic characters in English. For example, the symbol <2> is morphographic: it represents the phonemes /tu/ and the meaning 'two.' The same character is used with the same meaning but different pronunciations in different languages (e.g., in Spanish, <2> is pronounced [dos], and in German, [tsvai]). It is simply a character that has a particular meaning associated with it, but that says nothing about its pronunciation.

An example from a truly morphographic system, traditional Chinese characters, is given in (3a), in which each character stands for a word as a whole; another example from

---

[2]It should be noted that some Chinese texts are now written horizontally, from left to right, as is done in English, instead of the traditional vertical, from right to left. Can you imagine switching to reading English vertically from right to left? Try it below:

```
h  s  t  d
a  e  h  o
r  e  i  e
d  m  s  s
```

Chinese is given in (3b), in which each character stands for a morpheme that makes up a longer word.

(3) Chinese morphographs

    a. 與   狼   共   舞
       with   wolf(s) together dance   'Dancing with Wolves'
      (The Chinese translation of a movie name)

    b. 發   展
       expand extend   'to develop'
      (A longer word in Chinese)]

Traditionally, people have often thought that morphographic writing systems used symbols stylized from earlier **pictograms** (i.e., pictures drawn to express ideas) that do not convey any information about the sound of the word at all. In a dichotomous categorization of writing systems (i.e., sound-based versus meaning-based), these morphographic systems are thus categorized as meaning-based. This view, however, is true only of the earliest stage in the historical development of the morphographic writing systems. As these systems develop, a very large proportion of the morphographs come to represent the sound, as well as the meaning, of the words.

Let us use the Chinese writing system as an example. In early Chinese writing the concepts of 'above' and 'below' were represented by drawing a shorter line above or below a longer horizontal line (see (4)).

(4) Examples of morphographs in early Chinese: 'above' is on the left; 'below' is on the right.

        —   —
      —   —

Note that these two morphographs do not indicate the pronunciation of the two words. It did not take long for people to realize that representing concepts solely in this way was insufficient. Hence, morphographs began to be borrowed based on their phonetic value alone to represent concepts that did not formerly have a written representation and concepts that were not easily expressed otherwise. For instance, the Chinese character 來 was developed from a pictogram of wheat to represent the idea 'wheat.' Later on, this character 來, meaning 'wheat,' was borrowed to represent the concept 'come,' simply because these two concepts shared the same pronunciation (*[ləg][3] in early Chinese). This method is known as the **rebus principle**—borrowing a symbol only for the phonetic value that it encodes. To help illustrate, try to read the picture on your left (an eye), and the picture on your right (a sea):

(5) Illustrating the rebus principle in English

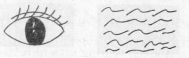

As you say [aɪ si], you probably don't mean 'eye sea' (which doesn't make much sense), but rather 'I see.' By the same token, the character 來 is like the pictures of *eye* and *sea*. That is, you look at the character 來 and say it out loud, and you mean 'come.'

---

[3]The asterisk * indicates that the pronunciation is a historical reconstruction for early Chinese. Details about historical reconstruction can be found in File 12.7.

As a matter of fact, combining a phonetic and a semantic component to create new characters to represent ideas has been extremely productive in the historical development of the Chinese writing system. The majority of Chinese characters have been created this way. [Statistics show that 81.2% of the Chinese characters in C.E. 100 in the Han dynasty (Norman (1988: 267)), and 90% of the Chinese characters today (DeFrancis 1984) have both a phonetic and a semantic component.] For instance, the character 來 above has become the phonetic component of other words, while the semantic component of these words is indicated by the non-來 part (or the radical) of the characters (see (6a); more examples are given in (6b)).

(6) Combining a phonetic and a semantic component to create new characters to represent concepts in Chinese. (The numbers after the segments are Chao-type tone numbers, with '5' denoting the highest pitch in the pitch range, and '1' the lowest (see Section 2.5.4); neutral tone is indicated by the number '0.')

a. Examples using 來 'wheat (in early Chinese)/come' as the phonetic component (pronunciations given in present-day Mandarin Chinese)

Meaning Component	Phonetic Component	Written Form and Pronunciation	Word Meaning
木 'wood'	+ 來 [lai^{35}]	→ 楋 [lai^{35}]	'large-leaved dogwood'
金 'gold'	+ 來 [lai^{35}]	→ 鋶 [lai^{35}]	'rhenium'
山 'mountain'	+ 來 [lai^{35}]	→ 崍 [lai^{35}]	'Qionglai' (name of a mountain)
水 'water'	+ 來 [lai^{35}]	→ 淶 [lai^{35}]	'Laishui' (name of a river in the north of China)
目 'eye'	+ 來 [lai^{35}]	→ 睐 [lai^{35}]	'to squint'

b. Examples using 馬 'horse' as the phonetic component (pronunciations given in present-day Mandarin Chinese)

Meaning Component	Phonetic Component	Written Form and Pronunciation	Word Meaning
口 'mouth'	+ 馬 [ma^{214}]	→ 嗎 [ma^{0}]	question particle
口 'mouth'	+ 馬 [ma^{214}]	→ 罵 [ma^{51}]	'to scold'
女 'woman'	+ 馬 [ma^{214}]	→ 媽 [ma^{55}]	'mother'
虫 'insect'	+ 馬 [ma^{214}]	→ 螞 [ma^{214}]	'ant/leech/locust'
玉 'jade'	+ 馬 [ma^{214}]	→ 瑪 [ma^{214}]	'agate'

As you can see from these examples, the traditional view that the morphographic writing system of Chinese (and other languages such as Egyptian) is solely meaning-based is not accurate. Perhaps a better way to characterize a given writing system is to evaluate it on a continuum where purely sound-based and purely meaning-based are two extremes (DeFrancis 2002). For a writing system such as Chinese, in which a large proportion of the morphographs represent **both** the sound and the meaning of the words, it is obvious that placing it at the meaning-based extreme of the continuum is not appropriate. When compared to the phonographic systems of the next section, however, it is clear that there is a distinct and significant meaning-based component to these systems.

Morphographic writing systems have been developed independently in separate parts of the world and are the oldest type of writing. Besides the Chinese writing system, the hieroglyphic writing of ancient Egypt and the cuneiform writing of ancient Mesopotamia were morphographic in their earliest form, although they too each became modified to include sound-based elements as they were utilized by succeeding generations. Both of these latter writing systems were invented at least 5,000 years ago, like Chinese, and survived for thousands of years.

13.4.4 Phonographic Writing Systems

Phonographic systems, by contrast, are more heavily weighted toward the sound-based end of the continuum. Again, however, this classification must be taken only loosely, for it is not the case that there is a one-to-one correspondence between graphemes and sounds in many phonographic systems (as was mentioned in File 2.1 in the context of discussing phonetic transcription systems). For example, you probably think of English as a phonographic system, especially if you were taught to "sound words out" when you came across an unfamiliar word in reading. If you think about it, however, you will see that even in a phonographic system like English, there is a heavy reliance on knowledge of the morphemes themselves in order to actually read a text. For example, the grapheme sequences <through> and <though> are pronounced as [θɹu] and [ðoʊ], respectively: although they differ in writing by only a single character, they do not, in fact, share a single phoneme! You can think of these sequences as being (arbitrary) graphic representations of the whole morphemes— while these sequences obviously historically derived from more direct sound representations of the words, they have become dependent on the reader's knowledge of the meanings to be recognizable (see File 12.3 on sound change). This is exactly analogous to the development of meaning-based pictograms into sound- and meaning-based characters that we saw in the section on morphographic writing above.

a. Syllabic (Moraic) Writing Systems. One type of phonographic writing system uses characters to represent particular sequences of sounds. Because each character is usually a syllable, such systems are often called syllabic writing systems, and the total set of characters that are used for a given language is often referred to as a **syllabary.** This nomenclature can be somewhat misleading in that it is not always the case that every possible syllable in the language is represented with a separate character; some syllables may have to be written using multiple characters, with the understanding that some characters are pronounced as extra sounds in a syllable rather than as separate syllables in their own right.[4]

Syllabaries have been used for languages such as Ancient Persian, Sanskrit, Japanese, and Cherokee. Japanese is particularly interesting because it actually uses three separate writing systems, two phonographic syllabaries (called *hiragana* and *katakana,* but known collectively as *kana*) and one morphographic system (called *kanji*), which consists of borrowed morphographic characters from Chinese. Although any word can be written using characters from the syllabaries, there are systematic ways of using the three writing systems. As a rough generalization, traditional Japanese writing normally uses a combination of syllabic symbols from the hiragana for function morphemes and morphographic characters from kanji for content morphemes. Katakana are normally used for western loanwords, for onomatopoeic words, and for emphasis. (7) shows some examples of the kana symbols.

---

[4]A more accurate term for these writing systems is *moraic;* each character represents a *mora,* a unit of timing somewhat similar to a syllable. We will not try to address the differences between syllables and moras in this book.

(7) Examples of some of the corresponding syllables in hiragana and katakana

Hiragana						Katakana				
だ	ぢ	づ	で	ど		ダ	ヂ	ヅ	デ	ド
[da]	[dzi]	[dzu]	[de]	[do]		[da]	[dzi]	[dzu]	[de]	[do]
わ			を	ん		ワ			ヲ	ン
[wa]			[wo]	[n][5]		[wa]			[wo]	[n]

The examples in (8) show the representation for the word 'telephone' by hiragana, katakana, and kanji. In each of the kana, the first two symbols represent [de] and [n], and the third represents [wa]. In the kanji, the two symbols are Chinese characters that stand for the morphemes meaning 'electricity' and 'words,' respectively.

(8) The word 'telephone' written in Japanese using hiragana, katakana, and kanji

Hiragana	Katakana	Kanji
でんわ	デンワ	電話
[den wa]	[den wa]	[den wa]

b. Phonemic Writing Systems (Alphabets, Abjads, and Abugidas). The other main type of phonographic writing system uses characters that represent individual sounds, that is, letters that represent phonemes. Each of the syllables that make up the words of a language is, in turn, composed of one or more speech sounds and therefore one or more letters. Since there are just a limited number of speech sounds used by any given language, there are fewer unique speech sounds than unique syllables in a language. Therefore, it stands to reason that a phonemic writing system requires fewer characters than a syllabic writing system.

Phonemic writing systems may not represent all of the phonemes used in the spoken language. Systems that do represent all the phonemes, both consonants and vowels, are said to use an **alphabet.** Systems that represent only the consonants but not the vowels are called **abjads.** Finally, systems that represent the consonants with full symbols and the vowels with extra marks (called **diacritics**) on the consonants are called **abugidas.** There are no systems where only the vowels are represented, without the consonants.

Devanāgarī, the script used to write Sanskrit, Hindi, Marathi, and Nepali; Gujarātī, the script used to write Gujarātī and Kacchi; and Bengali, the script used to write Assamese and Bengali, are examples of abugidas. These languages are all Indo-Aryan languages spoken in South Asia; they all use scripts that are descended from the ancient Brāhmī script. In these systems, all symbols automatically have a following vowel sound (usually a short [a] or [ə]), unless another vowel symbol is used. So, the symbol क all by itself is pronounced as the syllable /ka/. If a different vowel is necessary, then the symbol is marked in a specific way, as shown in (9). The vowels are each marked the same way regardless of the consonant they are associated with.

(9) Syllables in Devanāgarī starting with [k]

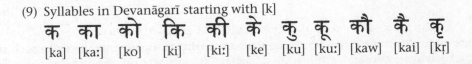

क   का   को   कि   की   के   कु   कू   कौ   कै   कृ
[ka] [kaː] [ko] [ki] [kiː] [ke] [ku] [kuː] [kaw] [kai] [kr̩]

---

[5]Note that this [n] and the one for Katakana is used only for the final [n] of a syllable.

Vowels in initial position have distinct forms. The vowel symbols in (10) are used only in initial position; otherwise, vowels are marked on the preceding consonant.

(10) Initial vowel symbols in Devanāgarī

अ आ इ ई उ ऊ ए ओ
[a] [aː] [i] [iː] [u] [uː] [e] [o]

In (11), you can see how a Devanāgarī word is built up from various symbols. Devanāgarī is (mostly) written from left to right.

(11) Writing the word [gadʒena] 'elephant' in Devanāgarī

ग जे न गजेन
[ga] [dʒe] [na] [gadʒena]

Arabic and Hebrew writings, on the other hand, are traditionally considered examples of abjads. An example is shown in the Hebrew words in (12). (Note that Hebrew is written from right to left.) It might at first seem that writing without vowels would be very difficult to read, but one's knowledge of the language usually allows one to "fill in" the vowels by observing the overall context of a sentence. This is illustrated by the following example from English, in which only the consonants are written: *Ths sntnc s wrttn wth th vwl smbls lft t.*[6]

(12) Some Hebrew words

Hebrew Orthography and Letter-by-Letter IPA	Full IPA Transcription of of the Pronunciation	English Gloss
גמל lmg	[gamal]	'camel'
מברשת tʃ ɣvm	[mivɣeʃet]	'brush'
סלם ml s	[sulam]	'ladder'
מדפסת t s pdm	[madpeset]	'printer'

As you might expect, however, writing only the consonants of words can create ambiguities. Thus, both the Arabic and the Hebrew writing systems do also have diacritics for the vowels, which are sometimes inserted to more explicitly indicate the pronunciation of the words. In (13), the Hebrew word 'ladder' from (12) is repeated, but using vowel diacritics to indicate the full pronunciation. Because it is an abjad, however, these vowel diacritics are not necessary.

(13) The word 'ladder' in Hebrew containing vowel diacritics

סֻלָּם [sulam] 'ladder'
m aḷ u s

Finally, there are several different alphabets used throughout the world today, the one most familiar probably being the Roman (Latin) alphabet used to write such diverse

---

[6]For comparison, try reading the same sentence with only the vowels: *i eee i ie i e oe o e ou.* The difficulty in reading just the vowels explains why no such writing systems exist!

languages as English, Swahili, and Turkish. The Roman alphabet is a variant of an early Greek alphabet used by Greek colonists south of Rome and by the Etruscans. Later on, this Greek alphabet was adapted by Slavic speakers to form the Cyrillic alphabet. (14) provides a list of the symbols of the Cyrillic alphabet used to write Russian. Slightly different versions of the Cyrillic alphabet are used to write other Slavic languages such as Serbian, Bulgarian, and Ukrainian (some Slavic languages, such as Polish and Czech, use the Roman alphabet). The Cyrillic alphabet is also used to write some non-Slavic languages of the former Soviet Union (e.g., Moldovan, a Romance language, and Uzbek, a Turkic language).

(14) The Cyrillic alphabet used for Russian (both capital and lowercase letters are given)

Аа	[a]	Кк	[k]	Хх	[x]
Бб	[b]	Лл	[l]	Цц	[ts]
Вв	[v]	Мm	[m]	Чч	[tʃ]
Гг	[g]	Нн	[n]	Шш	[ʃ]
Дд	[d]	Оo	[o]	Щщ	[ʃʲ]
Ее	[je]	Пп	[p]	Ъъ	'hard sign'
Ёё	[jo]	Рр	[r]	Ыы	[ɨ]
Жж	[dʒ]	Сс	[s]	Ьь	'soft sign'
Зз	[z]	Тт	[t]	Ээ	[ɛ]
Ии	[i]	Уу	[u]	ІОю	[ju]
Йй	[j]	Фф	[f]	Яя	[ja]

In the Cyrillic alphabet, notice that the "hard sign" and the "soft sign" usually have no pronunciation of their own. Instead of being symbols for separate phonemes, they indicate something about the preceding consonant. The "soft sign" indicates that the preceding consonant is unpredictably palatalized (see Section 3.2.3 for a discussion of palatalization), and it appears at the syllable boundaries after the palatalized consonant (see (15) for examples). Another way to mark palatalization is to use a different vowel sign: notice that there are four vowel symbols in (14) that represent [jV] (where V is any vowel). Generally, a sequence of a palatalized consonant plus a vowel are written with a consonant and one of these special vowel symbols, though there are cases where both the consonant **and** the vowel are marked with palatalization—in which case the consonant is palatalized and then followed by a palatal glide (see (15) for examples).

(15) Examples of Russian orthography

	Russian Orthography	Phonemic IPA Transcription	English Gloss
No palatalization	дома	/doma/	'at home'
	лучше	/lutʃʃe/	'better, rather'
Palatalization marked on the consonant (with the soft sign)	семь	/sʲemʲ/	'seven'
	больше	/bolʲʃe/	'more'
Palatalization marked on the vowel (using a special vowel symbol)	семя	/sʲemʲa/	'seed'
	любовь	/lʲubovʲ/	'love'
Palatalization marked on both the consonant and the vowel	семья	/sʲemʲja/	'family'
	колье	/kolʲje/	'necklace'

The "hard sign" is used to mark that a consonant is not palatalized in a context where you might expect it to be. The default assumption, however, is that a consonant is not palatalized unless it is followed by a soft sign or is inherently palatal, so the hard sign is used much less often than the soft sign.

13.4.5 Historical Evolution

Morphographic writing systems were the first type developed. The first characters developed for such systems were simple **pictograms**. Pictograms are merely stylized drawings of concrete objects. As an example, the Ancient Mesopotamian (Sumerian), Ancient Egyptian, and Ancient Chinese writing systems used the pictograms in (16).

(16) Comparison of some pictograms

	Sumerian	**Egyptian**	**Chinese**
'man'			
'ox'			
'star'			
'sun'			
'water'			
'road'			

A refinement that was soon made in each of these ancient writing systems was the semantic extension of the original pictograms. This means that the original pictograms came to be used not just to refer to the concrete objects they originally pictured but also to refer to activities and abstract concepts associated with those objects. For instance, the Ancient Egyptian hieroglyphs in (17) were used to refer to activities or concepts that were not directly picturable. At the point where such semantic extension has taken place, the characters of a writing system are considered morphograms, rather than pictograms, because they are used to represent all types of words—abstract nouns, verbs, adjectives, and so on—as well as concrete nouns.

It is thought that phonographic writing systems were developed from morphographic writing systems. Although at first morphographic characters symbolized entire words, as time went on the conventional symbols used as morphograms came to be associated more closely with the pronunciations of the words they represented—this is known as phonological extension. This meant that in the minds of their users, the symbols began to represent sequences of sounds. Consequently, people used the symbols as characters to write sequences of sounds, or syllables, rather than whole words. For example, the Egyptians used the hieroglyphs in (18) to represent syllables.

(17) Semantic extension of some Egyptian hieroglyphs

	Original Significance	**Extension**
	'knife'	'to cut, slay'
	'fire'	'to cook, burn'
	'sail'	'wind, air'
	'man with arms down'	'submission'
	'man with arms raised'	'to pray, praise'
	'men grasping hands'	'friendship'

(18) Sound associations of some Egyptian hieroglyphs

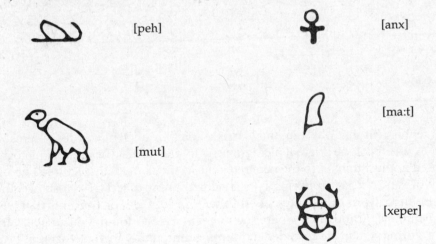

Also, some morphographic characters were used to refer to sequences of sounds in an abbreviated fashion. That is, they came to represent the first sound in the pronunciation of the word to which they originally referred. For example, the Egyptians originally used the symbol in (19) to represent an owl, the word for which was pronounced something like [mulok].

(19) Egyptian symbol for *owl* [mulok]

Eventually this hieroglyphic character came to indicate the sound [m]. There were similar developments in other originally morphographic writing systems, including the Mesopotamian cuneiform system and the Chinese systems.

The Semitic tribes living in the Sinai developed a system of writing based on the Egyptian usage of symbols to represent the first sound in the pronunciation of the word represented by the character. This eventually gave rise to the abjads now used in modern Hebrew and Arabic. For example, in the Semitic writing system, the character in (20a) represented an ox's head, and the character in (20b) represented a house.

(20) Semitic symbols for (a) 'ox' /ʔalef/ and (b) 'house' /bet/

   a. ⋉

   b. ৭

The Semitic words for these objects were something like /ʔalef/ and /bet/, respectively. Therefore, the Semites used the first symbol to write the glottal stop consonant /ʔ/, which began the word for 'ox,' and the second to write the bilabial stop consonant /b/, which began the word for 'house.' (Most of the characters in this alphabet were called by the names of the objects that they originally represented.)

The Phoenicians who used the Semitic abjad taught it to the Greeks, who adapted it for use in writing the words of their own language. Since Ancient Greek did not have some of the consonants used in the pronunciation of Semitic languages, the Greeks began employing some of the borrowed characters to write vowel sounds of their language. For example, since the glottal stop /ʔ/ was not used in the pronunciation of any Greek words, the symbol came to represent the vowel /a/ at the beginning of the borrowed word /ʔalef/, which the Greeks pronounced /alpʰa/ (which later became /alfa/). The Greeks borrowed all the names for the Phoenician characters along with the characters, adapting the pronunciation of each to Greek phonological patterns. They referred to the whole list of symbols by the Greek version of the names of the first two symbols in the list, namely, /alfa/ and /beta/, which is the source of the term *alphabet*. The Greek alphabet is shown in (21), along with the pronunciations of all the letters in modern Greek.

(21) The Greek alphabet

Greek Letters (Capital, Lowercase)	IPA Value	Greek Pronunciation of Letter Name	Greek Letters (Capital, Lowercase)	IPA Value	Greek Pronunciation of Letter Name
A a	[a]	[alfa]	N ν	[n]	[ni]
B β	[v]	[vita]	Ξ ξ	[ks]	[ksi]
Γ γ	[ɣ]	[ɣama]	O o	[o]	[omikron]
Δ δ	[ð]	[ðelta]	Π π	[p]	[pi]
E ε	[ɛ]	[epsilon]	P ρ	[r]	[ro]
Z ζ	[z]	[zita]	Σ σ ς	[s]	[siɣma]
H η	[i]	[ita]	T τ	[t]	[taf]
Θ θ	[θ]	[θita]	Y υ	[i]	[ipsilon]
I ι	[i]	[jota]	Φ φ	[f]	[fi]
K κ	[k]	[kapa]	X χ	[x]	[çi]
Λ λ	[l]	[lamða]	Ψ ψ	[ps]	[psi]
M μ	[m]	[mi]	Ω ω	[o]	[omeɣa]

Notice that, like the Roman alphabet for English, there is not a one-to-one correspondence between sounds and symbols in the Greek alphabet. For example, the sound [i] can be represented with the letters <η>, <ι>, or <υ>, depending on the word. As in English, many of these discrepancies are due to historical sound change (see File 12.3): these symbols did not all always stand for the sound [i].

Also interesting in the Greek alphabet is the use of two separate lowercase characters for the sound [s], both of which are called [siɣma]: <σ> and <ς>. The use of one or the other of these two characters is completely predictable: the first, <σ>, is used at the beginnings or in the middle of words, while the second, <ς>, is used at the ends of words. You can think of these as **allographs** of a single grapheme, just as we had allophones of phonemes (Chapter 3) and allomorphs of morphemes (Chapter 4). While this may seem unusual at first, we see the same phenomenon in any language that uses capital and lowercase letters. Capital letters in English, for example, appear only at the beginnings of sentences, at the beginnings of proper nouns, in acronyms, and a few other specialized places. Lowercase letters appear everywhere else. Thus, these two types of letters are also in complementary distribution and therefore allographic. Note that having capital and lowercase letters is not a requirement of alphabets or other phonographic writing systems: for example, Aramaic did not make this kind of distinction.

The Greek alphabet was adapted by the Romans. Thus, the alphabet we use today is referred to as the "Roman" alphabet. The Cyrillic alphabet seen in (14) was based on the Greek alphabet as well (see if you can figure out which characters in (14) correspond to the Greek letters shown in (21)). In fact, nearly all the alphabetic writing systems of the world can be traced directly or indirectly to the writing system of the Phoenicians.

We should note that not all phonographic writing systems are direct descendants of a particular morphographic system. For example, the Cherokee syllabary mentioned above was designed as a new writing system for the Cherokee language by Sequoyah. While Sequoyah did happen to use some characters that he had seen used for English writing, which ultimately can be traced back to pictograms like those in (20a) and (20b), it would not really be fair to say that the Cherokee syllabary itself derived from these symbols. Sequoyah was illiterate in English and certainly did not attach the same sound correspondences to the symbols that English-speakers do; and, of course, he was creating a syllabary instead of an alphabet.

In conclusion, then, we have seen that there are many different types of writing systems, each making use of different linguistic properties of the language they are representing. The common thread that unites them, however, is their ability to transfer fleeting spoken language into a more tangible and permanent form. This transfer of language from speech to writing has in turn allowed human culture to develop in a way that would be unimaginable without such systems.

Practice

File 13.1—Language and Identity

Exercises

1. Think about three social groups you belong to (e.g., in your family, at school, at work, as part of hobbies, etc.). Try to list characteristics of your speech that you think might be unique to each setting: for example, are there words, pronunciations, and so on, that you use only in one setting?

2. Explain why vowel centralization in Martha's Vineyard can best be understood in terms of a speaker's group identification rather than a particular isolated variable such as age, region, or ethnicity.

Discussion Questions

3. Based on what you have read in this file and your own experiences, why do you think that identity is so changeable or context-dependent? How much control do you think speakers have over how their identity is perceived? What kinds of things can speakers manipulate to affect this perception? Give examples.

4. Refer to the cartoon at the beginning of this chapter. What does the woman mean by "he's not my type"? What do you think she has based this judgment on? What role does language play in her making this judgment?

Activities

5. Refer to Exercise 1. Record yourself in each of the three different social situations you described in that exercise. Listen to the recordings: what elements differ by situation? Play parts of the recordings to someone who knows you well but who wasn't present during any of the recordings. Can he determine which situation each was recorded in? Try playing the same parts to a classmate who is less familiar with you—can she determine the different situations? What cues do you think people use to make these judgments?

6. Search online for dialect quizzes (some examples are the "Yankee or Dixie quiz," the quiz on "What kind of American English do you speak?," the "Yorkshire dialect quiz," etc.). Many of these quizzes will give you instant feedback on your word and pronunciation choices, labeling you as having a certain identity, usually related to region (e.g., "you are 44% Midwestern"). After taking the quiz, evaluate the label given to your answers. How accurate do you think the label is? Based on what you have read in this file (and other information on language variation, e.g., in Chapter 10), what do you think the percentages signify, if your score is represented with a percentage? In addition to

how well it identifies the region you grew up in or live in now, how well do you think it represents your "identity" as a whole? Would you want other people to have this impression of you? Why or why not?

File 13.2—Language and Power

Discussion Questions

7. Based on the material in this file, how do you think power relationships in a conversation are established? Give some concrete examples from your own experience. What cues do you think might be particularly indicative of someone exerting power as opposed to someone acquiescing? Are these cues inherent or socially determined?

Activities

8. You may be surprised to learn that there is no official language in the United States. All official government business in the United States is conducted in English, but no law requires this. English can nevertheless be considered the national language of the country, insofar as it is the most widely used. There has been much debate about whether English should be made the official language or not; some states have passed laws making it an official language in that state. Do some research to see which states have English as their only official language, which states include other languages, and which states do not have an official language at all. Gather information about why states have made the choices they have and what issues have been raised (e.g., issues dealing with immigration, economics, politics, history, culture, etc.). Set up a debate in your class, where half the class argues for making English the official language and half the class argues against this position.

9. Go to your school's library and research the "Deaf President Now" movement that took place at Gallaudet University in 1988. What is Gallaudet University? What were the students involved in this movement trying to accomplish? What originally led to their being upset? What were the consequences of their actions? How does the controversy underlying this story relate to the ideas in File 13.2?

File 13.3—Language and Thought

Exercises

10. Explain how the words a language has can appear to influence behavior; give at least one concrete example not found in the textbook.

11. Speculate as to what three reasons might be for why adult Pirahã speakers do not seem able to count objects in groups larger than three objects in any of the experiments done. How might experimenters try to tease apart these reasons to determine which is responsible for the behavior observed?

12. Explain why each of the words *tan, ruddy,* and *viridescent* would not be considered basic color terms of English, according to the definition of "basic color term" presented in this file.

Discussion Questions

13. One of the themes of both Chapter 10 and File 13.1 is the variability of language and how particular language varieties are associated with particular groups. How do you think this relates to the principle of linguistic relativity? For example, do you think that the fact that midwesterners tend to call sweetened carbonated beverages *pop* causes them to have a different worldview than northerners who use the term *soda*? Do you think that your worldview changes depending on what situation you are in (e.g., what register you are using or what identity you are trying to project with your language use)? Explain your answer.

14. Refer to the cartoon at the beginning of this chapter. Explain how someone could argue for the principle of linguistic relativity based on this cartoon by claiming that language is influencing the woman's decision not to date the man with the writing on his shirt. Do you think this is a valid argument? Why or why not?

15. What do color terms and direction terms have in common that makes them good candidates for testing the principle of linguistic relativity? Give an example of some other area that might prove to be a fruitful testing ground, and explain how you think it could be used as such.

16. In the discussion of absolute as opposed to relative systems of direction, the fact that English speakers actually have absolute directions (like *north* and *south*) in addition to relative directions (like *left* and *right*) was ignored. Why do you think English speakers in experiments like the ones done by Levinson and Brown (described in Section 13.3.4) tend to use their relative system rather than their absolute system? Does the fact that they have both systems available to them in their language affect the interpretation of the experiment with respect to the principle of linguistic relativity? Why or why not?

File 13.4—Writing Systems

Exercises

17. Consider the symbol <$>. Is it morphographic or phonographic? What sounds does it represent? What meaning does it represent?

18. The following texts all express the English words *itsy bitsy teeny weeny yellow polka dot bikini* but are written in three different (made-up) left-to-right scripts. Identify what kind of writing system (morphographic, syllabic, alphabet, abjad, abugida) each script is. Explain how you made each of your decisions.

a. το βτσ τν ων φλ πλκ δτ βκν

b. ♈× ⌘× ◆⊠ ◆⊠ ♌⌦ ■○ ♎ ♏✶⊠

c. ♋ ○ ♒ ⋊ ▢ ◎ ❖ ❧

19. Given that the symbol 巴 is pronounced as [pa] (tone omitted) in Chinese, take a look at the words (a) through (h) and try to answer the following questions.

a. 芭   **c.** 笆   **e.** 粑   **g.** 爸

b. 吧   **d.** 疤   **f.** 靶   **h.** 耙

i. If the words in (a)–(h) follow the same model as those in (6a) and (6b) in Section 13.4.3, how do you think these words are pronounced? (You can omit the tones of the words.)

ii. Do you think the eight words all share the same meaning?

iii. Given that 父 means 'father,' which one of the eight words is most likely to represent the word 'dad' in Chinese?

iv. For the word in (g), draw a table like those in (1) in Section 13.4.2 to demonstrate the relationship between the spoken language and its writing system.

20. Write the following Devanāgarī words in the Devanāgarī script. You will need to make use of the following symbols as well as those given in the text of Section 13.4.4.

ज	ज	द	ध	न	प	भ	म
[dʒa]	[ta]	[da]	[dʰa]	[na]	[pa]	[bʰa]	[ma]

य	ल	र	व	स	श	ह	ग
[ja]	[la]	[ra]	[va]	[sa]	[ʃa]	[ha]	[ga]

a. [vada:mi]   'I speak'
b. [a:judʰa:ni]   'weapons'
c. [nalena]   'by Nala'
d. [kr̥tamawna]   'silent'
e. [dha:vasi]   'you run'
f. [edʰate]   'he prospers'
g. [devana:gari:]   'Devanāgarī'

21. The following words are names of Greek gods and goddesses, written in Greek in the Greek alphabet. What are the names written in English in the Roman alphabet?

a. Ζευς
b. Αφροδιτη
c. Ποσειδωνας
d. Αθηνα
e. Αρης

22. Write the following words in the Cyrillic alphabet. It may help to write them out phonetically before you try to translate them to the Cyrillic! Remember, you are not trying to write these words in Russian, but simply trying to write the English words using the Cyrillic alphabet.

a. leg
b. cute
c. cheap
d. feud
e. jar

23. Refer to the cartoon at the beginning of this chapter. What do "QWERTY" and "ΦΦΞβΠΨ" refer to? Do you think they are simply references to a particular object (and, if so, what object?), or do you think they are being used as representative of a larger cultural phenomenon? Explain your answer.

24. Refer to the cartoon at the beginning of this chapter. On the man's t-shirt, there is a series of symbols. Based on what you know about the Greek alphabet, which symbol does not belong? Why do you think the cartoonist used this symbol?

Discussion Questions

25. Estimate the number of characters you think a typical morphographic writing system would have to have. How about a typical syllabic writing system? And an alphabetic writing system? How did you arrive at these figures?

26. How do you think newly introduced words are written in each of the three types of writing systems we have described above (morphographic, syllabic, phonemic)? Do you think that the systems reach consensus on the writing of new words with the same ease? Why or why not?

27. Given the phonetic values of the symbols given for the Cyrillic and the Greek writing systems (in (14) and (21) in the main text of File 13.4), can you think of English words that could not be written with one or the other of systems? If we were forced to use these systems instead of the Roman alphabet, what do you think people would do to solve the problem?

28. Explain why <σ> and <ç> are not contrastive in the Greek writing system. What sort of evidence would you need to show that they **were** contrastive?

Activities

29. You have been hired to develop a syllabic writing system for a language that contains only the following words: *hi, who, hay, die, do, day, cry, crew, crude, creed, creep, crudely, cruel, cruelly, creepy, daily, daylily*. You can assume that these words are pronounced as they are in your dialect of English. How many syllable types will be represented in your syllabary, and what will they be? If you were to try to expand the syllabary to be able to write all of English, what problems would you run into? How many characters do you think you would need?

Further Readings

File 13.1—Language and Identity

Mendoza-Denton, N. (2002). Language and identity. In P. Trudgill, J. K. Chambers & N. Schilling-Estes (Eds.), *The handbook of language variation and change* (pp. 475–99). Malden, MA: Blackwell.

File 13.2—Language and Power

Lakoff, R. T. (1990). *Talking power: The politics of language in our lives*. New York: Basic Books.
Mansour, G. (1993). *Multilingualism and nation building*. Clevedon [England]; Philadelphia: Multilingual Matters.
Nic Craith, M. (2006). *Europe and the politics of language: Citizens, migrants and outsiders*. Basingstoke [England]; New York: Palgrave Macmillan.

File 13.3—Language and Thought

Boroditsky, L. (2003). Linguistic relativity. In L. Nadel (Ed.), *Encyclopedia of cognitive science* (pp. 917–21). London: Macmillan Press.
Levinson, S. C. (1996). Language and space. *Annual Review of Anthropology* 25, 353–82.
Lucy, J. A. (1992). *Language diversity and thought: A reformulation of the linguistic relativity hypothesis*. Cambridge: Cambridge University Press.

Whorf, B. L. (1956). In J. B. Carroll (Ed.), *Language, thought, and reality: Selected writings of Benjamin Lee Whorf.* Cambridge, MA: The Massachusetts Institute of Technology Press.

File 13.4—Writing Systems

Coulmas, F. (1989). *The writing systems of the world.* Oxford: Blackwell.

DeFrancis, J. (1989). *Visible speech: The diverse oneness of writing systems.* Honolulu: The University of Hawaii Press.

Martin, J. (2000). *A linguistic comparison: Two notation systems for signed languages: Stokoe Notation and Sutton SignWriting.* Unpublished manuscript. Available online at http://www.signwriting.org/archive/docsl/sw0032-Stokoe-Sutton.pdf.

Ong, W. J. (1982). *Orality and literacy: The technologizing of the world.* London: Routledge.

Rogers, H. (2005). *Writing systems: A linguistic approach.* Malden, MA: Blackwell.

Sampson, G. (1985). *Writing systems: A linguistic introduction.* Palo Alto, CA: Stanford University Press.

CHAPTER

14

Animal Communication

"Yes, he can do tricks. When I say **SIT**
he sits... if he's already sitting."

Marmaduke: © United Feature Syndicate, Inc.

How Do Animals Communicate?

Humans are not the only creatures that communicate: in fact, almost all creatures have some sort of communication system, sometimes a very elaborate system. Are these systems comparable to human language? From what we know about how animals communicate in the wild, it seems that no other animal uses a system that we can call "language." Human language has a number of characteristics, and no other communication system has all of these characteristics. For example, dogs cannot talk about what will happen tomorrow or about the climate on another continent. Nevertheless, animal communication systems are often interesting to study in their own right.

A question that has interested many researchers and that is distinct from how animals naturally communicate in the wild is whether humans can teach animals to use language. A number of studies have been conducted to teach language to a variety of animals. The success of these attempts is still debated, but we can say that so far no animal can be taught human language to the same extent and degree of sophistication that a human child acquires it naturally without instruction.

Contents

Communication and Language

14.1.1 Design Features Revisited

The previous chapters have provided an introduction to various aspects of how humans use language to communicate. However, we are not the only species that communicates: most animals have some sort of communication system. All varieties of birds make short calls or sing songs; cats meow to be fed or let outside; dogs bark to announce the arrival of strangers or growl and bare their teeth to indicate their intent to attack; and so on. The fact that other animals send and receive messages is in evidence all around us. But can we call the communication systems of animals "language"?

Most people assume that only humans use "language"—it is something that sets us apart from all other creatures. But is it possible that when we examine animal communication systems, we will discover that our assumption that only humans use language was wrong? The task of comparing human communication with various animal communication systems is not an easy one. First, we need a suitable way to identify language on which to base our comparisons. Unfortunately, no definition seems to adequately define "language" or be agreeable to everyone. One approach to getting around this problem, suggested by the linguist Charles Hockett, is that we identify the requisite descriptive characteristics of language rather than attempt to define its fundamental nature. Hockett identified nine **design features,** introduced in File 1.4. Human language has all of these design features, but as far as we know, no animal communication system does. The following sections discuss Hockett's design features with respect to animal communication systems.

14.1.2 Design Features Shared by All Communication Systems

All communication systems have the following features in common:

Mode of communication refers to how a message is transmitted. Different animals transmit messages via different media. Many animals, for example, birds, whales, frogs, rattlesnakes, and crickets, use their bodies to produce sound to communicate. Some animals produce sounds that are not audible to humans. Elephants use infrasound—very low pitched sounds (below 20 Hz)—to send messages. These sounds can travel several miles and allow elephants to communicate over long distances. Bats and whistling moths, on the other hand, use ultrasound—very high pitched sounds (over 20,000 Hz)—to communicate. Such sounds do not travel very far, but not much energy is needed to produce them. Other animals use objects to produce the sounds they use for communication. Kangaroos, hares, and rabbits thump their hind legs on the ground as a warning signal, while the death-watch beetle bangs its head against wood to communicate.

Some animals communicate using visual cues. For example, dogs and apes use certain facial expressions and body postures to express submission, threat, playing, desire, and so on. Female rabbits use the white of their tail as a flag to lead their young to the safety of their burrows. Fireflies find mates by producing light, male spiders use elaborate gestures to inform a female that they are healthy and capable of mating, and fiddler crabs wave their claws to communicate.

Animals may also use touch to communicate. Monkeys hug, big cats and rhinos nuzzle each other, and bees use touch to communicate the location of a food source.

Other animals use odor to communicate. The best-known example of this kind of chemical communication is the pheromones used by many insects to attract mates. Ants use scent trails in order to communicate which path other ants in the colony should travel along.

Some fish and amphibians use electrical signals to communicate. These are often used to identify mates, broadcast territoriality, and regulate schooling behavior. Unlike sound, electrical signals don't get distorted when passing through different materials, for example, murky water.

Semanticity and **Pragmatic Function**, respectively, refer to the fact that signals in all communication systems have meaning and that all communication systems serve some useful purpose. The previous paragraphs have already mentioned many of the meanings conveyed by their animal communication systems. Since survival is the key function of animal communication systems, meaning of signals usually has to do with eating, mating, and other vital behaviors, such as deciding to fight or flee. Here are some (previously mentioned) examples: bees communicate the location of a food source, male spiders inform females that they are ready to mate, and dogs and apes communicate submission or threat.

14.1.3 Design Features Exhibited by Some Animal Communication Systems

Some, but not all, animal communication systems exhibit the following features:

Interchangeability refers to the ability to both send and receive messages. For example, every elephant can use infrasound to send messages and can also receive messages sent this way from other elephants. But not all animals can both send and receive signals. For example, the silkworm moth's chemical communication system does not display interchangeability with respect to mating. When the female is ready to mate, she secretes a chemical that males can trace back to her. The males themselves cannot secrete this chemical; they can only be receivers. On the other hand, for whistling moths, it is the males that send the signal (in this case to communicate messages about territory). Male whistling moths have a rough edge on their wings that they can rub together to make a sound; both males and females can hear and respond to these sounds.

Cultural transmission refers to the notion that at least some part of a communication system is learned through interaction with other users. In most organisms, the actual signal code itself is innate, or genetically programmed, so an individual can no more learn a new signal code than it can grow an extra eye. For example, fireflies are not taught how to produce or interpret their light displays; they are born with these abilities and perform them naturally and instinctively at the appropriate time. Likewise, cow birds lay their eggs in other birds' nests and therefore are not raised around adult cow birds. However, they nevertheless grow up to produce cow bird calls and not the calls of the birds raising them. This means that their calls are fully innate.

However, for some animals, aspects of their communication systems seem to be learned. For example, regional dialectal variation (see File 10.3) has been discovered in a number of bird species' songs, in killer whales' communication, and also in chimpanzee gestures. Dialectal variation indicates that there has been cultural transmission in these cases because the birds learn their dialect from hearing other birds singing, killer whales learn from hearing the clicking and whistling of other killer whales, and chimpanzees learn from seeing other chimpanzees using the specific gestures. These behaviors are not genetically encoded: if a young killer whale is raised in a pod of whales it is not related to, it will learn the communication system of the pod it is living with, not the communication system of its mother's pod.

In some cases, the division between what is culturally transmitted and what is not is less clear. In experiments with finches, juvenile finches that were isolated until adulthood were able to make simple calls, indicating that finch calls are somewhat innate, but their calls were not as complex as those of finches raised in groups. These experiments suggest that finches have a critical period for song acquisition, indicating that some aspects of finch call making are transmitted culturally (see File 8.1 for critical periods in humans). Those finches that were not exposed to calls early in life exhibited the aspects of calls that are innate but did not exhibit the aspects of calls that are culturally transmitted.

Arbitrariness means that the form of a symbol is not logically related to its meaning or function. However, since most animal systems use iconic signals that in some way directly represent their meaning, most animal signals are not arbitrary. For instance, when a dog bares its teeth to indicate it is ready to attack, the signal (bared teeth) is directly related to its meaning ('I will bite you'). Likewise, a dog may roll over and show its belly in order to indicate submission: this is an iconic way for the dog to indicate that it is making itself vulnerable. Many animals, including several species of snake, lizard, and frog, will stand up taller, puff out their features, or otherwise make themselves look larger in order to signify that they are making a threat: since larger individuals are often better able to win in a physical confrontation, using size to indicate threat is also iconic.

However, not all signals animals use are iconic. For example, the dorsal region of the male western fence lizard turns different shades of blue to indicate territoriality. A darker blue indicates territorial ownership and the lizard's willingness to fight to keep its territory. A lighter blue indicates that the lizard does not consider a territory its own. It is used when walking across another male's territory to indicate that the lizard is not challenging the other's territorial ownership. Here, the color blue does not iconically represent owning a territory. However, western fence lizards also use iconic signals to communicate: they make themselves look bigger (by turning sideways) to indicate threat. Thus, animal communication systems can include both iconic and arbitrary signals.

Discreteness refers to the property of having complex messages that are built up out of smaller parts. The messages in most animal communication systems that we are familiar with do not have this property. Each message is an indivisible unit. However, limited discreteness can be found in some communication systems. One example is the way in which bees dance, which is built up of smaller parts: the dance pattern, the direction, and the vivacity of the dance, each of which contributes different information to the message. The bees' dance will be described in detail in the next file.

14.1.4 Design Features That Are Not Found in Animal Communication Systems

Only human language exhibits the following features:

Displacement refers to the ability to communicate about things that are not present in space or time. No animal communication system appears to display this feature. However, there is some debate as to whether bees (see File 14.2) and some apes exhibit it to a limited degree. For example, Menzel and his colleagues (2002) studied spatial memory in bonobos. They used road signs with arbitrary symbols (**lexigrams**) that described where in a forest food was hidden. The bonobo Kanzi could use the information on the sign to find the hidden food, even though it could not be seen from the location of the road sign. Thus, even though the food was not present in space, Kanzi used information on the sign to determine its location. At first sight, this suggests that bonobos can understand messages about things not present in space. This is based on interpreting the road signs' messages as something like 'there's a food source hidden at this location.' This translation assumes a message **about** a distant, invisible object. But the message can be represented differently— more simply, for example, 'perform this behavior now,' that is, 'go to this location now.' This is no different from most messages sent in animal systems and does not involve communicating about things that are not present. Thus, we don't know if Kanzi understands the signs in terms of food being hidden somewhere, which would indicate displacement, or in terms of an order to perform a certain behavior. In other words, we don't know if Kanzi interprets the messages as representing objects that are not present or as an instruction to go somewhere. Thus, it is unclear whether bonobos (as well as bees) exhibit limited displacement, or whether they do not possess this feature to any degree.

Productivity refers to the property of a language that allows for the rule-based expression of an infinite number of messages, including the expression of novel ideas. In practical terms, it refers to the ability of an individual to produce and understand messages that the individual has not been exposed to before by applying rules and combining together discrete components of the language in new ways.

In all animal communication systems, the number of signals is fixed. Even though the signals in some animal communication systems are complex, there is no mechanism for systematically combining discrete units in new ways to create new signals. For example, some species of birds and whales have songs composed of different units that are combined in various ways. However, it seems that regardless of which order the units appear in, the song still has the same meaning. That is, while these birds and whales do use different combinations of discrete units, they do not seem to use the units to create signals with novel meanings or to convey novel ideas. These systems are thus called closed communication systems.

14.1.5 What the Design Features Show Us about Animal Communication

In the comparison of human language with animal communication systems, a debate has arisen over whether human language and other systems differ **qualitatively** or **quantitatively.** If there were merely a quantitative difference, then we would expect to find an animal communication system that possesses all nine of these features, but with some expressed to a lesser degree than in human language. If, on the other hand, human language and other communication systems differ qualitatively, we would not expect to find an animal communication system that possesses each and every design feature. However, it is sometimes difficult to decide whether an animal communication system displays a feature to a certain extent or not at all, as the displacement example above shows.

At any rate, we can say that a communication system must have all of the design features to be considered a language, and that no animal communication system has been identified to date that meets this criterion.

Animal Communication in the Wild

14.2.1 Bee Communication

In File 14.1 we claimed that no animal communication system is qualitatively the same as human language because no animal system with which we are familiar possesses all of Hockett's design features. In this file we will investigate three animal communication systems in a little more detail: that of an Italian species of honeybee, that of the European robin, and that of the rhesus monkey. These investigations will describe how these species communicate in the wild and will provide further support for the claim that, although enormously complex, animal systems are quite different from human language.

We will begin by discussing honey bees. When a forager bee returns to the hive, if it has located a source of food, it does a dance that communicates certain information about that source to other members of the colony. The dancing behavior may assume one of three possible patterns: round, sickle, and tail-wagging. The determining factor in the choice of dance pattern is the distance of the food source from the hive. The round dance indicates locations near the hive, within 20 feet or so. The sickle dance indicates locations at an intermediate distance from the hive, approximately 20 to 60 feet. The tail-wagging dance is for distances that exceed 60 feet or so.

In all the dances, the bee alights on a wall of the hive and moves through the appropriate pattern. For the round dance, the bee's motion depicts a circle. The only semantic information imparted by the round dance other than the approximate distance from the hive to the food source is the quality of the food source. This is indicated by the number of repetitions of the basic pattern that the bee executes and the vivacity with which it performs the dance. This feature is true of all three patterns. To perform the sickle dance, the bee traces out a sickle-shaped figure eight on the wall. The angle formed by the open end of the sickle intersecting with an imaginary vertical line down the wall of the hive is the same angle as the angle of the food source from the sun. Thus, the shape of the sickle dance imparts information about the approximate distance, direction, and quality (see (1)).

(1) The sickle dance. In this case the food source is 20 to 60 feet from the hive.

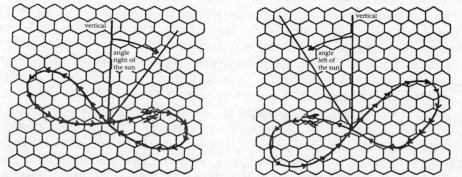

Reprinted with permission from Fromkin and Rodman, *An Introduction to Language,* 2nd edition (1978), p. 42.

In the tail-wagging dance, the bee's movement again describes a circle, but this time the circle is interrupted when the bee cuts across the circle doing a tail-wagging action. The tail-wagging dance imparts all the information of the sickle dance (in this case it is the angle between a vertical line and the tail-wagging path that communicates the angle to the sun), with one important addition. The number of repetitions per minute of the basic pattern of the dance indicates the precise distance: the slower the repetition rate, the greater the distance (see (2)).

(2) The tail-wagging dance. The number of times per minute the bee dances a complete pattern (1–2–1–3) indicates the distance of the food source.

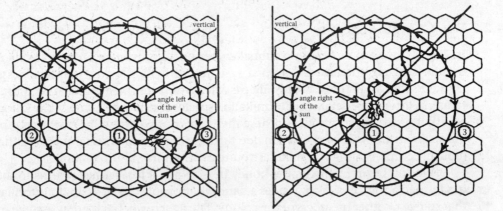

Reprinted with permission from Fromkin and Rodman, *An Introduction to Language,* 2nd edition (1978), p. 43.

The bees' dance is an effective system of communication that is capable, in principle, of infinitely many different messages. In this sense the bees' dances are infinitely variable, like human language. But unlike human language, the communication system of the bees has limited semantic value: the topics that bees can communicate about are limited. For example, an experimenter forced a bee to walk to a food source. When the bee returned to the hive, it indicated a distance 25 times farther away than the food source actually was. The bee had no way of communicating the special circumstances or taking them into account in its message. This absence of **creativity** makes the bees' dance qualitatively different from human language.

The bees' dance gives us a chance to illustrate another very interesting property that every natural human language of the world possesses, as previously discussed in Files 1.4 and 14.1. This property is the arbitrariness of the linguistic sign. When we say that a linguistic sign is arbitrary, it means that there is no inherent connection between the linguistic form and its corresponding linguistic meaning. What about the bees' dance? What are the forms of the signs, and to what meanings do they correspond? Are the relationships arbitrary or non-arbitrary? Consider the tail-wagging dance. One form is the vivacity of the dance, with a corresponding meaning 'quality of food source.' The relationship is arbitrary, for there is nothing inherent about vivacity that indicates good or bad quality. Because the relationship is arbitrary, there is no *a priori* way of telling what the form means.

What about distance? The question here is more complicated. Remember that the slower the repetition rate, the greater the distance. On the surface this relationship may seem arbitrary, but let's use a little physics to reword the relationship: the longer it takes to complete the basic pattern, the longer it will take a bee to fly to the source. Thus, we see that this sign is in some sense non-arbitrary. Similarly, the direction-determining aspect of the dance is obviously non-arbitrary, since the angle of the dance mirrors the angle to the food source. Therefore, we see that bee dances have both arbitrary and iconic (non-arbitrary) components to their signs.

14.2.2 Bird Communication

Birds communicate using both calls and songs. Calls are typically short, simple sounds that may warn of predators, express aggression, coordinate flight activity, or accompany feeding or nesting behavior. Flight calls, for example, are typically short sounds, the place of origin of which is easy to pinpoint: they allow the bird flock to stay together more easily. Sounds warning of predators, on the other hand, are typically thin, high-pitched, and difficult to locate. They allow birds to warn other members of the group of predators without giving away their location. We can see that these bird calls are not completely arbitrary; rather, the calls are functionally related to the meaning they convey: the calls that imply the meaning 'locate me' are easy to locate, whereas the calls that imply the meaning 'I don't want to be found' are difficult to locate.

Bird song is different from bird calls. In most species, only males sing, often to delimit their territory or attract a mate. Unlike calls, songs are largely seasonal. But like calls, the songs of certain species of birds have definite meanings. One song may mean 'let's build a nest together'; another song may mean 'go get some worms for the babies'; and so on. But the bird cannot make up a new song to cope with a new situation.

Scientists who have studied the songs of the European robin found that the songs are very complicated indeed. But, interestingly, the complications have little effect on the message that is being conveyed. The song that was studied was the one that signaled the robin's possession of a certain territory. The scientists found that rival robins paid attention only to the rate of alternation between high-pitched and low-pitched notes, but that which of the two tones came first didn't matter at all. A higher rate of alternation shows a greater intention to defend the territory. Thus, a robin's message varies only to the extent of expressing how strongly the robin feels about his possession and how much he is prepared to defend it and start a family in that territory. This means that the robin is creative in his ability to sing the same thing in many different ways, but not creative in his ability to use the same units of the system to express many different utterances, each with a different meaning. In other words, there is evidence that certain birds combine parts of their songs in different orders, but there is no evidence that different meanings are associated with this recombination.

14.2.3 Primate Communication

Many species of animals have communication systems that are much more complex than one might imagine but that still appear to be very different from human language. Studies of non-human primates such as the vervet and rhesus monkeys, studied both in the wild and in captivity, have revealed elaborate systems of vocal and facial communication that are almost invariably triggered by proximal external stimuli, such as the presence of predators or food sources. Vervet monkeys have been observed to use a variety of alarm calls to warn each other of different kinds of predators. A vervet monkey that emits a loud bark communicates to the rest of the group that a leopard has been spotted. This type of alarm call sends everybody up to the trees. A short, interrupted, usually two-part, cough-like sound means that an eagle is in the vicinity, and monkeys immediately look up and then hurry to take cover under thick bushes. If a snake has been seen by a member of the troupe, he or she will make a soft whirring noise that immediately prompts everybody to stand up and look around the grass cautiously.

Other types of vervet monkey calls deal with social hierarchy arguments, mating rituals, and territorial disputes between different groups of monkeys. This limited "vocabulary" of monkey calls is rigid and fixed. There have been some claims that some "cheating" monkeys might emit an alarm call in the absence of a predator in order to monopolize a food source by sending everybody else to seek shelter. Such reports indicate that the monkeys are able to use their limited array of calls for different purposes (either to give a genuine warning, or just to clear the area for selfish reasons). These instances of "cheating" indicate that the monkeys are aware of the behavioral effects that their calls have on other members of the troupe. However, these cases do not represent novel utterances or new signals. In fact, if we were to provide the gloss of 'Hey, everybody go climb a tree' instead of 'Hey, everybody, there's a leopard,' then it would be totally reasonable to expect the same call used in two different sets of circumstances. Most animal communication systems do not have the sophistication to use the same signal for different purposes in this way, but even a double usage like this doesn't come close to mirroring the complexity of human language.

A recent study of rhesus monkey calls has also revealed a humanlike ability to enhance auditory perception of vocal signals with visual cues. In (3), we can see two different types of rhesus monkey calls and the accompanying facial expressions. The picture on the left represents a cooing call, and the picture on the right a threat call. Cooing calls are long tonal sounds, and threat calls are short and pulsating, cough-like sounds. The study revealed that rhesus monkeys are able to recognize the correspondence between the particular call and the appropriate facial expression. This is a very humanlike ability.

(3) Facial expressions, waveforms, and spectrograms of rhesus monkeys' cooing (left) and threat (right) calls

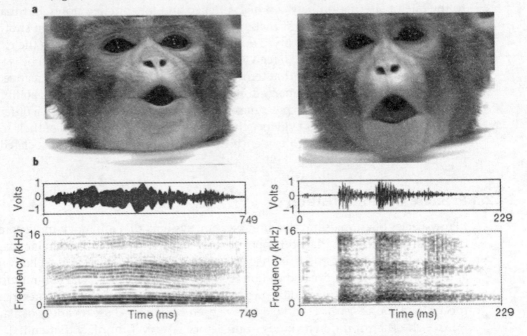

The great apes (gorillas, chimpanzees, bonobos, and orangutans) also communicate with facial expressions, gestures, and calls to express anger, dominance, fear, danger, acceptance in a group, and the like. These are also humanlike behaviors. However, as complex and humanlike as these systems may seem, they lack displacement and productivity: Apes do not communicate about things that are not physically present, nor can they combine their independent gestures or calls in novel ways to create new meanings.

14.2.4 Concluding Remarks

The philosopher and mathematician René Descartes pointed out more than three hundred years ago, in his "Discourse on Method," that the communication systems of animals are qualitatively different from the language used by humans:

> It is a very remarkable fact that there are none [among people] so depraved and stupid, without even excepting idiots, that they cannot arrange different words together, forming of them a statement by which they make known their thoughts; while, on the other hand, there is no other animal, however perfect and fortunately circumstanced it may be, which can do the same.

Descartes went on to state that one of the major differences between humans and animals is that human use of language is not just an immediate response to external, or even internal, emotional stimuli, as are the grunts and gestures of animals.

All the studies of animal communication systems provide evidence for Descartes's distinction between the fixed stimulus-bound messages of animals and the creative linguistic ability possessed by humans. However, even though animal communication systems are not like human languages, they are nevertheless frequently very complex, interesting to study, and different from human languages in fascinating ways.

Can Animals Be Taught Language?

14.3.1 Attempts to Teach Animals Language

The previous file discussed how animals communicate in the wild. As far as we know, no naturally occurring animal communication system is either qualitatively or quantitatively equivalent to human language. But just because animals do not use or acquire language naturally does not necessarily mean that they cannot be taught. This file describes attempts to teach primates language.

14.3.2 Primate Studies

The great apes (gorillas, chimpanzees, bonobos, and orangutans) are very intelligent creatures and *Homo sapiens*' nearest relatives in the animal kingdom. Chimpanzees, for example, share close to 99% of their genetic material with human beings. This biological similarity of ape and human, as well as the apes' intelligence, has prompted some scientists to wonder if language could be taught to apes, even though ape language does not occur naturally (see File 14.2). Many such projects have been conducted, most in the past thirty years or so. The ape used most often has been the chimpanzee, mainly because they are most easily available. They are also considered to be one of the most intelligent of the great apes. Orangutans, gorillas, and bonobos have also been used in some studies.

These experiments have generated both exuberance and disappointment, and a rigorous debate about the interpretation of their results continues to the present day. On the one hand, there are still some scientists who maintain that they have indeed taught an ape to use human language. On the other, many scientists dispute this claim and have proposed alternative explanations for the behaviors other researchers assumed could only have been language use. We will return to this debate later.

a. Early Projects. The first prominent experiment conducted on the linguistic capacity of great apes in the United States took place in the 1930s. W. N. and L. A. Kellogg wanted to raise a baby chimpanzee in a human environment to determine whether the chimp would acquire language on its own, just as a human child does, merely by virtue of being exposed to it. They decided not to give training or "forcible teaching" to Gua, the chimp they acquired at seven and a half months, other than that which would be given a human infant. Gua was raised alongside the Kelloggs' newborn son, Donald, and the development of the chimp was compared to the boy's. W. Kellogg stated that his intent was to determine how much of human language ability derived from heredity and how much from education. He reasoned, a bit naïvely in retrospect, that what the chimp could not learn would be those aspects of language that a human inherently knows. Kellogg admitted one violation of this program when, at one point, he attempted to mold Gua's lips in an effort to teach her to say *papa*. This effort, lasting several months, proved unsuccessful. The duration of the Kelloggs' experiment was rather short (only nine months) in comparison to those that were to follow.

In the 1950s, Keith and Cathy Hayes decided to raise Viki, a female chimp, also as much like a human child as possible, believing that with a proper upbringing, a chimp could learn language. The Hayeses believed that they could teach Viki to speak, even though doubt was emerging at the time about whether the chimpanzee's vocal anatomy could even produce human speech sounds. The Hayeses, however, believed that the vocal tract of the chimp was similar enough to a human's for it to be able to articulate human sounds. They had no aversion to "training," and their program included first teaching Viki to vocalize on demand (this took five weeks), and then shaping her lips with their hands into various configurations that yielded consonant sounds. After three years, Viki could "speak" three words—*cup, mama,* and *papa*—although they were accompanied by a "heavy chimp accent"; it sounded as if Viki were whispering. The Hayeses reported that Viki could "understand" many words, but they offered no experimental proof of this. The Kelloggs' and Hayeses' experiments were not viewed by scientists as successful attempts to teach language to apes. Three words are not very many when one is trying to prove human language capability.

Allen and Beatrice Gardner believed, contrary to the Hayeses, that chimps were not capable of producing human speech sounds, so they felt that trying to teach a chimp to speak was fruitless. Since chimps are manually dexterous and use gestures to communicate naturally, the Gardners decided to teach American Sign Language (ASL) to a chimp they named Washoe. Washoe was not raised as a human infant but was brought up with minimal confinement in a stimulating atmosphere. Spoken English was not allowed in her presence because the Gardners feared she would come to understand spoken language first and not be motivated to learn ASL. Like Viki, Washoe also received deliberate training. Objects were presented to her, and the trainers molded Washoe's hands into the shapes for their signs. Eventually, in order to be rewarded, she had to produce the signs herself and to produce them with greater and greater accuracy. The experiment was considered at the time to be a great success. By the time Washoe was five years old, she had learned 132 signs. More important, she supposedly exhibited some amount of productivity in her communication by inventing her own novel combinations such as *dirty Roger,* where *dirty* was used as an expletive, and *water bird,* upon seeing a swan on a lake.

The Gardners' insight about the vocal limitations of the chimp has been noted by every researcher since. Subsequent endeavors have all involved simplified versions of either a signed language or visual signs such as **lexigrams,** symbols composed of geometric shapes used to represent words.

Anne and David Premack began in 1966 to work with a chimpanzee named Sarah. Their methods were quite a bit different from those discussed above. Rather than treat the chimp like a human child, David Premack decided to try to find and use the best possible training procedure. The "language" used was also atypical. Instead of a simplified version of ASL, Premack used differently shaped and colored plastic chips. With each chip he arbitrarily associated an English word. Communication between the trainers and Sarah involved placing these chips on the "language board." Sarah was taught how to do one type of "sentence" at a time. Typically, her task was to choose an appropriate chip from a choice of two or to carry out a task indicated on the language board. Premack intended to teach Sarah the names of objects as well as the names of categories of objects. He originally claimed to have taught her 130 symbols, including category names such as color and concepts such as *same* and *different.* Premack also claimed that Sarah learned the word *insert.* As proof of this, Premack offered that in one task, when Sarah saw *Sarah banana pail insert* on her language board, she correctly executed the task.

Duane Rumbaugh wanted to design an ape language experiment with as much of the training taken out of the hands of human trainers as possible. He reasoned that if the training were automated, one could avoid cueing the animal, and the training could be more efficient and constant. So he and his associates designed a computer that would do the training. The computer could execute certain commands, such as dispensing food or displaying slides in response to an operator giving proper commands. Commands were given by lighting up symbols of an invented "language." Like the Gardners with Washoe, Rumbaugh used lexigrams—various combinations of nine different geometric figures, such as a big circle, a little circle, and a large X—as the language the operator of the machine would use. This operator was, of course, a chimp; her name was Lana. Lana did learn to use the keyboard quite well and managed to make the computer execute various commands, and Rumbaugh thought that he had succeeded in teaching a chimp some human language.

In 1972 Francine Patterson began to teach ASL to a gorilla named Koko. This project has been one of the longest lasting of its kind, and Patterson has made some of the most dramatic claims for such a project's success. According to Patterson, Koko knows several hundred signs and has invented many of her own combinations, such as *finger bracelet* for 'ring.' Koko also supposedly uses her signs to insult people and things she doesn't like. After being reprimanded one day, for example, Koko called Patterson a *dirty toilet devil*. In addition, Koko is reported to understand spoken English. The evidence given by Patterson to support this claim is that Koko occasionally rhymes, putting together such signs as *bear* and *hair* even though the signs themselves have no visual similarity to each other. Koko also substitutes homonyms for words when she cannot think of the sign, such as *eye* for *I* or *know* for *no*. Although Koko has exhibited a remarkable grasp of many linguistic properties, she does not yet seem to have displayed the abilities necessary to justify Patterson's claim that "Koko is the first of her species to have acquired human language."

b. Criticisms of the Early Projects. The results and conclusions of these projects have been critically questioned on two fronts. The first to criticize the projects was a researcher named Herbert Terrace. His criticism was based on a critical review of his own project to teach a chimpanzee the use of grammar. He then critically reviewed other projects and found similar shortcomings.

In the late 1970s, Terrace began his project, which was similar to that of the Gardners, with a chimpanzee he humorously named Nim Chimpsky (hoping that when Nim learned language, the joke would be on Noam Chomsky, the noted linguist who claimed such a thing was impossible). Terrace's concern was to prove that a chimp could acquire and display some use of grammar. Terrace believed, as did most researchers at the time, that evidence of human language capability was the use of grammar and not just the use of signs. (This is still important today, but as we will see below, current researchers are concentrating on the way signs are used by animals.) By the time Nim was four years old, he had acquired 125 signs based on ASL and had combined them in various ways, and Terrace felt that Nim had acquired human language abilities as well.

This project was the first to videotape all interactions between chimp and trainer, however, and it was on reviewing these tapes that Terrace decided he must reverse his initial claim and instead acknowledge that the ape's use of signs was very different from human language. He noted that there were many dissimilarities between Nim's and a human child's acquisition of "language." Nim, for example, almost never initiated signing. Upon reviewing the tapes, Terrace found that only 12% of Nim's signs were spontaneous, and a full 40% were mere repetitions of what the trainer had just signed. This subtle interaction was never noticed by the trainer at the time. In addition, Nim's spontaneous signing was invariably a request for food or social reward; he never made unsolicited statements or asked questions. Quite unlike a human child, he did not display turn-taking behavior and was more likely to interrupt his trainer's signing than not. There was also no evidence that Nim knew any grammar. His combinations had variable word order, and, more importantly, Nim rarely went beyond two-word combinations. Even when he did, the additional signs added no new information. For example, Nim's longest utterance was *give orange me give eat orange me eat orange give me eat orange give me you.*

Terrace called into question the results of all previous experiments. He reviewed tapes of Washoe and Koko and concluded that they too had been cued by their trainers. He and others leveled even more serious criticisms of the Premack project, arguing that the training procedure taught problem solving and not language and that Premack's conclusions were not well founded, given his experimental design and his results. Consider Premack's claim that Sarah learned the word *insert* because she could correctly insert a banana in a pail when seeing *Sarah banana pail insert* on her language board. When the word *insert* was tested against the word *give,* however, Sarah could not distinguish the two. Premack likewise claimed that Sarah knew the prepositions *on* and *in* but never administered a test where Sarah would have to distinguish one from the other. Following instructions did not have to involve Sarah's understanding a sentence on the language board, but rather her recognizing, for example, a banana chip and a pail chip and imitating what she had been trained to do in the first stage of the test—in this case, insert the banana in the pail (a banana couldn't go *on* an upright pail).

c. More Recent Projects. Terrace's revelations had a great effect on the field of animal language studies. Funding for projects was thereafter hard to come by, and many scientists responded with new cynicism to any and all claims of animal language researchers. Researcher Sue Savage-Rumbaugh maintains that both the initial easy acceptance of claims in this field and the post-Terrace cynicism are too extreme.

She has begun another project with several apes, but the focus of her work is quite different. She believes that looking for evidence of grammatical capabilities in apes as Terrace did was far too premature. She considers a more fundamental question: when apes use a sign, do they know what it **means**? This question is by no means easy to answer, and it is ironic that the early researchers took it for granted that when an ape produced a sign, it was using it in the same way humans do, as an arbitrary symbol to represent something. It is precisely this use of the symbol that Savage-Rumbaugh has considered and researched.

Note that this approach represents a departure from the attempt to assess animal language capabilities in terms of descriptive "design features," such as productivity and displacement. Human language does have these features that distinguish it from other communication systems, but the use of symbols also distinguishes human language from the natural animal communication systems discussed in Files 14.1 and 14.2. Understanding the concept of 'symbol' is difficult, partly because symbol use is innate to us. The use of a symbol involves a special relationship with at least three components. First, there is the physical, external form of a word such as *tree*—either ink on a page in the shape of the letters <tree> or a spoken word with a particular phonological form. Second, many words have reference. Reference is the relationship of the form to a real tree somewhere. Third, there is the mental representation we have for the word *tree,* an idea of tree that is called up when we hear, say, see, or think of the word *tree.* Note that "mental representation" does not mean 'image' or 'picture'—not every word can have one of these either (see File 6.2). Mental representations have an existence separate from reference and can be manipulated independently from reference. Thus, we can think and talk about things like invisibility for which we do not have a mental image, but for which we do have a mental representation.

No one disputes that humans use their words in this way. Furthermore, no one disputes that in many cases animals have been able to associate a phonological or visual form of a sign with a referent. But how are we to know whether an ape, when it uses a sign in the same way we might, really has a mental representation for it? Savage-Rumbaugh has suggested that in all previous experiments, apes were not using their signs symbolically. She argues that apes had merely learned to associate certain behaviors (making or seeing a particular sign) with certain consequences (e.g., getting something to eat)—similar to a dog, for example, which, upon hearing the word *walk,* knows it's going to get to go for a walk. This is an extremely subtle distinction for humans to perceive, since the use of symbols comes naturally to us. We interpret other creatures' signals to us in the same way we interpret those from each other, but that doesn't necessarily mean they're intended in the same way. For this reason, Savage-Rumbaugh has pointed out the necessity of proper experiments that prove that an ape has truly acquired a word in the same way a human has. She has criticized the claims made about previous projects either because they were not based on testing with proper controls or because use of symbols had not been tested at all. In addition, Savage-Rumbaugh reasoned that because apes had not learned to use symbols given the training techniques used previously (which had assumed that the symbol aspect of sign use would come naturally), apes must specifically and intentionally be taught to use symbols first, before tests could be informatively administered.

How could Savage-Rumbaugh determine whether such instruction was successful: how can one find evidence of a mental phenomenon? One must still look for it in the behavior of the animal or in the "processes of the exchange" with the trainer, but one must be more discriminating about what counts as evidence. Savage-Rumbaugh and her colleagues have worked extensively with two male chimpanzees, Sherman and Austin, attempting to teach them language skills with the computer and the lexigrams used with Lana. They have found that use of symbols by humans is not a single holistic phenomenon but rather a complex of independent abilities and behaviors. For example, the ability to produce a symbol was found to be composed of at least three separate abilities. Using the association of a lexigram and an object to request the object is only one of these (and a display of this ability does not prove the user has a mental representation for the symbol). Naming is a second relevant behavior, which involves providing the lexigram associated with an object without the expectation of consuming or receiving that object. The third ability involved in symbol use is called comprehension of the symbol. It involves linking the symbol to its referent. One might find it difficult to separate these three, but they each had to be taught separately to the chimpanzee, and the presence of one ability could not be assumed because of the presence of another.

Savage-Rumbaugh also points out the extreme importance of a fourth aspect of symbol use and human communication that had previously been overlooked: the role of the receiver or listener. This in itself was also found to comprise its own complex of skills and behaviors, each of which had to be taught separately to Sherman and Austin. Savage-Rumbaugh claims to have been successful at teaching the chimps these skills as well as the links between them (the coordination that occurs naturally in humans).

Furthermore, she has acknowledged Terrace's criticisms of other projects but maintains that Sherman and Austin do not evidence Nim's shortcomings. She maintains that they take turns, their utterances are not imitations of their trainers, and that they produce messages not only when they are elicited, but at other times as well.

This project certainly has made real progress both in clarifying what human language skills are and in investigating our ability to teach them to apes. Criticisms have been leveled, of course. Some suggest that, again, the apes have been skillfully trained but still neither comprehend what they are saying nor use their signs symbolically. After all, it is perhaps impossible to know whether another creature has a mental representation for a word. Savage-Rumbaugh might respond that this criticism is a reflection of a cynical attitude rather than scientific considerations. However, given past experience and the tendency to overinterpret, there is a need to scrutinize the claims in this field.

Savage-Rumbaugh's most recently begun project must be mentioned. She has started to work with another species of ape, the bonobo, *Pan paniscus,* which she claims is more intelligent than the common chimpanzee, *Pan troglodytes,* which she had used in all of her other projects. She claims that the bonobo she has been working with, Kanzi, has learned to comprehend spoken English just by being exposed to it and has spontaneously begun to use the keyboard with lexigrams to make requests and comment on his environment. Savage-Rumbaugh reports both anecdotal observations and the results of tests that might substantiate these astonishing claims. Again, these newest claims are difficult to accept without further confirmation based on carefully controlled experimentation and the objective scrutiny that was advocated at the inception of the Sherman and Austin project.

Practice

File 14.1—Communication and Language

Exercises

1. Refer to the *Marmaduke* cartoon at the beginning of this chapter to answer the following questions:

　i. Based on the comic, do you think Marmaduke understands the command *Sit*? What would you need to know to determine whether Marmaduke understands the command or not?

　ii. What are some of the ways that dogs communicate with their owners? Based on your answer, which design features are present in dogs' communication with humans? (Be careful that you don't confuse the design features that may be present when humans communicate with their dogs!)

2. The file mentions that when a dog bares its teeth, it indicates that it is ready to attack. Compare this with humans baring their teeth when they are smiling. What does it mean when we smile? Does it mean that we are ready to attack? Is that arbitrary or iconic? How do dogs probably interpret smiling in a person they don't know?

3. Many people insist that their dogs, cats, or other pets are able to understand what they want and to communicate with them. There is no doubt that our pets are often able to meld very well into our lives. There is also no doubt that often there is at least some level of communication between people and their pets. Based on what you have read in File 14.1, however, how would you refute a person's claim that her dog or cat "knows exactly what I mean when I talk to him"?

4. Refer to the communication chain diagram in File 1.2. Although all animal communication systems have a mode of communication, semanticity, and a pragmatic function, not all three of these are required to make the communication chain work. Which are, and which aren't? Explain your answers.

5. A male peacock has a brightly colored tail that can be fanned out behind him. He uses this fanning behavior in order to attract mates: females are attracted to males that have particularly full and vibrant tail displays. Are the females responding to something that is iconic or something that is arbitrary? Explain your answer.

6. A wolf is able to express subtle gradations of emotion by different positions of the ears, the lips, and the tail. There are eleven postures of the tail that express such emotions as self-confidence, confident threat, lack of tension, uncertain threat, depression, defensiveness, active submission, and complete submission. This system seems to be complex.

Suppose there were a thousand different emotions that the wolf could express in this way. Would you then say that a wolf had a language similar to a human's? Why or why not?

Discussion Questions

7. In File 14.1, many modes of communication are introduced. What are some reasons that a certain mode of communication might be well suited to some species but not to others?

8. Think about the following situation: two male crayfish fight with each other. One of them wins and a female crayfish chooses the winner as her mate. Who is communicating with whom in this situation? Are the males communicating with each other? Or are they using the other in order to communicate with the female? Explain your answer.

File 14.2—Animal Communication in the Wild

Exercises

9. Consider the bee communication system described in this file and answer the questions. Be sure to discuss all nine design features.
    i. Which design features does the system display? Please explain.
    ii. Which design features does the system clearly not display? Please explain.
    iii. For which design features does the file not provide you with enough evidence or information to decide whether the feature is present in the communication system or not? What would you need to know about the system to make a decision? What would the system have to be like in order for the feature to be present?

10. Consider the bird communication systems described in this file, and answer parts (i) and (ii) from Exercise 9.

11. Consider the primate communication systems described in this file, and answer parts (i) and (ii) from Exercise 9.

Activities

12. Use the Internet, an encyclopedia, an animal behavior text, or other resource to investigate a natural animal communication system other than the ones described in File 14.2. Describe this system relative to the design features outlined in File 14.1.

File 14.3—Can Animals Be Taught Language?

Exercises

13. Refer to the *Marmaduke* cartoon at the beginning of this chapter. Imagine that you wanted to teach Marmaduke language. Consider how you would go about doing this, and then answer questions (i)–(iii).
    i. What mode of communication would you choose to teach Marmaduke? Why?
    ii. If you tried to teach Marmaduke symbols and a simple syntax, how would you test whether he had learned to combine the symbols to form different messages?
    iii. Do you think Marmaduke would be better at comprehending or producing both symbols and simple syntax? Why do you think so?

14. There are transcripts of several "chats" with Koko the Gorilla available online. Pick a chat from the following links, and answer questions (i)–(viii):

> www.koko.org/world/talk_aol.html
> www.geocities.com/RainForest/Vines/4451/KokoLiveChat.html

i. What is Koko's longest utterance in the chat? What is Koko's average length of utterance, that is, how many words on average do Koko's utterances have? (You can estimate this.)

ii. About what percentage of the time did you understand Koko's utterances without any help from Dr. Patterson? About what percentage of the time did you need her to interpret for Koko?

iii. How relevant were Koko's utterances?

iv. Did Koko interrupt other speakers frequently or rarely?

v. What are the main topics that Koko talks about? What, if anything, does this reveal about her language use?

vi. Does Koko ever seem to repeat or imitate Dr. Patterson's signs? About how frequently does she do so?

vii. Do you find evidence that Koko really knows the meaning of the signs she uses? If so, what kinds of evidence do you find? Please give specific examples.

viii. Compare your answers to (i)–(vii) with the sorts of responses you would give after reading the transcript of a conversation between humans. Based on this comparison, do you think Koko can really use language? Justify your answer. Explain both the things she does that do seem to model language use and the ways in which her behavior is dissimilar from human language use.

Discussion Questions

15. In File 14.3, a distinction is often drawn between teaching an animal language and teaching an animal to use language. However, the distinction between these two terms is never clearly defined. Based not only on what you have read in File 14.3 but also on your studies of language and linguistics throughout the book so far, what would you say is the difference between teaching an animal language and merely teaching an animal to use language?

16. The work that Terrace did and his interpretation of his results raise doubts about the entire enterprise of trying to teach human language to animals. As a result, there was a loss of funding for this sort of work. Such responses are very common in the scientific community: those who fund grants only have so much money to give, and understandably they generally try to underwrite projects that have a high level of support within the community. Suppose, though, that there were an unlimited amount of monetary funding. Do you think, following pronouncements such as Terrace's, that it is appropriate to reduce the amount of effort put into researching a particular task?

17. Throughout this book, we have presented both signed and spoken modalities of human language. Both are equally authentic and natural modes of human communication. Presumably, then, the choice of whether to train an ape using one or the other of these two types of language is not particularly relevant to whether we conclude that it has, in fact, learned language. Now consider the case of lexigrams. Does using lexigrams to communicate have any less authenticity than either speech or signing? Why do you think so?

18. Suppose that apes can master some aspects of productivity (such as Koko creating the word FINGER-BRACELET for 'ring' and Washoe using WATER BIRD for 'swan.' If they have the cognitive capacity to put discrete units together in new ways, why do you think that we haven't found examples of productivity in apes' natural communication systems?

19. **i.** Savage-Rumbaugh claims that if we are able to teach an ape to use symbols (using her three-part definition), it will be a more important indication of its ability to use language than would use of grammar. Do you agree?

 ii. Suppose that we were able to teach a hypothetical animal—let's say a super-intelligent mutant guinea pig—to productively put together complex grammatical utterances using consistent word order, function words, and so on, but that the guinea pig was unable to use signs symbolically. Would you say that the guinea pig had a better command of language or a worse command of language than a bonobo who understood the symbolism of language but who did not have a grasp of a grammatical system?

20. Researchers have by and large concluded that—even if apes can be taught to use elements of human language—they cannot acquire human language naturally in the way that human children do. Imagine that on some alien planet we were to discover a new species of animal. Further imagine that these animals never learned language naturally (either growing up in communities with each other or growing up in a home with humans as a human child would) but that following instruction, the aliens mastered language use completely. That is, they exhibited language use encompassing all of the design features and full use of symbols: they could hold conversations, write speeches, tell jokes, and so on. How would you describe the linguistic abilities of these aliens? Would you say that their linguistic abilities (after training) were as genuine as those of humans, or would you say that they were still lacking in some way? Why would you make this judgment?

CHAPTER
15

Language and Computers

What Is Computational Linguistics?

B oth computers and people can be considered information processing systems. A number of the processing tasks that humans carry out with language can be automated to some degree on a computer: recognizing words in speech, pronouncing these words, translating from one language to another, and so on. Language processing in humans is, as we have seen, incredibly complex (Chapter 9), so it isn't currently possible to give machines the full conversational skills of a human being. However, programming a computer to work with language—written or spoken—can nonetheless be viewed as creating a (limited) model of language processing. Computers are therefore ideal for testing linguists' theories about language processing, because programming a computer requires explicitly specifying all details of an operation. By programming a computer according to our current understanding of various linguistic phenomena and then observing how well the computer's behavior mirrors human behavior, we can get a better idea of how good our models of those linguistic phenomena are.

Of course, there are also practical applications to giving computers language processing ability: even limited abilities can smooth the interactions between machines and their human users. Computers are useful for such applications as teaching and business.

Contents

586

FILE 15.1

Speech Synthesis

15.1.1 Synthesized Speech

Speech synthesis is the use of a machine, usually a computer, to produce humanlike speech. Artificial speech can be produced in several ways: by playing prerecorded utterances and phrases, called **canned speech;** by piecing together smaller recorded units of speech into new utterances; or by creating speech "from scratch," which is called **synthesized speech.** Not too many years ago, talking machines were found only in science fiction stories. Now they are found in many items in our daily lives, such as cars, elevators, automatic lottery machines, answering machines, telephone customer service centers, and automated grocery checkout lanes. In fact, you may have grown up playing with toys that talk. Many commercial machines that talk use canned speech, which is of little interest to linguists because the use of canned speech does not require language processing: it comes preprocessed. On the other hand, machines that talk using synthesized speech are of the utmost interest to linguists because synthesizing speech provides an opportunity to test our understanding of language and to apply knowledge that has been gained through linguistic investigation. Comparing synthesized speech with speech produced by people is a very rigorous test of how thorough our knowledge of language and speech is.

Synthesized speech should be intelligible and sound natural. **Intelligibility** refers to how well listeners can recognize and understand the individual sounds or words generated by the synthesis system. **Naturalness** refers to how much the synthesized speech sounds like the speech of an actual person. Speech that does not sound natural is usually reported to sound "robotic" and unpleasant. Usually, as a synthesized speech sample gets longer, it becomes less natural sounding. Linguists and computer scientists who work on speech synthesis use a variety of tests, often pertaining to speech perception, to achieve the highest levels of intelligibility and naturalness.

15.1.2 The Earliest Synthesis Machines

The very first speech synthesizers were mechanical. In 1779, Russian scientist Christian Gottlieb Kratzenstein built five acoustic resonators that could produce the five vowels /a/, /e/, /i/, /o/, /u/. In 1791, Hungarian Wolfgang Von Kemplen constructed a machine that could produce both consonants and vowel sounds. The earliest electronic speech synthesizer seems to have been made in the early 1920s by J. Q. Stewart, who put together circuitry that gave vowel-like formants to the sound generated by a buzzer (see File 2.6 for an explanation of formants). The 1930s saw the appearance of the "Voder," a device something like an electronic organ. An operator could change the pitch of the voice-source by pushing a pedal while turning various frequencies on and off with the buttons on a keyboard. The output of this machine, if the operator was a virtuoso, was marginally intelligible.

The 1950s saw the advent and extensive use of the "Pattern Playback" machine in research on speech perception. This machine took spectrograms (a kind of visual representation of sound waves; see File 2.6) as its input, which a researcher painted on a clear piece of plastic. The machine "read" these spectrograms by shining light through the plastic and producing the sounds indicated by the images. Literally hundreds of experiments were performed using pattern playback machines, forming the basis of much of the present research on speech perception. The ghostly sounds that this machine emitted were estimated to be between 85% and 95% intelligible, depending on how good the painted spectrograms were.

Later electronic speech synthesizers differed crucially from these early ones in one primary respect. Whereas the early ones took a tremendously rich and complicated description of the sound to be produced as input, later machines were designed to take into account only the types of sounds humans emit as speech. By greatly limiting the types of sounds the machines produced, the amount of information the machines needed to produce the appropriate sound was reduced.

15.1.3 Articulatory Synthesis

The earliest speech synthesizers were designed only to mimic the sounds of human speech, regardless of the process through which those sounds were produced. **Articulatory synthesis,** on the other hand, is a synthesis technique that generates speech "from scratch" based on computational models of the shape of the human vocal tract and the articulation processes. Most articulatory synthesis systems have not been very successful, because there are too many as-yet-unanswered questions about the vocal tract and articulation processes. For a long time, however, articulatory synthesis was thought of as the most promising way to synthesize speech because it most closely models the way humans produce sounds.

Early synthesizers of this kind included OVE (Orator Verbis Electris) and PAT (Parametric Artificial Talker), developed in the 1950s and 1960s. They were made of circuitry that imitated various aspects of sounds produced in the vocal tract. Both machines were based on the **source-filter theory** of speech production, which claims that there are two independent parts to the production of speech sounds.

The first part consists of some mechanism that creates a basic sound, and is therefore called the **source.** The second part, called the **filter,** shapes the sound created by the source into the different sounds we recognize as speech sounds, such as the vowels [i] and [u] or the consonants [l], [s], or [t]. For example, in human speech, the sound [i] is produced by combining a periodic sound wave created by air flowing through the vibrating vocal folds (the source) with a particular oral tract configuration that involves the tongue being in a high front position (the filter). See Chapter 2 for a description of how vowels and consonants are made by human speakers.

Both OVE and PAT were designed to directly mimic human speech production, by having some source that produced a basic sound similar to those produced by humans, and having some method of filtering this basic sound into the particular speech sounds needed. Using this technique, the OVE II was the first synthesizer that could produce an utterance that was indistinguishable from that of a real male speaker, though this production involved a long series of manipulations and settings by a human guide.

However, speech generated in this manner, "from scratch," rarely sounds natural. The main problems involve the accurate production of voicing, frication, intonation, sentence stress, and timing. For example, the characteristics of voicing are extremely complex and change continuously, depending on the thickness and consistency of the vocal folds, how close the speaker places the vocal folds to one another during voicing, and how much air is being pumped through the larynx. Other aspects of speech are equally complex and therefore difficult to generate from scratch.

15.1.4 Concatenative Synthesis

Concatenative synthesis is the most commonly used speech synthesis technology today because it generates very natural sounding speech. Unlike the systems introduced in the previous section, concatenative synthesis uses recorded speech, which eliminates the major problems that articulatory synthesis faced. Most commercial speech synthesis systems now start by recording speech, and then they manipulate the speech samples. Since high-quality sound recordings are extremely bulky (even if only small sound segments are stored), a synthesizer may need a lot of storage space. Thus, only recently—with the advent of computer technology that allows affordable storage of large amounts of data—has it become practical to use recorded data for speech synthesis.

Concatenative synthesis works by first stringing together (concatenating) pieces of recorded speech and then smoothing the boundaries between them. One kind of concatenative synthesis is called **unit selection synthesis.** The units, as discussed below, vary in size depending on the application.

The basic idea of unit selection synthesis is to take large samples of speech and build a database of smaller units from these speech samples. These units are then concatenated to create words or sentences that were not originally recorded. The process begins by recording real speech, usually predetermined sentences, in a quiet environment. The recorded sentences are segmented into smaller units, which may be individual sounds, diphones (discussed below), syllables, morphemes, words, phrases, or some combination of these units. There will often be many samples of the same sound unit, recorded in differing contexts, for example, at the beginning of a sentence and at the end of a sentence. After segmentation, each unit receives an index label that includes information about its pitch, duration, neighboring sounds, and other relevant data. When generating speech, the system uses a complex algorithm to choose the best units from the database, matching the sound and context of the new utterance as well as it can to the sound-context pairs available in the database. Unit selection synthesis is successful at creating natural sounding speech because it uses a large number of well-indexed units extracted from natural speech. In other words, it sounds like human speech because it is derived from human speech.

The question remains as to what type of speech segments to use for the best-sounding synthesis. On the one hand, large segments of recorded speech, such as complete sentences, will sound the most natural when played back in full. However, most applications will require too many distinct sentences for this to be practical. Segmenting speech at the word level is useful for many applications in which the same words are often repeated. If enough words are present in the database, a very large number of sentences can be produced by concatenating the words in various arrangements. By including words that have been recorded multiple times, with intonation for both declarative and interrogative sentences, the system can be quite expressive. However, only words that have been recorded will ever be produced. To solve this problem and allow for new words to be pronounced, speech can be segmented at the level of the phoneme (see Chapter 3). When a new word is requested, the system will go through steps to find the appropriate allophones, concatenate them, and pronounce the word.

Even more successful than phoneme synthesis is **diphone synthesis.** Diphones are pairs of adjacent sounds: the end of one phone attached to the beginning of the next phone. The image in (1) represents all of the diphones in a stream of speech with four adjacent sounds. Connecting phones in the middle, as happens when we string together two diphones, is usually more successful than stringing together two different sounds. The resulting synthesized speech sounds more natural, because it accounts for effects of coarticulation (where overlapping sounds affect each other).

(1) | Sound 1 | Sound 2 | Sound 3 | Sound 4 |
    | Diphone 1| Diphone 2 | Diphone 3 | Diphone 4 | Diphone 5 |

Concatenative synthesis is especially successful when applied to one particular domain, or topic, such as travel information or weather reports. **Domain-specific synthesis** systems create utterances from prerecorded words and phrases that closely match the words and phrases that will be synthesized. At the generation step, large segments such as words or phrases may be chosen from the database, increasing the naturalness of the speech. Generating new utterances is also possible using smaller segments, such as diphones, collected from the same recordings. If the vocabulary and sentence structure of the generated speech remain close to those of the speech that was recorded, the result will be very natural sounding.

Why is it important to choose sounds or words with their immediate context in mind? Two main reasons are the duration of sounds and the intonation of words and phrases. Certain sounds, especially vowels, vary in duration depending on where in a word they occur. The duration and intonation of full words depend on where in a sentence or phrase they occur. This is illustrated below with the word *Tom* in different contexts.

(2) Hi, I'm Tom.
     Are you Tom?
     Tom! Please stop crying!
     Tom went to the store.
     Sam, Tom, and Sue went to the store.
     Sam, Sue, and Tom went to the store.

If you read the examples aloud, you will see how the intonation of *Tom* differs in each sentence. You may notice that the duration of the vowel changes, too. So, if we want to generate the word *Tom* as the subject of a declarative sentence, it will be best if we can choose a speech sample of *Tom* where it was recorded serving the same grammatical function. The same holds true for smaller and larger sound segments.

15.1.5 Text-To-Speech Synthesis

Many speech synthesizers accept symbolic input, for instance, a phrase written in IPA or some other phonetic alphabet. Using the IPA can tell a speech synthesizer exactly which phonemes or diphones to select. However, it is more convenient for us to use ordinary written language to tell the synthesizer what words or phrases to generate. In **Text-To-Speech Synthesis** (TTS), speech is generated directly from text entered with normal orthography (spelling). For the following discussion, assume that we are using a concatenative synthesis system and diphone segments to produce the speech. If the system is given a phrase to produce, it must decide which series of diphones will best represent that phrase.

If the system will be required to pronounce only a limited number of words, and that number is relatively small, then simple word-to-pronunciation rules can be stored in the system. That is, the computer is told, for each sequence of letters, which sequence of sounds should be produced. If only one pronunciation per word is stored, then each word will always be pronounced the same way, using the same diphone segments from the database. If more than one pronunciation is stored for a given word, then the system might decide which pronunciation to use based on the context of that word in a phrase.

If the vocabulary is quite large, or even unlimited, then there must be rules that describe how to pronounce words in general based on how they are spelled. For some words, and in some languages, this is easy, because certain words are "spelled the way they sound," with one letter representing each sound. In English, however, there are sounds that are represented by multiple letters, and many letters represent more than one sound (see File 2.1). These inconsistencies mean that spelling-to-sound rules are often inadequate. As a result, systems that use spelling-to-sound rules usually include an **exceptions dictionary,** which lists the correct pronunciation of words that do not follow the rules.

Having taken care of spelling inconsistencies, what can be done about **heteronyms**? These are words that can be pronounced in two or more ways, although they are spelled only one way. For instance, there are many words like *record* that can be used as a verb or a noun and have different pronunciations based on their usage, as illustrated in (3).

(3) We may record this call for quality assurance.
   My mom doesn't know about technology. She calls a CD a record.

In the first case, where *record* is a verb, the first vowel is [ə] and the stress is on the second syllable. In the second case, where *record* is a noun, the first vowel is [ɛ] and takes the stress. This is a common type of alternation in English, and there are many others. So, a good, wide-domain TTS system must be able to detect the syntactic structure of a sentence, and thereby the grammatical role of each word, in order to pronounce the words correctly.

In summary, a TTS system will carry out some combination of the following steps to convert a word from normal spelling representation to a pronounceable representation: look up the word in a complete pronunciation dictionary; look up the word in an exceptions dictionary; use spelling-to-sound rules to generate a pronunciation; detect the grammatical role of the word to choose an appropriate pronunciation from a set. A further necessity of a TTS system, not explored here, is assigning and adjusting for the intonation of individual words and phrases.

15.1.6 Applications of Speech Synthesis

One research application of speech synthesis is testing our knowledge about speech production and recognition. For instance, a phonologist might use speech synthesis technology in the following way. When a researcher is faced with some phonemic contrast that is peculiar or unlike contrasts that linguists have seen before, synthesizing the relevant phones and then testing how native speakers perceive the synthesized speech is one of way of testing hypotheses about what that contrast might be. The linguist conducting the experiment would look to see which synthesized sounds were perceived as one phoneme and which were perceived as the other. We have only begun to tap the research value of speech synthesis, and there are many other research applications yet to be explored.

Commercially, various manufacturers have given voices to their products. Systems designed to help teach children to read are available today. Many telephone customer service centers use synthesized speech either for complete interactions or to direct a customer to the appropriate service representative. Weather channels also frequently use synthesized speech, allowing them to report the weather in many different areas, at all hours of the day, without paying people to read all of those reports. Interactive course registration systems are in use at many universities. Computer companies also find attractive the enhanced appeal of home and business computers that can "talk." Concatenative synthesis is used in a number of these applications, along with playback of prerecorded phrases and sentences in some instances. (Other applications use only canned speech.)

Perhaps more important, though not as well funded, are uses of synthesis in various devices to aid the physically handicapped. One such use is for the vocally handicapped. The American Speech and Hearing Association estimates that there are around 1.5 million nonspeaking people in the United States alone (not including those deaf individuals who are in principle able to speak): people who have lost the use of their larynx through injury or disease, for instance. Modern speaking aids allow anyone who can use a keyboard to be able to communicate vocally.

A similar application is reading aids. The number of people in the United States who cannot read normal newspaper print, even with corrective glasses, is about as high as the number of vocally impaired. For this segment of the population, machines that read printed text aloud are of great use, as are talking clocks, thermometers, calculators, and other commonplace objects.

FILE 15.2

Automatic Speech Recognition

15.2.1 The Nature of Speech Recognition

Talking to computers has been a standard of science fiction for many decades. Many of the linguistic and engineering challenges involved in machines' understanding speech remain to be solved, but the dream of having computers understand what we say is slowly becoming reality. True speech understanding entails many different levels of linguistic processing, so **automatic speech recognition** is usually defined more narrowly as the conversion of an acoustic speech waveform into text. Put another way, automatic speech recognition is the process through which a computer takes sounds of speech and converts them into words of some particular language. Dealing with the meaning of those words, once recognized, is usually handled by other computer programs (see File 15.3).

Although today's speech recognition systems cannot perform as well as many of the computers of science fiction, current technology is already finding use in many applications. For example, automatic speech recognition is used in telephone applications that allow customers to enter or request information verbally (e.g., calling to find the status of an airplane flight) or for call routing (e.g., "Operator, please"). Automatic speech recognition is also useful for dictation (e.g., producing a transcription of a spoken document). Being able to interact with computers through voice instead of depending on a keyboard is desirable in environments that require a user's hands to control equipment or demand that visual attention be focused elsewhere (e.g., flying a fighter jet in combat).

15.2.2 The Noisy Channel Model

The basic architecture for speech recognition software is built on a view of language processing called the **noisy channel model.** The insight guiding this model involves treating speech input as if it has been passed through a communication channel that garbles the speech waveform, producing a "noisy" or distorted version of the original words spoken. By modeling the distortion, its effects can be removed, and the original signal can be reconstructed.

In speech recognition, **noise** refers to variations in pronunciation that distort words' canonical form. For example, the canonical pronunciations of *did* and *you* are [dɪd] and [ju], but in an utterance like "Did you go yet?" those two words may be pronounced something like [dɪdʒu] (e.g., [dɪdʒugoʊjɛt]). Other sources of noise include acoustic variation introduced by the microphone or telephone network that the computer program gets its information from. Accounting for this variability makes it possible to decode a noisy utterance and retrieve the original intended phonemes.

In practical terms, speech recognizers solve the noisy channel problem by comparing an input speech waveform to a huge number of potential sentences and choosing the one that is most likely to have generated the input signal. Speech is highly variable, and uncertainty is an inherent part of the comparison process. Therefore, speech recognizers rely on a number of components designed to handle specific portions of the recognition process.

These components work together to provide the best guess at what a person originally said and produce the final recognized text.

15.2.3 Components of an Automatic Speech Recognition System

A typical speech recognition system consists of several components, each layered on top of the previous. Here is a brief overview of the four main components. At the base is a signal processing component responsible for converting a speech waveform into a numeric representation that can be used for further processing. An acoustic model provides a way to map energy in the speech waveform onto phonemes. Pronunciation and language models describe the sound and word sequences that the recognizer is likely to encounter. We will now go through each component in more detail.

    a. Signal Processing. The first step in the speech recognition process involves recording the speech waveform with a microphone and storing it in a manner that is suitable for further processing by a computer. Measurements of the speech signal are taken every 10 to 20 milliseconds, and these measurements are transformed into a digital representation of acoustic features that expresses information about the amount of energy present at different frequencies. One purpose of this acoustic feature extraction is to separate two kinds of information in the waveform: information about vocal tract characteristics (e.g., pitch, speaker identity, etc.) and information that corresponds to phonetic segments (e.g., the acoustic differences that distinguish [p] from [b]). This portion of the speech recognition process can be seen as an application of the source-filter theory of speech production (see Section 15.1.3). The output of the signal processing stage is a compact, numeric representation of the energy values in the original speech waveform.

    b. Acoustic Modeling. The second step in converting an acoustic waveform into words is mapping the energy values extracted during the signal processing stage onto symbols for phones. In order to carry out this conversion, the computer needs access to a model of what different phones' energy levels are like. An acoustic model of phones is typically created by automatically aligning a large set of audio recordings of speech with phonetic transcriptions that have been prepared for this purpose. The resulting data set—the mapping between segments of sound in the recording and symbols in the transcription—is used to compute how often particular energy values are associated with each phone. Because speech is so variable, similar energy values may be associated with more than one phone. Instead of relying on only one possible association from energy values to phones, speech recognition systems use a probabilistic calculation of the most likely mapping from a set of acoustic measurements to a phone label. This approach allows for some flexibility in dealing with uncertain energy measurements.

    Because energy measurements are taken at such short time intervals, it is also useful to break sound segments down into smaller parts and map the energy values onto those smaller parts instead of taking the phoneme as a whole. Most speech recognition systems break phones down into three parts: an onset (beginning), a middle, and an offset (end). Treating portions of a phone separately makes it possible to map them onto the acoustic measurements more accurately. The energy values in the onset and offset of a phone vary due to co-articulation effects from preceding or following phones, while the energy in the middle portion is relatively stable, regardless of the environment in which the phone is produced.

    c. Pronunciation Modeling. Because of the inherent uncertainty in identifying individual phones, speech recognizers rely on knowledge of which sequences of phones are most likely in some given language. This knowledge can be used to filter out unlikely sound sequences. For example, [n] and [ŋ] are relatively similar in terms of their energy characteristics, and a speech recognizer may tend to confuse them. However, no English words start with [ŋ], while many words start with [n]. Knowledge of this sort can help a speech recognizer assign the correct label even when the acoustic information is not sufficiently reliable.

Building a pronunciation model is fairly straightforward and mainly involves using a pronunciation dictionary to obtain the phonetic sequences that correspond to orthographic words. Alternate pronunciations may be given in cases where such information would be considered helpful. For example, in giving phone numbers it is possible to pronounce the digit <0> as [ziɹoʊ] or [oʊ], and having both pronunciations in the pronunciation model will improve recognition accuracy.

d. Language Modeling. Like acoustic modeling and pronunciation modeling, language modeling involves calculating the probability of sequences. In the case of language modeling, we are interested in calculating the probability of word sequences. For example, a language model may tell us that people are more likely to say *drive a car* than to say *drive a call,* and this information can be used by a speech recognizer to make choices about words.

Most speech recognizers use the probability of sequences of one, two, or three consecutively occurring words (called unigram, bigram, and trigram sequences, respectively). Calculating probable word sequences involves little more than counting how often each sequence occurs in a corpus (a collection of language samples; see File 15.5). Calculating unigram probabilities simply requires counting how often each word occurs in a corpus, and dividing by the total number of words. More-frequent words have a higher unigram probability. A similar calculation is performed to calculate bigram and trigram probabilities.

A language model can be calculated from any text, but it is most helpful to derive the model from text that represents the kinds of things people using the speech recognizer are likely to say. For example, knowing the probability of word sequences from the works of Shakespeare will not help a speech recognizer used for transcribing medical documents. In this case, it is better to calculate probable word sequences from similar medical documents.

e. Putting It All Together. In order to actually perform speech recognition, the output of each of the modules described above is composed in order to complete the mapping from an acoustic speech waveform to a string of recognized words. First, an input speech waveform is recorded by a microphone and converted to a sequence of acoustic features (signal processing). These acoustic features are combined with the acoustic model to generate the likelihood of individual phones (acoustic modeling). Next, the pronunciation model is applied to the proposed phonetic sequences to filter out the ones that do not correspond to actual words (pronunciation modeling). Finally, the language model is applied to this large set of possible words to filter out unlikely combinations and choose the sequence that is most likely to make sense (language modeling). Integrating these components provides an efficient way to examine many possible sound and word combinations at the same time and minimize the effort spent considering unlikely sentences.

15.2.4 Types of Speech Recognition Systems

Speech recognition systems can be categorized according to several parameters. In some cases, such as data entry or dictation, the recognized words may be the final product of the recognizer. In other cases, recognizing the words spoken may be the first step in some further natural language processing. For example, natural language dialogue systems require speech recognition as a first step toward extracting the meaning of what a user says. In such systems, recognized words must be mapped onto a recognition grammar that specifies what commands the computer should carry out in response to user input. Some of the other parameters that characterize speech recognition systems are given below.

a. Speaking Mode. A speech recognition system may accept only isolated word input or continuous speech input. Isolated word systems limit user response to single-word answers (e.g., cell phones that map names to phone numbers), or require the user to pause after each word. Continuous speech systems allow freer input and are designed to recognize running speech. Recognition accuracy is usually higher for isolated word systems, because the task is more constrained and there is less potential for ambiguity.

b. Vocabulary Size. Speech recognizers may have small (fewer than 20 words) or large (more than 20,000 words) vocabularies. Generally, recognition accuracy is higher for small vocabulary systems. A large vocabulary system that allows continuous speech input will face a more difficult recognition task due to the fact that at any given point, lots of words are potential recognition candidates.

c. Speaker Enrollment. A speech recognition system may be speaker dependent or speaker independent. A speaker-dependent system requires that a user train the system to recognize only his voice, whereas a speaker-independent system does not require such training. Recognition accuracy is generally higher for speaker-dependent systems, since there is less variability in an individual's speech than in the speech of a larger population. Typically, dictation software enrolls its users so as to provide higher-quality output for a single speaker, whereas a system providing flight information via the telephone to anyone who calls cannot use speaker enrollment since new people call the system every day.

15.2.5 Problems in Speech Recognition

The main difficulties for speech recognition revolve around the tremendous variability associated with the acoustic signal. This variability comes from several sources. At the acoustic level, any change in the physical environment such as changing the position of the microphone, echoes, background noise, or using a different microphone can have substantial effect on the acoustic signal. Whereas people accommodate these differences largely without even noticing, they are problematic for current speech recognition systems.

Phonetic variability (both among different speakers and even within the same person's speech) is another challenge for automatic speech recognition. For example, the phoneme /t/ is usually pronounced quite differently in words such as *tool, tree, still, butter,* and *button,* and these differences have to be accounted for explicitly in a speech recognizer. Sociophonetic pronunciation differences (e.g., File 10.2) or foreign accents (File 3.3) account for another source of variability that is difficult for speech recognizers to deal with.

Differences in vocal tract size and shape also affect the acoustics of the speech signal. For example, the energy characteristics of a vowel produced by a woman are somewhat different from the typical energy characteristics of the same vowel spoken by a man, and speech recognizers must have a way of adjusting to these differences. Within-speaker variability, such as differences in voice quality that arise from having a cold or being tired, or speaking rate and changes in speaking style (e.g., carefully enunciated versus casual speech), also impacts recognition accuracy.

15.2.6 Future Directions

In addition to current research aimed at improving speech recognition accuracy, researchers are also looking at ways to extend the capabilities of future speech recognition systems. One area of research involves detecting emotion in people's speech. Our tone of voice conveys lots of information that is potentially useful for a speech recognition system to know about. For example, it would be useful for a commercial speech recognition system to detect when a customer gets angry or frustrated, so that the system can immediately refer the customer to a customer representative. A related area of research concerns detecting which words are emphasized, since emphasized words are usually more likely to contain new topical information than words that are not emphasized.

Other researchers are interested in using knowledge of grammar to aid the recognition process. For example, it may help to know that encountering a determiner followed by a noun (e.g., *the* DET *computer* N) is more likely than encountering a determiner followed by a verb. This type of information can help a speech recognizer eliminate some types of recognition errors. Similarly, using semantic knowledge to guide the recognition process can help a system focus on words that make sense in the context of what it has already recognized.

Communicating with Computers

15.3.1 Interacting with Computers Using Natural Language

Computers are tools that humans use for various tasks. However, the way we use computers often differs in an important way from the way we use other tools such as a hammer or a backhoe: someone who uses a computer interacts with the computer. When this interaction involves giving and receiving information, it makes sense to talk about *communicating* with a computer.

For humans, natural language is the most familiar, convenient, and efficient method of communication in most situations. Therefore, it is clearly desirable for people to be able to use natural language to interact with computers. However, as is the case for many tasks, what is effortless for people can be extremely difficult for computers. Computers have been around for over sixty years, but systems allowing effective natural language communication with them are relatively new. This file will discuss such systems and some of the issues and difficulties that arise in developing them.

15.3.2 Interactive Text-Based Systems

One of the first computer programs that could carry on a conversation using a natural language (in this case, English) was a program called ELIZA, which was created in 1966 by Joseph Weizenbaum and was designed to carry on dialogue parodying a psychotherapy session. ELIZA is text based, meaning that the user types input in using a keyboard and ELIZA responds on the screen. Here is a sample conversation with ELIZA:

(1) 1. User: I am stressed.
  2. ELIZA: How long have you been stressed?
  3. User: Since I started writing this chapter.
  4. ELIZA: Can you elaborate on that?
  5. User: I can't stop thinking about human-computer interaction.
  6. ELIZA: Have you tried?
  7. User: No I guess not really.
  8. ELIZA: You are being a bit negative.
  9. User: Well what can I do to change my attitude?
  10. ELIZA: Why do you say your attitude?
  11. User: Because you said I was being negative.

ELIZA may appear to understand the user, but, in fact, the program works by simply looking for basic patterns in the user input and constructing responses in response to those patterns. Here is an example of one of ELIZA's strategies in action:

(2) User: I was once the captain of a ship.
    ELIZA: Why do you tell me you were once the captain of a ship just now?

> User: I was never good at soccer.
> ELIZA: Why do you tell me you were never good at soccer just now?

All ELIZA has to do to generate the responses in (2) is to look for the pattern *I was* [OTHER-WORDS] in what the user types and respond with *Why do you tell me you were* [OTHER-WORDS] *just now,* copying the OTHER-WORDS part verbatim from the input to the reply. The program need not know anything about ships or soccer, or even recognize these words. This technique is called **word spotting**: the program focuses on words it knows, like *I was,* and ignores ones it doesn't. Another example of ELIZA's word-spotting strategies occurs in lines 7–8 in example (1); the reply *You are being a bit negative* is triggered by spotting the negative words *no* and *not* in the input.

Clearly, communication with ELIZA barely counts as communication at all. Intuitively, the strategies she uses seem like a kind of cheating. But the really deficient aspect of interaction with ELIZA is that a user can't get any useful behavior or information by talking to her.

More useful programs have been created that use the same simple pattern-matching strategies to engage in productive communication. For instance, there are several "bots" (short for robots) designed to communicate about "Multi-User Dungeons," a kind of Internet role-playing game, that can give informative replies to questions about who is playing and how long they have been playing, how to use the game, etc. Here is an example conversation with a program called *Julia* written by Michael Mauldin:

(3) User: Where are we?
    Julia: We are in "The Inter Nexus"
    User: Who is here?
    Julia: Well Lenny, I see 8 players awake here:
            guest byte MadraRua Leda Lenny Mandi TheHighMage Samuel
    User: Who is asleep here?
    Julia: Well Lenny, I see 1 player asleep here: Jacques

Unlike ELIZA, Julia can recognize words she knows, such as the question *Where are we?*, retrieve the appropriate information from a database, and report it, resulting in productive, informative communication.

Programs like this perform better when their use is restricted to a **limited domain.** For instance, Julia can only give information pertaining to the specific virtual world in which she and the user are interacting. The other systems we will see below all use similar restrictions; for example, a flight booking system will generally only know words likely to come up in conversations about booking flights.

15.3.3 Spoken-Language Dialogue Systems

The examples presented above involve interaction with a computer via typed text. A more challenging task is the development of **spoken language dialogue systems**. These are to be distinguished from other computer applications involving speech, such as the Text-To-Speech programs discussed in File 15.1, or interactive systems that produce but do not understand speech, such as touch-tone telephone services that present options verbally but requires the user to answer by pressing buttons. A spoken-language dialogue system will make use of strategies used by both of these less complex types of systems, but it will require other strategies as well.

Spoken-language dialogue systems differ from one another in their degree of sophistication. For instance, some can correctly handle only **isolated speech,** in which the user speaks the input clearly and without extraneous words (e.g., *yes*). Other more complex systems can deal with **continuous speech,** in which the input can be more like normal speech (e.g., *well, yes, I guess so*). Systems also differ as to whether or not they are confused by **barge-in,** where the impatient user interrupts and talks over the computer.

The advantages of having spoken-language dialogue systems are clear. By combining them with telephone technology, they can be used by people who are nowhere near the computer running the program. For many kinds of communication, it is cheaper for a company or an organization to use a computer to handle requests than to pay people to do so. Spoken input is often more familiar and convenient for users than having to spell out words on a telephone keypad or listen to a menu of options.

Most applications of spoken-dialogue systems in use today operate over telephone lines. Since the late 1980s, some U.S. telephone companies have used spoken-language dialogue systems to allow customers to place and accept or reject calls, use a calling card, and perform other services. A growing number of companies now use this technology to allow customers to access services by phone, for example, to place orders, request or cancel a service, or check an account status. Other automated services include inquiring about train and flight timetables and reserving flight and train tickets. An example from the CMU Darpa Communicator, an automated telephone-based dialogue system for booking flight information, is given in (4).

(4) System: Hello. Welcome to the Carnegie Mellon Communicator. Are you a registered user?
  User: Hi, this is Alex Rudnicky. I'd like to fly to Charleston, please.
  System: Hello, Dr. Rudnicky, I'm glad to hear from you again. You can ask me for help at any time. You can fly to Charleston in South Carolina or Charleston in West Virginia.
  User: South Carolina.
  System: A flight to Charleston. Departing Pittsburgh on what day?
  User: On the fifteenth.
  System: I'm sorry. I must have misheard the date . . . a flight on Tuesday, February fifteenth. Okay what day would you be traveling?
  User: On March fifteenth.
  System: Traveling on Wednesday, March fifteenth. One Moment Please . . . Let's see . . . flights from Pittsburgh to Charleston . . . if you'll just hold on, this shouldn't take too long . . . Gosh, the network has been slow all day . . . I'm glad you called, though . . . I'm not sure how long this will take . . . This has been a long day, but I'm glad you called . . . hummmmm . . . this is taking longer than usual . . . I wonder if something is wrong . . . I'll bet the network is down again! I have a nonstop on US Airways departing Pittsburgh at eleven thirty five A.M., arrives Charleston at one thirty five P.M.
  User: How 'bout something later?
  System: The flight after that departs Pittsburgh at two ten P.M. arriving in Charleston at four ten P.M. Is that Okay?
  User: Okay, that's fine.
  System: Will you return to Pittsburgh from Charleston?
  User: Yes, on Saturday.
  System: Traveling on Saturday, March eighteenth. Okay I have a nonstop on US Airways departing Charleston at eleven oh five A.M. arrive Pittsburgh at one thirteen P.M. Do you want to take that?
  User: That's perfect. I'll take it.
  System: Do you need any hotel or car reservations?
  User: Yes, I'll need a car.
  System: No hotels. Do you need a car in Charleston?

User: Yes, please.

System: I've made a request for a car with Avis in Charleston. Do you want a summary of your trip?

User: Yes, please.

System: Your first flight is a US Airways flight 4072 leaving Pittsburgh at two ten P.M. on Wednesday, March fifteenth, arriving in Charleston at four ten P.M. Then, the next flight is a US Airways flight 4120 leaving Charleston at eleven oh five A.M. on Saturday, March eighteenth, arriving in Pittsburgh at one thirteen P.M. I've made no hotel reservations for your trip. I've requested a rental car in Charleston. Are you satisfied with this itinerary?

User: Yes.

System: Mail sent to air@cs.cmu.edu. Thank you for using the Carnegie Mellon Communicator. Please tell me any comments. When you're finished, just hang up.

As this example shows, the computer can give timetable information and book a flight in a way very much as a human travel agent might.

15.3.4 Components of a Spoken-Language Dialogue System

Take a closer look at the dialogue example in (4). What are the different components that must be present to allow such a dialogue to take place?

a. Automatic Speech Recognition. For computer programs that use a spoken interface (rather than a written interface), speech recognition is a necessary first step. As described in File 15.2, speech recognition involves the use of computers to transform spoken language into written (or computer-understandable) language. You may have already used a speech recognition system if you have been polled by a computer over the telephone or if you have a home computer with such capabilities. One system of speech recognition uses sound templates (or sound patterns) of individual words, which are matched to the incoming words through a microphone. For a very simple dialogue system in which the user will say a limited number of utterances, this strategy may suffice. This process is slow and limited, however, and may produce errors if a user's speech is not sufficiently similar to the templates stored in the system.

A more linguistic approach to speech recognition involves combining all the levels of linguistic knowledge (e.g., phonology, syntax, semantics, pragmatics) in order to allow speaker-independent understanding of continuous speech. In this case, speech recognition systems make use of acoustic cues to help figure out what sounds are being spoken. The sound waves themselves often don't contain enough information to determine what the words are. As a classic example, the phrase *How to recognize speech,* when spoken rapidly, sounds almost exactly like *How to wreck a nice beach.* Deciding which of the two possibilities is right generally requires further information, for example, what the topic of conversation is. The other parts of a spoken-language dialogue system can provide such information to help make such decisions. For instance, if the computer has just asked *What is your customer number?* the dialogue management component (see below) should expect the reply to contain words for numbers. This can help the speech recognizer decide that a sequence of sounds that could be understood as *tooth reef oar* should actually be understood as *two three four.*

b. Language Processing and Understanding. For some tasks, it is sufficient to use simple techniques such as word-spotting and pattern matching to process the user's input and use that simple input to accomplish a given task. Other tasks require that the computer reach more of an "understanding" of what the user says. This is true when the system asks the user an open-ended question such as "What seems to be the problem?" or "What can I do for you today?" When there is potential for a wide range of answers, the system must decipher not only the individual words, but the intention of the speaker. Often a deep analysis of the input is required, including building syntax trees to figure out the input's structure. Analyzing sentences syntactically is known as **parsing,** which is a difficult and sometimes slow process. Syntactic rules alone are not sufficient to guide the parsing process. Semantics, pragmatics, context, and world knowledge must play a role as well. This is why limited-domain applications are often more successful than very broad applications; when the context of an utterance is known, it is easier to deduce the meaning of that utterance.

c. Dialogue Management. An important part of carrying on a conversation is keeping track of the context and what the topic of conversation is. Since a system such as a flight reservation application is really working together with the user toward the common goal of booking a flight, it needs to understand the **intentional structure** of the conversation. For instance, in (4), the main intention is to schedule a travel itinerary, but this goal can be achieved only by accomplishing certain subtasks. Thus, in (4), the subtask of determining the desired departure and arrival cities is undertaken first, followed by the task of determining the day and time of travel. The need to structure conversation in this way may seem so obvious as to be hardly worth mentioning; however, the computer needs to be told how to complete each step. The system needs this information in order to know how to interpret the user's input, how to reply to the user's input, and what kinds of questions it needs to ask of the user. A large part of the system design process is devoted to how the dialogue should "flow," which depends on the subgoals of the dialogue.

The dialogue management component may also be responsible for dealing with error recovery, that is, getting the conversation back on track after a misunderstanding, for example, one caused by a speech recognition problem. For example, the system in (4) simply asked for clarification (*I'm sorry. I must have misheard the date . . . Okay what day would you be traveling?*) when it was unable to make out what the user said.

d. Text Generation. Text generation involves the use of computers to respond to humans using natural language (whether it be written or synthesized into speech) by creating sentences that convey the relevant information. Just as was the case with text understanding, syntactic rules alone are not sufficient to generate meaningful text. A text generation program must know which real-world knowledge is relevant before it decides on such things as the type of sentence it should generate (e.g., question, statement), or what tenses, order, and types of words it should use.

Sometimes the system's replies need to be more than canned answers. Often, a system retrieves an answer to a user's question from a database and needs to explain that answer to the user. The answer will probably be in an internal computer language that the user cannot understand, so it is necessary for the computer to translate from this answer to a suitable sentence of natural language. For example, an answer from a database containing flight information may look like this in a system's internal language:

(5) DEP_AIRPORT	ARR_AIRPORT	AIRLINE	DEP_TIME	ARR_TIME
CMH	JFK	American	11:45am	14:30pm

This table cannot be read to the user the way it is. Rather, the information needs to be put into a sentence like *There is an American Airlines flight leaving Port Columbus at 11:45 A.M. and arriving at JFK at 2:30 P.M.* This is often accomplished via a template that looks something like this: "There is a/an AIRLINE flight leaving DEP_AIRPORT at DEP_TIME and arriving at ARR_AIRPORT at ARR_TIME." A system may have several different templates to express the same information in order to not sound repetitive or to stress some information over other information. More complex systems use syntactic trees rather than templates to construct sentences, in a process analogous to parsing.

e. Speech Synthesis. Finally, if the computer program is one that interacts in spoken language rather than written language, the words that make up the generated text must be converted into a sequence of sounds. This process is discussed in greater detail in File 15.1.

15.3.5 Evaluation of Interactive Systems

Especially for commercial systems, the ultimate test of success is customer satisfaction. The best way to measure satisfaction is to have people who do not know anything about the application try to use it. Data can be recorded on how often the users get the results they need (e.g., the right flight information in a timetable system), how long it takes to do so, how many times the system misunderstands the input, and so on. The users can also answer questionnaires about their experiences that can be used to guide improvements. Experiments that test interactive text-based systems are important for commercial applications, because satisfaction can be affected by unexpected factors, such as whether users tend to have a preference for a male or a female voice. Such factors have no bearing on linguistic principles at work in the system per se, but they do have a profound effect on how useful the software eventually turns out to be.

However, interactive systems can become large and complex, and this creates a problem for testing. The system needs to be functional before it can be tested in realistic situations, but the information gained from such testing is much more useful if it is available early on to guide development. Once an application is up and running, many aspects of it can be hard to change. A common solution is the use of **Wizard of Oz simulations,** in which the users think they are interacting with the actual computer system, but in fact (in the manner of the wizard from Frank Baum's book), a hidden human controller simulates some aspects of the system. For example, the system developers may be interested in testing whether users prefer to have some kinds of information repeated twice. The experiment can be set up so that the "wizard" can hear the user and then choose a response that a Text-To-Speech component speaks aloud back to the user. In this way, both confirmation options can be tried, and the developer gains feedback about the human-computer interaction without fully building the system. Then the results of the experiments can be built into the final version of the program.

FILE 15.4

==

Machine Translation

15.4.1 What Is Machine Translation?

The existence of a large number of diverse languages and cultures makes for a much more interesting world, but at the same time it poses a problem when texts in one language need to be read in another. The task of converting the contents of a text written in one language (the **source language**) into a text in another language (the **target language**) is referred to as **translation**.

The need for translation may arise not only in the case of literary works but also in the world of international business, where all kinds of reports, legal documents, instruction manuals, technical documents, and correspondence must be routinely, rapidly, and accurately translated. **Machine Translation** (MT)—the use of computers to carry out translation—has recently emerged as a viable alternative to human translators for such business and technical translating needs. Two main factors make MT an attractive alternative. First, with increasing globalization, the volume of business-oriented translation has increased so much in recent years that often there aren't enough translators to meet the demand. Second, and perhaps more pressing, human translators can be extremely expensive. For example, a translation into English of a Japanese technical document of moderate difficulty could cost up to 30 cents a word, so that a standard double-spaced page containing 300 words would cost $90.

From the user's point of view, speed, accuracy, and cost of translation are the main issues, and MT's goal is to optimize these elements: to provide accurate translations at high speed and a very low cost. Although many commercial MT systems exist today—some of them fairly successful—the fact remains that not enough is known about language and the process of translation to enable a computer to duplicate the efforts of a human being. In this file, we consider what the process of translation involves and how computers are made to approximate this process.

15.4.2 The Translation Problem

Suppose that you are a translator, and that you work with Japanese and English. Given a sentence in Japanese, how would you proceed? First, you must understand the content of the text. To do this, you would have to consult a physical or mental dictionary to assign meanings to the words, and you would have to parse the structure correctly, assigning meaning to the whole sentence. Your decisions about the meanings you assign to each word and the correct parse will depend on "common sense" and on several syntactic, semantic, and pragmatic factors. Having understood the sentence, your next step would be to create a sentence in English that is equivalent in meaning. Again, you would look up English equivalents of the Japanese words in a physical or mental dictionary and construct a grammatical English sentence using those words. This process sounds so deceptively simple that many scientists and philosophers were fooled into believing it could be easily mechanized.

To appreciate the difficulty involved in translation, let us consider a simple example:

your job is to translate into English a sentence from a car repair manual written in Japanese. Suppose that the Japanese text instructs the reader to remove the front wheels. As it happens, Japanese does not have a plural marker to refer to more than one wheel, like the -s in *wheels*. The Japanese text may say either something like 'remove both front wheel,' or it may just say something like 'remove front wheel.' In the former case, there will be no problem in translating the sentence into English with the plural *wheels* because the word for 'both' is present in the Japanese version. But in the latter case, only the context can tell the translator whether the instruction is to remove a single front wheel or both front wheels. This would involve extralinguistic knowledge about the particular procedure: does it require the removal of both the front wheels or not? This sort of knowledge is extremely difficult, some say impossible, to encode in an MT system.

Another simple example is the problem of lexical ambiguity. In German, there are two words that correspond to English *wall*, with *Mauer* referring to an external wall and *Wand* referring to an internal wall. A human translator translating from English to German would know which one to use from the context, but encoding this information into an MT system is not an easy task. In a real translation, such problems (and many others) appear so frequently that mechanizing translation appears to require simulating general human intelligence in addition to knowledge of language.

Perhaps the first person to try to automate the translation process was a Russian named Petr Smirnov-Troyanskii. In 1933 he developed a three-step process: (1) analysis of the source language, (2) the conversion of source language sequences into target language sequences, and (3) the synthesis of these target language sequences into a normal target language form. These three stages form the conceptual basis of most MT systems today, with conversion, the second stage, receiving the focus of attention.

In the United States, the first steps toward building MT systems culminated in a public demonstration at Georgetown University in 1954. Although this MT system was very modest in scope, it sparked a great deal of interest, and large-scale funding became available for MT research. Over the following decade, however, it soon became apparent that the main aim of achieving **fully automatic high-quality translation** (FAHQT) was far from being achieved. Growing criticism of the MT effort resulted in government sponsors of MT research forming the Automatic Language Processing Advisory Committee (ALPAC) in 1964. This committee came to the strong conclusion that useful MT had no "immediate or predictable prospect." The ALPAC report turned out to be very influential, and funding for MT research in the United States was effectively cut off for subsequent years, although research continued in other countries. It wasn't until 1985 that MT was revived in the United States, this revival being due largely to successful efforts in Japan and Europe, improvements in computer technology and developments in linguistics, and more realistic expectations about the goals of MT: instead of aiming for FAHQT, the emphasis shifted to machine-aided human translation, and human-aided machine translation.

15.4.3 MT System Design

In developing an MT system, several design decisions need to be made at the start that will determine the details of the final working system. The design decisions discussed below do not constitute a complete list; other factors, like the choice of a linguistic theory or framework and certain computational decisions, also play an important role (see the additional reading suggested in File 15.6).

First, the designers need to decide whether the system will be fully or partly automatic. A fully automatic system would, in principle, not require any human intervention in the translation process: given a source language text, the MT system would output an accurate translation in the target language. However, as the discussion above shows, this is rarely a realistic goal. Partial automation is a more practical approach, and one that most systems use. In partial automation, the source language text can first be **pre-edited** by a person, so as to "prime" it for the MT system. Typically, pre-editing involves rewriting the source language text into a **controlled language,** which has fewer ambiguities and simpler syntactic patterns, or marking the source language text to indicate word boundaries, proper names, plurals, and so on. Pre-editing can be performed by anyone fluent in the source language; it does not need to be performed by a bilingual or a translator. Thus, this sort of design can be cost- and resource-effective.

A system can also be designed to be **interactive,** so that it turns to a person to resolve ambiguities (such as the singular-plural problem discussed above). Finally, the output of the system can be **post-edited.** Here, a person revises the machine's output, either correcting errors due to ambiguities in the source text (e.g., converting wrong instances of singular nouns to plurals), or converting the translated text into an idiomatic version of the target language. While these two tasks must be carried out by a bilingual, they are less time-intensive than translating a document from scratch.

Another major consideration is the proposed application of the system. Will the system serve to translate texts in a particular technical or business field, or will it be for general use? Generally, the more limited the type of document, the easier it is to design the system, since a more restricted field allows the use of a smaller lexicon and less variation in syntactic patterns.

A third consideration is whether to build a **multilingual** system, involving more than one language pair, or a **bilingual** one, which deals with only one language pair. Bilingual systems may be bi-directional, carrying out translation in either direction for the language pair chosen (e.g., Japanese to English, or English to Japanese), or unidirectional (e.g., Japanese to English only). A real-life example of a multilingual system is the European Commission's Eurotra project, which aims to translate nine languages in all directions—that is, 72 language pairs!

Another consideration is which translation approach to adopt. MT systems in operation today use one of three strategies. The oldest one (1950s to early 1960s) is known as **direct translation.** In this approach, the MT system is designed for bilingual, unidirectional translation; every word is translated, and then some reordering is performed based on morphological and syntactic rules of the target language in order to produce the finished text. The English sentence *He bought two white houses,* for example, would be translated into Spanish as shown in (1).

(1) Direct translation

Source language text:	He	bought	two	white	houses
Breakdown in source language:	He	buy	two	white	house
Dictionary look-up:	El	comprar	dos	blanco	casa
Adaptation to target language:	El	compró	dos	casas	blancas

As you can see, the translation in (1) required that the translation software know words of English and Spanish, rules about word order (such as whether adjectives come before or after nouns), and rules about agreement and morphology (such as how to mark the past tense). The example in (1) suggests that direct translation is fairly effective, and in some cases it can be. However, direct translation does not include any attempt at parsing or semantic analysis. The result is, predictably, unsatisfactory, as shown in the Russian-to-English examples in (2) and (3).

(2) Vcera my tselyi cas katalis' na lodke.
   Yesterday we the entire hour rolled themselves on a boat.
   Intended: Yesterday we went out boating for a whole hour.

(3) Ona navarila scei na nescol' ko dnei.
   It welded on cabbage soups on several days.
   Intended: She cooked enough cabbage soup for several days.

As computer science and linguistic theory developed, an improved method was proposed whereby the source language text is first translated into an intermediate abstract representation that contains sufficient information in it to allow the creation of a target language text. This is referred to as the **interlingua** method. This method is an improvement over the direct method, because it allows the creation of multilingual systems with relative ease: for every language, we only need to have a method for analyzing the language into an intermediate representation and a way to generate the language from this intermediate representation; the intermediate representation is common to all the language pairs, as the representation in (4) illustrates.

(4) Interlingua method

```
Language 1                                      Language 1
Language 2 ————→ interlingua ————→ Language 2
Language 3                                      Language 3
etc.                                            etc.
```

However, with this method the problem is that creating a common intermediate representation, or interlingua, is a very difficult task, even for related languages such as English and German. In spite of the emergence of sophisticated syntactic and semantic theories of natural language over the last 40 years or so, we simply do not yet know enough about language to create an interlingua for MT systems.

In response to the difficulties encountered in attempts to create language-independent intermediate representations, one solution is to have language-dependent ones. Such a strategy is called the **transfer** method. In this case, the source text is analyzed to produce a source language intermediate representation, which is then transferred to a target language intermediate representation, and then the target language text is generated. Although the transfer method involves more steps, it is more effective than the interlingua method because language-dependent intermediate representations are easier to create. Because the system is automated, the extra steps increase the time to produce a translation only a small amount.

A central issue in designing MT systems has been the lack of an adequate theory of translation, which in turn rests on the development of satisfactory linguistic theories. But some MT researchers dispute the central role of linguistics in MT systems, and alternative strategies range from example-based MT (the use of large amounts of pre-translated parallel texts of the source and target languages) to statistics-based MT (e.g., using probability to determine the likelihood that a word in the source language corresponds to a word or words in the target language). The trend most recently, however, has been toward hybrid or mixed systems, that is, systems that are based on more than one principle (linguistics, examples, statistics).

MT systems still have a long way to go, but there have been some success stories. One such case is the Canadian METEO system for translating English-language weather reports into French. In Canada, a bilingual country, weather bulletins must be produced in both languages, but translating weather bulletins is an extremely boring and repetitive job. The METEO system was installed in 1976 and has been producing accurate translations ever since; as of 1997, METEO translates some 30 million words a year with 93% accuracy. It succeeds precisely because the range of expressions found in weather reports is very limited; this illustrates the fact, mentioned earlier, that restricted types of documents are easier for designing MT systems. As we continue to learn more about language and develop more complete theories of how language works, we will be able to develop machine translation software that is increasingly reliable and easy to use.

Corpus Linguistics

15.5.1 What Is a Corpus?

So far in this chapter, we have discussed ways that we can apply our knowledge of various structural components of language—for example, phonetics, syntax, and semantics—in order to create machines that are able to produce or interpret human language in some way. We have seen that these applications have a wide variety of uses. However, there is a second side to computational linguistics: using computer programs to help us analyze language. Computers have the ability to process a large amount of data in a relatively short period of time, so we can use computers to find patterns in linguistic data much more rapidly than we could if we had to examine those data manually. Using computers therefore allows us to test hypotheses about language and linguistic rules more quickly. Using computers to analyze linguistic data has also made it more practical to think about linguistic rules in a new way.

Traditionally, linguists have tried to describe and analyze linguistic rules as though, for any linguistic form, either that rule has been followed or else it has not been followed. This approach would say, for example, that in syntax, sentences are either grammatical or not; in morphology, words are either well formed or not; and in pragmatics, utterances are either felicitous or not. According to this traditional view, "proper" linguistic description is a matter of being able to discern and then state the rules that distinguish the set of well-formed linguistic forms from the set that is not. Recently, some linguistic investigation has begun to depart from this binary "acceptable-or-unacceptable" tradition. Of late, the statistical properties of language have received more and more attention for the insights they may bring to theoretical issues, especially in phonology and syntax. Psycholinguists have also long been interested in the effects that frequency (of words, phonemes, etc.) has on human language processing. Finally, computational applications such as **natural language processing** (NLP) and speech recognition have placed more emphasis on incorporating statistical models of language into theoretical frameworks.

The central insight here is that certain types of linguistic forms (phones, syllables, words, phrases, or sentences) appear more frequently than others. Thus, instead of saying that a certain construction is "acceptable" or "unacceptable," we may want to say that it is "relatively common" or "relatively rare." However, this insight by itself is of quite limited use without some idea of just how frequent particular linguistic phenomena are. How might these frequencies be calculated? Ideally, we might follow around an individual for his entire life and record all the language he ever experiences—but obviously, this is impractical. An approximation to this is to gather up a more or less representative sample of language (either spoken or written) and use statistics over this sample as estimates for the language as a whole. A collected body of text is called a **corpus** (plural *corpora*), from the Latin word for 'body.' A linguistic corpus is a collection of linguistic materials (written, spoken, or some combination) appropriate for specific purposes of research, such as data analysis, training, and testing. **Corpus linguistics** involves the design and the annotation of corpus materials that are required for specific purposes.

15.5.2 Kinds of Corpora

Because different kinds of corpora are more or less appropriate for different tasks, one must differentiate various types of corpora, based on what the source material is and on what kinds of extra-linguistic information are added.

a. Source of the Corpus. Corpora can be composed from spoken, signed, or written language. As written documents are comparatively easy to obtain and store electronically, the vast majority of corpora are composed of written texts. Often, then, we find corpora composed entirely of news texts like the *Wall Street Journal* or composed of various books, stories, technical reports, and other written varieties of language. However, because many linguists are interested in how people speak (see File 1.3 on speech and writing), there is a great demand for corpora composed of speech. Corpora may also be composed from a combination of speech and writing. The British National Corpus, for example, contains about 90% written text and 10% spoken—the larger portion of written text due to the fact that it is much easier to obtain.

In addition, corpora can be classified by genre of source material. Because news text is very common and easy to obtain, it is often used as the source for corpora. For example, one English corpus consists of *Wall Street Journal* text from the early 1990s; one Chinese corpus consists of texts collected from newspapers in mainland China, Hong Kong, and Taiwan, also from the early 1990s. Most very large corpora are of this type, particularly in less commonly studied languages.

Of course, news text does not provide a very broad picture of how language is used, so there have been initiatives to create so-called **balanced corpora,** corpora which try to remain balanced between different genres. The Brown corpus, for example, contains newspaper stories, but also scientific papers, western stories, and so on. Although such corpora are often quite small (the Brown corpus contains only a million words), they are often more useful for accurate pictures of relative frequencies of words than news-heavy corpora.

Most of these corpora tend to capture language in one particular time or place. For the most part, they are frozen, meaning that once a specified amount of texts has been collected and annotated, the corpus is complete; this is called a **reference corpus.** Another possibility is to have a **monitor corpus:** as new texts continue to be written or spoken, a monitor corpus continues to grow, gathering more and more data.

We can also find corpora in many languages. Usually, this means that we find the same text written in two or more languages. The Hansard corpus, for example, contains French and English versions of the same Canadian parliamentary session. There are also several corpora, such as the MULTEXT corpus, which contain more than two languages. The MULTEXT-East corpus, for example, has George Orwell's book *1984* written in English and in seven Eastern European languages.

Although a corpus could theoretically contain multiple unaligned texts in different languages, texts that contain the same sentences written in different languages are more useful data for applications such as machine translation. Such texts are commonly called **bi-texts.** A corpus containing bi-texts is called a **parallel corpus.** It is useful for a machine translation system to see the same thing written in two different languages, because it can use this information to learn what words and syntactic patterns correspond to each other in each language. In German and English bi-texts, for example, the machine translation system can use the information that every time *I* occurs in the English text, *ich* occurs in the German text. However, matching the corresponding parts of the corpus accurately (known as aligning the corpus) is a nontrivial task that has only recently become practical to perform automatically.

b. Levels of Annotation. Linguistics is generally divided into several subfields, all studying a particular aspect of language (see the topics covered in the table of contents in this book). Likewise, corpora can be made to show different kinds of linguistically relevant information, called **representations**. For example, the word *chair* is a third-person singular noun. Each representation receives a label called **annotation.** For example, the fact that *chair* is a third-person singular noun can be labeled as "chair_3SN." One of the most common annotations is lexical category. Each word in the corpus is given a lexical category label (e.g., noun, verb, adjective, etc.). But we can have other labels, such as a word's function in the sentence (e.g., subject or direct object), the phonetic transcription, or the word's root (e.g., *dog* is the root of *dogs*). Additionally, more complicated annotation, such as the syntactic tree structure of a sentence, can be included in a corpus. Often, this kind of representation builds off of lexical category annotation. These corpora usually require many years to develop, and they also require a way to encode the more complicated annotations.

Additional kinds of annotation are possible for spoken corpora. Most spoken corpora include at least a transcription of the audio and/or visual recording, typically a word-by-word transcription in standard spelling. An example is the British National Corpus, which uses standard spelling and also renders words like *gotta, um,* and so forth.

Some spoken corpora use phonetic transcription to render spoken words or use both regular spelling and phonetic transcription alongside speech. Phonetic transcription provides information on which segments (or phones) were actually uttered. A variety of phonetic encodings are possible here, depending on the needs of the end-users (often programs as well as people), who may require input using limited characters, one-letter-per-sound, or other constraints. For example, *gotta go* could be written as [ɡɑɾə ɡoʊ] (IPA), [gA4@ go] (Sampa encoding), or [g aa dx ax g ow] (DARPA encoding).

Recently, information about *suprasegmentals* (prosodic elements) such as intonation and phrasing has been transcribed as well. In a number of corpora, the ToBI (for **To**nes and **B**reak **I**ndices) system for prosodic transcription is used (see File 2.5).

Syntactic, phonetic, and especially prosodic annotation are rare because they are time-intensive and they require a person trained in syntax, phonetic transcription, or prosodic transcription, respectively. The Corpus of Spoken Dutch (Corpus Gesproken Nederlands), for example, contains syntactic, phonetic, and prosodic annotation. It was constructed between 1998 and 2004. All of the almost 9 million spoken words were transcribed using standard Dutch spelling. About 1 million words received additional phonetic annotation, and the same number of words received additional syntactic annotation. Fewer than 250,000 words were transcribed prosodically. These numbers illustrate how difficult and time-consuming corpus annotation is.

Most corpus annotation is done first with a specially designed computer program and then is carefully hand-checked afterwards. Improving the quality of both of these steps is crucial to getting accurate data for other applications and has become an interesting natural-language processing task in its own right.

Practice

File 15.1—Speech Synthesis

Exercises

1. File 15.1 mentions that TTS systems use spelling-to-sound rules to generate the pro-nunciation for some words. This process is used for words that have rule-governed pronunciation. For example, <ou> is usually pronounced [aʊ] as in *mouse*. However, <ou> in *bought* is pronounced [ɔ]. The rule a TTS system uses to account for *bought* is something like "pronounce <ou> as [ɔ] if it is followed by <ght>."

   i. Write pronunciation rules that would allow the TTS system to produce the words in parts (a)–(e) correctly. (Focus on the letter <c> in part (a) and on the vowels in parts (b)–(e).)

   ii. Some of the words are irregular and cannot be pronounced correctly using spelling-to-sound rules. Which are they, and how would a TTS system pronounce them, ac-cording to the rules that you gave for part (i)? How can you make the TTS system pronounce them correctly?

   a. call, cab, cake, cone, cob, cinder, city, cell, cent, cello
   b. zoo, boo, moon, spoon, food, room, good, stood, book
   c. tough, rough, plough, enough, cough, bough
   d. mould, could, would, should
   e. bone, home, rode, stove, dove, love, done, move

Activities

2. Go to one of the following Web sites and answer questions (i)–(iii):

   http://www.research.att.com/~ttsweb/tts/demo.php
   http://www.lhsl.com/realspeak/demo/
   http://www.naturalvoices.att.com/

   i. Try to construct input that the speech synthesizer cannot say correctly. You may type in words, full sentences, even song lyrics if you like. Describe how the system mispronounces it, and venture a guess as to why the system may have a problem with the input you chose.

   ii. For the input that the speech synthesizer did say correctly, were there any instances that impressed you? If so, explain why you were impressed. If not, say why you were not impressed even though the output was correct.

   iii. Repeat Exercises (i) and (ii) using a different speech synthesizer. How do the two systems compare? Which system do you think is better? Why?

3. RUTH (Rutgers University Talking Head) is an animated talking face. Go to the following Web site and view the sample animation created with RUTH. Then answer questions (i)–(iv).

http://www.cs.rutgers.edu/~village/ruth/

 i. Did RUTH's speech sound natural? Was it intelligible? Based on your judgment of how natural and intelligible RUTH sounds, what kind of speech synthesis system might RUTH be using? Justify your answer.
 ii. In order for us to see and hear RUTH, natural-looking head- and eye-movements, facial expressions, as well as lip movements need to be simulated. How natural does RUTH look? Which movements or expressions look unnatural? How so?
 iii. Simulating appropriate lip movements to accompany speech is called visual speech synthesis. Appropriate lip movements are important because, if done correctly, they aid the perception of synthesized speech (which can sometimes be hard to understand). Listen to the animation again, this time without looking at RUTH. Do you think that RUTH's lip movements help you understand the system's speech?
 iv. A problem of visual speech synthesis is co-articulation. If you wanted to synthesize lip movements, how would you deal with the problem of co-articulation? What are the advantages or disadvantages of your approach?

File 15.2—Automatic Speech Recognition

Discussion Question

4. IBM's ViaVoice is dictation software that purports to write down whatever you say. The product description claims that ViaVoice allows you to write a ten-page report in one hour.
 i. What type of speech recognition system would be needed to write a ten-page report in an hour? How error-prone do you think such a system would be? (Think about speaking mode, vocabulary size, and speaker enrollment.)
 ii. Once the system has recognized the words that you produced, how do you think it can convert the input into written text? What kinds of words are especially problematic for this task?

File 15.3—Communicating with Computers

Exercises

5. Not only can we communicate with computers, we can also use the computer to communicate with other people, for example, via e-mail. A common problem for e-mail users is spam (unwanted, unsolicited e-mails). Many people use a spam filter to redirect or throw away unwanted messages. Refer to the *Rhymes with Orange* cartoon at the beginning of this chapter to answer questions (i)–(iii).
 i. Explain how spelling the word *Viagra* as <V!2AGGRA> might let it pass through a spam filter.
 ii. How might you design a spam filter that would not allow words like <V!2AGGRA> to pass through?
 iii. Why does Hilary Price (the cartoonist) think that the tactics that get messages through spam filters would hurt sales? What does this reflect about the notions of language prescriptivism (Chapter 1) and prestige (Chapter 10)?

6. Some people believe that computers, and also cell phones, have changed written communication among people. How is the language of instant messages or text messages different from that of traditional letters? Give examples. Which features of written and spoken communication do instant messaging and text messaging have? Which do they resemble more closely: written communication or spoken communication? Justify your answer.

Activities

7. Try out ELIZA at the following Web site and answer questions (i) and (ii):

   http://www-ai.ijs.si/eliza/eliza.html

   i. Try to figure out some of the strategies ELIZA uses to formulate replies to your input. What information does ELIZA need to extract from your input to do this? What parts can ELIZA just copy verbatim?

   ii. Sometimes ELIZA's strategies don't work. For instance, one strategy for replying to a question is simply to say *Does that question interest you?*

   User: When will the Yankees win the pennant?
   ELIZA: Does that question interest you?

   ELIZA assumes that this is a question because it begins with the question word *when*. However, it is possible to trick ELIZA by using declarative sentences with *when*:

   User: When I sneeze, I see stars.
   ELIZA: Does that question interest you?

   Here ELIZA's response is not appropriate, because the user's input was not a question. Find other examples of inappropriate responses that Eliza gives to various input, and try to explain what ELIZA's strategy is and how it fails.

8. Try out the Nuance automated information system at 1-800-555-TELL (a toll-free call in the United States). Answer questions (i)–(iv) about the system.
   i. Can the system handle continuous speech or only isolated speech? Give an example.
   ii. Can the system handle barge-in?
   iii. How are misunderstandings dealt with?
   iv. Do you think the system uses simple techniques like word-spotting, or does it make more sophisticated analyses of its input? Why do you think so?

9. Listen to the dialogue given in example (4) of File 15.3 by going to the following link. Then answer questions (i)–(iv).

   http://festvox.org/ldom/ldom_com.html

   i. How natural and intelligible is the system's speech? How well does the conversation "flow"? Give examples.
   ii. What features of the system are intended to make it appear like a real person? Give examples.
   iii. Listen to how the system pronounces the e-mail address at the end of the dialogue. How is it different from the rest of the speech? What does this tell you about the kind of speech synthesis the system might be using?
   iv. How well does the system understand the user's speech? Do you think the user has to speak more clearly than he usually would?

File 15.4—Machine Translation
Activities

10. Go to one of the free online MT systems available at the following URLs:

> http://babelfish.altavista.com/
> http://www.freetranslation.com/
> http://www.worldlingo.com/products_services/worldlingo_translator.html
> http://www.translation.net/instrans.html
> http://www.translate.ru

    i. Use the system to translate some English text into a foreign language, and then translate it back into English. Does the result differ from the original? How?

    ii. Find a Web page that is written in one of the languages that the system can translate from, preferably a language that you don't know. To find such a Web page, you can use a search engine and set the search language to, for example, *Spanish*. Then search for any word or topic you like, such as *computer, rock,* or the name of a famous person.

    iii. Now, use the MT system to translate (part of) the Web page you found in (ii) into English. Is the translation comprehensible? Is the English text good enough to publish? Is it at least good enough so that you can understand what the page is about and follow the discussion?

    iv. Repeat exercises (i) and (ii) using a different MT system. How do the two systems compare with each other? Which system do you think is better? Why?

File 15.5—Corpus Linguistics
Exercise

11. Imagine you are given a corpus of English literary texts. Your professor has asked you to develop a way to do the following four things automatically. In which order would you want them to be done? Why?

    a. Find the subjects, direct objects, and indirect objects (if applicable) in each sentence.
    b. Build a syntactic tree for each sentence, so as to show which words combine together to form noun phrases, prepositional phrases, verb phrases, sentences, and so on.
    c. Give a part-of-speech tag to each word in each sentence.
    d. Produce the root for each word in the corpus.

Discussion Questions

12. Imagine you have collected fifteen hours of spoken dialogue for linguistic research. It is up to you to transcribe the speech you recorded.

    i. What advantages/disadvantages are there to using phonetic transcription to transcribe a spoken corpus? For example, if a person wanted to search for a particular word, would the word be easier to find in a phonetically transcribed corpus or in a corpus transcribed using English spelling? What kinds of research might IPA transcriptions be useful for?

    ii. Think about other ways that your corpus could be transcribed. Propose a different way to transcribe your corpus.

    iii. What advantages does your transcription system have, and what kinds of research would it be useful for?

13. A portion of the British National Corpus (BNC), the BNC-Sampler, contains 50% written and 50% spoken language. Why would the corpus designers choose an even split between spoken and written language? Is it a fair, or balanced, representation of language use overall? Would a corpus that contained 90% spoken language or 90% written language be more representative of language use? Why do you think so?

Activity

14. Search the British National Corpus by going to the following Web site and answer questions (i)–(ii).

http://www.natcorp.ox.ac.uk/

i. Find out which are the most frequent color terms in the English language: select at least ten color terms, and check the BNC for the terms' frequencies. Which are the color terms used most frequently in the corpus? Do you think the BNC accurately captures which color terms are frequently used in English? Why or why not?

ii. The word *tie* can be a noun or a verb. Find out whether it is used more frequently as a noun or as a verb: search the BNC for the word *tie* and examine the first fifty entries. (*Note:* This activity assumes that the first fifty entries are representative of the remaining entries.) How many times is *tie* used as a verb, and how many times is it used as a noun? When used as a verb, does *tie* always mean the same thing? Similarly, when used as a noun, does *tie* always mean the same thing? Why does searching just for *tie* not give you a complete picture of the relative frequencies with which *tie* is used as a verb or a noun? Which words would you have to include in your search to get a more accurate picture?

Further Readings

Kurzweil, Raymond. "When will HAL understand what we are saying? Computer speech recognition and understanding." *HAL's Legacy: 2001's Computer as Dream and Reality.* David G. Stork (ed.). Cambridge, MA: MIT Press, 1997.

Lenat, Douglas B. "I'm sorry Dave, I'm afraid I can't do that: How could HAL use language?" *HAL's Legacy: 2001's Computer as Dream and Reality.* David G. Stork (ed.). Cambridge, MA: MIT Press, 1997.

CHAPTER

16

Practical Applications

What Can You Do with Linguistics?

The past fifteen chapters have presented an introduction to the study of language and linguistics. You may now be wondering about ways in which linguistics is applied. Actor Robin Williams, in speaking about his children, once quipped "I want to introduce . . . Zachary, the linguist. He does very good. He's going to open a Syntax Repair Shop." Presumably this is not actually what Zachary will end up doing, as there's no such thing as a Syntax Repair Shop. There are, however, plenty of other applications of the study of linguistics. A few of these, though by no means all, will be described in the files that follow.

Contents

Language Education

16.1.1 Job Description

Under normal circumstances, infants and young children seem to effortlessly acquire one or more native languages. However, later in life, language acquisition becomes more difficult for most people. Additionally, many people learn a second language in a classroom environment, rather than by being immersed in the language. This is where the language teacher comes in. This file focuses on teaching a foreign language to teenagers and adults.

Language teachers work in a variety of different settings: at middle and high schools, at immersion schools, at universities, at special language schools and institutes, as teachers in a foreign country, or as private teachers and tutors. In a school or university setting, language teachers usually teach students who all have the same linguistic background, but at language schools and institutes or as private instructors they may teach students with a variety of different native languages. Depending on the setting and goal of the course(s), a teacher may teach several different classes or teach the same students for several hours every day.

Several factors determine how a teacher will teach a class. Sometimes the company or institution employing the teacher has certain requirements, for example, that all classes be taught using only the foreign language. A second factor is the level of the class: in introductory-level classes, the teacher may focus on teaching vocabulary and grammar, but there might be a different focus in advanced classes. When talking to beginning students, the teacher will have to use simple grammar and basic vocabulary. In more advanced classes, many students already have a good command of the grammar and a sufficiently large vocabulary base. Here the teacher may focus more on class discussions or reading literature. Finally, the goal of the class influences the way it is taught. Sometimes classes are intended to teach students only one aspect of a foreign language, for example, pronunciation classes or classes that teach reading scholarly literature in a foreign language. The goal of the majority of classes, however, is to teach students how to communicate in the foreign language. In many classes, all four language-related skills are taught: speaking, listening, reading, and writing.

The most common teaching methodology today is probably the **communicative approach.** This approach focuses on speaking and listening skills. Furthermore, getting the message across is considered more important than having perfect grammar. Typical activities include role playing, games, and information gap activities. In the latter, students receive only partial information about a certain topic or task and have to talk to other students to get the missing information. Classes taught using the communicative approach are usually student-centered: instead of having the teacher lecture while the students absorb, the teacher functions more as a guide or coach. He or she introduces grammar and activities and is available for questions. However, the students are expected to do much of the speaking. Every teaching methodology is based on a different philosophy as to how languages are acquired. The communicative approach is based on the belief that people learn languages through interaction with other speakers.

Apart from choosing a particular teaching methodology (or having one chosen by a company or an institution), a language teacher must be able to adapt to different learning styles and temperaments. This is especially important in a classroom setting that is not lecture oriented, in which students get actively involved.

The preceding discussion has focused on the time teachers spend in the classroom. However, much time is spent preparing classes (choosing or developing activities that ideally develop all four language-related skills and adapt to different learning styles, deciding how to introduce new grammar and vocabulary, using the frequently limited amount of time effectively, etc.), writing quizzes and exams, and grading.

16.1.2 Job Qualifications

Of course, the most important qualification for a language teacher is the ability to speak the language he or she wants to teach. It can be the teacher's native language or a second or foreign language. A number of language schools, however, accept only native speakers of a language as instructors.

There are also a number of degrees that often help and are sometimes required for certain teaching positions. In particular, a degree in a foreign language, applied linguistics, English as a second language (ESL), or education is desirable. For most full-time language education jobs, one of these degrees is needed. For example, some states in the United States require a Master's in Education to teach foreign languages at the middle or high school levels, and many language schools offering ESL classes expect certification in ESL.

However, language teaching is also something that can be done as a part-time job, free-lance, or for just a couple of hours each week. There are many opportunities, such as offering private lessons or teaching in continuing education programs. In these cases, a degree is often not required, especially if the instructor is a native speaker of the language being taught.

16.1.3 Language Education and Linguistics

A degree in linguistics is not necessary to teach foreign languages. However, knowledge of the linguistic principles of the language you want to teach is very helpful. For example, if you were teaching English pronunciation, it would be useful to be able to inform your students (usually using layman's terminology) that the regular plural morpheme has three different pronunciations: [s] as in [kæts] *cats,* [z] as in [dɑgz] *dogs,* and [əz] as in [bɹɪdʒəz] *bridges* (see File 3.2). Most students will probably figure out that the plural morpheme in *bridges* sounds different from the one in *dogs,* but many may not realize that the plural morphemes in *cats* and *dogs* are also pronounced differently. And it is up to the language teacher to point out such distinctions and explain the rules that govern the differences in pronunciation. Understanding that these differences are rule-governed and being able to teach your students the rule makes their task of learning the language much easier than it would be if they simply had to memorize lists of words that used different pronunciations of the morpheme.

Apart from such structural issues that are directly related to the language you are teaching, there are some more general areas of linguistic knowledge that can be helpful in teaching a language. For example, knowledge of theories of second-language acquisition and characteristics of foreign language learners (see File 8.5) will help you understand why your students make the mistakes they make and how your teaching can most effectively handle this. Knowledge of sociolinguistics, especially variation, will also help you prepare students to communicate with native speakers of the language. For example, students need to be aware that there is variation and that, even after years of learning a language, they may come across a speaker they cannot understand. This is especially important for languages such as German or Italian where there is so much dialectal variation that not even native speakers of the language can understand all of the dialects. Finally, a background in linguistics helps bridge the gap between the largely prescriptive rules that are commonly taught in the classroom and the linguistic reality of the language.

16.1.4 Resources

American Council of the Teaching of Foreign Languages
<http://www.actfl.org>

International Association of Teachers of English as a Foreign Language
<http://www.iatefl.org>

American Sign Language Teachers Association
<http://www.aslta.org>

Language Teachers, Tutors, and Schools Marketplace
<http://www.language-school-teachers.com>

The Internet TESL Journal: For Teachers of English as a Second Language
<http://iteslj.org>

Foreign Language Associations Listed by State
<http://www.discoverfrance.net/France/Language/DF_lang_assn.shtml>

Dave's ESL Café:
<http://www.eslcafe.com>

Speech-Language Pathology and Audiology

16.2.1 Job Description

Throughout this book, we have described the study of language, from the physical properties of speech sounds to the ways in which they are organized meaningfully into words and used in context. The ability to understand and use language is important for successful interpersonal communication.

Some people, however, have a difficult time understanding or producing language and find it challenging to communicate with others. According to the American Speech-Language Hearing Association (ASHA), between 6 and 8 million people in the United States were diagnosed with some form of language impairment in 2006. **Speech-language pathologists** (SLPs) are professionals who are trained to diagnose speech and language problems and to help individuals become more effective communicators.

SLPs work with people who have difficulty with a wide range of language-related tasks, both physical and cognitive. These difficulties may be receptive (involving the comprehension of language), expressive (involving the production and articulation of language and speech), and/or pragmatic (involving the social aspects of language). SLPs work with children or adults, both those who were born with communication disorders and those who have acquired difficulty using speech and language as a result of illness or injury. They may also offer services for people who don't have any particular communication disorder, but who want to become more effective speakers by changing their pronunciation, vocabulary, or presentation style.

SLPs treat a variety of speech impairments, stemming from a variety of causes. A problem with articulation, for example, might arise from a congenital disorder, such as cerebral palsy and cleft lip and/or palate; from a neurodegenerative disorder, such as muscular dystrophy, amyotrophic lateral disease (ALS), or Parkinson's; from a developmental disorder, such as autism; or from trauma to the brain associated with a stroke or an accident. An SLP, therefore, must be well trained in all aspects of the study of language, from the theories we have introduced in this book to the physical, anatomical, and neurological foundations of language you might expect to read about in a biology text.

SLPs make use of a number of interventions, or techniques, to help the people they work with, including skills development in one or more areas of language: form (phonology, morphology, syntax); content (semantics); or function (pragmatics). Their approach to these areas may be spoken, written, signed, or augmented—that is, assisted by a computer or other device—or a combination.

Audiologists are similar to speech-language pathologists in that they work with people who have difficulty with language, but audiologists specialize in issues related to hearing, including the evaluation of normal and impaired hearing, hearing aid and assistive-listening technology, and the prevention of hearing loss. While some individuals are born with hearing impairment, many hearing problems are acquired as a result of accidents, illness, and noise exposure. Audiologists work closely with SLPs in order to provide rehabilitation services to individuals whose communication skills are impaired as a result of hearing loss.

Speech-language pathologists and audiologists may work in a variety of settings such as schools, hospitals, community clinics, corporations and businesses, colleges and universities, or private practices. When a person comes to an SLP or an audiologist for help, the first step is to determine whether there is evidence of a speech, language, or hearing problem by conducting a thorough evaluation. If results from the assessment show that the individual is functioning at a level below what is expected for a person of his or her age or potential, then therapy services may be recommended. The type and duration of speech-language therapy or audiological rehabilitation that is prescribed will depend on the nature of the problem and the characteristics of the patient. It is the responsibility of the treating SLP or audiologist to monitor the individual's progress to determine the effectiveness of the treatment.

16.2.2 Job Qualifications

Prospective candidates to the field of speech-language pathology or audiology might complete an undergraduate degree in Speech and Hearing Science, Communication Sciences and Disorders, Psychology, Linguistics, Education, Biology, English, or other fields. However, graduate training in Speech and Hearing Science, Communication Sciences and Disorders, or an equivalent program at an accredited postsecondary institution is required in order to become a licensed speech-language pathologist or audiologist in the United States. Clinical certification in speech-language pathology or audiology requires focused clinical training during graduate school, successful completion of a national (praxis) examination, and a supervised clinical experience (Clinical Fellowship Year [CFY]) after graduation. In addition to national certification through the American Speech-Language Hearing Association (ASHA), state licensure is also required. Additional certification may be necessary depending on the desired area of clinical focus. For example, school certification is necessary for public school employment, and a PhD is generally required for advanced research and teaching.

16.2.3 Resources

American Speech-Language-Hearing Association
<http://www.asha.org>

American Academy of Audiology
<http://www.audiology.org>

National Student Speech-Language-Hearing Association
<http://www.nsslha.org/nsslha>

Canadian Association of Speech-Language Pathologists and Audiologists
<http://www.caslpa.ca/english/careers/careers.asp>

The Corporate Speech Pathology Network
<http://www.corspan.org>

Speech-Language Pathology Resources
<http://www.speech-languagepathologist.org>

FILE 16.3

═════════════════════════════════

Language and Law

16.3.1 Legal Applications of Linguistics

One field in which there are many distinct applications for linguistic analysis is law. Although in general the legal professions—unlike several others discussed in this chapter—do not require explicit training in language or in linguistic analysis, an awareness of linguistic principles can nonetheless inform the work of many such professionals. Writing law, interpreting law, and determining whether a law has been followed in any particular case are all instances of analyzing language, because language is the medium in which our laws are encapsulated. In addition, there is a particular field of applied linguistics—forensic linguistics—in which the formal study of language is directly applied to matters of law and law enforcement.

16.3.2 Forensic Linguistics

Forensic linguistics is the application of linguistic analysis in judicial and law enforcement settings. A forensic linguist studies linguistic evidence from a criminal investigation, looking for patterns in the evidence that may shed light on how a crime was committed, or by whom. In this sense, forensic linguistics is similar to other types of forensic investigation: in each case, the goal is to use the information available in order to determine what is not immediately evident. Forensic linguists study any instance in which a particular use of language may shed light on an investigation. Evidence may include interviews conducted by law enforcement officers with witnesses or with suspects. In other cases, forensic linguists may study recordings made at the crime scenes themselves (for example, from surveillance equipment) or recordings of suspects in other situations. These recordings may be recovered from investigative work—answering-machine recordings, for example—or they may be garnered in sting investigations: investigations in which law enforcement officers set up recording equipment with the specific intent of capturing a suspect incriminating himself. In general, an audio recording is preferred, although in some cases a written transcript must suffice.

Once a recording is obtained, from whatever source, a forensic linguist may engage in different kinds of analysis depending on the goal. In some cases, it may be the linguist's responsibility to determine who the speakers are, for example, by using phonological clues. In other cases, the linguist's job will be to analyze a conversation in order to determine what the language use reveals about how a crime may have been committed. In these cases, the linguist will carefully investigate the turns in the conversation to determine who says what and in what context. Useful information may be derived from such details as who in a conversation talks more, who is responsible for controlling the topic of conversation, how often the topic of conversation changes, whether the speakers interrupt each other, whether they seem to understand each other, and so on. A forensic linguist needs to be familiar with issues of semantics and pragmatics as well as with sociolinguistic concerns. After analyzing and collecting evidence, a forensic linguist may then be called as an expert witness in the courtroom to discuss how certain conclusions were reached.

Although an important part of forensic linguistics is to help determine how a crime was committed or whether a suspect is innocent or guilty, forensic linguists are also involved in helping to ensure that justice is carried out properly. For example, in cases in which a suspect is a non-native English speaker, it is important to ensure that he is successfully made aware of his rights, even though he may not understand English. Likewise, if a translator is used in any interrogation, it is important to make sure that the nuances and implicatures used by both parties are understood by the other. These are processes that a forensic linguist may be asked to evaluate, in order to ascertain whether they were satisfactorily accomplished. Forensic linguists may also be called upon to determine whether an interrogation that led to an arrest was conducted fairly from a linguistic perspective: for example, whether leading questions used presuppositions that compelled suspects to inadvertently make claims they did not intend, or whether investigators drew too strong an implicature from something that a suspect may have said, leading to the arrest of someone against whom there was actually insufficient evidence.

Although it often falls to trained forensic linguists to do the sort of analysis outlined above, in fact, anyone involved in law enforcement needs to be aware of many principles of linguistics in order to ensure that sting investigations are designed to be maximally effective and that they are conducted properly, that interviews are conducted fairly, and that any communication with witnesses or suspects does not obstruct justice in any way.

16.3.3 Language in the Courtroom and Other Legal Proceedings

A domain for language use that has received much media attention—both through the many celebrity trials that have been in the news in recent years and through the large proliferation of court-themed television series—is the courtroom. Issues of language and power (see File 13.2) come out in how lawyers examine various witnesses. Although witnesses will likely be given much free rein to tell their story by the lawyer who has originally called them to the stand (in fact, law mandates that witnesses be asked open-ended questions in direct examination), they will not meet with such freedom on cross-examination. The cross-examining lawyer will want to control the types of answers that a witness can give, for example, by asking questions to which the answer can be only *yes* or *no*. This allows the cross-examining lawyer to choose how the story will be told, potentially using presuppositions in order to get witnesses to agree to his version of the story, and it also takes power away from the witness. Thus, the attorneys in the courtroom must be keenly aware of both how they and their adversaries use language and how those on the witness stand use language.

Finally, laws and legal documents themselves are composed of language. A critical component in the education of anyone who practices law is learning to use and interpret language according to pragmatic principles that differ rather markedly from those of standard discourse. The specialized language that is used, for example, in the preparation of contracts or wills adheres to conventions that are specific to those domains. Not only is there specialized vocabulary, as there is in any field, but also there is an attempt to avoid the use of the ambiguous language and implicature that pervades normal language use. Therefore, a background in linguistic analysis and a familiarity with thinking critically about language can benefit anyone in one of the legal professions.

16.3.4 Jobs Available and Job Qualifications

As you have seen from the preceding sections, there are many avenues that lead to careers in which an understanding of both linguistics and law will prove beneficial. These include law enforcement—itself a diverse field with many jobs, each with its own set of qualifications—and those who practice law: lawyers and judges. To practice law requires a law degree, generally three years of post-graduate education. Forensic linguists, like other linguists (see File 16.6), need a strong background in academic linguistics, but they also need a background in criminology, forensic science, or some related field. The exact degrees required, both what level of degree is required and in which fields, will be determined by the organization that employs the linguist.

Of course, even if you do not pursue one of these careers, it is almost certain that, in your endeavors to be a law-abiding citizen, at some point in your life you will have contracts that you will be expected to uphold; you will have to interpret what is required of you to submit your income taxes; you will be called upon to be a juror and evaluate criminal proceedings in which there may be linguistic evidence presented. Thus, recognizing the importance that language can play in legal proceedings is important for everyone.

16.3.5 Resources

International Association of Forensic Linguists
< http://www.iafl.org/>

The Forensic Linguistics Institute
<http://www.thetext.co.uk/>

International Association for Forensic Phonetics and Acoustics
<http://www.iafpa.net/>

The International Journal of Speech, Language, and the Law
<http://www.equinoxpub.com/journals/main.asp?jref=62>

Solan, L. (1993). *The language of judges: Language and legal discourse.* Chicago: University of Chicago Press.

Language in Advertising

16.4.1 Language and the Goals of Advertising

Advertising is a business in which language is used to persuade people to do things: to buy a particular product, to watch a certain television show, to donate to a given cause, to engage in a certain practice (such as getting a vaccine or not smoking), to go to some community function, to vote for someone, or to hold certain beliefs (for example, that a corporation is trustworthy or that a political philosophy is a good one). These specific goals of advertising are very different one from the next, yet advertisers use strikingly similar techniques to achieve each one. Depending on the medium—television, radio, billboard, newspaper, and so on—an advertiser may or may not have various tools available such as images, video, or sound. However, in almost every single advertising campaign, at one level or another language is used to convey a message. That means that advertisers must be very savvy users of language, regardless of whether they have any formal training in linguistics or language analysis.

On the one hand, understanding something of the language in advertising is useful for those who consider careers in marketing and advertisement or for those who may need to hire a marketing company to produce an advertisement. On the other hand, having a basic understanding of the language in advertising is useful to average consumers as well, as it can help us to discern the ways in which advertisers are trying to communicate with us and to disentangle any informative content that an advertisement may contain from the (often misleading) packaging that it comes in.

Successful advertisers must do at least three things. First, they must establish the trust of their audience so that the audience is compelled to pay attention to the content of the advertisement. Second, they must convey some message about what is being advertised. Finally, they must convince their audience to act in some way: to buy the target product, to vote for the target politician, or to do whatever else the advertiser has set as a goal. Language can be used to accomplish all three of these tasks, and often it takes rather subtle linguistic analysis—especially in the domain of pragmatics—in order to discern how the language of advertisements is used to manipulate its audiences.

16.4.2 Using Language to Establish Trust

Trust is obviously a critical part of almost any advertising campaign: if consumers believe that a company is not trustworthy for some reason, then the advertiser is much less likely to attain its goal. Advertisers use many strategies to establish consumer trust. In some cases, an advertiser may address the issue of trust outright. For example, McCormick, a company that sells spices and seasonings, has as its slogan "McCormick: the taste you trust." In a commercial during a recent Ohio political campaign, a woman says to a particular senatorial candidate, "I just don't trust you," suggesting that the candidate in question is not trustworthy (and thereby that the other candidate is more trustworthy). Both of these campaigns chose to explicitly connect the idea of trust to what they were advertising.

More often, though, the trustworthiness of a product or company is addressed indirectly, through an **implicature** (see File 7.3). One common strategy is to announce how long a company has been in business: a simple Internet search for the phrase, "in business since" results in over 1 million hits. This information is generally given at the very end of a commercial, following information about a product or service that the company offers. Recall that a fundamental principle of pragmatics is that people are expected to be cooperative when they communicate, and that part of being cooperative is making all contributions relevant to the topic at hand. At face value, the age of a company doesn't seem to be relevant at all, because the age of a company does not directly affect the quality of a product or service it provides. Therefore, there must be an implicature that we are supposed to derive from claims about the company's longevity. Based on the maxim of relevance, we infer that such claims are intended to mean that a company does something well enough to stay in business for an extended period of time.

At some level, though, trust is about more than saying that a product or company is trustworthy. Trust is also about forging a relationship between the audience and the advertiser or the product. One tool that advertisers often use in order to establish such a relationship is presupposition. Recall (from File 7.5) that a **presupposition** is an underlying assumption implicit in an utterance. Under ordinary circumstances, presuppositions are felicitous only when all participants in a discourse are familiar with the content of what is presupposed. Thus, by using a presupposition, an advertiser can create a feeling of common ground between itself and a consumer. (In examples (1)–(4), the presupposition triggers have been underlined in order to call attention to what the advertiser is presupposing.)

Consider the following example, a line that appears in commercials for the Midwest-based superstore Meijer:

(1) We're cutting prices <u>again</u>.
     (presupposes that prices have been cut before)

In (1), the presupposition trigger is the word *again:* it triggers the presupposition that prices have been cut before. Had the advertiser instead come right out and stated the presupposed content explicitly—"We have cut prices before, and we are cutting them again"—the content would have been much the same, but the effect would have been different. By choosing to presuppose the information that prices have been cut before, the advertiser suggests that there is a shared understanding between the advertiser and people watching the commercial that the viewers should have familiarity with previous price cuts. The advertiser expects viewers to know (implicitly) that a presupposition suggests that everyone is familiar with the presupposed content, and therefore hopes that viewers may accommodate: "Oh, yes, I suppose prices have been cut before, and that's the sort of thing that most people are aware of, so I should be aware of that too." Thus, the advertiser has ingeniously suggested not only that Meijer has cut prices before, but also that it does so with such regularity that the average consumer is generally familiar with this process. Any time that an advertiser uses a presupposition rather than an entailment to share information about a product, the advertiser is suggesting that the information should be considered general knowledge, and it is welcoming the consumer into the sphere of people who have this knowledge. When the advertiser instead chooses to entail the information, it loses the benefit of implicating that the information is commonly known (because of the maxim of quantity: give the amount of information appropriate to the situation).

In other cases, presuppositions are more personal, presupposing information not about what is being advertised, but rather about the consumer! The following is a sample line that could have come from any number of advertisements that air every season. The words *don't forget* are a mainstay in the vocabularies of many advertisers.

(2) Don't <u>forget</u> to come check out our super end-of-season close-out sale!
     (presupposes that you already intended to do so)

In (2), the advertiser might instead have said, "Come check out our sale," but were the advertiser to do so, consumers would recognize that they were being told to do something which they might not otherwise have intended to do. The wording in (2) is much gentler: it doesn't seem to be telling people to do something because the advertiser asked them to; rather it seems to be suggesting that they do something they intended to do anyway. Most people don't like to be told what to do, but we do like to be reminded of things that we might have forgotten. Lines like those in (2) establish the advertiser as helpful, rather than bossy. This is an artful way of ingratiating the consumer to the advertiser. Other advertisements contain lines such as (3).

(3) Let <u>them</u> know that you love <u>them</u>.
     (presupposes first that *them* refers to someone, and second that you love them; in other words, presupposes that you love someone)

The line in (3) is from a December holiday-time commercial: the advertiser is assuming that many television viewers will be in the process of buying holiday presents for loved ones. The advertisement takes advantage of this fact by presupposing that viewers have loved ones. Consider how an advertiser might have gotten around this presupposition. The advertisement could have said, "If there are people that you love, then let them know that you love them." But this phrasing would have seemed unusual at best and offensive at worst (by suggesting that perhaps a viewer did not have any loved ones). By instead presupposing that viewers of an advertisement have loved ones, the advertisers suggest that they know those viewers and are not strangers, thereby establishing a feeling of trust based on familiarity.

Some commercials take their use of presupposed material yet one step further, using a presupposition to single out members of a particular target audience. Consider (4) below.

(4) Trying to <u>quit</u> smoking <u>again</u>?
     (presupposes both that you smoke and that you have tried to quit before)

Unlike in (3), where the advertiser assumed that almost all viewers would have some loved one or other, in (4) the advertiser certainly does not presuppose that anywhere close to all of the viewers are smokers who have tried to quit in the past, but nonetheless only that group of people is being addressed. The advertiser certainly could have asked three questions instead of one: "Do you smoke? Have you tried to quit before? If so, are you trying again?" In so doing, the advertiser would gradually narrow down the target audience, involving every viewer in the process. But this is not the advertiser's goal. In this case, the advertiser wants to specifically target smokers who are trying to quit again, so the advertisement jumps right in to talk only to those people. By using presuppositions like those in (4), the advertiser hopes to establish a feeling of camaraderie with the target audience, to make a prospective client have the feeling "Wow; they are talking directly to me." A presupposition is thus also a tool that allows advertisers to make individuals feel singled out or special. Making people feel as though the advertiser knows them or understands them or their situation is yet one more way to establish a feeling of familiarity and trust.

16.4.3 Using Language to Convey a Message of Superiority

An advertiser's job isn't normally finished after establishing a relationship with the viewer. Ordinarily, the advertiser also wants to send a message about the superiority of whatever is being advertised. These claims can't be just blindly invented; advertisements are bound by law to be accurate. On the other hand, as enumerated in Chapter 7, the study of pragmatics has made clear that the same sentences can have very different meanings under different circumstances. There is a question, then, as to how to determine the accuracy of a message in advertising: should advertisers be responsible only for what their claims entail, or should they also be responsible for what they implicate? Usually, advertisers are held legally responsible only for the entailments. Much of the art of advertising, then, revolves around formulating claims that implicate a lot but entail little. Below we will investigate some of the more common techniques for accomplishing this goal.

One way to implicate a lot and entail little is to qualify very strong claims with adverbs or with modal auxiliaries (e.g., can, could, might, etc.) as happens in (5)–(9), where the qualifying word or words are underlined. In each of these cases, the maxim of quantity will encourage the audience of the advertisements to infer that a stronger claim is intended than the one that is actually entailed.

(5) Leaves dishes <u>virtually</u> spot free. (Cascade)

(6) Get <u>up to</u> ten times stronger hair. (Pantene ProV)

Upon hearing an advertisement that a dishwashing product leaves dishes "virtually spot free" a potential consumer may think that there will be no spots at all, but of course there is no way to measure what is meant by *virtually*. *Virtually* is a favorite word among advertisers: other advertisements may claim that a product will leave clothing "virtually static free" or that you will wait in line for "virtually no time at all," but such claims do not tell how many spots, how much static, or how long a wait should be expected. Similarly, after hearing (6), a prospective consumer might expect that using the particular Pantene conditioner will leave her hair "ten times stronger," or at least close to it, but in this case the qualifying term is *up to*. Amazingly, (6) is true even if no one who uses the shampoo gets stronger hair: it is true so long as no one has hair that becomes more than ten times stronger! Pantene has been subjected to legal questioning as a result of this claim, but there is no guarantee that similar claims won't be made in the future. The following three claims use modal verbs as qualifiers:

(7) If you choose to finance or lease your new GMAC vehicle someplace other than GMAC, you <u>might</u> find yourself waiting in line instead of coming out hugging one. (GMAC)

(8) There's another way for new homeowners to save money: the Allstate New House Discount. It <u>could</u> save you <u>up to</u> 15% on Allstate homeowners insurance. (Allstate)

(9) Vessicare <u>may</u> <u>help</u> effectively <u>manage</u> leakage. (Vessicare)

An observant consumer will notice that in (7) and (8), neither a short line nor savings on insurance is guaranteed. (Note that the words *up to* appear in (8) as well.) Finally, (9) contains two qualifiers. It is taken from an advertisement for a drug to treat people with an overactive bladder: these people presumably want to have no leakage at all; however, the commercial doesn't say that Vessicare will eliminate leakage, but rather only that it may be "managed" and, moreover, that Vessicare can only "help" to manage it. The term *managed* is not defined. In any case, the advertisement also does not guarantee that the drug will help to manage leakage (whatever that means)—only that it may.

One of the favorite ways of advertisers to implicate a lot while entailing little is to leave out the *than* clause or prepositional phrase in a comparative construction. For example, Campbell's Soup has advertised that its soups had "one-third less salt." The appropriate question to ask here is *One-third less salt than what?* Nowhere in the commercial is this question answered; the claim is always just "one-third less salt." By the maxim of relevance, the audience is inclined to fill out the comparative with the most likely choices, such as "one-third less salt than it used to have" or "one-third less salt than its competitors' soups." However, neither of these claims is entailed by Campbell's claim. All that is entailed is that their soup has one-third less salt than something. That something could be anything, including the Great Salt Lake. If you think that bringing up the Great Salt Lake is going overboard just a bit, the following should change your mind:

(10) When the Ford Motor Company advertised that the Ford LTD was 700% quieter, one might have presumed that the model was 700% quieter than some competing car or, at least, 700% quieter than some other model of Ford. But when the Federal Trade Commission demanded substantiation of the claim, the Ford Company "revealed that they meant the inside of the Ford was 700% quieter than the outside." (Bolinger 1980)

These open-ended comparatives are plentiful in the world of advertising. Here are a few more examples.

(11) a. More people sleep on Sealy Posturpedic.
b. Maytags are built to last longer and need fewer repairs.
c. More people are switching from ordinary dandruff shampoo to Selsun Blue.
d. Complete cat care for more years of healthy, contented purrs. (Iams)

A third favorite technique of advertisers is to make use of idiomatic language. An idiom is ambiguous between its literal and idiomatic readings, and the audience tends to lean toward the stronger of the two—that is, the reading that makes the stronger claim—because the weaker claim (the literal meaning) would be irrelevant given that the advertiser is attempting to persuade the listener to buy something. For example, Mercedes-Benz has claimed that its cars are "engineered like no other car in the world." On the idiomatic reading, Mercedes are engineered **better** than any other car in the world, but on the literal meaning, they're only engineered **differently** from any other car in the world. Every car can make that claim. Kenmore claims, "In one out of two American homes you'll find Kenmore appliances." The most natural reading is that 50 percent of American homes have Kenmore appliances. But there is another, more literal reading, by which there are two American homes in particular, one with Kenmore appliances and another without.

There are many similar methods that advertisers employ to achieve similar results, and a little attention to the language of advertising should help you to extend this list of tactics considerably. Here are a couple, in brief, to get you started. Be on the lookout for rhetorical questions (in which the advertiser merely implicates that the answer is *yes*). Likewise, watch for advertisers giving information that does not directly correlate to the quality of a product in any clear way or, worse, information that does not relate to the product at all. In such cases, an advertiser is almost always trying to use the maxim of relevance to implicate superiority without grounds for doing so. For example, if a particular Iams cat food contains more chicken, egg, and tuna than its competitors, does that necessarily make it a better cat food? Likewise, if Exxon tells its audience that it engages in environmental research, that doesn't mean that the gasoline it is advertising is any more environmentally friendly than that of its competitors.

16.4.4 Being a Savvy Interpreter of Advertising

We began this file by noting that people in the advertising industry must be savvy users of language in order to sell their products. After all, in many cases the products in competition with each other are very similar, so in order to suggest that one is superior to all of the others without saying something untrue requires the use of implicature. Even in cases such as political races in which the competitors may be quite different from one another, an advertisement should appeal to as many potential voters as possible, so the choice may be made not to emphasize particular substantive differences, but rather to use turns of language in order to make one candidate seem better than another.

In conclusion, we will simply reiterate that language users do not easily distinguish between the logical entailments of utterances and the implicatures drawn from them. Because advertisers are usually held responsible only for the logical entailments of their claims, they often craft their ads so that their audience draws implicatures that are favorable, yet false, ungrounded, irrelevant, or otherwise misleading in some way.

Codes and Code-Breaking

16.5.1 Code-Breaking

Government agencies involved in codes and code-breaking are among the largest employers of linguists and mathematicians. This happens because code-making and code-breaking are all about the discovery and exploitation of patterns in language and communication. Mathematicians are experts in the abstract study of patterns, while linguists are needed because the patterns are not completely abstract, but crucially involve the use of language. It is also helpful for code-breakers to have good foreign language skills since the secret messages might not be in English, but the analytical skills that you learn in linguistics classes are even more important.

16.5.2 Alice, Bob, and Eve

Codes exist because companies, governments, and private individuals want to create secret messages that can be read only by the intended recipients. The process of converting a text into a secret code is called **cryptography.** The original text is called the **plaintext,** and the encoded text is the **ciphertext.** There is a convention in cryptography that the message sender is called **Alice,** the intended recipient is called **Bob,** and both are trying to conceal the message from an eavesdropper who gets referred to as **Eve.** There are many ways for Alice and Bob to do this, ranging from simple schemes that can be understood in ten minutes and executed by hand to methods whose design relies on mathematics so advanced that no sane person would attempt to use them without the help of fast digital computers.

16.5.3 The Limits of Secrecy

In 1948 Claude Shannon, a Bell Laboratories communication researcher, managed to show that perfect secrecy is theoretically possible. The catch is that Alice and Bob need to share a key that is at least as long as the total amount of text that they plan to transmit. This is because for perfect secrecy, the key needs to be completely random. There cannot be any pattern. This means that every letter needs to be encoded in a different way, and that the key needs to include decoding information for every single letter, making the key at least as long as the message itself. Soviet embassies used a variant of Shannon's scheme called the **one-time pad** to communicate with their embassies during the Cold War. This is very secure, but it requires Alice to make two identical copies of a pad of completely random numbers and to send one copy to Bob ahead of time. This is no great problem for embassies, since they can arrange regular deliveries of one-time pads via the diplomatic bag (a shipping container that has diplomatic immunity from search or seizure), and then use the pads to send urgent messages. The diplomatic bag solves the **key distribution problem,** the problem of safely delivering the key to the intended receiver of the message. Modern computer-based systems have clever ways of getting round this problem. But if you need to work by hand and are not on the staff of an embassy, the practical difficulties of ensuring that both partners in the conversation have the same one-time pad are usually prohibitive. In any case, if you are a spy working in hostile territory, you are unlikely to be keen on being caught in possession of anything as incriminating as a one-time pad.

So, in practice, because the one-time pad is impractical, there is always some chance that Eve will manage to recover the message, because without it, perfect secrecy cannot be obtained. But Alice and Bob can do a lot to make her task harder. Instead of insisting on absolute secrecy, cryptographers aim to design codes that will resist Eve's efforts for long enough that the information that she eventually uncovers will be so old as to be of little practical value. If your goal is to win a baseball game by eavesdropping on the coded signals that the catcher is using to communicate with the pitcher, you want to break the code well before the game is over, and you want to make sure that the opposition does not suspect that you have broken the code, since it would be easy for them to change it if they did suspect.

16.5.4 Traffic Analysis

Sometimes you can gain useful information simply by looking at the pattern of who sends messages to whom. This is called **traffic analysis.** Suppose that you are an intelligence analyst working on criminal investigations, and you notice somebody who suddenly starts to get a lot of text messages from notorious drug traffickers. What does this mean? It could be that we are dealing with the planning phase of a smuggling operation, or that a law enforcement agent is setting up a sting, or that a journalist is researching an article on organized crime. Not all of these may be exactly what you are looking for, but it is clear that the traffic patterns are telling you something.

Traffic analysis is fairly easy to do, does not rely on the ability to actually break the code, and can yield useful information. It was used heavily throughout the twentieth century, and it is still important today, particularly because it is easier to automate than is the process of decoding and interpreting the actual messages themselves. Indeed, now that we have the Internet, it is likely that traffic analysis is going to be essential even if no codes are involved, simply because there are too many messages for anyone to read. Linguists who have studied **social networks** (see Section 10.4.4) are well placed to help out with traffic analysis, since they have highly relevant experience of thinking clearly about how to make sense of patterns of communication.

16.5.5 Keys

Almost all practical codes, whether simple or complex, rely on the idea that Alice and Bob have a shared secret, which Eve does not know. In cryptography, we call this shared secret a **key,** because it can be used to unlock the message. Unless Eve knows the key, or can work it out, the message will be incomprehensible. It is easy for Bob to decode the message, because he knows the secret. The key can be simple or complex, short or long. As mentioned above, long complex keys are preferable for secrecy, but hard to use in practice. It is much easier to memorize a short English word as your key than a 1024 character string of random-looking gibberish. Several common types of keys are described below.

a. Shift Ciphers. The easiest examples of codes are **ciphers,** in which individual letters of the original plaintext are substituted with symbols. The simplest kind of cipher is called the **shift cipher.** In a shift cipher the ciphertext is created by replacing the letters of the plaintext with a corresponding letter from an alphabet that has been shifted some number of places away from its normal order. For example, if the plaintext is SEND MORE TROOPS and we are using a one-letter shift, then the ciphertext (i.e., the message that you, the staff officer, might have received from your field commander) will be TFOE NPSF USPPQT. The correspondence between the plaintext alphabet and the ciphertext alphabet is shown in (1). Notice that the ciphertext equivalent for Z is A, because the ciphertext wraps around from Z to A when we run out of letters.

(1) Plaintext: ABCDEFGHIJKLMNOPQRSTUVWXYZ
     Ciphertext: BCDEFGHIJKLMNOPQRSTUVWXYZA

The difference between **decryption** and **decipherment** is that in decipherment you know the amount of the shift, whereas in decryption you do not. Decipherment is what Bob does; decryption is what Eve tries to do in order to solve an enemy code. Consider the ciphertext CPZPAPUNHBUAZJHUILHWYVISLT. For decryption, what we need to do is systematically explore different shifted alphabets until we find one that makes this look like English. Fortunately, there is a good way of doing this systematically. What you do is write the alphabet downwards, in columns, starting with the ciphertext letter. When you get to Z, wrap around back to A, as shown in (2). Then look for the horizontal line in (2) that makes this into good English words. This method for solving shift ciphers is called the **tabular method**.

(2) CPZPAPUNHBUAZJHUILHWYVISLT
     DQAQBQVOICVBAKIVJMIXZWJTMU
     ERBRCRWPJDWCBLJWKNJYAXKUNV
     FSCSDSXQKEXDCMKXLOKZBYLVOW
     GTDTETYRLFYEDNLYMPLACZMWPX
     HUEUFUZSMGZFEOMZNQMBDANXQY
     IVFVGVATNHAGFPNAORNCEBOYRZ
     JWGWHWBUOIBHGQOBPSODFCPZSA
     KXHXIXCVPJCIHRPCQTPEGDQATB
     LYIYJYDWQKDJISQDRUQFHERBUC
     MZJZKZEXRLEKJTRESVRGIFSCVD
     NAKALAFYSMFLKUSFTWSHJGTDWE
     OBLBMBGZTNGMLVTGUXTIKHUEXF
     PCMCNCHAUOHNMWUHVYUJLIVFYG
     QDNDODIBVPIONXVIWZVKMJWGZH
     REOEPEJCWQJPOYWJXAWLNKXHAI
     SFPFQFKDXRKQPZXKYBXMOLYIBJ
     TGQGRGLEYSLRQAYLZCYNPMZJCK
     UHRHSHMFZTMSRBZMADZOQNAKDL
     VISITINGAUNTSCANBEAPROBLEM
     WJTJUJOHBVOUTDBOCFBQSPCMFN
     XKUKVKPICWPVUECPDGCRTQDNGO
     YLVLWLQJDXQWVFDQEHDSUREOHP
     ZMWMXMRKEYRXWGERFIETVSFPIQ
     ANXNYNSLFZSYXHFSGJFUWTGQJR
     BOYOZOTMGATZYIGTHKGVXUHRKS

b. Monoalphabetic ciphers. We just introduced shift ciphers and showed you one way to solve them, by writing out the alphabet in columns below the plaintext. We're now going to practice frequency analysis, which is an alternative way of solving these ciphers. This method is overkill if you are sure that you are dealing with a shift cipher, but it is worthwhile because it generalizes beyond shift ciphers to any monoalphabetic substitution. In a monoalphabetic substitution we keep the idea that each letter always translates to the same letter in the ciphertext, but now the letters can occur in any order.

The basic idea of frequency analysis is to use the fact that some letters are more common than others. For example, the most common letter of English is <e>, while <x>, <j>,

<q>, and <z> are among the least common. The full letter-frequency breakdown for one nineteenth-century novel is shown in (3).

(3)

338,214 e	166,934 h	74,504 m	42,504 b	3,247 q
232,105 t	166,751 s	63,418 c	41,363 p	1,150 z
210,111 a	164,166 r	63,186 w	29,056 v	
207,579 o	112,708 d	62,045 f	16,295 k	
191,572 n	105,007 l	60,424 y	4,532 x	
182,630 i	77,320 u	51,694 g	4,179 j	

If a ciphertext is based on a monoalphabetic substitution, then there will be some letter that stands for <e>, and this is likely (but not completely certain) to occur frequently in the ciphertext. An enciphered version of an English short story (Conan Doyle's "A Case of Identity," from *The Adventures of Sherlock Holmes*) starts off like this:

(4) "ub zijn piqqcd." ajrz aminqcsg mcquia ja di ajf ch irfmin arzi cp fmi prni rh mra qczkrhka jf vjgin afniif, "qrpi ra rhprhrfiqb afnjhkin fmjh jhbfmrhk dmrsm fmi urhz cp ujh scyqz rhoihf. Di dcyqz hcf zjni fc schsiroi fmi fmrhka dmrsm jni nijqqb uini scuuchtqjsia cp ixrafihsi. rp di scyqz pqb cyf cp fmjf drhzcd mjhz rh mjhz, mcoin coin fmra knijf srfb, kihfqb niucoi fmi nccpa, jhz tiit rh jf fmi wyiin fmrhka dmrsm jni kcrhk ch, fmi afnjhki scrhsrzihsia, fmi tqjhhrhka, fmi sncaa-tyntcaia, fmi dchzinpyq

You can make a frequency table from the whole of this story (our ciphertext) and line this up with the frequency table from the novel in (3) (our plaintext). In other words, we guess that the most common letter in the ciphertext, which is <i>, corresponds to plaintext <e>, because <e> is almost always the most common letter in English. The frequency tables are shown in (5), and a more compact version of the letter correspondences is shown in (6).

(5)

Ciphertext		*Plaintext*		*Ciphertext*		*Plaintext*	
i	3657	e	338214	d	767	c	63418
f	2770	t	232105	s	687	w	63186
j	2364	a	210111	p	644	f	62045
c	2160	o	207579	b	600	y	60424
r	2050	n	191572	k	528	g	51694
h	1978	i	182630	t	430	b	42504
m	1955	h	166934	v	416	p	41363
a	1850	s	166751	o	324	v	29056
n	1685	r	164166	g	245	k	16295
z	1191	d	112708	x	32	x	4532
q	1163	l	105007	w	31	j	4179
y	869	u	77320	l	27	q	3247
u	828	m	74504	e	13	z	1150

(6) abcdefghijklmnopqrstuvwxyz
    syocztkieagqhrvflnwbmpjxud

Using the letter correspondence established above, we get the text in (7), which is not bad, but not perfect either. Not all the letters in (7) are in just the right place, but most of them are pretty close.

(7) "my dear felloc." sand sherlowk holmes as ce sat oi enther snde of the fnre ni hns lodgnigs at paker street, "lnfe ns nifnintely straiger thai aiythnig chnwh the mnid of

mai would niveit. ce could iot dare to woiwenve the thnigs chnwh are really mere wommoiblawes of exnsteiwe. nf ce would fly out of that cnidoc haid ni haid, hover over thns great wnty, geitly . . .

It is pretty easy to see that what should be the plaintext letters <i> and <n> are wrong. We have ciphertext <h> matched with plaintext <i>, and ciphertext <r> matched with plaintext <n>. Let's change this: for example, the third letter in the fourth word should be plaintext <i>, so we can match ciphertext <r> with <i>. The equivalences for <c> and <w> and also seem wrong. So let's change that too, and try a different part of the text as a check, which is shown in (8).

(8) . . . if we could fly out of that window hand in hand, hover over this great city, gently remove the roofs, and beeb in at the jueer things which are going on, the strange co-incidences, the blannings, the cross-burboses,

Now it looks as if <p> has been confused with <b> and <q> confused with <j>. Fix that and you have the original text from Conan Doyle's *Sherlock Holmes*. We have now solved the cipher. What have we learned, and how can we use what we have learned to guide us in studying language? The shift cipher was easy, because there were only a few possibilities to consider and an easy way to organize the process of exploring the possibilities. Many practical problems are like this: it is not hard to systematically try out all the possibilities, and once you have done that, the solution is obvious. But this isn't the case for general monoalphabetic ciphers, because the number of possibilities is too great to explore by hand (although not too great to explore with the help of a computer).

So, rather than trying all the possibilities, we looked for a **heuristic** (a principled method of trial-and-error) that would get us close to the correct solution. The heuristic that we used was the following: *Probably the pattern of letter frequencies in the transmitted text will be close to what we have seen before.* As we saw, simply applying the standard letter frequencies produced text that was nearly English. Once we had that, we were able to make sensible guesses about small changes that would make the text even more like English, and eventually the correct text emerged. There are many practical problems which are like this: hitting on a perfect solution right away is hard, but getting close to a solution is much easier.

We had it easy in comparison to real code-breakers, because we kept the word breaks. This can be a big help, so real codes will be written with no gaps between the words. In Renaissance Italy this was not so well known. Among other things, this made it possible for a code-breaker to get big hints by looking at the ends of words. In Italian, almost all words end in vowels, so the symbols that appear regularly at the ends of words are highly likely to be vowels.

16.5.6 Enigma

During the Second World War, a sophisticated generalization of the monoalphabetic cipher, called the Enigma, was used by the Axis forces to communicate secretly. The Enigma was a modified teletype machine with a typewriter keyboard. As the cipher clerk typed, the message passed through a series of plugs and rotors and was converted into a quite different letter which was sent in the message. When the message was received, the cipher clerk at the other end typed the encoded letter into his machine, whereupon the original letter would light up.

This was possible because the sender and the receiver had a shared secret: at the beginning of transmission both machines would be set to the same settings of the rotors and the plugboard. As the message was received, the rotors of the two machines moved in lockstep, always staying synchronized. In comparison to a monoalphabetic cipher, this is a very secure system, because the code keeps changing as the rotors move, so standard tricks like frequency analysis are of little use. Fortunately for the Allied war effort, Enigma did still have weaknesses, and its German users made a number of mistakes that allowed experts working at a secret code-breaking establishment in Bletchley Park, England, to crack the code. In the process, the staff at Bletchley Park, led by an astonishingly talented mathematician, Alan Turing, created a number of electromechanical and electronic machines that later played an important role in the development of the digital computer. Similar work by American code-breakers in the Pacific made it possible for U.S. commanders to gain advance knowledge of Japanese plans, including crucial information leading to the American naval victory at Midway. Overall, the information that was obtained from code-breaking does seem to have significantly shortened the war, and perhaps even changed its outcome.

As well as the mathematicians, there were linguists, translators, chess champions, and many others who turned out to have the peculiar combination of pattern recognition skills that was required by the work. Indeed, one of the things that recruiters looked for was an unusual ability to solve cryptic crosswords. There is little doubt that code-breaking is one of the areas in which careful study of language and persistent attention to detail has changed the world. This kind of work is now carried on by the National Security Agency and other government agencies.

16.5.7 Job Qualifications

Those wishing to work in cryptology may find it useful to complete an undergraduate degree in mathematics, computer science, statistics, (computational) linguistics, or other fields. However, many positions require graduate training in cryptology as part of a degree in mathematics, computer science, computational linguistics, or a related field.

16.5.8 Resources

International Association for Cryptologic Research
<http://www.iacr.org/>

Open Positions in Cryptology
<http://www.iacr.org/jobs/>

Journal of Cryptology
<http://www.iacr.org/jofc>

Cryptanalysis at the National Security Agency
<http://www.nsa.gov/careers/careers_8.cfm>

Cryptology Officer in the Navy
<http://www.navy.com/officer/cryptology>

Singh, S. (1999). *The code book*. New York: Anchor Books.

Stephenson, N. (2002). *Cryptonomicon*. New York: Harper Perennial (a fictional but informative and accurate account of British and American work on code-breaking in World War II).

FILE 16.6

═══════════════════════

Being a Linguist

16.6.1 Job Description

In the course of this book, we have introduced many of the ways in which language can be studied and have presented evidence from linguists about many different aspects of language. But from a practical standpoint, you may be wondering, what **is** a linguist? Where do linguists work? How did they get into their fields? What do they do on a daily basis? How could I become a linguist? While there are, of course, many different answers to these questions, this file will give you some idea of the possibilities that are out there.

Although someone who has been trained to be a linguist could be hired almost anywhere, there are two main types of jobs that most linguists enter: academia and industry. In academia, you will find linguists in many different university departments, from actual linguistics departments to anthropology, cognitive science, computer science, philosophy, psychology, sociology, speech and hearing, or language departments. Linguists in university settings, like other academics, are generally expected to do their own research, teach classes in their areas, and contribute service to the university.

Most linguists have a particular area of linguistic research that they focus on, but this could take many different forms: some linguists choose to study a particular language or language family (e.g., they could be a specialist in Bantu linguistics of all sorts); others choose a particular subfield of linguistics (e.g., they could be a syntactician, looking at the syntax of many different languages); and still others choose a particular aspect of language or language's interface with other phenomena (e.g., they could be a psycholinguist and focus on how humans process language). A linguist's area (or areas) of specialization will determine the types of research he or she does. Sociolinguists, for example, study how language interacts with society—so many sociolinguistic studies have involved doing interviews with native speakers of a language, to learn about both usage patterns and ideas about language and society. On the other hand, a formal semanticist might be interested in developing theoretical mathematical models of how language works, rather than doing fieldwork to collect new language data. Regardless of the particular focus of research, all linguists rely on already existing research and theories as well as collaboration with other researchers—so a lot of time is spent reading, writing, and discussing ideas and new lines of research.

In industrial settings, linguists may also be involved with a wide variety of linguistic areas, but the research they do is usually geared toward advancing a particular project that the company they work for has in mind, rather than doing research for its own sake. A computational linguist with training in phonetics, for example, might work at a communications company such as Nuance Communications or Voice Signal Technology to help improve automated speech recognition or computerized dialogue systems in particular types of software. A specialist in child language acquisition might be employed at a company that produces children's toys, such as LeapFrog or The Learning Journey, to help the company develop age-appropriate educational games and toys. Or a semanticist might find

637

a job working with a company that comes up with new names for products that convey particular ideas to their target audience, such as Brand Institute or NameBase.

16.6.2 Job Qualifications

The job qualifications for a linguist will vary depending on the type of job they are being hired for. Most academic linguists are required to have a PhD in linguistics or a closely related subfield; earning a PhD involves going to graduate school for about five years after finishing an undergraduate degree. Although having an undergraduate degree in a field related to language study may help prospective graduate students know what they want to study or find a graduate school that will most closely suit their needs, it is not usually necessary to have an undergraduate degree in linguistics or a particular language in order to be accepted into a linguistics graduate program.

To work in industry as a linguist, the requirements are much more varied. Some companies are simply looking for someone with a bachelor's or master's degree in general linguistics, with enough knowledge of language to be employed in a language-related area of the company (perhaps with additional training by the company). On the other hand, some companies are looking for a linguist with advanced PhD-level training in a particular field, to work on highly specialized projects.

16.6.3 Resources

Linguistic Society of America
<http://www.lsadc.org>

Linguist List
<http://www.linguistlist.org/>

Links for Linguists Looking for Jobs in the Industry
<http://ling.rutgers.edu/club/joblinks.html>

Jobs in the Social Science Fields: The Riley Guide
<http://www.rileyguide.com/social.html>

Macauley, M. (2006). *Surviving linguistics: A guide for graduate students*. Somerville, MA: Cascadilla Press.

Oaks, D. D. (1998). *Linguistics at work: A reader of applications*. Fort Worth: Harcourt Brace College Publishers.

FILE **16.7**

Practice

File 16.1—Language Education

Exercise

1. Imagine that you were teaching your native language to someone who doesn't speak it. Pick one grammatical characteristic of your language and describe how you would teach it. For example, how would you teach someone the past tense of English? Think about how you would explain the characteristic you chose, what activities you could do with your student, and what exercises you would give him or her as a homework assignment. (*Hint:* There are many teaching resources available online.)

Activity

2. Interview a foreign language instructor at your school about his or her job. Your interview may include the following questions:

   a. What is the instructor's educational background?
   b. What classes is the instructor teaching?
   c. What skills are emphasized in the classes?
   d. What teaching methodology does the instructor use? Why?
   e. What preparation work is involved in teaching the classes?
   f. How does the instructor deal with different learning styles?
   g. Does the instructor have exercises or activities that work particularly well? Why does the instructor think they work so well?

File 16.2—Speech-Language Pathology and Audiology

Discussion Questions

3. Some speech-language pathologists teach children how to articulate sounds. How might an SLP explain how to produce [s], [ʃ], [z], and [ʒ] to a child who is having difficulty with these sounds? What kinds of activities might the SLP use to practice these sounds with the child?

4. Some speech-language pathologists make use of "oral motor" exercises as part of their treatment plans for patients. Such exercises are designed to work on developing oral muscle coordination and strength in a nonspeech environment. For example, they might have a patient suck a very thick milkshake through a narrow straw or blow bubbles. Based on your knowledge of language and the types of disorders SLPs treat, what types of disorder do you think these exercises might be useful for? How effective do you think they are?

639

Activities

5. Find a practicing speech-language pathologist or audiologist. Interview him or her to find out what type of work they are doing. What sorts of patients do they see? What kinds of problems do they treat? What techniques do they use in treating them? Compare your answers with those of your classmates to get a sense of the diversity of jobs that speech-language pathologists and audiologists do.

File 16.3—Language and Law

Discussion Questions

6. Why would forensic linguists prefer to have access to an audio recording of any evidence they may have to examine, rather than a written transcript? (There are many reasons, so consider this question carefully: think about various levels of linguistic analysis that you have learned about during your study of linguistics.)

7. One intersection between the domains of language and the law that was not mentioned in this file is that of language crimes: cases in which specific kinds of use of language are illegal. These cases include slander (using language to negatively affect someone's image), perjury (using language to mislead while under oath), and placing a bomb threat (using language to suggest that there is an explosive device somewhere that it could cause a public threat—even if, in fact, there is no bomb).
  i. Why, do you believe, is each of these uses of language illegal in the United States?
  ii. In Chapter 13, we discussed the fact that in America there is a guarantee to freedom of speech. Do you believe that declaring certain kinds of language use to be crimes undermines that? Why, or why not?
  iii. What does the fact that these uses of language have been declared crimes tell us about the power that people perceive language to have? What does it tell us about speech acts and the sorts of actions that can be done using language?

Activities

8. A particularly famous legal case in which linguistic analysis played a large part was the impeachment trial of President Bill Clinton. Investigate the role that language analysis played. You should find information that you can connect back to what you have learned about various ideas of word meanings, descriptivism versus prescriptivism, entailment, and implicature.

9. Obtain a copy of a will or a contract that has been drawn up by a lawyer. (Examples are often available online.)
  i. Read the document and make note of places in which you believe that language is being used in a particular way that does not sound like "normal" discourse. Why do you believe that these particular words or constructions were used in writing the will or contract?
  ii. Speak with a lawyer whose duties include drawing up such documents, and determine whether your guesses were correct. Ask about what other specific uses of language—both words and constructions—are specifically chosen in writing wills and legal contracts.

10. Find out whether there are any forensic linguists practicing in your area. Set up an interview, or invite them to come to your class to discuss what they do. What sort of training did they receive? What other sorts of people (in law enforcement and in forensic investigation) do they work with, and how do they interact with these people? What kinds of cases have they investigated using language analysis? What sorts of cases have they testified in, and to what end? What sorts of linguistic analysis do they perform?

File 16.4—Language in Advertising

Exercises

11. The following advertising claims contain implicatures that are not entailed. Identify what these implicatures are. Explain why they are not entailments, and tell which Gricean maxims cause them to arise.

    a. "People from Ford prefer Chevy trucks." (*Ford* refers to Ford County.)

    b. "Interesting fact about what he took. Its decongestant lasts only 4 hours per dose, and it contains aspirin, which can upset your stomach. Contac lasts up to twelve hours per dose and does not contain aspirin." (*Hint:* What is entailed/implied about how long Contac lasts and whether or not it upsets your stomach?)

    c. "STP reduced engine lifter wear up to 68%." (Fine print at bottom of screen: "Results vary by type of car, oil, and driving.")

    d. "Isn't it time you got your health on the right course? Now you can cut back on cholesterol, cut back on sodium, cut back on fat, and still love the food you eat because now there's new Right Course from Stouffer's."

    e. No other pain reliever has been proven more effective against headaches than _____. (*Hint:* What has or has not been proven?)

    f. This calling plan can save you up to 15% over Midwestern Telephone.

    g. I'm concerned about my heart. Plenty of supplements contain selenium but only _____ has garlic.

    h. Presidential candidate John Smith is serious about air quality. He was governor of _____, one of the first states to pass legislation cracking down on coal-burning plants.

12. Several commercials for the Icy Hot Back Patch conclude, "Count on it." What does this line aim to communicate? Why do advertisers wish to communicate that message?

13. One advertiser that has had distinctive and well-known slogans for decades is McDonald's. Following are three:

    a. 1993: Do You Believe in Magic?
    b. 1997: Did Somebody Say McDonald's?
    c. 2000: We Love to See You Smile

      i. For each, tell what implicature(s) the advertiser was trying to convey.
      ii. What is a slogan? Why are slogans particularly useful in advertising campaigns?

Discussion Question

14. Should advertisers be responsible for the truth only of what their advertisements entail, or should they also be responsible for the truth of implicatures? If both, who should be responsible for determining what a given advertisement implicates, and how should it be determined?

Activities

15. Look at the advertising section in a newspaper, or watch a few commercial breaks on the television. Find examples of each the following. For each, record what was said, show how the implicated content is different from the entailed content, and explain the linguistic trick that the advertiser is using in order to persuade its audience to act in a certain way.

    a. A presupposition designed to establish camaraderie between the advertiser and consumer.

    b. A description using a comparative and lacking a *than* expression.

    c. An example of a word or phrase that qualifies a claim.

    d. A case in which a product is described as being "different" or "unique" in order to implicate that it is superior.

    e. An implicature that makes use of seemingly irrelevant information.

    f. An implicature indicating that purchasing or using a product will lead to some desired end.

16. Write an advertisement for something of your choosing: you may choose to write it as though it were going to be a printed advertisement or a commercial for the radio or television. Write the commercial three ways:

    i. First, write an advertisement that employs several of the tools described in this file, including both presuppositions and implicatures.

    ii. Second, rewrite your advertisement so that it has no presuppositions or so that all of the presuppositions are satisfied at the time of utterance.

    iii. Third, rewrite your advertisement so that all of the information that you can truthfully convey is entailed rather than implicated.

    iv. Which of the three versions do you think seems the most natural? Which seems most like the sort of advertisement you might come in contact with in the real world? Which do you think would do the best job at accomplishing its goal?

File 16.5—Codes and Code-Breaking

Exercises

17. **i.** Use the alphabets shown in (1) in File 16.5 to encipher the following plaintext: NO TROOPS AVAILABLE. Write down the ciphertext letters that you would send back to the field commander.

    ii. Use the same alphabets to decipher the following ciphertext from your field commander: XF XJMM EP PVS CFTU. Write down the corresponding plaintext.

18. Julius Caesar used a shift cipher like the one introduced in (1) in File 16.5, but his had a shift of 3 letters, not 1. We say that the key of the cipher in Exercise 17 is 1, whereas the key for this exercise is 3. (For shift ciphers the key is always a number, but for other ciphers the key might be a word or a sentence.) Make an alphabet table like the one given in (1) in File 16.5, but for Caesar's cipher.

    i. Use your table to encipher the following plaintext: THE BRITONS ARE REVOLTING.

    ii. Use your table to decipher JLYH WKHP D FXS RI WHD.

19. Decrypt the following message using the tabular method:

HXDBXUENMCQNLXMN

You will need to make a table like that in (2) in File 16.5, but with the new message at the top.
  i. How many different shift ciphers are there? (*Hint:* What does a shift of 26 do?)
  ii. Exactly how many possible monoalphabetic ciphers are there? Another way to think of this problem is to ask how many different orders are possible for the 26 letters of the English alphabet. Do you agree that there are too many possibilities to explore by hand?

Discussion Question

20. One of the "codes" used by the U.S. Marines during World War II that was never deciphered is Navajo, a Na-Dene language spoken today in areas of Arizona, New Mexico, Utah, and Colorado. At the time Navajo had no alphabet and was spoken by fewer than thirty non-Navajos. Why do you think Navajo "code" was never deciphered? To answer the question, think about how using a language not known to Eve is different from using encoded English.

File 16.6—Being a Linguist

Exercise

21. Pick a topic that was covered in this book that you find particularly interesting (e.g., phonetics, syntax, historical linguistics, etc.). Think of a question that you might wonder about related to that field (e.g., does Yeli Dnye have agglutinating morphology? Are all productions of [l] the same in American English?). Describe how you might go about investigating the answer(s) to this question.

Activity

22. Find a professor at your institution who describes himself as a linguist (remember, even if you do not have a department of linguistics, linguists may be found in language departments, psychology departments, etc.). Interview him to find out what type of research he is doing. How does this research tie in to the concepts you have learned about from this book?

Further Reading

Oaks, D. D. (1998). *Linguistics at work: A reader of applications.* Fort Worth: Harcourt Brace College Publishers.

APPENDIX

Answers to Example Exercises

File 3.6   Exercise 23—Phonology Exercise on Mokilese

Since there are no minimal pairs in the data where [i] and [i̥] are the only different sounds between the pair, and none where [u] and [u̥] are the only different sounds, we proceed to look for complementary distribution. To examine the environments more easily, we can list the sounds which surround the sounds in question.

(1)   [i̥]   [i]   [u̥]   [u]

      p_s   t_#   p_k   d_p

      k_s   k_#   s_p   #_d

      k_t   p_l   d_k

             p_d   l_dʒ

                            dʒ_k

If these allophones are in complementary distribution, the environment that precedes them does not appear to be the conditioning environment. For the pair [i̥] and [i], there is overlapping distribution, since they both can appear after [p] and [k]. Therefore, we cannot use the environment that precedes [i̥] and [i] to predict which allophone will occur. For the pair [u̥] and [u], the distribution is not overlapping. However, the sounds that precede [u] do not form a natural class, and although the sounds that precede [u̥] are all voiceless consonants, we should not assume that we have found the conditioning environment for [u̥]. This would mean that the conditioning environments for the two pairs of vowels ([u]-[u̥] and [i]-[i̥]) were different. This could happen, of course, but it is more likely that both are conditioned by the same environment, so we should continue to check out others.

     The environment that follows the sounds in question also does not appear to be the conditioning environment. The sounds [u̥] and [u] are in overlapping distribution. Both precede [k], and the environments which follow [i̥] form a natural class but present us with the same problem as the sounds following [u̥] (i.e., having to posit different conditioning environments for the two pairs). Before we give up the hypothesis that these pairs of sounds are in complementary distribution, we must examine another possibility: that the environment that occurs on both sides of the sounds in question is the conditioning environment.

     The sounds that surround [i̥] are voiceless, as are the sounds that surround [u̥]. In addition, neither [i] nor [u] is ever flanked on **both** sides by voiceless sounds. These two sets do not overlap; therefore, we have complementary distribution. This means that [i̥] and [i] are allophones of a single phoneme, as are [u̥] and [u]. We can state a rule that accounts for the distribution of these sounds:

(2)   [i] and [u] become voiceless between voiceless consonants

We can assume that /i/ and /u/ are the "basic" sounds because they are the ones that appear in a non-natural set of environments. (It would be difficult to write a rule saying that /i̥/ and

/ụ/ turn into [i] and [u] any time one of the sounds on either side of them is anything other than a voiceless segment.) Note that we cannot say that all vowels become voiceless between voiceless consonants as the word [kaskas] illustrates. However, we could make our rule more general by noting that [i] and [u] are both high vowels. Thus our rule becomes:

(3) High vowels become voiceless between voiceless consonants.

File 4.6   Exercise 24(a)—Morphology Exercise on Hierarchical Structure

Draw a tree diagram for the word *disappearance*.

The tree diagram is a representation of the structure of the word, so before you can draw a tree, you must determine what this structure is. That is, you must determine how many morphemes there are in the word and in what order they attach to one another. The word disappearance can be broken down into three morphemes, *dis-* (meaning roughly 'not'), *appear,* and *-ance* (a function morpheme that changes a verb into a noun).

   We must next determine whether *dis-* or *-ance* attaches first to *appear.* This can be done by listing and then analyzing words which have the prefix *dis-* and other words which have the suffix *-ance.* For example,

(4) a. disconnect   b. appearance
         disembark   endurance
         disbelieve   grievance
         disappear   acceptance
         disassociate   interference

When drawing up such lists, it is important to keep a couple of things in mind. First of all, choose words with only two morphemes (the one in question and one other). Second, the other morpheme should belong unambiguously to one part of speech. For example, words such as *disquiet* might be excluded, since *quiet* could be either an adjective or a verb. Third, make sure that the words you include have the morpheme in question. For example, the word *distant* has /dɪs/ in it, but this *dis* is not the same as that in *disappearance* since it cannot be analyzed as being a separate morpheme in this word.

   Now, we can determine the types of words that *dis-* and *-ance* attach to. *Connect, embark, believe, appear,* and *associate* are all verbs, so *dis-* must attach to verbs. Furthermore, since *disconnect, disembark,* and so on, are all verbs as well, *dis-* does not change the part of speech. *Endure, grieve, accept,* and *interfere* are all verbs, so *-ance* attaches to verbs as well. *Appearance, endurance,* and so on, are all nouns, so *-ance* changes verbs into nouns.

   Let's see how we can use these facts to determine the structure of *disappearance.* Let's consider all possible combinations (there are two in this case):

(5) a. appear + ance   b. dis + appear
         dis + appearance   disappear + ance

In (5a), *-ance* connects first to *appear,* then *dis-* connects to *appearance.* But this arrangement would violate the rules that govern how the affixes may attach. When *-ance* attaches to *appear,* it forms a noun. To say that *dis-* then connects to *appearance* violates the rule that *dis-* connects only to verbs. The arrangement in (5b), on the other hand, involves no violations of these rules. Therefore, we know that *dis-* must first attach to *appear,* and that then *-ance* attaches to *disappear.*

   The tree representing this structure is given at the top of the next page.

(6)

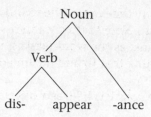

File 4.6   Exercise 29—Morphology Exercise on Isthmus Zapotec

i. The morpheme indicating possession is [s], indicating third-person singular is [be], and indicating second-person is [lu].

ii. The allomorphs for 'tortilla' are [geta] and [keta], for 'chicken' they are [bere] and [pere], and for 'rope' they are [doʔo] and [toʔo].

iii. The allomorphs that begin with a voiceless consonant are conditioned by a preceding voiceless consonant. The allomorphs that begin with a voiced consonant are conditioned by a preceding voiced consonant.

File 7.2   Exercise 13—Pragmatics Exercise on the Maxim of Quantity

This question asks you to construct a linguistic context for the question *Where did you grow up?* such that the answer *On the corner of Main Street and Minor Road* would be felicitous. In order to do this, you must think of a situation in which an answer with this level of specificity would be appropriate.

A sample solution is the following:

(7) "Oh, you grew up in Dayton? I used to live there, near where 70 and 75 meet. Where did you grow up?"

This linguistic environment establishes that both speakers know that the city they are talking about is Dayton and that the person asking the question has a basic understanding of the layout of Dayton. Therefore, it is appropriate for the person answering the question just to specify the street intersection in question without giving other additional information.

File 12.8   Exercise 35—Reconstruction Exercise on Middle Chinese

i. Protoforms:

Protolanguage	Gloss
*[kim]	'zither'
*[lat]	'spicy hot'
*[mɔk]	'lonesome'
*[lam]	'basket'
*[ɡip]	'worry'
*[lan]	'lazy'
*[pa]	'fear'

ii. Rules:

Mandarin	Hakka
*velar stops > palatal affricates / before [i]	none
*m > n / at the ends of words	none
*voiceless stops > Ø / at the ends of words	none

Explanation:

Total correspondence allows us to reconstruct the following sounds:

Protolanguage	Gloss
*[_i_]	'zither'
*[la_]	'spicy hot'
*[mɔ_]	'lonesome'
*[la_]	'basket'
*[_i_]	'worry'
*[lan]	'lazy'
*[pa]	'fear'

Position 1 in the 'zither' cognate set exhibits a [tʃ]-[k] alternation. Since [tʃ] is palatal and we know that it is very natural for "consonants to become palatalized before front vowels," we need to know if there is a front vowel in position 2. There is, so we reconstruct *[k] because doing so results in the most natural development. In the cognate set for 'worry,' we have a very similar choice. By the same reasoning we reconstruct *[g]. *[tʃ, dʒ], and *[k, g] are the natural classes of palatal affricates and velar stops, respectively. Therefore we can group these two sound changes together and use a single rule—making use of natural classes—to describe the change for both alternations.

In position 3 in the 'zither' cognate set, there is an [m]-[n] alternation. Neither direction of change is more natural. In such a case, we need to look at the other cognate sets. In the cognate set for 'lazy,' both languages have a word-final [n]. This information resolves the [m]-[n] alternation dilemma because sound change is regular. We must reconstruct *[m], because if we reconstructed *[n], then in Hakka we cannot account for a word-final [n] in [lan] 'lazy' and a word-final [m] in [kim] 'zither' with a regular sound change. This is particularly clear if we compare 'lazy' to 'basket.' Because 'lazy' must end in an [n] due to total correspondence, 'basket' cannot; if it did, one protoform *[lan] would have changed while the other one did not—an impossible situation! Of course, the change of *[m] to [n] in Mandarin only occurs word finally (because [mɔ] 'lonesome' begins with a [m]). We also need to put that condition on the rule.

In cognate sets 2, 3, and 5, there are [t]-Ø, [k]-Ø, and [p]-Ø alternations, respectively. [t,k,p] is a natural class (voiceless stops). Once again, we must reconstruct the voiceless stops and delete them in Mandarin in order to be able to posit regular sound changes. If we chose not to reconstruct the stops, we would have trouble predicting which stop would be added to the end of a word in Hakka. Worse yet, there would be no explanation for why there is no voiceless stop at the end of [pa] 'fear' in Hakka. This sound change too is limited to the ends of words, as the word-initial [p] in Mandarin [pa] 'fear' does not delete.

Glossary

≡≡≡≡≡≡

Note: Numbers in parentheses after headwords indicate the number of the file or section where the term is first introduced. See the index for a complete listing of references in the text.

A

Abjad (13.4.4)   The total set of characters used in a **phonemic writing system** that represents only consonants and not vowels.

Abugida (13.4.4)   The total set of characters used in a **phonemic writing system** that represents consonants with full symbols and vowels with **diacritics**.

Accent (10.1.1)   Characteristics of pronunciation inherent in every person's speech.

Accommodation (7.5.5)   See **Presupposition Accommodation**.

Acoustic Modeling (15.2.3)   In **automatic speech recognition,** the mapping of energy values extracted from recorded speech onto symbols for phones.

Acoustic Phonetics (2.0; 2.6.1)   Subfield of phonetics that is concerned with the physical characteristics of the sounds of speech. (See also **Articulatory Phonetics** and **Auditory Phonetics**.)

Acronym (12.4.3)   An abbreviation formed by taking the initial sounds (or letters) of the words of a phrase and uniting them to form a pronounceable word.

Active Construction of a Grammar Theory (8.1.1; 8.1.5)   Theory of child language which says that children acquire a language by inventing rules of grammar based on the speech around them. (See also **Reinforcement Theory, Imitation Theory, Connectionist Theory,** and **Social Interaction Theory**.)

Addition (9.3.3)   **Production error** involving the addition of extra units (out of the blue). (See also **Deletion**.)

Adjective (Adj) (5.3.2)   A word that is used to modify a noun.

Adstratum or **Adstratal Language** (11.1.3)   One of two or more languages in contact that mutually influence one another, owing to relatively equal degrees of power and prestige associated with the groups of speakers. (See also **Substratum** and **Superstratum**.)

Adverb (Adv) (5.3.2)   A word that is used to indicate manner, frequency, intensity, or other qualities of adjectives, adverbs, and verbs.

Affective Facial Expression (9.2.6)   Facial expression that conveys an emotion such as sadness, happiness, anger, fear, surprise, and so on. (See also **Linguistic Facial Expression**.)

Affix (4.1.2)   Bound **morpheme** that changes the meaning or syntactic function of the words to which it attaches. (See also **Prefix, Infix,** and **Suffix**.)

Affixation (4.2.1; 4.2.2)   Process of forming words by adding **affixes** to **morphemes**.

Affix-Stripping (9.5.2)   Hypothesis that each **morpheme** is stored individually in the **mental lexicon**.

Affricate (2.2.5)   Sound produced by complete obstruction of airflow followed by slight release of the **articulators,** allowing frication. An affricate can be thought of as a combination of a **stop** and a **fricative**.

Agent (5.2.2)   A **role** borne by a noun phrase in a sentence, which intentionally initiates some action.

Agglutinating (Language) (4.3.4)   A type of **synthetic language** in which the relationships between words in a sentence are indicated primarily by **bound morphemes**. In agglutinating languages, morphemes are joined together loosely so that it is easy to determine where the boundaries between morphemes are. (See also **Synthetic Language** and **Fusional Language**.)

Agglutination (4.3.4)   The putting together of **morphemes**. (See also **Agglutinating Language**.)

Agraphia (9.2.5)   Language disorder caused by damage to the **angular gyrus;** characterized by an inability to write words. Often accompanied by **alexia**.

Agreement (5.1.4)   Syntactic principle by which a certain word or words need to have a particular **form** (e.g., a morphological marking) in order to function in a sentence in a given way or in order to function with particular other words.

649

Airstream Mechanism (2.2.1)   Any of the various ways to produce a stream of moving air through the vocal tract for the production of speech sounds. Some major mechanisms are pulmonic, glottalic, and velar; each may be produced with an egressive or an ingressive airstream. (See also **Pulmonic Egressive Airstream Mechanism.**)

Alexia (9.2.5)   Language disorder caused by damage to the **angular gyrus;** characterized by an inability to read and comprehend written words. Often accompanied by **agraphia.**

Alice (16.5.2)   In **cryptography,** the sender of a message. (See also **Bob** and **Eve.**)

Allograph (13.4.6)   One of a set of nondistinctive ways of writing a particular **grapheme;** the distribution of allographs in a writing system is predictable.

Allomorph (4.5.1)   One of a set of nondistinctive realizations of a particular **morpheme** that have the same function and are phonetically similar.

Allophone (3.1.2)   One of a set of nondistinctive realizations of the same **phoneme.**

Alphabet (13.4.4)   The total set of characters used in a **phonemic writing system** that represents both consonants and vowels with full symbols.

Alphabetic Writing System (13.4.2)   See **Phonemic Writing System.**

Alternation (3.1.3; 4.2.6; 12.7.2)   In phonology, a difference between two or more phonetic forms that one might expect to be related. In morphology, the morphological process that uses morpheme-internal modifications to make new words or morphological distinctions.

Alveolar (Speech Sound) (2.2.4) Term used to refer to sounds produced by raising the front of the tongue toward the **alveolar ridge.**

Alveolar Ridge (2.2.4)   Bony structure located just behind the upper front teeth.

Ambiguity (*adjective:* **ambiguous**) (4.4.2; 5.1.5)   Property of words, phrases, or sentences that have two or more meanings. (See also **Lexical Ambiguity** and **Structural Ambiguity.**)

Analogy or **Analogical Change** (12.4.1)   A type of historical change in a grammar that involves the influence of one form or group of forms on another, causing one group of forms to become more like the other.

Analytic (Language) (4.3.1; 4.3.2)   Type of language in which most words consist of one morpheme and sentences are composed of sequences of these free morphemes. Grammatical relationships are often indicated by word order. Examples are Chinese and Vietnamese. (Also known as an isolating language.)

Angular Gyrus (9.1.2)   Language center of the brain located between Wernicke's area and the visual cortex, responsible for converting visual stimuli to auditory stimuli, and vice versa.

Annotation (15.5.2)   Labeling of linguistically relevant information (e.g., in a **corpus**) such as **lexical category,** syntactic function, thematic **role,** and so on.

Anomalous (5.2.1; 6.3.3)   See **Semantically Anomalous.**

Anosognosia (9.2.3)   Any **aphasia** in which the aphasic is unaware that he has aphasia. Frequent in Wernicke's aphasics who often seem to believe their speech is interpretable by others when in fact it is not. (See also **Wernicke's Aphasia.**)

Anthropological Linguistics (13.0)   The study of the relationship between language and culture.

Anticipation (9.3.3)   **Production error** in which a later unit is substituted for an earlier unit or in which a later unit is added earlier in an utterance. (See also **Perseveration.**)

Anti-Intersection Adjective (6.5.3)   Adjective that picks out a set of items that are not members of the set denoted by the noun being modified.

Antonymy or **Antonym** (6.3.2)   Words that are in some sense opposite in meaning. (See also **Gradable Antonyms, Complementary Antonyms, Converses,** and **Reverses.**)

Aphasia (9.2.1)   Inability to perceive, process, or produce language because of physical damage to the brain. (See also **Broca's Aphasia, Conduction Aphasia,** and **Wernicke's Aphasia.**)

Applied Linguistics (16.1.2; 16.3.1)   The application of the methods and results of linguistic research to such areas as language teaching; national language policies; lexicography; translation; and language in politics, advertising, classrooms, and courts.

***a*-Prefixing** (10.3.7)   The process of attaching the prefix *a-* to the beginning of certain verbs in English, as in *a-running.*

Arbitrariness (1.4.7; 14.1.1)   In relation to language, refers to the fact that a word's meaning is not predictable from its linguistic form, nor is its form dictated by its meaning. (See also **Design Features.**)

Arcuate Fasciculus (9.1.2)   A bundle of nerve fibers in the brain that connects **Wernicke's area** and **Broca's area** and allows sharing of information between them.

Articulation (2.2.1)   The motion or positioning of some part of the **vocal tract** (often, but not always, a muscular part such as the tongue or lips) with respect to some other surface of the vocal tract in the production of a speech sound. (See also **Articulators.**)

Articulators (2.2.1)   The parts of the **vocal tract** that are used to produce speech sounds (e.g., lips, tongue, velum).

Articulatory Description (2.2.1)   For an **auditory-vocal language,** the description of the motion or positioning of the parts of the vocal tract that are responsible for the production of a speech sound. (See also **Place of Articulation, Manner of Articulation, Voicing, Height, Frontness, Rounding,** and **Tenseness**.) For a **visual-gestural language,** the description of the motions or positioning of the hands, arms, and relevant facial expressions. (See also **Location, Movement, Handshape, Orientation,** and **Linguistic Facial Expression**.)

Articulatory Gesture (2.2.1; 8.2.1)   A movement of a speech organ in the production of speech, for example, the movement of the velum for the production of a nasal consonant.

Articulatory Phonetics (2.0; 2.2.1)   Subfield of phonetics concerned with the production of speech sounds. (See also **Acoustic Phonetics** and **Auditory Phonetics**.)

Articulatory Synthesis (15.1.3)   Generating speech "from scratch" based on computational models of the shape of the human vocal tract and natural articulation processes.

Artificial Language (1.4.11)   See **Constructed Language**.

Aspiration (2.6.5; 3.1.3)   A puff of air that follows the release of a consonant when there is a delay in the onset of voicing. Symbolized by a superscript <h> (e.g., [p^h]).

Assimilation (3.2.3; 12.3.3)   A process by which a sound becomes more like a nearby sound in terms of some feature(s).

Attention Getter (8.4.2)   Word or phrase used to initiate an address to children.

Attention Holder (8.4.2)   A tactic used to maintain children's attention for extended amounts of time.

Audiologist (16.1.2)   A professional who specializes in issues related to hearing, including the evaluation of normal and impaired hearing, hearing aid and assistive-listening technology, and the prevention of hearing loss. (See also **Speech-Language Pathologist**.)

Auditory Cortex (9.1.2)   Language center of the brain located next to the **Sylvian fissure;** responsible for receiving or identifying auditory signals and converting them into a form interpretable by other language centers of the brain.

Auditory Phonetics (2.0)   Subfield of phonetics concerned with the perception of speech sounds. (See also **Acoustic Phonetics, Phonetics,** and **Articulatory Phonetics**.)

Auditory-Vocal Language (1.5.1)   Language with a spoken **modality** (produced with the voice and interpreted auditorially). (See also **Visual Gestural Language**.)

Aural-Oral Language (1.5.1)   See **Auditory-Vocal Language**.

Automatic Speech Recognition (15.2.1)   The conversion of an acoustic speech waveform into text. The steps involved are **acoustic modeling,** **pronunciation modeling,** and **language modeling**.

Auxiliary Verb (Aux) (5.3.3)   Verb whose function is primarily to add grammatical information to an utterance, usually indicating tense, aspect, or other grammatical information that is not conveyed by the main verb of the sentence.

B

Babbling (*verb:* **Babble**) (8.2.2)   A phase in child language acquisition during which the child produces meaningless sequences of consonants and vowels. Generally begins around the age of six months.

Back (Vowel) (2.3.3)   An articulation for which the highest point of the tongue is held at the back of the oral cavity.

Back Formation (12.4.2)   Word formation process in which a new base form is created from an apparently similar form.

Backing (12.3.6)   A type of sound change (either diachronic or synchronic) in which a **front** vowel sound becomes a **back** sound. (See also **Fronting**.)

Balanced Corpus (15.5.2)   A **corpus** that tries to remain balanced between different genres by including articles from different sections in the newspaper, scientific papers, and other diverse sources.

Barge-In (15.3.3)   The act of users interrupting and talking over the computer, which may confuse some spoken language dialogue systems.

Basic Allophone (3.5.2)   The **allophone** of a **phoneme** that is used when none of the change-inducing conditions are fulfilled. Of a set of allophones, it is generally least limited in where it can occur. (Also termed the elsewhere allophone. See also **Restricted Allophone**.)

Bidialectal (10.1.4)   Having mastery of two dialects.

Bilabial (Speech Sound) (2.2.4)   Sound produced by bringing both lips together.

Bilingual (*noun:* **Bilingualism**) (8.5.1; 11.1.3; 11.5.1; 15.4.3)   State of commanding two languages; having **linguistic competence** in two languages. In **machine translation,** a system that can translate between only one language pair.

Bilingual Mixed Language (11.1.4)   Language in which different aspects of linguistic structure derive from different languages, resulting in a high degree of bilingualism among speakers. (Also called an intertwined language.)

Bi-Text (15.5.2)   Text that contains the same material written in different languages.

Blend (9.3.3; 12.4.3)   In speech production, a production error in which two words "fuse" into a single item. In language change, a new word created by combining the parts of two different words, usually the beginning of one word and the end of another.

Bob (16.5.2)   In **cryptography,** the intended recipient of a message. (See also **Alice** and **Eve.**)

Borrowing (11.0; 11.1.2)   Process by which one language adopts words, phrases, or grammatical structures from another language.

Bound Morpheme (4.1.5)   Morpheme that always attaches to other morphemes, never existing as a word itself. (See also **Affix** and **Free Morpheme.**)

Bound Root (4.1.5)   Morpheme that has some associated basic meaning, but that is unable to stand alone as a word in its own right.

Broca's Aphasia (9.2.2)   Inability to plan the motor sequences used in speech or sign owing to damage to **Broca's area** of the brain.

Broca's Area (9.1.2)   The region of the brain located at the base of the motor cortex in the left hemisphere. (See also **Broca's Aphasia.**)

Bundle of Isoglosses (10.3.2)   A set of **isoglosses** surrounding the same geographic region or distinguishing the same group of speakers, marking a particular **language variety.**

C

Calque (11.1.2)   See **Loan Translation.**

Canned Speech (15.1.1)   Speech synthesized from prerecorded phrases and sentences.

Canonical Babbling (8.2.2)   The continuous repetition of sequences of vowels and consonants like [mamama] by infants. (Also called repeated babbling.)

Categorical Perception (9.4.2)   Phenomenon by which people perceive entities differently after learning to categorize them: differences within categories are compressed, and differences across categories are expanded.

Centralization (13.1.5)   Process by which a speaker's pronunciation of a vowel approaches that of the central vowels [ə] or [ʌ].

Child-Directed Speech (8.1.7; 8.4.1)   Speech used by parents or caregivers when communicating with young children or infants. In many Western societies, child-directed speech is slow and high-pitched and has many repetitions, simplified syntax, exaggerated intonation, and a simple and concrete vocabulary.

Cipher (16.5.5)   A **code** in which symbols are substituted for individual characters of the original **plaintext.** (See also **Shift Cipher** and **Monoalphabetic Cipher.**)

Ciphertext (16.5.2)   In **cryptography,** the encoded text. (See also **Plaintext.**)

Circumlocution (9.2.3)   Descriptions of a word's meaning, used when a speaker is unable to name the intended word.

Classical Malapropism (9.3.3)   Competence error in which a speaker regularly uses a semantically incorrect word in place of a phonetically similar word. (See also **Malapropism.**)

Clear [l] (2.4.6)   An [l] produced with the tongue

body down and the tongue-tip up, as in *Lee* [li] in English. (See also **Dark [l].**)

Clipping (12.4.3)   Process of creating new words by shortening a longer word.

Closed Lexical Category (5.3.1)   **Lexical category** in which the members are fairly rigidly established and additions are made very seldom and only over long periods of time. (See also **Function Word** and **Open Lexical Category.**)

Co-articulation (2.2.6)   The adjustment of articulation of a segment to accommodate the phonetic environment it is produced in.

Code (1.5.2, 16.5)   A way of representing a language by replacing units of the language (morphemes, words, or written characters) with different symbols, yet preserving the structure of the original language. (See also **Cipher.**)

Code-Switching (8.5.2; 11.0; 11.5.2)   Using words or structural elements from more than one language within the same conversation (or even within a single sentence or phrase).

Cognate (12.7.4)   One of two or more words that descend from the same source. Usually similar in both form and meaning.

Cognate Set (12.7.4)   A group of **cognate** words that derive from the same source.

Cohort (9.5.4)   In the **cohort model** of lexical access, the cohort is the set of all the words that remain on the "list of possible words" as the auditory input progresses.

Cohort Model (9.5.4)   Model of lexical access in which possible words in the **mental lexicon** are identified based on the initial sounds of the word; impossible words are eliminated as the auditory input progresses. A word is accessed once all other competitor words are eliminated.

Coinage (12.4.3)   Process of creating new words without employing any other word or word part already in existence. Words are created "out of thin air."

Common Slang (10.1.1)   A type of **slang** that is fairly neutral and is simply informal, everyday language. (See also **In-Group Slang.**)

Communication Chain (1.2.2)   The process through which information is communicated, consisting of an information source, transmitter, signal, receiver, and destination.

Communicative Approach (16.1.1)   Foreign language teaching methodology that focuses on developing students' communication skills.

Communicative Isolation (10.1.2)   Situation in which a group of speakers forms a coherent speech community relatively isolated from speakers outside that community.

Community of Practice (10.4.4)   A group of people who come together to share some activity or lifestyle.

Comparative Method (12.7.3)   A technique that compares words of similar form and meaning in languages that are assumed to be related, in order to establish historical relationships among them. (Also known as comparative reconstruction. See also **Internal Reconstruction**.)

Competence (1.2.1; 9.3.3; 9.6.1)   See **Linguistic Competence**.

Complementary Antonyms (6.3.2)   Pair of **antonyms** such that everything must be described by the first word, the second word, or neither; and such that saying of something that it is not a member of the set denoted by the first word implicates that it is in the set denoted by the second word. (See also **Gradable Antonyms**, **Converses**, and **Reverses**.)

Complementary Distribution (3.1.3)   The occurrence of sounds in a language such that they are never found in the same phonetic environment. Sounds that are in complementary distribution are **allophones** of the same **phoneme**.

Complexive Concept (8.3.5)   A term used in the study of child language acquisition. A group of items (abstract or concrete) that a child refers to with a single word for which it is not possible to single out any one unifying property.

Componential Analysis (6.3.3)   See **Lexical Decomposition**.

Compositional Semantics (6.1.2)   The study of meanings of entire phrases or sentences as determined by the words that compose them and their syntactic structure.

Compositionality (6.5.1)   See **Principle of Compositionality**.

Compounding (4.2.4)   Word formation process by which words are formed through combining two or more independent words.

Compression (2.6.2)   Physical phenomenon resulting in a higher concentration of air molecules within a given space. (See also **Rarefaction**.)

Concatenative Synthesis (15.1.4)   In speech synthesis, stringing together (concatenating) and then smoothing pieces of recorded speech.

Conditioned Head-Turn Procedure (HT) (8.2.1)   Experimental technique usually used with infants between five and eighteen months with two phases: conditioning and testing. During the conditioning phase, the infant learns to associate a change in sound with the activation of visual reinforcers, first presented at the same time and then in succession, such that the infant begins to anticipate the appearance of the visual reinforcers and look at them before they are activated. During the testing phase, when the infant looks to the visual reinforcers immediately after a change in sound, it suggests that the infant has perceived the change in sound, thereby demonstrating the ability to discriminate between the two sounds involved.

Conditioned Sound Change (12.3.3)   Sound change that occurs under the influence of nearby sounds.

Conditioning Environment (3.2)   Neighboring sounds of a given sound that cause it to undergo a change.

Conduction Aphasia (9.2.4)   Type of **aphasia** caused by damage to the **arcuate fasciculus**. Patients use fluent but meaningless speech and cannot repeat utterances, but they are able to comprehend the speech of others.

Conjunction (Conj) (5.3.3)   **Function word** that joins words or phrases of the same category.

Connectionist Theory (8.1.1; 8.1.6)   Theory of language acquisition which claims that children learn language through neural connections in the brain. A child develops such connections through exposure to language and by using language. (See also **Imitation Theory, Reinforcement Theory, Active Construction of a Grammar Theory**, and **Social Interaction Theory**.)

Constant Reference (6.2.2)   Reference of a term (word or phrase) that always picks out or refers to the same object. (See also **Variable Reference**.)

Constituent (5.1.5; 5.5.1)   Grouping of words that form a discrete coherent syntactic unit.

Constituent Structure (5.1.5)   The relationship between **constituents** in a sentence. (See also **Phrase Structure Rule** and **Hierarchical Structure**.)

Constriction (2.2.1)   A narrowing in the vocal tract cause by articulator movement.

Constructed Language (1.4.11)   A language that has been designed by an individual or a group of individuals for some particular purpose, such as use in a fictional world or for international communication, but that did not originate as the native language of any speech community. (See also **Natural Language**.)

Contact (11.0)   See **Language Contact**.

Contact Situation (11.1.1)   Social situation in which speakers of distinct language varieties are brought together by social and/or economic factors such as settlement, trade, or relocation.

Content Morpheme (4.1.5)   Morpheme that carries semantic content (as opposed to merely performing a grammatical function). (See also **Function Morpheme**.)

Content Word (4.1.5; 5.3.1)   A word that has a particular identifiable meaning and contributes significantly to the meaning of a word or phrase in which it appears: content words are members of **open lexical categories**. (See also **Function Word**.)

Context (7.1.4; 9.5.5)   The set of circumstances in which an utterance is uttered. (See also **Linguistic Context, Social Context**, and **Situational Context**.)

Context Effect (9.5.5)   In speech recognition, the additional ease with which a word may be accessed owing to related meanings of the words preceding it.

Continuous Speech (2.1.4; 15.3.3)   See **Running Speech**.

Contralaterality (*adjective:* **Contralateral**) (9.1.4)   Property of the brain such that one side of the body is controlled by the opposite hemisphere of the brain: the left hemisphere controls the right side of the body, and the right hemisphere controls the left side of the body.

Contrastive (3.1.2)   A term used to describe two sounds that can be used to differentiate words in a language. (See also **Noncontrastive**.)

Contrastive Distribution (3.1.3)   The occurrence of sounds in a language such that their use distinguishes between the meanings of the words in which they appear, indicating that those sounds are **phonemes** of the language in question. Sounds that are in contrastive distribution are **allophones** of different phonemes. (See also **Overlapping Distribution**.)

Controlled Language (15.4.3)   In machine translation, a subset of natural languages which have been edited for ease of processing by a machine so as to have fewer ambiguities and simpler syntactic patterns.

Conventionalized (*noun:* **Convention**) (1.4.7) Established, commonly agreed upon, or operating a certain way according to common practice. When a grammatical rule is conventionalized, it is commonly established that that rule is a part of the **mental grammar** of speakers of the language. When an **arbitrary** relationship between a linguistic sign and its meaning is conventionalized, the linguistic sign bears a constant relationship to its denotation not due to any natural relationship, but rather because people consistently use that linguistic sign to convey that meaning.

Conversational Analysis (13.1.4)   See **Discourse Analysis.**

Conversational Turn (8.4.3)   The contribution to a conversation made by one speaker from the time that she takes the floor from another speaker to the time that she passes the floor on to another speaker. (See also **Conversational Turn Taking**.)

Conversational Turn Taking (8.4.3)   A basic form of organizing conversations in which only one person speaks at any given time and then passes the floor to another person by means of an indicator such as a pause or a glance. (See also **Conversational Turn**.)

Converses (6.3.2)   **Antonyms** in which the first word of the pair suggests a point of view opposite to that of the second word. (See also **Complementary Antonyms, Gradable Antonyms,** and **Reverses**.)

Conversion (12.4.3)   A word created by shifting the **lexical category** of a word to a different category without changing the form of the word.

Cooperative Principle (7.2.1)   Principle formulated by the philosopher H. P. Grice, stating that underlying a conversation is the understanding that what one says is intended to contribute to the purposes of the conversation. (See also **Gricean Maxims**.)

Copula Absence (10.4.5)   The absence of inflected present-tense forms of the verb *to be* in sentences for which **Standard American English** would use an inflected form.

Corpus (*plural:* **Corpora**) (15.5.1)   A collected body of text (or, less frequently, of recorded speech with or without a transcription).

Corpus Callosum (9.1.2)   Bundle of nerve fibers connecting the two hemispheres of the brain for the purpose of exchanging information between the two halves.

Corpus Linguistics (15.5.1)   Subfield of linguistics involving the design and annotation of **corpus** materials that are required for specific purposes.

Correspondence (12.7.3)   See **Sound Correspondence**.

Cortex (9.1.2)   Outer surface of the brain responsible for many of the brain's cognitive abilities or functions.

Counterfactual (6.4.2)   Describes a possible state of affairs that differs from the actual state of affairs in some particular way; a sentence that describes such a counterfactual state.

Covert Prestige (10.1.4)   Type of **prestige** that exists among members of non-standard speech communities that defines how people should speak in order to be considered members of those particular communities.

Creole (Language) (11.0; 11.1.4; 11.4.1)   A language that developed from contact between speakers of different languages and that serves as the primary means of communication for a particular group of speakers.

Critical Period (8.1.2)   Age span, usually described as lasting from birth to the onset of puberty, during which children must have exposure to language and must build the critical brain structures necessary in order to gain native speaker competence in a language.

Cryptography (16.5.2)   The process of converting a text into a **code**.

Crystallization (*verb:* **Crystallize**) (11.3.1)   The process through which a **pidgin** establishes regular grammatical **conventions**.

Cultural Transmission (1.4.6; 14.1.1)   Property of a communication system referring to the fact that at least some aspects of it are learned through interaction with other users of the system. (See also **Design Features**.)

D

Dark [l] (2.4.6)   An [l] produced with the tongue body up, moving toward the velum, and the tongue-tip down. The dark [l] is more accurately described as velarized, which is transcribed as [ɫ] (See also **Clear [l]** and **Velarized.**)

Dead Language (11.6.3)   A language that does not have any speakers. (Also called extinct language. See also **Dormant Language.**)

Decipherment (16.5.5)   In cryptography, decoding a message knowing the **key.** This is what **Bob** does. (See also **Decryption.**)

Declarative (7.4.6)   A sentence **form** that literally makes a statement. (In English, declarative sentences have a subject that precedes the predicate.) (See also **Imperative** and **Interrogative.**)

Decryption (16.5.5)   In cryptography, decoding a message without knowing the **key.** This is what **Eve** tries to do with an encoded message. (See also **Decipherment.**)

Degradation (12.6.4)   Semantic change by which a word acquires a more pejorative meaning over time. (See also **Elevation.**)

Deictic (Expression) (7.1.3; 8.3.5)   Word or expression that takes its meaning relative to the time, place, and speaker of the utterance.

Deletion (3.2.3; 5.5.3; 12.3.3)   In phonology, a process by which a sound present in the phonemic form (or underlying form) is removed from the phonetic form in certain environments. (See also **Insertion.**) In syntax, a test for constituency in which a group of words is left out of a sentence to see whether the remaining words constitute a grammatical sentence. In speech production, a production error involving the inadvertent omission of units. (See also **Addition.**)

Dental (Speech Sound) (2.2.6)   Sound produced by raising the front of the tongue toward the teeth.

Derivation (3.2.4; 4.1.2)   In phonology, a process by which an underlying form is changed as phonological rules act upon it. In morphology, a morphological process that changes a word's **lexical category** or its meaning in some predictable way.

Descriptive Grammar (1.2.5)   Objective description of a speaker's knowledge of a language (competence) based on their use of the language (performance). (See also **Prescriptive Grammar.**)

Design Features (of Language) (1.4.1; 14.1.1)   A set of nine descriptive characteristics of language, first introduced by the linguist Charles Hockett. Each design feature is a condition necessary for a communication system to be considered language. (See also **Mode of Communication, Semanticity, Pragmatic Function, Interchangeability, Cultural Transmission, Arbitrariness, Discreteness, Displacement,** and **Productivity.**)

Determiner (Det) (5.3.3)   A closed set of morphemes that indicate something about the nouns they appear with, such as definiteness, quantity, or ownership.

Diachronic Analysis (12.1.1)   Analysis of language change through time (from the Greek *dia* = 'across'; *chronos* = 'time'). See also **Synchronic Analysis.**)

Diacritic (13.4.4)   An extra mark on a written symbol, representing either some other characteristic of its pronunciation (in a phonetic transcription system) or a vowel (in an **abugida**).

Dialect (10.1.1)   A variety of a language defined by both geographical factors and social factors, such as class, religion, and ethnicity.

Dialect Continuum (10.1.1)   Situation in which a large number of contiguous dialects exist, each mutually intelligible with the next, but with the dialects at either end of the continuum being not mutually intelligible.

Dialectologist (10.3.2)   A person who studies **Regional Dialects** and **Regional Variation.**

Dialectology (10.3.2)   The study of regional dialects.

Dichotic Listening Task (9.1.4)   Experiment that presents two different sounds (speech and/or nonspeech) simultaneously, one in each ear. Participants indicate which sound they have heard.

Diglossia (11.5.2)   Traditionally, a situation in which one variety of a language is used for more **prestigious** functions, and another variety of the same language is used for less prestigious functions. Now refers to any situation in which two distinct languages or dialects are used for different functions within one society.

Diphone (15.1.4)   Pairs of adjacent speech sounds. (See also **Diphone Synthesis.**)

Diphone Synthesis (15.1.4)   In speech synthesis, a kind of **concatenative synthesis** that uses **diphones** to synthesize speech.

Diphthong (2.1.3; 2.3.6)   A complex vowel, composed of a sequence of two different configurations of the vocal organs. (See also **Monophthong.**)

Diphthongization (12.3.3)   Change of a simple vowel sound to a complex one. Process by which a **monophthong** becomes a **diphthong.**

Direct Speech Act (7.4.5)   Utterance that performs its function in a direct and literal manner. (See also **Indirect Speech Act** and **Performative Speech Act.**)

Direct Translation (15.4.3)   The oldest approach (1950s to early 1960s) to **machine translation,** employing word-for-word unidirectional translation between two languages.

Discourse Analysis (13.1.4)   The study of the use of language in a discourse or conversation. Discourse analysts examine the structure of the information flow of speech, the interdependencies of sentences in speech, and other aspects of language use.

Discreteness (1.4.8; 14.1.1)   The property of some communication systems by which complex messages may be built up out of smaller parts. (See also **Design Features** and **Duality of Patterning**.)

Displacement (1.4.9; 14.1.1)   The property of some communication systems that allows them to be used to communicate about things, actions, and ideas that are not present at the place or time where communication is taking place. (See also **Design Features**.)

Dissimilation (3.2.3; 12.3.3)   Process by which two nearby sounds become less alike with respect to some feature.

Distribution (3.1.3)   The set of phonetic environments in which a sound occurs. (See also **Overlapping Distribution, Complementary Distribution,** and **Contrastive Distribution**.)

Domain-Specific Synthesis (15.1.4)   In speech synthesis, a kind of **concatenative synthesis** for use in one particular area of application only. Utterances are created from prerecorded words and phrases that closely match the words and phrases that will be synthesized. New utterances can also be created using smaller segments, such as **diphones**, collected from the same recordings. (See also **Limited Domain**.)

Dominant Hand (3.3.2)   In a **visual-gestural language,** for a given speaker, whichever hand performs all one-handed signs and has more freedom of movement in two-handed signs.

Dormant Language (11.6.3)   A term used to label dead languages by people who believe they may be revived.

Double Modal (10.3.6)   The use of two modals in a single verb phrase, as in *might could* or *might should*.

Duality of Patterning (1.4.8)   Property of a language that allows the same meaningless units to combine in multiple ways in order to produce multiple meaningful larger units. (See also **Discreteness**.)

Dynamic Palatography (2.2.6)   Experimental method that tracks the contacts and contact patterns between the tongue and the hard palate over time.

E

Edge Tone (2.5.3)   A change in **fundamental frequency** at the end of a phrase, for example, to indicate a question or statement. (See also **Intonation**.)

Ejective (2.4.6)   Consonant sound produced by compressing air in the mouth or pharynx while the **glottis** remains closed, and then releasing. It is also called glottalic or **glottalized** sound, transcribed with a superscripted glottal stop following the segment involved, for example, [p$^{\textipa{P}}$].

Elevation (12.6.4)   Semantic change by which words take on a grander or more positive connotation over time. (See also **Degradation**.)

Ellipsis (5.5.3)   See **Deletion** (in syntax).

Emblematic Language (10.4.5)   A particular language variety used to refer symbolically to a particular cultural heritage or identity.

Endangered Language (11.5.1)   A language that has very few speakers left. (See also **Language Death**.)

Entailment (*verb:* **Entail**) (6.5.4; 7.3.1)   A relationship between two sentences such that if the first is true, the second must be true.

Environment (3.5.2)   The contexts that precede and follow a sound.

Eponym (12.4.3)   A word (such as a place name, an invention, or an activity) that is based on the name of a person or people somehow connected with the word.

ERP (Event-Related Potentials) (9.7.2)   Technique for determining which physical sensations or activities activate which parts of the brain by mapping areas of increased blood flow in the brain.

Error Recovery (15.3.4)   A function of the dialogue management component in a **spoken language dialogue system** which gets the conversation in question back on track after a misunderstanding, for example, one caused by a speech recognition problem.

Eve (16.5.2)   In **cryptography**, an eavesdropper from whom **Alice** and **Bob** are trying to conceal a message.

Exceptions Dictionary (15.1.5)   In **text-to-speech synthesis**, a dictionary that lists the correct pronunciation of words that do not follow a language's standard rules for pronunciation.

Existence Presupposition (7.5.1)   The **presupposition** that an item referred to in discourse exists.

Expanded Pidgin (11.3.1)   **Pidgin** whose use is not limited to certain social settings. An expanded pidgin is a full language, unlike a **prototypical pidgin**.

Experiencer (5.2.2)   **Role** of a noun phrase that refers to an animate being (person or animal) that has some kind of perceptual or mental experience, such as seeing, hearing, knowing, and so on, in a sentence.

Extension (6.3.2; 12.6.2)   In semantics, the set of objects, ideas, and so on, that a word may be used to refer to. (See also **Referent**.) In language change, a diachronic semantic change by which the set of appropriate contexts or referents for a word increases. (See also **Metaphorical Extension** and **Reduction**.)

Extinct Language (11.6.3)   See **Dead Language**.

Extralinguistic Factor (10.1.2)   A factor influencing language variation not based in linguistic structure, such as region, socioeconomic status, ethnicity, and so on.

Eye-Tracking (9.7.4)   Experimental protocol in which participants' eye movements (where the eyes are looking at any given time) are recorded, allowing researchers to draw conclusions about processing.

F

Family Tree Theory (12.2.2)   Theory formulated by August Schleicher that says that languages change in regular, recognizable ways and that similarities among languages are due to a "genetic" relationship among them.

Felicitous (7.1.5)   Describes an utterance that is appropriate for the context in which it is uttered. (See also **Felicity Conditions** and **Infelicitous**.)

Felicity Conditions (7.4.2)   The circumstances required to render a particular variety of **speech act** felicitous. (See also **Felicitous** and **Infelicitous**.)

Feral Child (8.1.2)   Child who grew up in the wild without care by human adults, often with animals.

Filter (15.1.3)   In speech synthesis, the mechanism through which a basic sound from the source is shaped to create particular speech sounds. (See also **Source-Filter Theory**.)

First-Language (L1) Acquisition (8.1; 8.2; 8.3)   The process by which children acquire the lexicon and grammatical rules of their native language. (In the case of native bilinguals, both languages are acquired as first languages.) (See also **Second-Language (L2) Acquisition**.)

Fissure (9.1.2)   Depression in the **cortex** of the brain's hemispheres that serves as a physical boundary for the identification of different sections of the brain. (See also **Gyrus**.)

Flap (2.2.5)   A sound produced by bringing two articulators together very quickly.

Flout (a **Gricean Maxim**) (7.2.3)   To break one of the **Gricean maxims** intentionally in order to convey a particular message that is often counter to or seemingly unrelated to what is actually said.

fMRI (functional Magnetic Resonance Imaging) (9.7.2)   Technique that detects changes in electrical activity in the brain at the millisecond level.

Folk Etymology (12.4.2)   The reanalysis of a word or phrase (usually an unfamiliar one) into a word or phrase composed of more commonly known words.

Foreign Accent (8.5.4)   An **accent** that is marked by the phonology of another language or other languages that are more familiar to the speaker.

Forensic Linguistics (16.3.3)   Application of linguistic evidence in judicial and law enforcement settings.

Form (1.4.7)   The **structure** or shape of any particular linguistic items, from individual segments to sentences. May also be used to denote the item itself.

Formal Language (1.4.11)   A communication system, such as one of the many systems of logical notation or most computer languages, that has both semantic and syntactic rules and that encodes ideas with symbols that represent particular meanings, but that could never be the native language of a human.

Formant (2.6.4)   Resonant frequency that amplifies some groups of harmonics above others; appears as a dark band on a **spectrogram**.

Formation (4.2.1)   See **Word Formation Process**.

Fortition (3.2.2)   See **Strengthening**.

Fossilization (8.5.4)   Process through which forms from a speaker's non-native language usage become fixed (generally in a way that would be considered ungrammatical by a native speaker) and do not change, even after years of instruction.

Founder Principle (10.3.3)   The principle by which the **language variety** spoken by the first group of people in a particular community (the "founders" of the community) is entrenched and becomes the basis for the community's language variety.

Free Morpheme (4.1.5)   **Morpheme** that can stand alone as a word. (See also **Sound Morpheme**.)

Free Variation (3.1.4)   Term used to refer to two sounds that occur in overlapping environments but cause no distinction in the meaning of their respective words.

Frequency Effect (9.5.5)   Additional ease with which a word is accessed owing to its repeated occurrence in the discourse or context.

Frication (2.2.5)   A turbulent, hissing mouth noise that is produced by forming a nearly complete obstruction of the vocal tract. The opening through which the air escapes is very small, and as a result a turbulent noise is produced. (See also **Fricative**.)

Fricative (2.2.5)   Sound made by forming a nearly complete obstruction of the airstream so that when air passes through the small passage, turbulent airflow (i.e., **frication**) is produced.

Front (Vowel) (2.3.3)   An articulation where the highest point of the tongue is held in the front of the oral cavity.

Frontal Lobe (9.1.2)   Area of the brain concerned with higher thinking and language production.

Fronting (12.3.7)   A type of sound change (either diachronic or synchronic) in which a **back** vowel sound becomes a **front** sound. (See also **Backing**.)

Frontness (2.3.1)   A property of the production of vowels having to do with how advanced or retracted the body of the tongue is. (Sometimes called backness; also called tongue advancement.)

Full Listing Hypothesis (9.5.2)   Hypothesis that every word is stored as a separate entry in the mental **lexicon**.

Fully Automatic High-Quality Translation (FAHQT) (15.4.2)   Very accurate machine translation that is performed completely automatically, without any guidance from human users.

Function Morpheme (4.1.5)   Morpheme that provides information about the grammatical relationships between words in a sentence. (See also **Content Morpheme.**)

Function Word (4.1.6, 5.3.1)   A word whose primary purpose is to indicate the role of other words or phrases within a phrase or sentence and that has very little meaning outside of this grammatical purpose: function words are members of **closed lexical categories.** (See also **Content Word.**)

Fundamental Frequency (2.6.3)   The rate at which the vocal folds vibrate during voicing. The frequency of repetition of a periodic wave. Closely related to pitch.

Fusional (Language) (4.3.5)   A type of **synthetic language** in which the relationships between the words in a sentence are indicated by **bound morphemes** that are difficult to separate from the stem. (See also **Synthetic Language** and **Agglutinating Language.**)

G

Garden Path Effect (9.6.2)   Phenomenon by which people are fooled into thinking a sentence has a different structure than it actually does because of an apparent **ambiguity.**

Glide (2.2.5)   Sound produced with a constriction in the vocal tract that is only slightly more constricted than that for vowels.

Globally Ambiguous (9.6.2)   Sentences in which **structural ambiguity** is not resolved by the end of the sentence.

Glottal (Speech Sound) (2.2.4)   Sounds produced at the **glottis.**

Glottalized (2.4.6)   Sounds that are produced with creaky voice, or sounds that are produced with a simultaneous glottal stop.

Glottis (2.2.3)   The space between the vocal folds. (See also **Voicing** and **Larynx.**)

Gradable Antonyms (6.3.2)   Words that are **antonyms** and denote opposite ends of a scale. (Also known as gradable pairs and as scalar antonyms. See also **Complementary Antonyms, Converses,** and **Reverses.**)

Grammar (1.2.3; 1.3.3)   A system of linguistic elements and rules. (See also **Descriptive Grammar** and **Prescriptive Grammar.**)

Grammatical (1.2.3; 5.1.2)   Linguistic forms (such as words, phrases, or sentences) that have been composed in such a way as to adhere to the rules of some particular language as determined by the speakers of that language; only the judgments of native speakers can determine whether or not a particular form is grammatical. (See also **Ungrammatical.**)

Grapheme (13.4.2)   An individual symbol used for writing; may represent a segment, a syllable, a morpheme, or some other unit of linguistic structure.

Gricean Maxim (7.2.1)   One of a set of conversational rules that regulate conversation by enforcing compliance with the **Cooperative Principle.**

Gyrus (*plural:* **Gyri**) (9.1.2)   Bumps in the **cortex** of the brain's hemispheres. (See also **Fissure.**)

H

Habitual *be* (10.4.5)   The use of an uninflected form of the verb *to be* to indicate that a state or activity is habitual.

Handshape (2.7.5)   A type of **prime** in a **visual-gestural language:** the configuration of the hands and fingers during a sign.

Harmonic (2.6.3)   Overtone of the **fundamental frequency** of the vocal tract; multiple of the fundamental frequency.

Head (5.4.2; 5.6.2)   The constituent verb from which a phrase is named and which determines the syntactic properties of the phrase (e.g., in a verb phrase, the head is the verb; in a noun phrase, the head is the noun).

Head-Final (Language) (5.6.2)   A syntactic type of language in which the **head** word of a phrase appears at the end of the phrase.

Head-Initial (Language) (5.6.2)   A syntactic type of language in which the **head** word of a phrase appears at the beginning of the phrase.

Height (2.3.1)   A property of the production of vowels having to do with how high or low the body of the tongue is.

Hemisphere (9.1.2)   One of two nearly symmetrical halves of the brain. (See also **Left Hemisphere** and **Right Hemisphere.**)

Hemispherectomy (9.1.4)   An operation in which one **hemisphere** or part of one hemisphere is surgically removed from the brain.

Heuristic (16.5.5)   A principled method of trial-and-error.

Hierarchical Structure (4.2.1; 5.1.5)   The dominance relationship among elements in a word, phrase, or sentence. (See also **Constituent Structure.**)

High (Vowel) (2.3.1)   An articulation in which the tongue is held at a relatively high (i.e., neither low nor mid) area of the oral cavity.

High Amplitude Sucking (HAS) (8.2.1)   Experimental technique used to study sound discrimination in infants from birth to about six months. Infants are given a special pacifier that is connected to a sound-generating system. Each suck on the pacifier generates a noise, and infant's sucking behavior is used to draw conclusions about discrimination abilities.

Historical Linguistics (12.1.1)   The study of how languages change through time; the study of how languages are historically related to one another.

Holophrase (8.3.2)   A one-word sentence.

Holophrastic Stage (8.3.2)   See **One-Word Stage**.

Homesign (System) (8.1.2)   A rudimentary visual-gestural communication system (not a language) that is developed and used by deaf children and their families when a signed language is not made available for their communication.

Homophone (*adjective:* **Homophonous**) (4.1.4)   One of two or more distinct words or morphemes with the same pronunciation but different meanings.

Hypercorrection (10.1.4)   The act of producing nonstandard forms by way of false analogy to standard forms.

Hypernym (6.3.2)   A more general term: a word whose denotation always includes the set of things denoted by some **hyponym**.

Hyponym (6.3.2)   A more specific term: a word whose denotation is always included in the set of things denoted by some **hypernym**.

Hyponymy (6.3.2)   Property of two words such that the set of things denoted by one word is a subset of the set of things denoted by the other word. (See also **Hypernym** and **Hyponym**.)

I

Iconicity (*adjective:* **Iconic**) (1.4.7)   Relationship between **form** and meaning such that the form of a word bears a resemblance to its meaning. (See also **Arbitrary** and **Onomatopoeia**.)

Idiolect (10.1.1)   The language variety of an individual speaker.

Idiom (6.5.1)   Fixed sequence of words with a fixed meaning that is not composed of the literal meanings of the individual words.

Imitation Theory (8.1.1; 8.1.3)   Child language acquisition theory that claims that children acquire language by listening to the speech around them and reproducing what they hear. (See also **Active Construction of a Grammar Theory, Reinforcement Theory, Connectionist Theory,** and **Social Interaction Theory**.)

Immediate Source (11.2.1)   In **borrowing** situations, the language from which a word has been directly borrowed (rather than some earlier source language for the word). (See also **Ultimate Source**.)

Imperative (7.4.6)   A sentence **form** that literally gives a command. (In English, imperative sentences begin with a bare verb stem and do not have an explicitly named subject.) (See also **Declarative** and **Interrogative**.)

Implication (*verb:* **Imply**) (7.3.2)   An idea that is communicated indirectly (either through language or otherwise) but that is not **entailed**.

Implicational Law (3.4.2)   Observation about language universals that takes the form of an implication (e.g., if A then B, meaning that if a language has feature A, then we can expect it to have feature B).

Implicature (*verb:* **Implicate**) (7.3.2; 16.4.2)   An idea that is communicated based on the way that language is used and on what speakers know about language use rather than on what is directly **entailed**.

Impressionistic Phonetic Transcription (2.1.1)   A method of writing down speech sounds with the intent of capturing how they are pronounced (e.g., by using a phonetic alphabet). Usually based simply on how the sounds are perceived when heard without any special analysis.

Incorporation (4.3.6)   Morphological process by which several distinct semantic components are combined into a single word in a **polysynthetic language**.

Indirect Speech Act (7.4.5)   Utterance that performs its function in an indirect and nonliteral manner. (See also **Direct Speech Act**.)

Individual Bilingualism (11.5.1)   The ability of a person to speak more than one language.

Infant-Directed Speech (8.4.1)   See **Child-Directed Speech**.

Infelicitous (7.1.5)   Describes an utterance that is not appropriate for the context in which it is uttered. Infelicity can result from a violation of one of the **Gricean maxims**, from the lack of fulfillment of some **felicity condition**, from an unsatisfied **presupposition**, or from some other source. An infelicitous utterance is marked with a pound sign. (See also **Felicitous**.)

Inference (*verb:* **Infer**) (7.2.2; 7.3.2)   A conclusion that is drawn from an **implication** or an **implicature**.

Infix (4.2.2)   A type of **bound morpheme** that is inserted into the middle of the stem. (See also **Affix, Prefix,** and **Suffix**.)

Inflection (4.1.3)   Modification of a word to express a grammatical relationship to other words in the sentence.

Information Content (6.1.1)   The information conveyed by or contained in a linguistic unit such as a phrase, sentence, or utterance.

In-Group Slang (10.1.1)   A type of **slang** that is associated with a particular group at a particular time. (See also **Common Slang**.)

Initial Cohort (9.5.4)   In the **cohort model** of lexical access, the words that are activated as possible candidates when the first sound of a word is perceived.

Innateness Hypothesis (8.1.1; 8.1.2)   A hypothesis that humans are generally predisposed to learn and use language.

Input (4.4.1)   The linguistic **form** before the application of a rule or a set of rules. (See also **Output**.)

Insertion (3.2.3; 12.3.3)   Phonological process by

which a segment not present in the phonemic (or underlying) form is added in the phonetic form. (See also **Deletion**.)

Instrument (5.2.2)   The **role** of a noun phrase denoting a thing used for an action.

Intelligible (*noun:* **Intelligibility**) (15.1.1)   Capable of being understood. (See also **Mutual Intelligibility**.) In speech synthesis, how well listeners can make out the individual sounds or words generated by the synthesis system.

Intension (6.1.1)   See **Sense**.

Intensity of Contact (11.1.3)   Level of contact between speakers of different languages, determined by the duration of the linguistic contact and the amount of interaction among the speakers.

Intentional Structure (15.3.4)   The organization of discourse segments' purposes and their interrelationships.

Interactive (15.4.3)   Computer systems that interact with a human user to obtain data and to give results or information.

Interchangeability (1.4.5; 14.1.1)   Property of some communication systems in which all users can both send and receive messages (as opposed to other systems, in which some individuals can only send messages and others can only receive messages). (See also **Design Features**.)

Interdental (Speech Sound) (2.2.4)   Sound produced by positioning the tip of the tongue between the upper and lower teeth.

Interlingua (15.4.3)   In machine translation, a language-independent "intermediate" language constructed to represent important linguistic properties (such as syntactic and semantic properties) that are necessary for the automatic translation from a **source language** into the **target language**(s). (See also **Transfer Method**.)

Internal Reconstruction (12.7.2)   Method of analysis used to hypothesize about a language's history by comparing forms that are assumed to be related within a single language. (See also **Comparative Method**.)

Internal Variation (10.0)   Property (of languages) of having more than one way of expressing the same meaning.

Interpreting (15.4.1)   The process of rendering one language into another, usually in spoken or signed form (rather than in writing).

Interrogative (7.4.6)   A sentence **form** that literally asks a question. (In English, interrogative sentences have an auxiliary verb that precedes the subject.) (See also **Imperative** and **Declarative**.)

Intersective Adjective (6.5.3)   **Adjective** whose denotation picks out a set of **referents** independently from the set of referents denoted by the noun being modified.

Intertwined Language (11.1.4)   See **Bilingual Mixed Language**.

Intonation (2.5.1; 9.6.2)   Commonly refers to the pattern of pitch movements across a stretch of speech such as a sentence. The meaning of a sentence can depend in part on the intonation contour of the sentence. (See also **Pitch Accent** and **Edge Tone**.)

Intransitive Verb (5.6.2)   **Verb** that takes only subject noun phrases and no object noun phrases. (See **Transitive Verb**.)

Isogloss (10.3.2)   A line drawn on a dialect map marking the boundary of an area where a particular linguistic feature is found.

Isolated Speech (15.3.3)   With regard to speech recognition software, clear speech input without extraneous words.

Isolating (Language) (4.3.2)   See **Analytic Language**.

J

Jargon (7.2.2; 10.1.1)   Speech usually associated with or used within a particular occupation, hobby, or sport. (Also known as technical language.) (In **contact situations**, see **Prepidgin Jargon**.)

K

Key (16.5.5)   In cryptography, the secret or code that can decode the message.

Key Distribution Problem (16.5.3)   The problem of safely delivering the **key** that allows deciphering an encoded message to the intended receiver of the message.

L

/l/-Vocalization (10.3.8)   The process of pronouncing syllable-final /l/ as a vowel or a **glide**.

Labiodental (Speech Sound) (2.2.4)   Sound produced by making contact between the lower lip and the upper teeth.

Lack of Invariance (9.4.1)   Problem in speech perception because no sound is ever produced exactly the same way twice.

Language (1.0)   An abstract cognitive system that uniquely allows humans to produce and comprehend meaningful utterances. (See also **Natural Language, Constructed Language,** and **Formal Language**.)

Language Acquisition (1.2.3, 9.0)   See **First-Language Acquisition** and **Second-Language Acquisition**.

Language Center (9.1.2)   Parts of the **cortex** of the brain that, as far as we know, are used only for the production and comprehension of language.

Language Choice (11.5.2)   A bilingual or multilingual person's decision—often politically, socially, or personally motivated—to speak a certain language in a certain situation.

Language Contact (11.0)   Situation in which groups of speakers of different languages come into contact with one another.

Language Convergence (11.0; 11.1.4)   The process by which two or more languages in contact become increasingly similar in both grammar and lexicon.

Language Death (11.0; 11.1.4; 11.6.1)   The complete demise of a language; a dead language no longer has any speakers. (See also **Endangered Language.**)

Language Endangerment (11.6.1)   See **Endangered Language.**

Language Family (12.0)   A group of related languages, in the sense that they come from common origins.

Language Mixing (8.5.2)   See **Code-Switching.**

Language Modeling (15.2.3)   In **automatic speech recognition**, filtering out unlikely word sequences.

Language Shift (11.0; 11.1.4)   The process by which a group of speakers abandons their native language in favor of another language.

Language Variation (1.2.4; 10.0)   Property of any linguistic phenomenon that can differ in different contexts according to factors such as geography, social class, gender, age, and so on.

Language Variety (10.1.1)   Any form of language characterized by systematic features. Varieties can range from **idiolects** to **dialects** to distinct **languages.**

Larynx (2.2.2)   Cartilage and muscle located at the top of the trachea and containing the vocal folds; commonly referred to as the voicebox. (See also **Glottis.**)

Late Closure (9.6.2)   Proposed universal parsing principle that suggests that incoming material is incorporated into the clause or phrase currently being processed if possible. (See also **Syntactic Parsing.**)

Lateralization (9.1.4)   Specialization of the brain **hemispheres** for different cognitive functions.

Lax (vowel) (2.3.5)   Vowel sound that has a less peripheral position in the vowel space. (See also **Tense.**)

Left Hemisphere (9.1.2)   The left side of the brain; the location of many language-controlling parts of the brain for most people; receives and controls nerve input from the right half of the body. (See also **Right Hemisphere.**)

Length (2.5.2)   Increased duration of segments. (See also **Suprasegmental Feature.**)

Lenition (3.2.3)   See **Weakening.**

Lexical Ambiguity (9.5.6)   A situation in which a lexical item (a word) has two or more meanings. (See also **Structural Ambiguity.**)

Lexical Bias Effect (9.3.3)   Describes the fact that phonological errors give rise to real words more often than chance would predict.

Lexical Borrowing (11.1.2; 11.2.1)   Process of adopting words or phrases from another language. (See also **Borrowing.**)

Lexical Category (4.1.1; 5.1.3)   Class of words grouped together based on morphological and syntactic properties. (Traditionally known as part of speech.)

Lexical Decision (9.7.3)   An experimental protocol in which a participant is asked to identify stimuli as words or nonwords and the decision time is measured.

Lexical Decomposition (6.3.3)   A way of analyzing lexical meaning by breaking a word's meanings into more basic parts. (Also called componential analysis.)

Lexical Processing (9.5.1)   The task of recognizing single whole words.

Lexical Semantics (6.1.2)   The study of the meaning of individual words.

Lexicon (1.2.4; 4.1.1; 6.3.1; 9.3.3; 9.5.1)   Mental list of the words in a language, including information about their meaning, grammatical function, pronunciation, and other properties that a speaker must know in order to use a word properly.

Lexifier (11.3.2)   The language that provides most of the vocabulary of a **pidgin**. (See also **Superstratum Language.**)

Lexigram (14.3.2)   Visual symbols used as part of a system for communication between humans and trained animals (generally apes). Lexigram communication shares several properties of language but is not as complex.

Limited Domain (15.3.2)   A restricted scope of application.

Linguist (1.1.4)   Someone who studies the structure of language and its use.

Linguistic Competence (1.2.1; 9.3.3; 9.6.1)   What we know when we know a language; the unconscious knowledge that a speaker of a language has about her or his native language. (See also **Linguistic Performance.**)

Linguistic Context (7.1.4)   The linguistic environment in which an utterance is uttered: specifically, the discourse that has immediately preceded the utterance in question. (See also **Context, Social Context,** and **Situational Context.**)

Linguistic Determinism (13.3.3)   A stronger version of the principle of **linguistic relativity** that claims that a society is in some way confined by its language, that language actually determines thought and culture.

Linguistic Facial Expression (2.7.7; 9.2.6)   Facial expressions that are part of a **visual-gestural**

language's grammar. (See also **Affective Facial Expression**.)

Linguistic Performance (1.2.1)   The observable use of language. The actualization of one's **linguistic competence**.

Linguistic Relativity (13.3.1)   The hypothesis (generally associated with Benjamin Lee Whorf) that the worldview of a speech community is subtly conditioned by the structure of its language. (See also **Linguistic Determinism**.)

Linguistic Sign (1.4.7)   The combination of a linguistic **form** with a meaning.

Linguistic Universal (8.1.2)   Property believed to be held in common by all **natural languages**.

Linguistics (1.1.4)   The scientific study of language.

Liquid (2.2.5)   Consonant sound produced by an obstruction of airflow that is less narrow than that of **stops** or **fricatives**, but more narrow than that of **glides**.

Loan Translation (11.1.2)   Phrase borrowed into a language by way of a word-for-word translation into native morphemes. (Also called a calque.)

Loanword (11.1.2)   Word borrowed from one language into another. (See also **Borrowing**.)

Lobe (9.1.2)   An area in a hemisphere of the brain. (See also **Temporal Lobe, Frontal Lobe, Occipital Lobe,** and **Parietal Lobe**.)

Location (2.7.3)   A type of **prime** in a **visual-gestural language**: where the sign takes place.

Logographic Writing System (13.4.2)   See **Morphographic Writing System**.

Low (Vowel) (2.3.1)   An articulation where the tongue is held at a relatively low (i.e., neither high nor mid) area of the oral cavity.

Lowering (12.3.5)   A type of sound change (either diachronic or synchronic) in which a **high** or **mid** sound becomes a lower sound. (See also **Raising**.)

M

Machine Translation (MT) (15.4.1)   Use of computers to translate from one language to another.

Malapropism (9.3.3)   **Performance error** by which a speaker uses a semantically incorrect word in place of a phonetically similar word. (See also **Classical Malapropism**.)

Manner of Articulation (2.2.5)   Term used to refer to how the airstream is modified by the articulators in the vocal tract to produce a sound.

Manual-Gestural Language (1.5.1)   See **Visual-Gestural Language**.

Maxim (for Cooperative Conversation) (7.2.1)   See **Gricean Maxims**.

McGurk Effect (9.4.4)   Effect illustrating that we rely not only on an acoustic signal in the perception of speech, but also on visual information. Occurs when a video showing a person produc-

ing one sound is dubbed with a sound-recording of the production of a different sound, and an observer's perception of the sound is affected by both kinds of input.

Mental Grammar (1.2.3)   The knowledge that a speaker has in his mind about the rules of his native language.

Mental Image Definition (6.2.5)   A conception of a word's meaning based on the picture that a language user has in his head upon thinking of that word.

Mental Lexicon (1.2.4; 4.1.1; 6.3.1; 9.3.3; 9.5.1)   See **Lexicon**.

Metaphorical Extension (12.6.2)   An expansion of the meaning of a word to include an object or concept that is like the original **referent** in some metaphorical sense rather than a literal sense. (See also **Extension**.)

Metathesis (3.2.3; 9.3.3; 12.3.3)   Switching of the order of two sounds, each taking the place of the other.

Mid (Vowel) (2.3.2)   An articulation in which the tongue is held at a relatively middle (i.e., neither high nor low) area of the oral cavity.

Minimal Pair (3.1.3)   Two words that differ only by a single sound in the same position and that have different meanings.

Mixed Language (11.0)   See **Bilingual Mixed Language**.

Modality (1.4.2; 1.5.1)   See **Mode of Communication**. (See also **Auditory-Vocal Language** and **Visual-Gestural Language**.)

Mode of Communication (1.4.2; 14.1.1)   Means through which a message is transmitted for any given communication system. (See also **Design Features**.)

Monitor Corpus (15.5.2)   A **corpus** that is continually growing. As new texts continue to be written or spoken, the corpus continues to grow, gathering more and more data. (See also **Reference Corpus**.)

Monoalphabetic Cipher (16.5.5)   A **cipher** in which the letters of the **plaintext** are each replaced with a randomly selected corresponding letter from a character set, such that each letter of the plaintext always translates to the same letter in the **ciphertext**.

Monophthong (2.1.3)   A simple vowel, composed of a single configuration of the vocal organs. (See also **Diphthong**.)

Monophthongization (12.3.3)   Vowel change from a conplex vowel sound to a simple vowel sound; vowel change from a **diphthong** to a monophthong.

Moraic Writing System (13.4.2)   See **Syllabic Writing System**.

Morpheme (4.1.4)   Smallest linguistic unit that has a meaning or grammatical function.

Morphographic Writing System (13.4.2)   A

writing system that relies predominantly on the representation of the meanings of words. Each symbol usually represents a morpheme. Sometimes referred to as logographic. (See also **Phonographic Writing System.**)

Morphology (1.2.2; 4.0; 4.1.3)   The study of how words are constructed out of **morphemes** or marked via other processes.

Motor Cortex (9.1.2)   Language center of the brain located in the upper middle of each **hemisphere,** perpendicular to the **Sylvian fissure**; responsible for sending impulses to the muscles.

Movement (2.7.4; 5.5.4)   With regard to the phonetics of **visual-gestural languages,** a **prime**: whether the hands move during a sign, and if so, the path or type of that motion. In syntax, a test for syntactic constituency in which a group of words is relocated to a different position in a sentence to see whether the resulting string of words is also a grammatical sentence. (See also **Topicalization.**) Also a process for establishing word order in a sentence that is a component of many syntactic theories (which are not discussed in this book).

Multilingual (*noun*: **Multilingualism**) (8.5.1; 11.5.1 15.2.3)   The state of commanding three or more languages; having **linguistic competence** in three or more languages. In **machine translation,** a system that can translate between more than two languages.

Multiple Negation (10.3.7; 10.4.5)   The process of using more than one marker of negation when only one such marker would be used in **Standard American English.**

Mutual Intelligibility (10.1.1)   Situation in which speakers of different language varieties are able to understand and communicate with one another. (See also **Intelligibility.**)

N

Naming Task (9.7.3)   A task in which a participant responds to a stimulus by saying the word for the stimulus aloud while an experimenter measures the response time.

Nasal (Speech Sound) or **Nasal Stop** (2.2.5)   Sound produced by making a complete obstruction of the airflow in the oral cavity and by lowering the velum to allow air to pass through the nasal cavity, unlike **oral stops.**

Nasalized (Vowel) (2.4.2)   Vowel produced while lowering the velum to allow air to pass through the nasal cavity.

Native Language (L1) Interference (1.2.5; 11.0; 11.1.3)   The process of carrying over features from one's native language into another language, usually in **language contact** or **second-language acquisition** situations.

Nativization (11.4.1)   Process by which some variety of speech that was no one's native language

is learned by children in a speech community as their first language.

Natural Class (3.2.2)   Group of sounds in a language that satisfy a given description to the exclusion of other sounds in that language.

Natural Language (1.4.11)   A language that has evolved naturally in a speech community. (See also **Constructed Language.**)

Natural Language Processing (NLP) (15.5.1)   The ability of computers to analyze, parse, interpret, and generate **natural language** (thereby allowing humans to interact with computers using natural language instead of formal computer languages).

Naturalness (15.1.1)   In speech synthesis, how much the synthesized speech sounds like the speech of an actual person.

Near-Minimal Pair (3.5.2)   Similar to a **minimal pair,** but whereas the words in a minimal pair are identical apart from the **contrastive** sounds, the words in a near-minimal pair are only **almost** identical, apart from the contrastive sounds.

Neglected Child (8.1.2)   A child who is neglected by caretakers, often resulting in significantly lower exposure to language as a child.

Neurolinguistics (9.0; 9.1.1)   The study of the neural and electrochemical bases of language development and use.

Node (5.4.3)   In a **phrase structure tree,** any point at which a branch terminates or joins another branch. Nodes are labeled according to the type of constituent (word or phrase) that is beneath that node in the tree.

Noise (1.2.2)   Interference in the **communication chain.**

Noisy Channel Model (15.2.2)   In automatic speech recognition, modeling variations in pronunciation that distort the words' canonical form. By modeling the distortion, its effects can be removed and the original signal reconstructed.

Nonarbitrariness (1.4.7)   Direct correspondence between the physical properties of a **form** and the meaning that the form refers to. (See also **Arbitrary.**)

Noncontrastive (3.1.2)   A term used to describe two sounds that are not used to differentiate words in a language. (See also **Contrastive.**)

Non-Intersection Adjective (6.5.3)   **Adjective** that picks out a subset of things denoted by the noun it modifies but that does not, in and of itself, pick out any particular set of things.

Nonstandard Dialect (10.1.4)   Any variety of a language not considered to be representative of the **prestige** or standard variety. (See also **Standard Dialect.**)

Northern Cities Shift (10.3.4)   The systematic rotation of the vowel space found in speakers in the northern region of the United States.

Noun (N) (5.3.2)   A word that refers to real, imaginary, or abstract objects, places, actions, or events.

Nucleus (2.1.3)   See **Syllable Nucleus.**

O

Object (5.2.2)   The position occupied by a noun phrase in English typically immediately after the verb in the sentence.

Obligatory Rule (3.2.5)   **Rule** that applies in the speech of all speakers of a language or dialect, regardless of style or rate of speech. (See also **Optional Rule.**)

Obstruent (3.2.2)   A **natural class** of sounds produced with an obstruction of the airflow in the oral cavity while the nasal cavity is closed off. Includes **oral stops, fricatives,** and **affricates.** (See also **Sonorant.**)

Occipital Lobe (9.1.2)   Area of the brain associated with many aspects of vision.

Offline Task (9.7.3)   Any task that measures the final result of a process but not what happens during the process. (See also **Online Task.**)

One-Time Pad (16.5.3)   A very secure method to send encoded messages. **Alice** makes two identical copies of a pad of completely random numbers and sends one copy to **Bob** ahead of time. The pad is then used at a later time to encode and decipher a message.

One-Word Stage (8.3.2)   Stage in **first-language acquisition** during which children can produce only one word at a time. (Also called the holophrastic stage.)

Online Task (9.7.4)   Any task that is designed to reveal what happens during a process and when during the process it happens. (See also **Offline Task.**)

Onomatopoeia (1.4.7)   **Iconic** use of words that are imitative of sounds occurring in nature or that have meanings that are associated with such sounds.

Open Lexical Category (5.3.1)   **Lexical category** into which new members are often introduced. (See also **Content Word** and **Closed Lexical Category.**)

Optional Rule (3.2.5)   Phonological, morphological, or syntactic **rule** that may or may not apply in an individual's speech. (See also **Obligatory Rule.**)

Oral Stop (2.2.5)   Sound produced by completely obstructing the airstream in the oral cavity and then quickly releasing the constriction to allow the air to escape. Made with the **velum** raised so that no air escapes through the nose, unlike **nasal stops.**

Oralist Education (13.3.3)   A pedagogic theory for teaching deaf children that suggests that they should be taught using predominantly (or exclusively) spoken language rather than signed language.

Orientation (2.7.6)   A type of **prime** in a **visual-gestural language:** the direction that the hand or hands are facing during a sign; may also include whether there is contact between the hands and how that contact takes place.

Output (4.4.1)   The linguistic form obtained after an application of a rule or a set of rules. (See also **Input.**)

Overextension (8.3.5)   In the study of child language acquisition, a relationship between child and adult perception of word meaning: the child's application of a given word has a wider range than the application of the same word in adult language. (See also **Underextension.**)

Overgeneralization (8.3.4)   In the study of child language acquisition, a relationship between child and adult application of rules relative to certain contexts: a process in which children extend the application of linguistic rules to contexts beyond those in the adult language.

Overlapping Distribution (3.1.4)   The occurrence of sounds in the same phonetic environments. (See also **Contrastive Distribution** and **Free Variation.**)

Overt Prestige (10.1.4)   Type of **prestige** attached to a particular variety of language by the community at large that defines how people should speak in order to gain status in the wider community.

P

Palatal (Speech Sound) (2.2.4)   Sound made by raising the body of the tongue toward the hard part of the roof of the mouth (i.e., the hard **palate**).

Palatalization (3.2.3)   A process wherein a sound takes on a **palatal** place of articulation, usually in **assimilation** to **high** or **mid** front vowels like [i] or [e].

Palatalized (2.4.6)   A term used to describe the articulation of a sound which involves the tongue moving toward the hard **palate.**

Palate (2.2.4)   Bony portion of the roof of the mouth (also known as the hard palate), extending from the **alveolar ridge** to the **velum.**

Palatography (2.1.1)   Experimental method that shows the contact between the tongue and the roof of the mouth. Can be **static** or **dynamic.**

Paradigm (12.4.1)   A set of grammatically (i.e., inflectionally) related forms all stemming from a common **root.**

Paradigm Leveling (12.4.1)   A type of morphological change in which irregular members of a **paradigm** become regulated through **analogy.**

Parallel (9.3.2)   Pertains to a model of speech processing in which different stages are all processed simultaneously and influence each other. (See also **Serial**.)

Parallel Corpus (15.5.2)   A **corpus** including texts that contain the same sentences written in different languages.

Parameter (2.7.2; 9.3.4)   In signed languages, aspects of articulation that describe **primes**.

Parietal Lobe (9.1.2)   Area of the brain that is least involved in language perception and production.

Parsing (9.6.1)   See **Syntactic Parsing**.

Part of Speech (4.1.1; 5.1.3)   See **Lexical Category**.

Partial Reduplication (4.2.5)   Morphological **reduplication** in which only part of a morpheme is reduplicated. (See also **Total Reduplication**.)

Patient (5.2.2)   The entity that is acted upon in a sentence. (See also **Role**.)

Performance (1.2.1)   See **Linguistic Performance**.

Performance Error (1.2.1)   Errors in language production or comprehension including hesitations and slips of the tongue. (See also **Linguistic Performance**.)

Performative Speech Act (7.4.3)   A **speech act** that employs a **performative verb**.

Performative Verb (7.4.3)   A verb that denotes a linguistic action; a verb that is used to perform the act that it names. (See also **Performative Speech Act**.)

Periodic Wave (2.6.2)   Sound wave that repeats itself at regular intervals.

Perseveration (9.3.3)   **Production error** in which an earlier unit is substituted for a later unit or in which an earlier unit is added later in an utterance. (See also **Anticipation**.)

Pharynx (2.2.5; 2.4.5)   The part of the oral tract above the **larynx** but behind the **uvula**. Commonly referred to as the throat.

Pharynx Wall (2.2.5)   The wall of the part of the oral tract above the **larynx** but behind the **uvula**. (See **Pharynx**.)

Phone (2.1.2)   A speech sound. Phones are written in square brackets, for example, [t].

Phoneme (3.1.2)   A class of speech sounds identified by a native speaker as the same sound; a mental entity (or category) related to various **allophones** by **phonological rules**. Phonemes are written between slashes, for example, /t/.

Phonemic Restoration (9.4.5)   Hearing a sound that was not actually produced, because the sound fits in the context of the utterance.

Phonemic Sound Change (12.3.4)   A sound change that results in a change in the phonological system of a language, often through the addition or deletion of a **phoneme**.

Phonemic Writing System (13.4.2)   A **phonographic writing system** in which each symbol represents a single **segment** like a consonant or a vowel. (Also known as an alphabetic writing system. See also **Alphabet, Abugida,** and **Abjad**.)

Phonetic Sound Change (12.3.4)   Change in the pronunciation of **allophones** which has no effect on the phonological inventory of a language.

Phonetics (1.1.3; 2.0)   The study of the minimal units of language (e.g., the sounds of spoken language). (See also **Articulatory Phonetics, Acoustic Phonetics,** and **Auditory Phonetics**.)

Phonographic Writing System (13.4.2)   A writing system that relies predominantly on the representation of the sounds of words. (See also **Phonemic, Syllabic,** and **Morphographic Writing Systems**.)

Phonological Rule (3.2.1)   The description of a relationship between a **phoneme** and its **allophones** and the conditioning environment in which the allophone appears. (See also **Rule**.)

Phonology (1.2.2; 3.0)   The study of the sound system of a language; how the particular sounds contrast in each language to form an integrated system for encoding information and how such systems differ from one language to another.

Phonotactic Constraint (3.3.1; 9.3.3)   Restriction on possible combinations of sounds. (See also **Sound Substitution**.)

Phrase (5.1.5; 5.4.2)   A group of words that work together to create a single syntactic **constituent**, generally larger than a single word, but smaller than a sentence.

Phrase Structure Rule (5.4.4)   **Rule** that shows the possible (i.e., **grammatical**) relationships between phrasal categories and the words or phrasal categories they are made from.

Phrase Structure Tree (5.4.3)   A visual means of representing the syntactic structure of a **phrase** or sentence.

Pictogram (13.4.6)   Stylized drawing of concrete objects used as characters in certain writing systems to represent the idea of the object iconically.

Pidgin (Language) (11.0; 11.1.4; 11.3.1)   A simplified language that develops in **contact situations** in which speakers previously shared no common language. (See also **Prototypical Pidgin** and **Expanded Pidgin**.)

Pitch Accent (2.5.3, 7.5.3)   A change in **fundamental frequency** used to put prominence on a particular word in an utterance. (See also **Edge Tone** and **Intonation**.)

Place of Articulation (2.2.4)   Place in the vocal tract where the **constriction** for the production of a speech sound is made by the **articulators**.

Plaintext (16.5.2)   In **cryptography,** the original, non-encoded text. (See also **Ciphertext**.)

Polysynthetic (Language) (4.3.6)   A type of language that attaches several **affixes** to a **stem** to indicate grammatical relationships.

Popular Etymology (12.4.2)   See **Folk Etymology.**

Possible Scenario (6.4.2)   One of many possible ways in which the world could be, had things turned out slightly differently than they in fact did.

Postposition (5.6.2)   A grammatical **function word** that follows the phrase with which it is associated in order to give information about grammatical relations. (See also **Preposition.**)

Power (11.1.3)   The influence or control a person, group, or nation has over others.

Pragmatic Function (1.4.4; 14.1.1)   The useful purpose of any given communication system. (See also **Design Features.**)

Pragmatics (1.2.2)   The study of how **context** affects language use: both whether or not a particular utterance is **felicitous** in a given context and how the context affects that utterance's meaning or interpretation.

Pre-Editing (15.4.3)   In partially automated **machine translation,** the process of rewriting the source text in simpler, less ambiguous language or marking the text to indicate word boundaries, proper names, plurals, and other features that will need to be addressed during the translation process.

Prefix (4.1.4; 4.2.2)   **Affix** that attaches to the beginning of a **stem.** (See also **Suffix.**)

Prepidgin Jargon (11.3.1)   An extremely rudimentary and variable type of language formed in the earlier stages of **contact situations.**

Preposition (Prep) (5.3.3)   A grammatical **function word** that precedes the phrase with which it is associated in order to give information about grammatical relations. (See also **Postposition.**)

Prescriptive Grammar (1.3.3)   A set of rules designed to give instructions regarding the "correct" or "proper" way to speak or write. (See also **Descriptive Grammar.**)

Prescriptive Standard (10.1.4)   The standard by which a society makes judgments of "right" or "wrong."

Prestige (*adjective:* **Prestigious**) (10.1.4; 11.1.3)   Having high standing or respect in a community. Can be **overt** or **covert.**

Presupposition (7.5.1, 16.4.2)   An underlying assumption that a speaker believes (and that the speaker behaves as though other participants in the discourse believe) prior to making an utterance. In order for an utterance to make sense or for it to be debatable, any presuppositions must be either **satisfied** or accommodated. (See also **Presupposition Accommodation.**)

Presupposition Accommodation (7.5.5)   The process by which participants in a discourse decide to accept (and not question) information that is presupposed by a sentence uttered in the discourse, even though the **presupposition** was not **satisfied** prior to the utterance.

Presupposition Trigger (7.5.2)   A word or phrase that typically indicates that a sentence has a **presupposition;** a word or phrase whose meaning generates presuppositions.

Prime (2.7.2; 9.7.3)   With regard to **visual-gestural languages,** a fundamental element, equivalent in many ways to a **phoneme** in an **auditory-vocal language,** with the exception that primes are produced simultaneously, whereas phonemes can be produced only sequentially. (See also **Location, Movement, Handshape, Orientation,** and **Linguistic Facial Expression.**) In language processing, the stimulus presented in a priming task right before the stimulus of interest. (See also **Target.**)

Priming (9.7.3)   Any experimental task in which participants are presented with a stimulus right before the stimulus of interest in order to see how or whether presentation of the earlier stimulus affects response to the stimulus of interest. (See also **Prime** and **Target.**)

Principle of Compositionality (6.5.1)   Principle stating that the meaning of a sentence is determined by the meaning of its words and by the syntactic structure in which they are combined.

Production Error (9.3.3)   Inadvertent flaws in a speaker's use of his or her language: "slips of the tongue" or "slips of the hands."

Productive (4.1.6)   Describes a **rule** (such as a morphological rule stating under what circumstances an affix may be added to a stem) that can be applied in novel situations to produce novel grammatical forms.

Productivity (1.4.10; 14.1.1)   The ability of a communication system (unique to human language) for novel **forms,** which may encode novel ideas, to be produced and understood. (See also **Design Features.**) Of a **rule,** the ability of that rule to apply in a new situation in order to create a novel form.

Pronoun (Pron) (5.3.3)   A closed lexical class of words that may stand in for a noun phrase or refer to some entity previously mentioned or assumed in the discourse.

Pronunciation Modeling (15.2.3)   In **automatic speech recognition,** the filtering out of unlikely phoneme sequences.

Proper Noun (8.3.5)   Name that denotes a particular individual person, place, or company, etc.

Proportional Analogy (12.4.1)   A type of morphological change caused by the influence of one pair of morphologically related words on another. (See also **Analogical Change.**)

Prosodic Break (9.6.2)   **Intonational** cues in the speech continuum that cause the parser to divide the continuum into discrete units.

Protoform (12.7.3)   A **reconstructed form** of a word.

Proto-Indo-European (PIE) (12.7.3)   The single ancestor of most of today's languages of Europe and India.

Protolanguage (12.2.2)   An earlier common ancestor of similar languages.

Prototype (6.2.5)   For any given **set,** a member that exhibits the typical qualities of the members of some set.

Prototypical Pidgin (11.3.1)   **Pidgin** that emerges rather abruptly in **contact situations** in which the contact is limited to particular social settings (such as trade). A prototypical pidgin has a reduced linguistic structure, but may evolve into an **expanded pidgin.**

Psycholinguistics (9.0; 9.1.1)   The study of the brain and how it functions in the production, perception, comprehension, storage, and acquisition of language.

Pulmonic Egressive Airstream Mechanism (2.2.1)   **Airstream mechanism** that produces speech sounds by modifying the stream of air forced out of the lungs and passed through the oral and/or nasal cavities.

Pure Intersection (6.5.3)   The relationship between the denotations of an **adjective** and a **noun** such that each picks out a particular group of things, and the denotation of the phrase that results from modifying the noun with the adjective is all of the things that are in both the **set** denoted by the adjective and the set denoted by the noun.

R

Raising (12.3.4)   A type of sound change (either synchronic or diachronic) in which a **low** or **mid** vowel sound becomes a higher sound. (See also **Lowering.**)

Rarefaction (2.6.2)   Physical phenomenon by which air molecules become less concentrated within a given space (i.e., pressure decreases). (See also **Compression.**)

Rebus Principle (13.4.3)   A principle found in some writing systems whereby a picture of a particular object is used to represent the sounds (but not the meaning) of the name of that object.

Recency Effect (9.5.5)   A psycholinguistic phenomenon whereby word recognition or production occurs faster owing to recent exposure to that word.

Recipient (5.2.2)   In a sentence, a **role** designating the individual that comes into possession of something (either something physical or something abstract).

Reconstructed Form (12.7.3)   Hypothetical word form recreated through **reconstruction.**

Reconstruction (*verb:* **Reconstruct**) (12.2.2)   The process of recreating earlier forms of a language or a protolanguage, through either the **comparative method** or **internal reconstruction.**

Recursion (5.4.6)   Property of languages allowing for the repeated application of a **rule,** yielding infinitely long sentences or an infinite number of sentences.

Reduction (12.6.3)   Semantic change by which the set of appropriate contexts or **referents** for a word decreases. (See also **Extension.**)

Reduplicant (4.2.5)   The morpheme or part of a morpheme that is repeated in **reduplication.**

Reduplication (4.2.5)   Process of forming new words by doubling either an entire word (**total reduplication**) or part of a word (**partial reduplication**).

Reference Corpus (15.5.2)   A **corpus** that captures language in one particular time or place. That is, once a specified amount of texts have been collected and annotated, the corpus is complete. (See also **Monitor Corpus.**)

Referent (6.2.2)   A particular entity (idea, object, etc.) to which a word or linguistic expression relates. (See also **Extension**).

Regional Dialect (10.3.1)   Variety of language defined by region or geography.

Regional Variation (10.3.2)   **Internal variation** of a language based on region or geography.

Register (10.1.3)   See **Speech Style.**

Regularity Hypothesis (12.2.2)   The assumption that speech sounds change in regular, recognizable ways.

Reinforcement Theory (8.1.1; 8.1.4)   Theory of child language acquisition which says that children learn to speak like adults because they are praised, rewarded, or otherwise reinforced when they use the right forms and are corrected when they use the wrong ones. (See also **Active Construction of a Grammar Theory, Connectionist Theory, Social Interaction Theory,** and **Imitation Theory.**)

Relatedness Hypothesis (12.2.2)   The hypothesis that similarities among certain languages may be due to a genetic relationship among them, that is, due to their coming from common origins.

Relational Term (8.3.5)   See **Relative Intersection.**

Relative Intersection (6.5.3)   Type of relationship between **adjective** denotation and **noun** denotation such that the adjective picks out a **set** of things relative to the set of things denoted by the noun that it is modifying and relative to the context in which it is being used. (See also **Subsective Adjective** and **Non-Intersection Adjective.**)

Repeated Babbling (8.2.2)   See **Canonical Babbling.**

Representation (15.5.2)   A symbolic presentation of elements of linguistic structure, as, for
example, a **phrase structure tree** or another presentation of linguistically relevant information,
for example, the tags in a **corpus**.

Restricted Allophone (3.5.2)   The **allophone** of
a **phoneme** that appears in a more limited set
of phonetic environments. (See also **Basic
Allophone**.)

Retroflex (2.2.5)   Sound produced by curling the
tip of the tongue back behind the **alveolar ridge**
usually to the top of the mouth.

Reverses (6.3.2)   Antonyms in which one word in
the pair suggests movement that "undoes" the
movement suggested by the other. (See also **Complementary Antonyms**, **Gradable Antonyms**, and
Converses.)

Right Hemisphere (9.1.2)   The right half of the
brain, which is in charge of processing music,
perceiving nonlinguistic sounds, and performing
tasks that require visual and spatial skills or pattern recognition; receives and controls nerve input from the left half of the body. (See also **Left
Hemisphere**.)

Role (5.2.2)   In a relationship that a sentence describes, the function served by the thing denoted
by some constituent (such as **agent, patient,
instrument, theme, experiencer, source,** or
recipient).

Root (4.1.2)   The **free morpheme** or **bound root**
in a word to which other **affixes** attach or on
which all morphological processes act. (See also
Stem.)

Rounded (Vowel) (2.3.4)   An articulation in
which the lips are pursed or rounded. (See also
Rounding.)

Rounding (2.3.1)   A property of the production of
vowels having to do with whether the lips are
rounded or not.

Rule (1.2.4)   A formal statement of an observed
generalization about patterns in language. (See
also **Phonological Rule** and **Phrase Structure
Rule**.)

Running Speech (2.1.4; 15.3.3)   The usual form
of spoken language, with all the words and
phrases run together (without pauses in between
them). (Also called continuous speech.)

S

SAE (10.1.4)   See **Standard American English**.

Sagittal Section (2.2.4)   A cross section of the
human head, designed to show a side view of the
vocal anatomy.

Satisfaction (of a Presupposition) (7.5.1)   Describes a state of affairs in which the content of a
presupposition is known and agreed upon by the
participants in a discourse prior to the utterance
of the sentence that contains the presupposition.

Satisfied (7.5.1)   Of a **presupposition**, being such

that the participants in a discourse know and believe the contents of the presupposition prior to
the utterance of a sentence containing it.

Scalar Antonyms   See **Gradable Antonyms**.

Second-Language (L2) Acquisition (8.5.1;
8.5.4; 11.1.3)   Acquisition of a second language
as a teenager or adult (after the **critical period**).
(See also **First-Language (L1) Acquisition**.)

Segment (2.1.3)   An individual unit of the speech
stream; statements can be further subdivided
into consonants and vowels.

Self-Paced Reading (9.7.4)   An experimental
protocol in which participants read a sentence in
small chunks, usually one word at a time, and
push a button to move on to the next word or
chunk of words.

Semantic Association Network (9.5.5)   A system that organizes words into a web in which
words are interconnected based on different
kinds of meaning relationships; one aspect of
how words are organized in the mental **lexicon**.

Semantic Feature (6.3.3)   A condition that must
be met in order for something to be a member of
the **set** denoted by a particular word.

Semantically Anomalous (5.2.1; 6.3.3)   A string
of words that follows the grammatical **rules** of a
language but that nevertheless fails to "make
sense" because of inconsistencies, incompatibili-
ties, or contradictions in the meanings of the
words. Semantic anomalies are marked with an
exclamation point.

Semanticity (1.4.3; 14.1.1)   Property of having
signals that convey a meaning, shared by all
communication systems. (See also **Design
Features**.)

Semantics (1.2.2; 6.0; 6.1.1)   The study of linguistic meaning. (See also **Lexical Semantics** and
Compositional Semantics.)

Semi-Speaker (11.6.2)   A person who does not
speak a language fluently.

Sense (6.1.1)   The aspect of a word's meaning that
is independent of what it may refer to in the real
world: speakers' mental conception of the word's
meaning. (Also called intension.)

Sequential Bilingualism (8.5.1)   Bilingualism
in which the second language is acquired as a
young child. (See also **Simultaneous
Bilingualism**.)

Serial (9.3.2)   Pertains to a model of speech processing in which different stages of the model
form a series or succession, each influencing only
those that follow. (See also **Parallel**.)

Set (6.3.2)   A collection of items of some sort. The
items in a set are not ordered, nor do they need
to be related to each other in any particular way;
however, normally sets are used to discuss all of
the items that do have some particular property
in common, such as the property of being denoted by a particular word.

Shift (9.3.3) In the study of language change, a series of organized diachronic sound changes that occur when a group of similar sounds undergoes a phonological change that conditions further changes in another group of sounds. In speech production, a production error in which a linguistic unit is moved from one location to another.

Shift Cipher (16.5.5) A **cipher** in which the letters of the **plaintext** are replaced with a corresponding letter from an alphabet that has been shifted some number of places away from its normal order.

Sibilant (3.2.4) A member of the **natural class** of sounds that are characterized by a high-pitched hissing quality.

Sign Language or **Signed Language** (1.5.1) See **Visual-Gestural Language.**

Simultaneous Affix (4.2.3) An **affix** that is articulated at the same time as some other affix or affixes in a word's **stem**; exist only in **visual-gestural languages.**

Simultaneous Bilingualism (8.5.1) **Bilingualism** in which both languages are acquired from infancy. (See also **Sequential Bilingualism.**)

Sister Terms (6.3.2) Words that are at the same level of any given hierarchy of sets of **semantic features.**

Situational Context (7.1.4) The aspect of an utterance's **context** that includes such information as where the speakers are, who is speaking, what is going on around them, and what is going on in the world that all speakers can reasonably be expected to be aware of. (See also **Linguistic Context** and **Social Context.**)

Slang (10.1.1) Words or expressions used in informal settings, often to indicate membership in a particular social group. (See also **Common Slang** and **In-Group Slang.**)

Social Context (7.1.4) The aspect of an utterance's **context** that includes information about the social relationships between participants in the discourse, what their status is relative to each other, and so on. (See also **Linguistic Context** and **Situational Context.**)

Social Dialect (10.3.1; 10.4.1) Variety of a language defined by social factors such as age, religion, ethnicity, or socioeconomic status.

Social Interaction Theory (8.1.1; 8.1.7) Theory of language acquisition that claims that children acquire language through social interaction—in particular with older children and adults—and prompt their caregivers to supply them with the appropriate language experience they need. (See also **Imitation Theory, Reinforcement Theory, Active Construction of a Grammar Theory,** and **Connectionist Theory.**)

Social Network (10.4.4, 16.5.4) A social structure which indicates the ways in which individuals or organizations are connected.

Societal Bilingualism (11.5.1) Phenomenon in which **bilingualism** is the norm for a group of people.

Societal Multilingualism (11.5.1) Phenomenon in which **multilingualism** is the norm for a group of people.

Sociolinguistics (10.1.1) The study of the interrelationships of language and social structure, of linguistic variation, and of attitudes toward language.

Sonorant (3.2.2) Sound (usually voiced) produced with a relatively open passage of air flow. **Nasals, liquids, glides,** and vowels are all sonorants. (See also **Obstruent.**)

Sound Correspondence (12.7.3) Sounds that occur in similar positions in words that are believed to be related. (See also **Reconstruct.**)

Sound Spectrograph (2.1.1) See **Spectrograph.**

Sound Substitution (3.3.2) A process whereby sounds that already exist in a language are used to replace sounds that do not exist in the language when borrowing or when a speaker is trying to pronounce a foreign word. (See also **Phonotactic Constraints.**)

Sound Symbolism (1.4.7) Phenomenon by which certain sounds are evocative of a particular meaning.

Source (5.2.2; 15.3.3) As a thematic **role,** the location where something starts out, or a former owner. In speech synthesis, the mechanism that creates a basic sound. (See also **Source-Filter Theory.**)

Source Language (SL) (15.4.1) In translation and interpretation, the language that is going to be translated into the **target language(s).**

Source-Filter Theory (15.1.3) Theory of speech production claiming that there are two elements in the production of speech sounds: the **source** and the **filter.**

Southern Shift (10.3.6) The systematic rotation of the vowel space found in speakers in the South region of the United States.

Spectrogram (2.2.3; 2.6.4) A three-dimensional representation of sound in which the vertical axis represents frequency, the horizontal axis represents time, and the darkness of shading represents amplitude.

Spectrograph (2.1.1) Equipment that generates **spectrograms** from speech input.

Speech (1.5.1) **Utterances** of any language—both **auditory-vocal languages** and **visual-gestural languages.** (May sometimes be used to refer specifically to utterances of auditory-vocal languages; however, this is not the most commonly intended meaning of the term and applies in this book only when auditory-vocal languages and visual-gestural languages are being directly contrasted with one another.)

Speech Act (7.4.0) Actions that are performed

only through using language: a term that describes the use of speech emphasizing the speaker's intention or goal in producing an utterance. (See also **Direct Speech Act, Indirect Speech Act,** and **Performative Speech Act.**)

Speech Communication Chain (1.2.2)   See **Communication Chain.**

Speech Community (10.1.2)   A group of people speaking the same **dialect,** usually defined by factors such as geographical distribution, age, gender, and socioeconomic status.

Speech-Language Pathologist (SLP) (16.2.1)   A professional who is trained to diagnose speech and language problems and to help individuals become more effective communicators. (See also **Audiologist.**)

Speech Perception (9.4.1)   The processes involved in understanding speech and sign. (See also **Speech Production.**)

Speech Production (9.3.1)   The processes involved in producing speech and sign. (See also **Speech Perception.**)

Speech Recognition (15.2.1)   See **Automatic Speech Recognition.**

Speech Style (10.1.3)   Way of speaking marked by degrees of formality (i.e., formal versus informal, casual versus careful). (Also called register.)

Speech Synthesis (15.1.1)   The use of computers and sound-generating devices for the creation of speech sounds that approximate the acoustic characteristics of human speech.

Speech-To-Speech Machine Translation (15.4.1)   The use of computers to translate spoken text from one language into another.

Split-Brain Patient (9.1.4)   Individual whose **corpus callosum** has been surgically disconnected (a procedure once commonly used in the treatment of severe epilepsy).

Spoken Language (1.5.1)   See **Auditory-Vocal Language.**

Spoken Language Dialogue System (15.3.3)   System that allows interaction with a computer via speech.

Spoonerism (9.3.3)   **Production error** in which the first sounds of two separate words are switched. (See also **Metathesis.**)

Sprachbund (11.1.4)   A group of several languages spoken in close proximity that may influence each other. (See also **Language Convergence.**)

Standard American English (SAE) (10.1.4)   The **standard dialect** of English spoken in the United States.

Standard Dialect (10.1.4)   The variety of a language used by political leaders, the media, and speakers of higher socioeconomic classes. The variety taught in schools. The variety of a language associated with **prestige.** See also **Nonstandard Dialect.**)

Static Palatography (2.2.6)   Experimental method that displays the contact resulting from a single articulatory gesture between the tongue and the hard **palate.**

Stem (4.1.2)   The base (which may consist of one or more morphemes) on which a given morphological process acts. The stem always includes the **root,** and it may include one or more other **affixes.**

Stop (2.2.5)   See **Nasal** and **Oral Stop.**

Strengthening (3.2.3)   A process through which sounds are made "stronger" according to some criterion. (See also **Weakening.**)

Stress (2.5.5)   A property of syllables; a stressed syllable is more prominent than an unstressed one, due to having greater loudness, longer duration, different pitch, or full vowels.

Structural Ambiguity (5.1.5; 9.6.2)   A characteristic of **phrases** that have more than one possible **constituent structure** and therefore more than one semantic interpretation. (See also **Lexical Ambiguity.**)

Structural Borrowing (11.1.2)   Process of adopting grammatical structures from another language. (See also **Borrowing.**)

Structure (4.4.1; 5.1.5)   The sequential and hierarchical organization of linguistic units.

Style (10.1.3)   See **Speech Style.**

Style Shifting (10.1.3)   Process of automatically adjusting from one **speech style** to another.

Subglottal System (2.2.2)   The part of the respiratory system located below the **larynx.**

Subject (5.2.2)   The position occupied by a noun phrase immediately before the verb in English.

Subsective Adjective (6.5.3)   Adjective that derives its meaning by picking out a subset of the things from the set of things denoted by the noun being modified. (See also **Relative Intersection** and **Non-Intersection Adjective.**)

Substitution (5.5.2; 9.3.3)   In syntax, a test for constituency in which a group of words is replaced with a simple word or phrase. In language processing, a production error in which one unit is replaced with another.

Substrate Influence (11.0; 11.1.3)   See **Native Language (L1) Interference.**

Substratum or **Substratal Language** (11.1.3; 11.3.2)   In a contact situation, the native language of speakers of a politically and economically non-dominant group. (See also **Adstratum** and **Superstratum.**)

Suffix (4.1.4; 4.2.2)   **Affix** that attaches to the end of a **stem.** (See also **Prefix.**)

Superstrate Influence (11.1.3)   The process of carrying over features from a second language or contact language into the speaker's native language.

Superstratum or **Superstratal Language** (11.1.3; 11.3.2)   The **target language** in a language contact situation; the language associated with the politically and economically dominant group. (See also **Adstratum** and **Substratum**.)

Suppletion (*adjective:* **Suppletive**) (4.2.7)   A morphological process between forms of a word wherein one form cannot be phonologically or morphologically derived from the other.

Suprasegmental (Feature) (2.1.3; 2.5.1)   A phonetic characteristic of speech sounds, such as **length, intonation, tone,** or **stress,** that "rides on top of" segmental features. Must usually be identified by comparison to the same feature on other sounds or strings of sounds.

Syllabary (13.4.4)   The set of characters used in a given **syllabic writing system.**

Syllabic Consonant (2.2.5)   A consonant that is a **syllable nucleus** and takes on the function of the vowel in that particular syllable.

Syllabic Writing System (13.4.2)   A **phonographic writing system** in which each symbol represents roughly one syllable of the language. Usually such systems actually represent the moras in a language and therefore may also be called moraic systems.

Syllable Nucleus (*plural:* **Nuclei**) (2.1.3)   The core element of a syllable, carrying **stress, length,** and pitch (**tone**). It usually consists of a vowel sound or **syllabic consonant.**

Sylvian Fissure (9.1.2)   A large horizontal fold located in the middle of each **hemisphere** of the brain that separates the **temporal lobe** from the **frontal lobe** of the brain.

Synchronic Analysis (12.1.1)   Analysis of a language at a particular point in time. (See also **Diachronic Analysis**.)

Synonymy or **Synonym** (6.3.2)   Property of words that have the same denotation.

Syntactic Category (5.1.3)   See **Lexical Category**.

Syntactic Parsing (9.6.1)   The analysis (by a human or computer) of the syntactic structure of a sentence that is heard or read: reconstructing a **hierarchical structure** from a flat sequence of words.

Syntax (1.2.2; 5.0)   The study of the way in which **phrases** and sentences are constructed from smaller units called **constituents;** how sentences are related to each other.

Synthesized Speech (15.1.1)   Speech generated by concatenating small speech units or artificially generating speech.

Synthetic (Language) (4.3.1; 4.3.3)   Language in which **affixes** are attached to other morphemes, so that a word may be made up of several meaningful elements. (See also **Agglutinating Language** and **Fusional Language**.)

T

Tabular Method (16.5.5)   A method for solving **shift ciphers.**

Target (9.7.3)   In **priming** tasks, the stimulus of interest that follows the **prime.**

Target Language (TL) (15.4.1)   In translation and interpretation, the language that some text is translated into. (See also **Source Language**.) In contact situations, the language associated with the politically and economically dominant group. (See also **Superstratum Language**.)

Telegraphic Stage (8.3.3)   A phase during child language acquisition in which children use utterances composed primarily of **content words.**

Telegraphic Utterances (8.3.3)   Utterances containing primarily **content words** (in the style of a telegram with many function words and function morphemes left out).

Temporal Lobe (9.1.2)   Area in the brain associated with the perception and recognition of auditory stimuli.

Temporary Ambiguity (9.6.2)   **Structural ambiguity** that is present up until some point during the processing of a sentence but that is resolved by the end of the sentence (because, in fact, only one of the original parses is consistent with the entire sequence of words).

Tense (Vowel) (2.3.5)   Vowel sound that has a more peripheral position in the vowel space. (See also **Lax**.)

Tenseness (2.3.1)   A property of the production of vowels having to do with whether the vowel was made with a **tense** or a **lax** gesture.

Text-To-Speech Synthesis (TTS) (15.1.5)   In **speech synthesis,** generating speech directly from text entered with normal orthography.

Theme (5.2.2)   In a sentence, the **role** of a noun phrase denoting a thing that has a property that is being referred to or that undergoes a movement or a change.

Tone (2.5.4)   Pitch at which the syllable of a word is pronounced; can make a difference in meaning. (See also **Tone Language** and **Suprasegmental Feature**.)

Tone Language (2.5.4)   Language that uses pitch contrast on syllables to signal a difference in word meaning.

Topicalization (5.5.6, 10.4.5)   A syntactic process by which (in English) a **constituent** moves to the beginning of a sentence in order to indicate that it tells the topic under discussion. Also, a test for syntactic constituency in which a group of words is relocated to the beginning of a sentence.

Total Reduplication (4.2.5)   **Reduplication** in which an entire morpheme is repeated. (See also **Partial Reduplication**.)

Trachea (2.2.3)   The windpipe; the tube between the **larynx** and the lungs through which air travels.

Traffic Analysis (16.5.4)   The study of the pattern of who sends messages to whom.

Transfer (8.5.4; 11.0; 11.1.3)   The influence of

one's native language on the learning of subsequent languages (which can facilitate or inhibit the learning of the second language). (See also **Native Language (L1) Interference.**)

Transfer Method (15.4.3)   In **machine translation,** a strategy to have language-dependent "intermediate" languages that represent important linguistic properties (such as syntactic and semantic properties) that are necessary for the automatic translation from a **source language** into the **target language**(s). (See also **Interlingua.**)

Transitive Verb (5.6.2)   **Verb** that takes both a subject noun phrase and an object noun phrase. (See also **Intransitive Verb.**)

Translation (15.4.1)   The work or the process of rendering one language into another.

Trigger (7.5.2)   See **Presupposition Trigger.**

Trill (2.4.6)   A sound produced by bringing two **articulators** together in a series of quick taps.

Truth Conditions (6.4.1)   The way that the world has to be in order for a statement to be interpreted as true.

Truth Value (6.4.3)   The truth of a sentence: always either true or false.

Two-Word Stage (8.3.3)   Stage in first-language acquisition at which children produce two-word utterances in addition to one-word utterances.

Typology (5.6.1)   Study of how grammars of various languages are similar to and different from each other.

U

Ultimate Source (11.2.1)   In **borrowing** situations, the language from which a borrowed word originated (regardless of its **immediate source**).

Unconditioned Sound Change (12.3.3)   Sound change that occurs without influence from neighboring sounds.

Underextension (8.3.5)   Application of a word to a smaller set of objects than is appropriate for mature adult speech or the usual definition of the word. (See also **Overextension.**)

Ungrammatical (5.1.2)   Linguistic **forms** (such as words, phrases, or sentences) that violate the (descriptive) rules of some particular language. An ungrammatical form is marked with an asterisk.

Uniqueness Point (9.5.4)   Point in the articulation of a word at which the word can be uniquely identified relative to all other words in the language that may begin with the same sound or sequence of sounds.

Unit Selection Synthesis (15.1.4)   A kind of **concatenative synthesis** that uses large samples of speech and builds a database of smaller units from these speech samples which are then put together in order to synthesize speech.

Universal Grammar (8.1.2)   The theory that posits a set of grammatical characteristics shared by all **natural languages.** Also, the name of this set of shared characteristics. (See also **Linguistic Universal.**)

Unparsable (9.6.2)   Describes a phrase or sentence that is grammatical, yet for which a person is unable to determine the syntactic structure, often due to the **garden path effect.** (See also **Syntactic Parsing.**)

Unrounded (Vowel) (2.3.4)   An articulation in which the lips are spread or not rounded. (See also **Rounded.**)

Usage-Based Definition (6.2.7)   A definition for a word based on the way that the word is used by speakers of a language.

Utterance (7.1.2)   A speech event: a particular occurrence of a person speaking or signing. Also, the content—words, phrases, or sentences—of what is said. Utterances are represented by the use of quotation marks.

Uvula (2.4.5)   The small fleshy mass that hangs down at the back of the throat; used to produce uvular consonants.

V

Variable Reference (6.2.2)   Reference of a term (word or phrase) that does not always pick out or refer to the same object. (See also **Constant Reference.**)

Variation (1.2.4; 10.0)   See **Language Variation.**

Variegated Babbling (8.2.2)   Production of meaningless consonant-vowel sequences by infants.

Variety (10.1.1)   See **Language Variety.**

Velar (Speech Sound) (2.2.4)   Sound produced by raising the back of the tongue toward the soft part of the roof of the mouth (i.e., the **velum** or soft **palate**).

Velarized (2.4.6)   A term describing a secondary articulation of a speech sound that is produced with the tongue body moving toward the **velum.** For example, the [l] in the English word *eel* [il] is velarized. (See also **Dark [l].**)

Velum (2.2.4)   Soft part of the roof of the mouth behind the hard **palate,** also known as the soft palate. When the velum is raised, the passage between the **pharynx** (throat) and the nasal cavity is closed. When it is lowered, air escapes from the nose, and a **nasal** sound is produced.

Verb (V) (5.3.2)   A word that refers to an action, event, process, or state of being.

Visual Cortex (9.1.2)   Area of the brain located at the lower back of each **hemisphere** responsible for receiving and interpreting visual stimuli and said to store pictorial images.

Visual-Gestural Language (1.5.1)   Language with a signed **modality** (produced with gestures of the hands, arms, and face; and interpreted visually). (See also **Auditory Vocal Language.**)

Vocal Folds (2.2.3)   Folds of muscle in the **larynx**

responsible for creating **voiced** sounds when they vibrate. (See also **Glottis** and **Voicing**.)

Vocal Tract (2.2.2)   The entire air passage above the **larynx**, consisting of the **pharynx**, oral cavity, and nasal cavity.

Vocalization (10.3.8)   The process of pronouncing a non-vowel as a vowel.

Voice Onset Time (VOT) (8.2.1; 9.4.2)   The length of time between the release of a consonant and the onset of voicing, that is, when the vocal folds start vibrating.

Voiced (2.2.3)   A term describing sounds made with the vocal folds vibrating.

Voiceless (2.2.3)   A term describing sounds made without the vocal folds vibrating.

Voicing (2.2.3)   Vibration of the approximated vocal folds caused by air passing through them. When the vocal folds vibrate, a voiced sound is produced; when the vocal folds do not vibrate, a voiceless sound is produced.

Vowel Harmony (3.2.3)   Long-distance assimilation between vowels.

Vowel Space (2.3.5)   Range of possible vowel sounds of a language from the high front vowel to the high back vowel. Languages and dialects choose a subset of the vowel space but do not exploit all possibilities.

W

Wave Theory (12.2.2)   The theory describing the gradual spread of change throughout a dialect, language, or group of languages, similar to a wave expanding on the surface of a pond from the point where a pebble (i.e., the source of the change) has been tossed in.

Weakening (3.2.3)   A process through which sounds are made "weaker" according to some criterion. (See also **Strengthening**.)

Wernicke's Aphasia (9.2.3)   A speech disorder, commonly associated with brain damage to **Wernicke's area**, that involves the inability to understand linguistic input.

Wernicke's Area (9.1.2)   A region of the brain found in the **left hemisphere** at or around the posterior end of the **Sylvian fissure**.

Whorf Hypothesis (13.3.1)   See **Linguistic Relativity**.

Wizard of Oz Simulations (15.3.5)   A technique used for **spoken dialogue system** development in which participants are told that they will interact with a computer system through a natural language interface, but in fact they interact with a human operator (i.e., the "wizard"). This allows testing aspects of how humans will interact with a dialogue system before the system is developed.

Word Formation Process (4.2.1)   The combination of **morphemes** according to rules of the language in question to make new words or forms of words.

Word Spotting (15.3.2)   In interactive computer systems, a technique in which the computer program focuses on words it knows and ignores ones it doesn't know.

Writing (1.3.2; 13.4.1)   Creating visual symbols on a surface to record linguistic forms; the representation of language in a physical medium other than sound.

X

X-Ray Photography (2.1.1; 2.3.7)   X-rays used in conjunction with sound film. The use of this technique can reveal the details of the functioning of the vocal apparatus. The entirety of how a sound is produced is revealed and can actually be seen as it happens.

Selected Bibliography

1946. *Hawai'i Tribune Herald,* November 2.

Aitchinson, J. 1976. *The articulate mammal: An introduction to psycholinguistics.* London: Hutchinson and Co.

Akmajian, A., D. P. Demers, and R. M. Harnish. 1984. *Linguistics: An introduction to language and communication.* Cambridge, MA: MIT Press.

Aronoff, M., I. Meir, and W. Sandler. 2005. The paradox of sign language morphology. *Language* 81:302–44.

Aronoff, M., and J. Rees-Miller. 2003. *The handbook of linguistics, Blackwell handbooks in linguistics.* Oxford; Malden, MA: Blackwell.

Ash, S. 2003. A national survey of North American dialects. In *Needed research in American dialects,* edited by D. Preston. Durham, NC: American Dialect Society, Duke University Press.

Auer, P. 1995. The pragmatics of code-switching: A sequential approach. In *One speaker, two languages: Cross-disciplinary perspectives on code-switching,* edited by L. Milroy and P. Muysken. Cambridge: Cambridge University Press.

Avrutin, S. 2001. Linguistics and agrammatism. *GLOT International* 5:3–11.

Bailey, G., and J. Tillery. 2006. Sounds of the South. In *American voices: How dialects differ from coast to coast,* edited by W. Wolfram and B. Ward. Oxford: Blackwell.

Baker, C., and R. Battison. 1980. *Sign language and the Deaf community: Essays in honor of William C. Stokoe.* Silver Spring, MD: National Association of the Deaf.

Baker, C., and D. Cokely. 1980. *American Sign Language: A teacher's resource text on grammar and culture.* Silver Spring, MD: T. J. Publishers.

Baldwin, D. 2003. Miami language reclamation: From ground zero. In *Speaker series, no. 24,* edited by K. Jamsen and E. Oliver. Minneapolis: University of Minnesota.

Bayles, K. 1981. *Linguistics: An introduction to language and communication.* Cambridge, MA: MIT Press.

Beck, R. B. 1969. Ethnographic interview by Peggy Dycus. Miami, OK: Miami Tribal Library.

Becker, J. 1984. Multilingual word processing. *Scientific American* (July):96–107.

Benson, L. D., ed. 1987. *The Riverside Chaucer.* 3rd ed. Boston: Houghton Mifflin.

Berko Gleason, J. 2005. *The development of language.* 6th ed. Boston: Pearson.

Berko Gleason, J., and N. B. Ratner, eds. 1998. *Psycholinguistics.* 2nd ed. Forth Worth: Harcourt College Publishers.

Berlin, B., and P. Kay. 1969. *Basic color terms: Their universality and evolution.* Berkeley: University of California Press.

Bickerton, D. 1983. Creole languages. *Scientific American* 249 (1):116–22.

Blackburn, B. 1993. *Words fail us: Good English and other lost causes.* Toronto: McClelland & Stewart, Inc.

Bloomfield, L. 1933. *Language.* New York: Holt.

Boas, F. 1966. Introduction. In *Handbook of American Indian languages,* edited by F. Boas. Lincoln: University of Nebraska Press.

Bolinger, D. L. 1980. *Language, the loaded weapon: The use and abuse of language today.* London, New York: Longman.

Bongaerts, T., C. van Summeren, B. Planken, and E. Schils. 1997. Age and ultimate attainment in the pronunciation of a foreign language. *Studies in Second Language Acquisition* 19:447–65.

Bonvillain, N. 1997. Cross-cultural studies of language and gender. In *Language, culture, and communication: The meaning of messages.* Upper Saddle River, NJ: Prentice Hall.

Boroditsky, L. 2003. Linguistic relativity. In *Encyclopedia of cognitive science,* edited by L. Nadel. London: Macmillan Press.

Bosch, L., and N. Sebastian-Galles. 2001. Evidence of early language discrimination abilities in infants from bilingual environments. *Infancy* 2 (1):29–49.

Braine, M. D. S. 1971. The acquisition of language in infant and child. In *The learning of language,* edited by C. E. Reed. New York: Appleton-Century-Crofts.

Brandes, P. D., and J. Brewer. 1977. *Dialect clash in America: Issues and answers.* Metuchen, NJ: Scarecrow Press.

Brentari, D. 2002. Modality differences in sign language phonology and morphophonemics. In *Modality in language and linguistic theory,* edited by R. Meier, D. Quinto, and K. Cormier. Cambridge: Cambridge University Press.

Broch, I., and E. H. Jahr. 1984. Russenorsk: A new look at the Russo-Norwegian pidgin in northern Norway. In *Scandinavian language contacts,* edited by P. S. Ureland and I. Clarkson. Cambridge: Cambridge University Press.

Brown, P., and S. C. Levinson. 1993. Explorations in Mayan cognition. *Working Papers No. 24 Cognitive Anthropology Research Group, Nijmegen.*

Brown, R. 1973. Development of the first language in the human species. *American Psychology* 28:395–403.

———. 1973. *A first language: The early stages.* Cambridge, MA: Harvard University Press.

Bucholtz, M., and K. Hall. 2005. Identity and interaction: A sociocultural linguistic approach. *Discourse Studies* 7 (4–5):585–614.

Buffington, A., and P. Barba. 1965. *A Pennsylvania German grammar.* Allentown, PA: Schlechter.

Burling, R. 1973. *English in black and white.* Orlando, FL: Holt, Rinehart and Winston.

Butterworth, B. 1983. Lexical representation. In *Language production,* edited by B. Butterworth. London: Academic Press.

Cameron, D., F. McAlinden, and K. O'Leary. 1989. Lakoff in context: The social and linguistic functions of tag questions. In *Women in their speech communities: New perspectives on language and sex,* edited by J. Coates and D. Cameron. New York: Longman.

Cameron, R. 2006. Words of the windy city (Chicago). In *American voices: How dialects differ from coast to coast,* edited by W. Wolfram and B. Ward. Oxford: Blackwell.

Carroll, D. W. 2004. *Psychology of language.* 4th ed. Belmont, CA: Wadsworth/Thomson Learning.

Carver, C. M. 1989. *American regional dialects: A word geography.* Ann Arbor: University of Michigan Press.

Chun, E. W. 2001. The construction of white, black, and Korean American identities through African American Vernacular English. *Journal of Linguistic Anthropology* 11 (1):52–64.

Clark, E. V. 1993. *The lexicon in acquisition.* Cambridge: Cambridge University Press.

———. 1995. Later lexical development and word formation. In *The handbook of child language,* edited by P. Fletcher and B. MacWhinney. Oxford: Basil Blackwell.

Clark, R. 1983. Social contexts of early South Pacific pidgins. In *The social contexts of creolization,* edited by E. Woolford and W. Washabaugh. Ann Arbor: Karoma.

Coates, J. 1993. *Women, men, and language.* New York: Longman.

Cole, R., J. Mariani, H. Uszkoreit, G. B. Varile, A. Zaenen, and A. Zampolli. 1997. *Survey of the state of the art in the human language technology.* Cambridge: Cambridge University Press.

Columbus, F. 1974. *Introductory workbook in historical phonology.* 5th ed. Cambridge, MA: Slavica.

Conklin, N. F., and M. A. Lourie. 1983. *A host of tongues: Language communities in the United States.* New York: Free Press.

Conn, J. 2006. Dialects in the mist (Portland, OR). In *American voices: How dialects differ from coast to coast,* edited by W. Wolfram and B. Ward. Oxford: Blackwell.

Corina, D. P., U. Bellugi, and J. Reilly. 1999. Neuropsychological studies of linguistic and affective facial expressions in deaf signers. *Language and Speech* 42 (2–3):307–31.

Costello, E. 1983. *Signing: How to speak with your hands.* New York: Bantam.

Coulmas, F. 1989. *The writing systems of the world.* Oxford: Blackwell.

Cowan, W., and J. Rakusan. 1980. *Source book for linguistics.* Amsterdam: John Benjamins.

Cran, W., and R. MacNeil. 2005. Do you speak American? Public Broadcasting System.

Crystal, D. 1987. *The Cambridge encyclopedia of language.* Cambridge: Cambridge University Press.

———. 2000. *Language death.* Cambridge: Cambridge University Press.

de Saussure, F. 1959. *A course in general linguistics.* Translated by W. Baskin. Edited by C. Bally and A. Sechehaye. New York: Philosophical Library.

DeCasper, A. J., and M. J. Spence. 1986. Prenatal maternal speech influences newborns' perception of speech sounds. *Infant behavior and development* 9:133–50.

DeFrancis, J. 1984. *The Chinese language: Fact and fantasy.* Honolulu: University of Hawaii Press.

——. 1989. *Visible speech: The diverse oneness of writing systems*. Honolulu: University of Hawaii Press.

——. 2002. The ideographic myth. In *Difficult characters*, edited by M. S. Erbaugh. Columbus, OH: National East Asian Language Resource Center, The Ohio State University.

Descartes, R. 2006. *A discourse on the method*. Translated by I. Maclean, *Oxford world's classics*. Oxford: Oxford University Press.

Dodsworth, R. 2005. Attribute networking: A technique for modeling social perceptions. *The Journal of Sociolinguistics* 9 (2):225–53.

Doyle, A. C., and C. Morley. 1930. *The complete Sherlock Holmes*. Garden City, NY: Doubleday.

Duchnowski, D. 1999. Chicano English: Language issues and their relationship to culture. In *Virtual International Classroom*. Available online: http://courses.wcsu.edu/valkommen/dawn.htm.

Durian, D. 2004. The social stratification of (str) in Columbus, OH department stores. Unpublished manuscript. Available online: http://www.ling.osu.edu/~ddurian/strsscds.pdf.

Durian, D., and A. Smith. 2005. Fronter, lower, and (shorter): The trajectory of /aw/ and /ow/ in Columbus, OH. Paper read at NWAV 34, New York City, NY.

Early 1900s statistical records tell story. 2002. *Aatotankiki Myaamiaki (The quarterly newspaper of the Miami Nation)*.

Eckert, P. 2004. California vowels. Unpublished manuscript. Available online: http://www.stanford.edu/~eckert/vowels.html.

Eckert, P., and S. McConnell-Ginet. 1992. Think practically and look locally: Language and gender as community based practice. *Annual Review of Anthropology* 21:461–90.

——. 1995. Constructing meaning, constructing selves. In *Gender articulated: Language and the socially constructed self*, edited by K. Hall and M. Bucholtz. New York: Routledge.

Eckert, P., and N. Mendoza-Denton. 2006. Getting real in the golden state (California). In *American voices: How dialects differ from coast to coast*, edited by W. Wolfram and B. Ward. Oxford: Blackwell.

Edwards, J. R. 1979. *Language and disadvantage*. London: Edward Arnold.

Eisikovits, E. 1988. Girl-talk/boy-talk: Sex differences in adolescent speech. In *Australian English*, edited by P. Collins and D. Blair. St. Lucia: University of Queensland Press.

Enninger, W., and J. Raith. 1988. Varieties, variation, and convergences in the linguistic repertoire of the Old Order Amish in Kent County, Delaware. In *Variation and convergence: Studies in social dialectology*, edited by P. Auer and A. di Luizo. Berlin: Mouton de Gruyter.

Evans, J., L. Workman, P. Mayer, and K. Crowley. 2002. Differential bilingual laterality: Mythical monster found in Wales. *Brain and Language* 83 (2):291–99.

Everett, D. L. 2005. Cultural constraints on grammar and cognition in Pirahã: Another look at the design features of human language. *Current Anthropology* 47:143–45.

Fantini, A. E. 1985. *Language acquisition of a bilingual child: A sociolinguistic perspective (to age ten)*. Clevedon [England]: Multilingual Matters.

Fasold, R. W., and J. Connor-Linton. 2006. *An introduction to language and linguistics*. Cambridge: Cambridge University Press.

Fernald, A. 1992. Human maternal vocalizations to infants as biologically relevant signals: An evolutionary perspective. In *The adapted mind: Evolutionary psychology and the generation of culture*, edited by J. H. Barkow, L. Cosmides, and J. Tooby. Oxford: Oxford University Press.

Fought, C. 2006. Talkin' with mi gente (Chicano English). In *American voices: How dialects differ from coast to coast*, edited by W. Wolfram and B. Ward. Oxford: Blackwell.

Fraser, G. 2006. *Sorry, I don't speak French: Confronting the Canadian crisis that won't go away*. Toronto: McClelland and Stewart.

Freed, A. 1992. We understand perfectly: A critique of Tannen's view of cross-sex communication. In *Locating power: Proceedings of the 2nd Berkeley Women and Language Conference*, edited by K. Hall, M. Bucholtz, and B. Moonwomon. Berkeley: Berkeley Women and Language Group.

Fromkin, V. 1971. The non-anomalous nature of anomalous utterances. *Language* 47:27–52.

——. 1988. Sign languages: Evidence for language universals and the linguistic capacity of the brain. *Sign Language Studies* (Summer):115–27.

Fromkin, V., and R. Rodman. 1978. *An introduction to language*. 2nd ed. Fort Worth: Harcourt Collins.

Fuller, J. M. 1997. Pennsylvania Dutch with a southern touch: A theoretical model of language contact and language change. PhD dissertation, University of South Carolina.

——. 1999. The role of English in Pennsylvania German development: Best supporting actress? *American Speech* 74 (1):38–55.

Gal, S. 1978. Variation and change in patterns of speaking: Language shift in Austria. In *Linguistic variation: Models and methods*, edited by D. Sankoff. New York: Academic Press.

Gardner, H. 1975. *The shattered mind*. New York: Knopf.

Garnica, O. 1977. Some prosodic and paralinguistic features of speech to young children. In *Talking to children: Language input and acquisition,* edited by C. E. Snow and C. A. Ferguson. Cambridge: Cambridge University Press.

Gelb, I. J. 1963. *A study of writing.* Chicago: University of Chicago Press.

Geschwind, N. 1979. Specializations of the human brain. *Scientific American* 241 (3):180–99.

Ghazanfar, A. A., and N. K. Logothetis. 2003. Neuroperception: Facial expressions linked to monkey calls. *Nature* 423 (6943):937–38.

Giddens, A. 1989. *Sociology.* Cambridge: Polity.

Gleason, H. A., Jr. 1955, renewed 1983. *Descriptive linguistics.* Orlando, FL: Holt, Rinehart and Winston, Inc.

Goodluck, H. 1991. *Language acquisition: A linguistic introduction.* Cambridge, MA: Blackwell.

Goodwin, M. H. 1990. *He-said-she-said: Talk as social organization among black children.* Bloomington: Indiana University Press.

Gordon, P. 2004. Numerical cognition without words: Evidence from Amazonia. *Science* 306:496–99.

Gordon, R. G., ed. 2005. *Ethnologue: Languages of the world.* 15th ed. Dallas, TX: SIL International. Online version: http://www.ethnologue.com/.

Graddol, D., and J. Swann. 1989. *Gender voices.* Oxford: Basil Blackwell.

Green, L. 2004. African American English. In *Language in the USA,* edited by E. Finegan and J. Rickford. Cambridge: Cambridge University Press.

Grenoble, L., and L. Whaley. 2005. *Saving languages: An introduction to language revitalization.* Cambridge: Cambridge University Press.

Grice, H. P. 1989 [1975]. *Logic and conversation: Studies in the way of words.* Cambridge, MA: Harvard University Press.

Groce, N. E. 1985. *Everyone here spoke sign language: Hereditary deafness on Martha's Vineyard.* Cambridge, MA: Harvard University Press.

Grosjean, F. 1979. A study in timing in a manual and a spoken language: American Sign Language and English. *Journal of Psycholinguistic Research* 8:379–405.

Gumperz, J. J., and R. Wilson. 1971. Convergence and creolization: A case from the Indo-Aryan/Dravidian border in India. In *Pidginization and creolization of languages,* edited by D. H. Hymes. Cambridge: Cambridge University Press.

Hankamer, J. 1989. Morphological parsing and the lexicon. In *Lexical representation and process,* edited by W. Marslen-Wilson. Cambridge, MA: MIT Press.

Harrison, J. 1999. Research rescues language of the Miami. *Indianapolis Star,* November 27.

Harvard dialect survey. 2002. Available online: http://cfprod01.imt.uwm.edu/Dept/FLL/linguistics/dialect/.

Heller, M. 1982. Negotiations of language choice in Montreal. In *Language and social identity,* edited by J. J. Gumperz. Cambridge: Cambridge University Press.

Hinton, L. 1993. *Flutes of fire: The Indian languages of California.* 2nd ed. Berkeley: Heyday Books.

Hock, H. 1991. *Principles of historical linguistics.* 2nd ed. Berlin, New York: Mouton de Gruyter.

Hockett, C. F. 1966. The problem of universals in language. In *Universals of language,* edited by J. H. Greenberg. Cambridge, MA: MIT Press.

Hoffmann, C. 1998. *An introduction to bilingualism.* London, New York: Longman.

Holm, J. 1988. *Pidgins and creoles.* Vol. 1. Cambridge: Cambridge University Press.

Hopkins, C. D. 1999. Design features for electric communication. *The Journal of Experimental Biology* 202:1217–28.

Hurford, J. R., and B. Heasley. 1983. *Semantics: A coursebook.* Cambridge: Cambridge University Press.

Hutchins, W. J., and H. Somers. 1992. *An introduction to machine translation.* San Diego: Academic Press.

Jahr, E. H. 1996. On the pidgin status of Russenorsk. In *Language contact in the Arctic: Northern pidgins and contact languages,* edited by E. H. Jahr and I. Broch. Berlin: Mouton de Gruyter.

James, D., and S. Clarke. 1992. Interruptions, gender, and power: A critical review of the literature. In *Locating power: Proceedings of the 2nd Berkeley Women and Language Conference,* edited by K. Hall, M. Bucholtz, and B. Moonwomon. Berkeley: Berkeley Women and Language Group.

Jay, T. B. 2003. *The psychology of language.* 2nd ed. Upper Saddle River, NJ: Prentice Hall.

Jeffers, R. R., and I. Lehiste. 1979. *Principles and methods for historical linguistics.* Cambridge, MA: MIT Press.

Johnstone, B., N. Bhasin, and D. Wittkofski. 2002. 'Dahntahn' Pittsburgh: Monophthongal /aw/ and representations of localness in southwestern Pennsylvania. *American Speech* 77 (2):148–66.

Jurafsky, D., and J. H. Martin. 2000. *Speech and language processing: An introduction to natural language processing, computational linguistics, and speech recognition.* Upper Saddle River, NJ: Prentice Hall.

Keenan, E. 1974. Norm-makers and norm-breakers: Uses of speech by men and women in a Malagasy community. In *Explorations in the ethnography of speaking*, edited by R. Bauman and J. Sherzer. New York: Cambridge University Press.

Keesing, R. 1988. *Melanesian pidgin and the oceanic substrate*. Palo Alto, CA: Stanford University Press.

Keiser, S. H. 1999. Language contact phenomena in Pennsylvania German: A literature review. Unpublished manuscript. Columbus, OH.

Khedr, E. M., E. Hamed, A. Said, and J. Basahi. 2002. Handedness and language cerebral lateralization. *European Journal of Applied Physiology* 87 (4–5):469–73.

Klatt, D. H. 1987. Review of text-to-speech conversion for English. *Journal of the Acoustical Society of America* 82 (3):737–93.

Klima, E. S., and U. Bellugi. 1979. *The signs of language*. Cambridge, MA: Harvard University Press.

Kurath, H. 1949. *A word geography of the eastern United States*. Ann Arbor: University of Michigan Press.

Labov, W. 1966. *The social stratification of English in New York City*. Washington, DC: Center for Applied Linguistics.

———. 1972. *Sociolinguistic patterns*. Philadelphia: University of Pennsylvania Press.

———. 1990. The intersection of sex and social class in the course of linguistic change. *Language Variation and Change* 2:205–54.

Labov, W., S. Ash, and C. Boberg, eds. 2005. *Atlas of North American English: Phonetics, phonology, and sound change*. Berlin, New York: Mouton de Gruyter.

Ladefoged, P. 1971. *Preliminaries of linguistic phonetics*. Chicago: University of Chicago Press.

———. 1996. *Elements of acoustic phonetics*. 2nd ed. Chicago: University of Chicago Press. Original edition, 1962.

———. 2001. *Vowels and consonants: An introduction to the sounds of languages*. Malden, MA: Blackwell.

Ladefoged, P., and I. Maddieson. 1996. *The sounds of the world's languages, Phonological theory*. Oxford, UK; Cambridge, MA: Blackwell.

Lakoff, R. T. 1975. *Language and a woman's place*. New York: Harper & Row.

———. 1990. *Talking power: The politics of language in our lives*. New York: Basic Books.

Lane, H., R. Hoffmeister, and B. Bahan. 1996. *A journey into the DEAF-WORLD*. San Diego: DawnSign Press.

Lehiste, I. 1988. *Lectures on language contact*. Cambridge, MA: MIT Press.

Lenneberg, E. H. 1967. *Biological foundations of language*. New York: John Wiley and Sons.

Lenneberg, E. H., and J. M. Roberts. 1956. The language of experience: A study in methodology. *International Journal of American Linguistics* 22 (2, part 2, Memoir 13).

Leopold, W. F. 1947. *Speech development of a bilingual child: A linguist's record*. Vol. II: Sound-learning in the first two years. Evanston, IL: Northwestern University Press.

LePage, R. B., and A. Tabouret-Keller. 1985. *Acts of identity: Creole-based approaches to language and ethnicity*. Cambridge: Cambridge University Press.

Levelt, W. J. M. 1989. *Speaking: From intention to articulation*. Cambridge, MA: MIT Press.

Levinson, S. C. 1996. Frames of reference and Molyneux's question: Crosslinguistic evidence. In *Language and space*, edited by P. Bloom, M. Peterson, L. Nadel, and M. Garrett. Cambridge, MA: MIT Press

———. 1996. Language and space. *Annual Review of Anthropology* 25:353–82.

Lieberman, P., and S. E. Blumstein. 1988. *Speech physiology, speech perception, and acoustic phonetics, Cambridge studies in speech science and communication*. Cambridge: Cambridge University Press.

Louden, M. 1997. Linguistic structure and sociolinguistic identity in Pennsylvania German society. In *Language and lives: Essays in honor of Werner Enninger*, edited by J. Dow and M. Wolff. New York: Peter Lang.

Lowth, R. 1762. *A short introduction to English grammar, with critical notes*. London: Printed by J. Hughs for A. Millar and R. and J. Dodsley.

Lucas, C., R. Bayley, R. Reed, and A. Wulf. 2001. Lexical variation in African American and white signing. *American Speech* 76 (4):339–60.

Lucy, J. A. 1992. *Language diversity and thought: A reformulation of the linguistic relativity hypothesis*. Edited by K. H. Basso, J. J. Gumperz, S. B. Heath, D. H. Hymes, J. T. Irvine, W. Klein, S. C. Levinson, E. Ochs, B. Rigsby, and M. Silverstein, *Studies in the social and cultural foundation of language*. Cambridge: Cambridge University Press.

Lyons, J. 1995. *Linguistic semantics: An introduction*. Cambridge: Cambridge University Press.

Macauley, M. 2006. *Surviving linguistics: A guide for graduate students*. Somerville, MA: Cascadilla Press.

Macnamara, J. 1969. How can one measure the extent of a person's bilingual proficiency? In *Description and measurement of bilingualism*, edited by L. Kelly. Toronto: University of Toronto Press.

Mallinson, C., B. Childs, B. Anderson, and N. Hutchinson. 2006. If these hills could talk (Smoky Mountains). In *American voices: How dialects differ from coast to coast,* edited by W. Wolfram and B. Ward. Oxford: Blackwell.

Malotki, E. 1983. *Hopi time: A linguistic analysis of the temporal concepts in the Hopi language.* Berlin and New York: Mouton.

Maltz, D. N., and R. Borker. 1982. A cultural approach to male-female miscommunication. In *Language and social identity,* edited by J. J. Gumperz. Cambridge: Cambridge University Press.

Mansour, G. 1993. *Multilingualism and nation building.* Clevedon [England]; Philadelphia: Multilingual Matters.

Martin, J. 2000. A linguistic comparison: Two notation systems for signed languages: Stokoe Notation and Sutton SignWriting. Available online: http://www.signwriting.org/archive/docs1/sw0032-Stokoe-Sutton.pdf.

McConchie, A. 2002. The great soda pop controversy. Available online: http://www.popvssoda.com/.

McConnell-Ginet, S., R. Borker, and N. Furman, eds. 1980. *Women and language in literature and society.* New York: Praeger.

McCrum, R., W. Cran, and R. MacNeil. 1986. *The story of English.* New York: Viking Penguin.

McGurk, H., and J. MacDonald. 1976. Hearing lips and seeing voices. *Nature* 264:746–48.

McKay, S. L., and S.-l. C. Wong. 1988. *Language diversity: Problem or resource?* New York: Newbury House.

Mendoza-Denton, N. 1995. Pregnant pauses: Silence and authority in the Anita Hill-Clarence Thomas hearings. In *Gender articulated: Language and the socially constructed self,* edited by K. Hall and M. Bucholtz. New York: Routledge.

———. 1997. Chicana/Mexicana identity and linguistic variation: An ethnographic and sociolinguistic study of gang affiliation in an urban high school. PhD dissertation, Stanford University.

———. 2002. Language and identity. In *The handbook of language variation and change,* edited by P. Trudgill, J. K. Chambers, and N. Schilling-Estes. Malden, MA: Blackwell.

Menzel, C. R., E. S. Savage-Rumbaugh, and E. W. Menzel, Jr. 2002. Bonobo (*pan paniscus*) spatial memory and communication in a 20-hectare forest. *International Journal of Primatology* 23 (3):601–19.

Miller, G. A. 1996. *The science of words.* New York: Scientific American Library.

Millward, C. M. 1989. *A biography of the English language.* Orlando, FL: Holt, Rinehart and Winston.

Morgan, M. 1996. Conversational signifying: Grammar and indirectness among African American women. In *Interaction and grammar,* edited by E. Ochs, E. A. Schegloff, and S. Thompson. New York: Cambridge University Press.

Moss, B. J., and K. Walters. 1993. Rethinking diversity: Axes of difference in the writing classroom. In *Theory and practice in the teaching of writing: Rethinking the discipline,* edited by L. Odell. Carbondale: Southern Illinois University Press.

Murray, T. E. 1993. Positive *anymore* in the Midwest. In *"Heartland" English,* edited by T. C. Frazer. Tuscaloosa: The University of Alabama Press.

Murray, T. E., T. C. Frazer, and B. L. Simon. 1996. *Needs* + past participle in American English. *American Speech* 71 (3):255–71.

Myers-Scotton, C. 1990. Intersections between social motivations and structural processing in code-switching. In *Papers for the workshop on constraints, conditions, and models.* Strasbourg: European Science Foundation.

Mühlhäusler, P. 1986. *Pidgin and creole linguistics.* Oxford and New York: Basil Blackwell.

Newport, E., H. Gleitman, and L. R. Gleitman. 1977. Mother, I'd rather do it myself: Some effects and noneffects of maternal speech style. In *Talking to children: Language input and acquisition,* edited by C. E. Snow and C. A. Ferguson. Cambridge: Cambridge University Press.

Nic Craith, M. 2006. *Europe and the politics of language: Citizens, migrants and outsiders, Palgrave studies in minority languages and communities.* Basingstoke [England]; New York: Palgrave Macmillan.

Nichols, P. 1983. Linguistic options and choices for black women in the rural South. In *Language, gender, and society,* edited by B. Thorne, C. Kramarae, and N. Henley. Rowley, MA: Newbury House.

Nida, E. A. 1949. *Morphology: The descriptive analysis of words.* 2nd ed. Ann Arbor: University of Michigan Press.

Norman, J. 1988. *Chinese.* Cambridge: Cambridge University Press.

O'Barr, W., and B. Atkins. 1980. 'Women's language' or 'powerless language'? In *Women and language in literature and society,* edited by S. McConnell-Ginet, R. Borker, and N. Furman. New York: Praeger.

O'Grady, W., and M. Dobrovolsky. 1989. *Contemporary linguistics: An introduction.* New York: St. Martin's Press.

Oaks, D. D. 1998. *Linguistics at work: A reader of applications.* Fort Worth: Harcourt Brace College Publishers.

Obler, L. K., and K. Gjerlow. 1999. *Language and the brain*. Cambridge: Cambridge University Press.

Ong, W. J. 1982. *Orality and literacy: The technologizing of the world*. Edited by T. Hawkes, *New accents*. London: Routledge.

Osherson, D. N., and H. Lasnik, eds. 1990. *An invitation to cognitive science: Language*. Vol. 1. Cambridge, MA: MIT Press.

Padden, C. A., and D. M. Perlmutter. 1987. American Sign Language and the architecture of phonological theory. *Natural Language and Linguistic Theory* 5:335–75.

Pearson, B. L. 1977. *Workbook in linguistic concepts*. New York: McGraw-Hill.

Pearson, B. Z., S. C. Fernández, W. Lewedeg, and D. K. Oller. 1997. The relation of input factors to lexical learning by bilingual infants. *Applied Psycholinguistics* 18:41–58.

Penfield, J., and J. Ornstein-Galicia. 1985. *Chicano English: An ethnic contact dialect, Varieties of English around the world*. Amsterdam: John Benjamins.

Perlmutter, D. M. 1992. Sonority and syllable structure in American Sign Language. *Linguistic Inquiry* 23:407–42.

Phillips, J. R. 1973. Syntax and vocabulary of mothers' speech to young children: Age and sex comparisons. *Child Development* 44:182–85.

Poser, W. 1994. Review of Smalley et al. *Phonology* 11:365–69.

Pullum, G. K. 1997. Language that dare not speak its name. *Nature* 386:321–22.

Purnell, T., W. J. Idsardi, and J. Baugh. 1999. Perceptual and phonetic experiments on American English dialect identification. *Journal of Language and Social Psychology* 18 (1):10–30.

Pyles, T., and J. Algeo. 1970. *English: An introduction to language*. New York: Harcourt Brace.

Rickford, J. 1997. Suite for ebony and phonics. *Discover* (December):82–87.

———. 1998. *African-American Vernacular English*. Oxford: Blackwell.

Rickford, J., and F. McNair-Knox. 1994. Addressee- and topic- influenced style shift: A quantitative sociolinguistic study. In *Sociolinguistic perspectives on register,* edited by D. Biber and E. Finegan. New York: Oxford University Press.

Roberts, J., N. Nagy, and C. Boberg. 2006. Yakking with the Yankees (New England). In *American voices: How dialects differ from coast to coast,* edited by W. Wolfram and B. Ward. Oxford: Blackwell.

Roberts-Kohno, R. R. 2000. Kikamba phonology and morphology. PhD thesis, Department of Linguistics, The Ohio State University, Columbus, OH.

Rogers, H. 2005. *Writing systems: A linguistic approach, Blackwell textbooks in linguistics*. Malden, MA: Blackwell.

Romaine, S. 1988. *Pidgin and creole languages*. London and New York: Longman.

Sachs, J., and M. Johnson. 1976. Language development of a hearing child of deaf parents. In *Baby talk and infant speech,* edited by W. von Raffler-Engel and Y. Lebrun. Amsterdam: Swets & Zeitlinger.

Sampson, G. 1985. *Writing systems: A linguistic introduction*. Palo Alto, CA: Stanford University Press.

Sandler, W., and D. Lillo Martin. 2001. Natural sign languages. In *Handbook of linguistics,* edited by M. Aronoff and J. Rees-Miller. Oxford: Blackwell.

Sapir, E. 1949 [1921]. *Language: An introduction to the study of speech*. New York: Harcourt, Brace, and Company.

Scott, W., ed. 1808. *The works of John Dryden*. 18 vols. Vol. 6. London: Printed by James Ballantyne and Co. for William Miller, Albemarle St.

Senghas, A., and M. Coppola. 2001. Children creating language. *Psychological Science* 12 (4):323–28.

Shannon, C. E., and W. Weaver. 1949. *The mathematical theory of communication*. Urbana-Champaign: University of Illinois Press.

Shroyer, E. H., and S. P. Shroyer. 1984. *Signs across America: A look at regional differences in American Sign Language*. Washington, DC: Gallaudet College Press.

Shuy, R. W. 2005. *Creating language crimes: How law enforcement uses (and misuses) language*. Oxford; New York: Oxford University Press.

Silva-Corvalán, C. 2004. Spanish in the Southwest. In *Language in the USA,* edited by E. Finegan and J. Rickford. Cambridge: Cambridge University Press.

Simon, B. L. 2006. Saying ya to the yoopers (Michigan's Upper Peninsula). In *American voices: How dialects differ from coast to coast,* edited by W. Wolfram and B. Ward. Oxford: Blackwell.

Singh, S. 1999. *The code book*. New York: Anchor Books.

Sinkov, A. 1998. *Elementary cryptanalysis: A mathematical approach*. Cambridge: Cambridge University Press.

Slobin, D. I. 1996. From "thought and language" to "thinking for speaking." In *Rethinking linguistic relativity,* edited by J. J. Gumperz and S. C. Levinson. Cambridge: Cambridge University Press.

Smalley, W., C. K. Vang, and G. Y. Yang. 1990. *Mother of writing: The origin and development of a Hmong messianic script*. Chicago: University of Chicago Press.

Smith, W. H. 1989. The morphological characteristics of verbs in Taiwan Sign Language. PhD dissertation, Department of Speech and Hearing Sciences, Indiana University.

Smith, W. H., and L.-f. Ting. 1979. *Shou neng sheng chyau (your hands can become a bridge)*. Taipei: Deaf Sign Language Research Association of the Republic of China.

Snow, C. E. 1977. The development of conversation between mothers and babies. *Journal of Child Language* 4:1–22.

Snow, C. E., A. Arlman-Rupp, Y. Hassing, J. Jobse, J. Jooksen, and J. Vorster. 1976. Mother's speech in three social classes. *Journal of Psycholinguistic Research* 5:1–20.

Solan, L. 1993. *The language of judges, Language and legal discourse*. Chicago: University of Chicago Press.

Springer, S., and G. Deutsch. 1981. *Left brain, right brain*. San Francisco: W. H. Freeman.

Stephenson, N. 2002. *Cryptonomicon*. New York: Harper Perennial.

Strand, E. 1999. Uncovering the role of gender stereotypes in speech perception. *Journal of Language and Social Psychology* 18 (1):86–99.

Taft, M., and K. Forster. 1975. Lexical storage and retrieval of prefixed words. *Journal of Verbal Learning and Verbal Behavior* 14:638–47.

Tannen, D. 1991. *You just don't understand: Women and men in conversation*. London: Virago.

Thomas, E. R. 1993. The use of the *all* + comparative structure. In *"Heartland" English*, edited by T. C. Frazer. Tuscaloosa: The University of Alabama Press.

———. 2001. *An acoustic analysis of vowel variation in New World English*. Durham, NC: Duke University Press.

Thomason, S. G., and T. Kaufman. 1988. *Language contact, creolization, and genetic linguistics*. Berkeley and Los Angeles: University of California Press.

Thorne, B., C. Kramarae, and N. Henley, eds. 1983. *Language, gender, and society*. Rowley, MA: Newbury House.

Todd, L. 1971. *Some day been dey: West African pidgin folktales*. London: Routledge and Kegan Paul.

Trudgill, P. 1972. Sex, covert prestige, and linguistic change in the urban British English of Norwich. *Language in Society* 1:179–95.

———. 1974. *The social differentiation of English in Norwich*. Cambridge: Cambridge University Press.

Vannest, J., and J. E. Boland. 1999. Lexical morphology and lexical access. *Brain and Language* 68:324–32.

Vikingstad, E. M., K. P. George, A. F. Johnson, and Y. Cao. 2000. Cortical language lateralization in right handed normal subjects using functional magnetic resonance imaging. *Journal of the Neurological Sciences* 175 (1):17–27.

von Wattenwyl, A., and H. Zollinger. 1978. The color lexica of two American Indian languages, Quechi and Misquitto: A critical contribution to the application of the Whorf hypothesis to color naming. *International Journal of American Linguistics* 44:56–68.

Waksler, R. 2001. A new *all* in conversation. *American Speech* 76 (2):128–38.

Warren, R. M., and R. P. Warren. 1970. Auditory illusions and confusions. *Scientific American* (December):30–36.

Weinrich, U. 1968. *Languages in contact*. The Hague: Mouton.

West, C., and D. Zimmerman. 1991. Doing gender. In *The social construction of gender*, edited by J. Lorber and S. Farrell. London: Sage.

Whatley, E. 1981. Language among Black Americans. In *Language in the USA*, edited by E. Finegan and J. Rickford. Cambridge: Cambridge University Press.

Whorf, B. L. 1956. In *Language, thought, and reality: Selected writings of Benjamin Lee Whorf*, edited by J. B. Carroll. Cambridge, MA: MIT Press.

Williams, R. 2005. Cecil B. DeMille Golden Globe Lifetime Achievement Award acceptance speech. Available online: http://www.ruggedelegantliving.com/sf/a/003420.html.

Winford, D. 2003. *An introduction to contact linguistics, Language in society*. Malden, MA: Blackwell.

Wohlgemuth, J. 1999. *Grammatical categories and their realisations in Tok Pisin of Papua New Guinea*. Available online: http://www.linguist.de/TokPisin/tp02-en.htm.

Wolfram, W. 1969. *A linguistic description of Detroit Negro speech*. Washington, DC: Center for Applied Linguistics.

———. 1991. *Dialects and American English*. Englewood Cliffs, NJ: Prentice Hall.

———. 2006. From the brickhouse to the swamp (Lumbee Vernacular English). In *American voices: How dialects differ from coast to coast*, edited by W. Wolfram and B. Ward. Oxford: Blackwell.

Wolfram, W., and D. Christian. 1976. *Appalachian speech*. Washington, DC: Center for Applied Linguistics.

Wolfram, W., and C. Dannenberg. 1999. Dialect identity and a tri-ethnic context: The case of Lumbee American Indian English. *English World Wide* 20:79–116.

Wolfram, W., C. Dannenberg, S. Knick, and L. Oxendine. 2002. *Fine in the world: Lumbee language in time and place*. Raleigh: NC State Humanity Extension Program Publications.

Wolfram, W., and N. Schilling-Estes. 2005. *American English*. 2nd ed. Oxford: Blackwell.

Wolfram, W., and B. Ward, eds. 2006. *American voices: How dialects differ from coast to coast*. Oxford: Blackwell.

Yule, G. 1996. *The study of language*. 2nd ed. Cambridge and New York: Cambridge University Press.

Zwicky, A. D. 1981. Styles. In *Styles and variables in English,* edited by T. Shopen and J. M. Williams. Cambridge, MA: Winthrop Publishers (Prentice-Hall).

Language Index

Subject Index

689

Examples of Phonetic Symbols Found in Standard American English

Note: Because English spelling does not have a one-to-one correspondence with sounds, underlining the letters in example words to show where a sound occurs can be difficult. For example, we have underlined the <ea> in *Leah* to indicate that there is a [j] between the [i] and the [ə]: [lijə]. For each symbol, think carefully about how the sound occurs in the example words.

a. Consonants
i. Non-Syllabic Consonants

Symbol	Sample Words
[p]	pit, tip, spit, hiccough, appear
[b]	ball, globe, amble, brick, bubble
[t]	tag, pat, stick, pterodactyl, stuffed
[d]	dip, card, drop, loved, batted
[k]	kit, scoot, character, critique
[g]	guard, bag, finger, designate, Pittsburgh
[ʔ]	hatrack, Batman
[f]	foot, laugh, philosophy, coffee, carafe
[v]	vest, dove, gravel, anvil, average
[θ]	through, wrath, thistle, ether, teeth
[ð]	the, their, mother, either, teethe
[s]	soap, psychology, packs, descent, peace
[z]	zip, roads, kisses, Xerox, design
[ʃ]	shy, mission, nation, glacial, sure
[ʒ]	measure, vision, azure, casualty, decision
[h]	who, hat, rehash, hole, whole
[tʃ]	choke, match, feature, righteous, constituent
[dʒ]	judge, George, Jell-O, region, residual
[m]	moose, lamb, smack, amnesty, ample
[n]	nap, design, snow, know, mnemonic
[ŋ]	lung, think, finger, singer, ankle
[l]	leaf, feel, Lloyd, mild, applaud
[ɹ]	reef, fear, Harris, prune, carp
[ɾ]	writer, butter, udder, clutter, cuter
[w]	with, swim, mowing, queen, twilight, gooey
[ʍ]	which, where, what, whale, why
[j]	you, beautiful, feud, use, Leah

ii. Syllabic Consonants

Symbol	Sample Words
[m̩]	possum, chasm, Adam, bottomless
[n̩]	button, chicken, lesson, kittenish
[l̩]	little, single, simple, stabilize
[ɹ̩]	ladder, singer, burp, percent

b. Vowels
i. Monophthongs (Simple Vowels)

Symbols	Examples
[i]	beat, we, believe, people, money
[ɪ]	bit, consist, injury, malignant, hymn
[ɛ]	bet, reception, says, guest, bury
[æ]	bat, laugh, anger, comrade, rally
[u]	boot, who, sewer, duty, through
[ʊ]	put, foot, butcher, could, boogie-woogie
[ɔ]	bought, caught, wrong, stalk, core
[ɑ]	pot, father, sergeant, honor, hospital
[ʌ]	but, tough, another, oven
[ə]	among, sofa

ii. Diphthongs (Complex Vowels)

Symbols	Examples
[aɪ]	bite, Stein, aisle, choir, island
[aʊ]	bout, brown, doubt, flower, loud
[ɔɪ]	boy, doily, rejoice, perestroika, annoy
[oʊ]	boat, beau, grow, though, over
[eɪ]	bait, reign, great, they, gauge

Consonants of Standard American English

The consonants of Standard American English, written with IPA symbols, classified by voicing, place of articulation, and manner of articulation:

		Place of Articulation												
Manner of Articulation		Bilabial		Labio-dental		Inter-dental		Alveolar		Palatal		Velar		Glottal	
	Stop	p	b					t	d			k	g	ʔ	
	Fricative			f	v	θ	ð	s	z	ʃ	ʒ			h	
	Affricate									tʃ	dʒ				
	Flap							ɾ							
	Nasal		m					n					ŋ		
	Lateral Liquid							l							
	Retroflex Liquid							ɹ							
	Glide	w̥	w								j				

State of the Glottis: Voiceless | Voiced

Vowels of Standard American English

The vowels of Standard American English, written with IPA symbols, presented using the traditional American classification system:

Monophthongs: Diphthongs:

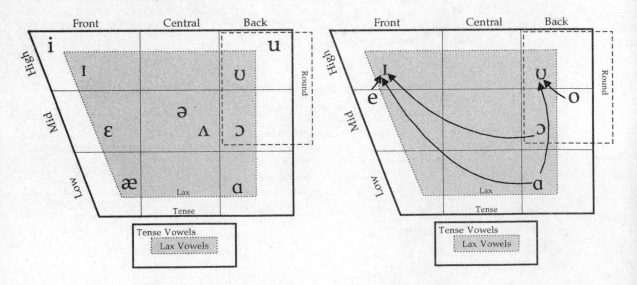

Tense Vowels
Lax Vowels